The Armed Forces of Asia

Series editor: **Professor Desmond Ball**, Strategic and Defence Studies Centre, Australian National University

This groundbreaking series is the first to examine the military capabilities of nations in Asia. Spanning the arc from Pakistan in the west to the Russian Far East in the north, each book provides a succinct survey of each service of the armed forces, including territorial and paramilitary formations. Written by military and defence strategy experts from around the world, the books assess the role of the armed forces in relation to national defence and security policy, and their social, political and economic functions. Up-to-the-minute research is drawn upon to present, in many cases, the first unclassified accounts of nations' defensive and offensive capabilities, as well as the ambitions of sectors within the armed forces establishments.

The Armed Forces of Asia series

You Ji	*China*
Stanley Weeks &	*The USA in the Asia-*
Charles Meconis	*Pacific Region*

Forthcoming titles

David Horner	*Australia*
Andrew Selth	*Burma*
Vijai K Nair and K K Hazari	*India*
Akio Watanabe & Naoko Sajima	*Japan*
Joon Num Mak &	
Russ Swinnerton	*Malaysia*
Joseph Bermudez Jr	*North Korea*
Pervaiz Iqbal Cheema	*Pakistan*
Ron May	*Papua New Guinea*
Carolina G Hernandez &	
Gina Pattugalan	*Philippines*
Tim Huxley	*Singapore*
Taeho Kim	*South Korea*
Andrew N D Yang	*Taiwan*
Noel Adams	*Thailand*
Carlyle Thayer	*Vietnam*

THE ARMED FORCES OF RUSSIA IN ASIA

GREG AUSTIN and
ALEXEY D. MURAVIEV

I.B.Tauris *Publishers*
LONDON • NEW YORK

Published in 2000 by I.B.Tauris & Co Ltd
Victoria House, Bloomsbury Square, London WC1B 4DZ
175 Fifth Avenue, New York NY 10010
Website: http://www.ibtauris.com

In the United States and Canada distributed by St. Martin's Press
175 Fifth Avenue, New York NY 10010

ISBN 1 86064 505 4 hardback
ISBN 1 86064 485 6 paperback

A full CIP record for this book is available from the British Library
A full CIP record for this book is available from the Library of
Congress

Library of Congress catalog card: available

Manufactured in Malaysia

Foreword

The Armed Forces of Russia goes to print as Russia is making a most important political transition. Parliamentary elections scheduled for the end of 1999 and Presidential elections scheduled for June 2000 will be landmark events for Russia's future and the future of its armed forces. But the book also goes to print as Russia unleashes a brutal assault on one of its own communities after a series of bomb attacks in Moscow that destroyed whole apartment blocks. This mix of promise and tragedy facing ordinary Russians and their men and women in uniform in late 1999 is probably one of the main conclusions readers will take away from *The Armed Forces of Russia.*

Russia's armed forces, like the country itself, are in dynamic and volatile evolution. *The Armed Forces of Russia* offers an account of the main features of this evolution over the decade since the end of the Cold War and the eight years since the break-up of the USSR. But, as part of the 'Armed Forces of Asia' series, the main purpose of the book is to provide a snapshot of the armed forces at the end of the 1990s as they affect Asia–Pacific strategic relationships. The book reviews Russia's strategic policies and its armed forces to answer two questions: what does Russia want to do with its military power in the region; and what *could* Russia do with its military power in that region? Notwithstanding this Asia–Pacific brief, the book offers an account which I believe will be of broad appeal to anyone interested in Russian strategy and military affairs.

The authors, Greg Austin and Alexey Muraviev, have pooled their talents very effectively in this book. Austin's career over two decades as an outside observer of Soviet strategic affairs and Muraviev's life experience as a young man inside the new Russia provide a synergy of ideas and research that an individual scholar would find almost impossible to match in the time period in which this book was written. The currency of the information on the military forces, although there had to be a clear cut-off date, is impressive as is the array of sources used. The use by the two authors of Russian language materials has significantly enriched the work.

If Russia's political system is able to develop relatively smoothly and some check on deteriorating public order and public morals can be made, then we should expect Russia's armed forces to undergo a steady consolidation. As the authors point out, since military reform began in earnest in 1997, the gains have been impressive. We have seen the unification of the two air forces into one, unification of space and missile assets into one force, creation of units of constant readiness, creation of unified territorial commands and a large-scale restructuring of higher military education. We have also seen the operational deployment of a new strategic nuclear missile system and the rolling out of a new advanced fighter.

Russia is and will remain a great power in the Asia–Pacific. Moreover, Russia's strategic policies in Europe, the Middle East and Central Asia will continue to have significant impact on the security interests of most countries of the Asia–Pacific. *The Armed Forces of Russia* will give its readers an accurate and comprehensive picture of how the armed forces of Russia fit into this picture.

Desmond Ball
Strategic & Defence Studies Centre
Australian National University
Canberra
November 1999

Contents

Foreword   v
List of maps, tables and figures   viii
About the authors   x
Preface   xii
Acknowledgements   xv
Note on transliteration and citation of sources   xvi
List of abbreviations   xvii

 1 Russia: rebuilding the state, reconstituting the nation   1
 2 Russia east of the Ural Mountains   39
 3 National strategic policy   62
 4 Strategic policy in the Asia–Pacific   96
 5 Military doctrine and force posture   130
 6 Nuclear forces   182
 7 Naval forces   204
 8 Air forces   234
 9 Ground forces   257
10 Military industry and regional arms sales   287
Conclusion   314

Appendix   319
Notes   323
Bibliography   380
Index   389

List of maps, tables and figures

Maps

1	Military districts	xix
2	Administrative divisions of Russia east of the Urals	xx
3	Heartland: the Volga Basin	xxi
4	Russia–US maritime border	xxii
5	Chechnia and neighbouring administrative units of Russia and Georgia	22
6	Relief	45
7	Vegetation and land use	46
8	Defence industries and major east–west rail links	48
9	Disputed Kuril Islands	109

Tables

1.1	Republic populations self-identifying as Russian in 1989	9
1.2	1995 State Duma elections—results by bloc and party	16
1.3	State Duma elections 1993 and 1995 national lists	17
1.4	State Duma number of seats by party after 1993 and 1995 elections	17
1.5	Results in presidential elections 1996 first and second rounds	18
1.6	Economic indicators (percentage of previous year) 1992–96	33
2.1	Nationality populations in selected administrative units east of the Urals	40
2.2	1995 parliamentary elections—eastern Russia results for single member seats	58

2.3 1995 parliamentary elections—eastern Russia results
     for national lists   59
6.1 Strategic nuclear forces   187
7.1 Changes in composition of the Pacific Fleet surface
     force order of battle 1990–98   208
7.2 Changes in composition of the Pacific Fleet
     submarine force order of battle 1990–98   218
7.3 Pacific Fleet Naval Aviation 1998   221
8.1 Service shares in mission execution in a conventional
     war   239
8.2 Tactical combat aircraft of the RFAF order of battle   241
8.3 Military aircraft production 1990–97   248
9.1 Comparison of Soviet and Russian ground forces 1991
     and 1998   262
9.2 Ground forces formations in military districts east of
     the Ural Mountains in 1998   269
9.3 Ground forces equipment holdings east of the Ural
     Mountains   282
9.4 Major ground forces equipment 1998–99   282
10.1 Russian/Soviet systems in India's order of battle:
     selected categories   299

Figures

5.1 Membership of Security Council   149
5.2 Organisation chart: Security Council Staff   150
5.3 Organisation chart: Supreme Command and General
     Staff   165
6.1 Organisation chart: Unified Command Strategic
     Deterrent Forces   200
7.1 Organisation chart: Navy   214
8.1 Organisation chart: Air Force   240
9.1 Organisation chart: Main Directorate of the ground
     forces   260

About the authors

Greg Austin has spent more than twenty years working on Asia–Pacific security, with about half that time spent studying Soviet or Chinese activities in the region for the Australian Department of Defence. His doctoral dissertation was on Soviet military doctrine, for which he conducted research at the Institute of Military History in Moscow. More recently, he has worked in the Research School of Pacific and Asian Studies at the Australian National University, where his publications have included *China's Ocean Frontier—International Law, Military Force and National Development* (1998) and an edited volume, *Missile Diplomacy and Taiwan's Future: Innovations in Politics and Military Power* (1997). He has worked in a variety of professional appointments in the field of international affairs, including adviser to an Australian government minister, foreign affairs correspondent for the *Sydney Morning Herald*, secretary of the Foreign Affairs and Defence Committee of Australia's Senate, and in a diplomatic assignment in Hong Kong. He is currently a Fellow in the Public Policy Program of the Asia–Pacific School of Economics and Management.

Alexey D. Muraviev did his undergraduate studies at Moscow State University. He is currently undertaking PhD studies at the School of Social Sciences, Curtin University of Technology, Perth, Western Australia. He is researching the role of naval power in Russia's foreign policy in the Asia–Pacific in the 1990s. He is the author of 'Responses to NATO's Eastward Expansion by the Russian Federation', published by the Strategic and Defence Studies Centre, Canberra. His work has appeared in *Morskoi sbornik* [Naval Digest] and *Indian Ocean Review*.

*This book is dedicated to
the memory of Alexey's grandfather*

Piotr Afanasievich Bolotintsev

*officer of the Soviet Armed Forces
and veteran of the Great Patriotic War*

and

to the life of Greg's father

Colin Douglas Austin

*who saw war service in the Australian Army
North Africa and New Guinea campaigns*

Preface

Four of Russia's six military districts border Asian[1] states (see Map 1). When the Russian Federation became an independent state, the distance between its capital, Moscow, and the closest neighbouring state in Asia, Kazakhstan, was cut to about 1000 km (see Map 3). Russia's heartland in the lower reaches of the Volga River, where famous cities such as Astrakhan, Volgograd (Stalingrad) and Saratov are located, lies within 100–200 km of the new Asian border for about 1000 km of the river's length. The newly independent Central Asian states to Russia's south have become the target of a new strategic competition involving Russia, Turkey, Saudi Arabia, Iran and more recently the USA. China and Japan have been showing considerable interest in the resources of the region.

East of the Ural Mountains, Russia has land or riverine borders with China (4000 km in the eastern sector and about 55 km in the western sector just west of Mongolia), Kazakhstan (6846 km), Mongolia (3441 km), and North Korea (19 km). Russia's leaders remain seriously concerned about the possibility of Chinese transmigration into their sparsely populated Far East. Russia also has ocean borders with Japan, with which it has a territorial dispute (see Map 9). It shares a fairly peaceful and cooperative border with the USA in the Bering Strait (see Map 4). Russia has considerable maritime spaces to patrol in the north-west Pacific and Arctic. The Korean Peninsula, which lies immediately adjacent to Russian Far East territory, is the most serious potential flashpoint in East Asia. Thus, Russia's strategic concerns in Asia have taken on a variety of new dimensions while longer-standing ones remain.

As part of the Armed Forces of Asia series, this book assesses the plans, operations and capabilities of the Russian Federation's armed forces in those parts of Asia covered by the series: that is, East Asia, South Asia and the North Pacific. The main focus is therefore on Russian forces deployed east of the Ural Mountains— in the three military districts north of China, Mongolia, and the eastern part of Kazakhstan: the Ural, Siberian, and Far East Military Districts. The area covered by this book approximates to the geographic planning regions of West Siberia, East Siberia, and the Far East, but it also includes Sverdlovsk, Cheliabinsk and Kurgan provinces[2] which lie just to the east of the Ural Mountains (see Map 2). The book uses the term 'eastern Russia' to refer to this area east of the Urals. (The term Far East in Russian usage refers, as indicated, to only that fourth part of the area east of the Urals that is contiguous with the Pacific Ocean.) The book does not focus on Russian military forces in those parts of European Russia that border on Asian countries—that is, in the area between the Caspian Sea and the Black Sea, and the areas north of the western half of Kazakhstan. The book refers to this area as southern Russia, as does common Russian usage.

But the book also discusses a number of topical subjects which relate directly to Russian military strategy, Russian military power and the state of the armed forces at the national level. The national strategic policies and capacities of Russia are reviewed because the strategic posture of any state is primarily nationally based, before unique regional considerations are taken into account. Moreover, forces from European Russia could be redeployed to specific contingencies in the Asia–Pacific region. The book comprises ten chapters. Chapter 1 reviews the evolution of Russia from the end of the Soviet era in 1991 to early May 1999, with reference to domestic politics, state structure, the national economy and national identity. Chapter 2 provides an overview of the geography, economy and politics of Russia east of the Urals. Chapters 3 and 4 outline Russia's strategic policy, the former looking at the national picture and the policy toward Europe and areas south of Russia, with the latter looking more specifically at strategic policy in the East Asian region. Chapter 5 reviews military doctrine and national military posture, before the book moves in separate chapters to review nuclear forces (Chapter 6), naval forces (Chapter 7), air forces (Chapter 8) and ground forces (Chapter 9). The military posture and military organisation of Russia in the area east of the Ural Mountains is elaborated through these chapters within the context of national force structure and national strategy. Chapter 10 discusses the Russian military industry and arms sales by Russia to East Asia and South Asia. The book does not offer a comprehensive account of Russia's political relations with its neighbours or near neighbours in East and South Asia.

Thus the book progresses from an overview of the emergence of the new Russian state out of the collapse of the USSR through an analysis of the more important political, military and economic trends of later years, in order to document the formative influences on the armed forces of Russia east of the Urals at the end of the decade. The authors are conscious that the subject of each chapter of this book could be treated better in a separate book devoted exclusively to it. This book is intended in large part as an introductory work on some of the qualitative aspects of Russian military capacities and strategic policies at the time of publication. It is intended for the general reader or for specialists interested in international security policy and military forces of the Asia–Pacific regions.

The book has been written with a keen eye on its target audience, and has sought to provide considerable background where it has been judged appropriate. But the authors have been conscious equally of the large volume of journal articles and reports that are readily available on developments in the armed forces in the period to 1996, especially on issues as central to the future of the armed forces as civil–military relations—the capacity of the state to direct its military forces and rely on their obedient support. There is a large number of studies on the war in Chechnia. There are two excellent and complementary books on the development of the Russian armed forces: Baev's *The Russian Army in a Time of Troubles* (1996), and volume one of the three-volume set *The Armed Forces of the Former Soviet Union* (second edition, 1996) authored by Richard Woff. The authors of the current work see their contribution as providing the reader who specialises in Russian security affairs with a useful update on these works.

Up until the time of submission of the manuscript, the authors continued to include the most up-to-date material on major developments affecting Russia's military posture. The specific data on some of the other subjects covered, such as national economic and political developments, are not as current as May 1999, but the authors have made every effort to reflect the most important trends in place and visible by May 1999 in these other areas that affect Russian military posture.

The book reveals a continuing contest between negative legacies of the Cold War and fulfilment of the promise held out by its end. There has been a gradual transition to a qualitatively new pattern of international relations. According to the Paris Declaration of November 1990, Russia and the West are no longer adversaries. Many old conflict scenarios are no longer applicable, since they were based on the bipolar structure of a military confrontation which no longer exists. These circumstances should have greatly altered former approaches to many security problems, but elements of reciprocal mistrust and stereotypical ideas generated by the superpower confrontation during the Cold War still exist. Many in Russia, as in former adversaries of the USSR, remain hostage to their old perceptions. Most importantly, the damage inflicted on Russian society—largely by its own leaders—in the years since the end of the Cold War has created dangerously shifting ground in terms of national identity and national security. But then it would have taken leaders of almost superhuman capacity to overcome the economic ruin left behind by the collapse of the Soviet economy in the late 1980s and then of the Soviet state between 1990 and 1991.

Acknowledgements

The authors would like to acknowledge the research assistance of Dr Stephen Bates, Mr Michael Thomas, Mr Richard Prosen, and Mr Brendan Taylor; and the assistance of Mr Brett Kunkel and Mrs Robin Ward in editing the penultimate version of the draft manuscript prior to submission. Mr Ian Heyward of the Cartography Unit of the Research School of Pacific and Asian Studies at the Australian National University drew the high quality maps.

Note on transliteration of Russian and citation of sources

A modified Library of Congress system is used. Names of certain countries appear in a variety of forms, often as a result of transliteration of different languages. The following choices have been used: Azerbaijan, Kyrgyzstan, Tajikistan, Turkmenistan, and Uzbekistan. The masculine-form endings of personal names or place names are rendered simply with a *y* or *i*, as in Yevgeny or Primorski. The masculine-form endings for ship names are rendered in full with a *yi* or *ii* as appropriate, as in *Bezumnyi*.

The Russian vowel *e* at the start of a word is rendered as *ye*, as in Yeltsin. In the middle of names of persons or towns, the repeated *e* is also rendered as *ye*, as in Sergeyev. The soft sign (') is not used in Russian words that are transliterated in the text, such as *glasnost*; but the soft sign is rendered as usual in all footnote references or transliterated titles. Transliterations in bibliographical references repeat the original forms, rather than following the transliteration used in the text of this book.

The authors have relied on a wide variety of sources both in Russian and in translation. In many cases, the authors had access to certain issues of a particular periodical in Russian, and to other issues of the same periodical only in translation, usually through the US government's Foreign Broadcast Information Service (FBIS) or its Joint Publications Research Service (JPRS). The date of wire service releases or radio broadcasts carried or translated in FBIS or JPRS is the date in Greenwich of the time of the actual transmission. This sometimes creates references with document dates in FBIS or JPRS that are one day different in date from the date of transmission.

List of abbreviations

AAM	air-to-air missile
ABM	Anti-Ballistic Missile (Treaty)
AIFV	armoured infantry fighting vehicle
APEC	Asia Pacific Economic Cooperation forum
ARF	ASEAN Regional Forum
ASEAN	Association of Southeast Asian Nations
ASW	anti-submarine warfare
CBG	carrier battle group
CFE	Treaty on Conventional Forces in Europe
COMECON	Council for Mutual Economic Cooperation
CPRF	Communist Party of the Russian Federation
CPSU	Communist Party of the Soviet Union
DCR	Democratic Choice of Russia
DDG	guided missile destroyer
DIA	(US) Defense Intelligence Agency
ECM	electronic counter measures
EEZ	Exclusive Economic Zone
EU	European Union
EV	electronic version
FAPSI	Federal Government Communications and Information Agency
FBIS	(US) Foreign Broadcast Information Service
FFG	guided missile frigate
FPS	Federal Border Service
FSB	Federal Security Bureau
GATT	General Agreement on Tariffs and Trade
GRU	Main Intelligence Directorate
HPW	High Precision Weapons
IAEA	International Atomic Energy Agency
ICBM	inter-continental ballistic missile

IISS	International Institute of Strategic Studies
JDA	Japanese Defence Agency
JPRS	Joint Publications Research Service
KEDO	Korean Energy Development Organisation
KOR	Kaliningrad Special District
LDPR	Liberal Democratic Party of Russia
LPD	landing ship
LRA	long-range aviation
MBT	main battle tank
MTCR	missile technology control regime
MVD	Ministry of Internal Affairs
NATO	North Atlantic Treaty Organisation
NIS	newly independent states
NPT	(nuclear) Non-Proliferation Treaty
OSCE	Organisation for Security and Cooperation in Europe
PFNA	Pacific Fleet Naval Aviation
PWS	Party of Workers' Self-Management
RAS	Russian Academy of Sciences
RFAF	Russian Federation Air Force
RFN	Russian Federation Navy
RNI	Russia's Naval Infantry
ROH	Russia Our Home
RSFSR	Russian Soviet Federated Socialist Republic
RUSMEDRON	Russian Mediterranean Squadron
SAM	surface-to-air missile
SDF	Japanese Self-Defence Force
SLBM	submarine-launched ballistic missile
SMF	Strategic Missile Force
SOVINDRON	Soviet Indian Ocean Squadron
SSBN	nuclear-powered ballistic missile submarine
SSGN	nuclear-powered guided missile submarine
SSK/SSN	nuclear-powered submarine
START	Strategic Arms Reduction Treaty
TMD	theatre missile defence (system)
UN	United Nations
US/USA	United States of America
USSR	Union of Soviet Socialist Republics
VTA	Military Transport Aviation
WOR	Women of Russia

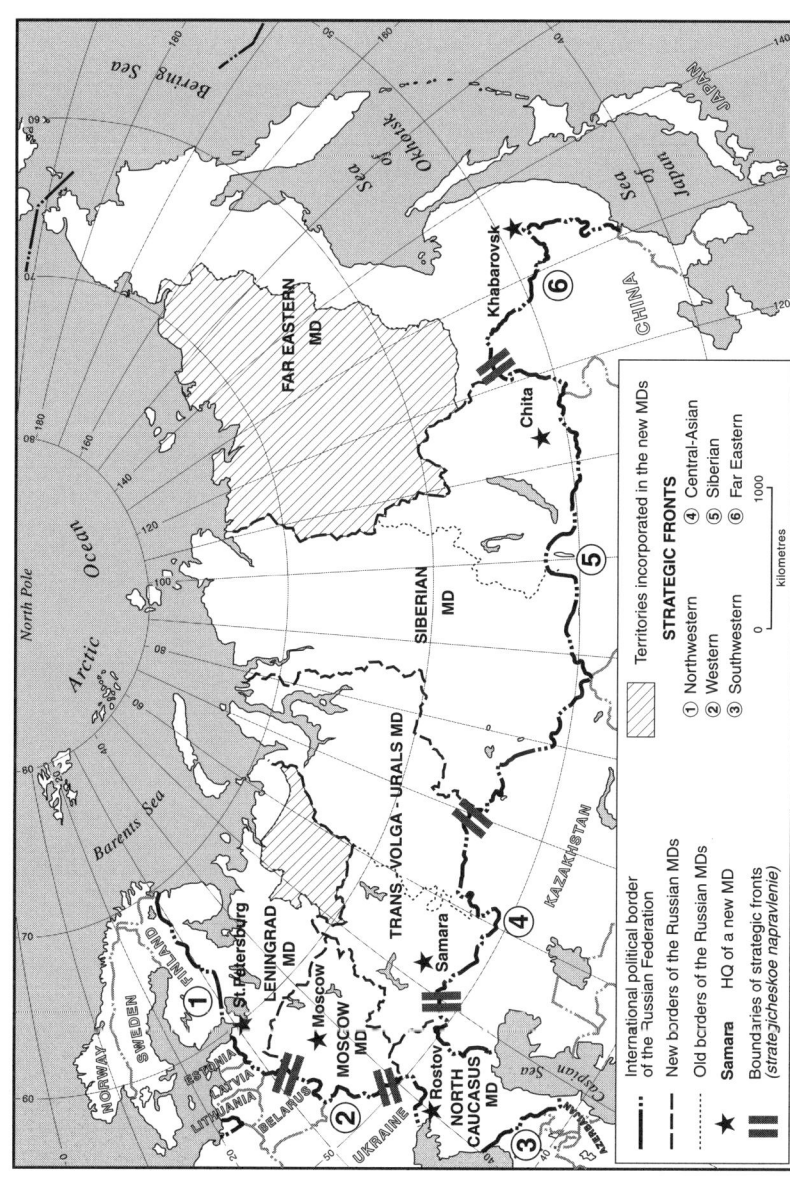

1. Military districts

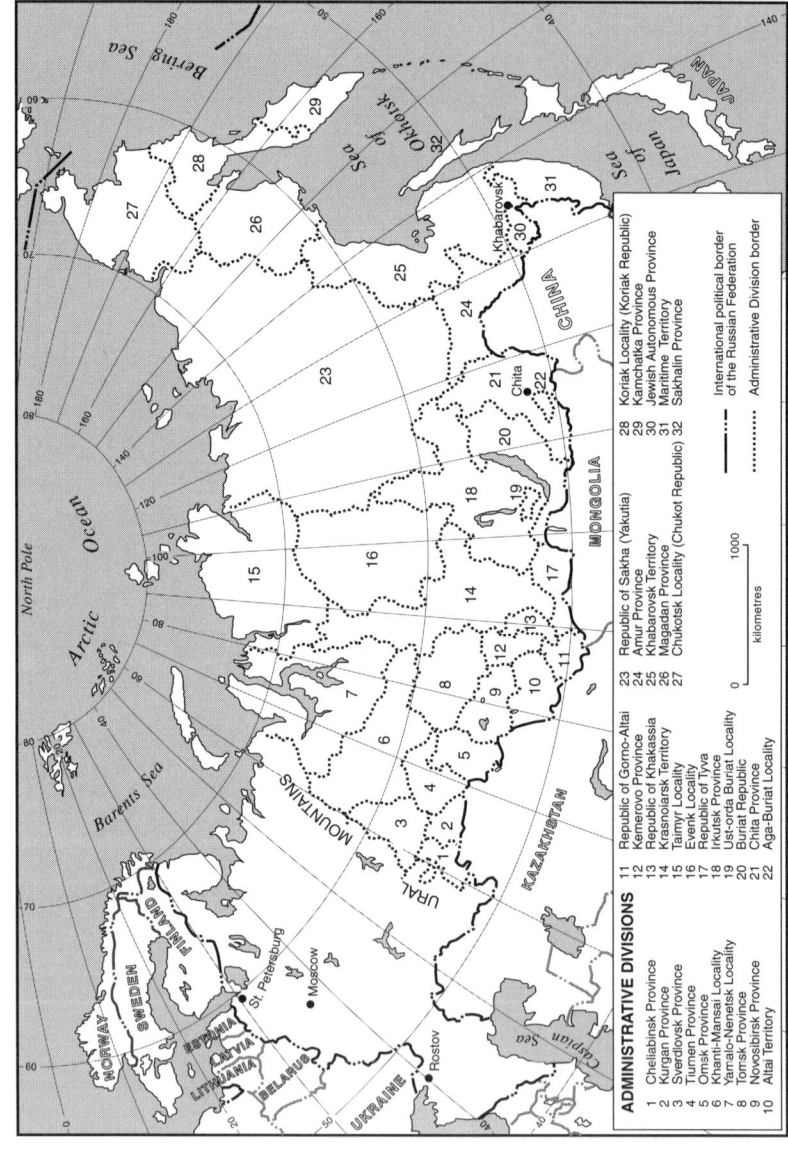

ADMINISTRATIVE DIVISIONS

1 Cheliabinsk Province
2 Kurgan Province
3 Sverdlovsk Province
4 Tiumen Province
5 Omsk Province
6 Khanti-Mansai Locality
7 Yamalo-Nenetsk Locality
8 Tomsk Province
9 Novosibirsk Province
10 Altai Territory

11 Republic of Gorno-Altai
12 Kemerovo Province
13 Republic of Khakassia
14 Krasnoiarsk Territory
15 Taimyr Locality
16 Evenk Locality
17 Republic of Tyva
18 Irkutsk Province
19 Ust-orda Buriat Locality
20 Buriat Republic
21 Chita Province
22 Aga-Buriat Locality

23 Republic of Sakha (Yakutia)
24 Amur Province
25 Khabarovsk Territory
26 Magadan Province
27 Chukotka Locality (Chukot Republic)

28 Koriak Locality (Koriak Republic)
29 Kamchatka Province
30 Jewish Autonomous Province
31 Maritime Territory
32 Sakhalin Province

———— International political border
of the Russian Federation

·········· Administrative Division border

0   1000
kilometres

2. **Administrative divisions of Russia east of the Urals**

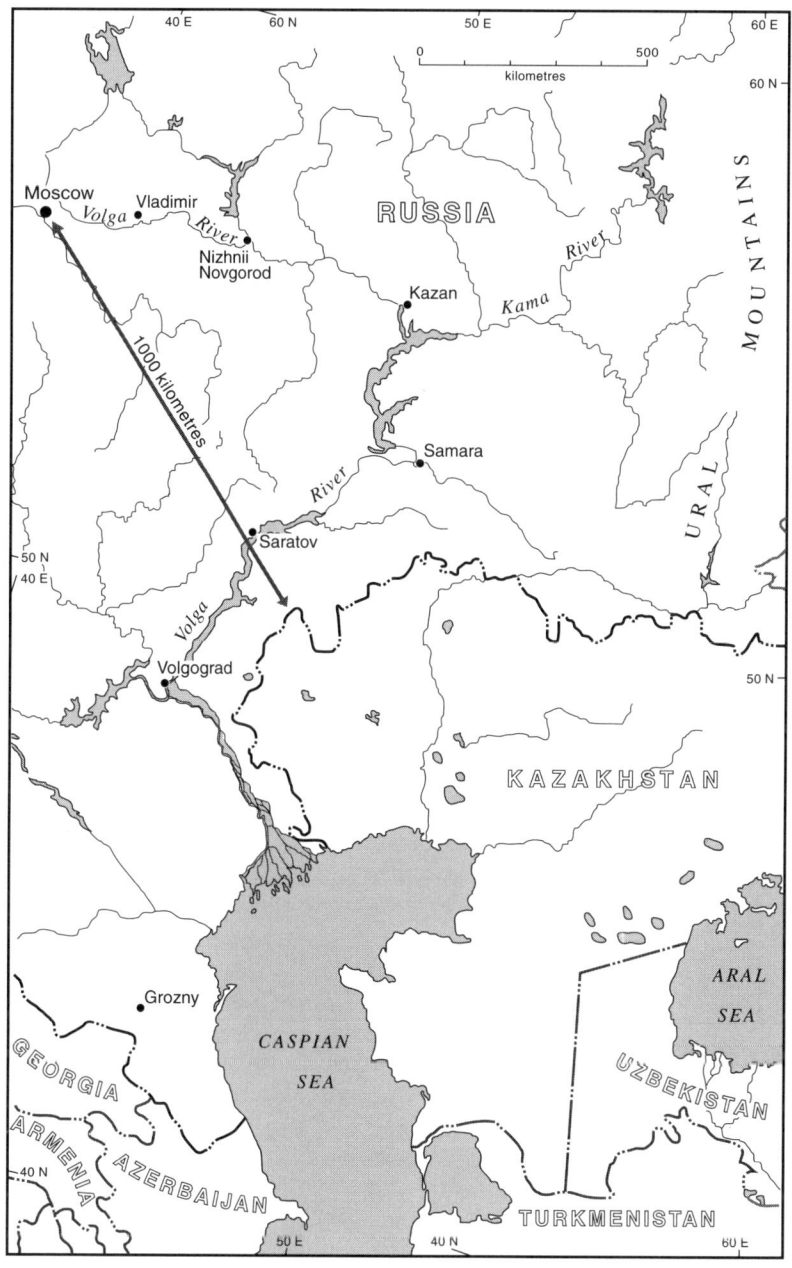

3. Heartland: the Volga Basin

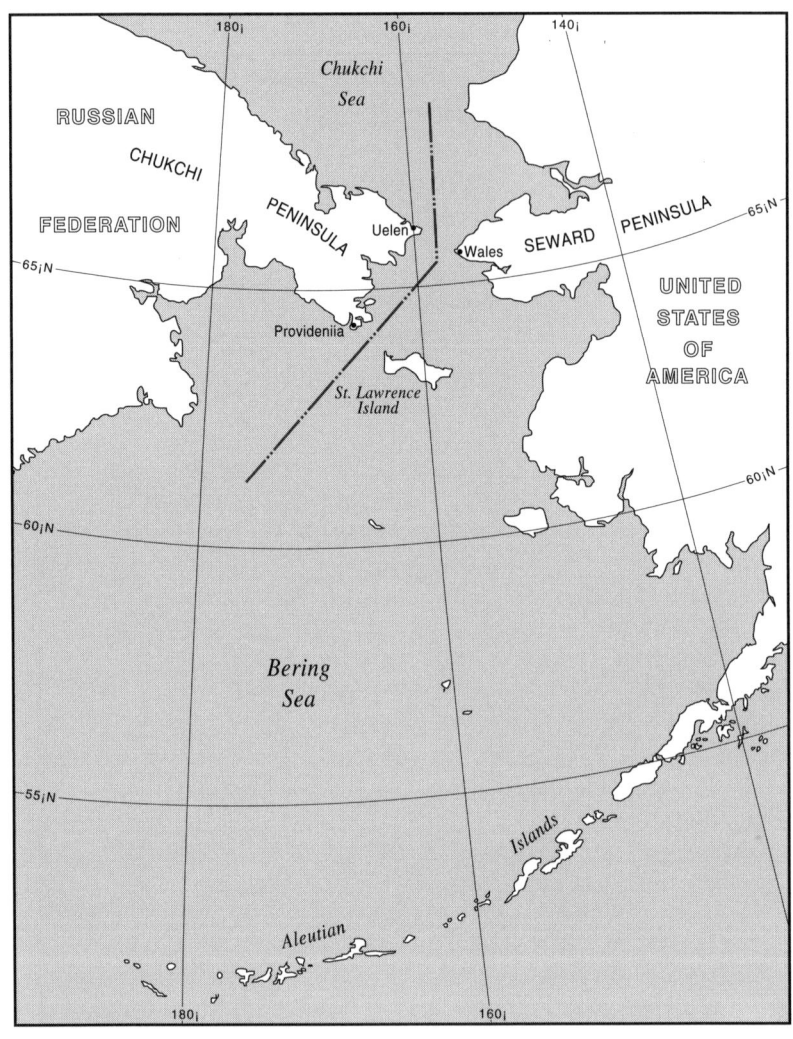

4. Russia–US maritime border

1

Russia: rebuilding the state, reconstituting the nation

When the mass terror and mass murder initiated by Iosif Stalin came to an end in 1953, his successors continued to rely on fear and repression. Several times in the three decades after 1953, Soviet leaders did contemplate some liberalisation of the political system but when it occurred, it did so slowly and fitfully, often with sharp regressions. Mikhail Gorbachev, who became leader of the Communist Party of the Soviet Union in 1985, began a new round of liberalisation that would bring about the collapse of his party and the state it ruled. This chapter reviews very briefly the history of the collapse of Communist Party power and the disintegration of the Union of Soviet Socialist Republics (USSR). It reviews the contest over a new national identity in the context of demographic, cultural, political, constitutional and economic considerations. This analysis pays close attention to the question of regionalism and the prospects for separatism in Russia. The final section of the chapter sketches very briefly some critical issues for the future of Russia: what happens in the transition to post-Yeltsin politics and what role the armed forces will play. This first chapter thus provides the framework against which subsequent chapters document and analyse the national strategic and military policies of Russia with particular reference to the Asia–Pacific region.

THE 1989 ELECTIONS: A DEMOCRATIC SURGE

In 1989, open and free elections came to Russia for the first time in seven decades. It could be argued that 'Russian politics was reborn'[1] but this is true more of popular participation in politics. Elite politics had been refined to the highest levels in the Soviet

1

era and the struggle between elite manipulation and popular participation would define domestic politics for the first decade of the new Russian state.

By gradually lifting the lid on criticism and providing for more free speech, Gorbachev provided a safer environment for popular participation in politics. No longer seized by the fear of life or limb, many Soviet citizens took up the challenge of politics with a passion. This was especially evident when Gorbachev provided for limited competition from non-Communists in the 1989 elections for the national parliament of the USSR, the Supreme Soviet. The leaders of the Communist Party believed that they could manipulate the elections largely for their own purposes of economic *perestroika* and limited political reform, but they unleashed a process which mortally wounded them. One of the techniques used by Gorbachev had been to promote *glasnost*,[2] a move designed to increase public discussion of local economic or political problems with a view to increasing pressure on officials to perform better. But the critique of the particular or local problems was so intense and so far-reaching that it became the critique of the national institutions which had created them.

The elections did not meet the Communist Party's expectations. Many leading Communists were defeated, replaced by non-Communist candidates with popular constituencies built on local issues or strong disaffection with the vagaries of Soviet life. The results disturbed the hitherto pro-Party allegiance of the Supreme Soviet. Communist leader Boris Yeltsin, by then expelled from the Politburo of the Party, won 90 per cent of the vote in the Moscow district of six million voters. The elections destroyed the paralysing effect of seventy years of totalitarian dictatorship. The results undermined the general conviction that political opposition to the Communist Party was futile and dangerous. Once this fundamental significance of the results was appreciated by many in the USSR, the 'country was rocked by an explosion of political activity'.[3] Many of the political alliances and ideologies active in Russia at the end of the 1990s sprang into existence in the immediate aftermath of the 1989 elections, before the collapse of the USSR.

This explosion of popular participation in politics enabled the Russian Republic, one of fifteen in the USSR, to deliver the fatal blow to Communist Party power. The end was expedited by a new spirit of anti-communism and democratisation that blossomed during complicated and protracted electoral processes for the republic-level legislature and local councils between December

1989 and May 1990. The campaigns in these elections over-whelmed existing Communist Party mechanisms designed to limit effective opposition. For example, the USSR Supreme Soviet did not lift the ban on non-Communist political parties until March 1990 after all candidates for the elections had registered, but this did not stop the eventual election of Yeltsin as Chairman of the Supreme Soviet of the Russian Republic.[4] He had become the focal point of anti-communism and the make-up of the Russian Republic's new parliament, also called the Supreme Soviet, was revolutionary in style, ideology and background.

On 12 June 1990, the Russian Supreme Soviet declared itself sovereign, but Yeltsin agreed to work together with the USSR government on a new treaty of federation for the USSR. From this point on, the political demise of the Communist Party was accom-panied by the political demise of the USSR as a sovereign state. The Baltic republics of Latvia, Lithuania and Estonia, which only became part of the USSR in August 1940, a year before they were occupied by the Nazis during the Second World War, had already postured vigorously for independence from Moscow. With the Russian Republic's declaration of independence, the union of republics crafted by Lenin in 1922 could not survive. The union fragmented with successive declarations of independence: Ukraine in July 1990, Tatarstan (part of the Russian Federation) in August, and the Dniester Moldavia Republic (Moldova) in September.

By December 1990, Gorbachev had called for a referendum on the future of the USSR. The referendum was held in March 1991 and recorded massive support for retention of a 'renewed federation of equal sovereign republics'.[5] In conjunction with the referendum on the future of the union, voters in the Russian Republic were asked, at Yeltsin's initiative, to approve the creation of a new post of President of the Russian Republic. The voters approved the new post, and Yeltsin won the resulting election on 12 June 1991 (the first anniversary of sovereignty) with 57.4 per cent of the vote.[6]

ANTI-DEMOCRACY: THE COUP OF AUGUST 1991

Within two weeks of Yeltsin's victory in the presidential election of the Russian Republic, and in advance of Gorbachev's foreshad-owed signature of a new union treaty, conservative forces in the Communist Party moved openly to depose Gorbachev. By 19 August, the conservatives resorted to military force in an

attempted coup under the leadership of a self-styled State Committee for the State of Emergency. The Committee comprised
some of the most powerful office-holders in the USSR—the Vice-
President, the Prime Minister, the chairman of the intelligence
service (the KGB), the Minister of Defence, the Minister of Internal
Affairs, and the deputy head of the Defence Council.[7] The aim of
the coup plotters was to restore the power of the Communist
Party, to restore the power of the central government of the USSR
over the republics, and to reverse other effects of political
liberalisation. The coup was defeated for a variety of reasons,
including the determination and clever political skills of people
like Yeltsin and his liberalising ally, Anatoly Sobchak, Mayor of
Leningrad; the depth of popular support for the targets of the coup,
such as Yeltsin and Sobchak; poor decision-making and command
by coup leaders after the coup was launched; and lack of resolve
from many senior and middle-ranking officers in the armed forces
to obey the coup orders when use of fatal force was ordered. One
study cites as an additional cause of the failure of the coup the
unfulfilled expectation by coup leaders that Party organisations
throughout the country would implement the emergency rule
with sufficient vigour to buttress the take-over in Moscow and
Leningrad.[8]

Before the coup was launched, Gorbachev was placed under
house arrest in Crimea and was denied communication with the
outside world. He remained there until the coup had been
defeated. He was therefore absent in action at the USSR's hour
of greatest crisis in several decades. By not having any hand in
the defeat of the coup, Gorbachev had been sidelined in the new
Russian politics. Moreover, the new union treaty which Gorbachev
had been planning to sign before the coup provided for a substantial reduction in the powers of the central USSR government, and
this reflected the decline of his personal authority even before the
coup.

RUSSIA AFTER 1991: TERRITORY, STATE, PEOPLE AND IDENTITY

Yeltsin, using the authority derived from his opposition to the
August coup and his position as the directly elected head of the
government of the Russian Republic, confronted the authority of
the central Soviet government head-on. In front of a national and
international television audience, Yeltsin mounted a vigorous

personal attack on Gorbachev face to face during a 'welcome back' meeting for Gorbachev on his return to Moscow from house arrest. In this move of masterful opportunism, Yeltsin destroyed Gorbachev's position, and along with it most remnants of central authority. By 1 December, people in Ukraine had voted for independence, rumours of a new coup attempt to restore Soviet power were mounting, and the union treaty which had been developed under Gorbachev's leadership was looking hopelessly inadequate.[9]

On 8 December 1991, the elected leaders of the three predominantly Slavic republics—Russia, Ukraine and Belarus—moved to dissolve the former union and create a new one. Meeting at Belovezh near Minsk in Belarus,[10] and having excluded Gorbachev, the three leaders agreed to form a new Commonwealth of Independent States (CIS) open to all former republics of the USSR.[11] This agreement formalised the independence of the former republics and the collapse of the central authority of the USSR government[12] but the Soviet central government took another three weeks to dissolve itself.

The three leaders meeting in Belovezh had quite differing presumptions of the relationships between Russia and the other republics.[13] In Russia, there was still some hope that it could retain a union in which it was 'more equal' than the other former union republics. A series of meetings and declarations ensued in subsequent weeks. On 21 December 1991, eight of the other twelve former republics joined the three founding members of the CIS to issue the Alma Ata Declaration which asserted complete equality for all members. The eight joining were the five Central Asian union republics, two of the Transcaucasus union republics, and Moldova.[14] Georgia and the three Baltic republics (Latvia, Lithuania and Estonia) were not signatories. By 25 December 1991, Gorbachev resigned from his post as President of the USSR and on 26 December the upper house of the USSR parliament (Soviet of the Republics of the Supreme Soviet) declared that the USSR no longer existed.[15] On 30 December 1991, the heads of state of the eleven CIS members signed a provisional agreement forming a council of heads of state and a council of heads of government. The agreement sought to put in place a basic framework for coordinating policy, but the future role and functions of the CIS would remain the focal point of intense political competition to the present day.

The Alma Ata Declaration registered common agreement that Russia would take the USSR's seat in both the General Assembly and the Security Council of the United Nations. Ukraine and

Belarus had been original members of the UN, and all three agreed to work toward obtaining full UN membership for the other signatories as independent, sovereign states. Through this process, but only after considerable difference of opinion both in the former USSR and in the international community, Russia became the successor state to the USSR in treaties, rights and obligations. These obligations included the foreign debts of the central government of the USSR, and the rights included the debts of foreign countries and foreign corporations owed to the USSR.

At the end of December 1991, Moscow was demoralised and confused. The country in whose name the people had suffered so much and to which they had given so much had ceased to exist almost overnight. The former international empire of the Soviet Union, the Warsaw Pact, had collapsed in 1989 along with the Berlin Wall, after a series of revolts and democratic elections. Millions of Russians were stranded in other republics and other Warsaw Pact countries. Many people were confused as to their new citizenship status, particularly those with parents of differing nationalities. The old values of Soviet society had already been swept aside by the leadership, and many of the people were struggling to catch up. The emergence of Western European style television in previous years had helped spread the morals revolution in a way that horrified many Soviet citizens. The former leaders of the USSR, ministers, deputy ministers and an entire civil service of the USSR had no clear future. Food was scarce, with suburban supermarkets carrying only two or three items. Milk and cheese were only available through special delivery, usually about every ten days to two weeks, and sausage would appear in the supermarkets about once a week. Salaries were not being paid, and where they were being paid, their value had been severely eroded by inflation. Most families had to live on their wits and their connections to feed themselves. They did so reasonably well, in a way that belied the extreme shortages of food in public outlets. Many pensioners without other means of support were nearly destitute because their stipend (fixed at Soviet rates) had long since lost the race with inflation. Old grandmothers lined the exits of some metro stations selling the last saleable, or not so saleable item from their houses to buy the next meal. The much-heralded humanitarian aid delivered from the USA and other Western countries, in which many Muscovites had placed considerable hope, had failed to solve the problems. Hyper-depression was setting in.[16] The decline in GDP in 1992 would reach 15 per cent.[17]

The transition for Russia was not going to be easy. The slate could not be wiped clean. There was an extremely bitter history to deal with, along with a complex web of economic and social relationships. The Russian Republic had all along positioned itself as the most powerful republic at the centre of the union and had presided over production specialisation in its former partner republics. With the collapse of the USSR, inter-republic trade relations on which all were highly dependent also collapsed. Foreign policy and security policy, including questions of owner-ship of the former Soviet armed forces, all had to be determined anew. Most importantly, many who rebelled in 1991 to finally defeat the USSR in its battle with Russian independence did not see themselves as revolutionaries until the coup attempt of 1991 began. They had no plans for the future, only a clear consciousness of what they opposed. The revolution of 1991 had been an ad hoc radicalisation of a program of gradual liberalisation, for which there had been little detail, little community consultation, and therefore no broad social consensus. It was a multi-dimensional 'insurgency',[18] a 'chaotic revolution from below' that had co-opted an impulse for reform from the regime.[19]

But the revolution did have some vision of a way forward, even if it was unelaborated: it was for Russia to be a normal, civilised country with a mixed economy.[20] The revolution marked the return to Russian politics of a philosophy of hope and a commitment to enlightened government that had eluded the people of Russia for most of the previous seven decades. But hope, like principle, is only a beacon in the distance. There were so many competing visions of the new Russia and of the princi-ples of social and economic organisation that the steps of 1991 into a new statehood for Russia were steps into the eye of a typhoon.

As one of the best studies on the new Russia has suggested, the events of 1991 may not have been a revolution as much as they were a 'devolution', representing the 'disintegration of the social order rather than its revolutionary transformation'.[21] The disintegration meant that in many respects the collapse of the USSR created fifteen cleared lots of territory on which struc-tures and social contracts of new states would be the subject of political contestation for a long time. Russia was to be just one of many states across this large part of the world occupied by the former USSR which would suffer the pangs of national reformation.

Territory and demographics

The Russian Federation inherited about 75 per cent of the territory of the former USSR (see Map 2). While this makes it bigger
than any other European state, most of the territory ruled from
Moscow is in Asia (about 75 per cent). Russia occupies about
one-eighth of the land territory on the planet. It shares land
borders along 20 139 km with fourteen states,[22] and has a coastline of 37 653 km.[23] Russia shares maritime borders with some of
its land neighbours but also with the USA and Japan. With the
break-up of the USSR, Russia was faced with a number of border
issues to resolve with former Soviet republics. It was in dispute
with Ukraine over the Crimean peninsula, which the Russian
Republic of the USSR had ceded to the Ukrainian Republic in
1954. Estonia claimed over 2000 sq km of territory under Russian
control, and Latvia disputed ownership of a portion of territory
ceded in 1944 to the USSR. Russia also had maritime boundary
issues to settle in the Caspian Sea.

In population size, Russia is the fifth-biggest country in the
world, after China, India, the USA and Indonesia. Russia retained
about 50 per cent of the population of the former USSR and much
of the community diversity. According to 1989 census data, Russia
had a population of 147 million,[24] of which 120 million identified
themselves as of Russian 'nationality'. In the USSR, the designation of 'nationality' was contrived as part of the central
government's efforts to control the huge diversity of community
groups inside the borders of the country. Outside the USSR, an
equivalent term might be 'ethnic group'. Some ten million people
in Russia identified their nationality in terms of other states
outside Russia, such as Ukraine (4 million), Germany (842 000),
Kazakhs (636 000) or Koreans (107 000). The remaining 17 million
non-Russians identified themselves with a nationality that did not
coincide with a sovereign state.

When Russia was one of the fifteen union republics of the
USSR, it was a multinational, federated state comprising a large
number of administrative units of several types: municipalities,
provinces, and minority nationality units either called republics
or autonomous regions. Russia was formally constituted as the
Russian Soviet Federated Socialist Republic (RSFSR). Even today,
strictly speaking, Russia as a political community is not the same
as the Russian Federation. At independence, the Russian Federation had 31 separate republics or autonomous regions outside the
territory of provinces or municipalities that are considered to be

'Russian', and another 11 nationalities with other forms of territorial autonomy. Few governments or writers acknowledge this distinction between Russia and the Russian Federation and use, as this book does, the term Russia interchangeably with the Russian Federation.

As mentioned above, a large number of 'Russians' were left living outside their country's borders in former republics of the USSR. In 1989, 25 million Russians, or 17 per cent of those who registered as of Russian nationality, lived in other Soviet republics. Table 1.1 gives some indication of the relative size of Russian communities in 1989. Although there has been considerable migration of Russians from the former republics, particularly the non-Slav republics, many Russians remained in the non-Slav republics, and these communities provide a continuing point of purchase for the Russian Federation over domestic politics in some of the newly independent states, and a source of serious political contention in others. At the very least, these Russian populations provide both a pretext and a potential fifth column for those political groups in the Russian Federation who harbour desires of restoring the Soviet Union or at least some new Russian empire on the territory of the old USSR.

Table 1.1 Republic populations self-identifying as Russian in 1989

Republic	Share of population (per cent)	Estimated total
Kazakhstan	37.8	6 227 000
Latvia	34.0	1 122 000
Estonia	30.3	474 000
Ukraine	22.1	11 355 000
Kyrgyzstan	21.5	916 000
Belarus	13.2	1 342 000
Moldova	13.0	562 000
Turkmenistan	9.5	333 000
Lithuania	9.4	344 000
Uzbekistan	8.3	1 653 000
Tajikistan	7.6	388 000
Georgia	6.3	341 000
Azerbaijan	5.6	391 000
Armenia	1.6	51 000

Russian identity: cultural and political

After the collapse of the USSR, there was serious competition within Russia for a new national identity, although this occurred mainly in the largest cities. As one writer observed in early 1992, the new Russia was 'in search of the very fundamentals of

statehood: frontiers, legitimacy, national identity, political institutions, and an economic system'.[25] A variety of groups emerged
who claimed to know and speak for the authentic Russian identity. The competing visions of this national identity were not as
simple as one might imagine. The Soviet period had created a
new vision of a Russian multinational identity (*rossiiskoe*, based
on the multinational, great power state of *Rossiia*), an identity
quite distinct from the medieval concept of *russkoe* (originating
in the Kievan state of Rus' in what is now Ukraine).[26]

The Russian Federated Republic set up under the Communist
regime embraced a diversity of communities each with such sharp
'national' identifications that a monochromatic national identity
was impossible. There was not a Russian community identity in
1991 in the same way as there existed a Ukrainian, Lithuanian
or Kazakh identity. These non-Russian communities subjugated
in the USSR had fought hard to retain a national identity, and
had in fact been supported by the Soviet state in doing so. For
these non-Russians, their nationality may have received its sharpest definition in their 'non-Russianness'. For those of Russian
nationality—which had been regarded as the leader of the nationalities in the USSR—there was confusion between 'Russianness'
and 'Soviet nationality'.

Nevertheless, most Russians had strong views of their
Russianness based on their very rich cultural heritage. A strong
sense of a Russian national myth had been perpetuated in the
notion that the Russian nationality was first among equals, both
in the former Soviet Union and within the Russian Federation. It
was to this national myth, or at least to variants of it, that
Russian citizens turned as the new state emerged. The variants
of the myth included the Orthodox church, folk culture, and
internationally recognised achievements in classical and modern
art, music, literature and the theatre. But there was also the more
recent history of the Great Patriotic War (1941–45), which most
people had absorbed as part of the national myth, which had once
been Soviet but was not going to be abandoned in new mythol-
ogies of the nation. That war had been the Russian nation's
greatest victory and its greatest tragedy.[27]

While the competition for a new Russian national identity at
first took on the appearance of salon debates of the early twenti-
eth century in which the Russian intelligentsia of the day had
taken much pride, a 'life and death' political struggle soon
emerged for a new constitutional foundation for Russia. Who
would rule the new Russia and on what terms? The struggle over

national identity was closely related to the war over an appropriate domestic political order for the new Russia. And here Russia was not well placed. As Rigby has pointed out, the socio-economic foundations which supported successful transitions from totalitarianism to democracy in Spain, Portugal and Chile did not exist in Russia. They had to be 'created at the same time as democracy itself' and 'in a context where not even the national basis of the state' was agreed.[28]

The first major battle in this war over what sort of state the new Russia would be was won by Yeltsin in October 1993 after long, bitter campaigns, and only after his resort to violence to end a stand-off between him (the elected President of the former RSFSR) and the parliament elected in 1989. Yeltsin had dismissed the parliament because it had become dominated by former Communists and other conservatives opposed to his radical programs. As a result of this violent confrontation, a new constitution was adopted and the 'first genuine multi-party elections' were held in Russia.[29]

When the new Constitution was approved in 1993, the authorities laid down in the preamble important markers for what they saw as elements of the desirable new national identity, but the proposed identity was sufficiently broad to contain something for most political forces in Russia—Communists and ultra-nationalists, as well as liberal democrats:

> We, the multinational people of the Russian Federation,
> united by a common destiny on our land,
> asserting human rights and freedoms and civil peace and concord,
> preserving historically established state unity,
> . . .
> revering the memory of our forebears who passed down to us love and respect for the Fatherland and faith in goodness and justice,
> reviving the sovereign statehood of Russia and asserting the immutability of its democratic foundations,
> seeking to ensure the well-being and prosperity of Russia,
> proceeding from our responsibility for our homeland to present and future generations,
> recognising ourselves as part of the world community . . . [30]

Above all else, what would most distinguish the new Russia from the USSR was what distinguished communism from all other major political ideologies—its view on private property. The Communist notion of a just society delivered by community or state ownership of the means of production was simply thrown out of the window. This was not the intended outcome of the top-down revolution in the USSR that Gorbachev had initiated with the goal of restructuring economic relations. He never imagined that his program would mean wholesale privatisation of the massive state ownership system. In the USSR, all industrial production was conducted by state enterprises, and up to 30 per cent of those had an absolute monopoly in their field of production—no other enterprise produced what they did.[31] In some specific industrial sectors, the degree of absolute monopoly was even higher—87 per cent of enterprises in machine-building were the sole producer of their output.[32]

The new government would base its turn away from the command economy to a market economy on its view of the need to liberate productive forces. The first tool of this process would be to provide new opportunities for personal wealth arising from personal ownership of the means of production. Personal ownership would take two forms: exclusive ownership or shared ownership (ranging from a simple partnership to joint stock companies). Beginning in June 1992, Russia began a program of privatisation of industrial enterprises. This encountered a variety of political obstacles and setbacks, but by September 1994, 80 per cent of the industrial workforce was employed in privatised enterprises.

A number of studies have concluded that the privatisation benefited those who held political power under Yeltsin, many of whom had held leading positions under the former Soviet regime—the *nomenklatura*.[33] One writer observed that lack of government control and supervision of the process 'allowed a small group of economic managers and nomenklatura capitalists to seize the lion's share of state property'.[34] One of the early Ministers of Privatisation was Anatoly Chubais, who subsequently became one of the most powerful men in Russia, presumably in part because of links he developed in his ministerial capacity. Former Prime Minister Viktor Chernomyrdin was also identified as a beneficiary of privatisation of state assets over which he had held control.

The impact of the process of theft of state property by the most powerful seriously undermined the legitimacy of the Yeltsin government. It also seriously undermined the credibility and legitimacy of efforts to rebuild a legal system which had all but collapsed. The criminality which emerged in society at large had been matched by the criminality of some of its leaders. In 1998, a committee of the State Duma recommended the parliament take greater control over privatisations of strategic industries in the light of a Duma investigation into possible illegalities in the privatisation of some of the country's biggest mineral enterprises, most of which are east of the Urals, and include the big oil conglomerates, Tiumen Oil and Sibneft.[35] The committee's concerns related to arbitrary exclusion of bidders and sale of shares below value, resulting in a net estimated loss to the state of US$2.7 billion.

Privatisation of agricultural land only began on 27 October 1993, when a presidential decree legalised the buying and selling of agricultural land for the first time in six decades.[36] Housing and other real estate were also privatised in these years and, in the absence of a highly developed legal system for the transfer and registration of titles, this process was open to grave abuse as well. In a number of cases, long-time residents were killed or forcibly removed from their apartments by criminal gangs wanting control of the property.

The second essential difference between the USSR and the emerging new Russia was a widely accepted need to re-order the relationship between the rights of the individual person in relation to the exercise of state power (though this reform has not been so readily accepted as privatisation and the restoration of individual property rights). The emergence of democratic liberalism in Russia after 1991 had taken place under the influence of 'nomenklatura politics', with former beneficiaries of the Soviet system as the main players. Freedom of speech and genuinely multi-party elections in 1993 have led to the emergence of effective pluralism and mass participation. The 1993 Constitution provides protections of the individual person similar to those found in the English *Magna Carta*, the British Bill of Rights, and their US counterparts. But so too did the 1977 Soviet Constitution. But as in any society, access to the most effective instruments of political power is heavily influenced by access to economic resources.

Thus, while the vision of a just society based on the rule of law is enshrined in the 1993 Constitution, the rule of law in Russia for most of the 1990s has been particularly weak. The influence of organised crime gangs has been one of the most serious problems, and the degree of entrenchment of this problem was illustrated in a late 1997 report that the Deputy Minister of the Interior would personally join 170 law enforcement officers already conducting investigations at one of the country's biggest auto manufacturing plants, Avtovaz in Togliatti, to recoup

2.85 trillion rubles in unpaid taxes, and to break the grip of mafia gangs on the factory, a situation which had resulted in 65 deaths of mafia figures or Avtovaz executives. The resulting investigation had led to charges for 29 murders and 217 other crimes, with more than 300 people charged.[37] Human rights abuses in Russia remain quite serious although they do not occur on anything near the scale that existed under the Soviet regime.[38]

Ideas among the people in Russia about the type of state they see themselves living in are varied but these have not moved as sharply from those of the Soviet era as the constitution suggests. This is reflected in continued support among a majority of voters, as demonstrated in election results and opinion polls, for older visions of a welfare state in which public order and personal security are dictated from above, and can be taken for granted. Most voters in Russia do not like the insecurity of having to compete for jobs in a deteriorating free market economy, and most do not like the threats to public order that have accompanied the free market reforms and the democratic liberalisation in the decade since 1989.

As the new Russian state was coming into existence and the Soviet order crumbled, the people of Russia and the Yeltsin administration had to make choices about national symbols, such as a flag, coat of arms, national anthem and possibly a state religion. These choices were made by the government, perhaps with a keen sense of what symbols might be commonly enough known to have some unifying power but certainly without any popular consultation. The choice of symbols was subsequently ratified in the plebiscite on the 1993 Constitution. Yeltsin's administration favoured a return to the past. The new flag and coat of arms were borrowed from imperial Russia. Elements of the flag of Russia under the tsars had survived anyway in the flag of the Russian Federated Republic of Soviet rule. The new coat of arms was the double-headed eagle of the tsars, complete with the crowns over each head.

In making these choices, it is not clear whether the government was considering the problems that potentially went with them. By casting back to these emblems, and by reviving a number of tsarist ceremonial devices, the Yeltsin administration was setting the scene for other groups to style themselves on tsarist-era models. One extreme right group, *Pamiat'*, styled itself on the 'Black Hundreds' or 'Black Companies' of pre-revolutionary Russia who were known for vicious attacks on Jews. But there were probably few other choices. National symbols must have some recognition factor and they must say something about the history of the nation. It is unlikely that any totally new symbols would have had any unifying effect at a time when Russians felt desperately in need of social cohesion.

In the bid to find national symbols, the Russian government rushed rather quickly to hold up the Russian Orthodox Church as a central national institution, because there was not much else to hold on to as a unifying force. The church itself responded as rapidly, keen to reassert the role it had held under the tsars. The rush to rebuild the Church of Christ the Saviour in central Moscow adjacent to the Kremlin, a church which had been demolished along with thousands of others under Stalin, was a sign of the new life found by the church after 1991. This close link between the church and the government has been demonstrated in several ways subsequently, not least in the 1997 decision by President Yeltsin, on the urging of the Russian Orthodox Church, to curb the activities of some 'foreign' religions in Russia. Yeltsin's move was clearly in violation of the Constitution.[39] Yet the church itself has an identity crisis, demonstrated in its insecurity in the face of foreign religions. Many Russians remain atheists, their inheritance from seven decades of Soviet rule, and not all Christians support the Orthodox Church, which was seriously tainted by its association with the Soviet regime, in particular its often very close association with the KGB.[40]

But the Yeltsin administration did not have exclusive rights to set a new national vision for the country behind which all citizens could unite. The search for a unifying national vision remains bitterly contested. If the formation of party blocs in the national parliament is a guide, there are five main visions of the new Russia: communist, social democrat, authoritarian nationalist, centre-right (statist or pragmatic nationalist), and liberal democrat. Table 1.2 shows the state of support for these parties in the share of votes cast in the 1995 State Duma elections.

All of these groups have considerable internal divisions and the loyalties of many individual members on a range of issues cannot be taken for granted. Only one of these parties, the Communist Party (CP), has possessed a nation-wide structure since 1991 and by 1994 few of these parties had participated in local elections.[42] Many parties have been organised around prominent political figures rather than a nation-wide membership or national structure. After 1993, the vision of reunifying the former USSR all but dissipated as an electorally significant issue.[43] Nationalism, often identified outside Russia as a possible impulse

Table 1.2 1995 State Duma elections—results by bloc and party

	(percentage share of votes cast)[41]	
Communist-aligned parties (C)	32.22	
Communist Party of Russian Federation		22.31
Working Russia		4.52
Agrarian Party of Russia		3.78
Authoritarian Nationalist parties (AN)	19.70	
Liberal Democratic Party of Russia		11.06
Congress of Russian Societies		4.29
Socialist Democrat parties (SD)	15.49	
Women of Russia		4.60
Party of Workers' Self-Management		4.01
Centre-Right parties (CR)	10.75	
Russia Our Home		9.89
Liberal-Democrat Parties (LD)	13.60	
Apple		6.93
Democratic Choice		3.90

for a belligerent and destabilising Russian foreign policy, now works itself out in national politics largely through a reasonably stabilised set of major political parties, even as one of these parties, the Liberal Democratic Party of Vladimir Zhirinovski, and minor fringe groups continue to act in domestic politics as a destabilising or unsettling source of ultra-nationalist agitation.

The Communist Party of the Russian Federation (CPRF), the most important communist party, is the direct successor to the Communist Party of the Soviet Union (CPSU), the party of Lenin, Stalin and Gorbachev. The CPRF is also the former party of Yeltsin and most others of his generation still active in politics. After Yeltsin's abolition in 1991 of the leading organs of the CPSU, such as the Politburo and Central Committee, was confirmed by the Constitutional Court in late 1992, the CPRF was able to rebuild itself on the rump organisational structure left intact by the court decision. It was also tremendously advantaged in the political struggle in a number of ways. It could 'draw on reserves of organisational and political experience matched by no other' party.[44] But just as importantly, there were many in Russia who still believed that the Communist Party, such as it was and had been, was the Russian way. For many, this was a fatalistic acceptance of the past; for others, it was protection of privilege; and for others, it was a commitment to the goals of communism, understood as rejection of private capitalism. The platform of the CPRF (still) holds that the 'capitalist mode of production has reached its natural limits'.[45] The 1995 CPRF program calls for 'balanced development of productive forces', 'qualitative transformation of outmoded models of production and utilisation', and a 'radical review of the system of social values and priorities of economic growth'.[46] The CPRF has opposed the principle of separation of powers which is written into the Constitution and favours a dominant legislature over the current provision in the Constitution for a dominant President.[47] Other communist-aligned parties include Working Russia, the Agrarian Party of Russia and Power to the People.

The broad support for the CPRF and its strong position have been reflected in increasingly impressive election results. The CPRF candidate scored 32 per cent support in the first round of the presidential ballot in 1996, and 40 per cent support in the second round; and the Party registered 22 per cent support in the 1995 State Duma elections compared with 14 per cent in 1993 elections. (For comparisons with the performance of other parties, see Tables 1.3, 1.4, 1.5.) The CPRF has clearly changed its platform to reflect the revolution in Russia and widespread hostility to CPSU rule over seven decades. One hard-line group, the Russian Communist Workers' Party, refused to rejoin the CPRF because the latter had adopted so-called 'social democratic' policies.[48]

Table 1.3 State Duma elections 1993 and 1995 national lists

Party	(percentage share of votes cast)	
	1993[49]	1995[50]
Communist Party of Russian Federation (C)	12.40	22.7
Liberal Democratic Party of Russia (N)	22.92	11.4
Russia Our Home (CR)	–	10.3
Apple (LD)	7.86	7.0
Agrarian Party of Russia (C)	7.99	3.8
Women of Russia (SR)	8.13	4.7
Russia's Choice (LD)	15.51	3.9

Table 1.4 State Duma number of seats by party after 1993 and 1995 elections[51]

Party	1993	1995
Communist Party of Russian Federation (C)	45	157
Liberal Democratic Party of Russia (N)	64	51
Russia Our Home (CR)	–	55
Apple (LD)	25	45
Agrarian Party of Russia (C)	55	20
Women of Russia (SR)	23	3
Russia's Choice (LD)	76	9
Other	162	110

Table 1.5 Results in presidential elections 1996 first and second rounds

Candidate	First round share	Second round share
Boris Yeltsin	35.28	53.82
Gennady Ziuganov	32.03	40.31
Aleksandr Lebed	14.52	–
Grigory Yavlinski	7.34	–
Vladimir Zhirinovski	5.70	–
For others or against both	5.13	4.83 against

The principal party in the authoritarian nationalist bloc is Vladimir Zhirinovski's Liberal Democratic Party of Russia (LDPR).[52] Gains by the Communist Party have eaten into support for the LDPR, whose share of the vote and share of seats declined between the 1993 and 1995 State Duma elections. The social democrat parties have two principal parties—Women of Russia (WOR), whose fortunes declined in the 1995 elections, and the Party of Workers' Self-Management (PWS). There at least eight other small parties or groups which together account for more electoral support than either WOR or PWS. Almost all electoral support for centre-right (statist) politics is taken by the party called Russia Our Home (ROH). The liberal democrat vote has been led by the Apple group, followed by Democratic Choice of Russia (DCR). There are a large number of independents in the State Duma. A former general in the armed forces, Aleksandr Lebed, who contested the 1996 presidential election and came third in the first round, formed his own political movement called Honour and Conscience (*chest' i sovest'*), which has campaigned on fairly vague policies of law and order, social discipline and support for the general trend of marketisation and cooperative policies with major Western powers.[53] After the first round of voting in the 1996 presidential election, Lebed and Yeltsin formed an alliance to ensure defeat of the Communist candidate in the second round.

State structure

The state structure of the new Russian Federation retains a number of structural features in common with the former Russian Soviet Federated Socialist Republic (RSFSR) when it was one of the 15 republics making up the USSR. For example, the boundaries of the 89 constituent parts of the Federation are much the same. But there have been important substantive and philosophical modifications in the state structure since the declaration of sovereignty on 12 June 1990.

The 1993 Constitution is explicitly rooted in the principle of separation of powers, with each branch (legislative, executive and judicial) guaranteed 'independence'. Provision is made for a Constitutional Court, as well as a Supreme Court, the latter being the highest court for the hearing of criminal, civil and administrative cases. In Article 80, the Constitution provides for a very powerful President,[54] who is 'guarantor of the Constitution . . . and of human and civil rights and freedoms'; who 'determines the basic guidelines of the state's domestic and foreign policy'; who is head of state and the leader in national security policy. Article 87 makes the President commander-in-chief of the armed forces. Legislation passed by the parliament can be vetoed by the President, but the veto can be overturned if two-thirds of the total number of deputies in the lower house vote for the rejected bill again (Article 107.3).

The Constitution provides for a bicameral parliament, called the Federal Assembly, made up of two chambers—a lower house, the State Duma, with 450 deputies, and an upper house, the Federation Council, with 180 members, made up of two representatives from each of the 89 component units of Russia, one representative of the Federal Assembly and one from the President. The term of the State Duma is set in the Constitution, while the 'procedure for forming the Federation Council' is established in federal laws, not in the Constitution (Article 96). In the Federation Council, the two representatives of each of the 89 units were elected until 1995 when a law was introduced making the governor of each of the 89 administrative units and the head of its legislature the two representatives for each unit.[55]

The State Duma has an effective system of committees and several of these address national security or foreign policy: committees on Defence, on Security, on International Affairs, on CIS Relations, and on Geopolitical Questions. The committees on Budget, Taxes, Banking and Finance and on Industry, Construction, Transport and Energy also address issues that affect foreign and defence policy.

Relations between the various arms of the Russian government are not stable, as various political forces struggle to exploit whatever position of power they might occupy. For example, as of 1997, there were disputes over the role of the upper house, the Council of the Federation, in amending the annual budget; and over the relationship between local municipal councils and their regional administrations (province, territory or locality).[56] There was a dispute over how governors of 'regions' should be elected by their component parts where the region is made up of two or more provinces, territories, or localities.[57] It will take several decades at least for the letter of the Constitution to be settled by the force of time-honoured convention. This struggle to define constitutional convention will be an important source of political tension regardless of the best will of the contending parties.

Separatism and regionalism within Russia

In its first decade as a sovereign country, Russia's federal structure has been a major source of political friction, leverage and competition. The outcome of the political contest over the status of regions or over the form of relations between Moscow and the regions will be central to the political future of Russia and its prosperity. In the politics of creating the Russian state on a ramshackle core of the collapsed Soviet super-state, most communities in Russia outside the big cities were very suspicious of the Kremlin. These communities began to rediscover their roots in their localities and to see their futures as tied up with the destiny of their locality.[58] But even before the final collapse, in each phase of the political struggle under Gorbachev, the regions had become important allies for one side or the other. Those vying for power in Moscow had to win the loyalties of the constituent parts, particularly the most powerful.[59] In their battle with each other, Yeltsin and Gorbachev contributed rather flagrantly to a process of regionalisation, with Yeltsin inviting the regions to 'take as much sovereignty as they could swallow', and Gorbachev holding out the prospect of making some regions into new union republics.[60] In Russia now, the opportunistic exploitation of regionalism for unrelated political advantage remains one of the most important political tactics.

The difficult relations between the federal government in Moscow and the regions is due in part to the way in which political and economic structures were set up in the Soviet period. But the more important cause of dispute since 1991 has been the collapse of political authority and legitimacy of the central government in Moscow, a process which has denied the multinational Russia any sort of smooth transition as a unified territorial entity. In the same way that Russia or Lithuania had declared itself sovereign (and therefore independent of Soviet central power), so too did a number of constituent parts of Russia declare their sovereignty, independence or autonomy, or promote themselves to 'republic' status within the Russian federation.

One substantial motive force for the growing regionalism in the country was nationalism in some of the 'nationality' republics of the Federation. This force that had led union republics of the former USSR to press for greater independence from Moscow and which led to the collapse of the USSR did not stop at the border of Russia. This nationalism has proved to be just as virulent in some places inside the Russian Federation, reaching its most violent form in the civil war in Chechnia, one of six Muslim nationality republics of the Russian Federation inside its southern border adjacent to the newly independent state of Georgia (see Map 5).

Between mid-1990 and August 1991, separatist Chechens succeeded in manoeuvring themselves into a position of strength and formal power in much of the Chechen-Ingush Republic sufficient to displace Russian authority in that part occupied predominantly by Chechens. In October 1991, Chechens declared their independence in this part of the Chechen-Ingush Republic and after that refused to recognise Russian authority.[61] By November, when Yeltsin decreed a state of emergency and sent MVD troops to restore Russian sovereignty, they were easily and painlessly rebuffed—and the Russian government was humiliated.[62] By June 1992, Russian military forces had withdrawn, leaving large amounts of their equipment and heavy arms. By November 1994, the Russian government was pushed into firmer action and as part of a wider strategy of regaining Chechnia sided with anti-separatist groups, at first politically but eventually through the supply of Russian military equipment and personnel. The opposition groups used this equipment and the personnel for a tank assault on Grozny, the capital of Chechnia, and this military operation was a complete failure. On 29 November, Russia decided to send formed units to Chechnia. On 31 December, a new battle for control of Grozny began and lasted for several weeks. On 26 January, the Russian armed forces turned the city over to troops of the Ministry of Internal Affairs.[63] But while the Russian forces had been victorious in the battle for Grozny, they could not win the war since they had no strategy and, in the end, no political will to defeat rebel forces in the mountainous countryside. After a violent terrorist attack by Chechens in Budennovsk in southern Russia in 1995, pressure from within the armed forces and in many parts of Russian society led the political leaders to agree to enter negotiations on a ceasefire.[64] Chechnia has effectively been independent since then.

5. Chechnia and neighbouring administrative units of Russia and Georgia

Russia's resort to military force in Chechnia had been part of a pattern followed both by the Soviet leadership in the dying days of its regime in a number of locations such as Vilnius, Baku and Tblisi, and by the Russian Federation government after 1991, both inside Russia and in other newly independent states of the former USSR. For example, in 1991 inside Russia, Russian forces successfully extinguished a revolt in the Ingush rump of the Chechen-Ingush Republic that followed Chechnia's declaration of independence. This dispute involved a military campaign by Ingush insurgents to detach a region of the neighbouring North Ossetia by force after the collapse of the Chechen-Ingush administration. On 31 October 1991, 8000 troops from the 76th Pskov airborne division, and special forces and police units, deployed to the region with a team of high-level military officers[65] with a clear mission of pre-emption of further troubles and pacification by deterrence. The troops subsequently placed themselves on the border between the insurgents' home territory (Ingushetia or South Ossetia) and the targeted region in North Ossetia called Prigorodny. Success in this type of operation has underpinned a continuing determination on the part of the Russian government to use force where it believes necessary to extinguish conflicts before they reach the stage of civil war that emerged in Chechnia.

The bloody war fought in the Republic of Chechnia after it declared independence from Russia is an extreme example of the manner in which regional politics is playing itself out, but there are diverse forms of this struggle going on in other places. Regionalism plays an important part in national politics and conceptions of the state. In 1996, Foreign Minister Yevgeny Primakov told a Duma committee that a 'strict definition and distribution of powers between bodies of state authority of the Russian Federation and its subjects is, probably, the most important problem of the construction of the Russian state at present'. He was commenting on activities by regional governments in the foreign policy sphere that run counter to Russian national policy. In a meeting with Russian regional governors, he said that Russia's federal make-up both benefits and complicates reforms. But he warned that there should be no tolerance for regions refusing to pay taxes to the federal government, or refusing to allow food to go out of their territory. He warned that unless this process of balkanisation of Russia stopped, 'we shall lose the single state'.[66] On another occasion, Primakov said: 'We lost the USSR, we shall never lose Russia.' The military option, though now seriously discredited because of Chechnia, remains on the table for Russia's leaders. For example, in May 1998, an airborne division based in Stavropol Territory was deployed to Dagestan, a national republic of the Russian Federation, to assist in disarming rebel groups after large riots in Makachkala on 20–21 May.[67] The 136th Infantry Brigade stationed there had been put on full alert in response to the riots on 21 May but it remained in its barracks at the time.[68] Checkpoints along the border between Dagestan and Chechnia were reinforced at that time.

Regionalism cuts two ways in Russia along boundaries which are for the most part hangovers from the Soviet era: first, along the boundaries of the constituent political units of the Russian Federation; and second, along the boundaries of large economic planning zones laid down in the Soviet era. Russia kept the formal state structure of the Russian Socialist Federated Soviet Republic (RSFSR) of the Soviet era. There are 89 constituent political units of Russia, organised in a federal structure, and these have a variety of Russian names which can best be translated as: province (*oblast*), territory (*krai*), locality (*okrug*), republic, autonomous locality, autonomous province,[69] and city of federal significance.[70] The different types represented a variety of statuses arising from Soviet modifications of tsarist-era administrative divisions. Under the current Russian Constitution, the rights of each component are notionally equal. Therefore, for ease of reference, this chapter uses the terms 'region' or 'subject of the federation' in several places as a generic descriptor for these 89 units.

The boundaries of the larger Soviet-era planning zones, often called macro-regions, have gained a new political prominence after 1991, mainly through the spontaneous creation of a regional association in Siberia by local authorities trying to find more leverage in their political battles with the national government in Moscow. The 11 zones which existed in the Soviet era have now been replaced by eight, whose boundaries either match those of previous zones or bring together some smaller zones. These regions are: Central (around Moscow), Northwest (Leningrad to Murmansk), Chernozem (Kursk to Voronezh), North Caucasus, Greater Volga, Urals, Siberian Accord, and Far East. At this level, regionalism is proving to have some positive effects, providing a sense of structure to an otherwise chaotic body politic. But the seven interregional associations apart from the Siberian Accord have been slow to develop because of unreconciled differences among their members. These associations were formed at Moscow's initiative after the Siberian Accord came into being, in an attempt to shape the nascent regionalism represented by the Siberian agreement. The Siberian Accord remains the most powerful macro-region, for reasons discussed later.

Separatism of the Chechen variety arises directly from the subordination of non-Slav, Muslim populations to Russian or Soviet cultural dominance over previous decades or centuries. Moscow was never likely to establish in a short space of time any new social contract to win the loyalty of these communities to compensate for past abuses. After 1991, many voices advocating separatism were raised in a number of the non-Russian nationality-based political units of Russia (21 republics, 10 autonomous localities and one autonomous province). A number of them have declared 'sovereignty', much as the Russian Federation did in 1989 to set in train the final collapse of the Soviet Union, but only in the Chechnia case did regional leaders take the declaration of sovereignty to its ultimate conclusion.

In many of these nationality-based political units, people of 'Russian nationality' are in a majority. Genuine separatist sentiment in any predominantly Russian region is not widespread. Threats of secession gain prominence in Russian areas when regional leaders are seeking to put pressure on Moscow. This was particularly the case before 1993. Secession of the Far East, often touted for political effect, is most unlikely given the huge imbalance in power between China and any putative new Far East Republic. The population imbalance between China and Russia in the border areas between Lake Baikal and the coast is about 120 million to 9 million. But there are less violent forms of regionalism apart from separatism that are being pursued with considerable vigour throughout Russia.

The most contentious issue between the federal government and the regions is the division of power between them, especially over tax and budgetary issues. More than 40 subjects of the federation have signed separate treaties delimiting authority between themselves and the federal government in spite of the existence of constitutional provisions and laws which are supposed to provide for a uniform regime applying to all. There are at least 26 such treaties creating special terms for tax collection. In more than half of the 89 regions, constitutional laws have been passed that conflict with the national constitution.

Political legitimacy of the national government remains weak because of the central government's failure to provide basic services and economic welfare, its failure to meet the social obligations of universal welfare made by the former Soviet state to Russian citizens, its failure to prevent the wholesale theft of state-owned enterprises, and its failure to provide basic public order. The Russian government has failed to meet most of its obligations under its part of the 'social contract'. The final collapse of Yeltsin's authority occurred in August 1998, after he faltered in his appointment of a new government to deal with the economic crisis, and this collapse means that structural defects in centre–region relations will not be repaired and are likely to be exacerbated over coming years. The federal government cannot improve its legitimacy without dramatic and sustained improvements in its revenue base and without effective redistribution of this revenue to nationally significant purposes.

Federal efforts to slow the flow of power away from Moscow have been largely reactive and have brought mixed results. Since the legal regime for the administration of centre–region relations has developed erratically and has not been enforced consistently, each new demand by either party sets in train a new set of negotiations, new compromises, and a new ad hoc arrangement. But the federal government has some leverage. There are 89 separate regions, and their leaders have generally preferred pressing their own parochial concerns rather than working in concert with others. The poverty of many parts of Russia also gives the federal government some leverage. By 1998, it was subsidising 81 of the 89 federation subjects in the form of cash transfers and loans. But the regions can exercise leverage over the centre on those occasions when it needs the cooperation of regional elites in order to implement many of its decisions.

A *modus vivendi* between the federal government and the federation subjects has been institutionalised to some limited extent through the macro-regions mentioned above and through a number of other political trends. As mentioned above, the method of selection of the 198 elected members of the upper house of the national parliament, the Federation Council, was changed in 1995 to provide for automatic membership for the 89 governors (elected heads of regional administrations) and the 89 heads of regional parliaments (*duma*). The direct elections, beginning in 1996, of the governors of provinces and territories gives the regional leaders considerable legitimacy in dealing with the federal government. In the 1996 presidential election, regional bosses played a key role in organising Yeltsin's victory and thereby established a political constituency where it counts—in the presidential administration—for more independent action by them.

Regionalisation can be seen as a normal part of the democratic evolution of Russia in that it dilutes the traditionally autocratic power of the national government,[72] but some of Russia's constitutional arrangements and other circumstances are probably not conducive to a functioning liberal democracy. Striking the right balance between powers of the centre and regions in a large federal state such as Russia is difficult, but a strong central government organised according to the principles of representative democracy, separation of powers, and a unifying pluralistic vision would appear to be minimum requirements. Without these, ballot box democracy inevitably produces little dictators and only a powerful central government can protect communities from misrule or from local seizure of power through non-democratic means. This is especially the case in a country as large as Russia and one with such little tradition of pluralistic democracy. Many governors have used popular election to rule with an iron hand and the greater autonomy of the regions has had the profound effect of strengthening that level of government. In a number of regions, fundamental questions about the distribution of economic and political power between executive and legislative branches have not been resolved. Moreover, the role of a presidential representative to each region is not clearly defined. In several regions, there is a rivalry between several centres of power representing either sectoral (agricultural, military, fuel and energy), territorial or ethnic lobbies. The decline of central authority in the regions also means that local authorities are now 'free' to choose people from the provinces as government officials instead of having them imposed by Moscow, and this has weakened the entire system of government administration throughout the country.

The Russian national economy has become fragmented, thereby undermining the effectiveness of policies designed for nationwide effect and imposing heavy burdens on the central government to develop highly differentiated regional policies. The large percentage of the economy that has become demonetised, perhaps as high as 75 per cent, according to one study, deters the formation of national markets. Similarly, housing shortages, the close link between the workplace and social services, and other constraints on labour mobility have tied most workers to their place of employment and impeded the development of regional and national labour markets. There are huge disparities in standards of living between the regions. Food prices have varied according to the region by as much as 1800 per cent, and consumer goods prices by as much as 1500 per cent. Some regions have banned food exports to other parts of Russia, imposed customs regimes on goods imported from other parts of Russia, or imposed their unique system of price controls. The gap between the richest and poorest regions is vast and is increasing. The average salary in Moscow is more than 17 times that of inhabitants of some of the poorer parts of the country.

Moscow City is the wealthiest and most powerful regional entity in Russia. In 1997, according to the Mayor of Moscow, Yury Luzhkov, 46 per cent of all money in the state budget was contributed by the city and that sort of contribution guarantees continued prominence to the capital in comparison to other regional governments. Moscow City will remain the focal point of national political struggle, but in coming years it will be challenged by several other centres of new wealth and new power. Apart from Moscow, there were seven other 'donor regions' supporting the other 81 regional units in 1998. Of this seven, there are four larger regions in Western Siberia that will increasingly be able to challenge the national government in its policy preferences. These are Sverdlovsk Province, Krasnoiarsk Territory, and the two autonomous regions of Khanti-Mansiisk and Yamalo-Nenetsk.

Of these four, Sverdlovsk and Krasnoiarsk regions can present substantial challenges to the national government's authority, though each has quite different characteristics in terms of political profile. Sverdlovsk Province, where Yeltsin had established his career in the Soviet era before moving to Moscow, is one of the regions which retains a very high percentage of Soviet-era officials.

Krasnoiarsk Territory is the second largest single territorial unit of the Russian Federation, and its government is now led by Aleksandr Lebed, who was elected as governor in 1998. Both Sverdlovsk Province and Krasnoiarsk Territory have been predominantly conservative in their voting preferences, usually supporting the Communist Party, the Zhirinovski party or Lebed's former party ahead of the liberal democrats.

Both Krasnoiarsk and Sverdlovsk regions have highly developed industrial capacities, although much of this is lying idle. Krasnoiarsk holds large strategic reserves of copper, nickel, precious metals, coal, non-ferrous metals and timber. It is also home to significant military units on its territory and this provides additional leverage of a particularly understated but powerful kind.

The closer a region is to the periphery of Russia and to major economic centres in other countries, the more able it will be to trade, and the more prosperous it is likely to become.[73] This is the emerging scenario for the Maritime Territory on the Pacific coast of Russia, which is not only contiguous with China's northeast but easily accessible by sea to the developed economies of Japan, Korea, the USA and Canada. Another factor likely to promote prosperity of a particular region will be the prominence of primary industry in its economy, with inefficient and noncompetitive secondary industry in most regions acting as more of a brake on prosperity for several years.[74] The southern warmer climates will probably do better than the northern colder areas since they will benefit from net immigration.

For many years to come, regionalism will continue to be used by political groups as one of several tools in their bid to capture political legitimacy and the reins of power. There is considerable likelihood that Lebed ran for election to the governorship of Krasnoiarsk to use that as a platform for national prominence in advance of the presidential election in the year 2000. Other national political figures have followed Lebed's example and won governorships.

Regionalism has important consequences for the political stability of Russia and for its prospects for a return to economic prosperity. Regionalism raises the prospect of some break-up of the Russian state, but this is not the most likely outcome in the short term. Nor is the possible break-up of the Russian state the most serious consequence of regionalism. In fact, some parts of Russia and maybe the Russian state itself could be better off in economic terms if there was some rationalisation of existing political boundaries. There are four more important consequences of regionalism in the short term:

- a gradual shift in economic and political power away from Moscow to a handful of the more prosperous or more independent regions;
- a reorienting of economic relations between border regions of Russia toward more prosperous neighbouring countries, including Mediterranean, Baltic and Pacific states;
- the frustration of efforts by the national government to bring cohesion to economic and fiscal policy; and
- the opportunistic exploitation of the issue of regional autonomy for unrelated political advantage

RUSSIAN PROSPERITY!

Russia is one of the richest and most self-sufficient countries in the world in terms of natural resources. It has the largest reserves of natural gas (45 per cent of world share), the third-largest reserves of coal (23 per cent of world share), and one of the largest reserves of oil outside the Middle East.[75] It is in the top five producers for iron ore, gold, zinc, copper, lead, mercury, nickel and hydropower. Russia's topography is diverse, with forest and woodland covering about 45 per cent, meadows and pastures covering about 5 per cent, and arable land covering only 8 per cent.[76] This underlying wealth and Russia's past as a great industrial power might have provided fairly solid foundations for economic prosperity of the new Russian state, but this was not to be the case.

In 1992, the government began to pursue a rigid economic strategy based on rejection of a social safety net (social democracy) in favour of almost absolute faith in 'real liberalism', a belief that abolition of the market constraints of communism and rapid privatisation would provide adequate economic forces not only to maintain the whole population through transition but also to support a positive improvement in general welfare in a short timeframe.[77] On 2 January 1992, the government lifted controls on most prices and on wages, and introduced a floating exchange rate as part of the 'shock therapy' approach to achieving economic stabilisation.[78] The idea was that the only way to overcome the chronic shortages and distortions in the economy created by decades of central control and state ownership was to cut everything loose: rapid liberalisation of prices, immediate removal of subsidies, sharp government expenditure cuts and sharp reductions in the money supply.[79] While some subsidies (in agriculture) and some price controls (for energy) remained, the policies were so severe that they soon came to be dubbed 'shock without therapy'.[80] The results included an increase of 245 per cent in the consumer price index (CPI) for the first month, which stabilised at about a 10 per cent monthly increase in August, before taking off again to a monthly 25 per cent before the end of 1992. By the end of 1992, prices had increased on average by 2200 per cent while wages had increased on average by only 1000 per cent.[81] Real income in 1992 was about one-third of the 1985 level.[82]

In March 1992, the new Russian state negotiated an IMF package of financial support which included a US$6 billion currency stabilisation fund, and a planned US$18 billion economic assistance package to be raised on a multilateral basis by the G–7.[83] The US$18 billion package included the rescheduling of US$2.5 billion in debt, US$4.5 billion in aid from international organisations, and US$11 billion in bilateral assistance to maintain trade.[84] By the end of April, it had become apparent that it would take several months to put the rouble stabilisation package together.[85] The exchange rate the IMF was aiming for was 80 roubles to the US dollar, but the Russian currency has never looked like recovering from its position then of 120. By January 1994, it had reached 1600 to the US dollar. The main goal of the shock therapy was stabilisation of the rouble and the emergence of convertibility—an outcome which still had not come to pass by 1998.

The radical policies implemented in early 1992 began to be softened within several months of their introduction under the pressure of parliament and industry.[86] By 14 December 1992, Yeltsin had removed the liberal Prime Minister, Yegor Gaidar, and replaced him with Viktor Chernomyrdin, whose instincts were closer to those of the former Soviet industrial ministries. But while Chernomyrdin softened some of the rhetoric and some of the policies, he did not in the end blunt the most radical reforms. He publicly backed the view that economic stabilisation could not occur by administrative fiat but only through the forces of the market.[87] One factor militating against a more measured and socially sympathetic set of economic policies by the government after 1991 was the lack of any organised and powerful groups representing workers' interests. The disintegration of Soviet power had not been accompanied by any moves amongst workers to organise as a political force. They remained vulnerable throughout the post-Soviet period because of the Soviet-era 'working class dependency on management'.[88]

Economic performance after 1992 and 1993 was not encouraging. In 1992, industrial production fell by about 20 per cent, having fallen by 11 per cent in 1991.[89] By 1993, there were 40 million Russians below the poverty line.[90] Government salaries and pensions dropped significantly in value. Consumer prices had increased by a factor of 255 (that is 25 500 per cent) between December 1991 and December 1993.[91] By 1994, according to official figures, unemployment was unnaturally low, with only 2 per cent of the workforce unemployed, but ILO sources put it at about 10 per cent.[92] The drop in average real wages between 1985 and 1995 was 50 per cent, although the drop was sharpest for the lowest paid, while incomes for the top 20 per cent actually increased between 1991 and 1994.[93] Groups affected most sharply included white collar workers such as doctors and teachers, while some blue collar groups, especially miners, were able to fare better. But for the most part, it has been blue collar workers who lost their jobs, even if some of their colleagues were able to keep theirs and get better salaries to boot. Employment patterns in the economy shifted substantially between 1992 and 1995, with large decreases in industry, transport, communications and science, while trade, catering, services, credit, finance and insurance showed big increases.[94]

The supply and demand situation for food and consumer goods fixed itself within a relatively short period because of a liberation from state controls and because of sharp drops in income. By 1994, according to Russian government statistics, the proportion of the population below the poverty line had fallen from 39 per cent in 1992 to 26 per cent. This rose again in 1995 to 29 per cent, and then fell again to about 25 per cent in 1996.[95] But this rebalancing came after severe hardships in the bigger cities through late 1991 and 1992. Moreover, the mix of food consumption changed for the poorer parts of the community. Between 1990 and 1994, national per capita consumption of bread, bread products and potatoes increased while for meat, milk and eggs, per capita consumption fell by about 25 per cent.[96] Life expectancy for men dropped from its already low 63.8 years to 57.3.[97] But women were the big losers in the rapid decline in daily living standards, since they constituted some 70 per cent of the poor and extremely poor, but only 27 per cent of the most prosperous section of the community.[98]

The economic pain continued for most Russians at a personal level until the time of writing. In mid-1997, the federal government foreshadowed moves to scrap a number of the social welfare benefits that have survived from the Soviet era, in part because it can no longer afford to pay them but also because there is no means test on the recipients. Arrears in social payments reached 12.5 trillion roubles in pensions, 13 trillion roubles in government workers' salaries, and 8 trillion roubles in child support.[99] The currency was not trusted, and many Russians kept their savings in US dollars. Life expectancy continued to fall, reaching 54 for men by 1998.[100] By 1997, Russia had dropped to 16th place in the world in GDP.[101]

Notwithstanding the sustained deprivation of large sections of the Russian community, especially through wage arrears and lower standards of living, by 1997 the worst seemed to have been passed, with the sharpest drops in GDP and productivity being confined to the first half of the 1990s, as Table 1.6 shows.

By early 1998, the IMF was claiming some success for its programs in Russia and hailing the stabilisation achieved by the Russian government: 'inflation has declined—from nearly 50 per cent in 1996 to about 15 per cent in 1997; the exchange rate has stayed within its predetermined band; and the balance of payments has remained broadly favorable'.[102] The private sector accounted for 70 per cent of Russian GDP and central financial institutions had been strengthened. This result was directly attributable to the political stability and continuity represented by the 1996 presidential election, combined with the unusual powers granted the Russian President in the Constitution. Russia's success in achieving some turn-around despite (or because of) significant absences by Yeltsin from his presidential duties was an encouraging sign. The IMF had flagged three areas for continued sustained reform: fiscal policy, especially tax collection; the weak banking sector; and 'crony capitalism'. But the promise of

Table 1.6 Economic indicators (percentage of previous year) 1992–96[103]

	1992	1993	1994	1995	1996 (first half)
GDP	85.5	91.3	87.4	96.0	95.5
Industrial production	82.0	85.9	79.1	97.0	96.0
Agricultural production	91.0	96.0	88.0	92.0	93.5
Capital investment	60.0	88.0	76.0	87.0	86.0

late 1997 and early 1998 was not fulfilled. GDP growth, which was positive in the last three quarters of 1997 and came in at zero in the first quarter 1998, fell dramatically to 7.6 per cent negative growth in the third quarter in 1998.[104] Annual GDP for 1998 was 4.6 per cent less than 1997.

A financial crisis hit Russia in late August and September 1998 under the prime ministerial stewardship of a 35-year-old, Sergei Kiriyenko, who had been thrust into the position only months earlier from a post as a junior minister, to replace the long-serving Chernomyrdin. In response to this crisis, Russia was forced back to the IMF for urgent support and negotiated stand-by financing of US$11.2 billion, announced on 17 August. By late 1998, and after the appointment as Prime Minister of the serving Foreign Minister, Yevgeny Primakov, the economy had started to decline again, with the IMF predicting negative growth of 1 per cent for 1998.[105] The government had not been able to repair its shaky tax system. The tax base shrank in the first part of the 1990s because of the large declines in production,[106] but continued to deteriorate because of the lack of effective tax enforcement.[107] By October 1998, the new Prime Minister became Russia's most popular politician and was trusted by 48 per cent of the country's population, not to mention many of the Communist Party deputies in the State Duma.[108] Primakov appointed two former high-ranking Communist Party members to the new ministry. The sorry state of Yeltsin's popularity at this time—he scored only 7 per cent support—was a reliable indicator of the legitimacy of his government in the eyes of the Russian people.[109]

By the end of April 1999, most Russian economic indicators were down on the previous year, especially industrial and agricultural production. Unemployment levels had also risen.[110] Inflation was stabilising (2–3 per cent per month in March and April), and there had been some climb back in production in the first quarter of 1999. But indicators of standard of living had fallen, the rouble exchange rate had slid further, and real incomes were still falling.

There was no joy for most Russian people in the economic fortunes of their country through 1998 and 1999.

The depth of the Russian economic collapse and the time period over which it has occurred mean that the country has suffered a hyper-depression. It will take Russia a long time to pull itself out of this hole. One assessment completed before the August 1998 crisis saw Russia even then as having a 'bleak economic status and a dismal outlook', and concluded that even with the most optimistic forecast for economic growth (2–3 per cent each year), it would take Russia decades to return to the standard of living that the USSR had at its peak.[111] The political program for 1999 and 2000 did not hold out any hope: parliamentary elections were scheduled for December 1999, but an impeachment resolution was pending against the President until May, when it failed to get the required number of votes for proceedings to go further. But in the meantime, Yeltsin had sacked yet another Prime Minister—the almost universally popular Primakov—securing the Duma's assent quickly to his new nominee, Minister of the Interior, Sergei Stepashin. However, even loyal Stepashin managed to stay in the office for only three months, and was replaced suddenly in early August 1999 by Vladimir Putin, Head of the Security Council and Chief of Russia's Federal Security Bureau (FSB), who was more loyal to Yeltsin. Such frequent changes of premiers in Russia can be explained by the growing power struggle before the year 2000 presidential elections, and desperate attempts by the Yeltsin administration to stay in power.

CRISIS?

The social and political implications of this sustained decline in living standards and of the incapacity of the government to stabilise economic production and social life are inescapable: Russia will have a new radical government before it has a more liberal one. There are strong foundations for the emergence of a xenophobic government in Russia, but there are several considerations which could well shape the ideology of a new government into a less dangerous variety.

First, while Russian popular attitudes show quite extremist and ill-informed tendencies, the lessons of 70 years of Communist rule and international confrontation are very powerful. The new extremist government, if one emerges, may well be of the Pinochet

Chilean variety—domestically repressive to restore economic and social order, but internationally conservative.

Second, there is not much respect in Russia for governments of any sort. Russians want the social benefits that big government produces but they are inherently suspicious of and independent of government.

Third, not everything is as it seemed according to national macroeconomic indicators. Some care should be taken in interpreting official Russian statistics, as they may not reveal an accurate picture in important aspects of people's lives. For example, declared income levels reflect in part an approach to tax-minimisation or lack of willingness to declare income derived by criminal methods, including corruption. Thus, Russia's GDP may in fact be anywhere between 22 and 50 per cent higher than the official statistics suggest.[112] The Mayor of Moscow, Luzhkov, claimed in late 1997 that the reforms had been carried on very well in the city, creating so many small and medium-sized businesses, that the unemployment problem in the city had been solved.[113] He also claimed that Moscow contributed about 40 per cent of all Russian central government revenue in 1997.

While many Russians remain in dire circumstances, most benefit from the black economy. Income levels cannot be equated with wage levels, since many of those people not paid wage arrears for months are still managing to feed their families. A former Minister of the Interior, Anatoly Kulikov, estimated the value of the black economy to be as high as 45 per cent of stated GDP, meaning that Russia is 50 per cent better off in gross terms than the statistics suggest. Kulikov, whose duties had included dealing with organised crime, described the influence of criminal gangs on the economy as a threat to its national security which if not eliminated would bring the country to its knees.[114]

This interpretation may underestimate the positive role of criminal gangs in consolidating a strong private sector economy in the circumstances where the legal regime is weak. Many Russian business leaders see the use of 'mafia' protectors to enforce contract compliance as the only effective tool in an area where the legal system has been almost totally ineffective. But corruption and criminality at the end of the day make consistent policy implementation very difficult and undermine any faith in the social order being advocated by the government. And this is Russia's greatest political weakness—lack of social cohesion behind a generally accepted vision of social order.

Fourth, there are powerful factors that tend toward social discipline rather than radicalism. In addition to all of the other economic burdens inherited by Russia from its communist past, perhaps the most serious and the most costly is the country's environmental devastation. According to two scholars, 'no other great industrial civilisation so systematically and so long poisoned its air, land, water and people. None so loudly proclaiming its efforts to improve public health and protect nature so degraded both.'[115] The prospect of further environmental catastrophes, particularly if control regimes for nuclear power stations or nuclear weapons are allowed to deteriorate, is one that most Russian citizens can appreciate and will act to prevent.

A descent into radicalism of the adventurous and internationally destabilising variety is not something that most Russians dream about on a daily basis. If power does shift from the popularly elected President, the future of the Russian state will be determined in large part by the response of those people who control the instruments of coercion. These can be found in a diversity of institutions, as chapter 5 indicates, which are dispersed between the armed forces, the Federal Security Bureau, and the Ministry of the Interior, not to mention other organisations like the border guards or the presidential security service. The history of military subservience to the political leadership in the Soviet period, or the history of failed attempts in 1991 and 1993 to resist presidential authority, are probably a poor guide to the future.[116]

In circumstances of the severely depressed conditions of the armed forces and the severely depressed personal situations of most members of the armed forces, Russia is as ripe for a political intervention in politics by the armed forces as any country might be. Only the spark is needed to set fire to the smouldering resentment within the armed forces. But the outcome of such actions need not be destabilising internationally. In fact, the most likely provocation for a direct military take-over or declaration of martial law would be a collapse of such residual government authority as exists, or a further threat of separatism such as that in Chechnia. And on these issues, there would not be much difference between the President's views and those of the military leadership. As divided as the officer corps in the armed forces is, there is not overwhelming support for radicals such as Zhirinovski. The balance of sentiment in the armed forces is probably in favour of the statists, represented by people like Luzhkov. His bloc *Otechestvo* (Fatherland) is winning more and more support from the military, especially among low- and middle-ranked officers. But Russia is definitely in the very dangerous situation where a small military revolt by extremists might lead to an avalanching collapse of authority in the armed forces as a whole in such a way as to ease the way to power of extremists with a radical international agenda.

CONCLUSION

Russia of the late 1990s remains a great power but it is severely hobbled. In governance it is a weak state in crisis. In social terms, it is a chaotic mix of hope and desperation, of order and lawlessness, of prosperity and poverty. There are many signs of consolidation of ordered, enlightened government, but this form of social organisation is still in open competition with despotic and repressive instincts in many political circles, including those closest to the so-called democrats in Yeltsin's immediate circle. Many people in Russia continue to suffer poverty and human rights abuses, even as others enrich themselves through clever capitalism or crime, or a combination of both. It remains to be seen whether the foundations for a liberal democratic, free market economy put in place by Yeltsin will be strong enough to withstand continuing pressure from political forces with a sharply contending vision of political order. The constitutional foundations of the Russian state have yet to be established by long observation of convention and principle. The written constitution, which in any country can only be the first step to institutionalised stability, was first promulgated in 1993—a mere seven years before the time of publication of this book. An entrenchment of liberal political ideas in Russia is the least likely direction for Russia in the next decade.

Russia remains susceptible to a sharp reorientation of foreign policy if more extremist political groups gain power through a coup or through an election. Both scenarios should be considered, but there are few signs that the extremists are sufficiently well placed to take power. The most powerful forces likely to succeed in replacing the Yeltsin administration in elections are those of the Communist Party, or a centre-right platform. The foreign policy of either group is more likely to be characterised by greater prickliness rather than by any return to the direct confrontation of a systemic kind that existed in the Cold War. Russia will still need international investment and international financial support regardless of whether Yeltsin remains in power. If a military coup were used to seize power, any sharp changes in policy in the medium term would be more likely to occur in domestic affairs, rather than in Russia's foreign policy.

2

Russia east of the
Ural Mountains

Russians first pushed across the Ural Mountains in the ninth
century, with the city of Novgorod being the primary Russian
influence, until it was replaced in this role by Muscovy as the
primary Russian influence in the fifteenth century. But for most
of the time between 1236 and 1465, Mongol or Tartar control was
pre-eminent in the southern parts of what is today eastern Russia.[1]
The more northerly parts were inhabited by smaller communities
of native peoples. By 1581 or 1582, Russia formally incorporated
parts of Western Siberia with the help of displaced Cossack
communities. By about 1650, Russian settlements had pushed to
the Amur River north of China, and the Pacific coast (Okhotsk
and Anadyrskii Ostrog in 1649). These settlements were in the
more inhospitable, northern reaches of what is today the Russian
Federation. In 1689, Russia reached a border agreement with
China in the Treaty of Nerchinsk. In the eighteenth century,
new settlements were built in Nizhne Kamchatsk (1703),
Petropavlovsk (1740) and Alaska (1784). By 1860, Russia had
become so strongly established in north Asia that it successfully
pressed China to sign the Treaty of Peking ceding large swathes
of territory in what is now the Maritime Territory (see Map 2).
Russia also became firmly established in Sakhalin and Alaska.
In 1867, Russia ceded Alaska to the USA.

Administrative units of Russia east of the Urals are shown on
Map 2. This eastern part of the country is thinly populated, with
about 20 per cent of the people but about 75 per cent of the territory
of the Federation. Three-quarters of the population live in the major
cities and towns. The largest cities east of the Urals are Novosibirsk
(1 400 000), Omsk (1 161 000), Tomsk (500 000), Krasnoiarsk
(914 000), Khabarovsk (600 000), Irkutsk (630 000), Vladivostok
(650 000) and Yekaterinburg (1 400 000). Many small cities were

Table 2.1   Nationality populations in selected administrative units east of the Urals

	Population	Percentage Russian
Province		
Jewish Autonomous	214 085	80
Territory		
Khabarovsk	1 811 828	77
Krasnoiarsk	3 605 454	86
Maritime	2 256 072	87
Locality		
Aga-Buriat	77 188	40
Chukotsk (Republic)	163 934	63
Evenk	24 769	68
Khanti-Mansai	1 282 396	66
Koriak (Republic)	39 940	64
Taimyr	55 803	67
Ust-Orda Buriat	135 870	56
Yamalo-Nenetsk	494 844	59
Republic		
Buriat	1 038 252	70
Gorno-Altai	190 831	63
Khakassia	566 861	80
Sakha (Yakutia)	1 094 065	50
Tyva	308 557	30

established exclusively for secret military factories. More than half of the 31 nationality-based republics or autonomous regions in the Russian Federation are east of the Urals, but they have quite small populations, and many have more Russians than non-Russians, as shown in Table 2.1.[2]

The more remote parts of eastern Russia have suffered sharp depopulation in recent years, with Magadan losing one-third of its people and Sakhalin losing 15 per cent.[3] With the formation of new states out of the former Soviet republics, many non-Russians working in Siberia and the Far East returned to their new countries. At the same time, the lifting of residency controls and opening of formerly closed cities, such as Vladivostok on 1 January 1992, allowed many people to enter the region seeking better economic fortunes. Some of the less inviting areas were rapidly depopulated, with a number of settlements becoming ghost-towns, while others actually grew in size.[4] In February 1995, Deputy Prime Minister Sergei Shakhrai warned that the region may well be so seriously depopulated within 20 years that Russia might lose parts of it to China, Japan or the USA, which he said were closely studying these regions with a view to organising their own settlements there.[5] In April 1995, he called for a program of 'great migration to Siberia', in order to reverse the decline in population. He advocated a system of incentives, including tax and transportation concessions.[6] A military review writing in 1997 identified the regions east of the Urals as the area most likely to be affected by military separatism arising from the serious discontent with service conditions for military personnel and the deterioration of the country's military posture.[7] Compared with the rest of Russia, these areas have relatively large military garrisons and relatively small non-military populations. In November 1998, former Prime Minister Yevgeny Primakov expressed the view that 'Russia cannot be great and will not remain a great power if we do not develop the Far East region'.[8]

FROM SOVIET TO RUSSIAN

Under Soviet rule, the region enjoyed a range of concessions to support the standard of living, but since 1991 many of these have disappeared. In spite of these concessions, the area east of the Urals had always been one of the USSR's two underdeveloped regions—the other being Central Asia. The Soviet government consistently lacked the political will to bring about more than a marginal increase in the region's share of national investment.[9] It was only in the extraction of raw materials that the economy enjoyed any significant advance relative to the rest of the country. The region consistently lagged 'hopelessly behind' the rest of the country in social indicators.[10] When the USSR paid more attention to regional development east of the Urals beginning in the 1970s, the economic performance of the region relative to the rest of the country actually deteriorated.[11] The Soviet system simply could not respond to the new specialised demands of the region. For example, as of 1988, less than 6 per cent of the equipment in the minerals-processing industry in east and west Siberia was found to be of world standard.[12]

The Soviet leadership paid personal attention to the region on several occasions, with Leonid Brezhnev, General Secretary of the Communist Party, making an extended tour in 1978 in the company of Konstantin Chernenko, a later General Secretary who was one of the region's few backers in Moscow. In July 1986, Gorbachev made a famous speech in Vladivostok which foreshadowed the hope for the city's future as a 'widely opened window on the East'. In September 1988, Gorbachev made an another exhortation in Krasnoiarsk for accelerated regional development because of the significance of the area east of the Urals 'for the fate of our state'. But it was quite clear then that rhetoric could not command the economy to move and one Russian expert concluded that even acceleration of development rates in the region 'will not remedy the situation'.[13]

Boris Yeltsin is the first supreme leader of Russia to have been born east of the Ural Mountains. His city of birth, Yekaterinburg (formerly Sverdlovsk), was one of the earliest provincial capitals to become politically active in the struggles between Gorbachev and Yeltsin. In November 1987, large public demonstrations protested Yeltsin's demotion from the Politburo of the Communist Party and soon after, a number of activist organisations sprang up in the city.[14] By 1989 and 1990, the same sort of activism emerged in regional politics in the Far East, with members of the Jewish and Korean nationalities looking for a new territorial and legal order.[15] Pressure mounted through 1991 but, as one scholar concluded in respect of the Far Eastern regionalists, they 'showed little readiness to relinquish the perquisites of dependence (food and fuel deliveries, subsidies from the Centre)'.[16]

But after the August 1991 coup, eastern Russia experienced most of the contradictory impulses that emerged elsewhere in Russia, from extreme nationalism to anti-Stalin commemorations of gulag victims, from radical environmentalism to criminally based entrepreneurship, and from nostalgic hopes for a return to the social security of the past (such as it was) to a rampant and free-wheeling embrace of the new.[17] Pre-revolutionary street names were reinstated and the Russian Orthodox Church became very popular.[18] No fewer than 27 newspapers were established in the Far East region alone after 1989, although not all survived.

ECONOMY AND INFRASTRUCTURE

As the USSR was collapsing and even after 1991, the areas east of the Urals suffered special hardships. Food became very expensive and production of major exports declined sharply because of wage payment problems. As one scholar described it, not only did Siberia and the Far East suffer economically because of structural bias in *perestroika* policies against its resource industries, but the 'shock therapy' economic policies pursued nationally by Moscow led to declining productivity and standards of living in the region.[19] The local economy collapsed in 1991 when Moscow liberalised prices and reduced subsidies, with power shortages becoming the norm. The armed forces in many places became the lifeline for communities.[20] The economic liberalisation has in a number of respects undermined the previous financial base of many of the cities. Omsk, for example, used to obtain two-thirds of its revenue from the local oil enterprises which were seen as 'local' and thought of themselves as 'local'. As the ownership changed and takeovers resulted in much larger parent companies operating in many parts of Russia, the headquarters of the once local companies were now in Moscow. Revenues to Omsk city authorities declined quickly to 40 per cent of the previous situation. The inevitable result was that new local taxes have been introduced to add to the burdens of seriously overburdened communities.

Siberia and the Far East remained among the poorest parts of the country in 1992 and 1993 in standard of living. When Yeltsin visited the Far East in 1992, he made no secret of his view of the backwardness of that area, using phrases such as 'This place is a dump'; 'Do you seriously live here?'; and 'Places like this make me ashamed to be Russian'.[21] Persistent calls can be heard to restore special treatment to eastern Russia to ease the burden of transition. These calls come from the highest levels of the parliament and the government, as well as from the regions themselves.[22] By 1995, some parts of eastern Russia had experienced even greater economic decline than the country as a whole, with Maritime and Kamchatka suffering an annual decline in industrial output in 1994 of almost 30 per cent, and Khabarovsk experiencing a decline of 41 per cent.[23] The next year, Kamchatka fared substantially better with a positive performance, while Magadan dropped sharply. Foreign investment has not provided the stimulus to domestic growth that many in Russia had put their hopes on. It was relatively small in scale, concentrated in non-productive sectors and heavily influenced by the instability in the investment regimes, in legal, political and economic aspects.[24]

The persistence of economic problems was manifested in a December 1996 emergency meeting of the board of the Siberian Accord which was told that the volume of manufactured production had fallen by two-thirds since 1991, that the defence enterprises were 'practically on their backs', that 550 000 people had been sent on unpaid leave, and that 40 per cent of the population in Siberia now lived below the poverty line.[25] The region has been seriously affected by strikes resulting from unpaid salaries. In July 1997, doctors in a town north of the Kuznetsk Basin (*Kuzbas*) went on strike and protested on the Trans-Siberian rail track for several hours because of unpaid wages going back several months.[26] In January 1998, mass strikes by 240 000 workers were held in the *Kuzbas* region to protest arrears on unpaid salaries since October 1996 and mine closures.[27] The strikes did not produce the desired responses and in February 1998, a series of hunger strikes protesting the unpaid wages were held, though with few positive results.[28] The company involved has been the subject of bankruptcy proceedings. In January 1998, the Prime Minister, Viktor Chernomyrdin, indicated that the Finance Ministry would need to treble its 1998 budget allocations to the sector to redress the problems.[29] The same month, more than 2500 miners in the Maritime Territory, joined by workers from a military plant, blocked the Trans-Siberian Railway at a station 43 km from Vladivostok for about 12 hours, in protest over unpaid wages and calling for the resignation of the government.[30]

There have been massive cuts to scientific institutes in the region, with the Siberian Academy of Sciences losing 3000 out of 12 000 personnel (25 per cent) between 1992 and 1997, and with plans announced in 1997 to cut about 20 per cent of the institutes working under the Siberian branch of the Russian Academy of Sciences (RAS).[31] The Siberian branch had not been cut as radically as institutes of the RAS in Moscow, because it has been very creative in establishing links with entrepreneurs and international foundations. According to one report, the number of former personnel who were forced out by cuts was almost matched by the number of new, usually much younger, specialists coming to work in the institutes and laboratories, because the Siberian branch was doing much better than its European Russia counterparts.[32]

Almost all of eastern Russia is north of 49°N, that is, more northerly than the US–Canada border. Almost none of the region benefits from the warm ocean currents and insular climates that can be found in similar latitudes in Europe (such as the south of England). In fact, cold ocean currents 'refrigerate' the Pacific coastline of Russia.[33] Much of eastern Russia is bounded in the north by 70°N, approximately the latitude of mainland Norway and mainland Alaska. The topography of eastern Russia includes Arctic desert, forested tundra, taiga and in some parts forested or grassy plains. The most common is heavily forested taiga (see Maps 6 and 7). There is very little arable land. Much of eastern Russia is covered with permafrost, and this increases the costs of construction.[34] Temperatures are extreme, with Siberia having an average annual air temperature of less than zero degrees centigrade.[35] In some parts of the Far East, temperatures reach –70°C.[36]

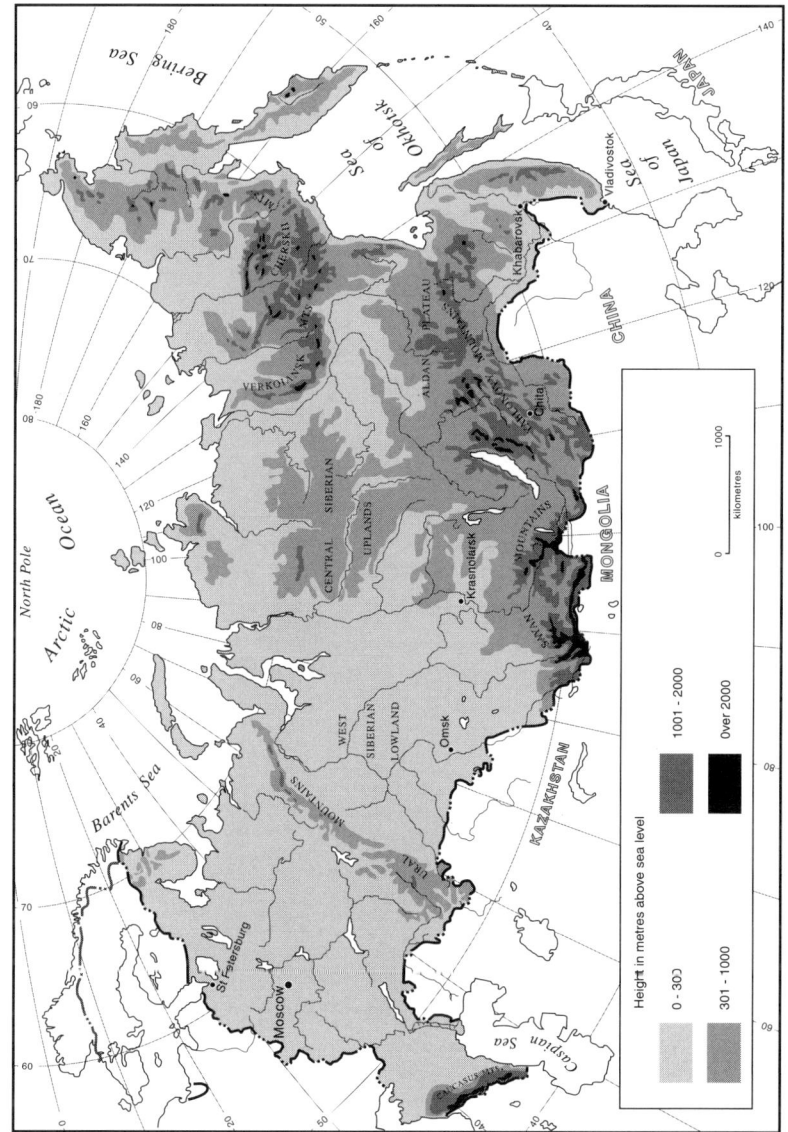

6. Relief

Height in metres above sea level

0 - 300

301 - 1000

1001 - 2000

Over 2000

kilometres

0   1000

North Pole

Arctic Ocean

Bering Sea

Sea of Okhotsk

Sea of Japan

JAPAN

Vladivostok

Khabarovsk

CHINA

Chita

MONGOLIA

KAZAKHSTAN

Barents Sea

Caspian Sea

St Petersburg

Moscow

Omsk

Krasnoyarsk

WEST SIBERIAN LOWLAND

CENTRAL SIBERIAN UPLANDS

VERKOYANSK

CHERSKY

ALDAN PLATEAU

STANOVOY MOUNTAINS

YABLONOVY MOUNTAINS

SAYAN MOUNTAINS

URAL MOUNTAINS

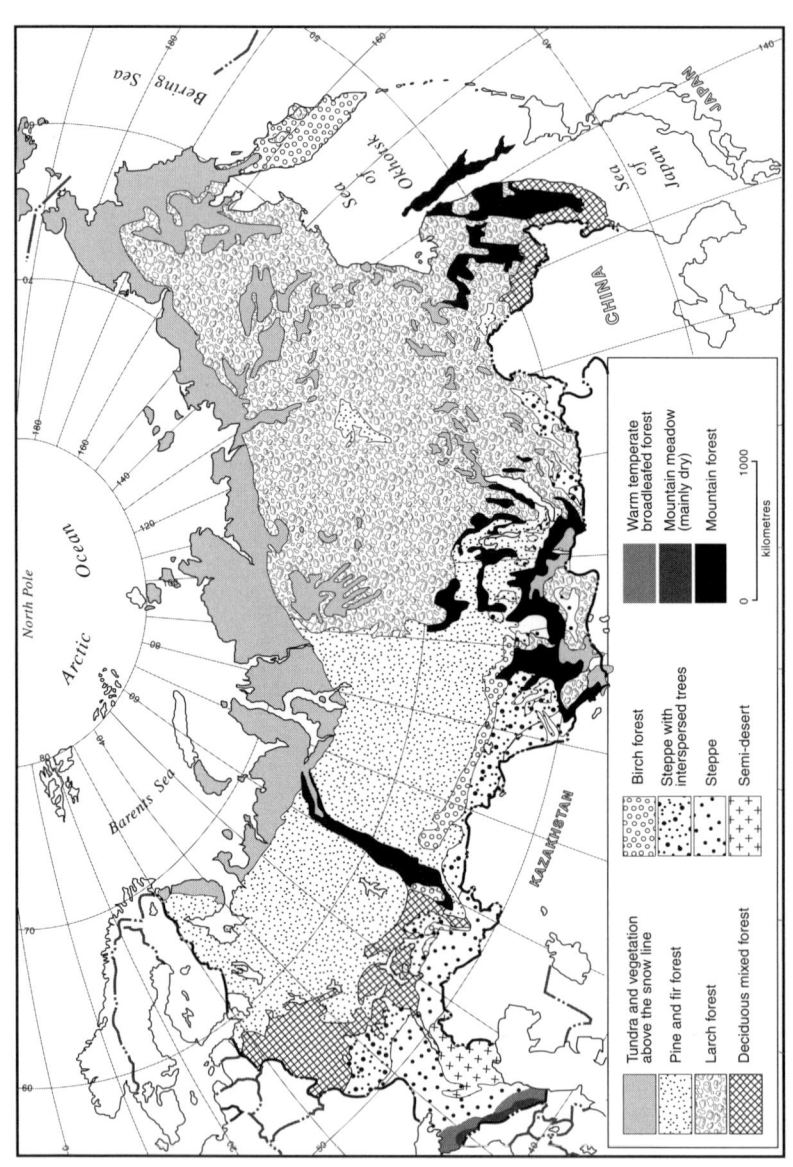

7. **Vegetation and land use**

Rivers in the south of Siberia are blocked with ice for five months of the year, but offer important hydropower potential because of their large size. Siberia is home to two of the biggest hydropower stations in the world.[37] Rivers in the Far East, such as the Amur, provide important transportation opportunities. The most habitable parts of eastern Russia are those in the south and the population densities are highest along the southern borders and the route of the Trans-Siberian Railway (see Map 8).

The forests of eastern Russia account for 57 per cent of the world's coniferous forest and 25 per cent of global wood resources. While stored carbon in these forested areas may only be about half that of the Amazon forest, the eastern Russia forest is the largest in the world. Northeast Asian countries, such as the Republic of Korea, have pursued commercial exploitation of this resource, but the forest has been protected to large degree by the difficulties of logging and transport operations.[38] Nevertheless, Russian scientists report that about 400 000 sq km of Siberian forest have been lost since the 1930s.[39] The Far East region is the main source of marine food production in Russia,[40] but the performance of this industry has also declined since 1992. Reinvestment is poor, vessels are in disrepair, crews are leaving for jobs that pay them, and a number of fishing crews have turned to the more lucrative activity of smuggling.[41]

Infrastructure in the region, especially roads, was and remains severely deficient. Major highways are rare and the only continuous land link between European Russia and Pacific Russia is the Trans-Siberian Railway. There is only one rail link across the border with China. Telecommunications infrastructure remains equally underdeveloped. There are other structural constraints, such as low labour force retention. There is an unhealthy dependence of the economy on commodities, principally oil and gas, non-ferrous metals and timber. For all of its contribution to the Soviet economy through massive exports of oil and gas, the West Siberia region saw little of the resulting wealth.[42]

Mining is the most valuable economic activity in eastern Russia, which has 75 per cent of the country's coal and 65 per cent of its oil, but many of the accessible deposits have already been exploited. For sustained income levels from mining, significant new investment will need to be made to exploit many of the less accessible deposits.[43] Annual diamond sales in 1998 from Russia's biggest producer, which operates in Sakha, netted more than US$1.3 billion in 1997. While this company expects increased production, it expects some of the potential profits to

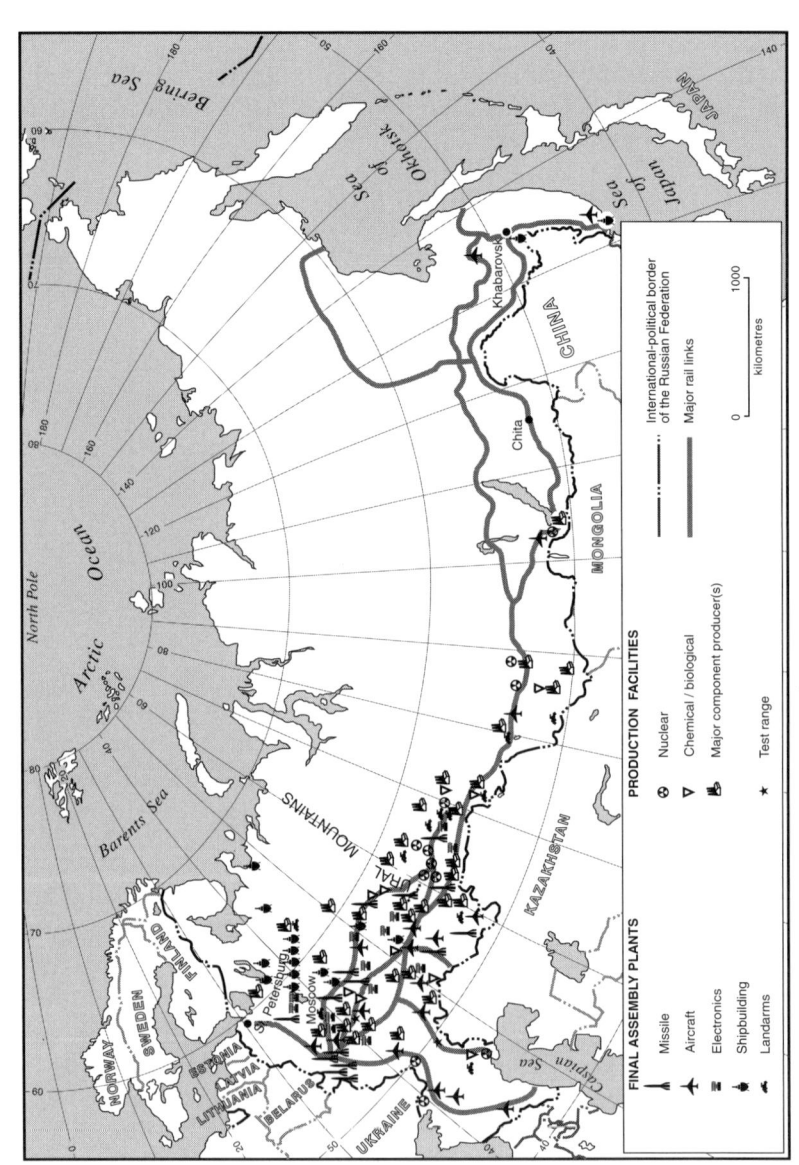

8. Defence industries and major east–west rail links

be affected by declining world prices. The company also expects to lay off workers and to cut capital construction costs by 40 per cent, in an effort to reduce its debt burden.[44]

Two-thirds of Russia's oil is extracted from western Siberia, in particular the Autonomous Locality of Khanti-Mansai.[45] In the last years of Soviet rule and the first years of the Russian Federation, this industry collapsed, with production dropping by half and little new investment. There was a near total clearing out of the State Scientific Research and Design Institute of the Oil and Gas Industry—losing 5800 personnel out of a workforce in the mid-1980s of 6000.[46]

Investment continues in oil and gas, with considerable interest from foreign companies in most phases of extraction, refining and marketing. In early 1998, Chevron signed a deal for worldwide marketing with a local producer in return for upgrading of the Russian refining plant; a gas compressor project for the Lugernetskoe gas field involving a Turkish sub-contractor and multi-national Bateman was reported ahead of schedule in early 1998; and Exxon has been negotiating for some time on a field in Sakhalin.[48] German and French companies are also active in gas development in eastern Russia because of depleted reserves in Western Europe.[49] Production in some fields has been increasing steadily in recent years, with Surgutneftegaz reporting 10.2 billion cubic metres (cu m) for 1997, compared with 9.7 billion cu m in 1996, and 8.4 billion cu m in 1995, with a reported increase in real revenues in the three years of 36.5 per cent.[50]

The Russian government is moving to corporatise a large number of existing ventures in oil and gas into several large conglomerates, with the aim of having them compete internationally with the majors. The first such merger occurred in early 1998, with a new company, Yuksi, bringing together Yukos and Sibneft, and two other companies controlled by them, Eastern Oil Company and the Eastern Siberian Oil and Gas Company. Revenues in 1997 for Yukos and Sibneft were reported at US$5.2 billion and US$3.1 billion respectively. Share prices for the firms participating in the merger rose on the news. Before the merger, Yukos had been planning to raise about US$9 billion for new investments, of which about US$2 billion would be raised inside Russia.[51]

The outlook for oil and gas production in Russia is good, with long-mooted plans for new developments coming much closer to fruition. For example, in late 1997, the Sakhalin–2 oil and gas field operation was set in motion after agreement on the US$10 billion project had been reached in 1994. The first exploratory rigs were due to arrive in the area in early 1998, and production to begin in 1999. The field will be operated by Sakhalin Energy, a consortium including Marathon (20 per cent), Mitsui (25 per cent), Mitsubishi (12.5 per cent) and Royal Dutch Shell (25 per cent).[52] New mining leases continue to be issued, and some are very promising, with Russia's biggest known goldfield, the Sukhoi Log in Irkutsk Province, only opened for bids in early 1998.[53]

Russia's production of coal has slumped badly, by as much as 50 per cent in 1997.[54] A number of low-productivity coal mines have been closed, and coal output in some areas of eastern Russia has dropped. For example, in Magadan Province, production in 1998 was projected to be 20 per cent below 1996 figures.[55] The projected decline can be accounted for in part by the mine closures. Other fields in the province will increase production slightly, but a decline in overall local demand will cap growth.

Accidents and long delays associated with poor maintenance continue to plague the mining industry. In January 1998, a copper smelter in Norilsk supplying 60 per cent of Russia's copper went out of action when a large part of the roof caved in. The plant officials intended to operate the plant without a roof, and repairs were expected to take five months.[56] In December 1997, a mine explosion killed 67 workers.

Capital markets are developing and becoming regularised, with one company in Yekaterinburg in early 1998 doubling its capital base to 2 billion roubles, and offering its executives share options for performance (one of the few companies in Russia to do so). The company has been audited by Ernst & Young for 1995 and 1996 and in January 1998, Ernst & Young was again appointed as auditor for 1997.[57] In late 1997, three forestry companies offered shares at auction, with only one attracting any bids.[58]

There have been some gains in the manufacturing sector. A watch and clock factory in Cheliabinsk, which was privatised in 1992 and which is majority owned by worker-held shares, reported steady growth in productivity by 1998, with 1997 output improving 30 per cent over 1996.[59] The Cheliabinsk Tractor Plant, privatised in 1992, increased production slightly in 1997, but the factory was looking for a much larger increase in 1998.[60] New industries have also been created, including some high-technology manufactures. An engineering plant in Cheliabinsk has begun production of fibre-optic cable using its own artificial quartz crystal technology and, while it needs significant new investment to proceed, it has already serviced orders from domestic clients.[61] A military space launch site in Amur Province was used to launch a US civil satellite on a converted nuclear missile launcher in late 1997[62] at a cost of US$6–8 million.[63] The launch site had been the USSR's easternmost ballistic missile launch complex and was converted to civil use under a presidential decree of 1 March 1996. The US launch was only the second directed from the revamped Svobodny cosmodrome, the first being a Russian military communications satellite. The local government of Yakutia protested the jettisoning of the second stage of the launch vehicle over its territory.[64]

The transport industry in eastern Russia, especially container movement along the Trans-Siberian Railway, is likely to pick up, but only slowly. By 1997, the cost of shipping containers to Europe from Japan via the railway was 40 per cent more expensive than by sea through the Suez Canal. Cargo volumes on the railway had slumped to one-fifth those carried in the 1980s.[65] This represented a loss to Russia of about US$800 million, according to a senior official from Nakhodka.[66] In March 1997, the countries most directly involved in the railway, which had been meeting in an informal coordinating group, decided to set up a permanent working group to better coordinate both policy and implementation of new measures. The group, known as the International Coordinating Council of the Trans-Siberian Railway, brings together Russia, Germany, Belarus, Poland, Hungary, Finland, South Korea and Japan.[67] In late 1997, Russia's Far East Shipping Company (FESCO) took out a loan from the European Bank for Reconstruction and Development for the purchase of three new container ships to service the rail link.[68] Russia has been working with users of the railway to speed up container traffic, expand volumes on the line, and to develop a plan for a 46-hour special container train service from Vladivostok to Budapest.[69] The former First Deputy Prime Minister, Boris Nemtsov, approved in July 1997 measures to reduce taxes, railway tariffs, border controls and customs inspections to improve operation of the railway.[70] Users of the railway must deal with the Belarus government as well as the Russian government, and announcement of the formation of a new union between Russia and Belarus increased hopes among railway executives in Nakhodka that there might be more harmonisation of fees by the two countries.[71]

International air routes in Siberia have not developed as rapidly as local officials had hoped, and a number of construction projects for new international airports have been stopped because of money problems. As of early 1997, an airport completed in Kemerovo in 1995 had never been used.[72]

Some parts of eastern Russia produce food, especially wheat. Annual wheat production in Siberia had peaked at 19 million tonnes, but in 1994 only 15 million tonnes had been produced. Between 1990 and 1993, per capita meat consumption fell from 75 kg to about 60 kg. Consumption of milk and dairy products fell by about 25 per cent.[73] Some parts of the region are food-rich, while others import almost all of their requirements.

Food distribution remains a serious problem, with two regions of western Siberia agreeing in September 1997 to forge closer economic ties, specifically to relieve fuel shortages in one and food shortages in the other: the two governors agreed to barter bread for coal on a regular basis. The two local administrations announced plans to build a freeway to link the main cities of each region.[74] By 1995, there was still no effective wholesale market for meat operating in Siberia, with the region exporting as much meat as it imported from elsewhere in Russia, but with residents being forced to pay much higher prices for the imported meat.[75] The Far East has suffered even more than Siberia from the post-Soviet collapse in food distribution to and from other parts of Russia.[76]

Environmental degradation is a serious problem in eastern Russia, with many parts of Siberia and the Urals region suffering nuclear contamination.[77] The Mayak plant near Cheliabinsk, which produced the nuclear material for the first Soviet nuclear bombs, has suffered three radiological accidents and left a large stock of radioactive waste.[78] The second of these accidents, in 1955, was the world's worst nuclear accident before Chernobyl in 1986. Lake Karachai is so contaminated that to stand by its shore for one hour is sufficient for a fatal dose of radiation. Even some major rivers flowing into the Arctic Ocean have been seriously contaminated, with the Yenesei having about 150 sites of nuclear contamination along a 500 km stretch. Other nuclear-related plants in eastern Russia were operated at Yekaterinburg, Krasnoiarsk and Tomsk.[79] Nizhniaia Tura, north of Yekaterinburg, used to have a very large nuclear warhead production facility.[80]

Atmospheric testing of 113 nuclear weapons at the Soviet test site in the Kazakh Soviet Republic in the 1940s and 1950s produced atmospheric fallout on parts of Siberia, affecting 40 villages where now about 78 000 people live. In 1996, the Russian government set in place a four-year program to alleviate the special problems of the affected areas, which report high incidence of cancers, high infant mortality and lower than normal life expectancy. The program of promised government funding is already seriously in deficit.[81] The islands of Novaia Zemlia just off the north coast of Siberia were the site of numerous military and non-military nuclear tests, and waters around the islands have been used as a dumping site for unimaginably high quantities of radioactive wastes, including as many as 15 retired or damaged nuclear reactors.[82]

Nuclear accidents have continued since the break-up of the USSR, with a major contamination accident reported in 1993 near Tomsk in the Siberian Chemical Combine.[83] This accident was assessed as Level 3 on the international seven-point scale—serious accident without exposure of personnel. When the radiation trail was identified and mapped, and pollution levels in the nearby river monitored, the government report concluded that there were no long-term harmful effects from the radiation leak.[84]

The situation with respect to the background radiation levels built up as the result of 40 years of nuclear operations at Tomsk is however startlingly different and extremely dangerous. An official Russian government report drafted in 1995 found that 'Elk living on the territory of the Siberian Chemical Combine have been so contaminated . . . that people using the meat of such animals in their diet have received dangerous doses of radiation'. The report identified significantly higher rates of biological abnormalities in people, animals and plants and attributed these to nuclear contamination. The report concluded that liquid radioactive wastes stored in the region 'represent a considerable ecological danger'. The report also mentioned that another accident at the Combine on 6 April 1994 showed that the relevant authorities 'are not ready to take large-scale action in emergency situations'. The report found that current normal operations were not resulting in additional nuclear contamination and that in many areas more distant from the Combine, radiation levels had been declining and in most areas were within allowable limits.[85]

The safe handling of nuclear reactors decommissioned under a US–Russia agreement on the cessation of plutonium production is becoming more serious with the passage of time. In 1996, Russian scientists who surveyed three reactors decommissioned from the Siberian Chemical Combine reported deteriorating conditions in the method of storage.[86]

Other forms of air and water pollution are serious in some parts of the region. The world's deepest freshwater lake, Lake Baikal, suffers chemical pollution and large organic waste disposal. One region has rates of lung disease almost 50 per cent higher than the national average. Air pollution is causing acid rain and degradation of reindeer pastures. Oil pipeline leaks are regular events (an estimated 11 000 per year in the 100 000 km of pipeline), and often pour millions of tonnes of oil onto the ground before they can be repaired.[87] Burning off of natural gas at the point of extraction causes serious ash fallout. Some rivers in summer run with continuous oil slicks.[88] Soil in many parts of Siberia is contaminated, with oil concentrations in some areas reaching one part in ten.

Most parts of the Far East region are free of the environmental hazards faced by Siberia and the Urals regions, and in several key measures (air pollution, soil and water degradation) the Far East has the lowest levels of all economic regions in Russia.[89] But it has its own problems, including overfishing of marine life, and pollution of water sources by timber-felling processes, leading to declines in fish spawning.[90]

Notwithstanding the range of political and economic problems facing eastern Russia today, the future looks particularly bright because of long-term projections for income from the region's mineral wealth, particularly natural gas. The government has set up a number of free economic zones, including in Nakhodka. A number of commentators have suggested that the political centre of gravity of Russia might shift toward those few regions where these resources are concentrated. There are already strong links between key figures in Moscow and leading commercial and political bodies in the key regions, such as Yamalo-Nenetsk and Khanti-Mansiisk.[91]

REGIONAL POLITICS

One of the more important aspects of regional politics in Russia, including east of the Urals, was the emergence of a system of regional administrators appointed directly by President Yeltsin. The formal title of these positions was 'head of administration' but they are often referred to as 'governors' in the press. In one of its earliest reforms, the central government in Moscow abolished all regional executive administrations which had operated under the legal authority of local 'soviets'.[92] Regional heads of administration appointed by Yeltsin were supervised by a nominated presidential representative. The appointed regional heads had the authority to appoint heads of smaller locality administrations.

Another aspect of regional politics was the move to create regional associations, based around the main planning regions. In

November 1990, the chairmen of regional soviets of three provinces, two territories and one autonomous republic in Siberia met in Kemerovo and signed an agreement setting up the Siberian Association. By 1994, the 19 administrative regions of East and West Siberia had joined the association.[93] While there has been talk from time to time of a separatist movement based around the association, it has operated almost exclusively as an economic grouping to coordinate and lobby for regional development. An important function is also to lobby in social policy areas, including public health.

Some parts of the Russian Federation made efforts to upgrade their formal legal status from province to republic in an effort to eliminate a number of the disadvantages they suffered relative to republics in areas like authority to levy and control tax revenue.[94] Sverdlovsk and Chita Provinces and Maritime Territory attempted to upgrade their status through declarations.

On 27–28 March 1992, a congress of Siberian deputies heard a number of calls for separation from Russia and eventually passed a resolution with a large majority calling for 'urgent and comprehensive measures for the decolonisation of Siberia'.[95] The motivation for growing regionalism in the local politics among the provinces and territories was not so much a desire to split with the Russian Federation, as the Chechen Republic had, but a desire to protest and correct discriminatory practices by the central government or unreasonable intervention by it in local affairs.[96] Another factor was that the power holders from the Soviet era saw manipulation of the regional autonomy issue as one the few cards they had to play if they were going to retain their positions and privileges.[97]

When it comes to regional politics of Russia, there is a fundamental distinction between the 21 autonomous republics which were established as part of the 'nationalities' policy in the Soviet era and most of the other administrative units (provinces and territories)[98] which were administered as more integral parts of the Soviet-era RSFSR.[99] As mentioned in chapter 1, the most famous of these republics is Chechnia, which had declared itself independent soon after the failed coup of August 1991. East of the Urals, there are five of these 21 republics, as well as an autonomous Jewish province and eight autonomous localities based around non-Russian communities. It is the loyalty of these non-Russian communities to the Federation that has caused most concern about the unity of the country but eastern Russia has not seen and is unlikely to see a secession of the Chechnia variety.

The outcome of the various moves for greater autonomy were heavily influenced at particular times by the ebb and flow of national political struggles. In April 1993, when Yeltsin was besieged in Moscow with serious political problems, the Siberian Association was powerful enough to resist his dismissal of two governors[100] and forced him to apologise for the move. After Yeltsin's attack on the Russian parliament in 1993, through which the Siberian Association had backed the parliament, Yeltsin eventually retaliated, forcing the retirement of one of the two governors and bringing the Association somewhat to heel.[101] In late 1993, Sverdlovsk Province sought to establish itself as the central authority in a new Urals republic comprising five other provinces. This bid failed but it aggravated tensions between Moscow and the regions, and resulted in the formation of a new national political party, Transformation of the Fatherland, by the unsuccessful regional administrator from Sverdlovsk.[102] Another particularly confrontational regional leader has been Evgeny Nazdratenko, a technocrat appointed by Yeltsin in 1993 as Governor of the Maritime Territory.

The mood east of the Urals for confrontation with Moscow was tempered somewhat after Yeltsin's victory over the former parliament in 1993 and there were clear signs that Moscow too was listening more to the legitimate economic and social demands of this region.[103] But not all parts of the region have abandoned their confrontations. In 1995, the governor of Khabarovsk Territory advocated the creation of a Far East Republic.[104] In August 1995, the national parliament passed a Law on Local Self-Government which laid down clear lines of responsibility for local legislatures or councils and the corresponding executive agencies.[105] Under a 1995 decree, elections for governors were scheduled for December 1996, and for the local legislatures in December 1997.[106] In the 1995 elections, eastern Russia returned 61 deputies from the 225 single member seats in the State Duma. (Another 225 are elected by proportional representation from party lists subject to a nationwide vote.)

Regional politics east of the Urals remains heavily influenced by national trends, but electoral sentiment in the region is singularly conservative (see Tables 2.2 and 2.3).[107] The distribution of seats according to political tendencies was as follows: Communist-aligned parties (C)—11; nationalists (N)—7; Socialist Reform (SR)—1; centre-right parties (CR)—3; and liberal democratic parties (LD)—7. The one constituency seat won by Zhirinovski's

Liberal Democratic Party, a nationalist party, was in eastern Russia.

In December 1997, the liberal democrat Apple group formed an alliance with a group led by Aleksandr Lebed, former National Security Adviser and presidential candidate in 1996, to field a common slate of candidates for local elections in Novosibirsk Province on the basis of their common opposition to the Communist Party and Zhirinovski's party.[108] The head of the Apple Group, Yavlinski, said in campaigning for these elections that if the joint slate did well in Novosibirsk there would be room to consider an alliance at the national level. In February 1998, Lebed announced he would stand in the 26 April 1998 election for governor of the Siberian territory of Krasnoiarsk as representative of the Popular Republican Party.[109] Lebed won this election.

The problems confronting Lebed in his administration of the Krasnoiarsk territory are typical for other regional administrations. In an interview for Moscow TV in September 1998, Lebed revealed that in his first three months, the territory had received only 4 per cent of the funds it felt it was due to receive from central authorities.[110] The day of the interview, there were strikes in more than 10 per cent of the schools in the territory. Lebed opined that 'all the old schemes of running the country from Moscow have become outdated forever'. He said he had been able to raise tax collection from 15 per cent of the planned target to 35 per cent, and that if he could reach 50 per cent, that would be satisfactory. There were 250 000 people on the payroll of the federal government in his territory and he was having to pay them from local funds because the central government was not paying them.

In eastern Russia, the administrations of the provinces, territories and localities (the component parts of the Federation) have been engaged in a power struggle with the mayors of the major cities and towns over the division of rights and responsibilities between them. In the Maritime Territory, this power struggle resulted in a running conflict between the governor of the territory and the mayor of Vladivostok, the latter having been dismissed by the governor and facing court charges which he said were trumped up by the governor to force him from his job. Similar battles had emerged in other cities throughout the region, prompting the Association of Siberian and Far East Cities to hold a meeting to protest the regular disputes and to write to the head of the Presidential Administration, Anatoly Chubais.[113] In 1996, most of the city administrations could have been classified as

Table 2.2   1995 Parliamentary elections—regional results for single member seats

	Party/bloc	Percentage of vote[111]
Amur	Independent/Local Groups	39.05
Cheliabinsk (182)	Congress of Russian Societies (N)	18.66
Cheliabinsk (183)	Democratic Choice (L)	21.61
Cheliabinsk (184)	Congress of Russian Societies (N)	37.09
Cheliabinsk (185)	Democratic Choice (L)	40.30
Cheliabinsk (186)	Congress of Russian Societies (N)	38.75
Chita (187)	Agrarian Party (C)	37.59
Chita (188)	Independent/Local Groups	21.74
Irkutsk (80)	Independents' Bloc	42.67
Irkutsk (81)	Independent/Local Groups	27.14
Irkutsk (82)	Russia Our Home (RC)	48.23
Irkutsk (83)	Agrarian Party (C)	38.90
Jewish Autonomous	Communist Party (C)	22.68
Kamchatka	Apple (L)	22.11
Kemerovo (88)	Communist Party (C)	33.16
Kemerovo (89)	Communist Party (C)	20.43
Kemerovo (90)	Independent/Local Groups	21.71
Kemerovo (91)	Independent/Local Groups	45.05
Kurgan	Independent/Local Groups	26.91
Magadan	Independent/Local Groups	41.82
Novosibirsk (124)	Agrarian Party (C)	34.94
Novosibirsk (125)	Independent/Local Groups	13.60
Novosibirsk (126)	Independent/Local Groups	15.10
Novosibirsk (127)	Liberal Democratic Party (N)	24.22
Omsk (128)	Power to the People (N)	21.06
Omsk (129)	Independent/Local Groups	38.29
Omsk (130)	Power to the People/Independent (N)	27.48
Sakhalin	Communist Party (C)	23.28
Sverdlovsk (161)	Apple (L)	17.09
Sverdlovsk (162)	Independent/Local Groups	29.14
Sverdlovsk (163)	Independent/Local Groups	21.68
Sverdlovsk (164)	Transformation of the Fatherland (RC)	17.01
Sverdlovsk (165)	Independent/Local Groups	25.01
Sverdlovsk (166)	Independent/Local Groups	19.41
Sverdlovsk(167)	Forward Russia (L)	30.22
Tomsk	Independent/Local Groups	21.47
Tiumen (178)	Independent/Local Groups	21.61
Tiumen (179)	Independent/Local Groups	20.56
Territory		
Khabarovsk (57)	Communist Party (C)	21.59
Khabarovsk (58)	Independent/Local Groups	16.76
Krasnoiarsk (45)	Congress of Russian Societies (N)	32.30
Krasnoiarsk (46)	Independent/Local Groups	35.17
Krasnoiarsk (47)	Agrarian Party (C)	31.41
Krasnoiarsk (48)	Democratic Choice (L)	14.28
Maritime (49)	Women of Russia (SR)	25.07
Maritime (50)	Independent/Local Groups	22.43
Maritime (51)	Communist Party (C)	43.50
Locality		
Aga-Buriat	Independent/Local Groups	37.39

	Party/bloc	Percentage of vote[111]
Chukotsk (Republic)	Independent/Local Groups	28.17
Evenk	Samovydvizhenie	14.89
Khanti-Mansai (221)	Independent/Local Groups	15.00
Khanti-Mansai (222)	Independent/Local Groups	15.26
Koriak (Republic)	Independent/Local Groups	17.98
Taimyr	Independent/Local Groups	26.22
Ust-Orda Buriat	Russia Our Home (RC)	43.05
Yamalo-Nenetsk	Samovydvizhenie	22.63
Republic		
Buryat	Independent/Local Groups	21.66
Gorno-Altai	Democratic Choice (L)	21.54
Khakassia	Independent/Local Groups	22.33
Sakha (Yakutia)	Power to the People (C)	24.69
Tyva	Our Home Russia (RC)	40.95

Table 2.3 1995 parliamentary elections—eastern Russia results for national lists

Province	CP	LDPR	ROH	Apple	Largest other[112]
Amur	161 456	59 707	16 360	15 504	27 100 (WOR)
Cheliabinsk	243 866	166 943	131 795	164 033	121 568 (CRS)
Chita	111 120	106 130	21 900	13 021	42 716 (CWR)
Irkutsk	163 458	162 729	86 140	68 487	72 635 (WOR)
Jewish Autonomous	20 937	10 355	4 525	4 075	6 301 (EMP)
Kamchatka	18 752	26 551	11 646	33 860	6 800 (WOR)
Kemerovo	632 911	166 583	46 217	38 048	93 027 (PWS)
Kurgan	120 328	106 175	37 642	17 102	44 111 (APR)
Magadan	12 565	22 308	8 157	7 630	6 808 (PWS)
Novosibirsk	287 141	243 893	96 943	78 308	68 815 (APR)
Omsk	164 862	164 163	67 329	36 740	87 036 (PTP)
Sakhalin	64 812	40 335	10 740	17 811	16 180 (WOR)
Sverdlovsk	149 356	166 644	150 761	120 362	218 676 (TOF)
Tomsk	87 233	48 678	42 515	48 165	32 125 (WOR)
Tiumen	84 877	61 352	52 174	24 312	32 433 (PWS)
Territory					
Khabarovsk	186 225	121 254	51 661	67 465	78 404 (PWS)
Krasnoiarsk	257 233	172 315	124 872	93 655	78 927 (WOR)
Maritime	177 643	193 235	33 089	91 764	61 786 (WOR)
Autonomous Locality					
Aga-Buriat	5 635	2 795	1 175	374	10 109 (APR)
Chukotsk (Republic)	4 448	5 371	7 018	2 625	3 066 (EMP)
Evenk	1 103	1 046	535	399	842 (EMP)
Khanti-Mansai	35 454	68 054	62 692	25 285	47 273 (PWS)
Koriak (Republic)	1 385	1 821	962	1 303	1 205 (EMP)
Taimyr	1 071	2 696	2 422	1 074	1 401 (EMP)
Ust-Orda Buryat	13 202	4 156	5 373	1 186	11 048 (APR)
Yamalo-Nenetsk	10 462	27 770	42 816	11 576	20 519 (PWS)
Autonomous Republic					
Buriat	483 832	45 418	145 466	16 613	123 239 (DCR)
Gorno-Altai	25 115	9 042	4 804	2 150	11 006 (APR)
Khakassia	47 836	31 804	9 491	8 979	14 445 (WOR)
Sakha (Yakutia)	68 622	26 511	53 577	14 136	29 145 (PTP)
Tyva	12 444	5 914	30 536	1 501	94 222 (APR)

'bankrupt' but have been able to operate on increasingly high budget deficits.[114]

By 1998, the regions of Russia were more autonomous or independent from Moscow than at any time, and most major political parties favoured all regions being treated on an equal footing, regardless of their original status in the RSFSR under Soviet rule. The regions continue to put pressure on Moscow to do more.[115] The mayors of the cities in Siberia and the Far East through the Association have lobbied the President and legislators to get the power to retain all income tax and land tax revenue. Yeltsin signed into law a bill on the Financial Foundations of Local Self-Government with which the mayors' association was broadly comfortable.[116]

CONCLUSION

Russia east of the Ural Mountains has huge economic potential, but largely in the extraction of raw materials. It has a poorly developed social infrastructure and a small population facing quite extreme circumstances. But as the country as a whole becomes much more reliant on raw material extraction as its main source of export earnings and as its main point of attraction for foreign investment, then the political centre of gravity for Russia as a whole will inevitably shift toward its eastern territories. The proximity of these regions to the dynamic economies of East Asia and major Pacific Rim economies, such as the USA, will also contribute to this shift. A political spirit is alive and well in these diverse regions, as events in Sverdlovsk Province and Krasnoiarsk and Maritime Territories demonstrate. Some observers would say that politics in these regions is closer to the common people than in the big cities or rural areas of European Russia. The area may be more politically conservative than the big cities west of the Urals, but this tendency is more likely to be the future of Russia than a liberal tendency. Any effort to mount an extra-legal challenge to the state in Russia is more likely to be successful in the east because of the great distances involved and poor infrastructure for moving military and police forces.

If Russia is unable to bring greater coherence to its regional policy and impose stricter discipline on regional leaders, the country is headed for even more serious problems of governance than it has endured in recent years. Former Prime Minister

Primakov took steps to co-opt the leaders of key regions like Sverdlovsk Province and Krasnoiarsk Territory into the central government. This has worked to some degree but eventually the leaders of these powerful regions will acquire more influence at the expense of the central government. The near future is more likely to bring a steady decline in centre–region relations rather than dramatic attempts to carve out complete independence from Russia. Good governance will not be restored in Russia for many years in the absence of a new authoritarian regime. The establishment of Lebed and people like him in positions of power in eastern Russia will remain a strong force for national unity, at the same time as providing a strong basis for challenging the authority of the centre.

3

National strategic policy

The intense domestic contest for the national identity of the Russian state and the struggle for legitimacy to create that identity have been sketched in chapter 1. One part of this contest about national identity concerned the vision of Russia's place in the world. Some insight was offered into the competing ideas about Russia's international identity and the political prospects of the advocates of particular positions. But for all of the heated debate and dramatic posturing by extremist parties, the initiative in strategic policy has remained squarely with the government. If the constitutional authority of the government relative to the State Duma is formidable in domestic policy, it is almost unassailable on foreign policy. The President and his administration set the general directions of policy about the geopolitical standing of Russia, about which countries should be allies, and about day to day responses to the country's security requirements. It is the aim of this chapter and the next to describe the government's choices and dispositions in strategic policy since 1991. This chapter concentrates on Russia's global aspirations and preoccupations and its regional strategic interests in Europe and Central Asia. Russia's strategic interests and preoccupations in the Asia–Pacific are the subject of the following chapter.

The choices of the Russian government in strategic policy have been clear and represent a continuation of the trends set in place by Gorbachev in the last years of the USSR. His 'new thinking' in strategic policy had already reoriented the strategic posture of the USSR well before its collapse in 1991. The Cold War had ended by 1989 and the Berlin Wall had been destroyed because the USSR had adopted a new defensive military doctrine. A series of summit meetings involving Gorbachev and Western leaders agreed upon a variety of measures for arms control, reduction of military forces and withdrawal of Soviet forces from Eastern Europe. Legislators and government officials in the USSR were looking to reduce defence spending, cut the armed forces in size, and introduce a professional force, as opposed to one based largely on conscription.[1] Notwithstanding considerable confusion, serious policy setbacks and notable exceptions, the general strategic disposition of the government of the successor state of Russia has been one of 'war avoidance', resolution of conflicts through peaceful means, and preference for a defensive military strategy. Questions remain about how far this disposition has been one of choice or necessity, and how much it has been the product of an unstable political consensus in the Russian government, but the basically defensive outline of the strategic policy of the new Russian state after 1991 has been very clear.

At the same time, there has been a shift in the rhetoric of Russian strategic policy away from more liberal and progressive positions. The 'new thinking' of Gorbachev's advisers was imbued with a spirit of common security and universal values and it rejected concepts like balance of power. By 1999, the Russian government was increasingly resorting to the more traditional approaches to diplomacy rooted in balance of power and concepts like 'national interest', and was paying less attention to concepts such as 'our common European home' that had been raised by Gorbachev and later on pursued by Andrei Kozyrev, first foreign minister of the newly born Russian Federation. Moreover, NATO's air campaign against Yugoslavia, Russia's traditional ally in the Balkans, only reinforced the opinion in Russia that its relations with the West should be reassessed.

It would be wrong to see strong intellectual coherence in the positions taken by any state over the full breadth of its foreign and defence policies. Russia does not have a highly developed ideology of foreign policy. Its strategic policy, like that of any state, is an imperfect mix of responses occasioned by necessity, threat or opportunity. Strategic policy can be shaped by domestic political imperatives as much as by external imperatives. Where costs and risks are low, a state may be more inclined to posture according to domestic political and emotional pressures. Where costs are higher, a state may be more inclined to take a cold and detached view and make a very hard-nosed calculation about the appropriate course of action. Without attempting to square the circle and to present Russia's strategic policy as a highly coherent and rationally developed set of preferences, this chapter sketches the country's response to its most important strategic problems.

Pragmatism, long considered in Western European tradition as the strength of any country's strategic policy, has been a marked characteristic of Russian policy since 1991. Russia's immediate geopolitical environment is characterised by states in crisis or not far from it. Russia itself has lurched from crisis to crisis since 1991. There is grim acceptance in Moscow that if Russia is to maintain any semblance of stability for itself, it must deal effectively with each set of problems as pragmatically as possible. There has been little support in the Russian government for the view that this diverse array of complex problems can be solved through adoption of some all-encompassing strategic posture premised on restoration of empire or return to policies of confrontation with other great powers. There is widespread support in the government for the view that the future of Russia's strategic environment depends on the ability to work with all of its available resources and with the cooperation of other great powers to stabilise existing crises and neutralise a number of latent crises.

This chapter and the next are at best an overview of Russia's strategic policy. There are numerous points of qualification or subtleties that might have been introduced on many of the issues raised, but Russia—as the largest country in the world, sharing borders with 16 countries, and still very much a great power with interests well beyond its borders—has a very large agenda in its strategic policy. As Alpo M. Rusi, a well-known European political scientist, has pointed out: 'Russia as an economic entity has fallen to secondary status but remains a great power militarily and politically.'[2] This chapter looks first at Russia's policy on its place in the world, before looking more closely at the strategic interests of Russia in the former Soviet republics. These newly independent states (NIS) remain Russia's single most important strategic preoccupation. The chapter reviews Russian reactions to the expansion of NATO in the context of Russia's attempts—largely ad hoc and reactive—to stabilise its immediate strategic environment in the wake of the break-up of the USSR. Chapter 4 deals with Russia's strategic policies in the Asia–Pacific. Arms control issues are canvassed briefly in this chapter but are addressed more fully in chapter 5 from the perspective of how they affect the structure and capacities of Russia's armed forces.

NEW RUSSIA AND INTERNATIONAL SOCIETY—FROM LIBERAL ROOTS TO GREAT POWER PRAGMATISM

After 1991, Russia had to make severe adjustments in its foreign policy toward the USA and other great powers, such as Japan and China. The Soviet relationship with the USA had defined much of world affairs for the previous five decades, and the new Russian state was not going to surrender this position of prominence. But in a much weakened position compared with the USSR in the 1970s and 1980s, the new Russia found it much more difficult to engage in the full range of issues from global arms control to regional security in places such as the Middle East or Southeast Asia. For its part, the USA pursued a three-track policy toward Russia: engagement, hedging and building relations with the non-Russian former republics of the USSR.[3] The USA remained suspicious and was keeping its powder dry at the same time as holding out the hand of friendship. Moreover, the USA was provoking Russian suspicions by actively courting strategic engagement of Russia's closest neighbours, such as Ukraine and Kazakhstan.[4]

The preferred strategic posture of the new Russian state in these circumstances was laid out in 1992 by the first Foreign Minister, Andrei Kozyrev, in an article in *Foreign Affairs*. Russia identified itself as a member of the international community of liberal democratic states working within established norms and institutions of international society. Russia's participation in that society would be undertaken in the spirit of a progressive interpretation of international law, rather than a conservative one. Kozyrev said that Russia now recognised that 'assurance of democracy is no longer an internal affair of states' and that the international community had an obligation to remove threats to democracy. Kozyrev rejected 'any unnatural military responsibility [for Russia] beyond its borders', thereby signalling an end to Russian pretensions to restoration of empire in the former Soviet republics or the former Warsaw Pact countries of Eastern Europe. He saw an evolution of NATO and the North Atlantic Cooperation Council as 'leading to openness and partnership in the military–strategic sphere'.[5]

The new Russia wanted very much to be a responsible member of the international community. It started to join many of the international organisations the USSR had shunned on ideological grounds. These included the International Monetary Fund, the World Bank and the General Agreement on Tariffs and

Trade. These moves were specifically identified by Kozyrev as helping to 'establish Russia as a reliable partner in the community of civilized states'.[6] Active participation in international organisations such as the Council of Europe and the Conference on Security and Cooperation in Europe[7] were also seen by the new government as contributing to the resolution of internal problems in the former Soviet republics, including Russia.

Even at his most liberal, Kozyrev had warned Western observers not to expect a consistent pattern of relations between Russia and its former partner republics in the USSR.[8] But equally he boasted that the lack of substance in the structures of the Commonwealth of Independent States (CIS) would mask the positive interactions between them as part of a geostrategic renovation of the Eurasian region. Kozyrev asserted that Russia's participation in the CIS would be based on the principle of complete equality, but reminded the world that 'Russia cannot afford to forget about the particular responsibility conferred upon it by history'. Kozyrev said he was referring to Russia's internationally recognised status as a nuclear weapons power which is a permanent member of the United Nations Security Council, and therefore a 'Great Power'.

Kozyrev believed that the new Russia was for the most part surrounded by 'friendly and positive external surroundings',[9] but he warned that the old attitudes of hostility were still powerful in Russia, that pressure from the 'managerial apparatus' and the 'military-industrial complex' for Russia to re-orient its foreign policy would continue and that the new liberal course in Russian policy did not yet have a 'reliable guarantee'.[10] His assessment about the lack of powerful enemies is important because it means that even though strong extremist forces have emerged inside the country, they have been denied one of the most powerful tools for the installation of an authoritarian or totalitarian regime—a hostile international environment.

By the end of 1992, the liberal democratic Kozyrev had become the loyal servant of his newly democratic country and was forced, along with the Yeltsin administration as a whole, to be more responsive, in rhetoric at least, to the majority views of powerful political forces which wanted a return to great power status for Russia somewhat akin to the role it had played in the nineteenth century. The debates turned on a variety of visions for new federal or union relations among the former Soviet republics. Some of these visions were based on imagined ethnic lines, Slavic versus Eurasian, or Central Asian, while others were based on economic considerations. Many in Russia feared that, if their new state were forced in international policy to defer to the USA and Western Europe out of economic and social weakness, any distinctive Russian culture would be swept away just as their Soviet identity had evaporated overnight. As one writer put it in 1995, 'the urge to recreate some sort of empire in the "geopolitical space" of what was once the Soviet Union is manifest in almost all shades of the Russian political spectrum'.[11] This renewed aspiration to great power status manifested itself as early as 1994 when Russia claimed successes in opposing proposals for NATO air strikes against Serbian forces in Bosnia, a position based almost exclusively on a resurrected notion of pan-Slavism; and when it claimed success in opposing membership of NATO for former Warsaw Pact members.[12] (Russian reactions to expansion of NATO are discussed later in this chapter.)

Although Russia retains its great power pretensions, its circle of interests has narrowed considerably and many more distant or less urgent issues with which it once concerned itself simply ceased to matter. This was largely a matter of lack of money, but it was also a condition forced on it by crises at home and in its immediate neighbourhood. Most Third World countries virtually fell off the screen as far as Russia's new foreign policy was concerned. The Middle East was an exception, especially in the Oslo–Madrid peace process, but Russia was only included in these talks as the result of US determination to prop up the new Russia's status as a great power. Within the Middle East, Iraq was a special case for sustained Russian attention, especially after the appointment of Yevgeny Primakov as Foreign Minister, because of the desire of Russia to posture against the appearance of a US free hand in the UN Security Council.

Several other Third World countries did remain high-priority targets of a more vigorous foreign policy. The richer countries, such as Iran or Malaysia, remained important as potential markets. The largely Muslim countries to the south of Russia (Iran, Turkey, Saudi Arabia, Iraq) remained important foreign policy targets because of concerns about Muslim separatism within the Russian Federation, civil disturbances in the former Soviet republics, and a variety of other strategic pressures. Even as early as 1991, many strategists in Moscow had identified the 'southern tier' of neighbouring Muslim countries as the most important source of serious threat to the USSR—more important even than NATO or China.

In 1995, especially in the light of the weak showing of liberal democrats in the State Duma elections, the internationalist influences on Russian foreign policy represented by Kozyrev were no longer politically viable for the Yeltsin administration. In fact, as early as 1993, Russia's political elite had become increasingly critical of Kozyrev's pro-Western attitudes. For example, Aleksei Arbatov, himself a liberal, argued that Kozyrev was 'selling out' Russia's national interests to the West.[13] After much criticism of Kozyrev by a range of political leaders in Russia, Yeltsin 'accepted his resignation' on 5 January 1996 and several days later replaced him with Primakov, the head of the Foreign Intelligence Service. Primakov had served as a journalist for the Communist Party newspaper *Pravda* in the Middle East in the 1960s, before transferring to academic work, where his output was typical of Soviet-style propagandistic studies of international affairs.

Primakov had risen under Gorbachev to become a Central Committee member, but after the August 1991 coup, he was appointed as a First Deputy Head of the KGB, before being appointed first to head the USSR's new Central Intelligence Service in November 1991, and then to head Russia's new Foreign Intelligence Service in December 1991. It was from this post that Primakov had taken the post of Foreign Minister. In an interview in December 1995, he had criticised Kozyrev for wanting, without regard to the cost to Russia, to move away from the Cold War 'to enter European society', taking a free ride on the backs of Western countries and 'following' them, when a more appropriate policy was to 'settle into normal relations with our former Cold War opponents but to keep these relations on a basis of equality'.[14] Primakov's appointment signalled a reorientation of Russian strategic policy away from pursuit of relations with the USA and NATO toward invigorated efforts to establish close relations with countries like China, Japan and countries of the Middle East.[15] Primakov sought to restore what he and many Russians saw as balance in Russia's posture, which had to them appeared to be unduly subservient to a very pushy, even strategically discomfiting USA.

Russian suspicions of the West, which had been gathering pace by 1996, had not overwhelmed their willingness to work with other great powers for a more stable international order. Russia was very keen to gain the support of other major powers to keep up its appearance of great power status. Primakov in particular vowed that he did not want a new confrontation with the West and that he did not want to harm US–Russia relations.[16] The declared policy of the Russian government by 1997 was that the main threats to Russian security were 'predominantly non-military', there was no external global threat, and the threat of internal secession could be met by allowing full internal autonomy for any region as long as the Russian Federation retained administrative control of foreign policy and foreign economic relations.[17] In May 1997, a number of events occurred which symbolised the new cooperative relationships in strategic policy: the Founding Act on Russia's Relations with NATO, the conclusion of the Russia–Belarus Treaty on union, agreement on a Russia–Ukraine treaty, and signing of a peace agreement between the Russian government and Chechnia.[18] By 1997, the USA succeeded in gaining Russia's acceptance—albeit reluctant—for membership in NATO of former Warsaw Pact allies Poland, Hungary and the Czech Republic.

Also in May 1997, Russia adopted a new 'blueprint' on national security (discussed further in chapter 5). On 17 December 1997, President Yeltsin signed an edict publicly promulgating the new doctrine under the title 'Russian Federation National Security Blueprint'. The document covered internal as well as external threats, and extended conceptions of security to embrace individual human security, ecological security and information warfare. The document has separate sections on Russia in the world community, Russia's national interests, threats to national security and safeguarding national security. It seeks in particular to resolve some of the institutional issues that had arisen in the preceding years since the promulgation of the Constitution. The blueprint 'formulates key directions and principles of state policy'. In the document, Russia moved to a view of comprehensive security that owed much more to the 'new thinking'[19] of the Gorbachev era than to anything in the Soviet period. A 1997 study by the prestigious Institute of National Security and Strategic Studies in Moscow characterised Russia's current strategic circumstances as heavily influenced by a new reliance on non-military means of ensuring military security and a new acceptance of large-scale economic integration in the international community of states.[20]

By 1998, Russia had been accepted as a member of the Asia–Pacific Economic Cooperation group, and the G–7 had been expanded to the G–8 to include Russia. It had been accepted to both after it had applied considerable diplomatic pressure and after other states accepted that even though Russian membership presented some important problems, it was better to include Russia as evidence of a commitment to work with it on problems of global governance. When Primakov was appointed as Prime Minister in September 1998, he told the Duma during confirmation discussions that it was not in Russia's interests to turn back to a path of confrontation and that a pro-American tag on one of the liberal members of the parliament was overly simplistic.[21] The Deputy Chairman of the Defence Committee of the State Duma, Aleksei Arbatov, asserted in 1998 that the imperialist aspirations of the former Soviet government had all but lost their appeal in Moscow: 'With the exception of a group of revanchist retired generals and militant marginal-politicians, nobody in the Russian political elite or strategic community evaluates the military needs of the country's armed forces in the spirit of restoration of the empire through force.'[22] The Defence Minister, Marshal Igor Sergeyev, observed in July 1998 that while Russia was opposed to the expansion of NATO because it carried a potential threat of undermining strategic stability in Europe, Russian cooperation with NATO was the best way of making sure that stability was maintained and that NATO itself was transformed into a 'truly effective' political system of 'Euro–Atlantic security'. He also emphasised Russia's preference for non-violent settlement of conflicts.[23] In January 1999, the Foreign Minister, Igor Ivanov, had expressed the view that even though there were irritants in the relationship with the USA, these could be overcome and should not be allowed to overshadow the whole relationship. He said that it was important to prevent disagreements from evolving into conflicts, and that the USA and Russia had a mutual obligation to maintain an international strategic partnership.[24] A few days later, he was talking of the 'concurring strategic interests' between the USA and Russia as the basis for US–Russian relations, and the importance of reaching compromise where there were disagreements.[25]

At the same time the basic directions or tenets of Russian strategic policy were under more serious challenge. Through 1998, Russia had found considerable difficulty with US approaches to international relations and regularly postured in opposition to a large variety of US initiatives. For example, Russia had opposed US plans for military action against Iraq to retaliate against Iraq's non-compliance with the inspection regime put in place by UN Security Council resolutions for destruction of Iraq's weapons of mass destruction. Russia was clearly dissatisfied that the USA was able to use its military power in this way and invoke the authority of the UN, but Russia's position conformed to a well-established pattern of opposition for opposition's sake. One concern appears to be that expressed by a journalist interviewing the head of Russia's Security Council in May 1997, commenting on the series of accords mentioned above: 'There is a view that as a result of the accords, Russia has lost face and dropped into the category of third-class states'.[26] But another concern felt by many Russian leaders, like the Defence Minister, Igor Sergeyev, was that the expansion of NATO was beginning to block Russia's efforts to re-establish some semblance of order in the CIS states and a working alliance among them.[27]

By early 1999, Russia was even more uncomfortable with US policies. In December 1998, in response to the US bombing of Iraq in Operation Desert Fox, Moscow recalled its ambassadors to the USA and the UK, and even threatened to deploy its Pacific Fleet warships to the Persian Gulf.[28] In January 1999, Russia's Foreign Minister, Igor Ivanov, called on the USA to avoid surprises and to stop bypassing the UN Security Council.[29] A widely respected military commentator, President of the Academy of Military Sciences, Makhmut Gareyev, observed that US and NATO policies were forcing Russia to 'revise the cardinal principles of its strategy to ensure the country's national security'.[30] He cited NATO's eastward expansion, the use of NATO forces in the Balkans for police functions, and US attempts to withdraw from the 1972 Anti-Ballistic Missile (ABM) Treaty.[31] This treaty is seen in Moscow, and by some foreign specialists, as a cornerstone of the strategic stability between the USA and the USSR that by 1986 allowed Gorbachev to recommend deep cuts in missile forces.

The bombing of Yugoslavia by NATO forces beginning in March 1999 was labelled by Russia as a 'barbarous' act contrary to international law. The bombing prompted Prime Minister Primakov to cancel a visit to the USA as his aircraft was over the Atlantic Ocean on its way to Washington. But the bombing was just one of a number of US policies causing Russia some serious concern. The USA had passed domestic legislation which sought extra-territorial effect by imposing sanctions on firms and research institutions in foreign countries which sold technologies considered in the US legislation to be strategically sensitive for a variety of reasons, some determined by non-proliferation goals and some determined by the politics of the receiving country. The USA also was looking to develop a theatre-missile defence system which, in the Russian view, would not only entrench US technological superiority in the military sphere but also threaten the

ABM Treaty and, as a consequence, the strategic nuclear parity between the two nuclear superpowers.

Important sections of the government of Russia were sounding a consistently ominous note about trends in US–Russian relations. For example, Viacheslav Trubnikov, head of Russia's Foreign Intelligence Service—which is responsible for the government's assessments of the international strategic circumstances of Russia —saw mainly negative aspects. He said that one of the main threats to Russia was the attempt of the USA to deny Russia its status as a great power and to achieve universal domination.[32] He saw US efforts to expand NATO into Eastern Europe and former Soviet republics as directly affecting Russia's security interests and demanded 'appropriate measures to counter the emergent threat'. He also identified the continued pursuit of advanced military technologies by unnamed countries, and the exploitation by unnamed countries of the Russian brain drain, as important security concerns. At the time of Primakov's appointment as Foreign Minister in 1996, Trubnikov was identified as essentially anti-American in disposition and, like Primakov, supportive of expanding Russia's relations with China to balance those with the USA.[33]

In response to the NATO bombing of Yugoslavia, the State Duma passed a resolution by 355 to 2 calling for a review of the country's military doctrine in the light of the new international strategic situation.[34] The Defence Minister, Igor Sergeyev, cited above in 1998 as sympathetic to Russia–NATO relations, said that the NATO action had destroyed relations with Russia and that all of the compromises made by Russia to NATO in recent years had amounted to nothing.[35]

On the other hand, there were still powerful voices, such as the new Foreign Minister, Igor Ivanov, appointed in 1998, saying that the key to Russian security lay in consideration of its responsibility for global stability as much as in consideration of the country's direct security. He said that Russia's security did not 'lie in arms race or the militarisation of the nation's economy' but in the maintenance of 'powerful armed forces with strong battle effectiveness'.[36] The Mayor of Moscow, Yury Luzhkov, a presidential aspirant with strong nationalist sentiments, opposed Russia's being drawn into any military response to the NATO action against Yugoslavia and advocated an early return to negotiations. He did say though that Russia should end its arms embargo and supply Yugoslavia with weapons if NATO deployed ground forces into Yugoslavia.[37] President Yeltsin said that the tragic mistake of the USA in Kosovo should not turn into a long crisis in US–Russia relations.[38]

The counter-currents in elite attitudes to Russian strategic policy had not resolved themselves by late 1999 and final resolution into a less contradictory, more unified set of strategic principles would have to wait for resolution of the political gridlock at the national level of government. If the more liberal elements have a decisive win in the parliamentary elections scheduled for December 1999 and the presidential elections due in 2000, then the strong pragmatic and non-offensive posture of Russia might remain intact. This would be the only circumstance in which pragmatism and a spirit of cooperation are likely to be preserved or, more correctly speaking, be restored. In all other scenarios, the trend of prickliness in strategic policy visible from as early as 1994 or 1995 is likely to intensify and may manifest itself in substantively confrontational postures.

FORMER SOVIET REPUBLICS

The most important influence on Russian foreign policy since 1991 has been the issue of dealing with the former union republics of the USSR and this has played itself out in different ways in political, economic and military dimensions. In spite of Russia's genuinely heartfelt acceptance in the early 1990s of principles of new strategic thinking toward former strategic adversaries such as the USA, Russia could not easily disconnect itself from its geopolitical past and its geopolitical instincts as a great power. This was evident in the statement on Russia's relations with the former union republics in Kozyrev's 1992 article discussed above. In 1993, Yeltsin went so far as to advocate in public the idea that the major powers should give Russia a special status as dominant power in the territory of the former Soviet Union, the guarantor or protector.[39] As Yeltsin was implying in this call, the break with the past structures of the USSR was not going to be as clean or easy as signing treaties between the newly independent, equal and sovereign states.

In some union republics, one of the biggest problems for Russia was simply to keep the peace in the transition from Soviet republic to full independence. Russia's efforts in this regard should be recognised as contributing to strategic stability among the newly independent states. Three examples stand out.

In 1991–92, political groups in South Ossetia, an administrative unit of the newly independent state of Georgia, had been seeking unification with their fellow Ossetians on the Russian side of the border in the region of North Ossetia. The two parts of Ossetia had been divided by the Soviet government between the union republic of Georgia and the Russian Soviet Federated Socialist Republic (RSFSR). After three years of intermittent fighting beginning in 1989 and involving relatively small forces numbering in the hundreds, a ceasefire was achieved in 1992 with the intervention of a Russian force of about 1000 personnel. By 1994, this force (a battalion from the Leningrad Military District) had been reduced to about 500 and it remained at that level as of 1998.[40]

Unlike operations in South Ossetia, the military operations of Russian forces in Moldova in 1991 and 1992 were not initially sanctioned or planned by the Russian government. By 1990, as a number of union republics of the USSR were declaring their sovereignty, two new states had declared their existence on the territory of the Union Republic of Moldova. In the subsequent civil disturbances and military clashes between the rival states, the USSR's 14th Army based there became both the potential peacemaker and a serious cause of further conflict.[41] In fact the 14th Army had fractured, with some elements supporting the rival sides. After the formal break-up of the USSR in 1991, the conflict in Moldova was caught up in the contest between political groups in the Russian Federation as well as in the interests of neighbouring states—in this case, Romania and Ukraine. By June 1992, Russian forces became more decisively involved in support of one of the warring factions and participated in an operation resulting in several hundred killed. This incident prompted the dispatch by Moscow of General Aleksandr Lebed[42] to take control of the situation. It appears that Lebed may have over-stepped his authority, or at least interpreted it creatively. He brought a standstill to clashes after taking operational command of some of the forces and engineering a brief and decisive military clash with the armed units opposing the 14th Army.[43] To achieve this, Lebed had to rely on support of airborne units already in Moldova or deployed there at his request.[44] In spite of several agreements implying eventual withdrawal of Russian forces, in 1999 they were still in Moldova, with the force comprising 2500 personnel in a variety of formations subordinated to the Moscow Military District.[45]

In Azerbaijan in February 1992, a small Russian force of regimental size, the 336th Motorised Infantry Regiment, joined forces in combat operations with separatists in the Nagorno-Karabakh autonomous locality who were fighting to be separated from the newly independent state of Azerbaijan. The people in Nagorno-Karabakh identified more closely with Armenia, another newly independent state on Azerbaijan's southwest border, and they wanted their autonomous locality to be merged with Armenia. The 336th Regiment comprised large numbers of Armenian nationality personnel. In March 1992, Russia dispatched airborne and special forces based in Azerbaijan to arrest the 336th (or at least its leaders). The involvement of Russian forces in the Armenia–Azerbaijan conflict and in earlier repressions in Azerbaijan in 1986 made their position there untenable and by September 1992, the former Soviet 4th Army in Azerbaijan was disbanded. By May 1993, the 104th Airborne Division was withdrawn to Ulianovsk in the Urals Military District.[46]

As the above examples suggest, Russia has not been interested in keeping the peace merely for its own sake. Russia has used its peace-keeping efforts in the former union republics to pursue its own geopolitical interests, especially its desire to reassert influence. It may have little expectation of reasserting its pre-eminence in traditional imperialist fashion by force, but it has not been averse to using what in the language of one writer must be called 'quasi-imperialist' methods when the opportunity arose.[47]

Two good examples of this were Georgia, a new state that had initially refused to join the Commonwealth of Independent States, and Tajikistan, where the government in power has been a more willing partner. In July 1992, after three years of separatist tension in the national Republic of Abkhazia within the newly independent Georgia, Abkhazia declared its independence. In the ensuing conflict, leaders of Russian military units which had been stationed in Georgia since before the collapse of the USSR sided with the Abkhazian rebels. They were encouraged in this by leaders of the Supreme Soviet (the hold-over parliament)[48] of the Russian Federation and quite probably by the military leadership in Moscow—while the Russian civilian government could not decide on a clear course of action. In February 1993, Russian military aircraft bombed Georgian forces which had taken over in the Abkhaz capital, and in March Russian ground forces and Cossack volunteers joined an Abkhazian attack on Sukhumi. In July 1993, a ceasefire was signed but clashes broke out again in September, and Abkhazian rebels succeeded in driving all Georgian forces from the territory. The Abkhazian success was the direct result of Russian military support and the opening of its border with Abkhazia to allow free flow of military equipment and mercenaries. By October 1993, Georgia had agreed to join the

CIS and from a position of weakness accepted in May 1994 a Russian peace-keeping force of three battalions (3000 troops), to be deployed along its internal border between Abkhazia and the rest of Georgia.[49]

The troubles in Tajikistan, which had begun in early 1990, had erupted into a civil war by May 1992 with Russian forces based in Tajikistan backing the incumbent government against opposition forces, but not on clear orders from the Russian government. The personnel of the units in the country were frustrating Russian government policy for a number of reasons. Some were backers of the Communist Party in its constitutional battles with Yeltsin, and some were traders in the military supplies over which they had control.[50] A number of important decisions on military actions were being made by lower level Russian officers in Tajikistan, not the government in Moscow. The situation was further complicated by the intrusion of other parties, notably the Russian population of Tajikistan and the government of Uzbekistan, which had intervened in the conflict with its own military forces. By May 1993, Russian official policy was to side with the government of Tajikistan, but only after its forces had already been actively engaged in doing just that, including the use of force against military and civilian targets alike. The two governments signed a Friendship Treaty in May. Sporadic military operations continued after that. More than 100 000 people may have been killed in this civil war.[51]

Russian ground forces and border units stationed in Tajikistan were based in large part on those that were stationed there at the time of the break-up of the USSR. Subsequent governments of Tajikistan did not take over the former Soviet units, as happened in many other former union republics. Tajikistan signed an agreement with Russia formalising the presence of the Russian forces until 1999 for common defence. These forces were the 201st Motorised Infantry Division (MID), with about 5000 personnel, which had been established in Tajikistan since 1943, and the border guards detachments. In August 1993, one month after 25 Russian border troops were killed on duty on the border with Afghanistan, Russia sent 10 000 reinforcements for the 201st, since it had been at low levels of manning and low levels of readiness. Two months later, in October, Russia organised a CIS-sponsored peace-keeping force, which was manned mostly by Russian personnel. The size of this force may have reached 35 000.[52] The mission of the Russian forces was to shore up a pro-Russian government under pressure from an Islamist political group and to protect the Tajikistan border from incursions from Afghanistan.[53]

By the end of 1998, there was active deliberation of withdrawing the 201st MID and a scaling down of Russian-supported border operations. (By 1998, total Russian personnel levels had shrunk to about 8000.)[54] Such consideration became possible after the brokering of a peace agreement in Tajikistan in 1997 and a marked reduction in cross-border incursions from Afghanistan. The reductions in Russian presence were also dictated by cost pressures and by the failure to develop an appropriate, durable regime for the interoperability of Russian and Tajikistan personnel in mixed units.[55]

As the Tajikistan experience shows, Russia's use of force in the newly independent states was not a sustainable policy in the light of the economic weakness of Russia and the policy preferences of its government. The 'quasi-imperialism' has been inconsistent in its implementation for most of the time since 1991. On many issues, Russia has been forced to deal with its newly independent neighbours as equals, even though Russia has held some particularly strong cards to play in these negotiations. This has been particularly evident in the sphere of economic relations.

The former Soviet republics wanted complete sovereign independence but the economic relationships that had grown between them over seven decades had been firmly based on the principle of 'trade specialisation' in a closed internal market. This involved concentration of production of specific items in one Soviet republic, quite often in the sole such factory in the entire country. When the newly independent states looked beyond the former Soviet Union for hard currency markets, the Soviet-era supply and pricing arrangements collapsed. For example, most of the machinery used in the USSR's oil industry was produced in other union republics outside the Russian Republic. The collapse of Soviet distribution agreements for this equipment contributed to a 30 per cent decline in oil production in Russia between 1990 and 1994.[56] Thus, the production relationships established by the former Soviet Union could not survive once the union collapsed. In the decade since, the failure by some of the former Soviet republics to rebuild production by relying on other markets or other sources of supply has created intense pressure for re-establishing some sort of economic union. This pressure has been strongest in Belarus, which in the Soviet period had been an 'assembly shop' for the USSR, with 5 per cent of its workforce employed in military industries.[57]

A second major problem in establishing normal relations among the newly independent states was what to do about the armed forces of the former USSR. Four agreements had been signed by CIS states in Minsk on 30 December 1991 to maintain a unified military posture. These were an Agreement on the Powers of the Highest Bodies of the Commonwealth of Independent States on Questions of Defence, an Agreement on Strategic Forces, an Agreement on Guarding Borders, and an Agreement on the Status of Border Forces.[58] The first agreement tried to vest in the Council of Heads of State the full range of executive powers that a national supreme commander might have in both peace and war for the preparation of strategic policy and the military forces to carry it out. The agreement established a Council of Defence similar to that which one might find in any national state.

The break-up of the Soviet armed forces among the newly independent states meant that Moscow was left in command of forces that contained some of the best but much of the worst. Strategic assets, such as the nuclear forces and the two main naval fleets, were largely based in the Russian Federation. Some of the newly independent countries, especially Belarus and Ukraine, got much of the best ground forces equipment and facilities because they had been on the front-line against NATO. Apart from two military districts east of the Urals (Transbaikal and Far East) which bordered China, most of the ground forces units that Russia was left with were rear garrison units, with correspondingly low levels of modern equipment and infrastructure. One estimate has it that the newly independent states inherited 13 combined-arms armies, four tank armies, two strategic missile armies, three air defence armies and five air armies.[59]

Within one or two months of the break-up of the USSR, it became apparent that the hope of maintaining a unified military posture would not be fulfilled, though it took several years for the final collapse of the unified force posture. By April 1992, Russia had announced plans to move ahead with independent policies for its armed forces after the failure of talks to retain a joint CIS force.[60] On 15 May 1992, a summit meeting of CIS states dedicated to military issues produced support for a new military alliance (the Tashkent Treaty) but it comprised only 6 of the 11 CIS members.[61] The summit was more successful in dealing with issues related to compliance with the Treaty on Conventional Forces in Europe, destruction of chemical weapons, collaboration in space, common use of CIS air space, and the establishment of a common high command for CIS border troops.

Russia found considerable difficulty coming to agreement with some of the former Soviet republics on how to divide previously common assets. The most bitter dispute on the division of military forces was with Ukraine over the Black Sea Fleet, with Ukraine seeking 85 per cent of the assets and 65 per cent of its personnel.[62] The small Caspian Sea Flotilla was divided more amicably among Russia, Azerbaijan and Kazakhstan. Nevertheless, the CIS military agreements signed on 30 December 1991 provided an important point of stabilisation in a number of spheres, especially in the control of nuclear weapons, on which a high degree of continuity was maintained while virtually all else was radically shifting ground. Ukraine, Kazakhstan and Belarus, the three new countries which had Soviet nuclear forces on their territory, pledged to honour nuclear weapons reduction treaties signed between the USA and the USSR. By June 1993, plans for joint armed forces in the CIS were abandoned, and CIS command structures were abolished.[63] A number of military cooperation agreements of more limited scope, most notably in air defence and border controls, were however subsequently put in place.[64]

A variety of agreements for civil cooperation were signed with only some CIS members as signatories—so-called 'mini-unions'.[65] For example, in 1995, Russia, Belarus, Kazakhstan and Kyrgyzstan signed an agreement on closer integration in the economic and humanitarian spheres.[66] The first three of these states had reached agreement in March 1996 on a customs union agreement, which Tajikistan moved to join early in 1998.[67] It was officially admitted into the customs union on 26 February 1999.[68] On 23 May 1997, Russia and Belarus signed a charter of union, seen by some as a charter of reunification, which accepts a 'common responsibility' for social security, creation of a common economic space, and the coordination of military and foreign policies. The charter set up a Supreme Council, comprising the Presidents of each state, an Executive Committee, and a Parliamentary assembly, all to be based in Moscow. The charter commits both states to recognition of basic human rights and the freedom of action of opposition political groups.[69] The union, which is open to other CIS states, does not envisage creation of a single superstate. Former national security adviser to Yeltsin, Aleksandr Lebed, described such a move to complete unity as a radical step which should be rejected. The possibility of complete federation of the two states of the former

Soviet Union should be approached gradually, he said.[70] Nationalists and great power restorationists, like Vladimir Zhirinovski,
welcomed the move as the first step toward re-assembly of the
former Soviet empire under Russian dominance. It was because of
this possibility inherent in the union agreement between Russia and
Belarus that a number of other former union republics lobbied hard
against it.[71] But the union had fairly broad support within Russia
based on the economic common sense of improved economic and
social policy coordination. The liberal democrats, led by Grigory
Yavlinski, had some months earlier walked out of the State Duma
in protest at the idea of union while the President of Belarus was
addressing the parliament.[72]

By March 1997, Yeltsin told a CIS summit that in spite of all
of the talk about integration and the signing of new documents,
'in reality those ties that continue to bind our states are now
being broken'.[73] Yeltsin warned that a dramatic improvement in
the spirit of cooperation and in the effectiveness of CIS mechanisms was needed to avoid the organisation's collapse. He
complained about disaffection with Russian peace-keeping efforts
in some of the newly independent central Asian or Transcaucasus
states, since it was mainly Russia which was bearing the burden
and he described military cooperation within the CIS as faltering
badly. In the CIS summit in October 1997, there were bitter
exchanges between Russian and some of the Transcaucasus members, such as Azerbaijan, because it was plain to all that many
of the CIS agreements were not working.[74] In 1998, Deputy Chairman of the State Duma Defence Committee, Aleksei Arbatov,
wrote that the 'CIS is an absurd hybrid of NATO, the European
Union and the UN, and it is not effective in any of its incarna-
tions'.[75] In December 1998, Russia's Defence Minister lost his
temper at a meeting of CIS ministers of defence and harangued
his colleagues to form a genuine and effective military alliance
in the face of a general military threat represented by US policy
on unilateral use of force and its repeated failure to cooperate
with Russia in major strategic decision-making in crisis situations
involving smaller countries, like Iraq.[76] But not all of his counterparts could agree with him, as some are actively pursuing closer
strategic relations with the USA.

In February 1999, two members of the Tashkent Treaty,
Uzbekistan and Azerbaijan, announced their withdrawal from the
treaty.[77] Moreover, Azerbaijan is threatening Moscow with closure
of its Russian-controlled, long-range, early-warning radar facility
(at Liaki). There is also speculation that Azerbaijan may agree to

the USA and Turkey using its military infrastructure for the deployment of their forces into the region.[78]

As fractionalised as Russia's relations with former Soviet republics are, many in Russia see these new states—of which eight are border states—as Russia's main strategic problem. There is growing concern in Russia about a further decline of its influence in the CIS and a consequent undermining of its national security. To the west, Russia is concerned that its neighbours (such as Ukraine, Latvia, Lithuania or Estonia) might become members of NATO. To the south, Russia is concerned about attempts to form a political bloc of newly independent states with a clearly pro-Western orientation: GUUAM (Georgia, Ukraine, Uzbekistan, Azerbaijan and Moldova), a move which Russia believes is strongly supported by Western powers.[79] Russia sees these countries as buffer states with the potential not only to protect Russia from the 'dark forces aroused by the Soviet Union in 1979' when it invaded Afghanistan[80] but also to infect parts of Russia with extremism based around the Islamic religion. Through the 1990s, Russia has seen itself in strategic competition in the southern tier with states like Turkey, Iran and Saudi Arabia. In the latter half of the 1990s, new concerns emerged about the expansion of US influence in southern tier states, such as Uzbekistan. The following sections provide a brief overview of Russia's strategic policy toward its European CIS neighbours and its southern CIS neighbours.

European newly independent states, Eastern Europe and the NATO problem

Russia's relations with its CIS neighbours in Europe have become intertwined with the broader question of the expansion of NATO. This process of entanglement of Russia's primary interest in its border states within a CIS framework and what it sees as an increasingly disturbing evolution of NATO has resulted in a dramatic transformation of Russia's attitudes toward Europe. In December 1991, Russia's main concerns were military disengagement from Eastern Europe and economic and political reintegration with Western Europe. By early 1999, as discussed above, Russia was very unhappy with the strategic architecture of Europe, the uses to which it was being put, and the lack of attention being given to what it regarded as Russia's strategic interests. A view of even the most dispassionate Russian observers was one of disillusionment, and this disillusionment was evident as early as the mid-1990s. It has been ably summarised by a scholar with a fairly positive disposition toward Russian cooperation with NATO and Europe who assessed in a 1996 work that US approaches to Russian association with NATO were increasingly being seen as a 'mockery, if not deception'. He said that there were grounds to believe that 'NATO's concept of partnership is "getting something for nothing", providing "photo opportunities" while demanding serious strategic concessions'.[81] By 1999, as mentioned above, Russia saw NATO policy not as genuine partnership but directed at pre-empting a successful reassertion of Russian geopolitical influence in the CIS states and therefore at weakening Russia.

Russia's interests in Europe have been severely complicated by the move of some its former East European allies to realign themselves decisively with NATO. As with the newly independent states (NIS) in the former Soviet republics, the former allies of the USSR in Eastern Europe[82] were among the most central preoccupations of Russian foreign policy in the first few years after 1991. But any enduring interest in Russia in these relationships was swept away by concerns with the domestic situation. The former Warsaw Pact allies assisted this evaporation of former bloc ties through their rapid reorientation of foreign policy toward integration with Western Europe. Bulgaria and Romania remained stranded in limbo, but Poland and Hungary moved decisively toward Western Europe, as did the Czech Republic and Slovakia, the successor states to Czechoslovakia. Ironically, given the serious breach between the USSR and Yugoslavia after 1948, it was this country—and the new states of Croatia and Bosnia that seceded from it—that took most of Russia's foreign policy attention in Eastern Europe in the 1990s. The former East Germany, the most powerful and loyal Soviet satellite state of all, had been absorbed into NATO through the unification of Germany.

The Russian Federation failed to prevent NATO's expansion, and this failure of policy has probably helped to colour their responses to the expansion. Russia's military and political leadership have repeatedly emphasised that the expansion of the alliance would feed Russian suspicions of some Western countries and force it to take 'adequate response measures'.[83] Russia saw the expansion of NATO as an effort by the USA and its allies to entrench the system of spheres of influence in Europe at a time when Russia had abandoned that concept—a move undertaken by Moscow, in its view, entirely of its own volition. Having lived for more than 40 years with the 'buffer zone' between the USSR and NATO provided by Soviet control of Eastern Europe, many in Moscow saw NATO's expansion into Central and Eastern Europe as absorbing the buffer zone and representing a threat to Russia's national interests and security. Russia took the view that NATO expansion would represent an effort to isolate it from Europe and the Euro–Atlantic community. The only appropriate response in Russia's view would be to reassert its historical spheres of influence. This would certainly mean closer economic and military cooperation with the former Soviet republics, now members of the CIS. During the 1996 conference on the military–political integration of the CIS states, former Russian Defence Minister Igor Rodionov argued for the creation of a military alliance between Russia and other CIS states to prevent the 'build-up of combat capability of foreign troops in regions adjacent to the external frontiers of the Commonwealth' in order to maintain the balance of forces.[84] Although not every CIS state supported Russia's idea,[85] Armenia, Belarus and Kazakhstan have strengthened their economic and military relations with Russia in this context. Furthermore, NATO military action against Yugoslavia somehow served as a stimulus to develop closer and stronger politico-military ties between some CIS members. In particular, Russia, Belarus, Armenia, Kazakhstan, Kyrgyzstan and Tajikistan not only confirmed their membership in the 1992 Tashkent Treaty, but also expressed their desire to deepen military integration, referring to the integration of air defence forces in the first instance.[86] Apart from condemning NATO's actions against Yugoslavia, the above-mentioned states and the Ukraine are planning to significantly expand their military relations in 1999 and beyond.[87]

In Russia's view, a new union or strategic alliance with Belarus is particularly important as a response to NATO's expansion. Situated on the frontier with Poland, it was not only the Soviet gateway to Central and Western Europe but also the 'western gate' to Russia for the invasions by France under Napoleon in 1812 and Germany under Hitler in 1941. Since the Baltic states are considered in Russia to be lost and relations with Ukraine have been strained, Belarus has been the main target of Russian policy in its efforts to retain a strategic window onto the West. For its part Belarus has been a more than willing ally since coming under the rule of President Aleksandr Lukashenko, a virulently anti-Western autocrat. Lukashenko has said that NATO should reckon with the interests of Belarus as a 'very mighty state', whose potential in common arms is greater than that of

Britain and Germany; and that failure to reckon with the interests of Belarus in pushing NATO eastwards 'would be just unwise and detrimental'.[88] In April 1997, as mentioned above, Russia and Belarus signed a treaty on union. Deeper bilateral military and political contacts with Belarus constitute a credible response by Moscow to the NATO enlargement, especially in the light of Minsk's tough stance on the issue. The two states have agreed to jointly use military installations in Belarus, to integrate air defences, to unite efforts in guarding Belarus' borders, and to effect joint defence measures in any case of outside aggression. During the official visit of Defence Minister Sergeyev to Belarus in late April 1999, both sides confirmed their desire to have a single defence order. In particular, Belarus will participate in Russia's 'Armaments—2001–05' program. Sergeyev also confirmed that a long-range, early warning radar facility near Baranovichi in Belarus would soon become fully operational, and that Russia and Belarus would finish the formation of a joint forces group in accord with earlier plans.[89]

Although relations with Ukraine have not been close, it is the strongest power after Russia among the former Soviet republics and Russia has viewed alliance with it as a potential counter to any substantive change in its security circumstances in Europe. This Russian position is somewhat complicated by several factors. Ukraine has been building its strategic policy on the principle of 'safety'—that is, distancing itself from Russia which it views as a potential threat to its independence. Russia's concerns about NATO expansion have been magnified by the fact that Ukraine has been a special target of diplomacy by NATO countries, especially the USA.[90] But Ukraine will not move quickly into a strategic alliance with the USA or NATO. In early 1999, Aleksandr Razumkov, Deputy Secretary of the Ukrainian National Security Council, stated that the question of Ukraine's possible membership of NATO will be hypothetical for at least the next ten years. There are basically three reasons for this: economic inability to meet NATO standards; unwillingness of about 70 per cent of Ukraine's population for its relations with NATO to be strengthened; and the risk of a radical reduction in economic cooperation by Russia.[91] As long as Ukraine has not irrevocably committed to NATO, Russia will still seek to shape its strategic dispositions positively. Although this will not be easy, Russia has three powerful levers: the close ties between manufacturing industries in the two countries; Ukraine's dependence on Russian natural resources, such as oil and gas; and the presence of 11 million ethnic Russians in Ukraine (more than 20 per cent of its population). Relations between Moscow and Kiiv were strengthened by the Russian Federal Assembly's ratification on 17 February 1999 of the Treaty of Friendship, Cooperation and Partnership between Russia and Ukraine, despite fierce opposition by some members, Luzhkov in particular. This followed ratification by the Ukrainian Parliament of an agreement about the division of the Soviet Black Sea Fleet and conditions for the Russian naval presence in Crimea. In addition, Ukraine has its own strategic problems which could push it closer to Russia. Relations with Romania over territorial disputes and the demarcation of territorial waters in the Black Sea have been difficult.[92]

A number of respected opinion leaders in Russia have taken a very dim view of the expansion of NATO, but many are prepared to see the best response as adjustment of Russian diplomacy and alliances in the newly independent states. Nevertheless, if any new NATO members allow forward stationing of US, British or German forces close to Russian territory, this may provoke a sharper reaction. As one widely respected military commentator has put it, 'Russia will view as a direct military threat the introduction of foreign troops to the territory of neighbouring countries of buildup in groupings of forces off its borders'.[93] Russia's potential responses to any such results of NATO expansion may include the threat of force against new NATO states (the Czech Republic, Hungary and Poland) or against other neighbouring countries still contemplating NATO membership, such as Ukraine or the Baltic states of Lithuania, Latvia and Estonia. During a visit to the Kaliningrad enclave in 1997, Russia's former Security Council secretary Ivan Rybkin stated: 'Those who think that our current economic difficulties and problems testify our impotence are wrong. We are strong enough to answer those who have lost all sense of reality.'[94]

New NATO members could be subject to selective air strikes against military installations and targets considered by Russia to be potentially dangerous to the nation's security. In February 1996, Viktor Mikhailov, at that time atomic energy minister and member of the Security Council, told reporters that Russia would destroy all sites of tactical nuclear weapons deployed by NATO in any East European country.[95] Although no plans for such deployment exist, this remark by a member of the Security Council indicates Russia's determination to use all means necessary to prevent the deployment of significant threatening forces near its borders. Russia is less likely to strike Hungarian or Czech territory, as these countries do not share any border with Russia. Apart from provoking a full NATO military response, any attack on targets in Hungary or the Czech Republic would badly damage Russia's international reputation and cause serious tensions with other East and Central European states via whose airspace such strikes would have to be delivered. Poland may be a different case especially if US *Patriot* complexes were deployed there. *Patriot* SAMs would not only deny Russia local air superiority but also threaten Russian ICBMs, and therefore upset the strategic nuclear balance.

Compared with the three new members of NATO, the Baltic states of Lithuania, Latvia and Estonia are quite different strategic entities from Russia's point of view. The first reason relates to the new strategic geography of Russia relative to the Baltic states. Their borders are within a very short distance of St Petersburg and Moscow. Military experts have estimated that the range of NATO's aircraft will extend far into the heartland of Russia if they operate from Baltic airfields.[96]

A second reason concerns access to the Kaliningrad enclave, which has no land routes connecting it to the rest of Russia. This enclave, to the west of Lithuania, is a former German territory which the Allied powers agreed in 1945 should be assigned to the USSR. It was, under Soviet rule, a part of the Russian Soviet Federated Socialist Republic and remained part of the Russian Federation after the collapse of the USSR. Its population is about one million. Short-term agreements have allowed Russia to transit via Belarus and Lithuania to Kaliningrad. However, since much of the Russian material crossing this route is military, Lithuania has raised objections to a treaty extension. Lithuania has also attempted to tie further agreements to its efforts to enter NATO— an explosive issue in itself for Moscow.

A third reason relates to the tensions between Russia and the Baltic states about the treatment of Russian ethnic minorities. In contrast to the unpopular war in Chechnia, the Russian military could be sure of broad public support for any measures undertaken to protect ethnic Russians in the Baltic states.[97] Russia has supported the independence of the three Baltic states because it has not seen them as a military threat and it has seen itself as capable of recapturing the states with military forces with little preparation if necessary.[98] It has also understood how important the continued independence of these states is to the USA.

By early 1999, Russia's new sensitivities to NATO expansion and developments in Europe suggest strongly that were any of the

Baltic states to join NATO they would be subject to considerable military pressure by Russia, possibly including full-scale military intervention.[99] If military forces from major NATO powers were stationed in the Baltics during peacetime, Russia would regard this as a direct military threat. It would be seen as an aggressive strategic deployment with only one purpose—to support future land, air and naval offensive operations against Russia.

Even if Russian leaders did not regard war as imminent, they would attach a fundamental strategic significance to NATO control of Baltic territory. This is particularly evident with respect to seaports. The independence of the Baltic states and Ukraine has substantially reduced the naval facilities available to Russia. The ports in the St Petersburg area of Russia are limited and vulnerable to easy blockade by an enemy power. Kaliningrad is also isolated and possibly not supportable in war from Russia proper. With its port easily subjected to enemy blockade, Kaliningrad is not seen by the Russian military as adding significantly to Russia's naval capacity in the Baltic Sea. In case of war Russia would need the ports of the Baltic states for its own use and certainly would seek to deny them to an enemy power. It could be assumed therefore that Russia's General Staff would plan on gaining control of these ports through military action at the start of any conflict with the West or even during a crisis period preceding the outbreak of large-scale war. This means that Russia already has some contingency plans for military operations in the Baltic states.

Although Russia's current conventional military capabilities are no longer sufficient to conduct military campaigns against countries of Poland's size, the Russian armed forces are still able to occupy and hold key centres in small countries such as Estonia, Latvia and Lithuania.[100] Russian ethnic minorities in the Baltic states could provide Russian troops with effective assistance (sabotaging communications, organising armed resistance behind the front lines). Russian planners have some doubts that in the event of a Russian attack on the Baltic states the major powers in NATO would defend them. First, if NATO were to open hostilities against Russia, it would risk a nuclear strike (according to Russian military doctrine). Second, historical experience shows that Western countries may not follow their alliance commitments if their national interests are threatened. Russian planners can envisage a situation where even if the Baltic states had joined NATO, the major NATO powers would prefer to exert strong diplomatic pressure on Russia and impose economic sanctions, rather than provoke direct military confrontation with Russia. The former

British ambassador to Poland, Sir Brian Barder, has raised some doubt about the ability of NATO to defend some of the potential new members, including even Poland, and he suggested that therefore NATO might be putting at risk the foundation of its alliance—the deterrent effect of the conviction that an attack on any NATO member would be regarded as an attack on all of them.[101]

Balkans

Outside the area of the former USSR, the only part of Europe which has been receptive to renewed Russian strategic overtures has been the Balkan peninsula—the area divided after the Treaty of Versailles between Greece, Bulgaria, Albania and Yugoslavia, which through the course of the 1990s has been rocked by the break-up of Yugoslavia into at least five states.[102]

After the Crimean War with Britain from 1853 to 1856, Russian conceptions of balance of power in Europe and of its security interests paid considerable attention to the Balkan peninsula. This strategic interest was overlain with cultural and religious concepts that were popular at the time, especially pan-Slavism and Orthodox Christian unity. Russia's particular strategic interest was control of the Dardanelles and the access to the Mediterranean from the Black Sea. With the USSR's control of Ukraine and its Cold War interests in Bulgaria, Yugoslavia and Greece, this powerful strategic interest remained in place until 1991, though the cultural and religious aspects had all but disappeared. With the collapse of the USSR and its control in Eastern Europe, Russian strategic geography might have been less concerned with the Balkans, but in some respects Moscow retained its sensitivity to strategic developments there. In Russia's desperate domestic search for cultural symbols, a number of groups resurrected the historic ideas of pan-Slavism and religious solidarity, and these have taken root in current Russian perceptions of the region. If the former republics of the USSR are viewed in Moscow as the country's 'first security belt', the Balkans form another.[103] The NATO bombing of Yugoslavia in 1999, coupled with strong historical animosities between Greece and Turkey, Greece and Macedonia, and Yugoslavia and its breakaway states, provide Russia significant opportunity for strategic counter-moves against NATO.

Bulgaria has emphasised that, in the present situation in Europe, a link with Russia is considered a strategic benefit.[104]

Bulgaria's Defence Minister Dimitri Pavlov has publicly supported Russia's views on European security issues, and described Bulgarian–Russian military cooperation as vital for Bulgarian security.[105] The NATO *Cascade* program, through which thousands of used heavy weapons were transferred to Greece and Turkey, has fuelled a small regional arms race and has led Bulgaria to express deep concern over the arms build-up in the Aegean area. Russia's immediate reaction was to supply Bulgaria with weapons to maintain the regional balance of forces. In 1996, Russia delivered a 'gift from the Russian government to Bulgaria', which included 100 T–72 main battle tanks (MBTs) and 100 BMP–1 armoured infantry fighting vehicles (AIFVs), formerly to be scrapped under the Conventional Forces in Europe (CFE) treaty.[106] In 1997, Russia provided Bulgaria with a government credit of $450 million 'on very favourable terms for the Bulgarian side' to finance the delivery of 14 MiG–29 *Fulcrums* and the upgrading of Bulgarian MiG–21 *Fishbeds*.[107]

Macedonia, a former province of Yugoslavia, has also received consideration as one of Russia's priority partners in the Balkans. During a 1997 meeting with the Russian Defence Minister, Igor Sergeyev, Macedonian counterpart Lazar Kitanovski stressed that there were no reasons against deeper cooperation between the nations: 'So far no serious problems have ever arisen between our countries'.[108] The parties agreed to sign a bilateral agreement on military cooperation, which was seen by some at the time as Macedonia's first step in its pro-Russian orientation in European politics. However, given the fact that governments of both Bulgaria and Macedonia have clear pro-Western and pro-NATO orientation, it will be surprising if there is any significant shift in the foreign policy of these countries. Consequently, it is unlikely that in the near future these countries will move closer to Russia in their foreign policy orientation.

Russia may also see its interests in the Balkans and the Caucasus as benefiting from the intensified bilateral problems between Greece and Turkey, both members of NATO. Russia's arms sales to Cyprus, which undermined the unquestionable military superiority of Turkey over the island, intensified the old conflict between Greece and Turkey.[109] Referring to the danger of 'violation of the military balance' on the island, Turkey is planning to strengthen its military presence there and even possibly to resort to a military operation for destroying the Russian air-defence missile (S–300) complexes the Greek Cypriots are planning to install.[110] If events take this turn, Turkish military action on

Cyprus will cause an immediate military reaction by Greece, which could lead to a military conflict between the two countries and a major crisis within the NATO alliance.

As of mid-1999, Russia was still working within the European consensus on the Balkan peninsula, especially with regard to Yugoslavia and the new states that had broken away from it. Russia had been part of a contact group of major European states negotiating with Yugoslavia on an end to the crisis in Kosovo. When NATO began bombing in March 1999, the Russian willingness to continue to work within the European mechanisms, like the Organisation for Security and Cooperation in Europe, was severely tested. The NATO move against Kosovo came just several weeks after the formal induction of Hungary, Poland and the Czech Republic as members of NATO. It is quite likely that eventually Russian cooperation will be won back if the major European powers and the USA can find appropriate diplomatic approaches.

Southern tier NIS

Russia's southern borders present much greater strategic challenges than its western borders, where Russia has five newly independent states, of which the two biggest are culturally close to Russian conceptions of national identity. A sixth newly independent state of the former USSR to the west of Russia is Moldova, but it is a small country nestled between Ukraine and Romania. On Russia's southern border, or close to it, there are eight newly independent states,[111] of which six are predominantly Muslim, but all of which have strong cultural identities quite different from those of Russia. Among these eight newly independent countries, Russia faces a wide variety of strategic relationships, opportunities and perceived threats. Russia's strategic relations with each of these eight countries are influenced by its perceptions of strategic competition with other major powers, either Turkey, Iran, or the USA. The strategic competition in these southern tier NIS plays directly into Russian insecurities about its national cohesion and about NATO expansion. For example, Russian media regularly carry stories of Turkish government support for the Chechen side in the civil war.[112] And the USA is seen to be vigorously pursuing a strategic foothold of some sort in this area.[113] By early 1999, Russian sources were predicting that Uzbekistan would leave the CIS Collective Security Treaty and sign up with NATO under the Partnership for Peace program.[114]

Armenia is Russia's most dependable partner in the Transcaucasus region to Russia's south. In the light of the increased cooperation between Azerbaijan and Turkey, Armenia staked its hopes on military cooperation with Moscow. It was the first of the CIS states to offer military bases on its territory to Russia. In May 1996, the two countries signed a number of bilateral accords in the military sphere, involving the creation of a single air defence, joint guarding of the Armenian–Turkish border, and Moscow's assistance in the development of the Armenian armed forces.[115]

Armenia has also backed Russia's position on the issue of NATO's expansion. According to the speaker of the Armenian National Assembly, 'this support is not only declarative, the agreement on Russian military bases in Armenia achieved by the two countries testifies to this'.[116] In 1999, Russia reinforced its small military presence in Armenia with several S–300B SAM complexes and 13 MiG–29 fighters.[117] During a visit to Armenia in February 1999, the mayor of Moscow, Yury Luzhkov, described Armenia as 'Russia's strategic partner'.[118] The Armenian government seems to be motivated both by its continuing confrontation with Azerbaijan and by Turkey's proximity.

Kazakhstan, because of its size and its history of relatively good relations with Russia since 1991, is probably one of Russia's main strategic partners among the southern tier NIS. The Kazakhstan government is a consistent advocate of a closer union with Russia—if only for geopolitical reasons. In early 1995, they agreed to form a joint grouping of Russian and Kazakh forces. Russia is also helping Kazakhstan to build and strengthen its own armed forces.[119] Tajikistan is another close ally of Russia's, in part because of Russian military support against anti-government forces since 1992, and in part because the country does not have its own military forces.

For Russia, its strategic circumstances in this area to its south have also been complicated by the vigorous engagement of the US and its allies in military operations against Iraq, both in the northern regions adjacent to Turkey and Iran, as well as in the Persian Gulf region. Russian instincts about this US military activity are not positive, even though at a diplomatic level Russia has been unable to curb US unilateral actions.

RUSSIA AND USE OF FORCE

It is true that Russia 'lacks the conditions necessary for a stable consensus on security policy'[120] but a more important observation would be that few in Russia have the stomach for war when there is so much disorder in their country and when the militarist policies practised by the Soviet regime as late as the 1980s have been widely discredited. The operations in Chechnia beginning in 1994 showed pretty quickly two things: that even the smallest states can effectively oppose Russian conventional forces with guerilla warfare; and that the Russian body politic has little truck with use of force in the sorts of circumstances that prevailed in Chechnia, even at the cost of loss of a small part of Russian territory. Thus, as one scholar has noted, it is possible to contrast the 'general neo-imperialist mood of the public' and its lack of willingness to act on it.[121] Within this spectrum of opinion, there is no decisive domestic opposition to Russian involvement in small peacekeeping operations or border security operations in former Soviet republics, such as Tajikistan.

However, with an eye to the future, it is important to acknowledge that Russia's strategic choices are subject to a number of dangerous dynamics. Past choices have not always been the outcome of a stable balance of political power and authority. The domestic political struggles and the instability in relations between the armed forces leadership and the government have resulted in a strategic policy characterised on occasion by uncertainty and inconsistency. Strategic policy appears to lurch from one side of the strategic spectrum to the other—from enlightened cooperation to great power chauvinism. On some occasions, the appearance of less cooperative positions was deceiving, since the government was looking to posture merely to appear responsive to certain anti-Western domestic constituencies, while seeking to prevent actual international impacts from the change in its rhetorical position. The Russian government has also used the appearance of being responsive to its more bellicose constituencies as a means of gaining leverage in international negotiations.

The inconsistency in Russian strategic policy might be viewed as normal for a country with a democratically elected parliament and president. But the inconsistency has been far greater than in a stable democracy, where changes to strategic policy are made fairly rarely and where a general underlying coherence can usually be seen as a result of the dominance of particular political parties with clear manifestos. Decision-making for strategic policy has been unusually personalised in the Russian administration around the personal staffs of the President, a circumstance aggravated by constant personnel changes in the various formal advisory bodies that have existed.

A second cause of the posture of opposition arises from the lack of institutional responsiveness within the Russian administrative system. While the Foreign Ministry remains better organised than most ministries, foreign policy takes in a range of political actors, including the armed forces. As the head of the Security Council observed in an interview in June 1997: 'Not everyone appreciates state discipline. If the Prime Minister has signed agreements and the President has signed a treaty, then be so kind to implement them.'[122]

Another important consideration is that Russia has been severely constrained in its strategic options by the pressures of reorganising daily life in the face of severe economic and social dislocation created by the collapse of the USSR, subsequent maladministration, and lack of political and social consensus. Thus, even had the government been inclined to pursue some of the extreme and aggressive postures that have been advocated, it would have found itself bereft of the resources to carry them through with much effect. In particular, the armed forces of Russia have not really been in a fit state to conduct war. This reality was clearly demonstrated in Russia's military defeat when it sought to reassert dominance over its breakaway republic of Chechnia between 1994 and 1996. This lack of strategic choice makes it difficult to be certain of the world view held by the leaders of Russia.

CONCLUSION

Russian strategic policy in the immediate aftermath of the creation of the new state was visibly based on liberal internationalist positions having more in common with the common security doctrines of Nordic countries like Sweden than with great powers like the USA. Within a short time, the government of President Yeltsin was forced to deal with a number of compelling emergencies in the newly independent states and these exigencies resulted in the resurfacing of great power tendencies in Russia's foreign policy. Pragmatism tinged with a visceral anti-Americanism began to define Russian foreign policy. As the President became progressively weaker in domestic politics, the need to play to a variety of chauvinist sentiments became more powerful. This resulted in the dismissal of an all-too-internationalist foreign minister and his replacement with an all-too-pragmatic intelligence apparatchik who had risen to prominence in the Soviet era.

The subsequent elevation of this apparatchik to the Prime Ministership cemented the trend in Russian strategic policy of greater distancing from the USA.

But there are two important aspects of Russian strategic policy between 1991 and 1999 that the atmospherics created by playing to the gallery of domestic politics have masked to some degree. First, there has been a fundamental reorientation away from postures of confrontation by Moscow and hence a significant reduction in external threats to Russian security compared with the Soviet era. Second, while Russia has retained significant diplomatic resources and has deployed these effectively on occasion in the years since 1991, it has in many respects not disposed of the levers of power that its Soviet predecessor could once boast of— substantial economic leverage and substantial military power. For a number of years Russia played the role of cooperative partner in the strategic policies of the developed world against smaller countries, such as Iran, Iraq and Libya, that threatened international order in a variety of ways.

Through a combination of circumstances, the good will displayed by Russia in the early 1990s in respect of its internationalist aspirations has been squandered. Some of this has been Russia's fault, and some of the blame must lie with the USA and its major allies. But most of the blame lies with the seventy years of Soviet rule. It would have taken a miracle for Russia after 1991 to have maintained the internationalist course in strategic policy promised so early in its existence. As old enmities and suspicions resurfaced in domestic politics, and were fuelled by sustained economic dislocation, Russian strategic policy reverted to the Soviet type. The idea of NATO expansion, once specifically approved by the Yeltsin government, and unambiguously put under offer by the Russian rejection of hegemony in Eastern Europe, suddenly began to take on ominous overtones in Moscow. Psychologies of defeat and inadequacy began to infect the cooperative and expansive spirit of Russian strategic policy.

As of mid-1999, the infection had not been defeated and was taking stronger hold. US actions around the world, but especially in the Balkans, offended Russian sensitivities so much that an era of renewed confrontation seemed possible. But as much as Russia railed against US hegemonic acts and threats to strategic stability, its record of behaviour showed few signs of return to a policy of sustained military or strategic confrontation with the USA. In fact, the former intelligence chief, Primakov, responsible for overseeing some of the shift in style and tone of Russian strategic policy after 1995, was continuing to rule out the viability of a return to any sustained confrontation with the USA. The trend at the end of the 1990s was not positive for sustained cooperative relations between Russia and the USA, but Russia faced so many strategic preoccupations, either domestically or in the newly independent states, that some confidence could be placed in a judgement that Russia would not undertake any threat to strategic stability, and would vigorously work to prevent any such threat.

In foreign policy, Russia has for one decade remained firmly committed to integration in the world community of states. Its influence in world policy councils has been severely constrained by its weak economy and domestic disorganisation. It has been able, however, to exercise its traditional influence in the UN Security Council and so is not entirely without political clout. Whatever transpires domestically, it will be difficult for Russia to rise above its huge domestic problems, or those on its immediate eastern and southern borders, to construct and implement a coherent and sustained policy of confrontation with the USA and its allies, or with the current system of global cooperative governance. But ad hoc forays to destabilise US interests or regional order in selected places could be easily undertaken by an extremist government or disaffected members of Russia's security forces. The Middle East will remain a particularly volatile area, and given its importance as a major source of oil for many industrialised countries, it will be in this area that Russian foreign policy moves under any new, extremist government would have to be watched most closely.

4

Strategic policy in the Asia–Pacific

If the western and southern neighbourhoods of Russia after 1991 have presented it with a wide a variety of strategic difficulties and foreign policy challenges, many of which remain in complex evolution, the eastern neighbourhood of Russia has been, by contrast, seen as full of strategic opportunity, foreign policy successes and resolution of long-standing disputes. When the first Foreign Minister of new Russia, Andrei Kozyrev, laid out the country's foreign policy for international observers in *Foreign Affairs* in 1992, he said that Russia's reforms were the only guarantee for its status as a great ('but normal') power in Eurasia—European, Asian, Siberian and Far Eastern. He foreshadowed an 'active Eastern policy', where he saw prospects for cooperation and reduction of tensions as considerable.[1] A senior Russian scholar has observed that Russia should pursue a 'pre-eminent' status on the Pacific Rim as a 'strategic alternative to exclusive reliance upon integration into Western economic and security structures'.[2] The Asia–Pacific region is seen as the main hope for Russia to invigorate its mineral exports from the resource-rich areas east of the Urals.[3] Lieutenant-General Leonid Ivashov in early 1997 expressed concerns about Russia's passiveness in the Asia–Pacific region and underlined the importance of greater active engagement in its affairs:

> Russia, busy resolving its own problems and sorting things out with the West, has so far made no attempts to participate in the development of a collective security policy for the Asia–Pacific region and took no part in the competition for its arms markets . . . Sooner or later, Russia will have to do so because in the 21st century, Russia's economic interests will begin to shift from the West to the East for objective reasons rather than the desires or reluctance of its presidents, parties and governments.

Moreover, major threats to Russian national security are also likely to come from the East. They will only increase if Russia tries to stay away from the Asia–Pacific economic processes.[4]

In February 1999, Russia's Foreign Minister, Igor Ivanov, repeated the well-known mantra that the Asia–Pacific region accounted for half of world GDP and 60 per cent of world trade, facts which he said 'spoke for themselves' about the importance of the region for Russia. He also observed that the region was a site of interaction of the interests of the four most important powers in the world: the USA, China, Japan and Russia, and that the Asian financial crisis of 1997 and 1998 had provoked a period of military–political instability in the region that might lead to the resurrection of old conflicts.[5] Russia saw itself as having a responsibility to maintain peace and stability in the region, but at the same time to ensure there was no weakening of Russia's position. Russia should, he said, participate directly in solving the most important regional problems.

But Russia's success in its eastern policies after 1991 has not removed several long-standing barriers to successful engagement by Moscow in the region's strategic affairs.[6] The first is that Russia has consistently seen itself as primarily a European power. The bulk of its population and its economic weight remain west of the Ural Mountains. According to the Deputy Foreign Minister speaking in March 1997, even as Russia paid closer attention to the east there was no prospect that Russian foreign policy would reduce its interest in other areas of foreign policy.[7] A second problem for Russia is that it has had to overcome several decades of being regarded in East Asia as an outsider or a hostile state, and treated either with derision or suspicion. Third, Russia's economic linkages with the developed countries of East Asia and the Pacific (Japan, USA) or the newly industrialising economies (South Korea, Taiwan, Hong Kong, Malaysia) have not been substantial.

This chapter reviews Russia's strategic posture toward the Asia–Pacific region and toward the countries most important in Russian perceptions: China, Japan, and the two Koreas. The chapter has a short section on other regional interests (Mongolia, Vietnam, ASEAN and India). It concludes with an assessment of the potential impact on strategic stability in the Asia–Pacific and global order of Russian efforts in the second half of the 1990s to engage India and China in some sort of 'anti-hegemonic' alliance designed to curb US unilateralism. It is largely in this context of great power relations that India has remained important to Russian strategic interests.

RUSSIA AND EAST ASIAN REGIONALISM

The political gulfs that existed between Moscow and many countries of the Asia–Pacific region were demonstrated consistently through the late 1980s when Soviet initiatives to develop its links there, such as Gorbachev's Vladivostok initiative in 1986,[8] were consistently rebuffed or treated 'politely'. After 1991, Russia intensified its efforts to build ties to these countries, and most responded positively in the light of Russia's move away from the strategic policies and military posture of the Soviet era. But even though attitudes were beginning to soften, and Russia's bilateral relationships in the region began to improve steadily, Russia was not regarded as a natural partner in the emerging regionalism that had led to the creation of the Asia Pacific Economic Cooperation (APEC) forum in 1989, and to its subsequent expansions in 1991 to include China (as well as Taiwan and Hong Kong) and 1994 to include Mexico, Peru and Chile. Other regional powers sought to exclude Russia on the grounds that it did not have the economic power and level of engagement in regional security issues sufficient to warrant its inclusion.

But Moscow had a long history of strategic engagement with the states of East Asia and most of its territory lay in Asia. It was not going to give up on its demands to be treated as a part of the region. Imperial Russia had been a Pacific naval power in the nineteenth century, and it had been one of the foreign interventionist powers in China, succeeding in the annexation of a large slice of Chinese territory (from Vladivostok to Magadan) as recently as 1858 and 1860. While Russian military power projection in East Asia collapsed with its defeat by Japan in the war of 1904–05, the USSR had made a number of successful and decisive strategic interventions in the region. Mongolia had been closely aligned to Moscow for most of the time since 1922. Moscow, as an ally of the USA, UK and China in the Second World War, was a signatory of the 1951 San Francisco Peace Treaty and therefore helped to shape the post-war settlements in East Asia. Moscow had a very close relationship with China through the Chinese Civil War beginning in the 1920s, and then sided decisively with the People's Republic of China from 1950 to 1960. Between 1954 and 1975 Moscow supported North Vietnam in its war against

South Vietnam and then the USA, finally entrenching a very close political, military and economic relationship with the unified Vietnam beginning in 1978. Moscow's close relationship with Vietnam supported the latter's invasion and occupation of Cambodia, its defence against Chinese invasion in 1979, and its subsequent pre-eminence in Laos and Cambodia through the 1980s. In return, the USSR gained access to military facilities in Vietnam that supported Soviet operations in the South China Sea, the Indian Ocean and Persian Gulf, and even intelligence collection in the South Pacific.

The new Russian state in 1992 was not going to take no for an answer in its effort to restore some strategic presence and influence in East Asia. The government applied its very skilled and determined diplomatic resources to the problem and, building on the improvements in its various bilateral relationships in the region (discussed below), Russia was able eventually to secure membership of important regional forums. Russia was an original member of the ASEAN Regional Forum (ARF)[9] when it was established in 1994; it became a member of the unofficial 'ASEAN plus' foreign ministers meeting in 1996; and in November 1998 it was admitted to APEC.

By 1998, however, a number of trends in regional affairs began to undercut the cooperative foundations of these new relationships in East Asia that Russia had first looked for in the early 1990s. These adverse trends arose from Russia's assessment of the significance of a number of developments: a deteriorating atmosphere in US–China relations; a consolidation and expansion of the arms sales relationship between Russia and China; a strengthening of the military relationship between the USA and Japan; the sustained push in Europe for NATO expansion; and growing mutuality between Russia and China in their opposition to the very strong unilateralist tendencies in US policy both in respect of use of force against other states (Iraq, Yugoslavia) and in respect of extraterritorial pretensions of new US legislation relating to proliferation of nuclear and missile technology.

By mid-1999, Russia's commitment to regional cooperative mechanisms remained firm and was in better shape than Russian relations with NATO after the bombing of Yugoslavia. But the Russian perception of the early 1990s that the Asia–Pacific region was relatively benign or even promising began to be replaced by a perception that here, too, dark and hostile forces may be turning against Russian interests. In this environment, Russia began to show considerable interest in expanding its strategic relations with China, North Korea and India. It still continued to work on improving relations with Japan and South Korea, but the sustained forward presence of US military forces in these two countries and efforts by the USA to upgrade this presence accompanied by threat of use of force against North Korea had by 1999 begun to push Russia into new strategic directions.

These issues are canvassed in further detail in the following discussion of Russia's most important bilateral strategic relationships in East and South Asia: China, Japan, North Korea, South Korea, Vietnam and India. But the most important consideration in Russia's approaches to all of these different countries is that Russia does not want a return to the confrontation of the Cold War—it merely wants its voice and its interests to be taken into account through a consultative process with the USA and other great powers.[10]

CHINA

There are two important aspects to Russia's strategic relationship with China—one at the global level of great power interactions and one arising from their contiguity as great powers. At the global level, the two countries can have a profound influence regardless of their relationship with each other; but the nature of the relationship has shaped global order. There were times of alliance, such as after 1941, when the USSR and the Republic of China became allies against Japan and Germany, or after 1950, when the USSR became an even firmer ally of the People's Republic of China. There were other times of sharp confrontation and great power politics, as in the 1920s and 1930s when the USSR was exercising concessional rights inside China and interfering in Chinese politics, or as in the 1960s, when the collapse of the Sino–Soviet alliance led to escalating border skirmishes resulting in a Soviet threat of pre-emptive nuclear attack on China. The adversarial military relationship between the USSR and China was still in evidence as late as 1979 when China invaded Vietnam, and the USSR took some military preparations in its border military districts. The suspicion and hostility continued through the early 1980s as Soviet naval deployments in the Western Pacific and in the South China Sea gathered pace and as the Soviet Pacific Fleet continued to receive the most modern warships in significant numbers. By the mid-1980s, the USSR devoted about 25 per cent of its peacetime military assets to eastern Russia, and the China border region. In particular, two powerful armoured groupings, comparable only to one stationed in East Germany, were deployed in Mongolia and the Transbaikal Military District to deter possible Chinese invasion. In fact, the Transbaikal MD was regarded as the most powerful military entity of the Soviet Armed Forces.

It is very difficult to separate the global and contiguous aspects of the interaction between Russia and China but it is probably the case that relations on the border serve as a very good indicator of the depth or closeness of political relations between the two countries at the global level. In 1960, when the USSR felt it was much more powerful than China, it was prepared to impose a complete interruption of cross-border contacts and exchanges. By contrast, in the 1990s, when Russia has had a greater economic need for contacts with this large and economically growing neighbour, and when both countries are beginning to look to each other for strategic support against US pre-eminence, cross-border relations have steadily improved.

A gradual easing of tension on the border between the USSR and China began about 1986, and this process helped a thawing in political relations which saw Gorbachev visit Beijing in May 1989—the first visit to China by a Soviet leader since 1960. Barter trade[11] was restored on the border with China in 1987, a move which set China in position to become one of the main suppliers of food and consumer goods to eastern Russia, and to become an important customer of manufactures from there, including trucks, steel products, and equipment for heavy industry.[12] An agreement on the promotion and protection of mutual investment was signed between the USSR and China in 1990.[13]

After 1991, when the two countries set border relations on a more solid footing with an agreement to settle the disputed eastern border within a specified timeframe, the growth in trans-border links has been dramatic. The two governments reached agreement to open the Amur River and others in the region to international shipping. In August 1992, for the first time, a ship travelled from Harbin in northern China via the Sungari River in China, then down the Amur River, before exiting to the sea and sailing to Japan. Local authorities have already undertaken important construction and upgrading work on roads and railways to facilitate cross-border trade. Freight and cargo handling facilities are also being upgraded.[14] But the atmosphere of the relationship was not positive for the first few years,[15] rather correct and cool.[16]

By 1997, cross-border relations had established an economic

momentum of their own independent of the strategic calculations of the two governments. As one of President Yeltsin's advisers observed, there were large mutual interests at stake in the Russia–China relationship that really had little to do with opposing NATO or with any sort of short-term political expediency.[17] For example, in December 1997, in a project of huge significance both for national development goals of both countries and for trans-border economic links, Russia exchanged letters of intent with China, South Korea, Mongolia and Japan to develop the Kovytka natural gas field 450 kilometres north of Irkutsk in Siberia, with a projected 4000-kilometre pipeline to pass through Mongolia. Production would commence in 2006 if a projected investment of US$11 billion was raised as planned. Annual production would be about 20 billion cubic metres (cu m) and last for about 30 years, although the field has been estimated to hold 1.5 trillion cu m. China and South Korea would receive about half of the projected production, with Russia taking the other half. The project would link the gas fields with Beijing and then Shandong and, by 2004, the Korean peninsula through undersea pipelines.[18] By December 1997, Russia and China had already spent US$20 million on a feasibility study.[19] Also in late 1997, the Russia–China Fisheries Commission agreed in late 1997 for China to take 85 000 tonnes in the Sea of Okhotsk in 1998, based in part on China's agreement to stop uncontrolled fishing in areas of the Okhotsk that did not lie within Russia's 200-nautical mile (nm) Exclusive Economic Zone (EEZ). The commission reached agreement that bilateral cooperation in fisheries should have three goals: stop poaching; cooperative work on promoting the most valuable freshwater species in the Amur and Ussuri rivers; and permission for Chinese boats to work inside Russia's 200-nm EEZ.[20] In late 1997, China and Russia were negotiating and expected to reach agreement on supply of electricity under a US$3 billion contract for construction of a power line from the Boguchany hydro-power plant in Siberia to northern China.[21] In early 1998, Russian commentators were expecting hundreds of Russian firms to benefit from a multi-billion dollar agreement with China on the provision of a nuclear power plant.[22] There is a highly developed set of twinning arrangements between towns and cities along the border, involving at least twelve on each side of the border. The degree of exchange has grown to include direct economic aid from Chinese local authorities to their Russian counterparts and direct investment by larger regional authorities of China in the Russian Far East.[23]

Transport and telecommunications links between Russian and Chinese border regions have also been improved. For example, in February 1998, a 16-lane vehicle crossing point was opened on the border with China at the village of Zabaikalsk as part of plans by the Russian government to develop a trade and industry centre at the village in an effort to stimulate trade with China.[24] Authorities claimed the crossing point could handle 10 000 people and about 10 000 tonnes of freight per day.

The improvements in political and economic relations across the border between Russia and China were accompanied by great strides in settlement of the boundary dispute between the two countries and in the establishment of some basic confidence-building measures in respect of military activities in the border region. These developments were made easier by the collapse of Russian military power after 1991 and by the break-up of the USSR into its constituent republics. China had a range of new incentives to work with Russia, not least of which was the need to prevent the newly independent state of Kazakhstan on China's western border from becoming a magnet for separatists in China's Xinjiang Autonomous Region, in which there were significant Kazakh communities disaffected with Chinese rule.

In December 1992, Moscow and Beijing signed a declaration for mutual reduction in armaments and for the development of more open military relations in the border areas. In 1993 and 1994, Russia and China exchanged naval visits. In 1994, the two countries issued a joint declaration which included a commitment to non-aggression, and exchanged basic data on military deployments in the border region. By 1996, Russia and China had signed an agreement on confidence-building measures along the border and in 1997, they joined a five-party agreement on reduction of forces in border areas along with Kazakhstan, Kyrgyzstan and Tajikistan. This treaty provided for a control regime for deployment of military forces within 200 kilometres of the borders. By 1998, the Sino–Russian border settlement was complete, with Russia ceding significant territory, including an island in the Amur River with an area of 175 square kilometres that had traditionally been used by Russians.[25]

The momentum in economic and political relations of the 1990s led Russian and China by the end of the decade to look at each other as strategic partners, a suitably anodyne term supposed to represent a relationship less than allies but something more than 'business as usual'. An important element of the bilateral relationship which represented a marked turn away from the period of bilateral confrontation of previous decades was the sale by Russia to China of sophisticated military hardware. (This is discussed later in chapter 10.) Russia and China began to invoke rhetoric of a 'confidential equal partnership' aimed at strategic cooperation in the next century because of Russian estimates that, by 2010, China would have the biggest GDP in the world and based on common interests arising from their contiguity.[26] Both governments insist that their strategic partnership is not aimed at third parties, and in fact both Russia and China were using similar terminology to describe the bilateral relationship with the USA (in China's case) or Japan (in Russia's case: 'creative partnership in keeping with strategic and geopolitical interests').

Yet, though this rhetoric may have had a relatively anodyne appearance, even when it was first being mooted Russia was prepared to allow it a deeper significance. This was put bluntly by the Foreign Minister, Yevgeny Primakov, in 1996, when he said that Russia and China need to be friends in order to avoid the impression that some countries lost the Cold War and to mitigate the circumstances of US unipolar dominance.[27] In April 1996, Russia and China issued a joint communique on opposing hegemony. By late 1998, Russia had begun to court China and India to join it in a more robust 'strategic partnership' to combat US unilateralism and pre-eminence. Russia's efforts to build a grand alliance in Asia for this purpose are discussed later in this chapter.

The improving border relations between Russia and China in the 1990s made their own contribution to the easing of strategic tensions and a slight drawing together of strategic interests, but the main cause of the change was the reorientation by both Russia and China away from policies of confrontation and strategic rivalry toward ones of internationalisation of the domestic economies and much greater openness of the domestic societies. In Russia's case, this reorientation had come about first from the changes in Soviet policy under Gorbachev but subsequently intensified under President Yeltsin. In China's case, this reorientation resulted from the change in Communist Party policy toward internationalisation of the economy and economic reform that had been set in train as early as 1978 by Deng Xiaoping. As long as these policy settings remain in place, then a solid foundation for an expansion of relations and an easing of tensions will exist. To the extent that Russia and China decide to step back from cooperation with the USA and its allies in order to combat US 'hegemonism', this will provide a further foundation for strategic cooperation.

The Russian Foreign Minister, Ivanov, expressed the view that by early 1999, Russia and China had reached a level of relations superior to anything in the past, and had created the basis for the dynamic development of the relationship into the future.[28] In particular, Russia saw the relationship with China as central to the outcome of the 'tense' [ostreishii] struggle to establish a multipolar world order over the efforts of the USA to carry out its policy of diktat, or hegemony.

But not all has been sweetness and light in the Russia–China relationship of the 1990s. Deep suspicions toward China remain in Russia and there are some fundamental differences in policy. In 1992, when Russia was at its most liberal internationalist position, it agreed to the BBC's use of two transmitters in eastern Russia to broadcast into China—a move regarded by the Chinese government as hostile and subversive.[29] In December 1996, when Russia's military forces were feeling besieged and vulnerable, the Russian Defence Minister created a diplomatic flurry when he made a speech to CIS members in which he said that China's military build-up constituted a sufficient threat to Russia and the CIS states to provide a solid reason for strengthening CIS military cooperation.[30]

Even the rapid growth in trans-border economic activity be-tween the two countries has caused concern in Moscow. There is a view that the relations between sub-national administrations and China may be developing too quickly or without appropriate consideration of national security issues.[31] This has led to increased pressure for greater central control of some of the activities. This would be against the trend of decentralisation that has characterised much of Russian politics since 1991. Moreover, some of the local authorities have argued that more decentralisa-tion is necessary to increase the economic vitality of the regions and therefore strengthen them against any creeping Chinese con-trol.[32] But even the local authorities have complained about the competitive effect on their own commercial interest of increased Chinese activity. This has occurred in respect of river shipping, with the Governor of the Maritime Territory complaining that it would undercut the importance of Vladivostok.[33]

The movement of people across the border with China, while economically important, has also become politically sensitive in Russia. After 1988, the first Chinese workers were permitted into Russia to work in timber and agriculture.[34] Though the numbers remained controlled and under 10 000 for several years,[35] by 1998 there had been an explosion of cross-border movements for long-term work (primarily in construction) and for business. This led to rising public concern about the possible transmigration of large Chinese populations into the region. In 1993 and 1994, a sustained media campaign supported by the administrations of Khabarovsk and Maritime Territories criticised the infiltration of the Far East by Chinese immigrants. The campaign developed such ferocity that it reportedly became a point of some tension between the governments of China and Russia.[36] In 1997, a presidential adviser went into print to discount the suggestions that up to two million Chinese citizens were now living in the Far East. He said that the number of legal Chinese residents was small, about 20 000, and that the number of illegal residents was about 180 000. But, he said, in historical perspective, this was small compared with the 500 000 Chinese who lived there in the period of close Soviet–Chinese relations after the Second World War. He reported that border guards had caught as many as 5000–6000 illegal residents in each of Maritime and Khabarovsk Territories and in Amur Province—in an unspecified period, but presumably since 1991. While the legitimate concerns of Russians about possible large-scale transmigration needed to be addressed and while there was still no adequate immigration regime, it was highly likely in his estimate that the Chinese government would not create a policy of supporting such transmigration at the expense of good relations with Russia.[37] Russia faces the special problem with the Chinese border that members of non-Chinese minorities, such as Kazakh and Kyrgyz, try to use the Russia–China border as a backdoor escape route to the new Central Asian countries, since China's border with those countries is closely guarded.[38]

Thus, Russia's strategic policy toward China at the end of the 1990s contains an essential contradiction. On the one hand, there have been many positive developments: the elimination of tension at the border level, deepening economic and political relations (including regular summit meetings), arms sales and a search for strategic cooperation against US unilateralism in global affairs. On the other hand, there is a reluctance to sell the most modern military technology to China and strong, visceral suspicions that in the longer term a more powerful China will by default or design look to retake the large underpopulated territories ceded to Russia under duress only 140 years ago. The main factors influencing the trend toward cooperative relations between the two countries have been collapse of Russian military power, the growth of China's economic power and the trends in domestic politics in both Russia and China. If these change significantly, then the strategic significance for Russia of the bilateral relationship is likely to change fundamentally.

JAPAN

Russia's strategic perspective of Japan for much of the time since 1951 has been coloured by two mutually reinforcing circumstances. First, Japan was a firm military ally of the USA for the entire Cold War period, not only through its consistent provision of military bases to US naval and air forces but also through its consistent diplomatic support to anti-communist and anti-Soviet positions. Japanese basing support for the powerful US Seventh Fleet brought US nuclear forces right to the doorstep of the USSR, and provided one of the principal obstacles to any Soviet assertion of military influence in Northeast Asia and the Western Pacific arising from its own massive naval build-up in the region through the 1970s and 1980s. Second, most Japanese officials looked down on Russia, initially for the way in which the USSR entered the war against Japan in 1945 and took territory that had been recognised as Japanese or had been ceded to Japan under international treaty; and subsequently because of the USSR's communist social system that over time proved itself no match for Japan's post-war economic recovery that placed it by the 1980s as the second most powerful economy in the world. The failure of the USSR and Japan to reach agreement on a bilateral peace treaty after the Second World War became an enduring symbol of the gulf in the bilateral relationship. There were short-lived periods of warming relations between the two countries, as in 1956 when they agreed on a solution to the territorial dispute over the Southern Kuril Islands (called 'Northern Territories' in Japan—see Map 3). In the 1970s, Japanese investors looked with great interest at the huge deposits of natural resources in the Far East, and the USSR was keen to capitalise on this interest, but the great promise was not matched by commitments, although some projects did get under way. In 1986, when Gorbachev launched the Vladivostok initiative in an attempt to break away from the Cold War hostilities, Japan was as lukewarm and suspicious about it as the USA and its other allies in the region.

As the USSR was going through its collapse, it was a beneficiary of early Japanese interest, but Japan did not really engage solidly with the new Russia for a number of years after 1991. Financial assistance to Russia beginning in 1990 looked substantial and promising. This included an emergency food assistance package announced on 18 December 1990 (US$10 billion in loans, US$8.3 million in food and medical assistance); a package announced on 8 October 1991 (US$50 billion in loans, trade insurance and export credits up to US$1.8 billion, and technical assistance in civil nuclear matters); a specific nuclear assistance grant of US$25 million announced on 2 July 1992; a grant of medical assistance for Chernobyl of US$21.7 million; and a grant of US$20 million to help retain nuclear engineers in Russia.[39] But this level of interest was not sustained and by early 1996 Japan's grant aid flows to Russia reached only US$381 million.[40] The trade credits of US$4.1 billion in the same period were perhaps more important. In spite of this willingness to offer some assistance, Japan remained uncertain about where Russia was headed, and this uncertainty was evidenced in 1992 by efforts to get closer to the European-based Conference on Security and Cooperation in Europe.[41]

The dispute over sovereignty of the Southern Kuril Islands (Kunashiri, Etorofu, Shikotan and a much smaller group of islets, called the Habomai group—see Map 9) became a source of more bitter contention in the early days of the new Russian government, when vigorous nationalist and extremist political forces emerged, thereby limiting the room for the Russian government even to maintain the status quo. For example, in March 1992, when Foreign Minister Kozyrev visited Tokyo to prepare for a visit by President Yeltsin, he told Japanese officials that extremist voices in Russia would make any return of the disputed territories difficult. They replied that Japanese economic aid to Russia would be imperilled if the islands were not returned.[42] In July 1992, a number of military leaders warned a special session of the Russian parliament that any concessions on the 'Northern Territories' by President Yeltsin in a planned visit to Tokyo would endanger the country's strategic interests.[43] Pressing economic circumstances emboldened Russia in 1992 to lease an area on one of the islands to a Hong Kong company (linked with a Japanese citizen) which wanted to develop a casino resort. The move prompted a protest from the Japanese government.[44]

Yet it was also at this time that the foundations of a future agreement with Japan to settle the dispute were laid. Russian Foreign Ministry officials briefed parliament in July 1992, and advocated the honouring of a 1956 agreement in which Russia agreed to return part of the disputed territory (the small Habomai group and Shikotan Island). While Japan wanted some psychological linkage between aid and resolution of the island dispute, it

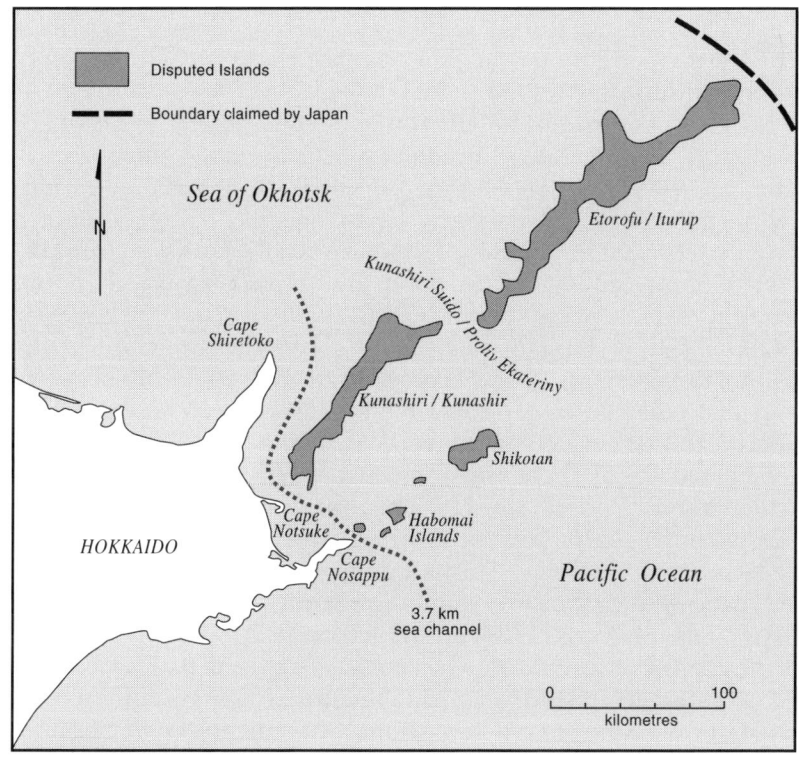

9. Disputed Kuril Islands

was keen to avoid an all-or-nothing policy.[45] In April 1992, a Japanese cabinet minister indicated that Japan might be prepared to settle for the terms of the 1956 agreement.[46] Japanese officials interpreted the 1956 agreement to mean that the USSR might return all of the disputed territories subject to improvements in bilateral relations.[47] By April 1992, Russia began to demilitarise the disputed islands, having already cut forces there by 30 per cent to 7000,[48] and this process of withdrawal of main force military units was completed in 1993 in advance of a visit to Japan by Yeltsin. (Border forces remained.)[49]

Between 1993 and 1996, relations developed in piecemeal fashion and with some setbacks. Japan offered Russia several low-interest loans for major infrastructure or resource projects in the Far East but these were not taken up because of lack of organisation in Russia.[50] In 1996, aviation talks between Russia and Japan broke down when officials of Japan's Defence Agency (JDA) refused to endorse a proposal to allow Russian civil aircraft to use a new international airport at Chitose, serving Sapporo in Hokkaido, reportedly on the grounds that there was an important military airbase nearby.[51]

By 1997, the international strategic environment had changed sufficiently and Russia's diplomacy had regained such greater coherence that Japan and Russia set about developing an entirely new relationship. For its part, Japan sought to give Russia a 'positive presence in [Japan's] diplomatic and security picture that is without precedent'.[52] The main factor pushing Japan in this direction was concern about China's growing military power, demonstrated in ballistic missile test launches toward Taiwan and live fire exercises in the Taiwan Strait in 1996. Other concerns have also emerged to reinforce for Japan the need to deal more directly and effectively with Russia at the global level. Japan became concerned about the implications of a US–China strategic partnership and about the US propensity to force its interpretations on other major powers in international forums.

As a result, high-level visits between the two countries gathered pace and important symbolic strides were made in the relationship. In early 1997, Deputy Foreign Minister responsible for the Asia–Pacific Region, Grigory Karasin, said that both Japan and Russia understood that the territorial issue could not be solved 'in a stroke or by sensational statements or demands'.[53] First Deputy Prime Minister Boris Nemtsov visited Tokyo in June 1997 to meet with Japanese ministers, including the Minister for Industry and Trade, with whom Nemtsov discussed greater cooperation in energy and transport. Japan was said to be looking to encourage involvement of its private sector in eastern Russia.[54] Japan is paying most attention to the Far East and the Transbaikal area, especially for resources. Major corporations involved in offshore exploration or development operations (in international consortiums) include Itochu, Marubeni, Mitsubishi and Mitsui.[55]

Russia has been willing to give rhetorical support at least to Japan's push for a greater role in international security affairs. In June 1997, Foreign Minister Primakov made a positive if non-committal statement to the effect that Japan's influence on international affairs was less than its economic potential suggested and that Russia looked to Tokyo to 'play a more positive role in international affairs'.[56] Primakov may have had his eye more on technological and economic impacts than security ones.

Russia is also looking to supply Japan with electricity under a US$2.5 billion project involving a line from southern Yakutia through Sakhalin to Japan. Officials of the two countries held

talks in November 1997.[57] In late 1997, commercial representatives from Russia and Japan were discussing the sale of
nuclear reprocessing technology by a plant near Cheliabinsk for
Japan's first domestic reprocessing plant scheduled to begin operations in 2002.[58]

In November 1997, Japan made an important breakthrough in
an informal summit ('no ties') between Yeltsin and Prime Minister
Hashimoto held in Krasnoiarsk—the first visit by a Japanese
Prime Minister to the USSR or Russia for 24 years—reacting to
the vigorous pace of high-level meetings between the USA and
China and the USA and Japan. But even at this meeting, as for
the last 20 years, Russia continued to place hope in Japanese
capital and technology for intensified exploitation of mineral
resources in Siberia, especially in oil and gas.[59] Even before the
meeting, the Russian Foreign Minister, Yevgeny Primakov, had
made plans to visit Japan after the summit to discuss joint
development of the disputed territories—in anticipation of some
breakthrough agreement at the summit. In the event, the leaders
reached agreement to work toward a peace treaty and resolution
of the territorial dispute by the year 2000.

Working relations for mutual economic gain improved steadily
in this atmosphere. In December 1997, officials of the two countries
reached in-principle agreement on an annual fish catch of 95 000
tonnes in each other's undisputed waters,[60] and up to 300 000
tonnes catch by Japan in waters around the disputed islands.[61] The
two sides could not agree on a quota for Japanese catch of
Kamchatka crabs in the waters around the disputed islands
because Russia insisted that the species was overfished.[62] In January 1998, Japan and Russia agreed to set up a working group on
the Trans-Siberian Railway to achieve the 'modernisation and full
scale revival' of the railway. The aim was to restore the transport
route to its levels of activity of the 1980s, which were some five
times higher than 1998 volumes.[63]

There are however substantial limitations on the development
of a strategically close relationship between Russia and Japan. As
rapidly as Russia–Japan political relations may have developed
after 1997, US–Japan security relations have been consolidated
and expanded in the same period. Beginning in April 1996, just
one month after China's military intimidation of Taiwan, the US
and Japan agreed on a package of measures to clarify operational
aspects of their alliance relationship in the event of conflict in
areas surrounding Japan.[64] Notwithstanding the trade disputation
between Japan and the USA, the two countries retain much more

in common than the things that divide them.[65] The US military presence in Japan remains of special interest or concern to many in Russia. This concern was exacerbated somewhat when the USS *Independence*, home-ported in Yokosuka naval base, Japan, made a visit to the northernmost of Japan's main islands, Hokkaido, in 1997.[66]

The involvement of Japan in efforts by the USA to establish a theatre missile defence (TMD) system are also viewed negatively in Moscow, on the grounds that the development would be a breach of the ABM Treaty on several counts.[67] Russian commentators and officials do not see the TMD system in Northeast Asia as a direct threat to Russia, but they see the moves as a shift backwards by the US–Japan alliance to some sort of Cold War footing. Apart from Russia's concerns about the impact of TMD on the ABM Treaty and the strategic nuclear relationship between Russia and the USA, Russia sees Japan's possible involvement as having the potential for it to spark either a new round of military build-ups in Northeast Asia or a new cycle of tension. Russia would like to see Japan winding back on its military ties with the USA in the light of the substantial reduction in Russian military power in Northeast Asia. Another important impediment in strategic ties between Russia and Japan remains the lack of intensive economic ties.

These sorts of rifts or points of dissension are likely to remain for some time. In particular, the territorial dispute will not be resolved by the year 2000 unless Japan abandons its claim to all of the disputed islands. Russia's Foreign Minister indicated in February 1999 that the 1956 joint declaration between the USSR and Japan is an 'active international agreement' that was ratified by the Soviet parliament.[68] This should imply that Russia has a binding commitment to hand over the Habomai group of islets and the island of Shikotan, as promised in the declaration, but in the same article asserting the continuing validity of the joint declaration, the Foreign Minister seemed to question what exactly the Habomai Islands comprised, and asserted Russia's immutable sovereignty over the 'lower Kuril chain' [*Malaia Kurisl'skaia griada*], implying that Shikotan was part of this designation. If Russia remains intransigent, Japan will have to abandon its claims or drop them in priority in its foreign policy if it wants to see any new type of strategic relations between it and Russia.

But as long as Japan is tying itself more tightly into the US global military alliance system, and as long as Japan continues to support US world order initiatives with which Russia is unhappy, there is little prospect of a substantial harmonisation of strategic relations with Russia. Many people in Russia remain hostile to the presence of US military forces on the country's doorstep. It is felt—unconsciously perhaps—as a painful reminder of the collapse of Soviet power.

KOREA

North Korea has only a 17-kilometre riverine border with Russia along the Tiumen River, but Russia's strategic position in Northeast Asia is seen in Moscow as being shaped in important ways by events on the peninsula. The war between Russia and Japan in 1904–05 was fought in part because of Russian resistance to Japan's interests in expanding its presence in Korea. The USSR was strategically engaged in the Korean peninsula since at least 1945, when its forces occupied the northern half and set up a communist government there. This involvement led the USSR to back the North Korean government in the invasion of South Korea in 1950. The USSR sent military forces to fight in Korea, especially pilots but also some ground troops, but did not commit fully to the defence of North Korea. This lack of firm commitment contributed in later years to a very mixed record of relations between the USSR and North Korea in the Cold War. A Treaty of Mutual Assistance, Friendship and Cooperation was signed in 1961 which committed the USSR to the defence of North Korea, and this underpinned a sustained military supply relationship between the two countries during much of the Cold War. But during the confrontation between the USSR and China in the 1960s and 1970s North Korea maintained relations with both countries. For most of the time, the relationship with China was warmer than that with the USSR, but still the USSR maintained working relations. The USSR certainly retained a very keen interest in Korea because of the presence of US military forces, and because of the possibility of the outbreak of a new war.

As the USSR's strategic policies began to soften in the 1980s, South Korea became a target of its diplomatic blandishments. It was South Korea, by then much wealthier and much more powerful militarily than for most of the time since the war, which was the most responsive of any East Asian country to the Vladivostok initiative of Mikhail Gorbachev in 1986. The reformist government of the USSR was keen to exploit the capital and technology newly available from its near neighbour to boost its flagging economy. Events moved quickly, in part because South Korea was keen to assert the influence that its new wealth potentially offered it, and almost overnight the government of South Korea became something of a wild card in Northeast Asian strategic relations. In 1990, Moscow formally recognised South Korea—the enemy of its ally, North Korea—and this move forced the People's Republic of China to follow suit. But just how much of a wild card South Korea had become in those years was revealed in 1996 by a former President of South Korea, No Tae-u, who said that under his administration, Seoul had canvassed with Moscow the possibiliy of taking out a 99-year lease on a part of eastern Russia to provide a solid resource base to underpin the process of Korean reunification.[69] These diplomatic moves provide some evidence of the degree to which in Moscow's view the military tension on the Korean peninsula had abated.

In line with the more internationalist and cooperative trends in Russian foreign policy in the first half of the 1990s, Russian relations with South Korea intensified. In 1993, discussion began on military cooperation, including exchange of warship visits and even plans for some joint military exercises. A presidential summit was held in Moscow in 1994. Economic and commercial relations looked very bright, with strong interest from leading South Korean firms in investment and sales in Russia. For a couple of years at least, Russia seemed to have stolen a march on the other three great powers with an interest in the Korean peninsula—China, the USA and Japan. But it was not long before the other three powers moved vigorously to catch up to Russian diplomacy. The weakness of the Russian economy in those years meant that Russia did not have available to it the sorts of economic levers available to the other three great powers.

Russia's virtual exclusion from the Korean strategic picture was confirmed as a result of the North Korean nuclear crisis beginning in 1994, when the USA threatened use of force if North Korea went ahead and developed nuclear weapons after it withdrew from the Nuclear Non-Proliferation Treaty, suspended inspection obligations, and looked like breaching an agreement reached with South Korea in 1991 not to manufacture nuclear weapons.[70] As a result of the crisis, two new international forums were established which excluded Russia. These were the Korean Energy Development Organisation (KEDO), a nuclear energy assistance program for North Korea set up in 1995 by the USA, Japan and South Korea to buy it out of its own unsupervised nuclear power program; and four-party talks on the Korean peninsula, involving North and South Korea, China and the USA, which were formally agreed to in 1997. North Korea had tried to keep Russia in the nuclear negotiations but Russia did not have the money to match South Korea's offer of two light water reactors and associated support.

Even as Russia was looking to maintain some sort of strategic leverage in the Korean peninsula, it was also pursuing its new foreign policy. It was not seeking to increase or exploit tensions in the Korean peninsula, rather to lend its weight in abating tensions. In 1995, it notified the North Korean government that it could not renew the 1961 treaty because it contained a commitment to the defence of North Korea in the event of an attack.[71] In 1997, Moscow and Pyongyang conducted talks about the renewal of military cooperation (excluding military assistance in the case of aggression, one of the basic provisions of the 1961 Treaty of Friendship, Cooperation and Mutual Assistance). As Russian Deputy Foreign Minister Grigory Karasin has pointed out, the new agreement will establish 'absolutely normal military and technical cooperation with North Korea'. Such cooperation may include supply of weapons, training and military exchanges, but will be restrained by either Russia's international commitments, or by its potential to cause an imbalance of forces on the Korean peninsula.[72] By early 1999, a new treaty was agreed, but only after Russia had consistently refused to include in it a reference supportive of North Korea's vision of a confederal solution to the problem of reunification with South Korea. The signature of the treaty could not belie the lack of substance in the relationship between the two countries. Nor could it conceal important differences of policy. Russia was still committed to its position agreed with the USA of opposing missile sales by North Korea to areas of tension; and North Korea was illegally purchasing Russian military equipment and smuggling it across the border.[73] Russia denies suggestions in Western countries that it has sent experts and computer equipment to North Korea to help its missile and nuclear weapons programs.[74]

But the new treaty was one of a number of signs that had emerged by mid-1999 that relations between the two countries were beginning to warm up. New commonalities of interest between Russia and North Korea were beginning to appear. Russia opposed the overbearing approach by the USA in its demand for challenge inspections of suspect nuclear sites,[75] and Russia believed that the USA was exaggerating North Korea's nuclear and missile potential for the sake of raising tension in the region and achieving certain military expenditure goals, such as funding for TMD.[76]

At the same time, Russia began to suffer something of a downward turn in its relations with South Korea. This was caused in part by economic problems: Russia could not repay a debt of US$1.8 billion and South Korea needed the money badly. In 1998, two-way trade dropped by 25 per cent compared with 1997.[77] But there were many continuing positive aspects of relations between Russia and South Korea: in April 1999, they signed a new nuclear energy cooperation agreement;[78] there had been some limited arms transfers from Russia as part of the debt repayment; talks continued on a shipping treaty which would increase the access of Russian ships to South Korean ports[79]; talks on resource development continued; and Russia continued to offer South Korea some of its most advanced weapons, including S–300 anti-aircraft missiles and Su–35 aircraft. South Korea supported Russia's inclusion in new regional economic cooperation arrangements in Northeast Asia.

It may be fair to pose the question, as some commentators have, whether Russia may not be drifting back toward solidarity with governments in confrontation with the USA simply for the sake of opposing the USA and whether on the Korean peninsula this means a weakening of the relationship with South Korea in favour of the North.[80] But the answer to those questions will depend on trends in Russian strategic policy more generally, rather than on events in the Korean peninsula. As long as Russia remains preoccupied with its domestic circumstances and with high-priority strategic problems in the newly independent states or in Europe or the Middle East, it is unlikely to allow itself too much anxiety about its current lack of leverage on the Korean peninsula. It will work steadily within its current strategic orientation to expand cooperative relations, through proposals like six-party talks (to bring Russia and Japan into the existing four-party talks)[81] or proposals from South Korea for a Northeast Asia free trade regime involving Russia, China, Japan and the two Koreas.[82] War in Korea would probably force a change, but even then Russian interests would be, as they have been in Kosovo in early 1999, to stop the war rather than exploit it for strategic advantage. As in Kosovo in April and May 1999, Russia is unlikely to seek to intervene militarily in Korea, so its strategic leverage in Korea will remain relatively insignificant.

OTHER REGIONAL INTERESTS

Russia sees important strategic interests engaged in other states in the Asia–Pacific region, especially Mongolia, Vietnam and India. It also sees ASEAN as a group as an important target of its diplomacy in asserting Russian great power standing and keeping abreast to the extent possible with moves made by the other East Asian great powers (USA, Japan and China) toward ASEAN.

Mongolia has been of some strategic significance to both Russia (or USSR) and China throughout this century. For most of the time, Mongolia has seen its security as best served by close relations with the USSR rather than China. When relations between the two great powers were not confrontational, as in the 1950s, Mongolia was able to enjoy relatively good relations with both. It signed a defence treaty with China in 1960, while having one with the USSR that went back to the 1930s. As relations worsened between its two powerful neighbours, Mongolia's relations with China also worsened—in part because of concern about Chinese designs to reunify Mongolia (once called 'Outer Mongolia') with China's own Inner Mongolia. Mongolia and the USSR became firm military allies, signing a new defence treaty in 1966 that allowed the stationing of Soviet forces there. The USSR based five ground forces divisions and some air assets there for most of the 1970s and 1980s.

As relations between the USSR and China began to improve in the late 1980s, so the strategic importance of Mongolia to Russia began to decline. It began to withdraw its military forces there in 1989, a process completed in 1992. Mongolia began to pursue more vigorous independent diplomacy, and signed a new treaty on friendly relations with China in 1994. But even so, Mongolia appears to have more of an eye to Russian diplomatic and strategic interests and works closely with it in international forums.

In 1997, Russia and Mongolia signed a treaty on cooperation between their armed forces. In April 1998, they further agreed on direct contacts between the Transbaikal Military District and the Armed Forces of Mongolia with a view to fostering low-level cooperation in maintenance and repair, observing of exercises, and social exchanges.[83]

As a relatively poor country, Mongolia will however have to take advantage of the potential existing in closer cross-border links with the more prosperous China. As long as Russia and

China are not pursuing confrontational policies, Mongolia will have a relatively low profile in Russian strategic calculations. The one exception to this relates to Russian concerns about long-term population movement from China into the depopulating eastern regions of Russia. Russia and Mongolia will continue to have very businesslike relations on this issue of border control.[84]

Russia's strategic interests in Vietnam declined sharply after 1991, but it still retains some residual interests, not least of which is continued access to intelligence collection facilities at Cam Ranh Bay. (Soviet naval activities out of Cam Ranh Bay had all but ceased by 1991.) For its part, Vietnam has been willing to keep up some military relations with Russia, in large part because it was the only major power with which it had any useful relations. The Socialist Republic of Vietnam, unified in 1975 after North Vietnam completed its war of national liberation, became an important ally of Moscow in its confrontation with China after 1975.

The hostile relations between the USSR and China had made themselves felt during the fighting of the Vietnam War, but Russia maintained strong support for North Vietnam through much of the Sino–Soviet confrontation. This support had three primary foundations: the first was part of the global contest with China for supremacy in the world communist movement; a second was the value of having a close ally on China's southern borders; and a third was commitment to a policy of support for communist governments or rebel forces against US-supported non-communist governments or forces (as long as this was relatively low-risk).

The USSR provided North Vietnam with military supplies for the war against the South and on some occasions deployed air defence units to Hanoi and other locations to help North Vietnam defend against US air attacks. Soviet commitment was not absolute, however, and its willingness to sacrifice Vietnamese interests on occasion for the pursuit of its strategic policies at the global level left China with some openings during the Vietnam War.

After 1975, the USSR developed such a close relationship with Vietnam that this became one of the motivations for China's invasion of Vietnam in 1979. This invasion allowed the USSR to become even closer, leading to the establishment of the Soviet naval facility in Cam Ranh Bay that supported substantial naval deployments to Indian Ocean crises beginning in late 1979 and continuing through the 1980s. Vietnam gained almost the same status as the USSR's Eastern European allies and Cuba. As Russia abandoned communism very abruptly, the ties with Vietnam simply became a burden from the past, with Vietnam owing Russia billions of dollars. In the second half of the 1990s, as Vietnam itself moved to reform communism and looked more to Japan and then the USA for investment and trade, and as Vietnam normalised its relations with China, any special commonality in the strategic interests of Russia and Vietnam evaporated. Still, the Vietnamese political leadership continues to consider Russia as its strategic partner in the Asia–Pacific region; this was emphasised during the official visit of Russia's Defence Minister Sergeyev to Vietnam in October 1998.[85]

The principal value to Russia of Vietnam in the 1990s has been as a foundation for re-establishing a vigorous diplomacy in the Asia–Pacific and for reasserting great power status. This has been achieved through reliance on extensive contacts established through decades of close relations, through Russian ability to exploit Vietnam's debt burden, and through Vietnam's interest in leasing fees for continued access, albeit limited, to Cam Ranh Bay. During the October 1998 visit of Russia's military delegation to Vietnam, both sides discussed the future terms of Russia's lease of the Cam Ranh Bay naval facility.[86]

The countries of ASEAN, like the organisation itself, have become part of Russia's effort to rebuild its great power status in the Asia–Pacific. This strategy, as mentioned earlier in the chapter, has had some notable successes. For some countries of ASEAN, a non-communist and relatively weak Russia has proved for certain purposes to be a useful diplomatic foil to the otherwise intrusive pressures from the USA and long-term concerns about China. But this relationship is more at the conceptual level and has had few, if any, operational implications except to facilitate Russia's joining a variety of regional forums. Russia has become a supplier of military equipment on a very modest scale to Malaysia, the country in the region most interested in creating the impression of strategic independence from its traditional sources of military equipment imports. Russia's diplomacy toward and strategic interests in ASEAN and its members will remain relatively benign as long as Russia maintains a non-confrontational posture toward other great powers interested in the region.

India had never been a military ally of the USSR in the way that Vietnam had been, nor a strategic adversary of the USSR in the way that China had been, for two reasons. South Asia was geographically remote from the main theatres where the military aspects of the Cold War and the Sino–Soviet confrontation had played themselves out. But more importantly, India was relatively meticulous in its efforts not to fall to the blandishments of one side or the other. One reason why India had this luxury was that by 1971, as the military dimension of these two great confrontations was expanding to many parts of the world, the political geography of South Asia had been resolved in such a way as to establish India's undisputed regional superiority. In that year, India intervened in East Pakistan in support of the creation of the new state of Bangladesh, thus crippling the only state in South Asia capable of matching India in strategic power.

India did enjoy close political relations with the USSR and a close military supply relationship, because the two countries shared important strategic interests. The USSR's adversaries were those of India. India was locked into a strategic rivalry with China because of a territorial dispute with it that had led to a short war in 1962; because of China's acquisition of nuclear weapons beginning in 1964; because of China's growing support for Pakistan, including the possible transfer of nuclear weapons technology; and because of China's efforts in the international community to coopt the non-aligned movement (a joint creation of India and China in 1955) for radical communist purposes.

Similarly, but to a lesser extent, India was uncomfortable with US strategic policy, beginning as early as 1971 when the USA sent a naval task force into the Bay of Bengal in an unsuccessful effort to intimidate India during its intervention in East Pakistan. But India also opposed US military support for Pakistan, which had commenced as early as 1959 in the creation of a military alliance drawing together Iran, Pakistan and Turkey in the Central Treaty Organisation, but which continued on a sporadic basis since that time. India did not condemn the Soviet invasion of Afghanistan in 1979 in part because of the close military relationship between Pakistan and the USA.

Since the collapse of the USSR, India has seen little value in Russia except as a continuing source of important items in its military inventory. Russia has sought repayment of its debts from India and opposed India's efforts to become a nuclear weapons power. For Russia, India has had little to offer as long as Moscow was preoccupied with events at home, in the newly independent states, in Eastern Europe, on its southern borders, and in East Asia. India simply comes a long way down the list of Russia's strategic priorities.

RUSSIAN EFFORTS TO CREATE A GRAND ALLIANCE IN ASIA

India gained new prominence for Russia after 1995 as it sought ways to curb US unilateralism. Leading figures in Russia have canvassed a range of alliance options for the country as a means of combating US pressure on a number of policy fronts. Russia, India and China (the Big Three) all feel that they have been pushed around by the USA in recent years in the processes of international decision-making, with the USA able either to engineer their support or to buy their support. This has occurred in many areas of international policy, two of the most prominent being UN Security Council votes and in agreements on missile and nuclear proliferation. But all three countries see danger signs in US decisions to use force against weaker countries, like Yugoslavia and Iraq, without Security Council support. US pressure has also come through legislative intrusions into areas central to domestic sovereignty, such as economic austerity measures and nuclear exports, or defence policy and human rights. The advocates of new international partnerships to constrain the USA say they want a world in which all of the great powers have an equal say rather than one in which the United States is able to exploit its dominating position.

This international goal, while sincerely felt, conceals less conscious desires at the domestic level. On Russia's part, pursuit of a new anti-Americanism is seen as one way to restore the clout, prestige and national unity of purpose lost by Russia in the decade since the Berlin Wall was breached. For India, a new anti-Americanism on the part of the government is rooted in widespread disaffection with the social and religious impacts of economic globalisation. For China, the domestic sensitivities owe more to the regime's anxiety about pressures for political liberalisation, but many Chinese feel the same loss of unique national identity in the face of powerful external forces they see as both homogenising and essentially American. These domestic constituencies will keep the pressure on the three governments to work together to reduce US freedom of manoeuvre and US diplomatic success.

The possibility of the creation of a triangular alliance between Russia, China and India has been discussed since the early 1990s and gained new prominence in late 1998 amidst the deterioration of relations among the great powers. During an official visit to India in December 1998, Russia's Premier Yevgeny Primakov called for the creation of a strategic alliance of Russia, China and

India.[87] At that time, Moscow's invitation to Beijing and New Delhi was largely regarded as an attempt to deliver a firm response to the US bombing of Iraq.[88] However, while in December 1998 India's Prime Minister Vajpayee was very cautious about Primakov's proposal, in response to the Balkans crisis of early 1999 Vajpayee suggested the time may have come to give serious thought to the idea of the strategic triangle.[89] NATO air strikes against Yugoslavia further fuelled speculation about the emergence of a new strategic alliance in Asia, with condemnation of NATO's actions by Russia, India and China: Russian representative to the UN Sergei Lavrov pointed out that commonality of positions about such a significant issue (war in the Balkans) could stimulate the development of alliance relations among the three states.[90]

For Russia, a new alliance structure directed against the USA would give ideological coherence to an otherwise reactive and pragmatic foreign policy, and to an otherwise contested national identity. Options canvassed have included an alliance with either China or India; a trilateral alliance with both China and India; and an alliance with the more radical Muslim states, such as Iran or Iraq. With the exception of Iraq, most of these potential allies are not particularly interested in closer relations with Russia except on one or two issues, such as transfer of Russia's technology or opposing the USA in international decision-making, especially the UN Security Council. A change in government in Russia, and even in some of the other countries, would be needed for a seriously combative alliance of a military kind to be formed.

If the other partners were willing, Russia would probably enter any of these alliances without hesitation as long as appropriate words could be found to invest the alliance with huge symbolic intent but with little substantive commitment. The scope of such alliances must be quite narrow since the current Russian government has no intention of embarking on a sustained confrontation with the USA or a sustained challenge to international order. At worst, Russia may step up its current policy of recalcitrance with the USA on issues such as Security Council votes, weapons proliferation issues, or arms control. In doing so, Russia would attempt to quarantine its relations with US allies from the effects of its anti-US posture. It would do so by combining prickliness toward the USA on the one hand with cooperative approaches toward institutions of international order (UN, OSCE, EU), or towards single powers allied with the USA (Germany, France, Japan) on the other hand. But Russian leaders accept that in an era of US strategic pre-eminence, a policy of confrontation with the USA would seriously reduce Russia's ability to deal with other great powers. Advocates in Russia of new alliances rarely discuss the need to combat or confront Western European countries or Japan.

There would need to be a change of government in Moscow for Russia to use any new alliance to embark on a sustained confrontational course. While a radical change in the Russian government is not likely, the political situation is sufficiently unstable and polarised to throw up such a change with relatively little warning. The country is in serious political and economic circumstances after a decade of reform and ruin; and elections for the parliament in 1999 and for the President in 2000 provide the appropriate opportunity for a radical change—as does the existing incapacity of President Boris Yeltsin. Radical change would however more likely come through illegal or unconstitutional means than through elections. Another circumstance that could push Russia to pursue radical options is if any state on its borders, such as Ukraine, joined NATO. This is the event most likely to push Russia to seek some form of 'strategic break-out' through alliance with US enemies or rivals.

The current government in China remains firmly opposed to a formal alliance with Russia, but a group of serving and retired military leaders has lobbied the leadership for China to form a new alliance with a number of states, including Russia. The main goal for China would be to constrain US pressure on it on a wide variety of fronts, from domestic economic and social policy to the most fundamental aspects of China's political order. This pressure from the USA has been described by a Chinese minister as 'World War Three without smoke' and other Chinese leaders are convinced that important parts of the US government are engaged in a war against Communist Party rule. China would like to push the USA out of its position of pre-eminence in military, economic and technological power—a position that allows the USA to hold out the carrot of access to capital and advanced technology as a means of forcing compliance on a variety of policies. Chinese leaders argue for an international order more along the lines of a concert of great powers working conservatively toward commonly accepted goals in a framework they describe as 'genuine multipolarity'. But China's interest in any enhanced alliance relationship with Russia does not include a desire for military confrontation.

China's leaders see strong disincentives against a formal alliance with Russia. Most importantly, China's leaders are prepared to accept for some time the continued strategic pre-eminence of the USA for fear that the alternative, a sudden change in international order, might create such instability as to threaten a fragile domestic order and the country's ambitious development goals. A weak Russia has very little to offer China beyond access to military technology that has already been accessible through the existing 'strategic partnership', and as Russian military industrial capacity continues to decline, even this attraction will continue to decline. China does have strong interest in getting access to Russia's best brains in the fields of technology, but since Russian technology levels are falling further behind those of the USA, Western Europe and Japan, this will not be a strong attraction for any more robust alliance with Russia. China does have much to gain in a major reorientation of its own military industry through some program of joint development with the Russian counterpart. This would be more acceptable than it has been in the past since China would now be the stronger partner, but to the extent that Chinese elites resent US pressure they see the preferred alternative as splendid independence, not closer association with a potentially collapsing state such as Russia.

A radical change of government in China would produce a different set of preferences. The more likely short-term prospect if a radical change in government occurred is for a repressive, bellicose and chauvinistic government. Such a government would look to engage Russia in confrontation with the USA over its support for Taiwan, over US forces in Japan, but especially over the Persian Gulf and access to oil, since that is one of the main vulnerabilities of Japan and the USA. China would intensify its efforts to divide the USA and its West European allies, but this may be difficult in circumstances of alliance with a more belligerent Russia. A major confrontation with the USA and Japan would force China to confront a unifying NATO and a collapse of East Asian regionalism in APEC and the ASEAN Regional Forum. In circumstances of a more robust and recalcitrant alliance between Russia and China, the preferences of most NATO and ASEAN states would be to side with the USA and Japan, not with Russia and China.

The most visible manifestation of a Russia–China alliance would be a return to Cold War gridlock in international organisations. This would hurt those two countries more than it would affect the USA. If Russia and China pursued this course the two countries would have to confront the prospect of being turned out of these organisations or being denied effective privileges of membership. Since 1989, the two countries have actively courted a number of important international organisations, such as the IMF, GATT and APEC. But China has a powerful card up its sleeve to play in any developing alliance strategy directed at the USA. A threat by China to disrupt existing economic links with Japan and the USA would send powerful shock waves through both economies.

Russia's alliance relationship with India—though not deep—has been the main one to survive the collapse of the USSR. The alliance comprises little more than a formal structure (a 1971 Friendship Treaty) and military co-production arrangements. The current government of India has important interests that some of its leaders believe might be served through an enhanced alliance with Russia. These are quite similar to the goals China would see in alliance with Russia: a means of resisting US pressure on issues of domestic political, economic and social order. There are important resonances between the underlying philosophy of the BJP in India and the dilemma facing Russia: both are looking for a way of giving coherence to an otherwise confused national identity in the face of traumatising engagement with forces of economic liberalisation or internationalisation.

India has a special interest in opposing US pressure in the field of military posture, in terms of missile and nuclear weapons development—but current governments in Russia and China have not differed substantially from the US position on these issues. An enhanced Russian alliance with India would force Russia to give greater support to India's policies for greater international stature. Russia would certainly come under pressure to demonstrate at least tacit support for India in its vision of China as a strategic competitor or enemy.

Russia, China and India do have common security and military interests that would underpin a military alliance. Russia wants to stop the expansion of NATO or at least be seen to have a strategic counter-move available in response to it. If the USA were removed from its position of global pre-eminence, China would feel less threatened and may have a free hand to deal with Taiwan. India would like to undermine US positions in South Asia as well as the Persian Gulf and Indian Ocean regions. India would like to break up what it sees as US–Chinese strategic partnership, and it has a special interest in opposing US pressure on military policy (missile and nuclear weapons development). Russia is already an active partner of both countries in the provision of military technology and weapons systems. These relationships are expanding.

A Russia–China–India alliance could arise only in circumstances vastly different from those that exist at the time of writing. If Russia and China had decided on an alliance relationship, they would see little merit in including India since it brings few strategic assets to the table. Russia and China would see themselves as giving great power status to a country neither regard as worthy of that. India has no strategic purchase on the main areas of US interest, either in terms of geographical interests (Western Europe and Northeast Asia) or resources. The one exception to this would be India's capacity to threaten oil supply from the Persian Gulf through aggressive naval and air operations. India does retain some leadership capacity in Third World or North–South contexts, and a tripartite alliance could be most effective in leading a Third World revolt on debt repayment or an embargo on export of strategic materials.

But a policy of contestation with the USA would seriously reduce the ability of Russia, China and India to deal with other great powers. In pursuing non-cooperative relations with the USA in areas it has identified as important, the three countries might have to bear large costs in organisations where the USA and its close partners (Germany, Japan, Britain and France) have considerable strength, such as the IMF, the World Bank and GATT. If the three countries attempted to renege on international undertakings made in the last decade on issues such as open economic policy, environmental protection or military security, they would pay large costs with close US partners. Since Russia, China and India have actively courted US, European and Japanese technology and capital, a new posture of confrontation by them in international organisations would hurt them more than the USA.

If Russia, China and India went down the path of vigorous contest with the USA in international organisations, they would find it very hard to turn the clock back on the last decade of greater international intrusiveness and globalisation. This intrusiveness is now enshrined in treaties like the Treaty on Conventional Forces in Europe Treaty, the Chemical Weapons Convention, and the UN sanctions regime against Iraq. The USA is a convenient target of propaganda but it has not been the only perpetrator of globalisation, the only possessor of capitalist economic power, or the only advocate of greater intrusiveness of international regimes. It is unlikely that the three could mobilise enough international support to revise existing treaties or other commitments against the unified opposition of US, the EU and Japan.

The domestic pressures in each of the three countries for change in policy to a comprehensive, combative partnership against the USA will probably continue to gain ground. The political ideologies that could bring about a major shift in policy are well formed and have substantial support. The political situation in each of the countries is sufficiently unstable or polarised to throw up such a change with relatively little warning. It is easy to identify credible scenarios that might push each of the three countries to such positions. If any state on Russia's border, such as Latvia or Estonia, joined NATO, this could push Russia to seek some form of counter-measure through a combative alliance with China or India. Escalation of hostilities in Kosovo or the former Yugoslav Republic of Macedonia might provoke a similar reaction. China, already on the cusp of a political crisis, would be pushed to a strong anti-US position if Japan makes more substantial moves toward planning joint combat operations with the USA, theatre missile defence, or forward deployment. If Taiwan provoked a major confrontation with the mainland, China and the USA would quickly be at loggerheads and might well seek Russian support. For India, a shift in US policy more decisively toward military support of Pakistan or toward more comprehensive sanctions on India could provoke a shift to more combative postures toward the USA.

The dire threat of a new Russia–China–India military alliance directed at US interests remains distant, and a number of powerful constraints remain in place even for quite limited coordination of anti-US positions by all of the Big Three. Nevertheless, the prospects must be for an increase in efforts by each of them, in partnership with whoever is willing, to hobble the accretion of US power and to contain the cultural onslaught of globalising influences identified with the USA.

The USA shows no signs of abating the determined, often aggressive pursuit of its foreign policy objectives, so an escalating spiral of reaction and counter-action with each of the Big Three is inevitable. The intensity and consequences of this inevitable spiral of reaction will depend on the ability of major players, including the USA, the EU and Japan, to provide the necessary circuit-breaking measures or incentives for Russia, China and India to step back from sustained and damaging confrontations. The bombing of Yugoslavia by NATO in 1999 is the complete opposite of a circuit-breaker.

Russia would be most successful in any new alliance strategy if it pursued two great strategic vulnerabilities of the USA which come together in the Persian Gulf. These are US economic dependence on sustained oil supply to several of its major trading partners or important allies; and US exposure to terrorism by political groups living in the region or associating themselves with targets of US policy in the region.

A more purposeful anti-US alliance strategy centred on radical Muslim states might provide pay-offs for Russia in its efforts to deal with restive Muslim communities within the Russian Federation or with civil disorder in former Soviet republics. This would be a high-risk strategy in terms of potential costs in relations with West European countries and Muslim countries, like Turkey, which are very important to stability in Russia's Muslim Caucasus region. But Russia would have considerable flexibility in how it conducted any alliance targeted at these two US vulnerabilities. Russia could modulate its conduct quite successfully while maintaining some appearances of cooperativeness. This has been the style of Moscow's policy on Iraq for most of the time since 1990. The reliance of China and India on Persian Gulf oil would be a complicating factor in any Russian alliance strategy designed to exploit US vulnerabilities associated with the Persian Gulf.

CONCLUSION

Diplomats and military planners in Moscow now face the most propitious circumstances in East Asia that have existed for nearly a century. No major power is seeking a military confrontation with their country; most states are seeking mutually beneficial economic links; and there are few strong hostilities toward Russia in the region. In fact, in some countries of the region, such as Vietnam and India, Russia is viewed quite favourably. The positive strategic circumstances in which Russia now finds itself in the Asia–Pacific are in large part due to the abandonment of Cold War policies of military confrontation by Moscow, China and the USA. As long as the great powers of Asia persist with these policies, Russia should have few strategic concerns in the region and its strategic efforts will be directed to building mutually beneficial relationships in social and economic domains.

There remain several points of unresolved tension in East Asia where the potential exists for Russian strategic responses to take on a more combative manifestation. These will be limited however by Russia's lack of strategic levers relative to the other great powers. Russia's strategic circumstances in Asia may be the most benign it has faced for a century, but in terms of its ability to project power and influence, Moscow is at its weakest point for at least seventy years. There has been some marshalling of diplomatic and economic resources by Russia in the second half of the 1990s to good effect in pursuit of policies of economic interchange and peaceful resolution of disputes, but few signs that Russia has strategic leverage for a more combative posture against any of the other great powers. If Russia were to succeed in forming a new grand alliance with India and China, then Russia's strategic weight would count for a lot more, but few countries in the Asia–Pacific would view this positively and Russia would lose more in economic terms than it would gain in political terms.

The main substantial threat to a continued beneficial strategic engagement by Russia in a prosperous and integrating East Asia will be the manner in which the USA pursues its own strategic purposes and the way in which Russia evaluates its position relative to the USA on a global basis. Global strategic confrontation may have faded and may well remain almost non-existent, but global strategic relationships never cease to exist. They can either be nourished or abused. The extent to which countries of the Asia–Pacific and Russia continue to work together to build new and positive relationships will remain the only true, if obvious, test of how long Russia will face a benign strategic environment in the region. If great powers in the Asia–Pacific neglect Russia, or if Russia has unreasonable expectations, then there will be a gradual slide toward renewed strategic confrontation over the next ten to fifteen years.

5

Military doctrine and force posture

Yeltsin announced the formal establishment of the new Russian military forces by presidential decree on 7 May 1992, two days before the anniversary of the defeat of Germany in the Second World War. The choice of date reflected the Russian government's declared intent to 'safeguard the continuity of the best combatant and heroic traditions of the Russian army'.[1] By harking back to the memories of the Great Patriotic War or Great Fatherland War,[2] as the Russians described their part of the Second World War, Yeltsin was invoking not only 47 years of vigorous Soviet propaganda that kept memories of the war prominent in domestic order as a legitimiser of Soviet rule, but he was also invoking the very deep, often bitter memories of the sufferings of the populace as a powerful symbol of national unity.

The new armed forces of Russia, as for the country as a whole, had to find new symbols and ceremonials to complement their role as the guardians of a new state established on the basis of rejection of the Soviet period. This was particularly difficult for the armed forces, and for veterans, since the military victory over Germany at the cost of 20 million war dead was the one symbolic point at which the Soviet regime had enjoyed near-universal support since 1945. But the Yeltsin government acted quickly on some changes, returning to the symbols of the Tsarist era and ceremonies of the Russian Orthodox Church. For example, in May 1992 the government announced that the Russian Navy would reinstitute the former Tsarist naval ensign, the Cross of St Andrew.[3] By December 1992, army aviation regiments had begun replacing the Red Star on their aircraft with the emblem of the double-headed eagle.[4] Within a short period of time, graduating naval cadets would go to church to pray before receiving their commissions. But a number of symbols and referent points from the Soviet era were to remain, and many Soviet war heroes and Soviet units are commemorated in the Russian armed forces symbology today. For example, when the name of the city of Leningrad was changed to St Petersburg, the armed forces did not change the name of the Leningrad Military District. Because of the siege of Leningrad in the war the military historic significance was just too great to abandon it. *Red Star* remained the name of the newspaper of the Ministry of Defence.

But the position in society and politics of the new armed forces, and therefore their institutional structure, was to be vastly different from that enjoyed by their Soviet-era forebears. On the one hand, the Russian armed forces would not be able to dominate the formulation of strategic policy and thus would not command the resources the Soviet military had. On the other hand, their everyday influence on politics would be more powerful. The Soviet armed forces had benefited from a highly organised system of military science and military production which combined to take the country from the ruins of war in 1945 to military superpower status by the end of the 1960s. This achievement was facilitated by the country's policies of state ownership of production, a centralised economic planning system, an ideology of confrontation with the USA and its allies, and simultaneous promotion of ideologies of scientific determinism and state militarism. Another important factor was the resource base, both natural and human, provided by membership in the USSR of the fourteen sister republics apart from the Russian Soviet Federated Socialist Republic (RSFSR). By 1991, every one of these major underpinnnings of Soviet military power had collapsed.

The impact on the military posture of the new Russian Federation was immediate and profound. Russia retained only 8 of the USSR's 16 military districts and lost the majority of the USSR's most capable military units which had been stationed in the newly independent states to the west and southwest (Ukraine, Belarus, Georgia).[5] In the three years after 1991, Russia had to absorb a redeployment of military forces from the former Warsaw Pact states and former Soviet republics involving 29 infantry, tank or airborne divisions, 51 missile, artillery and SAM brigades, 66 fixed-wing and helicopter regiments and more than 300 000 personnel (accompanied by 900 000 family members).[6] Large stretches of Russia's international border were left unguarded, including some 9000 kilometres on the strategically sensitive northern and western approaches to St Petersburg and Moscow.

The impact of the collapse on the military doctrine of the

new Russian Federation would prove to be as profound as it was on force posture, but not as immediate. Russia's first and highest priority after 1991 was to cope with the financial, social and domestic political aspects of the convulsion in the armed forces. Compared with these problems, the issue of determining the operational military doctrines of the new state did not attract the attention of the highest levels of the political leadership. But work did continue on military doctrine, and the reorientation of strategic doctrine at the rhetorical level had been relatively simple. As mentioned in chapter 2, the new Russia adopted non-confrontational policies and a defensive posture, and sought resolution of international disputes by peaceful means. But this transition was made easier in political terms by the physical realities of a military force that had been ripped apart, and by the failure of the Russian government to provide a rational and sustained program of defence spending.

In most countries, the relationship between doctrine and military posture is not always a direct one. Governments rarely fund the armed forces to the level that operational doctrines dictate, and in peacetime they make trade-offs between mobilisation time of military forces and competing budget priorities for non-military purposes. Operational doctrine concerns wartime readiness levels, wartime deployment locations and the actual conduct of war. None of these are possible in peacetime, so military forces must constantly operate at some remove from their doctrinal precepts. In Russia after 1991, all of the factors that maximise the distance between peacetime posture and the precepts of military doctrine came into play.

Chapters 3 and 4 sketched the myriad strategic problems Russia has faced since 1991. In military operational terms and planning terms, each of these problems carried its own substantial demands. Russia wanted to maintain a great power posture relative to the USA, but also wanted to honour the arms control commitments of the former USSR. The government had to provide internal security forces in a way not even imagined in the Soviet period. It had to provide peacekeeping in the former Soviet republics, and more recently it has had to deal with the prospect of NATO forces forward-deployed in Poland. In addition, however, Russia has sought to avoid relegation to an even lower position in the military technology stakes, and desperately sought to keep abreast of new military advances, in fields like information warfare and space technology. Russia wanted to keep alive the highly formalised approach to military science that its military officers identified most closely with the USSR's superpower status.

Writing in 1993, a respected strategic analyst, Aleksei Arbatov, suggested that the Russian armed forces may be destined within ten to fifteen years to look much as the Chinese armed forces looked in the 1970s—'large, technologically backward, and supported by a few hundred vulnerable nuclear weapons linked to an inadequate C^3I system'.[7] He suggested that radical reductions in size, major redeployments and extensive restructuring were essential if Russia's military capacities were to satisfy their tasks. He advocated further reductions in tanks in the western regions and a shift in the military centre of gravity of Russia from the west to the southern and eastern borders. He saw the Muslim-populated regions of the southern Volga as particularly vulnerable, but also identified the logistic vulnerabilities of the areas adjacent to China as cause for a heightened military posture there, including prepositioned supplies. He explicitly rejected the idea of a massive military presence opposite China, preferring a posture based on mobile and highly flexible forces which could simultaneously be prepared to move in response to a variety of contingencies in a variety of border areas.[8] Most Russian forces should be deployed, in his opinion, in the Moscow, Volga and Urals military districts. He saw the need to transfer some forces to the Far East and Eastern Siberia, but suggested a total of 5–7 heavy division equivalents to conform to the ceilings on forces within 100 kilometres of the border that Russia and China were at that time negotiating. Arbatov saw the Russian armed forces of the future as needing to be more powerful than those of Britain and France, prepared to fight on a 'come as you are basis', able to defend Russia against plausible threats, and seeing themselves as part of a democratic and market economy system.[9]

This chapter provides an overview of how the Russian government has responded to these various demands both in formulating its military doctrines and in shaping its national military posture. The fundamental conclusion is that the posture of the Russian armed forces will be characterised for the next decade at least by exclusive reliance on the forces in being, a 'come as you are' military posture.[10] The chapter reviews development of military doctrine; military reform policies (including defence spending); force structure; and military responses to NATO expansion and to emergencies in Russia's southern regions. It offers a very brief comment on new military concepts because the economic realities of Russia have not matched the ambitions of its military theoreticians. The final

section of the chapter reviews changes to regional military organisation, as they affect eastern Russia. The discussion in this chapter
provides necessary background to the discussion in subsequent
individual chapters on nuclear forces, navy, air force and ground
forces (chapters 6–9).

STRATEGIC DOCTRINE

The process of establishing new strategic and operational doctrines for the armed forces after 1991 has not been a smooth one.
It has been characterised by bitter disputes between individual
military leaders and their political masters, and between the
armed forces as an institution and other institutions in Russian
society. The role of doctrine in serving as a guide for the ordered
development of force structure in peacetime and in the determination of material requirements of the forces has been denied
through the sustained political and economic instability in the
country. This section traces some of the key developments in
the evolution of Russian military doctrine, highlighting the co-
existence of great power chauvinist tendencies with quite liberal
internationalist positions, and the eventual recognition in 1997
that Russia could not afford to delay radical reductions and
radical restructuring of the armed forces. It became apparent to
all, as Aleksei Arbatov has noted, that failure to achieve effective
military reform would result in a disaster for the country equivalent to the situation that would have emerged had Hitlerite
Germany succeeded in defeating the USSR.[11]

When the Russian armed forces were established in May 1992,
they not only inherited a five-year whirlwind of political turmoil,
but they inherited a radically altered set of doctrinal precepts and
a radically altered military geography to confront. As Garthoff
observed, the intrusion of Gorbachev's new thinking between 1986
and 1988, which replaced an offensive doctrine with a defensive,
war termination doctrine, was followed between 1988 and 1991
by agreement on conventional force reductions in Europe, the
collapse of the Warsaw Pact, and a new assessment in the USSR
that war with NATO was a very low likelihood.[12] Soviet military
leaders had just witnessed the triumph of high-technology US
forces in the Persian Gulf in January 1991; and then faced the
break-up of the USSR. This event meant that the Moscow Military
District now had a border with a foreign country,[13] a situation
not known in Russia in peacetime for nearly three hundred years

and a situation which all too readily evoked memories of the German invasion in 1941.

In May 1992, a draft military doctrine was released, based mostly on a document which the Soviet General Staff had begun to compile in late 1990. The doctrine had some hangovers from the Cold War, such as veiled allusions to a threat from NATO, but it was a document that faced Russia's new geopolitical and domestic circumstances reasonably well. The defensive aspect was central to it, although in subsequent debate on the draft, questions of the balance between use of nuclear forces and conventional forces—given Russia's seriously reduced capacities to field the latter—could not be easily resolved. The draft was opposed by the parliament, which had put forward its own military doctrine, but after Yeltsin closed it down with military force in October, he issued a decree on 2 November 1993 on the Basic Provisions of the Military Doctrine of the Russian Federation.[14] In December 1993, the new Russian parliament approved the military doctrine.[15] The full text of the doctrine was not published at the time, but an official account was released[16] which was reported to have about five pages of the final document missing.

The 1993 military doctrine showed much greater concern with local wars, especially in the newly independent states of the former USSR, than with any residual fears about NATO. These wars were identified as the primary threat to Russian security. The doctrine also provided for use of force by the government against civil uprisings within the country. War termination and defensive aspects of military posture were dominant. The document gave full recognition to the constraints imposed by Russia's new economic circumstances. The doctrine called for a force with greater mobility and tactical punch, at the same time as it asserted the strategic nuclear forces as the continuing foundation of the country's security.[17]

The new doctrine abandoned a commitment made by the former USSR under Gorbachev not to be the first to use nuclear weapons.[18] According to a widely respected military commentator, Major General Yury Kirshin, the aim of this change in Russian doctrine was primarily deterrent in nature, not to look toward using such weapons against non-nuclear weapons states, but to dissuade them from participation in acts of aggression against Russia.[19] This position was confirmed in discussions between NATO and Russia in March 1999 when Russia made plain that its new doctrine did not include a first strike prior to the outbreak of any other military hostilities.[20]

The doctrine identified the expansion of military blocs and alliances to the detriment of Russia as a threat to its national security, but this was interpreted by the more liberal military strategists according to the premises that former Warsaw Pact members had a right to make their own arrangements for national defence and that the expansion of NATO was not a threat to Russia since Russia did not view NATO as a threat. The expansion of any bloc or alliance would be viewed as a threat in any of the following circumstances: if armed forces were 'massed' on Russia's borders; if border conflicts or armed provocations occurred; or if foreign forces were introduced into the territory of foreign states contiguous with Russia.

The doctrine identified as a military danger to Russia any suppression of the rights of Russian citizens which constituted large minorities in the three former Baltic republics, and in Ukraine, Belarus and Kazakhstan. According to Kirshin, this recognition was not tantamount to reserving a right of military intervention by Russia in such cases, but rather indicating the significance with which Russia would regard such actions. He said that the preferred resolution of such problems would in Russia's view lie through organisations such as the Organisation for Security and Cooperation in Europe and the United Nations. According to another source, a secret foreign policy doctrine promulgated in April 1993 and the 1992 draft of the new military doctrine did specifically refer to possible Russian use of force to protect Russian minorities in neighbouring countries.

By 1996, doctrinal conceptions inside the General Staff began to get more specific about local war responses. It had been decided that military mobilisation would be guided in very general terms by the following propositions:

- a local conflict must be neutralised by the forces of one military district;
- a regional armed conflict must be neutralised by the forces of two or three military districts;
- in the case of the danger of aggression developing from a regional armed conflict into a large-scale war, Russia can be the first to use nuclear weapons to deal a disarming strike at military targets.[21]

By 1996, after the war in Chechnia, several years of deterioration in the armed forces, several years of economic crisis, and a growing conviction in Russia that its strategic circumstances had deteriorated since 1991, relevant authorities began work on a new military doctrine. The Security Council (established in 1992) started the process and in June 1996, after the appointment of General Igor Rodionov as Minister of Defence, the newly constituted Defence Council, co-existing with the Security Council, approved a series of propositions on military posture and force structure that would radically alter the armed forces.[22]

The new guidelines which addressed force structure in some detail, and the 1993 doctrine, were described by Aleksei Arbatov, who had become Deputy Chairman of the Defence Committee of the State Duma, as a 'treatise on the topic of modern wars and military art that is cut off from life'; and a 'broad set of wishes regarding what military capabilities it would be nice to have'.[23] The mentality of competition with the USA was still very strong in the military leadership and within the armed forces in general and this played itself out in the formulation of strategic doctrine, with advocates of such a position unable to break completely with a view that Russian armed forces should be developed on the basis of such strategic competition.

Through 1997, the tensions between the competing schools of thought were resolved to some degree in favour of the 'new thinkers'. On 17 December 1997, President Yeltsin promulgated a new national security blueprint which effectively updated the 1993 doctrine by expanding the scope of national security from narrow military interests to human security broadly defined: 'the security of the individual, society, and the state from external and internal threats of a political, economic, social, military, man-made, ecological, or informational' kind. The document, running to more than 10 000 words, has four sections: 'Russia within the World Community', 'Russia's National Interests', 'Threats to the National Security of the Russian Federation', and 'Safeguarding the Russian Federation's National Security'.[24]

In the section on Russia's position in the world community, the blueprint offers the judgement that the 'preconditions for demilitarizing international relations and strengthening the role of law in settling disputed international problems have been created, and the danger of direct aggression against the Russian Federation has decreased'. These conditions 'open up fundamentally new opportunities to mobilize resources to solve the country's internal problems'. Positive trends in relations between Russia and a number of CIS states and a variety of international organisations are noted. At the same time, this section of the blueprint railed against the threat posed by the expansion of NATO and the continuing desire of some unnamed states to see

Russia weakened. It also complained about Russia's exclusion from the Asia–Pacific economic integration processes.

In its following sentences, the document raised the threat posed by internal instability in remarking that the main cause was the persistence of 'crisis phenomena' in the economy. Declining production, declining investment, declining innovation and growing dependence on imports of food, equipment and technology were identified as major weaknesses. But the underlying potential, wealth and power of Russia, including its nuclear forces, would continue to guarantee the country's security and its role as an influential power in world affairs.

Russia's national interests, discussed in the second section of the blueprint, are described as the 'aggregate of the basic interests of the individual, society and the state'. All of these are served by the preservation of basic human rights and consolidation of democracy, social accord, and a spiritual renaissance. National interests embraced economic, political and international concerns as well as military ones. The document pays as much attention in this section to the fight against organised crime and to the need for social stability as it does to foreign policy or security policy. In foreign policy, strengthening the UN Security Council and other collaborative international mechanisms are counted as central national interests. The protection of the rights and livelihoods of Russians living outside Russia is identified as a national interest. In military policy, Russia's national interests are defined in terms of making the structure and support base of the armed forces conform more appropriately to the demands of social policy and economic reconstruction.

The third section distinguishes two sources of threats to national security, internal and external, but concentrates more on the former type—negative processes in the economy, the deterioration in inter-ethnic relations, and the polarisation of Russian society. The blueprint called for the creation of a national social strategy to combat these internal threats. Fear is expressed about the 'conquest of Russia's internal market by foreign firms' but a few lines later, the blueprint complains of a lack of large-scale investment in the economy. This section identifies a rapid deterioration in Russia's relative standing in the world of high technology because of a number of features, especially the brain-drain of specialists to more lucrative jobs in other countries. Environmental threats and the poor public health indicators for Russians are identified as contributing to Russia's weakened international position. The document expresses doubt about the ability of the Russian Federation to overcome systemic threats to its territorial cohesion and physical integrity. Regional separatism and associated conflicts receive close attention and the document sees 'deliberate and purposeful interference by foreign states and international organisations' in the internal affairs of Russia. Unnamed states are accused of aggravating these domestic conflicts, and conflict in CIS states, in order to reduce Russia's influence on its periphery.

The document says that the poor state of the armed forces threatens the country's security, and highlights a continuing failure to arrest the deterioration in military organisation, training, manning, equipment levels, readiness, provisioning and morale.

Turning to direct international threats, the most important judgement is that the 'threat of large-scale aggression against Russia is virtually absent in the foreseeable future'. But there are many low-level threats that Russia must deal with. These include:

- great power rivalry, including efforts by other states to counter Russia's efforts to consolidate its position in the multipolar world;
- local wars and armed conflicts close to the borders;
- proliferation of weapons of mass destruction, particularly in neighbouring countries;
- international terrorism, possibly using weapons of mass destruction;
- the retention of powerful military forces by great powers or their allies in regions adjacent to Russia;
- the threat of a new split in Europe as the result of NATO expansion;
- the technological upsurge of other leading world powers, particularly in new generations of military technology; and
- the intensifying activities of foreign intelligence services in Russia, particularly in commercial sectors, in ways that may be crippling the country's ability to rebuild and particularly in the distribution of information critical to the entire national economy.

But having declared that Russia is almost on its knees, the blueprint predicts confidently that 'the development of qualitatively new relations with the world's leading states and the virtual absence of the threat of large-scale aggression against Russia while its nuclear deterrent potential is preserved make it possible to redistribute the resources of the state and society to resolve acute domestic problems on a priority basis'.

The fourth section on safeguarding national security, the

longest section, outlines programmatic rather than detailed goals and these broad goals correspond fairly comprehensively to the list of low-level but very dangerous threats outlined in the preceding section. The blueprint emphasises the need for collective social responsibility if the threats are to be overcome, and it places individual security on the same level as security of the state.

The principles for use of force by Russia are set out as follows:

- Russia reserves the right to use all the forces and weapons systems at its disposal, including nuclear weapons, if armed aggression threatens the independent sovereign existence of the state;
- force must be applied in a decisive, consistent, and planned manner until conditions beneficial to Russia for the conclusion of peace are created;
- use of force must comply with the law and should only occur when all non-military measures for resolving the crisis have been exhausted or proved ineffective;
- use of force against civilians for domestic political objectives is not permitted, but use of force against armed groups posing a threat to national interests is permitted.

The Federal Intelligence Service is given the responsibility for coordinating threat assessment and monitoring of potential threats. The Federal Border Service is responsible for coordinating responses to threats to the Russian border, based on the presuppositions that there is a steady consolidation of the borders with contiguous states, that interstate border cooperation with Russia is increasing, and that collective security mechanisms will be implemented on the external borders of the CIS states.

Conscious of the potential for information warfare, the blueprint identifies the Federal Government Communications and Information Agency under the President as the coordinating body. It lays down the principles for implementation as:

- the establishment of a requisite balance between the need for free exchange of information and permissible restrictions;
- improvement of information infrastructure, through acceleration of the standardisation and use of the most advanced information technologies, taking account of Russia's becoming part of the global information infrastructure; and
- the formation of an appropriate legal base.

By August 1998, President Yeltsin had approved 'The Fundamentals (Concept) of State Policy in Defence Building until 2005'.

This document has not been published but according to extant accounts it is not so much an account of operational requirements according to likely future conflict scenarios, but a plan for the restructuring of the armed forces according to the depressed material, financial and social capacities of the Russian state. In announcing the President's approval of this document, the then Secretary of the Security Council, Andrei Kokoshin, revealed that a new military doctrine was to be drafted later that year.[25]

As of early May 1999, the new doctrine had not been published. One cause for the delay was that NATO planned to release a new military doctrine at its fiftieth anniversary summit in April 1999. In February 1999, the President of the Academy of Military Sciences, General Makhmut Gareyev, had reported that US actions and those of its NATO allies had forced Russia to revise the 'main provisions' of its military doctrine.[26] Gareyev cited NATO actions in the Balkans, US intention to renegotiate the ABM Treaty, and the US and NATO intention to 'influence the situation in any part of the globe at their own discretion'.

After the NATO summit, and in the light of the sustained NATO bombing of Yugoslavia over Russian objections, the Defence Minister, Sergeyev, announced that Russia would 'make adjustments in its national military doctrine, with due notice taken of the new NATO strategic concept adopted at its Washington summit'.[27] He said that NATO had forced Russia to 'revise many aspects in order to ensure our own military security'. Russia objected to provisions of the new NATO strategic concept that relate to use of force outside the NATO defensive area. Sergeyev foreshadowed adjustments in doctrine relating both to strategic nuclear forces and with general purpose forces. Russian television reported Sergeyev saying on another occasion that measures taken by Russia would relate to raising readiness levels, improving air defences, increasing CIS cooperation, and ensuring that at least 3.5 per cent of Russian GDP would be spent on the armed forces each year.[28]

The shape of the new military doctrine and its continuing authoritativeness will depend in large part on the outcome of domestic politics in coming years, especially the parliamentary elections due in December 1999 and the presidential election due in 2000. There are increasing signs however that the next version of the military doctrine will postulate the need for a new global opposition to US and NATO imposition of their will by force without reference to the UN Security Council. The military aspects of this opposition are likely to concentrate on alliance building and development of highly mobile forces, including a significant increase in special forces capabilities and psychological warfare forces.

It will be especially interesting to see if the President of the Academy of Military Sciences, Gareyev, has much influence in his support for the view that Russia is already at war: 'The new version of Russian military doctrine must single out separately the threat stemming from the long-range policy of certain international forces and powers aimed at depriving Russia of independence, infringing on its interests, undermining it from within, isolating it . . .' Gareyev asks rhetorically: 'If this is not war, what is it?'[29]

But the most important aspect of this new line of thinking by people like Gareyev is the proposed response to these pressures, given Russia's very weak military position: to resort to diplomatic and indirect methods of resolution of disputes, and to avoid being overly rigid in making claims about what national interests should be. A particular goal of the new strategic doctrine should be, in Gareyev's opinion, to support a 'fundamental normalisation of international relations'—by which he meant mobilising international support for greater respect for existing international law.

Through all of these deliberations about the broad foundations of Russia's strategic doctrine, there has been a consistent effort to come to terms with the military consequences of the need to fight local wars and military conflicts short of war, particularly on the periphery of Russia and on the borders of CIS states. A particular point of inquiry has been to illuminate methods of extinguishing local conflicts before they escalate. It can be expected that the new military doctrine will contain much more work on these questions than has appeared to date in the broadly programmatic statements of national strategic policy. Much work has been done on this in the military research institutes but not much of it has found its way into officially endorsed doctrine.

MATCHING DOCTRINE TO FORCE STRUCTURE: LITTLE CONSENSUS AND NO MONEY

One reason for the attempted coup against Gorbachev in August 1991 was to prevent the weakening of the USSR as a union of the republics that was foreshadowed in a new Union Treaty. In the minds of the coup leaders, and some of those senior military officers who supported them initially, saving the union meant protecting 'national security', preserving the gains of the Great Patriotic War, and therefore respecting and maintaining the special place of the armed forces in society, especially their historical traditions. The failure of the coup and the subsequent collapse of the union provoked the very outcome many officers had hoped to prevent. History left them in the impossible situation of re-establishing a national military force in circumstances where the Russian government wanted totally separate military forces of its own, but at the same time was pushing these to maintain high levels of cooperation with the 'break-away' military forces of other newly independent states of the former USSR under the framework of the Commonwealth of Independent States.

In creating its own armed forces, most Russian leaders hoped to emulate the Soviet model, at least in terms of military structure, but circumstances would deny them this outcome. Russia sought to maintain all the branches of the armed forces as before. These included five branches of the armed forces proper (strategic missile forces,[30] air forces, air defence forces, naval forces, and ground forces); other forces (border troops, Ministry of Interior troops, Ministry of Security troops, government communication troops, railroad troops, and civil defence troops). In subsequent years, additional military or paramilitary forces emerged, in some cases out of pre-existing special commissions that had existed in the Soviet era (troops for aerospace search and rescue), or in other cases out of new circumstances (Service for the Protection of the Russian President).

The development path of the Russian armed forces since 1991 has owed little to the formal documents or informal discussion of the strategic requirements for future war. Each year has brought new difficulties. In announcing the creation of the new Russian military force in 1992, the government somewhat ambitiously foreshadowed a seven-year transition plan due to be completed over three stages by 1999. Eight programs were announced, including demobilisation of conscripts, abolition of low-readiness units, introduction of volunteer service options, withdrawal of forces from neighbouring states, social security benefits for soldiers, destruction of a number of nuclear submarines, destruction of a number of strategic and tactical nuclear weapons, destruction of chemical weapons and some conventional weapons, and collection and destruction of weapons left on the seabed.[31] The staggering dimension and cost of these programs (more than 1000 million roubles) guaranteed that the new Russian armed forces would take at least a decade to achieve any sort of normalcy.

One important consideration favouring continuity in an otherwise destabilised military force in 1991 and 1992 was that over 95 per cent of the top Soviet officers (those in command of nuclear forces, theatre headquarters, superior commands, branches of the armed services, and other politically important posts) were Russian. About 75 per cent of the entire officer corps were from Russia, Ukraine or Belarus.[32] Thus, as the Russian forces were much smaller in number than their Soviet counterpart, there was actually a surplus of trained Russian officers for the forces available. This sort of advantage was to count for little as two overwhelming, inter-related, domestic factors, came into play: lack of consensus about restructuring and reform of the military, and lack of money.

Lack of consensus

The single most important cause of disunity in the national security policy apparatus is the uneasy, often conflictual relationship between the armed forces, the civilian leadership, and the parliament. In making the announcement establishing the armed forces in 1992, Yeltsin specifically highlighted the subordination of the armed forces to civil control. But he surrendered his post as Defence Minister *pro tem* in favour of a 44-year-old military officer, General Pavel Grachev, formerly First Deputy Minister of Defence of the USSR, who had served in Afghanistan.[33] The appointment of a serving military officer was a continuation of the practice for most of the Soviet period and flew in the face of demands from reform groups in the parliament and society to appoint a civilian, in line with practice in liberal democratic countries.[34]

The appointment of the first Minister of Defence for the new armed forces was given to a military officer out of recognition of the special role the armed forces had played in politics. The armed forces had already demonstrated on two occasions in 1991 their potential to make or break the new government of Russia: in their support of the coup against Gorbachev in August 1991 in its early stages before abandoning it, and in acquiescing in Yeltsin's moves against Gorbachev in December 1991 when the former negotiated the break-up of the USSR.[35] Grachev, a former commander of the airborne forces, had been instrumental in the collapse of the August 1991 coup after switching sides to Yeltsin when he came to the view that a military operation against the White House would be too costly in casualties on both sides.[36] In 1993, Yeltsin ordered the armed forces to attack the parliament building where a group of deputies had barricaded themselves after refusing to recognise his decree dissolving the parliament. The deputies, who included former Afghan war hero and Yeltsin's former Vice President, Aleksandr Rutskoi, were armed. Yeltsin had to plead for several hours with the military leadership to intervene and attack the rebels. When the attack was mounted, the forces used had been drawn from five different divisions near Moscow, and personnel selected were mostly officers or senior non-commissioned officers.[37]

The irony is that, although the armed forces have possessed this potential to be king-maker, they have not been able to capitalise on it in any significant way to secure even adequate basic food, wages, fuel and other logistic support for normal operations, let alone to secure funding for new equipment. For most of the time since 1992, the armed forces have been on a downhill slide in terms of effectiveness, cohesion, planning, size, and budgets. There are several reasons for this gap between the potential of the armed forces to act as king-maker and their deteriorating position, but one important one may well be that most members of the armed forces have not, as Lambeth points out, had the stomach to use force against civilians in domestic disputes.[38] More importantly perhaps, the military leadership had taken an institutional view that the armed forces should remain outside politics and this principle was incorporated in the 1993 Law on Defence.[39]

While the armed forces have not in the decade since 1989 been prepared to use violence[40] to overthrow the civilian government, the military leadership and its rank and file were to remain prominent in politics in one way or another for the entire decade. The uniformed services of all types, veterans of military service, and their potential allies in the military industrial sector, comprise a large percentage of the electorate.[41] But there is little quantitative evidence of the extent of support within the armed forces for particular parties or individual people. In late 1992, Defence Minister Grachev sought to justify some sort of political agitation by military personnel with a statement to parliament that the armed forces were 'on the side of law and the constitution' but that his political prominence was related merely to the fact the armed forces wanted to be heard on military issues.[42] If the personnel of the armed forces are united on any policies they are the ones that relate to deterioration in the status, capabilities and conditions of service of the forces. But on several occasions since 1992, military officers and a 'military constituency' have provided new focal points of power in Russian politics. This has been particularly the case when it comes to implementing presidential or administration decisions affecting the armed forces. There has been sustained and widespread rejection both of the administration's thinking and its specific orders by members of the armed forces who do not agree with them. Disobedient personnel have rarely been disciplined or dismissed as would be normal. Moreover, serving military officers, many senior ones included, regularly criticise government policies toward the armed forces in the press, and are happy to target Yeltsin personally for this criticism.

The 1993 Constitution provides for a variety of institutions and associated arrangements which position the armed forces in the body politic. But as the discussion in chapter 1 suggests, the written constitution is only a starting point, and the practice over subsequent years and decades will be a more reliable indicator of the exact nature of the political relationship between the armed forces and the body politic.

The following list of powers of the President in foreign affairs and defence shows that he is able to exercise greater independence of the parliament in these areas than the President of the USA, but the Russian President's powers are probably no greater than those of a Prime Minister in the UK, or in other Westminster systems. The President:

- is Head of State, and adopts policies to safeguard the sovereignty, independence and state integrity of Russia (Article 80).
- sets the basic guidelines of foreign policy (Article 80).
- forms and heads the Security Council of Russia (Article 83).[43]
- is the supreme commander of the armed forces (article 87).
- approves the military doctrine of the armed forces (Article 83).
- appoints and removes the high command of the armed forces (Article 83).
- appoints plenipotentiary representatives, ambassadors and other representatives 'following consultations' with relevant committees of the parliament (Article 83).
- can submit draft laws to the parliament, and signs and promulgates laws approved by the parliament (Article 84).
- can issue decrees and directives as long as they do not contravene the Constitution or federal laws (Article 90).
- can veto laws adopted by the parliament subject to an over-

ride which requires two-thirds of the total membership of both houses combined (Article 107).

- cannot veto a 'constitutional law', which requires support by three-quarters of the upper house and two-thirds of the lower house (Article 108).

Under Articles 87 and 88, he has the right to introduce martial law in parts of Russia or the whole country in the event of aggression or threat of aggression against Russia[44] or to declare a state of emergency in other circumstances laid down in Russian constitutional law. In accordance with the Law on Defence, the President approves the conceptions and plans for the construction of the armed forces and mobilisation of the economy and reserves when necessary.[45]

The Constitution gives some powers to the parliament in foreign affairs and defence. The Federation Council, or upper house, has the following powers:

- It 'decides the question of the possibility' of use of the armed forces outside Russia (Article 102).
- It confirms decrees of the President on martial law or a state of emergency (Article 102).
- It can initiate legislation (Article 104).
- It is obliged to review and approve all laws passed by the State Duma (lower house) that concern war and peace, the status and protection of Russia's borders, the ratification or denunciation of treaties, and budget measures (Article 106).

The State Duma, or lower house, has the function of adopting federal laws, subject to optional review by the Federation Council (Article 105) except for the instances mentioned above and included in Article 106. The Federal Assembly has developed little control over military expenditure, a situation suggesting the incomplete transformation from the Soviet style of military plan ning to one that exists to some degree in most democracies where the parliament has the main voice in military expenditures.[46] This lack of control by the parliament has been seen by one critic as contributing to disaffection in the armed forces because the members of the Assembly are judged to be more sympathetic than the leaders of the armed forces to the social needs of military personnel, such as the non-payment of their salaries and their poor living standards.

The executive government of Russia provided for in Articles 110–117, comprises the Prime Minister (appointed by the President), the Deputy Prime Ministers and ministers (appointed by the President on the Prime Minister's recommendation). The government has similar powers in foreign affairs and defence to those of a Westminster-style government. It implements measures to provide for defence, state security and the realisation of the country's foreign policy (Article 114). The government's decrees appear to have the power to override the Constitution, federal laws or decrees of the President unless the President chooses to rescind the particular government decree within 14 days (Article 115).

The Constitution provides for a Defence Council, as in the Soviet era. In wartime, this council becomes the headquarters of the Commander in Chief (the President). The main working arm of the council is the General Staff of the Armed Forces.[47] In 1996, Yeltsin established a 'Defence Council' which became an engine of reform for a couple of years, largely under the influence of the Minister of Defence and the General Staff, but by March 1998, it had been abolished by a presidential edict.[48] This edict passed the responsibility for military structural reform to the Security Council, and folded the staff of the Defence Council into one part of the Security Council, its Military Inspection Directorate.

The responsibilities of the Security Council have been spelled out in a number of laws and edicts, including in the 1997 blueprint, where they were described as follows:

- the timely identification of threats to national security and for the preparation of prompt decisions to avert emergencies;
- coordination of the country's national security apparatus in devising strategies to meet external or internal threats, including the realms of foreign policy and armed forces policy;
- monitoring of the implementation of strategy and policy in the national security arena;
- preparation of recommendations and proposals for the country's National Security Blueprint;
- the examination of questions of national security in all spheres, including economic, social, defence, border, informational, and ecological.[49]

The responsibilities had also been spelled out in a 1992 Law on Security, a 1996 presidential edict (No. 1024 of 10 July 1996), the 1998 edict abolishing the Defence Council, and a separate edict that year elaborating on the Security Council's constitutional role (No. 1418, 18 November 1998). The November edict identified the membership of the council as shown in Figure 5.1. The council is

Figure 5.1 Membership of Security Council

President

Permanent Members
   Prime Minister
   Secretary of the Council
   Minister of Foreign Affairs
   Director, Federal Security Bureau
   Minister of Defence

Members
   Minister for Nuclear Energy
   First Deputy Prime Ministers
   Minister of Finance
   Director of the Presidential Security Service
   Minister of Justice
   President of the Russian Academy of Sciences
   Director-General, Government Communications and Information Agency
   Minister of Internal Affairs
   Director, Federal Border Guards Service
   Director, Foreign Intelligence Service
   Minister for Civil Defence and Emergencies
   Head of the Presidential Administration
   Head of the State Duma
   Head of the Federation Council

Source: Presidential Edict No. 1418, 18 November 1998; *Krasnaia zvezda*, 15 April 1999, p. 1.

a particularly powerful organisation, with a large staff and a very wide mandate. Its structure is shown in Figure 5.2.

The Chechen operations in 1994–96 provoked a new level of political activism in the Russian armed forces, not only on account of the war but on account of the general deterioration in the professional and personal conditions under which military personnel were expected to operate.[50] The 4000–5000 Russian military deaths,[51] along with 75 000 other deaths, and the humiliating defeat 'inspired a rumbling antimilitaristic activism that is slowly gathering steam' and fresh calls for democratic standards of accountability in defence policy.[52] When Yeltsin ordered the armed forces into operations against the Chechen separatist forces in 1994, at least two generals disobeyed the order, one because he believed his forces were not prepared for such operations (most were conscripts), and the other because he believed that the armed forces should not be used in internal operations against fellow citizens.[53]

In the 1995 election campaign for the national parliament, the military leaders acted on their word to continue to agitate to be heard on military issues. They joined forces with the leaders of

Figure 5.2 Organisation chart: Security Council Staff

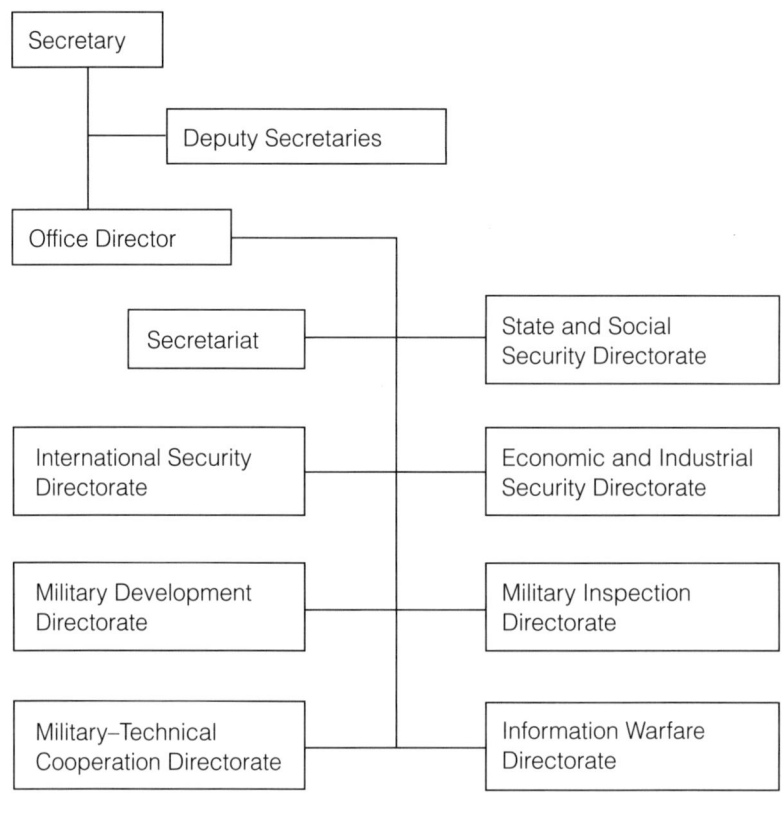

Source: Presidential Edict No. 333, 15 March 1999

military industrial enterprises in an effort to mobilise a faction in the new parliament in support of their interests. This effort included the nomination of some 370 serving or former military personnel as candidates—only two years after the armed forces leaders had banned any participation in political affairs by military personnel. This move in the 1995 campaign put considerable stress on the relationship between the military chiefs and the civilian government, who saw this as an assault on their legitimacy.[54]

But armed forces personnel distrusted the population for placing its faith in the political leadership; they distrusted the government for committing the armed forces to the war in Chechnia; and they distrusted other sections of the coercive forces, such as the Ministry of Interior troops, whose officers received on average twice the salaries of military personnel. Most of all, they did not have much trust in each other. The forces were seriously divided between reformers and conservatives, between elite forces and 'peripheral' forces, between supporters and opponents of the authorities, and between the supporters of one political party and the supporters of others.[55]

In these circumstances of deep division, the moves by the armed forces leadership to try to cultivate a common corporate military line among its participating personnel was probably a wise move that averted a serious split in the military.[56] In the end, there was not much difference in the 1995 elections between the positions of the political parties on military issues, with all of them wanting the same sort of consolidation of reforms and improvement of conditions of service as the politically active military personnel. Nevertheless, military sentiment seemed to polarise between Yavlinski's liberal democrats (Apple) and Zhirinovski's extreme nationalists (Russian Liberal Democratic Party). The Communist Party did not pay much attention. The most senior officers supported Yeltsin and the government, while many middle-ranking officers supported the Zhirinovski party.[57]

In the June 1996 presidential election, the military factor came into play in important ways, primarily through the emergence in the campaign of a strong military candidate, General Aleksandr Lebed. Since the election process involved two rounds of voting, with only the two leaders in the first round going through to a second round, the Yeltsin campaign sought to polarise the vote as much as possible in the first round between Yeltsin and the Communist Party contender, Gennady Ziuganov. This strategy was mainly intended to marginalise other challengers, but in the case of Lebed it meant forging an alliance. The goal was to direct anti-Yeltsin sentiment in the electorate to Lebed, but then have Lebed deliver his voters to Yeltsin in the third round on the strength of a promise of a high-level job for Lebed in the next Yeltsin administration.[58] Lebed's campaign was staffed with military officers and his support base, while not exclusively serving military officers, comprised people who saw the armed forces as perhaps the last hope to restore order and discipline in Russian society through special coercive measures, including the possible use of military force or a declaration of martial law.

After Yeltsin was re-elected in June 1996, he replaced Minister of Defence Grachev with General Igor Rodionov, who had been supported initially by Lebed, but who was not long in the job before his frustration made him as politically contentious as Grachev had become. But more importantly, the role of the Defence Ministry, never very powerful in the Soviet era, began to decline in the face of competition from other national-level bodies charged with security policy, such as the Security Council, headed by General Lebed since the June election, and a newly constituted Defence Council, designed to curb Lebed's power.[59] A major dispute between Lebed and the head of the Presidential Security Service resulted in Lebed's resignation less than a year after he was appointed.

At the end of 1996, the new Minister of Defence, Igor Rodionov, described himself as 'minister of a disintegrating army and a dying navy'.[60] In fact, by 1996 the armed forces were in a state of severe confusion on three fronts. The responsibility for defence policy was contested between a variety of political organisations and personalities; the armed forces had become highly politicised; and the organisational cohesion of the forces had almost disintegrated.[61] The lack of consensus was profound at three levels: between political leaders and military leaders, between military leaders and other elements of the forces, and between political leaders and the rank and file.

The appointment of yet another new Defence Minister, Igor Sergeyev, in May 1997 was necessary before President Yeltsin and his administration could finally put faith in the political commitment of the military leadership to radical restructuring and reform of the armed forces. Previous defence ministers had favoured sectional interests of parts of the armed forces over others. Grachev had favoured the airborne forces and ground forces, while Rodionov had favoured the strategic missile forces and called for the reduction of the airborne forces, the latter move provoking an angry response from Lebed, his former protégé. In August 1997, a former Commander in Chief of the ground forces complained that Rodionov had no rational approach to prioritising the budget allocations between the branches of the armed forces and was operating on the principle that 'everyone gets a little'.[62] Rodionov had expressly rejected such a proposition in an interview in February, in which he said absolutely highest priority had to be placed on maintaining the strategic missile forces in combat-capable condition, on the development of military space programs, and on defence against the potential aerospace threat.[63]

The institutional instability continued in August 1998, when Yeltsin sacked one of the more creative and progressive defence planners, Andrei Kokoshin, a civilian who had served as First Deputy Minister of Defence or Deputy Minister from 1992 to 1997, and had been elevated in May 1997 to head the Defence Council, and then in March 1998 to head the Security Council.[64]

The impact of this instability was obvious and inevitable. The seasoned observer of Russian and Soviet strategic policy, and a Deputy Chairman of the Defence Committee of the State Duma, Aleksei Arbatov, remarked that the decline in effective civilian control and supervision of the armed forces not only meant that overall direction of policy was faltering but also, and more dangerously, that the armed forces leadership was being pushed into extreme characterisations of external threat in order to bring maximum pressure to bear on the civilian government for both resources and effective administration.[65] Arbatov also complained about the government's lack of openness in security policy, saying that 'secrecy regarding the armed forces is almost the very same as in the USSR and has been toughened in recent times'.[66]

The personal disaffection of members of the armed forces, regardless of any of their political views about the President and his administration or about the best force posture of Russia, became both an issue in the reform process and an important obstacle to it. The massive shake-up of the armed forces created serious disaffection, widespread corruption and large-scale desertions. The leakage of weapons and other military equipment into society, especially for criminal uses, was substantial. The availability of former military weapons, and trained military personnel out of work, contributed both to the severity of the breakdown in public law and order and to the rise of armed groups challenging the constitutional authority of the Russian state. Commercial pressures began intruding on military order very soon after 1991, with the supreme command of the CIS forces banning participation by military command personnel or units of the forces in any business structures.[67] A ban was also imposed on selling military property through any military organisations except designated authorities. In 1992, the prevalence of crime in the forces, largely the illegal sale of equipment, was high, and although reductions were achieved in subsequent years, by 1995 the situation was still bad, with only about 40 per cent of the units of the forces untouched by serious crime.[68]

In 1991, the USSR had already recognised the collapsing morale in its armed forces and the desperately poor conditions of the troops, but this situation has continued to deteriorate in the Russian armed forces. As one set of problems has been addressed,

new ones have arisen. A parliamentary investigation which concluded in 1992 revealed that 5500 military personnel had died in
1991 and 98 700 had been injured, most from non-combat causes,
including physical assault from other military personnel.[69] A new
Law on Military Service was passed in 1993 to reduce the length of
service for conscripts in the navy from three years to two years and
for other services from two years to 18 months, but in 1995 Yeltsin
reversed this change. Opinion surveys in 1994 and 1995 revealed
high levels of dissatisfaction (from 50 per cent to 90 per cent) with
the Defence Minister and ultimately with President Yeltsin.[70] In
1996, a survey of field rank officers showed almost no support for
military operations against breakaway regions of the Russian
Federation.[71]

Conditions have been so bad in the forces and in society
generally that military personnel have recorded a high rate of
suicides, some 140 in the first six months of 1994.[72] In 1995,
military salaries for enlisted personnel were below the recognised
average subsistence level, and in some parts of Russia with
unusually high costs of living, the salaries were half or less of the
subsistence level.[73]

Poor morale has persisted in the armed forces, as more recent
examples of conditions of service from eastern Russia show. In
January 1997, the commander of the Siberian Military District sent
a telegram to President Yeltsin and Prime Minister Chernomyrdin
telling them that the situation among his forces was very poor
because of funding problems, and that many officers' families
did not have enough money to buy bread.[74] In May, the commander
resigned on health grounds.[75] In the Siberian Military district, one
major forced his subordinates to earn money outside the unit and
to give it to him, if they were to be spared beatings.[76] In August
1997 Sergeyev, after a visit to the Siberian Military District,
identified the payment of back wages as his highest priority.[77]

Power cut-offs have been normal because of the failure of
military units to pay the utilities companies, and these blackouts
have seriously affected the military readiness of a wide range of
units. For example, in February 1998 the local utility company,
Chita Power, cut off electric power to a military helicopter base
near the town of Nerchinsk in the former Transbaikal Military
District. The unit was in the process of combat training flights at
the time and commanders asserted that the three-hour power cut
endangered the lives of the pilots. Military barracks and houses
had no heat or light, and food was cooked in field kitchens.[78] The
same month, the power company in Chita cut supply to border

guards, leaving about 1000 kilometres of the border unprotected by powered surveillance devices, raising the prospect of a return to border patrols on horseback.[79] The power cuts were delivered in eight two-hour periods in 24 hours over several days. In early 1998, air defence troops in the Siberian MD were still suffering from shortages of housing, and unpaid ration allowances going back 11–12 months, although arrears for 1997 pay and other allowances had all been paid in full.[80] In March 1998, the government began a scheme for the issue of housing grants to service members from the Transbaikal Military District who were discharged to the reserves. Some 3000 military personnel in the district did not have their own housing at that time.

Such desperate living and working conditions for military personnel could only aggravate the sharp divisions between the armed forces and the political leadership about the appropriate directors for national security policy.

Lack of money

Between 1991 and 1997, there was a massive reduction in the scale of defence spending: by a factor of eight in real prices.[81] There was an equally massive shift in the composition of spending, from a three-quarter share going to equipment procurement (including development of new weapons) to a three-quarter share going to personnel costs.[82] Large proportions of the defence budget went to relocation of military personnel, thereby reducing funds available both for procurement and operations.[83] The budget problems, particularly the food problem, became a subject of international disgrace for Russia in 1993 when news broke of the death from pneumonia (aggravated by malnutrition) of four seamen in the Pacific Fleet.[84] In late 1992, *Aviation Week* reported that the air force had begun abandoning air bases.[85] In 1993, there were no funds for operational training, and in these years there was not even enough money to meet the relocation obligations of new housing.[86] In 1994, 70 per cent of planned military exercises had to be cancelled because of lack of fuel.[87]

The Russian Defence Ministry reported Chechen operations in 1995 to have cost 10 per cent of the 1995 budget, about 5.7 trillion roubles.[88] By the middle of the year, the deficit in the defence expenditure was 5 trillion roubles.[89] The 1995 defence budget had not provided for any expenditure for operations in Chechnia (1.5 trillion roubles), nor any money for the planned inflation adjustment for salaries.[90]

In September 1995, the Prime Minister signed an order preventing power stations from cutting power to military bases
regardless of the debts after power had been cut to a strategic
missile force base and a nuclear missile submarine base on two
separate occasions.[91]

In 1996, the armed forces did not receive some 30 per cent of
their allocated funds from the 1996 federal budget.[92] Within the
allocations received, even more serious distortions exist, with
some forces getting only about 40 per cent of food requirements,
according to the Ministry of Defence. Even so, official spending
by the armed forces in 1996 was 25 per cent higher than that
appropriated by the parliament.

By October 1997, officers' pay was running several months in
arrears[93] and most officers had not received non-salary components of their entitlements, such as housing allowance, for more
than one and a half years. For lieutenants, this meant a shortfall
of some 48 per cent of income.[94]

The Defence Minister, Rodionov, estimated that the 1997
budget would cover only one-third of the armed forces' necessary
expenses, but at that time spending on national security, including
spending on other security forces such as border troops, consumed
just under one-third of total central government expenditure.[95]

Writing in 1997, the Deputy Chairman of the Defence Committee of the State Duma, Aleksei Arbatov, estimated that the
two extreme options for adequate budgeting were to reduce the
armed forces to 100 000 personnel or to increase the military
budget to double the value of the entire Russian annual budget.[96]
Arbatov noted that the only way to reverse the trend toward
destruction of the armed forces was to implement 'large scale and
swift' cuts in the number of serving personnel. He warned that
radical measures were needed to save the army from final collapse
and therefore to save society from a grave threat. But radical
changes in personnel levels would require massive changes in the
structure and doctrine of the armed forces, he said. In particular,
there would have to be a 'narrowing of strategic missions'.

In spite of efforts to stabilise military spending, strategic
analysts in Moscow do not expect a favourable outcome in the
short term. In 1999, the defence budget reached only 2.34 per cent
of projected annual GDP (in contrast with Yeltsin's promise of
3.5 per cent) and represented 16.3 per cent of total government
expenditure.[97] By April 1999, just two months after the budget
was passed, Arbatov was calling for a 10 per cent supplementation
to take account of inflation.[98] As another of Russia's better known

strategic analysts, Sergei Rogov, has noted, GDP growth will not return on a stable basis until the middle of the next decade, and the prospects for military expenditure remained one of 'avalanching reductions'.[99] This view has been supported by internal studies within the General Staff.

Reform timetable: long delays, eventual reassertion

Apart from the two factors discussed above, one of the most powerful causes for the delay in substantive military reform was that the armed forces were consumed with major operational matters. Between 1991 and 1994 the armed forces were still in retreat from Eastern Europe and many of the newly independent states.[100] Just as the final withdrawals were complete, the armed forces went to war from December 1994 to January 1996 in Chechnia. With relief from the operational burdens and with victory in the presidential election of June 1996 behind him, Yeltsin and his administration turned more seriously to reform. The newly constituted Defence Council, and its Executive Secretary, Yury Baturin, began to press the issues, and Yeltsin instructed them in an edict of November 1996 'On Support Measures for Military Construction in the Russian Federation' to develop a concept for military development up to 2005.[101] It was to include funding measures, adoption of a new military doctrine, reform strategies, and resolution of command and control difficulties, especially between the General Staff and the High Command (the President) and between the various power ministries (Defence, Interior, Security), and between various functional, regional and service commands in the armed forces.

But it was not until 1997 that the Russian government began to make any serious inroads on narrowing the gap between doctrine and practice by at last pursuing sustained and comprehensive military reform. It took the removal of the Defence Minister, only in his job for less than a year, and removal of the Chief of the General Staff, to make this progress. As political battles raged over the preparation of the concept document, with Defence Minister Rodionov opposing efforts at substantive reform, Yeltsin and his aides moved against him and the Chief of the General Staff in May 1997, forcing the former out of the post in favour of General Igor Sergeyev. Yeltsin set a spending target for defence at that time of 3 to 3.5 per cent of GDP. He also set a deadline of two months for completion of the concept paper, and set up two new commissions: one under Prime Minister Victor

Chernomyrdin on military reform and military construction, and one under Deputy Prime Minister Anatoly Chubais on economic and financial support for the military reforms. By September 1997, Yeltsin had approved a two-page document on priority measures for the reform and restructuring of the armed forces.[102]
The main elements were:

- reduction of the armed forces to 1.2 million by 1 January 1999;
- merger of the Strategic Missile Forces (the ICBM force) and other military space forces;
- disestablishment of the High Command of the ground forces and its replacement by the Main Staff of the ground forces;
- unification of the Air Defence Forces and the air forces into a single Russian Federation Air Force by 1 January 1999;
- assigning to each military district by 1 January 1999 the status of an operational-strategic command for the corresponding strategic front and giving it operational command of all military and paramilitary forces in its borders;
- directing the government to ensure funding for these measures and for the social needs of military personnel released from service; and
- directing the Ministry of Defence to prepare before 1 January 1998 final draft edicts on the roles and functions of the ministry itself and the General Staff.

A number of substantive measures for reforms and restructuring followed, but still without formal approval of any new military doctrine which the President had ordered in 1996. In December 1997, the Ground Forces High Command was abolished, and its Main Directorate was converted into the Main Operational Directorate of the General Staff, where it became responsible for oversight of the entire reform program of the armed forces.[103] This reorganisation harked back to 1918 when a directorate of the same name was created in the staff of the Revolutionary Military Soviet of the republic. The new Main Operational Directorate of 1997 became the main policy organ within the armed forces, responsible for all matters with military implications, including such things as civil aviation agreements and use of Russian airspace. In January 1998, the appointment of a single commander of the air forces and air defence forces was announced.[104]

In late 1997, the merger of some military districts was foreshadowed, a move which had been mooted since 1995 and which would reduce the number of military districts in Russia from eight to six.[105] In eastern Russia, this meant a reduction in the number of MDs east of the Urals from four to three (Urals, Siberian and Far East). At the same time, the formation of new unified operational commands combining naval, air and ground forces in these MDs was also announced.

When in 1998 Yeltsin approved the more detailed concept paper he had commissioned in late 1996, 'The Fundamentals (Concept) of State Policy in Defence Building until 2005', it foreshadowed a transition over seven years to three branches in the armed forces corresponding to three spheres of warfare: land, aerospace and sea. There were to be two stages to the reform: the first to 2001 was to 'carry out a restructuring of the Armed Forces and convert them to a four service structure, optimise their composition and reduce their strength to 1.2 million'.[106] The second phase (2001–2005) was to concentrate on boosting the level of operational and combat training and improving command and control procedures. By 1999, Yeltsin had ordered the merging under one command of all of the strategic nuclear forces. These restructuring proposals, and others, are discussed in more detail in subsequent chapters.

But military reform has still not passed many of the basic institutional hurdles. By early 1999, there was still no single law providing a legal foundation for the organisation and operations of the armed forces beyond the provisions in the Constitution. Such a law had been foreshadowed in a presidential decree of 6 March 1992, and remained an urgent requirement given a proliferation of military and paramilitary forces under government control after 1991. In 1998, the Chief of the General Staff complained about the haphazard development of a variety of military and paramilitary forces operating under the auspices of some 20 different laws.[107] There were serious problems of duplication, lack of coordination, and incompatibility of command and control systems. Important steps were taken in late 1998 and early 1999, with the President approving an edict on the roles and functions of the Ministry of Defence and the General Staff.[108] In February 1999, Yeltsin drew a line and ordered the Defence Minister to complete the restructuring of the forces by the end of the year.[109]

Just as the government was intensifying its efforts to reform the armed forces through 1997 and 1998, the opposition within the country to the government's entire strategic policy was growing. This opposition led to the tabling in the State Duma in late 1998 of a resolution impeaching the President on charges which included damaging state security and weakening the state's

military power. This impeachment process is unlikely to be completed by the time Yeltsin seeks re-election, but his dismissal of
the Primakov government in May 1999 may provoke an alternative course to remove him. The State Duma approved a military
reform bill in February 1999, thus overriding a veto imposed by
the upper house, the Federation Council.

FORCE POSTURE: AN OVERVIEW

There are two types of military units in Russia: the armed forces,
and the 'other forces' not subject to the Minister of Defence.[110]
The armed forces are responsible for the protection of the state
and the inviolability of its borders, and in early 1999 there were
four services: the Strategic Missile Forces (SMF), the Russian
Federation Navy (RFN), the Russian Federation Air Force (RFAF),
and the Ground Forces. In addition, the Ministry of Defence has
about 200 000 personnel, including centrally controlled units for
electronic warfare, logistic support and training, and intelligence.
Military intelligence is conducted by the Main Intelligence Directorate (GRU) which is subordinated to the General Staff. Total
strength of the armed forces in 1998 was estimated by the
International Institute for Strategic Studies as 1.159 million,[111]
down from 1.7 million in 1997.[112] These figures compare with
some 3.4 million under the control of Moscow in the Soviet armed
forces in 1991.

There are at least six 'other forces', and some of these have
received substantial political and financial support, to the extent
that they have been seen as competitors for the armed forces
proper. Ministry of Internal Affairs[113] troops are responsible for
restoring order in the context of a domestic state of emergency
and at the end of 1998 numbered about 237 000. They were
organised into some 20 divisions, including four independent
special force divisions, 29 brigades including 10 independent
special force brigades, 65 regiments, including special motorised
units, and elite special forces units. The Interior Ministry forces
had 1700 armoured combat vehicles and their own aviation wing,
equipped with different types of fixed-wing aircraft and helicopters, including Il–76 *Candid* transport heavy-lifters, and several
Mi–24 *Hind* combat helicopters. The Federal Border Service[114] had
a force of 220 000 which was directly subordinate to the President,
and was deployed in seven frontier districts, as well as units in
the Arctic, Kaliningrad and Moscow. The forces were well

equipped, with armoured combat vehicles (1700), aircraft (80 fixed-wing and more than 200 helicopters) and patrol or coastal combatant boats (about 240). The forces also deployed eight icebreakers. The Forces for the Protection of the President of the Russian Federation, with 25 000 men, were organised in a Presidential Guard Regiment, one airborne regiment, and one mechanised infantry brigade.[115] Troops of the Federal Security Service[116] (successor to the KGB) amounted to 9000, including three special commando units (Alpha, Beta and Zenith).[117] The Ministry for Affairs of Civil Defence, Emergency Situations and Natural Disasters is based in part on the former Civil Defence Troops of the Soviet era and is responsible for military aspects of protection of the population in wartime, as well as civil disaster relief. The Federal Government Communications and Information Agency (FAPSI) provides information security, and in 1998 included about 54 000 personnel. The Border Guards Service has received special consideration in allowance, status and funding compared with the army, according to one source.[118] Ministry of Interior troops and troops of the Federal Intelligence Service operated in Chechnia where, even though their main function should have been lower level, clean-up operations, they did participate in several front-line combat actions alongside regular ground forces units.[119]

In line with the 1998 concept document, the Interior Ministry troops were to be transformed into a Federal Guard and lose a number of their functions and equipment; and become an entirely volunteer professional force.[120] In particular, the strength of the Interior troops was to be reduced by 54 000. Special motorised units, plus guards and escorts, have been cut or transferred to other ministries, such as the Ministry of Justice.[121] The seven Interior Troops Military Districts have been reduced to four (Central, North Caucasus, Trans-Volga and Siberian). The border guards would similarly be rationalised, with some functions cut out and some equipment to be transferred to the armed forces.[122] In May 1998, Yeltsin abolished the Federal Special Construction Service based on the former Railroad Construction Troops of the Soviet era. The personnel and functions were reassigned to the armed forces or to FAPSI.

Between 1997 and 1998, four Cossack units which had been formed as private associations after the collapse of the USSR were formally incorporated into the state structure of Russia through agreements between them and the President. These units, Transbaikal, Siberian, Terek and Orenburg Cossack communities, are supervised by the Main Directorate of Cossack Troops under the Presidential Administration, but will be provided with pay and weapons by those units with which they serve in the Border Guards Service, the Ministry of Defence, municipal militia, or the Ministry for Emergency Situations and Natural Disasters.[123]

In the armed forces proper, recruitment problems have been quite severe and have frustrated the declared intention of the government to move to an all-volunteer force. Educational standards and social profiles of conscripts have been deteriorating and conscript numbers have been declining sharply: in 1996, 530 000; in 1997 about 381 000; and in 1998 about 300 000. The term of service for conscripts is 24 months. From a process begun in December 1992 of contract employment of volunteers in the armed forces, with an initial signing of about 45 000 by April 1993, the proportion of volunteers by 1995 had grown to about 30 per cent in the non-officer grades.[124]

Yet there is little interest in Russia in military service—about one in ten young Russians would be prepared to serve in the forces.[125] In August 1998, the Defence Minister Sergeyev announced that it would be difficult to meet the President's goal (set in 1996) of achieving a fully professional (non-conscript) force by the year 2000 because of lack of funding.[126] He said that the armed forces would need an additional six billion roubles to make that change. According to Arbatov, writing in 1997, the transition to full contract (volunteer) service had by then already been postponed to 2005.[127] One source, a retired military officer who continues to publish on the subject, suggested in 1997 that the goal of 30 per cent as contracted service was never reached. It may have reached 25 per cent but had probably shrunk to 15 per cent.[128] This was borne out by figures released in late 1998 of 163 000 contract personnel.[129] There was a leakage of about 15–20 per cent of new contracted personnel because of lack of competence. Another cause was that draftees were cheaper than contract personnel, and military units facing budget difficulties were under pressure to dismiss the latter before draftees.[130]

Personnel shortages in the armed forces were persisting through 1998, with a deficit of about 12 per cent for officer billets and about 20 per cent for non-commissioned officers. Generals were in over-supply,[131] and that was after a cut of 20 per cent in the Russian general corps in 1998. In September 1998, Sergeyev revealed that in the previous five years three out of every five officers younger than 30 had left the service, and that in the first half of 1998 the figure was lower, although not much.[132]

The system of military registration both for conscription and for mobilisation in emergencies broke down in the period after 1991 and was only corrected on a legislative basis in December 1998 in a presidential decree which is to operate in accordance with existing legislation on military service, call-up and mobilisation. In the autumn 1998 draft, only 7 per cent of all those registered were called up (110 000 for the armed forces).[133] In the spring 1998 draft, about 40 000 of those called up refused to appear for service.

Some military leaders believe it will be impossible and unwise for Russia to move to a completely volunteer force. One of the main reasons they give to oppose this policy is that conscription is a powerful tool for breeding national consciousness in a multi-cultural or multinational state such as Russia.[134] One officer suggests a suitable balance might be 70 per cent contract personnel and 30 per cent draftees, and this figure was based in part on the likelihood that after 2005, the annual draft pool will have been cut to 380 000 men. According to a NATO study, the failure of Russia to manage its military personnel problems has resulted in a disastrous decline in combat capability of the ground forces.[135]

Women in the armed forces in 1998 numbered about 130 000, all of whom were volunteers. More than half of them had higher education, but only 2500 were officers.[136] Women rarely rise above the rank of major, and there was not a single female general. According to one source, some 75 had reached the rank of lieutenant colonel, and another 500 were majors. About 50 per cent of women officers were under 30 years of age; and the majority of women in the forces were non-commissioned officers.[137] Some 200 women have been decorated for recent service in combat operations. Most women serve as radio operators, communicators, map plotters, or logistics and medical personnel. About 500 were taking formal courses in higher military education institutions and another 400 were auditing such courses, a much higher figure than the 20–30 in Soviet days. Women who are fit for military service and who have certain specialisations are obliged under the December 1998 provisions to register for military service.

COMMAND AND CONTROL

As mentioned above, the President is the Supreme Commander of the Armed Forces, and he/she has authority over all other civilian and military personnel in this function, including the Minister of Defence, and including all other power ministries with paramilitary forces. This authority is promulgated specifically in the Law on Defence (No. 61 F–3, approved 31 March 1996) and reiterated in the Edict on the Ministry of Defence and the General Staff (No. 1357, 11 November 1998). The Minister of Defence is not the principal adviser to the President on security broadly defined or even on military security. His responsibilities relate to 'preparations for the armed defence of the Russian Federation, its territorial unity and the inviolability of its borders', the defeat of aggression directed against Russia, and the fulfilment of Russia's international obligations. He has a policy-coordinating role for the activities of other power ministries and paramilitary forces; a policy responsibility for the economic, social and technological foundations of national defence posture; and a responsibility to participate in international military cooperation. The Ministry of Defence 'participates' in the formulation of military doctrine but directs the conceptual work on force structure. On some issues, the minister is subordinate not only to the President, but also to the Prime Minister. But the minister is responsible, under the President, for direction and control of the armed forces. The General Staff supports the Defence Minister in all of these roles, and is the central point for policy development in these roles. The General Staff is also the central command point within the armed forces under the minister, and it is responsible for the operational command of all military and paramilitary forces in Russia. The Chief of the General Staff has full authority to issue any order or instruction to implement decisions of the minister. Figure 5.3 sets out the principal organisational links involved in command and control of the armed forces of Russia as set out in various government documents and plans, although some of these are still evolving or have yet to be fully implemented.

Specific arrangements for command and control have been a major target of the reform, with some restructuring in the Ministry of Defence and General Staff departments; moves to unify the whole national system through standardisation of equipment and procedures; and a shift to a territorial system for line command of all of the armed services and other forces within a particular military district which, as mentioned above, will be simultaneously designated as a unified operational command.[138] According to the Chief of the General Staff, two special features need attention in reform of command and control arrangements: developing security measures against information warfare tech-

Figure 5.3 Organisation chart: Supreme Command and General Staff

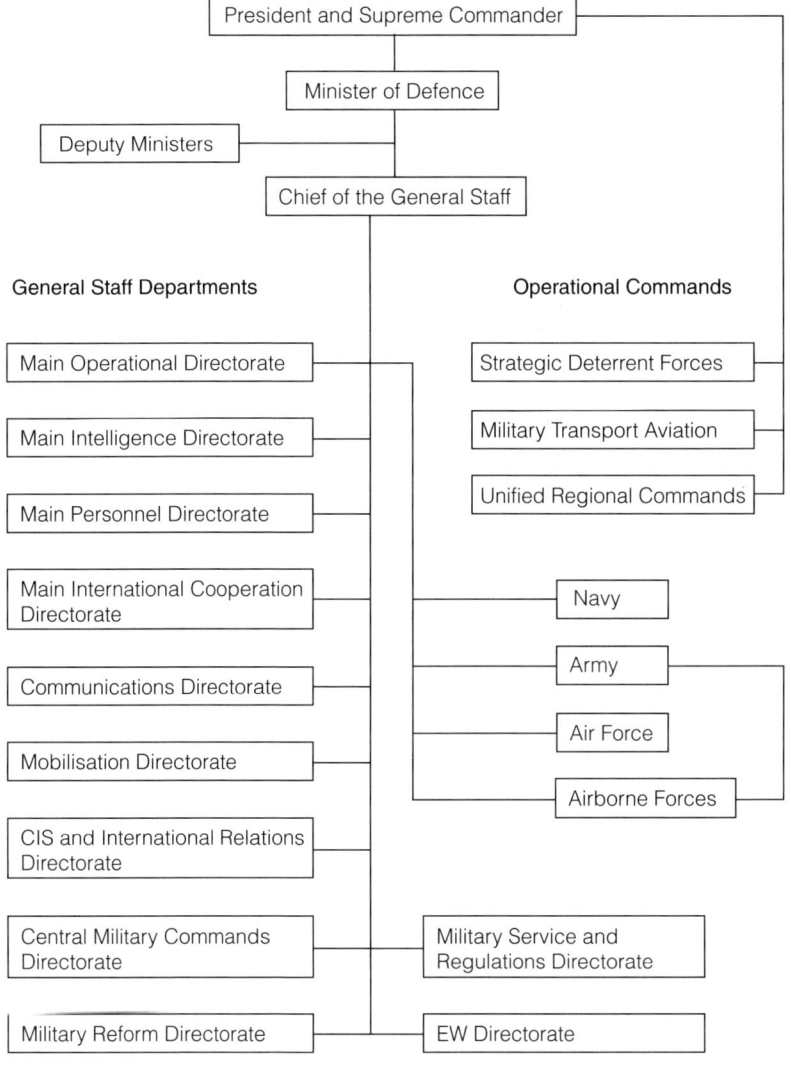

niques, and providing a command and control structure appropriate for Russian participation in 'supra-state' wars authorised by the United Nations.[139]

In exercises, a new emphasis has been placed on command and control for operation in local or regional wars. The main indicators of changed arrangements were strategic staff and command exercises 'Redut–95' and 'Redut–96', conducted with the participation of several military districts and formations of various services of the armed forces.[140] In particular, 'Redut–96' involved troops of the Leningrad MD, former Kaliningrad Special District (KOR) troops, and elements of the Moscow MD.[141] Based on the conclusions drawn from the exercises, MDs were granted the status of operational-strategic (operational-territorial) commands of the armed forces in the 'corresponding strategic directions', a measure which made the MDs more flexible in responding to possible threats in their zones of responsibility.[142] The purposes of this territorial reorganisation included: improving operational planning, improving coordination, centralising procedures for transition from a peacetime to wartime footing, and improving the quality of training. Under the shift to unified territorial command, the territorial commander will not have command functions over the paramilitary units for non-military functions. But the reforms have been designed to make it much easier for the armed forces proper to support the paramilitary forces in peacetime roles.

At the level of strategic command and control, much work remains to be done. As one officer put it, 'one of the main reasons for our disgraceful defeat in Chechnia was the complete lack of a unified operational-strategic leadership'.[143] The author of this view, a colonel in the General Staff Main Operations Directorate, reported that by November 1998 there was still no legislative basis for the existence and operations of the Supreme High Command and the State Defence Committee during wartime—beyond the constitutional provision that the President was Commander in Chief of the armed forces.

Rear services

The Rear Services Branch was a very strong part of the Soviet armed forces, having its own First Deputy Minister of Defence. In the Russian armed forces, while rear services remain very important, their institutional status has declined significantly since 1991. In undertaking reform in this area, the government has paid special attention to improving the management systems for all aspects of rear services, but financial management has been a particular target. The weakness in military accounting procedures has had a substantial negative effect on the implementation of reform.[145] But there will be moves to integrate the technical and rear services of all of the single services and paramilitary forces through the country. There have been three independent operations, each duplicating the other, in the armed forces, in the

Ministry of Interior troops and in the border guards. Not only had these three forces maintained separate hospitals, depots and other support structures independently of each other, but other paramilitary forces had actually begun setting up their own structures as well. A centralised system of purchasing would be established for all of the power ministries. Regional systems for the maintenance, repair and recycling of military equipment and property of all types would be established.

Doctrinal considerations have also been forcing a radical rethink of the role of rear services in ways that actually reduce the significance of the decline in size of this branch of the armed services. According to some specialists, new weapons actually reduce the level of survivability of rear services groupings and this decreases the impact on battle outcomes of the rear services.[146] At the same time, while a lower impact may be in prospect, there still needs to be considerable rear area and logistic support, and contemporary and prospective weapon systems will impose higher demands for concealment and deception, as well as high demands on engineering works. New techniques would have to be found, these specialists suggest, for reducing the time of supplying combat formations and ensuring the defence of rear service units in combat conditions.

Chemical weapons and chemical defence troops

In November 1997, President Yeltsin signed the bill of the Federal Assembly ratifying the Chemical Weapons Convention which prohibits the development, production, stockpiling, and use of chemical weapons, and which mandates their destruction. Russia has to begin destroying the weapons no later than November 1999 and must complete the process by 2007. The USSR had the largest stock of chemical weapons in the world and possessed the greatest capabilities for their use. Today, Russia's 40 000 tonnes of chemical agents still represent a great danger. The convention requires each state to fund the destruction and verification of destruction. A five-year extension on the destruction time frame is possible if the Executive Council of the Organisation for the Prohibition of Chemical Weapons, a group set up under the convention, agrees to grant it.

Russia plans to destroy its stocks close to the five current storage sites, a move which will reduce the risk of diversion of parts of it. The Russian government is not in a hurry to dispose of these stocks, its main argument being the cost of the destruction process (around $5 billion). In May 1998, Russia met with about 30 potential donor countries seeking foreign funds to assist.[147] As of March 1999, Russia had not secured any firm commitments, or established its own control organisation for the destruction task, as required by the convention, because of internal political disputes. US experts have suggested that the Russian government may be deliberately postponing the destruction. The US Defense Intelligence Agency (DIA) in 1996 reported that 'Russian officials probably believe they need a CW capability to deter other nations'.[148] But Russia's capacities to destroy its CW stocks are probably not substantial enough. The first experimental destruction unit built can only handle 350 tonnes per year.[149] Russia will almost certainly seek an extension of the time period allowed.

The projected elimination of chemical weapons has increased pressure on the existence of the Chemical Defence Troops, already suffering cutbacks under budget pressures experienced by the armed forces as a whole. There remain many civil and military tasks for these forces, which are also trained for defence against radiation and biological threats. As one officer noted, 'accidents at installations in the Ministry of Defence and the industrial complex and problems of military ecology are becoming no less important'.[150] He cited a variety of civil tasks, many to do with pollution emergencies, and one to do with checking the Moscow headquarters of the Japanese Aum Shinrikyo sect—the terrorist group responsible for a chemical attack in the Tokyo subway.

Biological weapons

The USSR signed the Biological Weapons Convention in 1972, but since the convention had no verification provisions, the USSR consistently breached its obligations under that treaty for two decades.[151] The BW program was kept secret, even after an incident in 1979 at the Sverdlovsk research facility, which caused an outbreak of anthrax.[152] Only in 1992 did Russia admit to developing an offensive program in violation of the convention. In 1992, President Yeltsin signed a decree that recommitted Russia to the convention. The 15th Directorate of the MoD responsible for the biological warfare programs was reorganised into the Biological Defence Directorate, which is now part of the Radiation, Chemical and Biological Defence Directorate, which is now part of the Radiation, Chemical and Biological Defence Troops (Voiska radiatsionnoi, khimicheskoi i biologicheskoi zachshity). According to Lieutenant-General Valentin Evstigneev, Chief of the

Biological Defence Directorate, Russia is no longer working on offensive biological warfare programs and is currently concentrating its efforts on the development of the defensive counter-agents/techniques to protect Russian troops and population against possible use of biological warfare.[153] But in 1994, defectors revealed an ongoing Russian BW program that was concentrating on a 'superplague' for which there is no antidote. President Yeltsin claimed he did not know of any such programs. Defectors supported Yeltsin's claim, implying that the military leadership was running the program on its own, without Yeltsin's knowledge and contrary to his explicit instructions. In 1997, US military sources revealed that a 'superplague' virus has been developed and successfully tested. That indicates that a Russian BW program possibly still exists.

Given the continuing secrecy of the program, Russia's BW assets are probably maintained as an absolute last resort counterstrike capability. They are almost certainly not seen as a deterrent. Biological warfare offers unique and significant advantages because of the ease of production of agents, the potential impact of their use, and the ability it offers to penetrate an enemy's defences. Biological agents are many times deadlier than chemical agents. For example, 10 grams of anthrax spores could kill as many people as one tonne of the nerve agent Sarin.[154] Using BW under the cover of an epidemic or natural disease occurrence provides an attacker with the potential for plausible denial. In this context, biological warfare offers greater possibilities of use than nuclear weapons. As Russia destroys its chemical weapons, it may come to rely more heavily on its BW capabilities to counterbalance the increasing conventional superiority of NATO and the USA. But a more likely explanation of the Russian BW program may be Russian fears of China and the large numbers of troops and people that it possesses. Biological weapons may be seen by some military planners as one of the most effective ways of stopping a massed Chinese military attack.

Military education

Major restructuring has occurred in the military education system, with the number of institutions cut by half and many others reorganised into large, multi-level training centres. After 1 April 1999, there were to be 55 higher institutions (8 academies, 11 universities and 36 colleges), and 84 technical schools.[155] Closures between 1992 and 1999 had only amounted to about 10 per cent of institutions even though the forces as a whole had shrunk by almost 70 per cent. Some schools had ten times as many instructors or staff as students. But most of the substantive questions about the future direction of military education remained under debate, a circumstance evidenced by the small number of closures (15) in the 1998 and 1999 measures. Many institutes had been merged, such as the very famous Frunze Academy (US War College equivalent) and the Armour Academy. A new Main Directorate to supervise all military training was created in the General Staff in 1997.[156]

MILITARY RESPONSES TO NATO EXPANSION

As discussed in chapter 3, Russia has been suspicious and critical of the expansion of NATO on a fairly consistent basis since the idea was first floated. NATO's increased military potential as the result of its enlargement and its use of force against Yugoslavia on two occasions in the 1990s have provided a powerful stimulus to modernisation of the Russian armed forces and to the political will to reform. In April 1999, the Defence Minister, Igor Sergeyev, declared that Russia would be adjusting its military posture in response to the new NATO strategic concept which provided for NATO military action outside its defensive area and without UN Security Council endorsement.[157]

The armed forces have been even more sensitive to NATO expansion than the government's official policy. This has been reflected in military exercises, military concept development and in military posture in ways that probably run slightly counter to national strategic policy. According to Aleksei Arbatov, Russian military plans still revolve to a large degree ('50–60 per cent') around contingencies related to a major war with the USA and NATO in the west and with the USA and Japan in the east. He saw this as rather natural since the armed forces had to consider capabilities, which took years to change, and not intentions, which could change overnight. He also felt that US military planners shared this adversarial strategic disposition with their Russian counterparts.[158] The development of war strategy by Russian Air Force planners is primarily influenced by their assessment of NATO and United States Air Force (USAF) capabilities.

Russian military leaders have never been comfortable with the NATO expansion in spite of some important cooperative milestones. Russia and the USA held their first joint naval exer-

cise in July 1992 in the Barents Sea[159] and in 1997 Russia and
NATO signed the Founding Act, which set down the basis of
military relations and created a NATO–Russia Permanent Joint
Council. But even as there were positive evaluations of this
process, by 1998 most Russian military leaders had become even
more uncomfortable. In January 1998, the Defence Minister,
Sergeyev, said that the idea of a NATO corps headquarters
(German, Danish and Polish) in Szczecin in Poland was a 'very
bad thing'.[160] Any new cooperative measure with NATO was being
painted in a negative light in the popular press. For example, in
September 1998, Russian forces exercised with a small NATO
force under the Partnership for Peace program in cooperation with
Uzbekistan, Kazakhstan and Kyrgyzstan, but even these activities
have been reported negatively in the Russian press as manifesting
US strategic interests in Central Asia that are inimical to Russian
interests.[161]

Russian military attitudes have been sharpened by the fact
that NATO's combined forces continue to grow while Russia
continues to cut its forces in accord with the Treaty on Conventional Forces in Europe (CFE) signed in 1990 between NATO and
the Warsaw Pact. Since 1994, citing various military, political and
economic concerns, Russia has been pressing for a relaxation of
equipment limits in Russia's southern and northwestern areas,
what have been termed the flank zones of the CFE treaty area.
In particular, Russian military leaders have wanted the CFE limits
changed to allow the stationing of more troops in the North
Caucasus Military District without reducing the strength on the
northern flank (Leningrad MD). In particular, Moscow wants
approximately 400 MBTs, 2400 armoured combat vehicles (ACVs)
and 800 artillery pieces above what is authorised in the North
Caucasus MD.[162] Furthermore, Russia did not meet an associated
commitment to destroy 14 500 pieces of equipment of types limited by the treaty east of the Urals.

In January 1997, new talks began in Vienna on CFE because
of Russia's disaffection with its restrictions on deployments given
new strategic requirements.[163] While these talks have been successful, NATO's expansion may create a situation in which Russia
implements its threat to withdraw from the CFE treaty and
to build up forces in European Russia, as a direct counter to
NATO.[164] The 1997 Founding Act between NATO and Russia does
not preclude such a build-up. According to the Deputy Foreign
Minister, Nikolai Afanasievski, Russia has retained 'freedom
of action' in such spheres as the deployment and stationing of

additional troops in European Russia. In other words, his view is that the Russian command can reinforce the western MDs according to its own judgement.[165] Any move by Russia to strengthen its conventional forces west of the Urals would put considerable pressure on the arms control and confidence-building regimes in Europe.

Russian strategic planners believe that a major military confrontation in Central and Eastern Europe would involve either engagement of conventional forces from eastern Russia or nuclear escalation. Some Russian sources see resort to nuclear escalation as more likely than redeployment of forces from eastern Russia.[166] In March 1999, Russian forces held a large exercise, called 'Air Bridge', premised on response to a NATO-sponsored operation against western Russia.[167] The exercise tested strategic redeployment of troops using military airlift assets and airborne assault, as well as mobilisation of heavy bomber assets as far away as Ukrainka in the Far East.

The NATO expansion and new pressures in the southern border regions have led to creation of new formations on the main strategic fronts. In particular, two air armies have been re-established in the Moscow and North Caucasus MDs.[168] But Russian planners only expect their air forces to be able to deny air superiority to an enemy and gain it themselves during a limited conflict, and not in a major war with NATO. This consideration probably had a big influence on talk of possible nuclear responses.

Another response by Russia to NATO's expansion has been seen in efforts to strengthen the Russian naval presence in the Mediterranean Sea, a region seen in Russia as within the traditional sphere of its interests.[169] Although the Russian Navy re-established the Russian Mediterranean Squadron in 1992,[170] a stronger Russian naval presence was re-established in 1996 with the three-month deployment of a task force, headed by the carrier *Admiral Kuznetsov*.[171] Since Mediterranean communications are vital for NATO's southern flank, a Russian naval presence there can reassure Moscow that at least it can monitor events and be in a position to make a fairly rapid, if low-level response.

After a period of some stagnation, the Baltic and Black Sea fleets resumed policies of strengthening their forces with major warships. The Black Sea Fleet will now make a greater contribution to Mediterranean naval groups, on a par with the Northern Fleet contributions, which had been the main source for Mediterranean operations in the Soviet era. The Black Sea Fleet also attempted to increase its potential to cope with the growing naval capabilities of Turkey. For example, in 1996 and 1997, the fleet commissioned two new vessels and reactivated the *Kynda*-class cruiser *Admiral Golovko*.[172] By the end of 1999, the flagship of the Black Sea Fleet, the guided-missile cruiser *Moskva*, will become operational after a prolonged refit. *Moskva* will eventually replace the aging *Golovko*.

In response to the potential expansion of NATO's naval assets in the Baltic by nearly 20 per cent through Poland's membership, the Russian Navy moved in 1996 to strengthen its Baltic and Northern Fleet by reactivating older ships and procuring new vessels. This shift in the naval balance in the Baltic was the likely motive for the transfer of the *Sovremennyi*-class destroyer *Bezuprechnyi* from the Northern Fleet to the Baltic Fleet in 1996.[173] The Baltic Fleet has also acquired new generation escort ships, the *Neustrashimyi*-class frigates.[174] In the Northern Fleet, the most powerful fleet in the Russian Navy, the *Kiev*-class carrier *Admiral Gorshkov* was reactivated.[175] Currently *Admiral Gorshkov* is undergoing refit in Severodvinsk. In 1998–99 the Northern Fleet also received the last *Ushakov* class nuclear-powered battle cruiser *Piotr Velikii* and the *Udaloi II* class destroyer *Admiral Chabanenko*. The deployment of *Piotr Velikii* to the Northern Fleet instead of the Pacific for which it had been intended serves as an indication that the Russian military is taking steps to reinforce its forces west of the Urals in response to NATO's growing military power.

But deploying additional forces in the western regions would not necessarily improve Russia's security relative to NATO. The Russian armed forces are not in a condition to wage a Soviet-style war by conducting large-scale, long-term strategic operations. The Russian armed forces could not repel a hypothetical large-scale attack using only conventional means of combat. If NATO was to launch a large-scale conventional campaign against Russia, or if Russia was involved in hostilities with a NATO member such as Poland, Russia has warned that it may be forced to use nuclear weapons. The circumstances in which this would be likely to occur have been set out by Russia:

- if a nuclear power launches extensive aggression against Russia or its allies;
- if aggression against Russia is launched by a non-nuclear country linked to a nuclear state by a military alliance; or
- if Russia has no other means to safeguard its independence and sovereignty.[176]

Russia will almost certainly continue to make adjustments in its military posture as if the expansion of NATO were a threat to it, even if it returns to more cooperative military relations with the Atlantic alliance. By mid-1999, one Russian commentator was predicting a sharp increase in Russian defence spending in response to NATO actions in Yugoslavia.[177] But other indicators suggest that Russia may not feel that its immediate responses to NATO expansion must be in military deployments in the western regions. Two strong indicators of the firming commitment to a different military posture came with the disbandment in September 1998 of the army group in Kaliningrad, the territorial enclave of Russia on the Baltic coast between Poland and Lithuania; and with the revelation that there had been a substantial decline in readiness through force reductions in the area round St Petersburg (site of a historic prolonged siege in the Second World War).[178]

MILITARY RESPONSES TO THE EMERGENCIES IN THE SOUTH

Russia's military responses to NATO have been conditioned in large part by the weaknesses in the country's military position in its southern regions and by its defeat in the war in Chechnia between 1994 and 1996. In its southern regions, Russia faces one of the most complex combinations of internal and external security problems now being experienced by any great power. By 1998, according to a Russian official source, the armed forces had more conventional military forces in the North Caucasus MD than in any other MD and more units on higher levels of readiness there than in other MDs.[179] The deployments in this region exceeded the limits set by the CFE Treaty for this area, but Russia was relying on its right under the treaty to hold higher levels in the region on a temporary basis. According to the IISS, the forces in the MD in 1998 comprised 54 500 personnel in two infantry divisions and one airborne division, three independent infantry brigades, one special forces brigade, one naval infantry regiment, and other air force and ground formations. There were about 300 fixed-wing ground-attack aircraft, and about 350 fixed-wing fighter aircraft.[180] The independent infantry brigades serve as garrison units in the major towns, like the 205th in Budennovsk. The Russian military posture in the southern regions must also take account of Russia's peacekeeping commitments in the newly independent states, like

Georgia and Armenia, where in 1998 there were about 15 000 Russian military personnel.

The largest single group deployed close to Chechnia is a force of more than 10 000 but this was comprised primarily of MVD troops (five independent special forces divisions) and militia (police) units.[181] Similarly, the air forces assembled there (Mi–8 and Mi–24 helicopters) included units of the RFAF as well as MVD. In the first half of 1999, the 58th Army based in the North Caucasus Military District was in a high state of readiness. Were offensive operations to resume against the Chechen forces (which are not large), the most likely form would be aerial bombardment and special operations. The ground forces do not have enough high-precision weapons to support a campaign. Their most accurate artillery pieces only have a range of 20 kilometres. According to Russian specialists, the special force units most appropriate to operations against the Chechen armed groups are in the MVD and the Federal Security Bureau, not the armed forces proper.

NEW MILITARY CONCEPTS

Notwithstanding the relative state of underdevelopment of officially approved military doctrine, the Russian armed forces have a fairly clear vision of the general direction in which they must head. There are three main directions: high-precision weapons, aerospace operations and information warfare, each of which must be mastered both for local wars and for large-scale great-power war.

As the Chief of the General Staff, Anatoly Kvashnin, summarised the goals: 'Today victory on the ground is impossible without superiority in air and space and without active information pressures'.[182] He acknowledged the argument of some specialists that victory was possible merely through the combined use of high-precision air strikes and psychological pressures derived in large part by information warfare. He said that the reform of the armed forces would be based on working toward this capability and establishing it in an 'integrated combat system'.

Kvashnin claimed that the Soviet air force had been heading in that direction from the mid-1980s, and that a viable foundation existed for information warfare in the Russian forces. He identified several fundamental requirements: the capability to obtain the fullest possible intelligence information, and to collate, analyse and distribute this through the shortest and most effective communications systems to the military decision-makers who need it; the potential to inflict damage in real-time or near real-time, both through effective integration of precision-strike capacities and information flows, and through reduction of the number of levels of troop command; and protection of the system as a whole and components of it from 'modern information counter-measures'. Kvashnin said the air force would be receiving priority in terms of achieving these sorts of goals, and the main aim of air force reform would be shortening the 'detect–destroy' cycle.[183]

MILITARY ORGANISATION EAST OF THE URAL MOUNTAINS

In the European parts of the USSR, the bulk of the armed forces had been deployed outside the Russian Republic, and the Russian armed forces' transition in Europe was therefore very complex. By contrast, in those parts of the USSR east of the Urals, most military assets were on the territory of the Russian Republic. For the military forces in these areas, the transition from the Soviet era to an independent Russia was therefore far less painful. In the early 1980s, about 25 per cent of the Soviet military effort went to meeting the China threat. This meant that about one-quarter of all conventional forces were deployed east of the Ural Mountains, including in the three Soviet republics of Kazakhstan, Kyrgyzstan, and Tajikistan, and in Mongolia. With the change in political geography after the collapse of the USSR, the proportion of its military forces that Moscow deployed east of the Urals rose to about 40 per cent, even as the national forces shrank. Under the Treaty on Conventional Forces in Europe, the majority of Russian forces must be located east of the Urals. The Siberian Air Defence District was until 1998 the most powerful in the country, with units stationed in ten separate administrative divisions.[184] The Siberian Military District was first established in 1865, according to Russian historians.[185] In discussions with the Chinese government on confidence-building measures in 1994, Defence Minister Grachev indicated that the Far East Military District was the most important of the four east of the Urals (and one of the four most important in the whole of Russia).[186]

The biggest change to military organisation east of the Urals has been the changes in military district boundaries and designation of the new MDs as strategic fronts, in which the MD commander has authority over all operational military forces and rear services (including mobilisation arrangements), and coordinating authority over paramilitary units of border forces and MVD. The incorporation of the Transbaikal MD into the Siberian MD meant that it would cover 42 per cent of Russian territory over four time zones, and about 1000 kilometres of international border.[187] One part of the Transbaikal MD (the Sakha Republic), which housed a number of rear support bases, was assigned to the Far East MD and not to the new Siberian MD (see Map 1). In January 1999, the first meeting of commanders of the new Siberian MD to discuss arrangements for the amalgamation with the former Transbaikal MD was held.[188] By early 1999, there were still few details on exactly how the merger of the Volga and Urals MDs would be put into place.[189]

Special considerations have been made for regions with specific military or geopolitical features, such as the Kamchatka peninsula, which are geographically remote or separated from the main concentrations of Russian air and ground power. With the continuous inappropriate financial coverage of military needs, supply and maintenance of troops in remote areas, and subordinated to different commands, had become an enormous burden. The first reorganisation of remote troop concentrations occurred on the territory of Russia's Kaliningrad enclave. In December 1997, troops of the 11th Guards Army, deployed in the former military administrative unit of *Kaliningradskii Osobyi Raion* (KOR or Kaliningrad Special District), were resubordinated to the command of the Baltic Fleet. In the view of the General Staff, this reorganisation has created an efficient mechanism, capable of ensuring national security in this strategically important region. The positive outcome of the Baltic experiment allowed the Russian Ministry of Defence to initiate a similar type of reorganisation in the Russian Far East. However, this military-administrative reorganisation was carried out on a grander scale, as it included troops of the Far Eastern Military District and the Pacific Fleet, deployed on the Kamchatka and Chukotka peninsulas.

By the end of May 1998 a new joint grouping of forces had been formed there and began its operation on 1 June. Russian military sources usually refer to the new formation as the Northeastern Group of Troops and Forces or sometimes more simply as the Kamchatka Group of Forces, because most of the reorganised troops are deployed on the Kamchatka peninsula. The newly formed group of forces has incorporated the Kamchatskaia Flotilla of the Pacific Fleet, the Pacific Fleet flotilla of nuclear-powered submarines (including SSBNs) based in Petropavlovsk-Kamchatski, one army corps of the Far Eastern MD, an independent air force/air defence division, coastal defence units, and other multi-purpose units and formations.

As the Chief of Staff of the Russian Navy, Admiral Igor Kasatonov, has emphasised, the point of creation of the new grouping in Russia's northeast was the 'assurance of the combat stability of sea-based strategic nuclear forces, and besides that, more reliable and firm management of all troops and forces concentrated there'.[190] The basing of SSBNs in Petropavlovsk-Kamchatski and their operations in the Sea of Okhotsk has played a decisive role in preventing any significant reductions of troops deployed on the Kamchatka peninsula. Back in 1996, Russia's former Defence Minister, General Igor Rodionov, had emphasised that there would be no 'sweeping' numerical reductions on Kamchatka, since Russian naval forces based there require protection and defence.[191] However, it became clear to the Russian Minister of Defence and the General Staff that some significant administrative changes had to be made.

In comparison with the reorganisation of the relatively compact KOR, the scale of the Kamchatka reorganisation brought quite a different level of complexity, especially in the context of the successful management of troops, garrisons and bases which are spread around an area of tens of thousands of square kilometres. Before the changes, troops and forces deployed in Kamchatka and Chukotka were subordinated to five commands of the previous four services of the armed forces: the Army, the Navy, the Air Force, and the Air Defence Force. Traditionally, troops deployed in Kamchatka and Chukotka could be provided with logistic support during only a relatively short period of the year, mainly during summer navigation. Each of the four services had to supply their troops independently, as well as to keep up their operational condition. Besides, subordination to different commands had created a very complex and 'irrational' system of troop management with many duplicated elements. The creation of an inappropriately large command superstructure made the system of coordination of different services very complex and time-consuming. It was considered particularly inappropriate to keep these command structures when the area of responsibility was so large. Modern warfare is characterised by the high intensity of the conflict and needs to have quicker response times through minimisation of command echelons. The Russian military leadership is trialling a new command system in Kamchatka which if successful will be used elsewhere.[192]

As with the KOR reorganisation, the new grouping is subordinated to the Commander of the Pacific Fleet Admiral Zakharenko (HQ in Vladivostok). The Commander of the Kamchatskaia Flotilla, Vice-Admiral Valery Dorogin, was appointed as the operational commander of the new joint group of forces. He will have three deputies: deputy for naval forces and chief of naval forces; deputy for ground and coastal defence troops and chief of those forces; and deputy for air forces and air defence and commander of the air district.[193] The unification of the management of the Kamchatka group under naval command raised the status and importance of the Pacific Fleet as Russia's main operational-strategic entity in the Far East.

The creation of the unified group has expanded the capabilities for operational support of the forces. In particular, it allowed the Russian command to optimise the logistic structures through elimination of duplicated and parallel structures, to rationalise and reduce the number of storage facilities and bases,[194] and to adequately distribute available resources among the troops. Centralised delivery of necessary supplies to garrisons and bases during the short period of summer navigation has already significantly reduced total expenditure on the maintenance of the forces in Kamchatka and Chukotka. Estimated savings from these measures reached 226 million roubles in less than one year.[195]

The same benefits have been found in recruitment for force elements in Kamchatka. Previously, each service had to recruit conscripts separately. In a situation where young Russians are not in a hurry to submit to conscription, there would often be an unbalanced distribution of available personnel between the four different services and some of the more important units in the remote territory were often undermanned. Now, the unified command is able to control the process of recruitment of new conscripts and distribute them on a priority basis.

Apart from central management, the unified command of the new joint group of forces will provide subordinated forces with a more centralised policy of maintaining the required combat readiness and effective mobilisation capabilities. In the view of the General Staff this situation will create more effective coordination of both combat training and operational use of troops on the Kamchatka front. From now on, the armed forces are planning to organise a process of combat training of the new grouping according to one strategic plan. The first testing of capabilities of the new operational entity took place in September 1998, during a joint exercise of the Pacific Fleet and ground and air units of the Kamchatka group subordinated to the fleet.[196] This exercise involved 14 surface combatants and submarines, including two Oscar–II class SSGNs, and five support ships, air assault and air defence units, S–300 SAM complexes and MiG–31 *Foxhound* aircraft, two infantry battalions and heavy artillery.[196] During four days of manoeuvres nearly 70 different exercises were performed on shore and at sea. It seems that the Russian military command were satisfied with the results of the exercises, not only for their military effectiveness but for the much lower cost.

CONCLUSION

Russia has adopted successive versions of a defensive military doctrine which sees a much reduced threat of major war compared with Soviet doctrine and which pays much more attention to local wars on the periphery of the country, or even within the country. The new doctrines place on Russia burdens of international citizenship, such as peacekeeping, that the USSR had not undertaken. The new doctrines enshrine ideas of economic and human security that underpin the defensive orientation of Russia's military doctrine. But the new doctrines also shift Russia's public position on use of nuclear weapons to provide for their use against grave threats to Russian territory in a conventional war. Moreover, the more liberal-inspired elements of the military doctrine sit beside other aspects which indicate that Russia retains some great-power chauvinism in the way it views the world. These aspects have come to the fore in threats by Russia to revise its military doctrine in the light of US unilateralism in use of military force and the expansion of NATO to the east. On both of these issues, Russia has been seeking to be heard but believes it has been ignored for more than five years.

The Russian government has not been successful in matching new military doctrines to its force structure because of the overwhelming weight of domestic political and economic circumstances, and because of the resistance of military leaders to substantial change. The log-jam of military reform was broken by 1997, and military reforms began in earnest, but the government has not been able to finance the armed forces or the reform program to the extent necessary.

In the chaos of unfunded military reform and a toughening

strategic attitudes toward the USA and NATO, Russian military leaders are looking for ways to stiffen their military posture in the west. There is not much they can do, but nor is there really a direct military threat there for them to posture against. Most military leaders will remain confident that they have sufficient nuclear forces to deter any adventurism by NATO. The more difficult problem for Russia's military leaders is how to respond in terms of force structure and deployments to the more immediate threats it faces or believes it faces in its southern border regions. There will have to be a more decisive shift than has occurred toward a force structure that is trained and equipped for small wars on Russia's periphery involving complex civil–military operations. On its eastern borders, Russian military posture is less problematic and the main issues have been how to adjust locally to the national level reforms.

6

Nuclear forces

Russia remains a nuclear superpower. No other state apart from the USA has the numbers, variety and advanced technology of Russia's nuclear forces. In circumstances where all other measures of Russian national power, save its resource base, have eroded, its nuclear forces have taken on a new and more threatening prominence in the country's strategic posture. Talk of limited nuclear war has surfaced in the armed forces in a way that was never possible in the Soviet period, but the discussion in the 1990s is far from coherent. At the same time, the general deterioration in conditions of service and standards of maintenance brought on by the sustained economic crisis in Russia have raised concerns about the safety both of nuclear materials and of the weapons themselves. This chapter reviews the situation of the Strategic Missile Forces (SMF) and the air component of Russia's nuclear triad. Discussion of the naval component of the triad is primarily reserved to the next chapter on the navy since much of Soviet and Russian naval development has revolved around protection of the nuclear missile submarines. This chapter begins with a brief account of the important shift in Russian nuclear doctrine away from 'no first use'. After reviewing the land-based intercontinental ballistic missile (ICBM) component within the SMF and the air-launched strategic forces, the chapter discusses briefly the bringing together of the three components of the nuclear triad under a unified operational command. There is also a brief comment on tactical nuclear weapons.

SHIFTING DOCTRINES

The Strategic Missile Force (SMF) was the only Soviet armed service not to take part in any hostilities. From their creation in

1959, the SMF's main purposes were deterrence of the US and NATO joint nuclear potentials, and the delivery of retaliatory strikes against Soviet opponents in case of nuclear war. From the late 1960s, the evolving military situation prompted a shift in Soviet nuclear requirements from seeking 'strategic superiority' to being satisfied with 'nuclear parity'. On a number of occasions, Soviet strategic nuclear forces were put on increased levels of alert. In 1982, the USSR was the first nuclear weapons state to declare that it would never be the first to use nuclear weapons, but this policy was never tested. This policy was repeatedly affirmed by Mikhail Gorbachev, who had probably had more of an instinctive appreciation of and commitment to it. This position had two important legs to it. First, it demonstrated some confidence in the ability of the USSR to achieve conventional force superiority over its NATO adversaries in central Europe. Second, it was a commitment that was unlikely to be tested, and if it was, then the circumstances would be such as to allow immediate repudiation of it. In the 1980s, Soviet military exercises consistently practised pre-emptive nuclear missile attack on enemy forces but there is little evidence that the Soviet leadership believed that a nuclear war was winnable. (There were a number of articles or statements by military propagandists supporting the proposition that nuclear war was winnable, but it is more than likely that the Soviet political leadership did not have a firm view—that their ideas about nuclear war were 'confused and confusing'.)[1]

After the collapse of the USSR in 1991, with the loss of superiority in conventional military capabilities over NATO, the Russian military–political leadership began to back away from this promise not to be the first to use nuclear weapons. As mentioned in the preceding chapter, in the 1993 military doctrine Moscow indicated that it would be the first to use nuclear weapons under certain circumstances.[2] Moreover, as the US intelligence community has pointed out, preparedness for nuclear war with the USA remains an important priority for Russia.[3]

The dramatic reduction of Russian conventional military capabilities from more than 4 million troops at the height of the Cold War down to just more than 1 million by 1999 has boosted the importance of the country's nuclear arsenal. As Commander of Russia's Strategic Missile Forces, Colonel-General Vladimir Yakovlev commented: 'in conditions of the known weakening of the conventional forces, the role of the nuclear deterrence factor is increasing'.[4] Yakovlev has identified the primary function of the strategic nuclear forces as deterrence of nuclear and conventional attack on Russia, or on its allies.[5]

Drastic changes in Russia's security environment in both Europe and Asia since 1993 have confirmed the conviction among Russian military strategists that the country should place a new reliance on retaining the threat of first use. NATO's decision to expand eastward only strengthened feelings in Russia of growing military vulnerability since its pre-existing conventional superiority over NATO was being turned into an overwhelming NATO conventional superiority over it. As even the more liberal Aleksei Arbatov has acknowledged, the nuclear forces 'chillingly' represent the main way for Russia to redress the conventional force superiority that NATO currently holds over it.[6]

Many Russian military theorists also believe that nuclear weapons provide the best answer for Russia against the higher-technology, conventionally armed weapons (precision-guided munitions) which have become an important part of Western military strategies. Russian military analysts fear that, in general war against Russia, the employment of conventional 'smart weapons' by Western nations could seriously weaken Russian strategic nuclear forces, leaving them with inadequate reply capacity.[7]

Besides, there is growing opinion across Russia's political spectrum that only substantial nuclear capabilities will help the country to maintain its status of a 'great power'. As a result, in 1997 Russia adopted a new 'nuclear-first-use' policy, under which it might resort to the employment of nuclear weapons, even during conventional conflict. As Russia's Security Council Secretary Ivan Rybkin commented: 'Naturally, we are not talking of a preventive nuclear strike, but if an aggressor starts a war against us with conventional armaments, then as part of our decisive reply, we could use nuclear weapons . . . we are reviewing political declarations of the past'.[8]

Rybkin pointed out that Russia's deeper reliance on its nuclear arsenal is explained both by the necessity to compensate for the deficiencies of the conventional forces, as well as the desire to create an effective preventive mechanism that will safeguard weakened Russia against possible hostile actions before the country's armed forces can successfully complete their reorganisation and modernisation. He said that it was necessary to stress the nuclear option so that 'military adventurers do not get tempted by the fact that at this stage our armed forces are being reformed and do not have the might they used to have'.[9] Russia is seeking to deter not only other nuclear powers, but also smaller states that might be tempted to launch any sort of aggression against Russia, including civil strife.

UNIFYING MISSILE AND SPACE FORCES: THE NEW SMF

After the collapse of the USSR the strategic nuclear forces available to Russia were reduced by more than one-third. In particular, groupings of ICBMs were based in Kazakhstan, Belarus and Ukraine. Under agreements with these countries and with the assistance of the USA, these ICBMs outside Russia were dismantled. About 2500 warheads were removed and transferred to Russia, and more than 20 000 tonnes of missile fuel was drained.[10] The completion dates for the transfers to Russia were 1995 for Kazakhstan, 1996 for Ukraine and 1997 for Belarus.[11] As of 1997, new housing in Russia for some 12 000 missile personnel transferred from the other countries had yet to be found.

On 16 July 1997, President Yeltsin signed a decree 'On Priority Measures to Reform the Armed Forces of the Russian Federation and Improve Their Structure'. One of the main provisions of that decree concerned the amalgamation of the Strategic Missile Forces,[12] the Military Space Forces,[13] and the Missile-Space Defence[14] into a single fighting service—the Strategic Missile Forces (SMF).[15] This measure would bring together missile armies, military units and establishments for the launch and control of spacecraft, early warning systems, boosters and spacecraft, and commands and formations of the missile-space defence. The new service began its operations on 1 November 1997. In early 1997, the manning level of the Strategic Missile Forces was only 85.3 per cent, which had forced personnel to work 20 to 25 per cent more shifts (110–130 days per year instead of 90–110).[16]

Under the new structure, information from space-based and ground-based missile warning systems will be fed directly to the central command post of the SMF, bypassing intermediary links. This will enable the Supreme Commander, as well as the High Command of Russia's Armed Forces to make quicker and more appropriate decisions on the potential violation of nuclear-missile stability and relate them to the combat crews of the missile complexes. The main idea of the integration is to centralise command and to reduce the number of control agencies and stations. The unification of the three branches into the single SMF is to be implemented in two stages: the first from 1997 to 2000, and the second after the year 2000. The ultimate aim, to be achieved by the years 2005–2010, is to raise the operational effectiveness and flexibility of control. The General Staff expects the measure to raise the effectiveness of retaliatory actions of the SMF by 50 per cent in the near future and still more over the longer term. Early results have been claimed, with assertions that the integration of the three original structures into one raised combat effectiveness of the integrated SMF by 15–20 per cent. Back in 1994, Andrei Kokoshin, then the First Deputy Minister for Defence, emphasised that the improvement of the command, control, and early-warning systems of the SMF was one of the priority measures of Russia's Ministry of Defence.[17]

Creation of the new unified service has already resulted in dissolution of nearly 60 military units and establishments, and elimination of duplicated structure. In the Plesetsk test range, there were two entirely separate command chains for two of the services that were being merged.[18] Nearly 6000 positions have been cut, including 237 management positions (in particular, 6 generals and 122 colonels).[19] Now the force will comprise one general per 1760 servicemen, a ratio similar to that of the US military (1:1200) and the *Bundeswehr* (1:1740). In comparison, the ratio within other Russian armed services is one general per 843 servicemen. Through the elimination of duplicative infrastructure and surplus management positions, the SMF has been reduced by 18 per cent in 1998 with expected savings of nearly 240 million roubles.[20] The integration has also reduced the number of research institutes and facilities, testing ranges and other establishments, and these measure have produced further savings. The General Staff expect that by the year 2000, the integration will save up to 7 per cent of the military budget.[21] By the end of 1998, the process had allowed a flow of 30 per cent more funds to upgrading the missile attack warning system than would have been possible otherwise.[22]

The integration is likely to stimulate the process of standardisation of weaponry and equipment of the new-look SMF, as well as the development of Russia's fourth-generation strategic missiles. The Soviet nuclear arsenal consisted of eleven types of strategic missiles. Currently, Russia's strategic forces are equipped with six types of missiles, including the most powerful ICBM in the world, the RS–20.[23] See Table 6.1.[24] The standardisation plans aim to reduce the number of ICBM missile launcher systems from six to one (*Topol*), and the number of booster rockets from eight to three.[25]

The strike component of the SMF is the ICBM force, deployed

Table 6.1 Strategic nuclear forces

Type	Launchers	Year deployed	No. of warheads
ICBMs			
SS–18	180	1979/1998	1800
SS–19	160	1979	960
SS–24	46	1987	460
SS–25	360	1985	360
SS–26	10	1998	10
Sub-total	756		3590
SLBMs			
SS–N–18	176 (11 SSBNs)	1978	528
SS–N–20	60 (3 SSBNs)	1983	600
SS–N–23	112 (7 SSBNs)	1986	448
Sub-total	348		1576
Bombers			
Tu–95	64 (ALCM/bombs)	1984	734
Tu–160	6 (ALCM/SRAM/bombs)	1987	72
Sub-total	70		806
Total	**1174**		**5972**

in four missile armies (Vladimir, Omsk, Orenburg and Chita) made up of 19 divisions[26] (nearly 100 regiments) equipped with 756 launchers and approximately 3635 nuclear warheads mounted on stationary and mobile systems (rail or road). The mobile systems, with no equivalent in other nuclear powers, are harder to detect, and more survivable for it, and therefore are the main foundation of the counter-value retaliatory strike mission.[27] Control and management of the SMF rests with the Central Command Post of the SMF, located in Vlasikha, near Moscow. A new underground command and control centre has been built in Kosvinski Mountain in the Ural Mountains.[28] Final authority for the employment of nuclear weapons rests with the Supreme Commander of Russia's Armed Forces (President).

The SMF currently comprises around 100 000 troops. Nearly all of these troops are highly trained officers who hold advanced degrees and who have been screened for reliability prior to acceptance into the SMF. The integration has allowed the SMF to increase manpower in some combat units and formations by 20–25 per cent, bringing them to full strength. Chronic budgetary shortfalls in recent years have made life of SMF personnel quite difficult and this has resulted in an increased number of early retirements and even suicides. Nevertheless, in spite of hardships, such as dramatically lower real wages which are not even paid in time, service in the SMF is still considered to be prestigious and there is still ongoing high competition for places in the SMF educational establishments.

The defensive component of the SMF (the former Missile Space Forces and Missile Space Defence) has about 21 000 personnel, 100 anti-ballistic missiles, a number of satellites and up to 20 related radar sites, including some sites newly constructed in former Soviet republics which are now independent states (Belarus, Azerbaijan, and Kazakhstan). This defensive component has been redesignated as the 3rd Independent Army of Missile Space Defence. According to an official source, the space orbital group of the integrated SMF consists of about 130 satellites of different types, of which about 80 are for military purposes.[29]

The space reconnaissance assets of the SMF are reported by many sources to be in very bad condition, and some specialists have called on the government to take emergency measures to prevent their total collapse.[30] One military writer reported in February 1999 that some 40 per cent of space intelligence assets are less than fully operational.[31] The rate of replacement of orbiting satellites had dropped more than five-fold to 1998, and some 68 per cent of satellites in use had outlived their rated life of type (compared with 45 per cent in 1992).[32] Still, the process of replacement of obsolescent military satellites is underway, though at a relatively slow rate. In July 1999, Colonel-General Anatoly Sitnov, Chief of Armaments of Russia's Armed Forces, announced that in 1999 the Russian MoD is planning to acquire 10 military satellites.[33] The launch facility at Baikonur is essentially obsolete, and the fact that it is in the newly independent state of Kazakhstan provides significant complexities in its operation. By 1997, 22 separate agreements had been signed with Kazakhstan to govern the operation by Russia of the facility, and at least nine major problems remained under negotiation.[34] Russia will retain control over Baikonur until at least 2004, but until then it will be administered by the Russian National Space Agency. The armed forces will retain control over the launch facilities on Russian territory at Plesetsk and Svobodny, a new facility in the Far East. All military satellites will be launched from these two facilities after Russia leaves Baikonur.[35]

In spite of these difficulties, the Commander of the SMF claimed that in 1998 the space assets of the Ministry of Defence completed all of their assigned tasks, including early warning regimes.[36] The SMF launched 12 military satellites and 13 civil satellites for the National Space Agency in 1998.[37] This information is credible given economies and external earnings that had been achieved by the appropriate authorities.[38]

The SMF is seen in Russia as a low expenditure security guarantee, taking only 6–8 per cent of the defence budget. The personnel of the SMF constitute less than 10 per cent of the overall strength of Russian military power, but it is the most cost-effective service within the armed forces. The SMF is the main element of Russia's strategic nuclear shield, providing about 50 per cent of the warheads and strategic delivery systems of Russia's total strategic nuclear forces. The SMF would be assigned to carry out the majority of Russia's strategic nuclear missions during war: they would be assigned at least 50 per cent of the combat tasks of Russia's nuclear triad in a retaliatory counter-value strike (*otvetnyi udar*) and up to 90 per cent in a counter-force strike (*otvetno-vstrechnyi udar*).[39] As a result of arms control negotiations and associated decisions, even if the START–II Treaty is not ratified, more than half of Russia's nuclear strategic capabilities will be concentrated in the sea-based component of the national nuclear triad, thus reducing the total stock of warheads of the land-based SMF down to approximately 35 per cent of Russia's total.

Some specialists have speculated about rapidly deteriorating control over Russia's nuclear arsenal and warned about the possibility of an unauthorised launch.[40] Russia's Defence Minister, Igor Rodionov, has even warned that the country faced a breakdown of its nuclear control systems.[41] The main dangers in contemplation in the popular press are that the service conditions or personal psychological conditions of the personnel may be so bad, or the equipment so old and so poorly maintained, that an unsanctioned launch could occur. However, these speculations have been vigorously denied by senior Russian military staff on several occasions. The readiness levels and security regimes in the SMF were assessed in June 1997 by their commander as reliable and up to the required standard.[42] At the end of 1998, the SMF combat readiness was assessed as very high (92 per cent).[43] There are a number of measures in place to prevent unsanctioned launch, including a system of monitoring of each regiment by two others.[44] These positive assessments have on occasions been supported by some of their US counterparts. The Commander-in-Chief of the US Strategic Command, General Eugene Habinger, told journalists that the Russian system of operational control of strategic missiles and nuclear warheads is 'as reliable as the American system', after he inspected some Russian nuclear facilities in 1998.[45] The maintenance and personnel standards in the Russian forces will need to be monitored for possible deterioration. Yet the main threat of accidental nuclear war probably remains the difficulties associated with the strict launch-on-warning protocols in the Russian (and US) forces which provide less than 15 minutes for the determination that a suspected nuclear strike by the other country is genuine.[46] Another concern about the Russian strategic nuclear force is that controls over unauthorised launch in the submarine fleet are weaker than for land-based systems: the 'General Staff cannot continuously monitor the status of the crew and missiles or use electronic links to override unauthorised launches'.[47] In February 1999, the US State Department expressed concerns about the reduced coverage by Russian early warning satellites, and suggested that Russian commanders aware of the reduced coverage might try to overcompensate in their assessment of any questionable event by assuming it to be an actual attack but without the capacity to verify it as such.[48]

Another problem for Russia's strategic nuclear forces is that most combat control and targeting systems for the SMF have been produced by Ukrainian enterprises (the *Iuzhmash* industrial complex and the Khartron firm).[49] Even some of Russia's currently operational missiles, such as RS–20 and RS–22,[49] were completely designed and produced by the Ukrainian enterprises.[51] To be dependent for strategic nuclear missile supply on another state, even a friendly one, is strategically inadmissible for Russia. But in the case of Ukraine, Russia's relations with it are far from good, so this dependency is totally unacceptable to Russia. Consequently, Russia is concentrating on both extension of service for ageing missiles, and the domestic development of a new-generation ballistic missile. Some politicians have made suggestions about the development of a Russian-made multiple warhead ICBM. However, this proposition was rejected by General Vladimir Yakovlev, because such a project would require 9–11 billion roubles and five to seven years for completion, circumstances which would be too demanding for the Russian economy, and not acceptable to the SMF.[52] Therefore, Russia has given priority to developing the same type of single-warhead silo missile.

Funding released from the integration of the three structures into a unified SMF has already allowed the SMF to finish the program of tests and start serial production of a new missile— the modernised RS–12M *Topol-M*[53] ICBM in early 1998. On 25 December 1997, the first two new *Topol* missiles were put on experimental combat duty in the 60th Red Banner Tamanskaia Division of the SMF, deployed in Tatishevo near Saratov.[54] They replaced ageing SS–19 ICBMs. On 30 December 1998, the 104th Missile Regiment of the 60th Missile Division of the 27th Vladimir Missile Army equipped with ten *Topols* was placed on combat duty—an event rightly regarded by many as one of the most remarkable achievements of the Russian armed forces in recent times.[55] On 22 October 1998, one of the *Topol* missiles exploded after being launched in a test firing, but a subsequent test flight in December 1998 was successful.[56] Another ten *Topol* missiles are likely to delivered and deployed in 1999. It is expected that research and design work will continue to raise the combat parameters of the new system and to train personnel in its combat use. The service life of a new missile is expected to be 20–25 years. Some Russian specialists claim that the missile is capable of penetrating any type of ABM defences, including those that are under development in the USA.[57]

Given inadequate financing and current capabilities of Russia's defence industries, the SMF will deploy the new system gradually. First of all, *Topol-M* will replace 270 silo-based SS–17, SS–18, SS–19 and SS–24 multiple-warhead ICBMs. Only 30 per cent of the planned production of the new missiles will be fitted into silos. After the year 2000, a road-mobile version of *Topol-M* will be put into service and up to 350 units of this type are expected to be deployed.[58] According to General Yakovlev, some 3.7 billion roubles are required to complete the *Topol-M* program. If the program is funded to this level, the SMF will be able to re-equip two or three regiments each year with new system by 2001, and three or four after 2001.[59] Two US specialists suggest that a more realistic rate might be one or two regiments (10–15 missiles) per year.[60] Serial production of the *Topol-M* system and its introduction in the SMF will allow the Russian military to complete the process of rationalisation and standardisation of the various types of missiles within the force.

The posture of Russia's nuclear forces has been heavily influenced by a number of arms control agreements initiated during the Soviet era. After a number of agreements during the Cold War to place ceilings on strategic nuclear weapons, the USSR and the USA began to move toward reduction of the nuclear arsenals. The first Strategic Arms Reduction Treaty (START–I) was signed in 1991 and subsequently required ratification and compliance from three new states (Belarus, Ukraine and Kazakhstan) as well as Russia. START–I has been fully implemented. On 17 June 1992,

Russia and the USA signed an agreement to eliminate heavy ICBMs and all other ICBMs with multiple warheads. Under this agreement, the two countries would cut their total number of warheads from the 6000 allowed under START–I to 3500 (or 3000).[61] In 1993, Russia and the USA signed the second treaty for reduction of strategic weapons, START–II, which provided for reduction of the number of warheads of the sides to 3800 and 4250 respectively by 1 January 2003. However, a further agreement signed in 1997 (the New York Protocol) has postponed the final achievement of START–II targets until 31 December 2007. According to START–II, Russia has to scrap all its multiple warhead ICBMs, and re-arm its 105 mobile SS–25 ICBMs with single warheads.[62] Within its START–II limit of 3800 warheads, Russian sources estimate that the country may keep operational between 500 and 800 single-warhead ICBMs, about 1750 warheads on multiple-warhead submarine-launched ballistic missiles (SLBMs) in some 20–25 strategic missile submarines, and the rest on strategic bombers. (Russia in 1998 had 806 warheads allocated to bombers). US specialists estimate that Russia's entire strategic nuclear force by 2010 or 2015 may have only 1300 to 2400 warheads, or even fewer.[63] (The START–II limit is 3800.)

The START–II Treaty has been ratified by the US Senate but has not yet been ratified by Russia's State Duma. Many Russian parliamentarians consider START–II an unequal treaty disadvantageous to Russia. The ratification delay reflects public opinion in Russia, which sees the treaty as offering several marked concessions to the USA and not taking into account Russia's economic difficulties in changing the structure of its strategic nuclear force.[64] The implementation of the START–II Treaty will change the whole appearance of Russia's nuclear shield, with a substantial shift from ground-based to sea-based nuclear forces. It will require eliminating or disarming all multiple warhead ICBMs (Russia's main strategic striking force) and the destruction of most of Russia's SS–18 silos at a great expense, while allowing the USA to retain its multiple warhead SLBMs (its main strategic force).[65]

Nevertheless, the Russian military leadership, in particular those in the SMF, strongly favour the ratification of START–II. They argue that the implementation of START–I leaves the US strategic forces with obvious superior striking capabilities. The realisation of START–II will reduce this gap. Besides, Russian military experts argue that regardless of the ratification status of START–II, Russia will not be able to maintain parity with the

USA at the levels allowed in START–I. For example, Head of the International Military Cooperation Directorate, Rear-Admiral Valentin Kuznetsov, has argued that even without ratifying START–II Russia will have to cut down its nuclear forces due to growing obsolescence: 'The existing MIRVed ICBMs and heavy ICBMs are subject to liquidation not so much because of the START–II Treaty, but as the result of the expiration not simply of their rated life of type, but the expiration of their extended periods of service.'[66] The service life of some 60 per cent of Russian ICBMs has already expired.[67] By the end of 2007, of today's 756 launchers, only about 250 launchers with 250 warheads will remain fit for combat duty. Others will not survive the 25-year-long life, which considerably exceeds the rated service life of 10 to 15 years. Given the highest possible build-up rate of the SMF armaments with the help of the new-generation cheap missiles and missiles with expired service lives, only 700 single-warhead ICBMs can be preserved in the SMF with as many warheads, and this is compatible with START II limits. It is still uncertain whether the navy will be able to maintain the required numbers of SSBNs, though the introduction of a new MIRVed SLBM system and the launch of a new class of SSBN might improve the overall situation slightly.[68] In October 1998, the Defence Committee of the State Duma, in cooperation with Ministry of Defence officials, drafted a new law which would prevent the SMF from falling victim to new budget pressures within the armed forces as a whole by identifying new SMF expenditures separately and mandating their allocation only for the SMF.[69] This legislation was premised on the crisis that Russia now faces in replacing its strategic forces even at START–II levels.

Therefore, the main argument of the Russian military leadership is that Russia should ratify START–II as soon as possible in order to restrain US nuclear capabilities at levels roughly comparable to what Russia can afford to field. They are also pressing for the signing and ratification of a START–III Treaty which would reduce nuclear arsenals of both sides down to 2000–2500 warheads. They also insist that Russia must reorient START–III negotiations to seek a further reduction in the number of warheads from 2000–2500 to 1000 or at most, 1500 warheads by the year 2007. This is the level that will be reached by Russia's strategic nuclear force. Even under START–III limits, Russia would retain massive retaliation capability against 50–100 economic centres in US territory.[70] Moreover, apart from losing the opportunity to lock the USA into nuclear parity with Russia, a refusal to ratify the START–II Treaty would have more damaging political consequences, with the USA and its European allies becoming increasingly suspicious of Russia's stand on the issue of nuclear disarmament. (Even when START–II obligations are fulfilled, Russia will have two to four times as many warheads as China, France and Britain combined.)[71]

Even after the ratification of the START–II and possibly START–III treaties, the SMF will continue to play a central role in Russian military posture. It will remain to be seen whether the mounting international opinion in favour of abolition of nuclear weapons and the 1995 decision by the International Court of Justice that parties to the Nuclear Non-Proliferation Treaty had an obligation to work toward their abolition[72] will eventually be felt in Russia (and the USA). One of Russia's well known and respected strategic analysts, Sergei Rogov, has dismissed this possibility as less likely than a long-term continuation of the status quo.[73] One of the most serious ironies of the new world nuclear order is that Russia was forced to sell the USA 500 tonnes of weapons grade plutonium to obtain US financial assistance to destroy its surplus nuclear warheads.[74]

AIR COMPONENT OF THE TRIAD

The airborne component of the Russian strategic deterrent forces (strategic bombers) traditionally appeared to be the least developed in terms of numerical strength or stockpile of nuclear warheads. Stalin's desire to create a powerful Soviet strategic bomber force had initially resulted in the intensive development of state-of-the-art aircraft in the early 1950s (M–4 *Bison*, Tu–95 *Bear*). However, the Kruschev era inflicted incredible damage on the technological levels of Soviet strategic aviation. Kruschev's obstinate belief in the power of ballistic missiles led to the reallocation of billions of roubles to the missile programs that could have paid for bombers. Only later did the Soviet leadership realise the importance of having considerable airborne strategic forces, or Long-Range Aviation (LRA),[75] as a strategic component of the Soviet air forces. An enormous effort was made by the USSR to develop and maintain an appropriate force of strategic bombers but it did not manage to reach the same level that the USA possessed during the Cold War and continued to enjoy at the end of the 1990s.

The collapse of the USSR further decreased the capacity of

the country's strategic bomber force. Its strength has fallen by over 20 000 men in the past five years[76] and a considerable number of the LRA's modern aircraft fell into the hands of the military of two of the newly independent states which were former Soviet republics. Two large groupings of the former Soviet LRA were based on the territory of Kazakhstan and Ukraine. As part of its claims to control the entire Soviet 'nuclear' heritage, Russia demanded the return of all strategic bombers based in these two new countries. After intensive negotiations, the Russian government came to an agreement with its Kazakh counterpart. As a result, the 40 *Bear*-H bombers (27 *Bear*-H6s and 13 *Bear*-H16s) were withdrawn to Russia, along with some 370 AS–15 ALCM warheads, in exchange for Russia's assistance to create Kazakhstan's, own armed forces. The successful transfer of nuclear systems and weapons (including strategic bombers) from Kazakhstan to Russia can be largely explained by the pro-Russian orientation of the Kazakhstan government, especially in the military sphere, at the time.

However, Ukraine became a serious obstacle. With the declaration of Ukraine's independence, a considerable number of modern strategic bombers were 'privatised' by the Ukrainian armed forces. That included the 184th Heavy Bomber Regiment (Priluki air base) equipped with 19 Tu–160 *Blackjack* bombers, and the 182nd Heavy Bomber Regiment (Uzin Air Base) with 27 Tu–95 aircraft.[77] Up until 1997 there was still hope that the Ukrainian bombers (or, as was later stated, some of them) would be transferred to Russia. The Russian side offered 12 MiG–29 and Su–27 fighters plus several transport planes as an exchange. However, political manoeuvres by Ukrainian nationalists during the previous six years, and ultimately the incredibly poor condition of the bombers, destroyed any chance of a resolution of the issue in Russia's favour. By 1997, Russia's former Air Force Commander General Pyotr Deinekin strongly objected to the transfer of the Ukrainian strategic bombers due to their bad condition.[78] Besides, an announcement in 1998 by the Secretary of the Ukrainian National Security and Defence Council, Vladimir Gorbulin, approving the liquidation of strategic bombers based in his country, made the prospect of the transfer of even small numbers of the aircraft seem quite remote.[79]

However, by mid-1999, the possibility of the transfer of some Ukrainian strategic bombers to Russia had changed dramatically. After an intensive period of consultations, it was announced that Ukraine is likely to transfer 8 Tu–160s and 2 Tu–95Ms to Russia as a form of partial compensation for Ukraine's $2 billion debt for Russia's gas. Russian pilots and engineers had already examined the aircraft and found them in working condition. If the transfer goes ahead, 10 bombers will be sent to the 22nd Bomber Division (Engels).[80]

If the transfer deal with Ukraine is accomplished, Russia's LRA capability will be significantly improved, since the Russian Air Force at present has only a limited number of operational strategic bombers capable of delivering airborne nuclear strikes. In 1994, two LRA armies, the 46th (HQ Smolensk) and the 30th (HQ Irkutsk) were disbanded, and the LRA shifted to a divisional structure. In late 1998, Russia's strategic bomber force comprised 75 aircraft and 816 nuclear warheads,[81] compared with 70 aircraft and 806 warheads in May 1999. The backbone of the LRA is the 22nd Guards Red Banner Donbass Heavy Bomber Division at the Engels Air Base (Saratov region). Its 121st Guards Regiment is equipped with six Tu–160 *Blackjack* strategic bombers, nicknamed by Russian pilots *Ilia Muromets*.[82] Apart from the *Blackjack* force, the LRA operates 29 *Bear*-H6 and 35 *Bear*-H16 heavy strategic bombers (Tu–95), all of which are capable of carrying cruise missiles for a total load of 800 missiles. Besides, it possesses 125 Tu–22M–3 intermediate-range bombers (plus 71 Tu–22Ms in the naval aviation), and 10 Tu–22M2/3 reconnaissance aircraft.[83] The tanker fleet consists of 20 Il–78 planes.

The warheads of the LRA are included in the 'Operational Plan of the Strategic Nuclear Forces of the Russian Federation', the basic document enumerating nuclear strikes in case of an all-out war. But in comparison with other assets of Russia's deterrent forces, the LRA has only a small number of warheads and its peacetime combat readiness is rather low. In case of nuclear war, the main strike was to be delivered by the SMF and the deployed SSBNs. Moreover, at the start of the 1990s, the USSR and the USA reached an agreement that their strategic bombers would stop flying along air borders of their 'potential enemy' with nuclear weapons embarked. Other major adjustments in national nuclear forces and the reorganisation of Russia's air forces have led to the formulation of new roles for the LRA. In March 1998, the newly appointed Commander of the LRA, Lieutenant-General Mikhail Oparin, underlined the main directions for development of Russia's strategic aviation for the next decade:

- maintenance of combat capacity at levels which will enable the LRA to fulfil its role in the national nuclear deterrence policy;

- adjusting LRA combat potential to the level which will allow the force in the shortest period of time to be ready to defend Russia's national interests and its security in continental or maritime theatres with the employment of conventional weapons; and
- substantial modernisation of operational aircraft, as well as the development of new-generation planes and systems.[84]

The pressures that led to the reorganisation of the air forces discussed in chapters 5 and 8 also resulted in changes to the structure of the LRA. By 1 May 1998, the LRA was reorganised into the 37th Strategic Air Army of the Supreme High Command.[85] However, due to its small size, the main change occurred in the command structure, with the Command of the LRA being reorganised into the Directorate of the Strategic Air Army within the administrative structure of the Air Force.[86] The control and management of the reorganised LRA from now on will be carried out from the Main Command Post of the integrated air force near Balashikha (Moscow region). The transfer of the command and control functions of the airborne component of Russia's nuclear triad was closely monitored by Russia's military leadership, which is another confirmation of how important for Moscow are its strategic nuclear forces.

Organisationally, the 37th Air Army of the Supreme High Command currently consists of two heavy bomber divisions, the 22nd Division based in Engels in western Russia and the 73rd Division based in Ukrainka (Amur Province) in eastern Russia. The 22nd Division comprises the 121st and 182nd Bomber Regiments and the 213th Guards Regiment of aerial tankers.[87] The 73rd Division comprises two Tu–95MS regiments (probably 123rd and 126th), redeployed to Ukrainka from Semipalatinsk in Kazakhstan.[88]

Some reductions have taken place. The unstable situation in the Caucasus, especially the continuing threat posed by Chechnia, forced the Russian command in May 1998 to close down one of Russia's largest LRA bases, the Mozdok Air Base, situated only 50 km from the Chechen border. In early February 1998, the Air Force Commander, Colonel-General Anatoly Kornukov, while inspecting the base, raised doubts about the necessity of having a strategic bomber base in the troubled region.[89] As it was announced, all combat-ready Tu–95 planes of the 182nd Regiment based before in Mozdok were to be relocated to the Engels Air Base.[90] The remaining aircraft were to be scrapped or canabalised for spare parts. The stockpile of 316 nuclear warheads in Mozdok has been transferred to different LRA facilities in Russia.

By the year 2000, 204 Russian bombers will have been destroyed, with as many as 134 of these decommissioned as a result of obsolescence, and only 70 destroyed as part of compliance with the Conventional Forces in Europe Treaty. The bombers remaining in the force can stay in service for another 20 or so years.[91] Nevertheless, Russia's LRA command anticipates the need to replace the ageing Tu–95MC and Tu–22M3 bombers after the year 2010 with a new-generation aircraft.[92]

In June 1997, General Deinekin announced that Russia is developing 'in tight secrecy' a new long-range aircraft which will replace the strategic bombers Tu–95 and Tu–160.[93] That information was confirmed this year by the new commander of the integrated RFAF, Colonel-General Anatoly Kornukov, who said in an interview with the armed forces newspaper *Krasnaia zvezda* that a decision has been made about the development of a new bomber.[94] Russian planners hope that the new bomber will be a subsonic aircraft which will incorporate Russian-developed 'Stealth' technology, and will be fielded after the year 2005.[95] However, in the near future, the air force and the LRA will focus their efforts on the radical modernisation of the Tu–95 and Tu–160. In particular, they will be re-equipped with new-generation 'smart' weapons systems (air-to-surface missiles, a unit such as the Kh–101 strategic cruise missile) under development.

There is also a possibility of the resumption of Tu–160 production, which had ceased in 1992. This assumption is based on the fact that in 1997 preparatory work began on restoration of the production line in the Kazan aviation plant.[96] In 1999, the Russian Air Force will finally receive one Tu–160, a unit which was under construction in Kazan at the time of the plant closure.[97]

Constant shortage of funds has resulted in the postponing or even cancelling of some expensive development programs for new aircraft and the concentration of funds on modernisation of aircraft already in service. This policy choice was evident in the decision by the Russian Federation Air Force (RFAF) to postpone the development of an 80-tonne intermediate-range bomber by the Sukhoi design bureau, known in the West as the T–60S program. Instead, the RFAF reallocated funds to the radical upgrade of the Tu–22M–3 fleet.[98] The early-model Tu–22M–2 *Backfire-B* will not be included in the program.[99] The Tu–22M–3 will receive new radar and missile systems, plus a terrain-following/terrain-avoidance capability to allow automatic flight at low level. This will permit the retention of the modernised *Backfire* in service until the year 2020. The decision to concentrate on the modernisation of the *Backfire-C* is the result of the new interest in the missions it might be able to carry out. With the likely ratification of START–II, Russia will have to increase its bomber force to maintain strategic parity with the USA. With the country's current inability to produce enough new bombers, more effective use of all types of existing LRA operational aircraft is essential. Russia has considerably more such bombers than the total number of comparable aircraft in China and France taken together. At a time when the Russian strategic bomber force is suffering from small numbers of operational aircraft, the fleet of Tu–22M–3s has become a major component of Russia's strategic nuclear forces.

The other major task facing the LRA is to maintain adequate levels of combat readiness of its forces, as well as high professionalism of its personnel. And here the LRA has faced the same problems as the RFAF as a whole: limits of fuel and, as a result, low flying hours for pilots;[199] constant problems with spare parts for aircraft and auxiliary equipment; and outflow of qualified pilots (especially at the rank of plane commander).

Nevertheless, it would be too soon to talk about the incapacity of the LRA to perform its missions. As the result of reorganisation, the LRA has managed to bring into working condition 90 per cent of all listed Tu–95MS, Tu–160, and Tu–22M–3 aircraft.[101] Apart from that, the intensity of combat training increased in 1998. For example, during a command-and-staff exercise held by the LRA commander in the Donbass heavy bomber division, pilots conducted more than 40 combat sorties, with two Tu–160s performing ultra-long-range flight to the North Pole area.[102] And later in the year, a large-scale, three-day exercise, headed by General Oparin, involved practically all units and formations of the 37th Air Army, plus a fleet of Il–78 in-flight refuellers and fighter units.[103] The environment of the exercise was designed to reproduce combat conditions as far as can be done. As the result of intensified training, the 37th Air Army was considered to be one of the best formations of the integrated RFAF in 1998.[104]

A NEW STRATEGIC COMMAND FOR RUSSIA

Toward the end of 1998, a proposal for the subordination of the strategic nuclear forces (ICBM, SLBM and bomber force) to a unified operational command authority was floated by the

Figure 6.1 Organisation chart: Unified Command Strategic Deterrent Forces

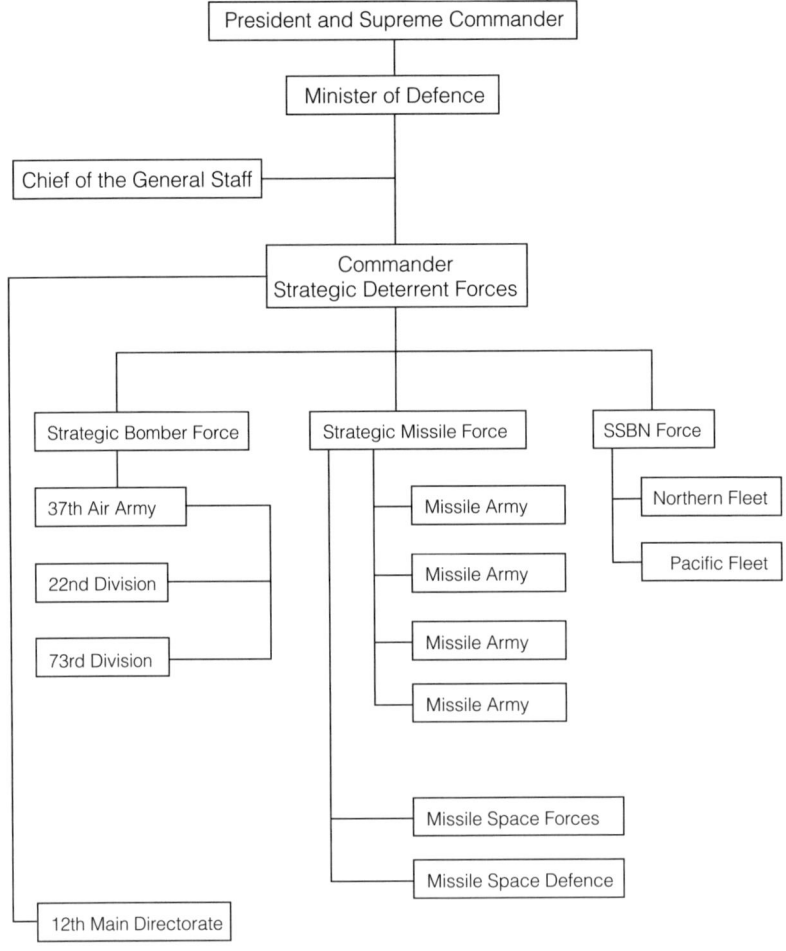

Minister of Defence with a view to its implementation after a discussion period. The new command would be designated as the Unified Command of the Strategic Deterrent Forces (OGK SSS after its title in Russian).[105] The proposal would involve loss of operational command authority for these forces from the three single services (SMF, navy and RFAF), which would retain other training and support functions. In 1991, Gorbachev had ordered a similar move. The proposed command line for the new forces is shown in Figure 6.1.

The 1998 proposal aroused sharp criticism within the policy community and the armed forces, primarily on the grounds that it would deny the single services (navy and RFAF) appropriate control over the assets they were responsible for fielding and heighten the propensity for Russia to consider a nuclear option. These arguments are somewhat spurious, since the measure involves only operational subordination and it would reduce the risk of unauthorised release of nuclear weapons. The proposed new command is modelled on the US Strategic Command and most in the defence policy community support it. Sergei Rogov has supported it as an important means of ensuring Russia has a second-strike response capacity.[106] But like many other projects, lack of financing has brought a halt to all work on the proposal, which had already been set in train toward implementation in February 1999.[107] President Yeltsin has approved the plan, so it will almost certainly be implemented eventually.

TACTICAL NUCLEAR WEAPONS

By February 1993, Russia announced its compliance with a promise made by President Gorbachev in 1991 to remove all tactical nuclear weapons from naval vessels, the number of such weapons having been estimated by Western sources at around 3600.[108] The Russian action matched a similar pledge by the USA.

Russian military leaders retain a wide variety of options for the employment of tactical nuclear weapons. As recently as 29 April 1999, the Security Council met to consider Russia's policy on this issue and others, and Yeltsin signed a decree reaffirming the country's concept for the development and use of non-strategic nuclear weapons.[109] This concept has not been published, but President Yeltsin has declared that Russia would only use nuclear weapons as an unavoidable last resort in cases of a critical threat to the national security of Russia or its allies [*v kachestve vynuzhdennoi krainei mery presecheniia kriticheskikh ugroz*].[110] The main use of tactical nuclear weapons is probably for defeating large groupings of enemy forces.[111] Russian forces continue to exercise for limited use of nuclear missiles for theatre purposes, usually to defeat an enemy invasion force. According to a Russian specialist, the country had about 10 000 tactical nuclear weapons in 1998.[112]

Russia may deploy tactical nuclear weapons along its western borders to counter the shift in the balance of forces on the Western front. In 1995, the Russian Institute for Defence Studies prepared a study entitled 'Conceptual Theses for a Strategy Countering the Principal External Threats to the National Security of the Russian Federation', which proposed to deploy Russian tactical nuclear weapons to the Western, Northwestern and Southwestern theatres of military operations to neutralise the threat coming from NATO's expansion.[113] Russian foreign minister Primakov emphasised that nuclear weapons will never appear on Belarussian territory 'in the absence of any threat of aggression against our two countries'.[114] However, the obvious implication was that if Russia considered itself threatened, it would deploy nuclear weapons in Belarus.

Russian specialists have proposed the development of new tactical nuclear weapons if NATO continues to expand in ways Russia regards as unacceptable. Options for Russia include restoring its arsenal of missiles of the *Pioneer* and *Oka* types, which were scrapped under the 1987 treaty on the elimination of intermediate range nuclear forces, and developing new-generation battlefield nuclear arms with relatively low capacity and reduced blast effects. Russian sources are also reporting that the new program for development policy does not rule out the possibility of developing new tactical nuclear warheads for the *Iskandr* tactical missile system, which is being built to replace the *Scud*.[115] These sources estimate that Russia could manufacture 10 000 'high-safety' small nuclear warheads for surface-to-surface missile, air assault and air defence.[116] Such programs could use material obtained from nuclear warheads dismantled under the START–I and START–II treaties. It is quite likely that some types of the proposed weaponry already exist. In 1995, Aleksei Yablokov, chairman of the Security Council's environmental commission, testified at parliamentary hearings that miniature nuclear weapons weighed 30 to 40 kilograms, whereas a spokesman for the Russian Ministry of Defence responded that the minimum weight of such warheads was 90 kilograms, thus acknowledging their existence.[117]

CONCLUSION

Russia has made important improvements in its strategic nuclear forces, both through the successful entry into service of the *Topol* missile and through significant structural reform. Budget support remains problematic, but relative to the cost of general purpose forces, the nuclear forces are not a great burden. Through the strategic arms limitation process, Russia will remain a nuclear power nominally on parity with the USA, and clearly well ahead of China, France and the UK. Since Russia does not have the wealth and economic cohesion to match unrestrained US strategic nuclear development, it will want to rely on the arms limitation and reduction process to lock the USA into parity with it. There has been a strengthening of interest in the armed forces of the great powers in the prospect of eliminating nuclear weapons, but for reasons of cost, and since Russia cannot afford the substitutes (high-precision conventional weapons), Russia will continue to stake its military security on nuclear weapons.

There is considerable room for concern about the shift in Russian strategic doctrine to greater reliance on nuclear weapons. The threshold for use of these weapons in war has been substantially lowered. The main saving grace is that no nuclear weapons power is likely to pose a threat to Russia in the medium term and no neighbouring state, save China, is likely to be able to mass enough forces to prompt Russia to that resort. And China has moved decisively away from policies of confrontation with Russia. There must also be concern about the security of the launch procedures for Russian weapons and of the warheads or fissionable materials, given the general deterioration in conditions in the armed forces as a whole. Russian military leaders have assured the world that they are being vigilant, and one can trust the commitment of the Russian military leadership to the principles and standards of security required. The simple reality is, though, that they do not have sufficient control or incentive mechanisms in place, and national loyalties have been so fractured, that some significant proliferation incident or unauthorised or inadvertent nuclear launch accident is, on the balance of probability, only a matter of time. If there is no reversal of the decline in the funding and state of the armed forces, then this probability will increase through the decade.

7

Naval forces

The use of Russian ground troops or air forces as an instrument of Russian strategic policy beyond its borders carries some risk of escalation to war. By contrast, use of naval power presents lower risk opportunities for power projection because of the freedom of movement of warships on the high seas, their associated international visibility, and the operational flexibility that naval forces can offer. For these reasons, Russia's military presence in the Asia–Pacific and its power projection capabilities there are largely identified with the Pacific Fleet which has, for nearly a century, sailed the Western Pacific Ocean in support of the country's political and military interests.[1]

While Russia or the USSR was certainly a keen competitor, it was never a dominant naval power in the Pacific. For nearly 50 years the USA has dominated, having defeated the powerful Japanese navy in the Second World War and having supplanted the British and the French naval presences as they surrendered their colonies in Asia. But within 20 years of the end of the war the US pre-eminence came under challenge. Beginning in 1965, the Soviet Pacific Fleet emerged as the largest and strongest single fleet in the Soviet Navy, to the point where within two decades it was able to challenge the dominance of the US Navy (USN) in the Pacific. Other Soviet maritime activities, especially fishing and shipping, began to expand correspondingly.[2]

Soviet naval posture in the Pacific stemmed from the desire to become a world maritime power. During the 1970s and 1980s, Western analysts had, by and large, reached a consensus which looked to constant and stable development of a strong Pacific Fleet. The unexpected collapse of the USSR brought confusion and disagreement as these analysts sought to reorganise their views on Pacific maritime security. In 1993, Ken Booth captured the new view on the future of Russian naval power, one which has since gained ground: 'The retreat from the global oceans by the Soviet Navy was well on course when the Soviet state collapsed, and there is no obvious reason why the Russian Kremlin should change the calculations'.[3] Booth saw the end result of the 'break-up, sales, and retrenchment' as leaving the Russian Navy a shadow of its Soviet predecessor. Similarly, a leading Indian strategic analyst, Jasjit Singh, described the Russian Navy of the 1990s as a force with extremely limited power projection capabilities.[4]

However, competing views on Russian naval power in the Pacific emerged at the same time, and these saw less of a 'retreat' and more of a continuity despite the upheavals in the country. US Admiral R. J. Kelly, at that time Commander-in-Chief of the US Pacific Fleet, observed in 1993 that, although the Russian Navy is out of the 'business of influencing world events with naval power . . . from a capability standpoint, they can still project power anywhere in Asian waters'.[5] He explained Russia's desire to stay engaged in Pacific affairs primarily by reference to its economic interests: 'The wealth of their country lies in Siberia and along the eastern shoreline. Years of industrialisation have exhausted most of the resources of the European side of the country, while on the Pacific side, vast deposits of minerals and oil lie untapped.' Prominent Australian maritime affairs specialist Commodore Sam Bateman, also writing in 1993, agreed: 'It seems likely . . . that the residual need for maritime forces will be particularly strong in Eastern Russia, with the likely outcome that the Russian Pacific Fleet will emerge as the most elite of all the Russian fleets with a concentration of professional expertise and the better ships and submarines'.[6]

This chapter will review the development of Russian naval power in the Pacific since 1991. It concludes that Russia has the potential to play a bigger role in Pacific affairs using its naval forces than some analysts have been prepared to admit. The chapter also documents trends in order of battle, budget support for the fleet, and operational readiness of its forces—trends which highlight the constraints on Russia's use of its Pacific Fleet both for power projection in peacetime and for sustained combat operations in war.

FROM SOVIET FLEET TO RUSSIAN FLEET: STRATEGIES, MISSIONS AND FORCES

By the time of the collapse of the USSR, the Pacific Fleet appeared the strongest of the four Soviet fleets: only the Northern Fleet came close to approximating its power. These two fleets each had two aircraft carriers, and together they supported the Soviet nuclear-powered ballistic missile submarine force. The Pacific Fleet, however, had more major surface combatants, large amphibious ships, mine warfare ships and approximately 28 per cent of the total aircraft inventory of the Soviet Navy. It had the largest contingent of naval infantry of the four fleets. These forces, with high level training similar to that of special forces, were assigned for support of Soviet political interests in the unstable states on the shores of the Pacific and Indian Oceans.[7] The Fleet had access to Vietnamese ports, and thus could station naval ships and supplies in Southeast Asia, improving the strength and speed of responses to changes of situation in the Indian Ocean.[8] This presence gave the USSR the capacity to project military power into the Pacific theatre[9] beyond its historic area of influence.

But the qualitative and quantitative improvement of naval forces in the Pacific after 1965 had been undertaken for other reasons. Soviet strategists had first sought forward deployments of the navy away from coastal waters in response to US deployment of nuclear-powered ballistic missile submarines (SSBNs) in the northern reaches of the Indian Ocean.[10] This deployment of the *Polaris* naval strategic nuclear missile system by the USA acted as a catalyst for accelerated development of ocean-going ships by the USSR to counter the threat. For the Pacific Fleet, this resulted in the deployment of its own SSBN force in the 1970s which targeted the United States, and surface forces to protect these SSBNs. These surface units included as centrepieces two *Kiev* class aircraft capable cruisers, *Minsk* and *Novorossiisk* deployed in 1979 and 1984 respectively, and the *Kirov* class heavy nuclear-powered missile cruiser *Frunze* deployed in 1985.[11] As Michael MccGwire has suggested, Soviet leaders came to attach new strategic importance to their Far East region as a result of the build-up of the Pacific Fleet and the progressive deployment in it of strategic nuclear submarines.[12]

In early 1992, immediately after the collapse of the USSR, the former Pacific Fleet was officially declared to be an asset of the combined forces of the Commonwealth of Independent States (CIS), but its location within Russia and the predominance of Russian personnel in it effectively made it a Russian fleet, and when the Russian armed forces were established in 1992 the CIS Pacific Fleet was renamed as the Russian Pacific Fleet.[13] Initially representing a sizeable portion of the entire ex-Soviet Navy, the Pacific Fleet has changed dramatically in its appearance and composition since 1992. In May of that year, when the Russian armed forces were established, the strength of the Pacific Fleet's conventional forces stood at 90 attack submarines, 45 large surface combatants, 380 small surface combatants, and 150 strike aircraft.[14] By May 1992, the headquarters of the fleet had been moved ashore and the flagship, *Admiral Seniavin*, had been removed from the order of battle.[15] At the same time, and as a sign of the changing times, the first public relations officer was appointed to the fleet.

Facing new economic realities and political objectives, the numbers of ships and personnel have been reduced by more than half. (Table 7.1 shows changes in the composition of the Pacific Fleet between 1990 and 1998.)

Even if Russia wanted to maintain its Soviet-era naval might, the national economy has been in no condition to support that task. During the Soviet era, the naval share of the defence budget was about 20 per cent, but by 1996 under the Russian government, the share had been cut to approximately 14 per cent[16] and the allocations actually flowing to the navy represented only 25 per cent of its requirements.[17] By 1996, the financing for naval ship-building had been slashed drastically, leading to a 60 per cent reduction in warship construction.[18]

Budget problems have been exacerbated by lack of easy access to repair facilities. The only major shipyard in the Far East is in the inland city of Komsomolsk on the Amur River, which is primarily a submarine construction facility, and the capacity of other local repair facilities is limited. The overwhelming majority of Soviet naval shipyards were located in the European part of the country, including in Ukraine, where the navy's most important repair facilities were located.[19] Historically, and even today, most of the fleet's combatants were constructed in the western ship-yards and were then transferred to the Pacific. The Pacific Fleet lost its two carriers, the *Minsk* and the *Novorossiisk*, as a result of inability to maintain them. It also lost two cruisers sent to Ukraine in the late 1980s for overhaul but retained by Ukraine after the dissolution of the USSR.[20]

The reductions, the worsening situation with finances, and the problems with maintenance and combat training had a very substantial impact on the Pacific Fleet's performance and its capabilities. According to Admiral Mikhail Zakharenko in 1997, when he was the Chief of Staff of the fleet, it could no longer fulfil all the tasks that it had ten to fifteen years previously.[21]

But there is no reason now for the Russian Federation to

Table 7.1 Changes in composition of the Pacific Fleet surface force order of battle 1990–98

1990: 41 ships

Cruisers (16)

Kara class	Nikolayev, Petropavlovsk, Tallin, Tashkent
Kiev class	Minsk, Novorossiisk
Kirov class	Frunze
Kresta–I class	Vladivostok, Sevastopol
Kresta–II class	Admiral Oktiabrskii, Marshal Voroshilov, Vasilyi Chapayev
Kynda class	Admiral Fokin, Variag
Sverdlov class	Admiral Seniavin, Aleksandr Suvorov

Destroyers (14)

Kashin class	Odarionnyi, Steregushchii, Strogyi, Sposobnyi
Kotlin class	Skrytnyi, Vozbuzhdionnyi
Sovremennyi class	Boyevoi, Osmotritelnyi, Stoikii
Udaloi class	Admiral Spiridonov, Admiral Tributs, Admiral Vinogradov, Admiral Zakharov, Simpferopol

Frigates (11)

Krivak–I class	Letuchii, Poryvistyi, Razumnyi, Raziashchiskii, Retivyi, Storozhevoi
Krivak–II class	Gordelivyi, Groziashchii, Revnostnyi, Rezkii, Rianyi

1998: 18 ships

Cruisers (4)

Ushakov class	Admiral Lazarev (formerly Frunze)
Slava class	Variag
Kara class	Nikolayev, Petropavlovsk*

Destroyers (11)

Sovremenny class	Bezboiaznennyi, Boyevoi, Burnyi, Bystryi, Osmotritelnyi,,* Stoikii*
Udaloi class	Admiral Panteleyev, Admiral Spiridonov*, Admiral Tributs*, Admiral Vinogradov, Marshal Shaposhnikov

Frigates (3)

Krivak–I class	Letuchii, Razumnyi, Storozhevoi**

Notes: * denotes non-operational in reserve but officially enlisted; ** Apart from 3 Krivak-I FFGs there are 7 Krivak-III FFGs of the border service which can be mobilised to naval service during wartime

sustain its navy at the Cold War level and the sizeable reductions in the fleet's force should not be seen as necessarily representing an equally large deterioration of Russian naval power in the Pacific.

The Soviet Navy in general, and the Pacific Fleet in particular, had an impracticable variety of types of warships. For example, in 1990 the Pacific Fleet had about 13 types of major surface combatants and 20 types of submarines, many of which had been designed to perform similar tasks.[22] This variety of platforms can be explained not by military–strategic necessity but by the corporate interests of the Soviet military–industrial complex, backed up by the Soviet political leadership. The navy was practically forced to order different classes of ships, each of them with some different types of equipment. The navy sometimes received semi-ready ships, and then had to spend significant resources for modifications to bring them to combat-ready status. As a result, by the mid-1980s, taking modifications into account, the Soviet Navy had nearly 250 different types of ship.[23] The maintenance of this large but diverse force imposed a heavy burden even for the financially stable Soviet Navy and the burden simply became untenable for its cash-strapped successor.

Moreover, rapid development of the qualitative characteristics of the Soviet Navy had not been accompanied by a corresponding development of on-shore infrastructure to provide ships with appropriate support. As a result, many of the ships exhausted their operational life much faster than should have been the case. The Pacific Fleet had been in an even more difficult position with on-shore infrastructure than the other Soviet fleets. The quantitative expansion of the Pacific Fleet from the 1970s to the 1980s was not backed up by similar improvements in its infrastructure. Even SSBNs, the navy's elite units, found sometimes they did not receive full logistic support, and major surface combatants were more poorly served. The Pacific Fleet's aircraft carriers, for example, did not have specifically designed piers for basing in their home ports and thus usually had to spend most of their 'shore time' in the roads.[24]

In these circumstances, the headquarters of the Russian Pacific Fleet, like the rest of the navy, adopted a realistic policy of scrapping older ships with the goal of having approximately 70 per cent of the force comprised of far more capable operational vessels of an average age of 10 to 15 years. Thus, the large reduction in naval forces in the Pacific can be seen also as an attempt by the navy to move towards qualitative improvements of the force through standardisation of types of ships and weaponry.

According to the so-called 'Gorshkov Doctrine', the Soviet Navy's primary goal was to confront the USN in remote sea areas of the world's oceans, and the rapid expansion of the 'blue-water' capabilities of the Soviet Navy in the 1970s certainly allowed the Soviet military to project its power into many distant areas. However, this mission in no way served Soviet national security priorities and constituted a completely unachievable task. Even during the Soviet Navy's finest hour, at the beginning of the 1980s when it reached unprecedented size and capabilities, the aggregate combat potential of US naval forces was at least two and a half times larger.[25]

Only in the late 1980s did the USSR begin to consider that its goal of offsetting the US global naval presence was inconsistent with political interests or, what is more important, with its emerging economic stagnation. By the late 1980s, the Pacific Fleet had cut back its out-of-area activities by almost half and major fleet exercises were being conducted in its coastal waters instead of the open oceans. The end of the Cold War and the collapse of the USSR had a further impact on Russian maritime strategy in the Pacific theatre. The crisis that hit the Russian economy after 1992 has meant that the operational activities of the fleet have dwindled even further. The Pacific Fleet of new Russia no longer sought to station a task group in the Indian Ocean and ceased the permanent basing of surface combatants and submarines at Cam Ranh Bay in Vietnam.

Nevertheless, these changes were not only the result of the worsening economic situation. The reduction of USN SSBN operations in the Pacific theatre lessened to some extent the importance of anti-submarine operations in open ocean areas, performed by large surface combatants and aircraft (Tu–142 Bear–F) which operated out to a range of 4000 km. The present Russian naval strategy attaches greater importance to short- and medium-range operations (up to 500 and 2000 km respectively), due to the increased number of USN submarines and surface ships equipped with Tomahawk cruise missiles, which have a range of 2500 km. Based on the experience of the Gulf War, Russian naval experts believe that one of the navy's primary tasks in wartime will be the defence of Russia's territory against possible massed attacks by sea-based high-precision weapons, such as cruise missiles from USN or NATO warships or carrier-borne aircraft.[26] Modern high-precision weapons can be launched against military targets in eastern Russia from the Bering Sea or the north-eastern part of the Pacific Ocean, approximately 1500 km east and south-east of Japan or the Kuril Islands. At the same time, Russian naval analysts also expect that the next generation of sea-launched cruise missiles entering service with the USN could have ranges up to 4500 km. Consequently, possible areas for launching attacks would include the Indian Ocean and the north-eastern Pacific as far away as the islands of Guam and Midway.[27] Growing concern about such dangers to Russia's security in the Pacific led the Russian armed forces to come up with some countermeasures, including the deployment of attack submarines (Oscar SSGNs) into the central Pacific in late 1995 to track USN carrier battle groups, sometimes operating at more than 7000 km from the Russian coast.

The shift in Russia's Pacific naval strategy towards the defence of littoral waters does not of itself represent a decline of Russia's naval combat strength in the Pacific, as analysts such as Ken Booth assumed at the beginning of the 1990s. Russia's change of emphasis towards the defence of littoral waters has resulted in Russian military planners paying greater attention to the Sea of Okhotsk and the Sea of Japan. In 1992, one of the senior officers of the Pacific Fleet, public relations officer Captain First Rank Viktor Ryzhkov stated: 'The seas lap our shores and can be the route for invasion by enemies . . . Additionally, our merchant and fishing vessels are actively operating in these seas and it is our duty to protect our ships'.[28] As long as Japan is militarily linked to the United States, any attacks on Russian Far Eastern bases and naval units, whether by air or sea, would most likely be mounted from bases in Japan. Strike forces, such as aircraft carriers, attack submarines, and an amphibious invasion force would have to approach Russian territory either via the Straits of Tsushima, or the Sea of Okhotsk.

There were several other reasons for the reduction of Russia's naval presence in remote areas. Contrary to the situation in the USN with its well-developed system of support bases throughout the world, which allows it to maintain a significant forward naval presence, the Soviet Navy did not have this kind of luxury. With the exception of a handful of foreign-based naval installations, Soviet naval deployments were largely dependent on either the navy's own replenishment fleet, or temporary use of ports and bases of the USSR's client states. As a result, and due to their vulnerability in wartime, Soviet naval task groups in the Mediterranean Sea or the Indian Ocean served more political objectives, rather than military purposes.

Another important reason that probably influenced decisions of the Russian military to keep its fleet close to home shores is the problem of ensuring air cover of naval forces during 'out-of-area' deployments. Even when the Pacific Fleet had two aircraft carriers, *Minsk* and *Novorossiisk*, this problem was not resolved. Despite initial expectations among Western defence analysts, the efficiency of these *Kiev* class VTOL carriers was limited. Their actual functions were more in line with their designation in Russian as 'aircraft-carrying heavy cruisers'.[29] They were primarily long-range ships designed to hunt down US SSBNs and support friendly battle groups. But in terms of providing air support and air cover for the fleet's battle force their air-strike capabilities were very limited, and in no way could be compared to those of the USN standard carrier air wing. Therefore, in present conditions, Russia's Pacific naval forces can rely for air cover only on land-based aviation and this obviously limits their effective operational range.

Changes in the security environment of the Asia–Pacific region raised new objectives for Russian naval forces. In particular, since the end of the Cold War, Russian ships have participated in UN peacekeeping operations and the overwhelming majority of Russian combatants assigned to these missions have been from the Pacific Fleet. In fact, participation in humanitarian and UN operations is one of the fleet's current priorities.[30] In accordance with this new policy, the fleet has undertaken several peace-keeping missions. Following the UN sanctions against Iraq, the Pacific Fleet sent in October 1992 an *Udaloi* class DDG, *Admiral Vinogradov*, to conduct patrols in the Persian Gulf under the UN flag, later replaced by the same-class DDG *Admiral Tributs*.[31]

Russia is also trying to play a more active, cooperative role in regional affairs by actively participating in other maritime activities, such as combating pirates. Beginning in 1992, the number of pirate attacks in the Far East increased seven-fold.[32] In 1993, Russian merchant ships had been threatened or attacked by pirates 16 times (out of 20 piracy incidents in total); 14 of these incidents having occurred near Chinese territorial waters.[33] In response to these attacks, the Pacific Fleet deployed a task group to the East China Sea, headed by *Kara* class CG *Petropavlovsk* with orders to protect merchant shipping in the area.[34] In 1994, the Pacific Fleet conducted naval exercises together with the US Navy in the East China Sea in order to develop joint efforts in combating piracy.[35]

These measures were an effective, if temporary, deterrent to piracy in the region and demonstrated the potential of the Russian Navy as an effective partner in a wider regional effort to contain local pirates. To combat piracy on a wider scale, the Pacific Fleet could assemble a special task group, comprising for example one *Udaloi* class DDG and *Ropucha* class LST with a couple of hundred marines on board. Such a force would be ideal for patrolling one of the regional trouble spots (such as the Hainan–Luzon–Hong Kong triangle) with an international mandate to protect commercial shipping.

Another significant change in Russia's naval policy in the Pacific has been the increased contact between its naval forces and their counterparts from other countries. The end of the Cold War allowed the Russian Federation to establish, in the words of Vice-Admiral Valery Chirkov, First Deputy Commander of the Pacific Fleet, 'the best possible' relations between the Pacific Fleet and its former opponents in the region.[36] In March 1992, for example, French helicopter–carrier *Jeanne d'Arc* visited Vladivostok. It became the first French warship to visit the Russian Far East in 74 years.[37] Since 1994, the Pacific Fleet and US naval forces in the Pacific have held an annual disaster relief exercise codenamed 'Cooperation From the Sea'.[38] This program aims to ease regional tensions and build up trust and understanding between the two navies, but can be said to have done so at only a fairly basic level.

As of July 1998, the Russian Navy was drawing up a naval strategy based on the 1997 Blueprint for National Security, acknowledged as the fundamental guidance document for naval development. The main operating assumption is that the navy should not be viewed by other countries as a threat.[39] The main goal of the navy had become deterrence, and the 'specific correlation of naval forces is not of decisive significance'.[40] One of the main missions of theatre naval forces is to localise or neutralise a conflict once it breaks out.

Compared with the other services, the structures of the navy have been less affected by the radical change from the Soviet era to the Russian Federation. Command and control arrangements in the navy remain much as they were in the Soviet period, and are shown in Figure 7.1.

OPERATIONAL UNITS

As in the Soviet era, Russia's Pacific Fleet consists of sea-based strategic deterrent forces, general-purpose surface and submarine forces, naval aviation, naval infantry and coastal defence, as well as support units, but significant reductions in size, strength and personnel have occurred. On paper, the fleet's order of battle in 1998 comprised 7 strategic nuclear-powered ballistic missile submarines, 19 general-purpose submarines, 39 principal surface combatants, approximately 100 smaller combatants, 96 combat aircraft and 80 combat helicopters. This respresented between 25 and 50 per cent of total Russian navy assets. Total naval assets in mid-1998 were said by the commander of Russia's navy to be 100 submarines, 70 major surface combatants, 250 coastal ships

Figure 7.1 Organisation chart: Navy

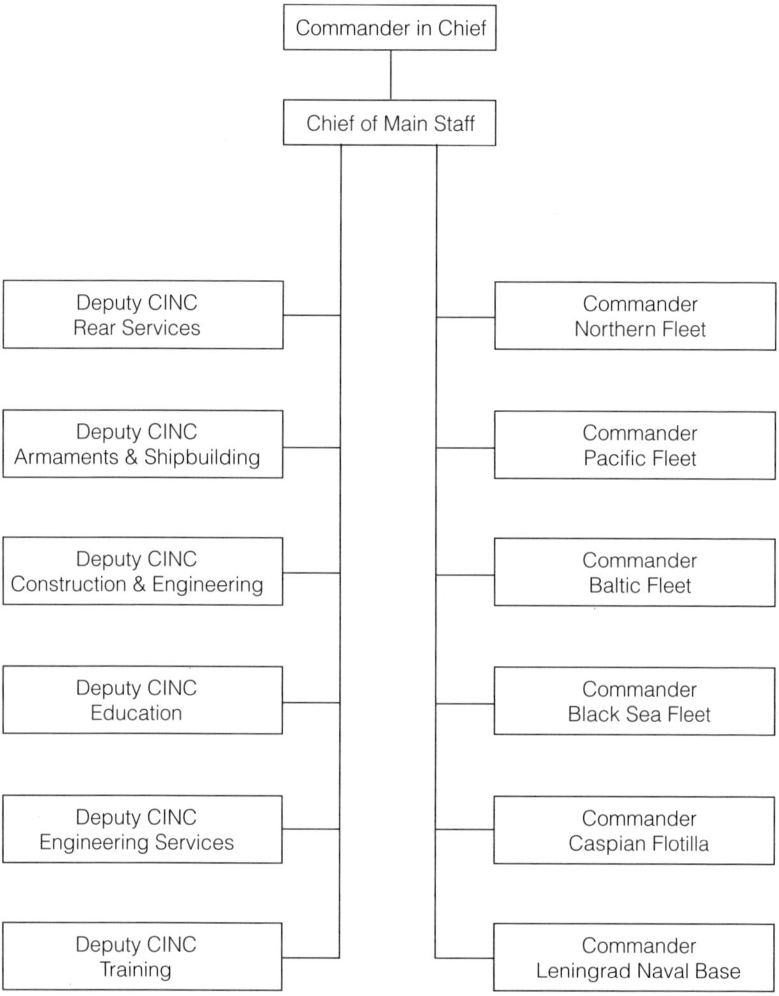

```
                        ┌─────────────────────────┐
                        │   Commander in Chief    │
                        └────────────┬────────────┘
                                     │
                        ┌────────────┴────────────┐
                        │   Chief of Main Staff   │
                        └────────────┬────────────┘
                                     │
  ┌──────────────────────┐          │          ┌──────────────────────┐
  │   Deputy CINC        │          │          │     Commander        │
  │   Rear Services      ├──────────┼──────────┤   Northern Fleet     │
  └──────────────────────┘          │          └──────────────────────┘

  ┌──────────────────────┐          │          ┌──────────────────────┐
  │   Deputy CINC        │          │          │     Commander        │
  │ Armaments & Shipbuilding ├──────┼──────────┤    Pacific Fleet     │
  └──────────────────────┘          │          └──────────────────────┘

  ┌──────────────────────┐          │          ┌──────────────────────┐
  │   Deputy CINC        │          │          │     Commander        │
  │ Construction & Engineering ├────┼──────────┤    Baltic Fleet      │
  └──────────────────────┘          │          └──────────────────────┘

  ┌──────────────────────┐          │          ┌──────────────────────┐
  │   Deputy CINC        │          │          │     Commander        │
  │   Education          ├──────────┼──────────┤   Black Sea Fleet    │
  └──────────────────────┘          │          └──────────────────────┘

  ┌──────────────────────┐          │          ┌──────────────────────┐
  │   Deputy CINC        │          │          │     Commander        │
  │ Engineering Services ├──────────┼──────────┤   Caspian Flotilla   │
  └──────────────────────┘          │          └──────────────────────┘

  ┌──────────────────────┐                     ┌──────────────────────┐
  │   Deputy CINC        │                     │     Commander        │
  │   Training           ├─────────────────────┤ Leningrad Naval Base │
  └──────────────────────┘                     └──────────────────────┘
```

or small naval combatants, and about 500 naval planes and helicopters.[41]

The fleet is divided into two major formations (flotillas): Primorskaia, which is based in Vladivostok where the fleet head-quarters is located; and Kamchatskaia, which is based in Petropavlovsk-Kamchatski. Vladivostok is the primary base of major surface combatants and miscellaneous vessels, while Petropavlovsk-Kamchatski is the main base for the submarine fleet, including all SSBNs. In the words of the fleet's Chief-of-Staff,

Vice-Admiral Viktor Fiodorov, it is practice now to form new fleet formations with ships of different classes[42] to 'deal with multi-purpose tasks: strike, anti-submarine, anti-mine and some others'.[43] The centrepiece of Russia's surface fleet in the Pacific remains the Squadron of Surface Ships [*eskadra nadvodnykh korablei*] which traditionally incorporates only the most powerful units of the surface fleet. The squadron is designated the 10th Operational Squadron and is based in Fokino on the Bay of Strelok. Currently, the squadron comprises *Sovremennyi* and *Udaloi* class guided missile destroyers, and only one operational guided missile cruiser, *Variag*, the fleet's flagship.

Major surface combatants[44]

Rapid enhancement of the surface fleet capabilities was the most remarkable development of Soviet Pacific naval power during the Cold War, and this was most impressive in the expansion of cruiser numbers.[45] The variety of types of cruisers ranged from old *Sverdlov* class gunships which first entered service in 1955 to *Kiev* class VTOL carriers which first entered service in 1979. However, the majority of them were designed for open ocean anti-submarine warfare.[46] With the reduction of long-range ASW operations of the Pacific Fleet due to the changes in Russia's naval strategy, severe cuts to fleet resources, and the growing difficulties of maintaining large numbers of outdated ships, the number of cruisers fell rapidly in the seven years after 1991—from seventeen to two—and only one of the two is operational.

The two cruisers, *Variag* and *Admiral Lazarev*, carry anti-ship missiles and are optimised for surface strike in a variety of environments. The one operational cruiser is the *Slava* class guided-missile cruiser *Variag*.[47] A relatively new ship, commissioned in 1989, it was transferred to the Pacific in October 1990.[48] Falling midway between the massive *Ushakov* cruiser and *Sovremennyi* class destroyer, the *Slava* class guided missile cruiser[49] is the second most powerful surface ship in the Russian Navy after the *Ushakov* class. *Variag's* primary armaments are eight twin missile launchers for SS-N–12 *Sandbox* missiles which can carry a nuclear or conventional (500 kg) warhead, have a range of 550 km, and are capable of destroying or disabling every surface vessel, including an aircraft carrier.[50] The *Slava* class cruiser would be used as the centrepiece of the fleet's battle group with the primary tasks of attacking carrier battle groups or acting as a formidable escort to other ships which it would screen with its comprehensive air defence systems.[51]

Admiral Lazarev is a 24 000 tonne *Ushakov* class heavy nuclear-powered missile cruiser[52] and is the most powerful ship the Pacific Fleet ever had. The ships of this class are the largest non-carrier surface combatants built since the Second World War. They have been called battle cruisers for their impressive size and very heavy armament.[53] Apart from serving as a flagship, they can serve as the lead ship of a naval task force by providing a screen in a high-threat environment through the 'deployment' of the powerful echeloned anti-ship and anti-air defences. *Lazarev* is an improved version of the *Admiral Ushakov* (formerly *Kirov* class).[54] Currently, *Lazarev* is non-operational because the ship's reactor needs refuelling and reconditioning. Western naval analysts are predicting that *Lazarev* will be decommissioned and scrapped like *Ushakov*, which was decommissioned from the Northern Fleet in late 1998. This assumption is based on the fact that ships of this class are very expensive to maintain and repair. Nevertheless, in comparison with *Ushakov*, *Lazarev* has standard equipment and weaponry which should reduce costs of repair. Besides, a decision by the navy to undertake repair of the *Lazarev*'s sister-ship, *Admiral Nakhimov* in the Northern Fleet, indicates a desire of the naval command to retain battle cruisers.[55] In July 1999, Ilia Klebanov, Deputy Prime Minister responsible for the military–industrial complex, supported the proposal to allocate resources for *Lazarev*'s refit and return into combat service.[56] If *Admiral Lazarev* is brought to operational status, the combat potential of the Pacific Fleet would be significantly increased.

Russia's destroyer force in the Pacific did not suffer such significant reductions as the cruisers. Today, the Pacific Fleet operates two types of guided missile destroyer: *Sovremennyi* class and *Udaloi* class which both first entered into service in the Pacific theatre in 1985. Deployment of the two new types of destroyer was part of the navy's policy to modernise and stand-ardise its surface fleet but no numerical expansion was planned. These new guided missile destroyers are larger and far more capable ships than their predecessors of the *Kashin*, *Kildin*, *Kotlin* and *Skoryi* classes. As Derek da Cunha commented, if these ships had been built in the 1960s, they would have been classified as cruisers.[57] Indeed, the *Sovremennyi* class destroyer can be roughly compared to the US *Ticonderoga* class guided missile cruiser. Armed with SS-N–22 *Sunburn* anti-ship cruise missiles[58] with a range of 120 km, and two sets of twin 130 mm automatic guns, the *Sovremennyi* class represents a very powerful surface strike ship. The *Udaloi* class is by contrast a first class anti-submarine combatant.[59] Armed with two single-barrel dual-purpose 100 mm guns, it carries two Ka–27 *Helix* helicopters, equipped with 55-km range SS-N–14 *Silex* missiles, rocket launchers and torpedoes, and is fitted with excellent underwater sensors. In comparison with their predecessors, both destroyer classes have larger fuel and storage capacity that increases their sustainability for operations during 'out-of-area' deployments. At present, four *Sovremennyi* class and three *Udaloi*–class destroyers are operational and very active, the remainder are in reserve, but still accountable. According to *Jane's*, some of those reserved combatants, *Admiral Tributs* in particular, may soon be reactivated.[60]

The Pacific Fleet's frigate force has been significantly reduced since 1991, leaving only three *Krivak–I* class guided missile frigates[61] available for combat duty. However, if needed, Russia's Pacific command can rely on seven *Krivak–III* guided missile frigates[62] which belong to Russia's border guards but which are still under naval control.

Submarines

The Russian Navy values submarines for their strike capabilities, mobility, secrecy of deployment, and ability to successfully implement the navy's primary task—to deny the use of the sea to the enemy.[63] This is especially relevant to the Pacific theatre with its vast distances and extreme depths, and submarines have traditionally been a main strike force of the Pacific Fleet, on a par with missile-carrying naval aviation. Prior to 1962, geographical distances of the Pacific theatre from major shipbuilding centres often resulted in limited numbers of major surface ships deployed in the Pacific. That was usually compensated for by the introduction of powerful submarines in bigger numbers. The value of submarines for the USSR's Pacific security became clear after the Komsomolsk shipyard became responsible for the production of ballistic missile and attack submarines for the Pacific Fleet in the mid-1970s.[64]

Since the introduction at the beginning of the 1970s of SSBN patrols, the Pacific Fleet's strategic submarine force has become an integral part of the Soviet strategic nuclear deterrent forces. Together with the strategic submarine force of the Northern Fleet, it represents a sea-borne branch of Russia's nuclear triad. In 1992, all Russian nuclear missile submarines that had been based

Table 7.2 Changes in composition of the Pacific Fleet submarine force order of battle 1990–98

	1990	1998
SSBN		
Delta–I	9	2
Delta–III	8	6
Yankee	8	–
SSGN		
Charlie–I/II	8	–
Echo–II	14	–
Oscar–II	–	6
SSN		
Akula	5	7
Echo–I	5	–
November	4	–
Victor–I	4	–
Victor–III	12	1
SSB		
Golf–II	6	–
SSG		
Juliet	6	–
SSK		
Foxtrot	13	–
Kilo	9	8
Whiskey	12	–
SSAC		
Golf 1	1	–
SST		
Bravo	1	–
ASGSS		
India	1	–

in Vladivostok were transferred to Rybachi (near Petropavlovsk-Kamchatski) which became the main SSBN base in the Pacific Fleet.[65] In 1998 and early 1999 the remaining *Delta–I* SSBNs were stationed in the Pavlovskoe SSBN base (Maritime Territory). However, with their forthcoming retirement, Russian Pacific SSBNs will be concentrated in Rybachi. Under new economic conditions, the fleet continues its policy of retiring old and technically obsolete boats, both nuclear and conventional, which do not meet modern requirements, leaving the force with fewer but far more capable submarines. Table 7.2 compares the order of battle for the Pacific Fleet submarine force in 1990 and 1998.

The backbone of Russia's sea-based strategic nuclear forces east of the Urals are *Delta–I* and *Delta–III* class SSBNs. The *Delta–I* class, which first entered service in the early 1970s and is the follow-on to the *Yankee* class, carries 12 SS-N–8[66] submarine launched ballistic missiles (SLBMs) with a range of more than 7500 km (4000 nautical miles). *The Delta–III* class SSBN, which first entered service in the late 1970s, carries 16 SS-N–18[67] SLBMs with a range of approximately 5000 nautical miles.[68] The long range of new missiles deployed on the *Delta* class SSBNs allowed the Soviet Navy to change the deployment areas of SSBNs in the Pacific theatre.

SSBNs of earlier types (*Hotel* or *Yankee*) with their short-range missiles had to operate in areas of the north-eastern Pacific, close to US coasts, in order to increase strike distance. However, the improved capabilities of *Delta* submarines allowed the Pacific Fleet to deploy them within enclosed seas (bastions), primarily in the Sea of Okhotsk, under the cover of friendly land-based aviation and anti-submarine forces. In 1998, the Sea of Okhotsk remained the main area of Russian SSBN patrols in the Pacific, with the Russian Navy regularly deploying one or two strategic submarines. These are supplemented by at least one SSBN in a state of full alert and preparedness for strategic missile launch at the home base at Rybachi. The Russian Navy will probably retire its last *Delta–I* SSBN by the year 2000, leaving *Delta–III* submarines as the only platforms for a sea-based strategic strike in the Pacific MTVD. There is some likelihood that all SSBNs will be withdrawn from the Pacific Fleet to concentrate the strategic submarine force in the Northern Fleet. In 1998, the SSBN force in the Pacific Fleet comprised 10 *Delta* submarines, each armed with 16 R–29R SLBMs (K–441, K–424, K–449, K–445, K–490, K–506, K–211, K–223, K–180, and K–433 listed in date order of commissioning between 1976 and 1981).[69] US specialists report that a figure of 10 operational SSBNs in the Pacific Fleet is too high.[70] Through 1998, operational deployment of the SSBNs was very low-level. As of early 1998, Russia was reportedly deploying only two SSBNs at any one time, since 20 out of 26 were not capable of putting to sea at all.[71] From May to August none were on patrol in any Soviet fleet because of safety concerns. By the end of the year, one in each of the two fleets was on patrol at sea, and one was on alert at pier-side.[72] The prospect is that there will only be about 13–15 SSBNs left in five to ten years, and in that case, they will almost certainly all be based in the Northern Fleet, leaving none in the Pacific.[73]

The most significant improvement of Pacific Fleet conventional strike capabilities in the 1990s has been the introduction and continuous deployment of the *Oscar–II* class nuclear-powered guided missile submarine (SSGN). The first *Oscar–II* became operational in the Soviet Navy in 1986 and the Pacific Fleet currently has six, based at Taria Bay near Petropavlovsk-Kamchtski. These huge submarines (nearly 14 000 tonnes in surface displacement) are considered to be one of the most powerful anti-shipping platforms in the world. Despite their enormous size, *Oscars* are very quiet and are capable of launching 24 SS-N-19 *Shipwreck* cruise missiles from long ranges. Designed to attack carrier battle groups, *Oscars* are considered to be the 'shock element' of Russia's general-purpose submarine force.

Russia's attack submarine forces in the Pacific comprise mainly two types: the nuclear-powered *Akula* and the conventional *Kilo* class boats. The remaining *Victor-III* class SSN, based in Pavlovskoe, is probably not operational and is likely to be retired in the next few years. That leaves the *Akula* as the only advanced nuclear-powered attack submarine within the Pacific Fleet. The *Kilo* class[74] has been deployed to defend maritime approaches in the Seas of Japan and Okhotsk, and along the Kuril chain. The *Akula* class[75] can be deployed practically anywhere in the Pacific to hunt down enemy SSBNs, though usually they operate along Russian ASW barriers where they can also be used to defend friendly SSBNs. All Pacific *Akulas* are based at Taria Bay, while *Kilos* are stationed in Fokino.

All attack submarines in service are in operational status. However, financial hardship has affected this once most prestigious branch of the navy, and only some of the in-service submarines are able to go to sea. In particular, the fleet is experiencing problems with supplies of storage batteries for the submarines.

Despite obvious reductions in strength, and scale of operations, the Russian submarine force continues to possess substantial capabilities, and continues to enjoy some privileged attention from the Russian Navy and the Ministry of Defence. According to the chief of the US naval intelligence, Rear Admiral Michael Cramer, the Russian submarine force 'is not suffering at all' the same hardships as other assets of Russia's armed forces.[76] In the Pacific theatre, the result of this policy has been a resumption of prolonged patrols by Russian nuclear submarines in waters distant from Russia. According to the US Navy, an *Oscar–II* class SSGN tracked USS *Independence* and *Abraham Lincoln* CBGs in September and November 1995 off Hawaii, followed by operations of an *Akula* class SSN off the north-west coast of the USA in December.[77] Today, the Pacific Fleet possesses a much smaller but more effective submarine force, with a substantially improved capability in anti-submarine and anti-ship warfare.

The Russian submarine force presents a catastrophic ecological threat. By 2000, some 100 nuclear submarines would have to be decommissioned, but it is unlikely that there will be enough money to do this safely, even though according to one account each one has the same contamination potential as the Chernobyl disaster.[78]

Naval aviation

Together with attack submarines, Pacific Fleet Naval Aviation (PFNA) is regarded by the Russian naval command as a main strike force in the Pacific, especially because of its missile-carrying aircraft. In fact, land-based aircraft are a very attractive means of sea denial because, if they have sufficient range, they can be concentrated very rapidly against maritime targets approaching from different directions. The PFNA is completely subordinate to the Fleet Command. The air arm consists of approximately 100 fixed-wing aircraft and 96 helicopters, most of which are based ashore (see Table 7.3).

The PFNA currently has four basic missions: anti-ship strike, fighter attack, reconnaissance and surveillance, and anti-submarine warfare. However, at present it largely performs only anti-submarine and reconnaissance missions, partly as a result of reductions in its aircraft strengths. Since 1992, some PFNA formations (regiments and squadrons) ceased to exist and others

Table 7.3 Pacific Fleet Naval Aviation 1988

Fixed-wing	**85 (total)**
Strike	
Tu–22	9
ASW	
Tu–142	27
Il–38	19
Fighter-Bombers	
Su–24	15
Reconnaissance/EW	
Tu–95, An–12	8
Communications	
Tu–142	7
Helicopters	**96 (total)**
ASW	
Ka–25/27, M–14	80
Other purpose	
Ka–29, Mi–14	16

have decreased in size; and some bases and airfields were abandoned or transferred to the civilians. The PFNA main strike force of missile-carrying aircraft has been sharply reduced, leaving only one regiment with nine Tu–22Ms, thus practically reducing it to the size of a squadron. At the beginning of the 1990s, Su–17C *Fitter* bombers were replaced by more capable Su–24 *Fencer* medium-range bombers.

With the decommissioning of the *Kiev* class carriers in 1991–92, the carrier-borne strike regiment (Yak–38) was brought ashore and re-equipped with the shore-based Su–25 *Frogfoot* but it was disbanded in 1996, leaving the Pacific Fleet with only one strike regiment (equipped with Su–24 aircraft). By 1995, the PFNA had lost most of its reconnaissance aircraft through the decommissioning of medium-range and short-range Tu–16R and RM *Badger* and long-range Tu–95 RT *Bear*, as a result of their obsolescence and the lack of money for their modernisation. Even the creation in 1993 of a separate reconnaissance squadron, equipped with medium-range Su–24M/MR aircraft with a range of up to 400 km did not completely resolve the problem. Since then, reconnaissance missions (especially long-range) have largely been carried out by missile- carrying aircraft and by anti-submarine aircraft, a state of affairs less than satisfactory to the naval command.[79] Air cover and air defence for naval operations in the proximity of Russian shores is provided by the aircraft of the Far East Military District— a force of approximately 300 fourth-generation interceptors such as the MiG–31 *Foxhound* and Su–27 *Flanker*.[80]

Naval aviation, like the rest of the Pacific Fleet, has really felt the consequences of radical defence budget cuts and the country's poor economic situation. This can be seen in an analysis of flight training in recent years. Owing to the low level of logistic support, especially in aviation fuel, the frequency and range of flights are constantly declining. With the reduction of aircraft by nearly half, limits on aviation fuel supplies have been cut by eight times. As a result, the average per-crew flight time fell by more than 200 per cent in 1997 in comparison with 1991. During the last two years naval air crews spent approximately 25 to 30 hours on average in the air, instead of the designated 100 to 150 hours.[81] Most of the crews, especially flight school graduates, have little chance of perfecting their flight skills due to the fuel restrictions and poor condition of some of the aircraft. In this situation, the naval aviation command focuses on maintaining combat preparedness of the most professional and prepared crews and flight instructors, even if that means sacrificing some training for new crews. Each regiment now has a limited number of crews and aircraft (usually no more than a squadron) which are fully combat-ready. They usually spend more time in the air, and most of these crews participate in the fleet's exercises, where they have a chance to improve their combat training. Despite difficulties of this kind, however, the PFNA remains a potentially capable force. Mobilisation for combat would probably require transfer of experienced pilots from the Northern Fleet.

Amphibious forces

Russian power projection capability in the Pacific is centred in the naval infantry,[82] an elite well-trained combat force of an estimated 14 000 troops. Pacific Fleet naval infantry were widely employed by the Soviet leadership in the Asia–Pacific region. Different contingents of Soviet marines were periodically deployed on board amphibious ships to the Indian Ocean, as part of the Soviet Indian Ocean Squadron (SOVINDRON); and naval infantry were stationed in Cam Ranh Bay and Dahlak (Ethiopia) installations. In no way can Russia's Naval Infantry (RNI) be compared to the US Marine Corps which outnumbers its Russian counterpart by twelve to one in personnel. The RNI has a rather different set of tasks to perform. Nearly 60 per cent of all RNI is concentrated in the Pacific Fleet and form one nominal 8000-strong division (the 55th Division) which mostly plays a defensive role. Pacific Fleet marines are assigned to participate in sea-borne assault operations, sabotage behind enemy lines, defence of vital coastal installations, and operations against enemy amphibious assaults.

The Pacific Fleet naval infantry is a heavily armed force, equipped with tracked and wheeled amphibious vehicles, including BTR–70 and BTR–80 armoured personnel carriers. It has 329 main battle tanks (T–72 and T–80), and 215 pieces of artillery, among them eighteen 152-mm 2S3 *Akatsia* self-propelled howitzers. Division air defence, provided previously by ZSU–23–4 *Shilka* self-propelled anti-aircraft guns, and short-range SA–9 *Gaskin* surface to air missiles (SAMs), was considerably improved in 1989 with the deployment of twenty SA–8 *Gecko* low- to medium-range SAMs.

During the battle for Grozny in Chechnia in January 1995, poor performance of the ground troops forced the Russian military command to form a combined grouping of the naval infantry force (from the Baltic, Northern and Pacific Fleets) for special operations.

The Pacific Fleet sent the 165th regiment of its 55th naval infantry division.[83] Despite the fact that conventional land combat and urban combat are not usually part of marine operations, the naval infantry demonstrated its professionalism, strong combat potential, and high mobility. In fact, during the Chechen campaign, Russian naval infantry proved to be among the few professionally trained and fully combat-ready formations within the Russian armed forces (on par with airborne troops, special forces,[84] and special units of the internal security forces). Perhaps this is the main reason for the decision to make Pacific Fleet naval infantry a core of Russia's mobile forces in the Far East.

Restructuring and the reduction of the fleet's size and strength have significantly reduced its amphibious lift capabilities. What was originally a division of amphibious ships has been reduced and reorganised into a brigade, and later on into a squadron,[85] leaving only three large amphibious ships fully operational and combat-ready.[86] The two *Ivan Rogov* class landing ships (LPD),[87] once the pride of the Soviet amphibious forces, had been withdrawn from operational duty with the Pacific Fleet by 1996–97. There was even speculation that the Indonesian Navy might purchase them, but later on these reports were denied. Still, the existing amphibious capability allows the Pacific Fleet to deploy approximately 500 marines, 20 main battle tanks, and 24 infantry fighting vehicles anywhere in the Asia–Pacific region, giving the armed forces some limited capacity to support Russian national interests during crisis situations.

Combat training

Russia's economic crisis and significant reductions in defence spending had a direct impact on the nature of combat training of the navy in general and the Pacific Fleet in particular. During Soviet times, when the navy enjoyed stable financing of its activities and did not experience any problems with fuel or logistic support, the naval command was able to conduct step-by-step training without any limits or restrictions. First, separate ships would go to sea to train crews in close-to-combat situations. Ships would then perfect their training as parts of tactical groups or multi-purpose formations. But after 1991, the navy had to reduce the intensity of out-of-area activities by 50 per cent, and naval activities in nearby areas by 20 to 30 per cent.[88] Only the naval component of Russia's nuclear triad—SSBNs—did not suffer much in terms of their operational activity. Budgetary restrictions and a change in the term of conscription in the navy from three to two years in 1992 created a situation where the navy had to change its views on combat training in order to prevent a fatal decline in the required level of combat readiness of its forces. The emphasis was given to base-training where the crew develop their skills through classroom learning and more book learning than previously of the ship's equipment and weaponry. After this, theoretical knowledge is complemented by practical experience during short but very intensive periods of exercises (usually twice a year). Since 1994, all Russian fleets have adopted a practice of multi-purpose deployments of their operational units in which the ships are able to exercise independently or in groups.

In 1996, the navy increased the intensity of multi-purpose deployments by adopting a policy of so-called *sbor-pokhod*— large-scale deployment of different fleet formations.[89] During *sbor-pokhod* the naval command has a chance of bringing more complexity into the fleet's combat training by creating, for example, engagement situations between several tactical groups, or by organising coordinated operations of different-purpose formations (major surface combatants, light missile craft, attack submarines and naval aviation). *Sbor-pokhod* usually takes place in spring and autumn, as a culmination of a base-training period. As the Deputy Commander of the Pacific Fleet, chief of combat training Vice-Admiral Valery Riazantsev pointed out:

> Analysis shows that multi-purpose training of ships at sea, held in the form of *sbor-pokhod* with the employment of the Fleet's Naval Aviation, coastal troops, electronic countermeasures, and reconnaissance units, is quite effective, and in the conditions of limited financing and the reductions of fuel limits—the only possible form of force training at sea.[90]

In the Pacific, the adoption of new principles of training have resulted in increased activity of the fleet's forces. In April 1996, the *sbor-pokhod* of the Pacific Fleet became the largest naval exercise held in Russia or the USSR for ten years. The manoeuvres, held over several days in areas of the Sea of Japan, Sea of Okhotsk and the Bering Sea, involved 69 warships and support vessels, and paratroopers and aviation of the Far East MD. Some 200 different exercise components were conducted.[91]

Out of eleven *sbor-pokhod* conducted by the Russian Navy in 1997, six were held by the Pacific Fleet and these involved in total almost 150 warships and 90 aircraft, plus combat units of the Far East MD.[92] The most intensive was the autumn exercise under the leadership of the Pacific Fleet Commander Vice-Admiral Zakharenko, held in the Seas of Okhotsk and Japan in late August and early September. More than 70 surface combatants, nuclear-powered and conventional submarines and support vessels, more than 30 aircraft, and naval infantry and coastal defence units conducted more than 200 separate exercises.[93] In the first half of 1999, the Pacific Fleet intensified its combat training, compared with the same period of 1998. In the period of March–June 1999, the Fleet staged three command-and-staff exercises, one of which was part of a strategic command-and-staff exercise held in the Far Eastern Military District in late March–early April 1999. All in all, around 40 combat surface ships (includig the flagship *Variag*), submarines and support vessels, and nearly 20 aircraft were involved in the exercises. An amphibious exercise, which involved the landing of a marine battalion, was conducted as part of the strategic command-and-staff exercise.[94]

Thus it can be concluded that despite the decline in financial and logistic support, the fleet is managing to maintain the required level of combat training, though the emphasis now is on ships and units that comprise the combat-ready nucleus of the fleet's forces. This level of training, though confined to a much smaller number of ships than in Soviet days, has ensured that the crews and ships involved are at high levels of combat readiness even if they are not practised in more complex operational circumstances.

Morale

Rapid negative changes in the socio-economic situation in Russia, radical reductions in the defence budget, and chronic lack of cash within the Russian armed forces, have caused a significant deterioration in the social conditions of Russian military personnel, especially in the navy. The Pacific Fleet, on a par with other Russian fleets, is suffering the consequences of the sudden demilitarisation of Russia that occurred in the early 1990s. Growing inflation on the one hand, and delayed compensatory measures of the government on the other, have led to the significant devaluation of wages of Russian naval officers. For example, at present, the average wage of officers (including the commander) of a Russian Pacific Fleet SSBN is lower than the wage of a trolley-bus driver in Moscow.[95] Many naval officers have to work after hours as loaders or taxi drivers just to feed their families.

Apart from inadequate wages, the housing problem is another

headache for the Pacific Fleet command. Housing has been the traditional Achilles heel of the Soviet military, but after the collapse of the USSR, the situation has significantly deteriorated. In 1998, more than 7000 families of Pacific Fleet officers did not have their own accommodation.[96] With practically no help coming from Moscow, the fleet has to handle this problem by itself, and can get little help from local authorities because of the fleet's huge debt to them. The housing problem will not be successfully resolved in the near future.

Another significant problem is the promotion process. With large reductions of ships and combat formations in the fleet, the prospects for getting a promotion have decreased accordingly. As former commander of the Pacific Fleet Admiral Vladimir Kuroyedov emphasised, usually naval officers resign not because of the lack of desire to defend their country, but 'because of impossibility of continuing to serve . . . The reason for their resignation is the condition of poverty in which they work'.[97]

However, many officers choose to stay, despite all the odds. This can be explained by two factors. First, many of them do not see any better alternative and they hope that soon the situation will improve, the prestige of the naval service will be restored, and the government will finally pay appropriate attention to its seamen. The second reason lies in the traditions of the Russian Navy, in the so-called *morskaia kul'tura* [maritime culture], which is still very strong in the Russian naval officer corps, and which is carefully preserved. The basis of this culture is dedicated loyalty to the navy and to Russia. As Admiral Kuroyedov has pointed out, only patriotism and devotion to duty helps Pacific Fleet personnel survive the hard times.[98] Only these factors can explain why the officers of one Pacific Fleet SSBN decided to put together their own miserable wages to buy paint and a computer for their submarine.[99] Thus while there has been a significant drop in a morale among some officers of the Pacific Fleet, there has not been an abandonment of commitment altogether.

PROSPECTS FOR DEVELOPMENT

The financial crisis that hit Russia in 1998 has forced the Russian naval command to revise its plans about the navy's development. During a press conference, held in the navy's General Staff, C-in-C of the Russian Navy Admiral Kuroyedov announced that the construction of new warships would be put on hold for a period of five years (up to the year 2003). Exceptions would be made for those ships already under construction.[100] Released funds would be concentrated on the maintenance of the fleet's operational warships, especially SSBNs.

This announcement did not come as a big surprise, because this approach correlates with the current reform plan for the Russian armed forces which had already projected a large-scale modernisation beginning only in the year 2005. During the first stage of the current reform plan (1997 to 2002), the Navy will look to optimise its size and strength in the context of new economic realities and Russia's newly adopted military doctrine. By the year 2000, the numerical strength of the Russian Navy will be reduced to 100 000 personnel, leaving Russia's two largest fleets, Northern and Pacific, with a 30 000-strong force each. The rest will be divided between the Baltic and Black Sea fleets, and the Caspian Flotilla. An optimisation of the navy's infrastructure is planned to allow the Russian naval command to increase the fighting capabilities of its forces through the deployment of new ships and weapons systems after the year 2005. The Russian Navy development strategy emphasises the improvement of the maritime strategic nuclear forces, multi-purpose surface ships and submarines.[101]

Due to the pressure on its share of Russia's defence budget, the navy is concentrating its near-term efforts on the development of only five major projects: for the surface fleet, a guided-missile destroyer and frigate (for both open-ocean and littoral operations); for the submarine force, a nuclear-powered ballistic missile class, a nuclear-powered attack class and a diesel-electric attack class.[102]

In accordance with the ratification of the START–II Treaty, Russia had planned to increase the share of nuclear warheads deployed with the naval component of Russia's strategic nuclear triad (SSBNs) from 33 per cent to 58 per cent.[103] To meet this requirement the navy has to maintain no less than twenty SSBNs with a total capacity to carry up to 1700 nuclear warheads.[104] Russian experts estimated that by the year 2003 Russia would have 24 SSBNs with a total capacity to carry nearly 1700 warheads.[105] The Russian Navy expected to achieve further improvements in its SSBN force by re-arming currently operational submarines with a new missile suite, and by replacing ageing boats with a new-generation SSBN of the *Borey* class. The first vessel of this series, *Yury Dolgorukii*, was laid down in 1996 in Severodvinsk, and the navy had expected to launch it around the year 2002. As of late 1998, construction of the lead vessel in this class has been suspended, pending re-design, and commissioning dates of beyond 2005 are now likely.[106] Construction work in the naval component of the strategic nuclear forces is in crisis, with some predictions that the deployment levels in the middle of the first decade of the next century will only provide Russia with half (or less) of its planned SLBM allocations under START–II.[107] As mentioned above it is likely that by 2005–2007, all Russian SSBNs will be withdrawn from the Pacific and based in the Northern Fleet. Russia may have as few as 10–15 operational SSBNs by 2003.[108]

Russia's military are still planning to finish construction and commissioning of the third generation of attack submarines (*Akula* class). The navy will complete the decommissioning of older types of nuclear and conventional submarines and will begin to receive two new types of attack submarines at the beginning of the 21st century: a fourth-generation *Severodvinsk* class SSN and *St Petersburg* class SSK.

It is expected that Russia's surface forces will receive a new type of guided-missile frigate—*Novik* class FFG. The lead vessel of this series, *Novik*, was launched at the end of 1997 and follow-on ships are now under construction in Kaliningrad. The *Novik* class FFG is viewed by the Russian Navy as a backbone of the future surface fleet. The Russian Navy also hopes to receive a new type of destroyer, though its design and characteristics are not yet known. If the economic situation and the level of technological development permit, the Navy has hopes to begin the construction and deployment of aircraft carriers by 2010 to 2015.[109]

The Russian Navy has learned from the troubled experience of its Soviet predecessor and will look to equip new surface and sub-surface units with unified types of weaponry and equipment to achieve a higher level of standardisation and integration. For example, the main armament of Russia's advanced frigate and destroyer will be one type of anti-ship missile suite, armed with SS-N-28 *Grom* cruise missiles (similar to the US *Tomahawk* missile).

As for the Pacific Fleet, the Russian Navy's near-term strategy is to preserve its sea-borne strategic nuclear forces, to maintain significant operational levels in its attack submarine force, and to maintain the ocean-going component of the surface fleet. Looking to an improvement in the national economic situation, Russia's naval leadership had hoped in 1995 to improve and even expand Pacific Fleet capabilities:

The basis of the fleets in the North and the Far East, from our point of view, would comprise multi-purpose nuclear submarines, aircraft-carrying and missile-carrying combatants, naval aviation and coastal troops. The specifics of the Pacific theatre require more scaled development of mobile forces for operations in the strait and island zones, in particular, specifically-designed amphibious assault ships.[110]

Russia's naval experts believe that the Pacific Fleet should have at least the same number of strategic and general-purpose submarines as it has now. Ideally, the nucleus of the surface fleet should include approximately two aircraft-carriers, one to two CG(N)s, two to three DDGs, two to three FFGs, plus a significant number of light missile, anti-submarine, patrol and mine-sweeping craft.[111]

After the August 1998 financial crisis, it is hard to see how the Russian Navy will be able to achieve these goals. The worsening economic situation and unstable financing of existing programs will certainly postpone realisation of some projects and will force a re-evaluation of strategies and development programs. Despite some optimism about Russia's plans to restore and even increase its naval might in the 21st century, it is clear that the Pacific naval command is no longer hopeful about the possibility of receiving new warships in the near future. In January 1998, the Pacific Fleet's Chief of Staff, Vice-Admiral Viktor Fiodorov, expressed the view that the commissioning of new warships was unlikely even then and he expected that the Pacific Fleet would have to continue operating with existing surface combatants and submarines.[112]

As recently as 1996, the Pacific Fleet had still hoped to get some new warships. It was expected that the surface forces would receive an *Ushakov* class CGN, *Piotr Velikii*, and a *Sovremennyi* class DDG, *Vazhnyi*.[113] However, *Piotr Velikii* joined the Northern Fleet in 1998[114] and, according to *Jane's Fighting Ships*, *Vazhnyi* was one of two *Sovremennyi* class DDGs bought by China, so eventually it will be deployed to the Pacific theatre but under another naval ensign and another name. Nevertheless, the Fleet command thinks that its surface force will not suffer much for at least two to three years as the age of the majority of operational surface combatants is only 10 to 15 years. The maintenance of operational warships will be carried out by regular check-ups on board and small repair works will be undertaken by the crew and the fleet's maintenance service without resorting to more costly repairs in workshops. Expensive spare parts will be canabalised from non-operational vessels.

If in the next few years no improvements are expected in the Pacific Fleet surface units, the situation is not the same with its submarine force. Despite evident hardships, one can observe continuous deployments of modern attack nuclear submarines to the Pacific. In July 1995, the fleet received its seventh *Akula* class SSN.[115] The most recent deployment was the transfer of the newest *Oscar–II* class SSGN *Tomsk* to Petropavlovsk-Kamchatski.[116] As of 1997, two more *Akula* class SSNs were under construction in the Komsomolsk shipyard, though it is not clear when the construction will be completed.[117]

Thus one can assume that the Pacific Fleet will maintain some significant capabilities in the foreseeable future. As Admiral Kelly pointed out, even if 'all modernisation ceases, they [Russians in the Pacific] will continue to have a powerful blue-water navy for some time'.[118]

The situation might get better for the Russian Pacific naval forces, as well as the rest of the navy, since President Yeltsin has approved the creation of a civilian agency to dismantle and scrap decommissioned nuclear-powered submarines.[119] The Pacific Fleet alone has 62 submarines waiting to be scrapped.[120] The upkeep, utilisation and security of decommissioned submarines had required substantial financial and human resources with practically no support from the government. During the period 1996 to 1997, the actual government allocations towards utilisation of nuclear submarines were only 16 per cent of the required amount.[121] With the navy now being relieved of that burden, and with cost savings from the liquidation of duplicate structures and units, and reductions of bases and other installations, the navy will be able to direct more funds towards the maintenance of the fleet's operational warships.

COMPARISON WITH REGIONAL FORCES

By the year 2000, the ratio of combat potentials of the Russian Navy and its US counterpart could be as low as 1:20 or 1:25 if the Russian government does not improve its policy towards naval development in the next few years. In contrast to the Russian Navy, the USN has relatively stable funding. For comparison, during the period 1995–96, the USN commissioned four improved *Los Angeles* class SSGNs and five *Arleigh Burke* class DDGs. During the same period the Russian Navy commissioned only two improved *Akula* class SSNs and one *Udaloi–II* class DDG.[122] In comparison with China, while the PLA Navy may have a 63-submarine force—the largest in the Pacific—its boats are very old, with as many as half no longer operational, and difficulty in communications (outdated equipment) keeps the boats close to shore. For some time, the Russian Navy will remain more than a match for its Chinese counterpart for a large variety of scenarios, the one exception being offensive operations close to the Chinese coast.

CONCLUSION

The Pacific Fleet has a long history of development by fits and starts, becoming rather powerful time and again, but with stagnation and decay setting in later on. After the collapse of the USSR, the navy—like the other services—suffered from budget cuts. A significant number of vessels and aircraft have been decommissioned; maintenance of equipment and the fleet's operational readiness have deteriorated; and deployment areas have been considerably reduced. However, Russia's Pacific Fleet has managed to survive as an integral operational–strategic entity in the Pacific basin.

Although the navy is shrinking in size, a qualitative modernisation is still slowly taking place. Notwithstanding new arrangements for unified (joint) operational commands operating on the basis of Military Districts, the organisational structure of the Pacific Fleet has remained essentially unchanged since the days of the USSR. It still reflects the strategic thinking of the past, when Russia's major adversaries were the Western sea powers, and the United States in particular. However, the Russian Navy is not abandoning its Pacific Fleet. Although now the Pacific Fleet is less powerful than the Northern Fleet, efforts have been made to increase its operational capabilities, mainly through the deployment of advanced submarines. Despite the changes, Russia's naval forces in the Pacific will sustain an option for involvement in regional maritime and other strategic affairs for many years to come.

Russia is aware of the growing importance of, and potential conflicts in, the Pacific region. Despite the severe economic crisis that hit some East Asian countries in 1997 and 1998, there are still good grounds to believe that East Asia will be one of the world's major economic and political centres in the first half of the next century and that maritime interests of great powers, particularly sea-borne trade and resource exploitation, will continue to grow. This fact is well understood by the world's leading nations. Therefore, it is in Russia's national interests to become more involved in the region's maritime affairs. Moreover, there is growing opinion within Russia that major threats to its national security are likely to come from the East.

If the Russian Federation wants to be one of the leading power centres of the 21st century, it needs to manifest itself as a great Pacific power, ensuring regional stability and peace. One of the best and most effective ways of demonstrating its power is by the use of naval forces.

Russia must also rely on its naval forces to defend its territorial interests, while dealing with other maritime issues, such as the ownership of seabed resources. Consequently, the Russian Pacific Fleet will need to continue to maintain substantial capabilities. The prospects for this in coming years now seem quite remote, since it will take Russia many years and enormous efforts to restore its navy in the Far East. Yet, if other great powers in the Pacific sustain the current tendency toward cooperative, non-belligerent policies, this will certainly reduce pressure on Russia to maintain large naval forces at high readiness levels for sustained combat.

8

Air forces

Once a very powerful force, comparable only to the US Air Force, the air forces of Russia today find themselves in the worst situation in their entire history. Constant underfunding and severe shortages with spare parts and aviation fuel have resulted in a substantial reduction in the size of the force, as well as a serious decline in the professional training of its personnel, especially combat pilots. Russia's air forces[1] are now passing through a very difficult transitional period. Russia lost vital elements of Soviet air force logistic support infrastructure to the newly independent states, together with a considerable number of modern aircraft. By the time of the collapse of the Soviet state, its air force had about 11 000 aircraft, including some 5000 combat and 700 military transport aeroplanes. The new Russian state received about 65 per cent of the USSR's aircraft and about 62 per cent of its combat aircraft. Some of the most advanced aircraft, such as Tu–95MS and Tu–160 strategic bombers, Su–27 fighters, and Il–78 tanker aircraft were left outside the Russian Federation. Russia's air forces also had to deal with withdrawal of aircraft from former republics of the USSR and from former Warsaw Pact members. This involved redeployment of units and formations and command and control centres to new locations virtually devoid of the required infrastructure. The numerous other problems have included continuous degradation of infrastructure in Russia,[2] loss of flying and combat experience of the large numbers of personnel leaving the service, and a sharply reduced number of operational aircraft. According to the assessments of foreign military experts, the Russian air forces are unable to engage in two strategic missions simultaneously.[3]

Constant inadequate funding of the air forces has resulted in serious financial difficulties in all areas, including salaries of the personnel and their social insurance system. Probably for the first time for 50 years air force pilots and other personnel could not get their wages for months, and on occasion have been driven to desperate measures to put pressure on the government to deliver. For example, in 1996 four MiG–31 pilots at the Yelisovo air base (Far East MD) went on a hunger strike to demand their back-pay overdue by several months.[4] Eventually, this particular incident was resolved by using emergency financial resources of the unit, but it provides a good indication of the environment in which the Russian air forces have to operate.

Budget pressures forced consideration of radical organisational restructuring as a means of addressing these complex management problems. But the change in Russia's strategic posture compared with the USSR, particularly the change from concern with superpower war to preoccupation with local wars and civil insurrection within Russia or on its borders, has also dictated a radical rethinking of what do with Russia's troubled air forces. In particular, combat operations by the air forces in Chechnia between 1994 and 1996 demonstrated to the military leadership how vital experience gained by the Soviet air forces during the Great Patriotic War had been lost. One example of this cited by the air force command was the greater need for special techniques providing appropriate air support to ground forces 'in conditions of complex combat in a large city'.[5]

The radical rethinking that resulted led to a decision to reorient the armed forces as a whole to more integrated operations according to the environment in which they operated (land, sea or air), as mentioned in chapter 5. In this process, the existence of two separate air forces—the Air Force [*Voenno-Vozdushnye Sily*] and Air Defence Force [*Voiska Protivovozdushnoi Oborony*]—was no longer regarded as acceptable. In accordance with President Yeltsin's decree of July 1997 on the 'Priority Measures to Reform the Armed Forces of the Russian Federation and Improve Their Structure',[6] the two independent services were to be transformed into a qualitatively new branch of the armed forces—the Russian Federation Air Force (RFAF)—by 1 January 1999. But this process, like all reform processes, has added new pressures to the already troubled air forces.

This chapter analyses the current state of and likely prospects for the RFAF, with special reference to units east of the Urals. After a brief comment on the current turmoil in development of air power concepts in Russia, the chapter pays considerable attention to the reorganisation of Russia's air forces from two separate services into a single Russian Federation Air Force (RFAF). This reorganisation is sufficiently radical, perhaps the most radical change in organisational structure anywhere in the entire Russian armed forces, that it will have profound effects on all other aspects of Russia's air power, including its presence and capabilities east of the Urals. The current and prospective circumstances of the air force in training and equipment are discussed.

CURRENT AIR POWER CONCEPTS

In recent years, Russia's military–political leadership have reconsidered the role and place of military aviation in modern strategic planning. In contrast to the views of Soviet military leaders in the 1970s and even the early 1980s, which strongly favoured the employment of ground force tank armies as a main shock force, military leaders of Russia in the 1990s have come to see the country's air force as the main strike component of Russia's forces in a conventional war. This shift in approach has emerged from Russian analyses of recent military conflicts, especially the Gulf War in 1991.

Success of the allies' air operations against Iraq during Operation Desert Storm served to re-ignite air power theory in the RFAF upper ranks, and in Russia's Ministry of Defence. Lieutenant-General Vladimir Vasiutin, deputy head of the leading air force institution, the Gagarin Air Force Academy, summarised the outcomes of recent conflicts and suggested that these dictated a reorientation of Russian strategy as follows:

> Experience gained by forces in recent military conflicts indicates that the outcome of any war is now decided by effective air attacks. The wars in the Persian Gulf and Lebanon, and other conflicts in recent years, provide ample proof that the outcome of individual operations or entire wars largely depends on aviation activity. Hence the nature of the operational training of the armed forces should be worked out in this direction.[7]

The RFAF is concentrating its efforts on preparations for a limited-scale war, where it can concentrate an appropriate number of combat-ready aircraft and prepared pilots to wage a successful air campaign. This correlates with a new concept of Russia's military doctrine. According to the provisions of a 1996 version of Russia's military doctrine:

- A local armed conflict must be neutralised by the forces of one military district, and
- A regional armed conflict must be neutralised by the forces of two or three military districts.[8]

Consequently, RFAF operational planning includes the redeployment of forces from one strategic sector (theatre of military operations or TVD[9] by its Russian initials) to another in order to build up a grouping of military aircraft sufficient to accomplish the abovementioned major tasks.

Despite the fact that Russia's military doctrine promulgated in the National Security Blueprint of 1997 places most emphasis on local or regional war—in other words limited-scale conflict— the RFAF Command still considers the possibility of a large-scale conventional war. The Commander in Chief, Colonel-General Anatoly Kornukov, formulated the basic strategic objective for the RFAF in the foreseeable future as follows:

> There is no immediate military threat to Russia in modern conditions, but military dangers still exist. In this case, territorial claims of other countries to Russia, and existing (potential) sources of local wars and armed conflicts in the near proximity of the CIS borders, and attempts of interference in internal affairs . . . Thus, in the 21st century, Russia's integrated Air Force should be prepared to execute missions not only in armed conflicts and local wars, but also in regional, and consequently, large-scale conventional war.[10]

However the balance between missions in current air power concepts and doctrine is far from settled, as a retired air force general observed in late 1997.[11] Kornukov reiterated this same point in March 1998: 'one of the primary theoretical problems [of the reorganisation] is the development of concepts for the operational employment' of the new integrated air force.[12]

Nevertheless, Kornukov identified 18 separate missions, a compilation of which is offered below. The order in which he identified them reveals something about the more defensive strategic dispositions both of the national government and the air force compared with declaratory doctrine of the Soviet era. The missions are to:

- detect the initiation of an enemy's airborne attack and provide warning to regional military and civil defence (1–2);
- gain and maintain air superiority (3),
- protect troops and rear services (4),

- provide support for operations by ground and naval forces (5),
- destroy enemy facilities and economic potential (6),
- disrupt enemy command and control at national and operational levels (7),
- destroy enemy military forces and reserves (8–11, 14–15),
- air-drop and airlift of troops (12–13),
- conduct strategic, operational and tactical aerial reconnaissance and monitor air use of border regions (16–17),
- accomplish special missions (18).

Kornukov tied the future of Russian national security to the ability of the government to fund an adequate air force and to the ability of the air force itself to further develop operational doctrine in line with the above missions.

CREATION OF AN INTEGRATED AIR FORCE

In the light of the country's persistent financial crisis after the mid-1990s, Russian specialists quickly came to the conclusion that if the government tried to preserve both the Air Force and the Air Defence Force as separate services, Russia would have 25 per cent fewer combat-ready aircraft by the year 2000 than it did then. By remaining separate, the air forces faced decline from multi-purpose and highly flexible services into ones with limited combat capabilities likely to be defeated in many scenarios of military conflict. Financial constraints would certainly make it impossible to increase the combat effectiveness of Russia's air forces while maintaining them as two separate services.

But developments in international affairs, strategy, military art and air power were also quite fundamental influences on the decision for integration. Military conflicts in recent years were interpreted in Moscow as dictating the need for significant air strike capabilities to achieve victory in a limited amount of time with minimum losses among friendly troops. The progress of a military campaign and the final outcome were now seen as being more dependent than before on results of air combat operations. At the same time, the ability of modern air forces to deploy with little warning and deliver massive surprise strikes raised the issue of having very flexible and centralised command and control mechanisms for all air force related assets.

Russian military strategists argued that the capabilities of the former Air Defence Force (ADF) were limited compared with the former Air Force (AF). The ADF assets did perform vital missions.

They could combat enemy air assault, support friendly air forces to gain air superiority, and provide appropriate air defence of the country's vital military and economic facilities and centres, and most populated areas. However, they were unable to destroy enemy ground troops, its air defence and naval forces, and were incapable of providing air support to friendly ground troops during their defensive and offensive operations.[13] By contrast, the Air Force was inherently more versatile. It was structured for much greater manoeuvre—for offensive operations as well as defensive. Table 8.1 shows in schematic form the deliberation of certain strategists[14] that where large-scale defensive operations against enemy air are not required—that is in circumstances of local or regional war on Russia's periphery or beyond—the ADF assets would be largely idle. Table 8.1 also reflects a very strong faith in the central role of air power relative to ground and naval forces in the sort of conventional warfare that Russia is likely to face. In seven out of twelve strategic operations, the share of an integrated air force would be more than 70 per cent.

Defence Minister, Marshal Igor Sergeyev, described basic principles of the reorganisation of the Air Force and the Air Defence Force into one fighting service:

- maximum reduction of management and duplicative structures of the two services;
- preservation of significant fighting capabilities of the combat units and formations directed at both defensive and offensive operations;
- maximum resolution of the problems associated with conditions of service of personnel;
- increasing the percentage of operational aircraft, equipment and weaponry; and

Table 8.1 Service shares in mission execution in a conventional war (%)[15]

Missions	GF	AF	ADF	Navy
Repel sudden aerospace attack	5	30	60	5
Neutralise enemy forces—ground	75	20	0	5
—air forces	3	80	15	2
—air defence forces	10	75	10	5
—naval	5	20	0	75
Prevent enemy reconstitution of forces	5	75	0	20
Win strategic air superiority	5	70	20	5
Weaken enemy military–economic potential	10	70	0	20
Disorganise enemy state and military controls	5	90	0	5
Repel and defeat enemy invasion	70	15	10	5
Protect communications and key areas	45	15	20	20

- bringing the personnel level of units/formations to full manning.[16]

Command and control arrangements and most lower level command structures were still being worked out through 1999, but based on a number of sources, the authors have concluded that the organisational structure of the RFAF closely approximates that shown in Figure 8.1.

It has been repeatedly pointed out by top Russian military officials that the integration of the Air Force and the Air Defence Force into one service is not just an ordinary force reduction measure but a very complex process of creating a very capable service with significantly improved 'qualitative parameters from the point of view of its combat effectiveness'.[17] Out of 8 billion roubles, provided by the government towards military reform at the beginning of 1998, 60–65 per cent were allocated to reform of the Air Force and the Air Defence Force.[18] This is a clear indication that the new RFAF occupies a special place within the Russian military machine, and the quick and successful reform of this service is one of the highest priorities for the country's military–political leadership.

As of 1 March 1998, the date of amalgamation of the two air forces, the RFAF had five tactical air armies and three air defence armies. Table 8.2 shows the aircraft composition of the RFAF in early 1998. Column 2 shows total for aircraft with units. More than 1000 combat aircraft are in store.

Figure 8.1 Organisation chart: Air Force

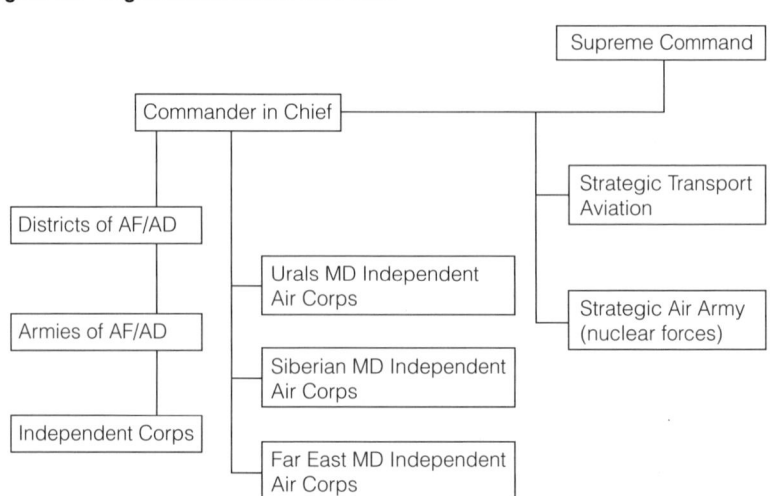

Table 8.2   Tactical combat aircraft of the RFAF order of battle [19]

Type	Total
Bombers/tactical aircraft	
Su–24 *Fencer*	475
Su–25 *Frogfoot*	250
Su–34	unknown
Fighters/interceptors	
MiG–23 *Fogger*	100
MiG–29 *Fulcrum*	315
MiG–31 *Foxhound*	425
Su–27 *Flanker*	375
Su–30 *Flanker*	5–7
Reconnaissance	
MiG–25 *Foxbat*	40
Su–24 *Fencer*	160
AWACS	
Il–76 *Candid*	20
Training	
MiG–23 *Fogger*	165
MiG–25 *Foxbat*	10
MiG–29 *Fulcrum*	100
Su–24 *Fencer*	95
Su–25 *Frogfoot*	30
Su–27 *Flanker*	10
L–39	1100
L–410/Tu–134	250
Combat helicopters	820

During reorganisation of the Air Force and the Air Defence Force, the combined strength of the personnel and non-military employees of the two services will be reduced by 200 000, including approximately 50 000 officers (40 generals).[20] Between January and May 1998, 496 units and formations (including 90 000 men) of the two services were disbanded.[21] However, the main emphasis has been on the reduction of duplicative management structures, non-vital logistic support units, including several engineering, automotive, and service battalions.[22] After the reductions, logistic and support units will amount to only 43 per cent of the total strength of the new RFAF[23] and combat units have been increased already to 52 per cent of the total RFAF personnel strength.[24] As the result of the unification of the command structures of the two services, 21 generals and 226 senior officers were cut[25] and an overall savings effect of 29.5 per cent of annual costs for the two commands was achieved.[26] The reorganisation also had a positive effect on the problem of undermanned combat units. By August 1998 the integrated RFAF was almost fully manned (98.7 per cent). By the end of 1998, it was expected that all units and formations of the RFAF would be fully manned (100 per cent).

The system of military education of the RFAF has also been reorganised. The total number of air force flying schools is to be reduced by 20 per cent, from 19 schools down to 14.[27] Training terms for pilots will be reduced from five to four years. The RFAF command believes that these measures will not affect the quality of training. From now on, flying schools will train their cadets only on combat aircraft: MiG–29, Su–25, and partially MiG–23, since existing training aircraft had not fulfilled initial expectations.[28] The RFAF expects to save approximately 65 billion roubles each year by reducing training terms.[29]

Another major benefit the RFAF gained from the reorganisation is the significant improvement in the quota of operational equipment and weaponry of the combat units. Before the reorganisation only half of the aircraft allocated to units were considered operational.[30] After the re-distribution of equipment and weaponry under the reorganisation, numbers of operational aircraft in units are expected to rise to 85 per cent of the total number.[31] Only modern types of combat aircraft will remain in service. In particular, fighter regiments equipped with MiG–31 *Foxhound*, Su–27 *Flanker*, and MiG–29 *Fulcrum* will be preserved.[32] In particular, combat-ready units and formations will receive later model aircraft from disbanded units. Earlier models will be removed from combat service and will be used as 'donors' for spare parts.

Structural composition of the integrated RFAF will change as well. The basic task of the RFAF structural reorganisation is the development of a centralised command and control structure for subordinated forces. All preserved or restructured units and formations of the new service have been reorganised into units designated as Armies, Corps or Divisions of the Air Forces and Air Defence Forces (AF/AD). Corps and divisions will be reinforced with fighter units. Currently, the RFAF comprises three AF/AD Armies (headquartered in St Petersburg, Rostov on the Don, and Khabarovsk), three AF/AD Corps (headquartered in Chita, Yekaterinburg, and Novosibirsk), and the Moscow AF/AD District.[33] They are directly subordinated to the RFAF Commander in Chief. On the operational level, each of these groupings is subordinated to the commander of a particular MD according to their location. In 1999 it was decided to re-establish the Urals AD Army on the basis of the Urals AF/AD Corps. Lieutenant-General Yury Bondarev, RFAF Deputy Commander, said that the decision was influenced by NATO's air campaign against Yugoslavia.[34]

As part of the reform of the air forces, the commands of the

Long-Range Aviation (LRA)[35] and the Military-Transport Aviation (VTA for its Russian initials)[36] have been disbanded. Forces of the LRA and the VTA have been reorganised into two separate armies: the 37th Air Army of the Supreme High Command (former LRA), and the 61st Air Army of the Supreme High Command (former VTA), both under the direct command of the RFAF.

As of early 1999, the 61st Air Army of the Supreme High Command comprises two divisions (nine air transport regiments).[37] With around 340–350 aircraft in its inventory, the 61st Air Army currently relies on three main types of aircraft: medium/long-range heavy-lift transports Il–76 *Candid* and ageing An–22 *Cock*, and the long-range heavy-lift An–124 *Condor*.[38] According to General Anatoly Kornukov, the 61st Air Army is now capable of air-lifting one airborne division, manned at peace-time standards, in two-and-a-half lifts. On wartime mobilisation, civil aircraft would significantly increase RFAF military transport capacity to enable the air-lifting of the entire wartime-manned airborne division at once.[39]

Ground-based air defence units have also been reorganised. The number of radar posts or stations on less vital strategic fronts has been reduced. Despite economic hardships, air defence troops received new up-to-date types of armaments, including the advanced long-range S–300PMU SAM,[40] the medium-range 9M38 *Buk*–M1 SAM,[41] and short-range 9K22 *Tunguska* missile complexes.[42] Since 31 December 1997 air defence troops of the ground forces have been reorganised into the Army Air Defence.[43] From now on, Army Air Defence will provide air defence not only for the ground forces but also for the airborne troops, and the naval infantry of the Russian Navy. For example, in the Far Eastern MD, Army Air Defence will take part in the protection of naval installations and facilities of the Pacific Fleet. According to the Chief of the Army Air Defence, Colonel-General Boris Dukhov, mobile well-equipped air defence groupings will be created on the territory of each MD.[44]

Personnel strength of the integrated RFAF in early 1998 was estimated at about 200 000 with 45 per cent of the enlisted personnel to be reduced as the result of the integration. It had approximately 1850 combat aircraft, out of which 1365 were potent fourth-generation planes: MiG–29 *Fulcrum*, MiG–31 *Fox-hound*, Su–25 *Frogfoot*, and Su–27 *Flanker* (see Table 8.2). Half of Russia's combat aircraft, around 900, are located east of the Urals.[45] According to the Russian sources, in 1997 the RFAF fielded 10 fighter regiments east of the Urals. One regiment was equipped with MiG–23 (40 aircraft), three with Su–27 (80 aircraft), and six with MiG–31 (180 aircraft).[46] Out of 1900 surface-to-air missile complexes (SAM) of the former Air Defence Force, 800 are modern models. Some 600 SAMs are deployed east of the Urals.[47]

Command and control functions of the integrated air force from now on will be carried out by the RFAF Central Command Post, formally a CCP of the Air Defence Force. This command post is located in the settlement Chernoye, near Moscow, and is commanded by an RFAF major-general.[48]

RFAF units and formations east of the Urals have been also reorganised. According to Kornukov, the strength of the Independent Urals AF/AD Corps (HQ Yekaterinburg) would be reduced by more than 50 per cent.[49] An Independent AF/AD Corps (HQ Chita) has been created on the basis of the reformed 33rd Air Army.[50] In the Far East Military District, two independent armies—an Air Army and an Air Defence Army—have been reorganised into one army, the 11th AF/AD army.[51] A number of fighter and transport regiments and logistic units have been reduced. In the Far Eastern MD, only one military airlift regiment will be preserved.[52] Some of the closed air bases and airfields have been handed over to the local authorities, and will be used for civilian purposes. For example, the air base Zolotaia Dolina [Golden Valley] near Nakhodka will be converted into an international airport.[53] It will provide services to the Nakhodka free economic zone.

As part of the air force reorganisation, the most modern equipment and weaponry have been redistributed to the preserved units and formations. However, this process did not just begin. Since the beginning of the early 1990s, as part of major reductions of conventional armaments in Russia's Siberian and Far Eastern MDs, the process of replacing ageing equipment and weaponry with modern equivalents has been taking place. For example, MiG–23 *Flogger* aircraft of the Guards Fighter Regiment located on the outskirts of Vladivostok were replaced with modern Su–27s in 1995.[54] With the release of substantial quantities of armaments as a result of the air forces' amalgamation, the process of re-equipping accelerated.

Most combat aircraft have been withdrawn from the Kuril Islands and Sakhalin Island. In 1993, Russia removed all MiG–23 fighters from the Burevestnik air base (Iturup Island in the territory disputed with Japan).[55] Only army aviation units will remain on the islands. In particular, at the end of 1998 a mixed helicopter detachment was formed for operations in the Kuril Islands area.[56]

Generally speaking, Russian tactical air power east of the Urals has been primarily concentrated on battlefield aviation or ground attack. The trouble is that more than 70 per cent of Russia's military aircraft are front-line planes. In 1998, the balance between fighter and strike aviation was approximately 3:1 in favour of fighters. Out of overall RFAF strength, tactical bombers comprise only 16–17 per cent, attack aircraft 10–11 per cent, and fighter planes 37–38 per cent. This disproportion could gradually reduce the RFAF's capability to fulfil one of its highest priority tasks— air support of the ground troops.[57] To solve the problem, the RFAF has been emphasising the development of new-generation strike aircraft, and substantial modernisation of existing aircraft (including fighters) to increase their strike capabilities. Also, based on the Great Patriotic War and the Afghan War experiences, the RFAF Command is inclined to think that partial employment of long-range aviation could be one solution for certain tactical tasks.[58]

COMBAT TRAINING

The RFAF Command has placed great expectations on the integration of the Air Defence Troops into the Air Force as a means of significantly improving the level of combat training of its personnel, especially pilots. The transformation of social and economic conditions in Russia after 1991 has had similar effects on the air forces as those felt by the armed forces in general. Apart from the radical decline in defence spending, fuel costs skyrocketed after price controls were lifted. Consequently, the air force, like other services, has been unable to buy enough fuel, and this has resulted in severe fuel shortages for combat training. Flying hours of combat pilots have been drastically reduced—from 120–130 hours per year (the Soviet standard) down to approximately 20–30 per year. As recently as 1997, RFAF fighter pilots were getting 40 flying hours a year; bomber and long-range aviation pilots 70–80 hours; and transport pilots 120–150 hours a year. By June–July 1998, the average flying hours in tactical aviation was 5–8 hours; long-range aviation 15–20 hours; and transport aviation 50 hours.[59] The intensity of flying operations in transport aviation can be explained by its involvement in commercial activities, an important means of obtaining additional finance for air force needs.

The lack of fighter pilot combat training brought the flying skills among some pilots to such a low level as to raise questions in the upper ranks of the RFAF about prohibiting use of some types of aircraft. For example, in 1997 Air Defence Force Commander, Colonel-General Viktor Prudnikov, thought about grounding all its MiG–31 interceptors. He argued that due to the complexity of flying the MiG–31, its aircrews should fly 100 hours a year as an average, instead of around 20.[60] If Prudnikov's proposed ban on flying were acted on, Russia's air defences would suffer a significant blow because the MIG–31 is a state-of-the-art, possibly the world's best, fighter. Lack of hours has not prevented the air forces east of the Urals from maintaining a high profile with some neighbouring countries. For example, during three hours in September 1995, four MiG–31s repeatedly threatened to violate Japanese air space in the island of Hokkaido, forcing the Japanese Air Force to deploy 10 fighters in response.[61]

High fuel costs are not the only obstacle affecting combat training of pilots. Severe shortages of spare parts, equipment and maintenance personnel have led to a decline in numbers of operational aircraft. The availability of aircraft has been so low that the RFAF is suffering from a substantial excess of pilots compared to the number of aircraft available. At the time of the USSR's collapse, the two air forces had roughly 5000 aircraft, with a pilot pool of 13 000–15 000 men—a maximum pilot/aircraft ratio of 3:1. By the time of the decision to integrate the two forces, this ratio had blown out to 5:1 in some units. As a result, the number of flying hours per pilot was below the required level, and the severe fuel shortages have made the problem even worse.

Under the circumstances, regimental commanders tried to achieve readiness standards by allocating available training hours to experienced air crews and neglecting the training of young pilots. Available fuel was thus directed at maintaining appropriate levels of professional skill of only a limited number of pilots and front-line aviation regiments were prepared to fulfil their combat tasks with only a limited number of aircrews. Especially difficult missions could therefore only have been performed by an even smaller number of pilots.

Therefore, one of the goals of the restructuring of the two air forces into one is a reduction in the pilot pool to the point of having three fully trained pilots for two aircraft. The RFAF plans to reduce the manning table of its 70 aircraft regiments by one-third. Since the RFAF Command prefers to keep older and better-trained pilots, this reduction will fall most heavily on younger inexperienced pilots, and the initial plan was to discharge some 365 young pilots.[62] By 1998, the average age of fighter pilots was 36, which is two years above the preferred level.[63] The RFAF hopes that with more funding and fuel released by the restructuring and integration, it can increase the intensity and scope of combat training and that it can return to normal levels of training for young pilots. In early 1998, the Deputy Commander-in-Chief, General Viktor Kot, expressed the expectation that by 1999 the annual average number of flying hours per pilot would be brought to 50 hours.[64] But he did not expect the RFAF to be able to restore professional training standards of its pilots to the 1991 level before the year 2001.

In response to the new concept of strategic re-deployment of aviation groupings from one strategic sector (TVD) to another, the RFAF conducted several experimental exercises. The first one took place in May 1993, when 10 Su–24s flew from Voronezh (in European Russia near the border with Ukraine) to Dzhida (Buriat Republic in the Russian Federation, near the border with Mongolia). A similar exercise was held at the end of 1997, when six Su–24s deployed from the Transbaikal area to the European TVD.[65] In both cases, aircraft groupings conducted live-fire exercises during the flight. In mid-1998, the RFAF conducted a more complex exercise on the deployment of a combat aircraft grouping from one TVD to another. It involved four Su–30s, two MiG–31 fighters, one A–50 AWACS aircraft, and two Il–78 flying tankers.[66] The grouping was deployed from the Savosleika air base (Niznegorodskaia Oblast) to the Arctic Circle area where they participated in a simulated repulsion of an air assault. Similar experimental exercises were held at the beginning of April 1999, when a group of combat aircraft (three Su–30s, three MiG–31s, a Tu–95MS strategic bomber, and an Il–78 aerial refueller) were deployed to the same area. As in 1998, the basic idea of this exercise was to develop principles of manoeuvre of air power from one theatre to another.[67] Other training in 1998 included 82 command-and-staff exercises, including a large-scale live-fire exercise of the 37th Air Army (Long-Range Aviation). Twelve fighter regiments also carried out live-fire exercises.[68]

MODERNISATION PROGRAM AND PROSPECTS FOR DEVELOPMENT

The military budget crisis has translated into severe reductions in aircraft orders by the air forces. According to Major-General

Nikolai Anisimov, Chief of the RFAF Financial-Economic Directorate, the Russian Air Force was able to purchase 77 aircraft (both fixed-wing and helicopters) in 1992; 66 in 1993; 29 in 1994; 31 in 1995; 19 in 1996; and 6 in 1997. No purchases were made in 1998.[69]

Production rates for military aircraft between 1995 and 1997 were very low, as Table 8.3 shows. Procurement rates for the Russian air forces have been even lower, since many of the aircraft produced have been sold to other governments. Between 1993 and 1997, no new MiG–29 aircraft were delivered to the Russian air forces.[70] With most of the third-generation aircraft expected to be retired by the year 2000, the RFAF might end up with a force of about 1400 combat aircraft by then (though they would be fourth-generation planes). Still, the RFAF expects to receive some new types of aircraft to replace its ageing third-generation planes. The budget constraints have forced the air forces to cancel some expensive prospective programs, such as the MiG MAPO[71] Project 1.42 (discussed later in this chapter).

The imbalance in strike and defensive capabilities, which has raised serious concerns in the upper ranks of the RFAF, will set the direction for much of the future development of Russian military aviation. Other high-priority development programs for the RFAF are as follows: substantial modernisation of the fourth-generation systems (MiG–29, Su–27 and Su–25); a new-generation tactical fighter-bomber (Su–34); a new transport aircraft; a fifth-generation fighter; a new generation of all-weather, high-precision weapons (HPW) systems; and adoption of a new attack helicopter. Several of these are elaborated below.

Table 8.3 Military aircraft production 1990–97[72]

	1990	1991	1992	1993	1994	1995	1996	1997
Bombers	40	30	20	10	2	2	1	0
Fighters/FGA	430	250	150	100	50	20	25	35
Transports	120	60	5	5	5	4	3	0
Helicopters[73]	450	350	175	150	100	95	75	70

Improving strike capabilities of the air force

In late 1997, the RFAF decided to proceed with modernisation of the operational MiG–29 fighter aircraft to the MiG–29SMT standard and assigned this project a high priority. According to Colonel-General Anatoly Sitnov, Chief of Armaments of Russia's Armed Forces, the MiG–29SMT complies with standards of a fifth-generation fighter.[74] The MiG–29 has been constantly criticised (especially by Western analysts) for a short operational range compared with that of heavy fighters.[75] As a result, the upgrade will extend the operating range of the aircraft from 1850 km (original MiG–29 range) up to 3500 km, which matches the range of heavy fighters. In addition to a new cockpit and the most advanced avionics,[76] the MiG–29SMT is fitted with new high-precision weapons systems, primarily the X–31A air-to-surface missile, which provides the aircraft with significantly improved strike capabilities. The combat load of the MiG–29SMT has increased from 2 tonnes to 4 tonnes.

Significantly increased combat potential of the modernised MiG–29, plus relatively cheap cost of conversion of earlier MiG–29 aircraft into the MiG–29SMT, has led to the decision of Russia's MoD to place an order for modernisation of up to 180 RFAF MiG–29s into a MiG–29SMT version.[77] Also, 124 MiG–29UB trainers will be converted into MiG–29UBTs.[78] Originally, the RFAF and MoD expected to upgrade 10–15 MiG–29s in 1998, with a goal of having up to 40 MiG–29SMTs by 2000.[79] However, due to the worsening economic situation in Russia in 1998, the RFAF probably received no more than three MiG–29SMTs that year.[80]

Nevertheless, it is likely that the RFAF and MoD will continue to push hard for the quick modernisation of the MiG–29 fleet. The RFAF expect 24 MiG–29s to be upgraded to the new standard in 1999.[81] The new version MiG–29 is to be the leader of Russia's front-line aviation until 2015 or 2020. As of August 1998, the RFAF commander, Colonel-General Kornukov, was still hoping that up to half of the planned MiG–29SMTs could be deployed by 2000.[82]

The RFAF also expects to convert some Su–27s into the Su–27P version which has superior air-to-surface capabilities, though it would be a limited number of aircraft, due to the costs involved.[83]. The MiG–31, Russia's heavy long-range interceptor, will be upgraded as well to give the aircraft a multi-role capability. The upgrade version of the MiG–31 is called MiG–31F. Apart from its traditional arsenal of different range air-to-air missiles (including the types still under development, such as R–77 *Adder*), the MiG–31F will be equipped with different types of air-to-surface missiles, among them Kh–31 anti-radar missile, and Kh–59M TV-guided missile.[84]

The RFAF has also placed orders for several Su–25TM attack aircraft, which features the *Phasotron Kopyo–25* multi-mode radar. In April 1998, Russia's armed forces were already operating three Su–25TMs with a further four expected in mid-1998.[85] The importance of acquisition by the RFAF of this aircraft comes from the fact it is considered to be the vital airborne 'shock' component of Russia's newly created rapid-deployment forces. Groupings of rapid-deployment forces, called 'units of constant combat readiness', have been organised in every military district. (This is discussed in chapter 9.) It is expected that the air element of each such grouping will consist of four Su–25TMs, 12 Su–25s, and several helicopter gunships.[86] Apart from the four Su–25TM aircraft ordered by the RFAF, 20 Su–25T aircraft built in a plant in Tblisi (Georgia) in 1990 and 1991 and transferred to Russia were to be converted into the Su–25TM version at the Ulan-Ude aircraft plant.

Another significant step taken by the RFAF to improve its strike capabilities was the acceptance into service of a new-generation tactical bomber—the Su–34 (also known in the West as Su–27IB). The development of the Su–34 for the RFAF is the highest priority combat aircraft program in Russia today. First flown in April 1990, this long-range interdiction aircraft has been designed to replace the Su–24, as well as the ageing MiG–27 and Su–17 aircraft. Key features of the Su–34 are its unrefuelled range of 4000 km and new avionics (multi-function phased-array radar with automatic terrain-following/terrain-avoidance for low-level attack profiles).[85] The Su–34 will give Russia's armed forces an enhanced capability to mount offensive tactical operations. The aircraft has been nicknamed *Platypus* because of its heavily armed 'twin-crew' side-by-side cockpit with an extensively redesigned nose.[88] Since its adoption by the RFAF in 1995, it has been in production at the Novosibirsk aircraft plant with a planned output of 15 units by 1998.[89] A reconnaissance version of the Su–34 is in development as well. It is set to replace the Su–24MR *Fencer-E* in this role. The new reconnaissance aircraft will be fitted with side-looking radar, SIGINT, TV, infra-red, laser and photo-reconnaissance equipment. This aircraft is unlikely to be commissioned until 2000.[90]

Improvement of airlift capability

A strategy of flexible response to possible security crises along the Russian perimeter, adopted as part of the new Russian military strategy, has raised the need for substantial air transport capability. Some indications of Russia's new airlift doctrine were observed during the 1994–96 Chechen War. Over half of the forces used in the conflict were airlifted to the theatre. In 1996, the commander of the military transport aviation (VTA), General Viacheslav Yefanov, described the future composition of the force. He said the RFAF was planning to adopt three new types of transport aircraft: Il–76MF, four-engine Il–106 heavylifters, and the twin-engine Tu–330 freighter.[91] However, since then the situation has changed. Plans for the Il–106 and Tu–330 appear to have been cancelled, and even the future of the Il–76MF, once the RFAF's favourite, was looking uncertain for some time. For now, the RFAF's surge airlift capability is estimated to be limited to one airborne division in two sorties of the entire VTA fleet.

The Il–76MF is a stretch, improved version of the Il–76 *Candid* heavy transport, a backbone of Russia's VTA. The maximum payload of the Il–76MF has been increased to 52 tonnes, and the range is 5200 km. The program was launched in 1992 and is being funded by the RFAF. In August 1995, at the Moscow International Air Show, it was announced that the RFAF would receive two IL–76MF in 1996 with more to follow later.[90] But now the prospects for the Il–76MF being adopted by the RFAF are uncertain, as suggested by general designer of the Ilyushin bureau, Academician Genrikh Novozhilov:

> The military, despite promising announcements, refer to the Il–76MF, from my point of view, rather coldly. But they talk a lot about the An–70. I have nothing against the machine of the *Antonov* bureau [in Ukraine], this is a really good aircraft, but I think it will be more efficient to support the domestic aircraft industry first, and then everybody else's.[93]

By 1999, there was renewed talk that the Il–76MF acquisitions would proceed, with General Kornukov suggesting that the 61st Air Army might acquire the first eight aircraft in two years time.[94]

Somewhat ironically, the An–70 medium-range transport seems to have brighter prospects even though it had been low priority for the RFAF. The An–70 was designed for the Soviet Air Force as a replacement of the An–12 *Cub*. But after the disintegration of the USSR, the project was taken over by Ukraine. Until recently, it had been assumed that the RFAF would abandon the An–70 project and focus on the production of domestically built aircraft, such as the Tu–330 as a replacement for the An–12 in particular. However, it is clear now that the RFAF is keen to make the An–70 its primary medium-range transport.[95] In 1998, Russia's President Boris Yeltsin and his Ukrainian counterpart, Leonid Kuchma, signed a joint declaration about the development of the An–70 for the air forces of the two states.[96] This project is seen as a flag-bearer for improvement in economic and scientific links between Russia and Ukraine. With a range of 7500 km, the An–70 has a maximum payload of 35 tonnes, and can accommodate up to 170 troops. It will be produced in both Ukraine and Russia (probably in Samara), thus leaving Russia some independence of the foreign supplier.

It is likely that the RFAF will adopt only one new type of military transport aircraft in the near future, the An–70. Current RFAF requirements are for the medium-range airlifter. Besides, since the An–70 project has been transferred into the sphere of inter-state relations, there is some hope that it will at least attract stable funding. In particular, General Kornukov expects to see the first An–70 aircraft in the military transport inventory only in three to four years time.[97] The rest of Russia's transport fleet will have to be modernised to prolong its operational life. While the RFAF now sees no point in modernising the An–22 due to its obsolescence, it has plans to extend the life of the Il–76 and An–124 fleets.

Development of a fifth-generation tactical fighter

Beginning in the late 1980s, leading design bureaus of the Soviet military aviation industry began work on a fifth-generation fighter for the air forces. The best known project outside the country was MiG's Multi-Role Front-Line Fighter (MFI).[98] Also known as Project 1.42, the MFI was designed in response to the US F–22 *Raptor* program. A prototype of the MFI was ready to start test flights in 1994, but the expense involved in the development of the aircraft forced its cancellation.[99]

The story of a new fifth-generation fighter for the RFAF took a new turn on 25 September 1997 when Sukhoi flew its S–37 *Berkut* demonstration-experimental aircraft with forward-swept wing configuration.[100] Though the S–37 is claimed to be an experimental aircraft to test new technologies, it indicates extensive R&D progress toward the development of a fifth-generation combat plane for the RFAF. Another surprise came in December 1998 when MiG MAPO finally presented its MFI.[99] MiG MAPO claims that their fighter is superior to the US F–22. The MFI has been built with technologies to reduce radar visibility, has a maximum speed of Mach 2.6, includes fifth-generation avionics and carries all weapons inside the aircraft to reduce radar visibility.[102]

Despite halts in funding by the RFAF for both the MFI and S–37 programs as a result of worsening economic conditions, the RFAF still expects to need a replacement for its front-line aircraft after about 2015 or 2020. Consequently, a fifth-generation fighter remains a stated requirement. And if both the MFI and S–37 are unlikely to be adopted by the RFAF, their test results will provide necessary data and technology for new programs which are under way. The best known program nowadays is a joint project by MiG and MAPO for a Light-Weight Front-Line Fighter (LFI),[103] an alternative version of the heavier MFI. The LFI program, also known as I–2000, is seen as a rival to the US Joint Strike Fighter project.[104] The project is intended to provide the RFAF with a new-generation fighter and air-support aircraft around 2005. The LFI is expected to have a unique aerodynamic configuration, it will incorporate Russian 'Stealth' technology, and it will have short-take-off and landing capabilities.

Development of new weapons systems

Apart from the development of new-generation air-superiority aircraft, the RFAF is concentrating its limited resources on the R&D of new-generation aircraft weapons systems. Special emphasis has been placed on the development of highly mobile missiles, including air-to-air backward-launched missiles. A backward-launched version of the R–73 (AA–11) air-to-air missile (AAM) has been developed and tested. An advanced ramjet-powered version of the R–77 (AA–12) AAM is under development—a competitor for the Future Medium Range Air-to-Air Missiles (FMRAAM) project of the US Air Force. Russian officials have stated that they are also developing AAM with ultra long-range (up to 400 km).[105]

The RFAF is also paying special attention to tactical problems associated with the possibility of using limited forces to perform an increased number of combat tasks. This is associated, first of all, with the advent of HPW that can selectively destroy targets on the principle 'a point strikes a mass'. According to Russian calculations, the use of HPW in conflicts of the second half of the 20th century increased by 3.5 times but during the 1994–96 Chechen campaign, Russia's combat aircraft used HPW only in 35 cases.[106] The main reason was bad weather conditions. As a result, the RFAF has placed an order for the development of all-weather air-to-surface HPW capable of destroying targets in complex static conditions and under high electronic counter measures (ECM).[107]

Adoption of a new combat helicopter

Since the early 1980s, the Soviet and then Russian armed forces have been asking the aviation industry to develop a new combat helicopter to replace the ageing Mi–24. Russia's leading helicopter design bureaus, Mil and Kamov, have each offered a potential replacement. Mil developed the two-seat Mi–28 *Havoc* attack helicopter (a later version is the Mi–28N), while Kamov developed the Ka–50 *Black Shark*[108] coaxial one-seat helicopter. After a fierce rivalry between the two bureaus, the Ka–50 was commissioned for service with Russia's armed forces in 1995.[109]

Black Shark is the first single-seat combat helicopter in the world. Since 1991, the *Progress* plant at Arsenev (Far East) has undertaken a serial production of the helicopters. Up to 20 have been fielded already with Russian ground force units. The government's defence order for 1998 included allocations to build 10, though it is unclear after the August financial crisis whether the government will be able to pay for them. Still, some reports suggest that RFAF will be able to get some in 1999. In particular, one helicopter regiment of the Far Eastern MD is scheduled to receive two by the end of 1999.[110] The Russian army however has a requirement for at least 60 per year, to replace its ageing Mi–24 fleet, but since stabilisation in the near future of financing for defence programs is unlikely, the replacement of *Hinds* with *Black Shark* will probably be a long process. In response to the army requirements, Kamov has developed a two-seat version of the Ka–50, the Ka–52 *Alligator*, which will probably be adopted for service by army aviation as well.

In July 1998, the Kamov Design Bureau showed a prototype of a new helicopter, developed according to the requirements of the Russian military—the Ka–60 lightweight multi-purpose combat helicopter. It is expected that Russia's MoD will place an order for Ka–60 helicopters as a cheaper alternative for pilot training (in terms of operating costs) than Mi–8s which are used now.[111] Production lines for the Ka–60 have been set up at the Ulan-Ude aircraft plant, and this indicates that the acquisition plans will go ahead. Hence, it can be assumed that the Russian army now considers the Kamov family of helicopters to be the backbone of its combat helicopter force.

CONCLUSION

Like the other Russian military services, the RFAF is passing through a difficult and painful period. With the dissolution of the Warsaw Pact and the disintegration of the Soviet state, the Russian air forces had to cope with several urgent problems, such as withdrawal of air force units from Central and Eastern Europe, Mongolia, and the territory of the former Soviet republics, and 'privatisation' of a significant proportion of the Soviet aviation heritage by the armed forces of the newly independent states. The radical 'demilitarisation' of Russia that occurred on the back of continuous economic decline of the country has had a very negative impact on Russian military aviation.

To redress these deficiencies and in response to new strategic circumstances, the two air forces that existed as separate services in the Soviet period (the Air Force and the Air Defence Force) have been reorganised into one—the integrated RFAF. The reorganisation has already created a more capable fighting force than that which existed in early 1998. Significant savings in expenditure created by the reorganisation should allow the RFAF to intensify combat training, and modernise the force. If the goals of the reorganisation continue to be met, the first decade of the 21st century will see Russia with a smaller but far more capable air force than it inherited in 1991.

Regardless of the projected large-scale re-equipment of the RFAF after 2003, some qualitative modernisation is slowly taking place even now. The emphasis is on enhancement of tactical strike capabilities. Despite some pessimistic prognoses made by Western analysts about future prospects for Russia's military aviation due to the critical condition of the Russian aviation industry, there are some positive signs. Flight tests of Sukhoi's revolutionary aircraft (S–37 *Berkut*) are some affirmation of the world-class and in some areas unique capabilities of Russia's military aviation industry, and it leaves room to believe that this industry has quite a few surprises to offer if the country's economic circumstances permit.

Despite the reductions in Russia's air power, the country still has substantial air force assets east of the Urals, consisting of mainly fourth-generation aircraft. The main changes have been in the composition of the force. The overwhelming majority of the combat aircraft based east of the Urals are tactical ground attack aircraft and there has been a marginal shift in balance toward front-line fighters. Still Russia's air power in Siberia and the Far East has significant strike capabilities. Taking into consideration the combined strength east of the Urals of the Long-Range Aviation units and strike components of the RFAF and Naval Aviation, one can conclude that Russia's theatre air strike capabilities continue to represent a very serious potential threat to any adversary. In case of serious military confrontation on its maritime periphery in the east, Russia's regional air power would be able to disrupt sea communications to the theatre. Russia's theatre-based Long-Range Aviation would be capable of delivering strikes to practically any country of the Asia–Pacific region. Consequently, Russia's air power east of the Urals remains among the most potent in the region and a formidable force to be reckoned with.

9

Ground forces

Russia's ground forces have been committed to operations outside the country to a far greater extent since 1991 than either the naval or air forces. At the same time, the ground forces have been more readily associated with domestic politics, either through operations such as the attack on the Parliament in 1993, or through their continuing potential to launch some sort of insurrection against the constitutional order and the government. The war in Chechnia between 1994 and 1996 was stark confirmation of both the high priority the current Russian government places on its ability to field capable ground forces and their domestic political role. These operational commitments and political sensitivities have been additional burdens the ground forces have had to bear at the same time as they have had to cope with the same tribulations being experienced by the navy and air force as a result of the collapse of the USSR—restructuring, sharply reduced budget support, and very low levels of procurement, training and personnel support. For the ground forces, the forced withdrawal of units from former Warsaw Pact members and from former Union Republics of the USSR was a far more demanding, more expensive and more debilitating process than it was for the air forces or the navy. On top of that, the ground forces were obliged under the terms of the 1990 Treaty on Conventional Forces in Europe (CFE) to destroy large quantities of equipment.

East of the Urals, ground forces units should have fared better than those in most other parts of the country because in this region the political geography did not change as drastically. The new Russia still shared a long border with China, and two of the front-line military districts of the Soviet era were still frontier military districts of the new Russia. In the west and south of Russia, the collapse of the USSR had meant that the new frontier military districts had been interior military districts charged largely with garrison or rear support functions. Yet the more combat-ready status of the military districts north of China, which had been and remained frontier military districts, could not be protected through eight years of transition. Russia's new strategic priorities on its Central Asian borders and with internal security have denied the forces in the east any special consideration of the sort they once enjoyed at the peak of Soviet power. Moreover, Moscow's international border with China has been reduced by half in length and Russia withdrew its forces from Mongolia. The military requirements for defence of national territory east of the Urals have changed substantially. As importantly, any threat from China has been considerably obviated by Moscow's new diplomacy toward China which began in the early 1980s and had reached a point in the late 1990s where Russia was prepared to sell China sophisticated military equipment and where some in Russia were prepared to consider the possibility of a renewed alliance with China. The dramatic changes in China's international policy in the last two decades have considerably reduced fears in Moscow about short- to medium-term military threats on the border with China.

The one newly independent state on Russia's border east of the Urals is Kazakhstan, the former republic with which Russia has the closest and easiest security relationships. One plus for the forces east of the Urals was that to comply with the CFE Treaty, large amounts of ground forces equipment, especially ammunition, were moved there. The general strategic picture created by these circumstances was sufficiently benign that in 1998, notwithstanding shortages of all kinds and low numbers, the ranking ground forces officer, General Yury Baluyevski, said that the troops based east of the Urals have an 'optimal structure'.[1]

This chapter offers a snapshot of the Russian ground forces based largely on reporting from 1997, 1998 and early 1999. The chapter provides some sense of the evolution of the ground forces from being part of the Soviet military to their position today in Russian military power. Issues canvassed include operations, formations, missions, personnel levels, equipment, and training. Where possible, the chapter focuses on the situation of the ground forces east of the Urals, although reporting on these units in available sources is not particularly extensive.

FROM SOVIET ARMY TO RUSSIAN ARMY

The impact of domestic politics on the ground forces has been substantial. This is the result in large part of the central position of land forces, also including paramilitary and security services, in domestic political order in Russia after 1991. The infantry, special forces and airborne capabilities[2] of the ground forces are more relevant to a wider range of civil operations than naval or air forces. The commander in chief of the ground forces in August 1991 was one of the principals in the attempted coup against Gorbachev. The senior officers of the ground forces have also been well positioned to resist government policies on reform of the armed forces because of the predominance of ground forces officers in the hierarchy of the armed forces as a whole, a circumstance inherited from the Soviet period and dictated by the USSR's status as a continental superpower. The pre-eminence of ground forces officers in the military hierarchy has also meant that they have been more exposed to the widespread corruption that has for many Russians become a necessary way of life.

By 1996, a number of these factors played out in the rhetoric surrounding the dismissal of the commander in chief of the ground forces who had occupied the post since 1991. He was relieved of his command as the result of allegations that he had spied for Chechnia, had illegal dealings with the Chechen mafia, and had illegally sold military goods. In his defence, he claimed the real reason for his dismissal was that he had opposed the former disgraced Defence Minister and others in the federal government on certain aspects of Chechnia policy and army reform.[3] Whatever the truth in that particular case, the ground forces have undergone major structural reform because of the tension between the senior officers in that service and the political leadership that the case revealed.

The ground forces are being subjected to the total reform plan for the armed forces as whole. For the ground forces, there are two phases: the first until 2001, the second until 2005.[4] In December 1997, the Ground Forces Command was abolished and command of this branch of the Russian armed forces was diffused between six separate organisations, all subordinated to a Deputy Minister of Defence. These were the Main Operations Directorate, the Main Combat Training Directorate, the Main Vehicle and Armour Directorate, Army Aviation, Air Defence, and Missile Forces and Artillery.[5] (The separate Main Directorate for Tank Troops was abolished.) The responsibilities of the Main Operational Directorate

Figure 9.1 Organisation chart: Main Directorate of the ground forces

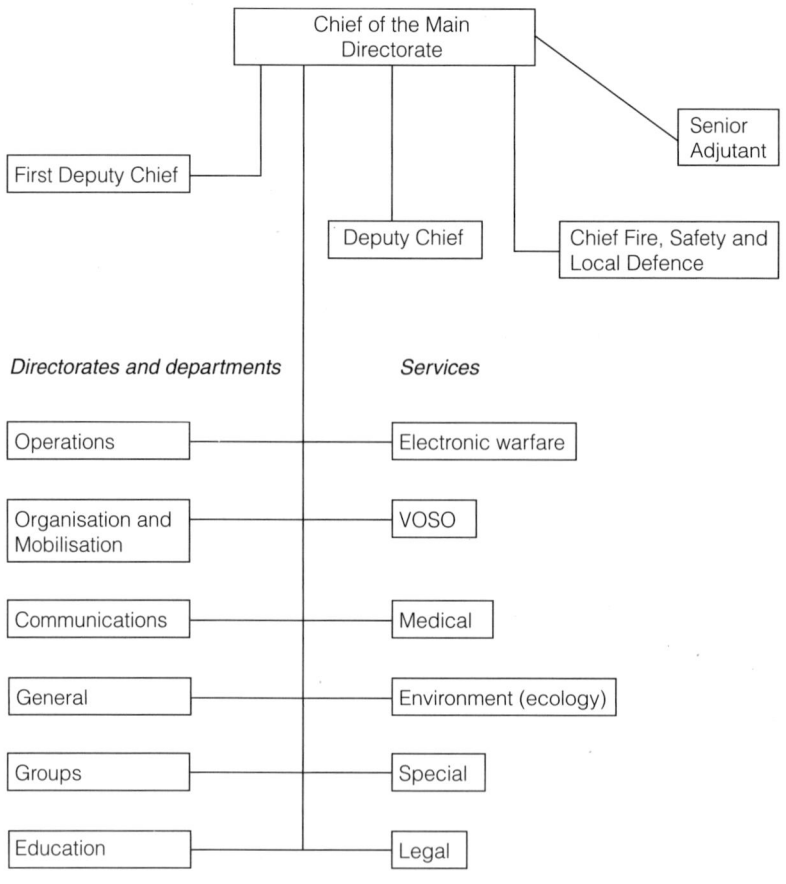

go in two directions. It is the senior planning agency of the ground forces and therefore is responsible for organisational development, formation and training of reserves, organisation of territorial defence, and command and control of military districts in wartime.[6] In this role, the Main Operational Directorate is often referred to simply as the Main Directorate. At the same time, the Main Operational Directorate has become fully integrated into the structure of the General Staff[7] and it is responsible for overall planning and policy for the armed forces as a whole, especially implementation of the reform policies and restructuring. The structure of the Main Operational Directorate as it shapes the ground forces is shown in Figure 9.1. Figure 5.3 shows the position of the Main Operational Directorate in the General Staff.

The direct subordination of the Main Operational Directorate to a deputy minister can be seen in some respects as a reflection of the value of closer civilian control of this politically sensitive branch of the armed forces. By removing the Ground Forces Command, the political leadership of the country has also effectively broken up the power of one of the main potential sources of unconstitutional usurpation of power. The decision to abolish the post of Commander-in-Chief of the Ground Forces has been interpreted by some as the 'elimination' of the once powerful army as a separate branch of the armed forces.[8] This occurred at the same time as the decision to shift to consolidation of existing branches of the armed forces into a three-component structure based on the three operating environments—land, sea and aerospace. Thus the abolition of the ground forces command has been regarded as 'nonsense' because it appears to conflict with this central aim.[9]

The position of Ground Forces Commander in Chief was not a consistent feature of the Soviet ground forces, and did not exist in the Second World War. It has not been necessary for military operational purposes, and with the creation of new territorially-based unified commands, there is no great need for such a post. The main purpose of the post was seen on different occasions as either a political opportunity or a political liability. It has been formed and abolished three times beginning in 1946 when it was first established.[10] It is more than likely that at some stage in the future it will be resurrected.

The ground forces of the USSR were large, some 200 divisions, and were structured, equipped, trained and located for major war mostly in the European theatre. Only some 25 per cent of ground forces units were east of the Urals. The majority of the most capable Soviet ground forces units were deployed in union republics of the USSR (Ukraine, Bielorussia, and the Baltic republics) or in Warsaw Pact states (East Germany, Poland and Czechoslovakia). Through break-up of the forces and disbandment of units that followed the collapse of the Warsaw Pact and then the USSR, and through financial stringencies imposed by Russia's economic depression, the number of ground forces divisions remaining to Russia had shrunk to around 24 by 1999. This represents a force almost one-eighth of its size in 1991. By early 1998, Russian official sources were reporting the personnel strength of the ground forces at about 400 000 after a precipitous slide from more than 600 000 in 1996.[11] By early 1999, the figure was 318 000, or 30 per cent of the armed forces.[12] This level of manning was described by the

Chief of the Main Operational Directorate of the General Staff as a critical level which should not be breached if Russia was to defend its vast territory.[13] Table 9.1 shows the scale of reduction of the size of the Russian ground forces by 1998 relative to those of the USSR in 1991 as estimated by the IISS.

Table 9.1 Comparison of Soviet and Russian ground forces 1991 and 1998[14]

	Soviet GF 1991	Russian GF 1998
Personnel	1 473 000	420 000
Tank divisions	46	6
Motorised infantry divisions	142	19
Airborne divisions	7	5
Artillery divisions	19	3
Special operations brigades	16	8 (5 operational)
Main battle tanks	61 500	15 559[15]
AIFV	28 000	26 300
APC	50 000	3 245
Artillery	66 880	15 700
SSM	1 723	316
Attack helicopters	2 050	1 000
Transport helicopters	1 510	1 300

OPERATIONS

Since 1991, the ground forces have participated in one small war and more than 20 civil–military or peacekeeping operations either inside Russia, in the former Soviet republics, or in more distant countries. Operations on the territory of the former USSR were not new for Moscow after 1991, but were part of an emerging pattern of military interventions that had begun in 1986 in Alma Ata in Kazakhstan. Operations followed in 1988 in Azerbaijan and Armenia, in 1989 in Georgia, in 1990 in Tajikistan and Kyrgyzstan, and in 1991 in Lithuania, Georgia and Moldova. This pattern of intervention must have emboldened the leaders of the ground forces in their decision to support the attempted coup against President Gorbachev in August 1991. Some of the more notable operations by Russian forces since 1991 were outlined briefly in chapter 4. Outside Russia, they include South Ossetia in Georgia for 18 months in 1991–92; Moldova for 11 months in 1991–92; Azerbaijan in 1992; Abkhazia in Georgia from 1992 to 1994; and Tajikistan since 1992. Inside Russia they include North Ossetia in 1992; Chechnia from December 1994 to August 1996; and Dagestan from May 1998. Russian ground forces involvement in UN peacekeeping operations is discussed in a later section in this chapter.

The operational commitments after 1991 have been particularly important in shaping Russian perspectives on the balance to be struck between planning for major inter-state wars and localised conflicts that have grown out of separatist tension or civil disturbances. The engagements have also sharpened Russian conceptions of how to use force in civil emergencies since almost all of them have been characterised by lack of proper military planning and lack of effectiveness. One analysis concluded that the use of military forces by Russia (or the former USSR) in civil conflicts in the decade prior to March 1998 had rarely been successful.[16] The ground forces had some limited success in containing conflict but very low levels of achievement in curtailing conflict or reducing tension. This was attributed to the lack of readiness for the missions, a circumstance which made failure likely and created conditions for aggravation of a conflict rather than creating conditions for hostilities to stop. The lack of readiness was seen as multi-dimensional, and included lack of policy structures and a legislative basis for coordination of various elements of the armed forces or security services involved; lack of military doctrine for such operations; no training exercises for such operations; and poor psychological preparation of the troops for operations against civilians. Notwithstanding the limited political success of military interventions of the sort described above, they have provided invaluable (if painful) lessons in combat operations and preparation for combat under conditions of poor readiness.[17]

Airborne units or personnel have been prominent in many of the peacekeeping operations. Airborne personnel have consistently staffed Russia's peacekeeping contingent to Yugoslavia, and an independent airborne brigade (1600 personnel) joined the UN force some time after its formation.[18] In summer 1999, Russia deployed its largest peacekeeping contingent to a foreign country outside the periphery of the former USSR. A 3600-strong brigade (some Russian sources refer to it as the 10th Independent Airborne Brigade) was deployed to Kosovo as part of the NATO-led KFOR peacekeeping force.[19] Airborne battalions have also served in peacekeeping missions in Slovenia and Abkhazia (Georgia). Short-duration operations by airborne units included the evacuation of the Russian embassy in Kabul in August 1992.

Units from east of the Urals were prominent in those deployed to Chechnia. Special purpose militia detachments from Krasnoiarsk[20] and a motorised infantry regiment from near Khabarovsk[21] were detailed for deployment in 1994 and 1995 to support the civil-military operation. These ground force units which had to conduct street operations in Grozny took high casualty rates, partly because that is normal for such operations (it is very difficult to train for them), but also because the Siberian troops had no training to speak of in preparation for the deployment.[22] Troops of the Ministry of Internal Affairs were also used in Chechnia for combat missions.

MISSIONS

The frequent use of the ground forces in operations since 1991 and the changes in Russia's strategic environment in the same period have led to substantial revisions of their missions, doctrines and planning. But it appears to be the case that ground forces theoreticians have not had the same luxury of time as their naval and air power counterparts to develop elaborate mission statements beyond some general principles. There also appears to have been much greater debate or at least much greater controversy over the roles of the ground forces compared with the naval and air forces. The ground forces have however had many more opportunities in practice than the other services to improve their strategies, doctrines and planning for operations. The main targets have been separatists or other insurrectionists; and the main emphasis has been on tactics for urban warfare and mountain warfare, two areas of Russian operations that have undergone a significant rejuvenation.

A 1997 analysis of the missions of the ground forces by the Chief of the Main Operations Directorate of the General Staff, Lieutenant-General Yury Baluyevski, probably remains a relatively reliable indicator of the main trends in thinking about the missions of this service, even though the author expressed them as 'personal views'. Baluyevski believed that ground forces would remain a substantial part of the armed forces of major powers and the 'main' service in the Russian forces. As important as air forces may now appear, the air was only a 'temporary habitat' and the activities to which military power is ultimately addressed are land-based. But the ground forces would be employed as one part of a highly integrated, highly mobile joint force designed to achieve theatre outcomes in reconnaissance, strike and electronic warfare. The goals would be deep strikes on enemy military forces.[23]

Baluyevski identified two main types of activities in war: joint operations, involving large units of other services; and special operations, under an all-arms commander in chief, but designed to support the goals of joint operations. Operations that might previously have been classified as defensive, counter-offensive or offensive, could now usefully be considered as of one type, a 'strategic theatre operation', because combat under modern conditions is highly dynamic. Operations will have to be designed with an eye to ensuring that the conflict as a whole can be settled on 'terms meeting national interests'.[24]

Baluyevski considered that a broad consensus now exists that the combat power of the ground forces must increase not by increasing the forces or the numbers of weapons involved in operations but by enhanced information warfare and enhanced electronic warfare. He concluded that a 'further increase in fire weapon density or in ammunition resourcing and consumption will not considerably enhance the efficiency' of ground forces. The force multiplier would be a 'marked improvement in real time information support of troops, especially their firing systems'. Modern warfare would be characterised by three features. First, the emerging trend toward the elimination of nuclear weapons meant that major powers would now look toward using high-power conventional weapons. Second, information superiority would become a primary goal. Third, high-precision weapons will provide the conditions for successful employment of the ground forces.[25]

Baluyevski suggested that pre-emption in information warfare and pre-emption in manoeuvre will be the determinants of success, and that there will no longer be a need for 'warring forces to come into direct contact' for the outcome of a conflict to be decided. He identified a new law of war: 'the dependence of the course and outcome of war on the balance between information potentials of the warring sides'.[26] A group of weapons designers involved in Russian tank design has expressed the view that the availability of high-precision weapons makes protracted war almost impossible.[27]

Russian doctrinal development has begun in some respects to imitate that of the US armed forces, and for the ground forces of Russia there has been much talk of the need to be victorious in a 'large-scale regional war'.[28]

Units of constant combat readiness

The General Staff drew several important lessons from the Chechnia operations which led them to devise a new mechanism for maintaining combat readiness: 'units of constant readiness'.

The main problems encountered in Chechnia that dictated subsequent interest in the creation of this new type of unit were that units staffed in haste had a poor level of preparation, teamwork and coordination; and that defects in equipment in understrength units had not been detected and had the predictable impact on operations.[29] The result was the creation of a new three-tier system of mobilisation. The first involves the units of constant readiness whose mission is to 'cover the state border' or localise a conflict in coordination with Ministry of Interior forces.[30] The second tier includes reduced-strength and cadre units, which perform mobilisation work and provide long-term storage of weapons and equipment. These units shift to a war footing according to prescribed schedules. The third tier comprises the strategic reserves. As of 1997, the head of the ground forces Main Directorate expressed concern that the ground forces had already fallen behind the level of permanent manning of units that is necessary to support a rapid mobilisation.[31]

Some constant readiness units were set up through 1997, preceding a formal announcement in March 1998. The move is a repudiation of efforts made under former Defence Minister Grachev to imitate the Soviet era standard of large numbers of divisions, many of which were dramatically understrength.[32] It had become impossible to maintain combat-ready forces across the breadth of the country's border regions as had been case in the USSR, so the Russian General Staff finally settled for having one or two combat-ready divisions in each of its military districts as the only way of giving coherence to force structure in the dire economic circumstances in which they found themselves.[33] The move will see more variation between the equipment and personnel standards for various divisions and regiments, according to their theatre-specific terrain and likely missions. The role of tank forces in the new units will be considerably reduced relative to their central place in Soviet doctrine.

The mission of the constant readiness units was to be capable of 'stamping out' local conflicts by being able to commence combat operations on 24 hours notice. According to General Anatoly Kvashnin, Chief of the General Staff, the mission of these units is to 'extinguish' possible border incidents or conflicts endangering Russia's security.[34] These units will act as an advance guard, to be followed by mobilised units normally held at lower strengths and lower levels of readiness. One or two formations of this type were to be formed in areas with the most probable threats. In making the announcement, the ground forces Main

Directorate revealed that the 4th Guards Kantemirovskaia Tank Division in the Moscow Military District had already been assigned such status and that it had several units already at permanent readiness, with the whole division to be brought to full readiness (described as 80 per cent wartime strength) by the end of 1998.[35]

According to a March 1998 report, the ground forces were to have between 8 and 11 constant readiness units.[36] In August 1998, the Defence Minister, Sergeyev, announced that there would be 10 units on 24-hour military alert by the end of the year: three general purpose divisions, three airborne divisions, and four general purpose brigades.[37] East of the Urals, the 84th Motorised Infantry Division at Novosibirsk in the Siberian MD was designated to become an elite unite under the reforms.[38] Other units to be designated with that status include: the 74th Motorised Infantry Brigade at Yurga in the Kemerovo region, a unit which served in Chechnia[39]; at least two motorised infantry regiments in the former Transbaikal MD (the Guards Tatsinsk Regiment and the Guards Smolensk Regiment[40]; and a regiment in the Urals MD visited by the Defence Minister in early 1998, which was reportedly staffed at 98 per cent of establishment.[41] This Urals MD regiment may be part of the 34th Simferopol Motorised Infantry Division based in Yekaterinburg that was designated as a constant combat readiness unit, according to a report of early 1998.[42] Also, there are reports that at least one motorised infantry division of the Far Eastern MD was given the status of being a constant combat readiness formation.[43] The government plans to increase the number of constant readiness units as economic circumstances permit.[44]

By November 1998, according to one report, four divisions of the new type had been brought up to full strength and full equipment levels (two in the North Caucasus MD; one infantry division and one airborne division in the Moscow MD), and four additional brigades (two in the North Caucasus MD, one in the Moscow MD; and one in the Siberian MD).[45] By early 1999, the General Staff was hoping to have up to 31 regiments in the designated 10 divisions up to this status.[46]

The optimistic reports about readiness levels in the newly designated units have been contradicted in part in another report attributed to the same officer at the same time saying that these units were only at 80 per cent of establishment in both personnel and equipment.[47] In December 1998, a senior artillery officer reported that his arm of the service was still trying to bring these units up to strength with equipment and personnel, and to provide adequate training.[48] A report from January 1999 indicated that officer and recruit levels in one of the designated regiments in the Urals MD meant that a better rubric for the unit would be 'periodic combat readiness'. After each call-up, one-quarter of the lower ranks were being replaced; and in one of the battalions, only two officers were graduates of two-year training courses.[49] A March 1999 report from official sources had only three divisions and four brigades (in the Moscow, Leningrad, North Caucasus and Siberian MDs) at the level of constant combat readiness.[50] In a tank regiment in the Urals MD that was designated constant readiness, by 1999 recruits from the spring 1997 call-up constituted 70 per cent of the enlisted members.[51] The concept of constant readiness units has also been challenged by serving officers as rather hollow in the absence of well organised logistics and a sound system of training.[52]

A special burden was being imposed on the designated units of constant combat readiness because their new status meant that they had become the showpiece of each military district, requiring them among other things to coordinate training for other units in the district. Other circumstances were imposing special burdens on the constant readiness units. In the North Caucasus, crime levels in the local communities were so high, and community relations so difficult, that the units stationed there had to be self-sufficient in food and other consumables.[53]

As for the second-tier units, there were reportedly 21 divisions and 10 brigades in reduced operations (10–50 per cent of personnel and 100 per cent in equipment) with a readiness level of 30 days. The 81st infantry regiment in the Volga MD, which had served in Chechnia, was to be converted to a reduced strength division, a move which its members saw as an insult to the sacrifices of its members in that war.[54] Third-tier units were on readiness warning of 30 days to three months, and are only likely to be used in case of large-scale attack on Russia.[55]

FORMATIONS AND ARMS OF THE GROUND FORCES

In line with the reform program for the armed forces as a whole, the ground forces are being resubordinated to a reduced number of military districts. The merger of the Transbaikal and Siberian MDs into one, to be called the Siberian MD, had occurred in 1998. A second merger (Urals and Volga) into a single MD had been expected at about the same time, but by early 1999, the date for that merger was put at 2000.[56] In line with the move toward creation of unified commands, the resubordination of the Kamchatka Army Corps to the Commander Pacific Fleet was due to have occurred by May 1998.[57] Almost all ground air defence regiments in the Siberian MD were to be disbanded as of May 1998, with only one SAM unit to remain, probably stationed in Novosibirsk.[58] Officers in one of the units (Barnaul in Altai) complained that the cost of relocating its modern equipment (S–300PM) would far outweigh the cost of keeping the unit on for a few years. They also warned that two SMF divisions would be vulnerable to attack as a result of their disbandment. Table 9.2 lists the formations in the ground forces east of the Ural Mountains in 1998, as recorded by IISS.

Table 9.2 Ground forces formations in military districts east of the Ural Mountains in 1998[59]

	Urals MD*	Siberian MD	Far East MD	Total all Russia
Airborne	0	1	1	5
Airborne bde	0	0	0	3
Spetsnaz	1	2	1	8
Tank divisions	1	3 (1 trg)	0	6
Tank bde/regt	1	0	0	1
Mot. inf. div	1	2	10 (2 trg)	19
Mot. inf. bde/regt	0	3	0	11
MG/arty or arty div	0	2	3	7
Arty bde/regt	2	10	9	32
ATK bde/regt	1	4	1	9
SAM bde/regt	0	2	5	21
SSM	1	2	3	13
Helo regt (assault t'port)	0	1	2	7
Helo regt (attack)	0	2	2	12
Helo regt (training)	0	0	0	7

Groups of forces

The Soviet practice of creating a 'group of forces' according to a territorial or operations deployment independent of a Military District headquarters has continued, with a joint force in the Kaliningrad enclave between Poland and Lithuania until September 1988 and one in the North Caucasus region.

Peacekeeping forces

In 1996, President Yeltsin ordered the creation of a standing peacekeeping force, leading to the designation of ground force units, such as the 27th Motorised Infantry Division in Orenburg province (Volga MD), as specialised peacekeeping units. According to an official source, in 1997 there were 17 infantry and 4 airborne battalions (more than 20 000 personnel) assigned for specialised peacekeeping operations on the periphery of Russia.[60] According to at least one report, the peacekeeping units—many of which are engaged in operations–were receiving higher priority than the constant readiness units.[61]

Peacekeeping operations were placing a serious strain on resources available to the ground forces. In 1998 the estimated cost of these operations was 512 million roubles, less than 1 per cent of the official defence outlays but unfunded in defence appropriations.[62] Apart from the running expenses of such operations, major equipment inventories were being written off as a result of use, illegal sale or theft. Troops involved in some international missions under UN auspices appear to be receiving special payments, up to US$1000 per month.[63]

It is unlikely that the wish of the former Defence Minister, General Rodionov, to reduce or eliminate commitments of the ground forces to contingency deployments in foreign countries can be satisfied. Nevertheless, his motivation was to prevent scarce resources being soaked up by ad hoc commitments abroad when the ground forces lacked funds even for basic training.[64]

Airborne and special forces

In Russia's current strategic circumstances, both internal and international, airborne and special forces have been particularly prominent and active, notwithstanding reductions in their total strength and abolition of a number of units, and a lowering in Russian military doctrine of the operational demands on these forces. Combined theatre level and strategic assault operations by airborne divisions in support of a front or army group of the sort planned in the Soviet era are now less likely. They are also less possible given the reduced capacity of the military transport aviation (see chapter 7) and reductions in the number of airborne units.

Through the 1990s, several different plans for the future use of the airborne forces surfaced, from their being a centrepiece of new ready reaction forces under central strategic command in 1992 to some of them being resubordinated to military district commanders in 1995.[65] By 1996, the Defence Minister was considering them for new operational–tactical missions.[66] By 1997, airborne units, still formally considered a strategic reserve, were only manned at about 70–85 per cent of authorised levels.[67] In 1997, the airborne forces had only one constant readiness special forces unit, the 45th Independent Brigade.[68] It was recognised by military leaders that some of the primary wartime missions which the airborne forces had been assigned in the Soviet period were no longer practicable. In the view of the commander of the airborne troops, Russia could no longer conduct the strategic offensive operations with ground forces in which the airborne forces had been assigned their primary function.[69] In a 1998 exercise involving 1725 troops of the 76th Airborne Division, the scenario involved reinforcement of border outposts and protection of the Russian border.[70] In March 1999, airborne units participated in a large-scale command and staff exercise of the 61st Air Army (military transport aviation) called *Vozdushnyi most–99* ['Air Bridge–99'] to test employment of the 'rapid reaction' force in a regional conflict. The exercise included the air-drop of 709 para-troopers, eight BMP–1 infantry fighting vehicles, and other equipment of the 331st Airborne Regiment of the 98th Airborne Division.[71]

The 'peacetime' missions of such units, either in international peacekeeping operations or in internal police actions against armed insurrection, were by this time receiving as much emphasis as their wartime roles.[72] The development strategy then was to identify three separate missions and to structure the airborne forces accordingly: general purpose forces (regular combat); peacekeeping forces; and special operations units. In approaching airborne forces in this way, the airborne command was prepared to allow its general purpose units to take their cuts ('reforms') along with the rest of the armed forces, but advocated that whatever the size of the airborne forces as a whole the government should maintain a standing peacekeeping airborne force of at least two independent brigades (each with five or six battalions) and should provide more budget support for special forces.

For a number of years, the airborne forces had not suffered as badly as many other components of the forces, having maintained a 2.5 per cent share of total armed forces personnel, a figure comparable with the share of airborne forces in US and UK forces. In 1996, a plan to resubordinate the airborne forces from direct strategic control of the President (and General Staff) to the Commander in Chief of the Ground Forces was announced, and this was implemented in March 1997. In 1998, when the post of Commander in Chief of the Ground Forces was abolished, this left the airborne forces back under the control of the Main Operations Directorate of the General Staff.

By 1 January 1999, the planned restructuring of the airborne forces had been completed. Reductions in 1997 and 1998 resulted in the loss of 14 000 personnel (including 2403 officers) to reach a total force strength of 32 000.[73] (This compares with about 70 000 in 1990.) By July 1998, there were four airborne divisions (106th Division at Tula, 98th Division at Ivanovo, 7th Kaunasskaia Division at Novorossiisk and 76th Svirskaia Division at Pskov) and one independent airborne brigade (31st at Ulianovsk). Each division had one or two battalions in constant readiness[74] or, according to other sources, one regiment in constant readiness.[75] (This 1998 order of battle of four divisions and one brigade compares with eight divisions and twelve independent brigades in 1991.)[76] According to Colonel-General Georgy Shpak, Commander of the Airborne Troops, by June 1999, the Airborne Troops had 10 regiments of constant combat readiness.[77]

One airborne division and eleven independent brigades were disestablished. East of the Urals, the 11th Air Assault Brigade stationed at Ulan Ude (Transbaikal MD) and the 83rd Air Assault Brigade stationed at Ussuriisk (Far East MD) were probably disestablished in 1998, along with the 100th Airborne Brigade at Abakan in Khakassia (Siberian MD), which was disbanded on 1 May 1998—when it was under the command of the brother of Aleksandr Lebed.[78] The airborne training centre in Omsk remained operational. The 345th Airborne Regiment is being withdrawn from Gadauta in Georgia and disbanded. But some 800 officers and warrant officers could not be discharged immediately because of the lack of funds to pay them out. The 104th Airborne Division has been reconstituted as the 31st Airborne Brigade and cut by more than 2500 personnel. The equipment displaced by this change was to be reassigned to other airborne units.

By the end of 1998, according to the commander of the airborne forces, all units were at their required peacetime manning levels[79]; and according to the officer responsible for airborne training, 98 per cent of training objectives for 1998 had been met.[80] Plans for some expansion of personnel strengths by 11 000 were in place even as the reform (reductions) of the airborne forces had been completed, with the commander, Colonel General Georgy Shpak, indicating that by 2006 he expected each division to have a third parachute regiment, bringing the total strength of the airborne forces to about 43 000.[81] However, according to Lieutenant-General

Nilolai Staskov, Chief of Staff of the Airborne Troops, in the near future the strength of the Airborne Troops will rise by 5600 troops, due to the increased involvement of Russian paratroopers in peacekeeping operations.[82]

Special forces are viewed by some in Russia as particularly important in contemporary warfare in light of the tendency of warring sides to avoid direct confrontation in joint force warfare.[83] Since special forces units have a central function in internal stability of the country, it would be natural for the leadership to maintain all of the special forces brigades in the ground forces at near to full strength. But these forces may not have received the attention of the Russian political leadership quite to the degree demanded by the country's strategic circumstances, especially its internal problems.

In fact, the domestic political circumstances, and the growth of paramilitary forces discussed in chapter 5, probably convinced the leadership that new or stronger special force units were the last thing they wanted in the ground forces. As one critic put it: 'We have every conceivable kind of "special forces" personnel today in every department, more than we know what to do with'.[84] The unidentified GRU officer making this criticism believed that the 'power departments' did not have the capabilities for the 'broad-scale anti-sabotage, anti-guerilla warfare' that the country required. He recommended joint forces be established based on GRU special forces, with the remaining airborne brigades to form a special operations command somewhat similar in inspiration and style to the US Special Forces Command. What was needed, he said, was greater recognition by the national government of the potential of special forces to resolve the internal problems of Russia. Operations such as that used by the US to capture General Noriega of Panama were needed, he said. One constraint was the lack of a legal basis for such operations inside Russia.

The mission of special forces units in the ground forces remains reconnaissance on enemy territory and destruction of enemy targets, not operations in support of civil authorities within Russia.[85] Each military district reportedly has special forces units. Three special forces brigades and one smaller unit were known to exist at several locations east of the Urals in the mid-1990s (Berdsk, Ussuriisk, Khabarovsk, and Kiakhta)[86] but their current status is unclear. In 1997, a special forces brigade subordinated to the GRU was identified in the Siberian MD.[87] (Like other units,

its personnel was not being paid on time, but they did receive their pay ahead of other military personnel.)

Tank forces

Once the pride of the Soviet ground forces, and a major part of theatre offensive strategies of Soviet generals, the tank forces have come to occupy a much lower profile in the Russian ground forces. One tank regiment reported that in 1998 its infantry battalion had been disbanded and that it no longer exercised with live fire. The new situation was that the 'tank regiment of a motorised infantry division can no longer be seen as an independent combat unit, as it was earlier'.[88]

Ground forces aviation

In the 1994–96 Chechnia campaign, ground forces air units flew some 50 000 missions, involving 35 000 flying hours.[89] This should suggest to the Russian leadership that one of the most central elements of the armed forces in the country's current strategic circumstances is army aviation, but as mentioned in chapter 8, army aviation has suffered very serious setbacks since 1991. By early 1998, this part of the ground forces was facing cuts of up to 60 per cent of its regiments.[90] In 1998, more than 2000 personnel (961 pilots and 1134 flight engineers and technical staff) were to be discharged.[91] Most army aviation engineer and pilot schools were being closed, with some 850 new graduates in 1998 unable to find jobs in their chosen specialisation. In 1998, some 2000 personnel (airmen and flight engineers) were to be retrenched. Since this element of the ground forces was only transferred from the air force in 1990, there may be some prospect that it will be resubordinated to the unified RFAF.

Cossack units

Cossack units[92] formed in the areas east of the Urals have a special significance. As the original colonisers of the region in the seventeenth century, and with their combat potential having been demonstrated in the Second World War, the re-establishment of Cossack military units based on rejuvenated Cossack communities is an important development affecting the ground forces of Russia. Although some units have been formed in the ground forces, most have been associated with the work of border forces. Nevertheless, they do represent an independent force that can be mobilised in support of ground operations in lower intensity conflict.

As early as 1991, the Cossack units began to be formed. An agreement was reached in February that year between the *ataman* (leader) of the Siberian Cossack troops and the Commander of the Siberian Military District on the formation of a Cossack motorised infantry regiment to be based near Omsk. In 1993, the unit was designated a brigade and was identified as part of the Omsk garrison.[93] Also in 1993, a group of Cossacks from several parts of Russia decided to establish the Khabarovsk Cossack troops in the Far East Military District, and were allocated military land and buildings of border units which were to be disbanded for the purpose of establishing a Cossack settlement.[94]

Between 1997 and 1998, four Cossack units which had been formed as private associations after the collapse of the USSR were formally incorporated into the state structure of Russia through agreements between them and the President. These units, Transbaikal, Siberian, Terek and Orenburg Cossack communities, are supervised by the Main Directorate of Cossack Troops under the Presidential Administration, but will be provided with pay and weapons by those units with which they serve in the Border Guards Service, the Ministry of Defence, municipal militia, of the Ministry of Emergencies.[95]

East of the Urals, members of the Ussuri, Transbaikal and Siberian Cossack communities are engaged in regional border patrols.[96] In June 1998, Ussuri Cossacks participated in joint naval, air and ground exercises in the Far East Military District. The ground component was carried out by border troops and MVD troops.[97] Currently, 15 units or formations of Russia's armed forces and 39 border guard posts are staffed with about 50 000 Cossacks.[98]

PERSONNEL ISSUES

According to the IISS estimates for 1997, no Russian ground force units were manned at more than 75 per cent of establishment strength.[99] IISS suggested that half of the 12 tank divisions, about two-thirds of the 24 motor rifle divisions, and all 5 of the airborne divisions were manned above 50 per cent of establishment. Independent brigades were probably also manned at or above 50 per cent of establishment. The remaining ground force units were probably kept at between 25 and 50 per cent of establishment.

In 1997, the 201st Motorised Infantry Division in Tajikistan represented something of an anomaly in personnel arrangements. It was manned almost entirely by contract soldiers, more than 20 per cent of whom had served in Afghanistan or operational deployments of Russian forces to civil emergencies after 1991.[100] But the retention rate of volunteers was very low, between 10 and 15 per cent in the first year. Only one in five in service in that division in 1997 believed that Russia was worth dying for.

Nevertheless, there were relatively high rates of satisfaction with the professionalism of colleagues in the division, and high dissatisfaction levels with the Russian government and the logistic support system. Russian soldiers were being subject to sporadic terrorist attacks in Tajikistan at that time, with 12 being killed there in the first six months of 1997. Yet even in the face of these difficulties, the 201st Division was considered to be the best-trained and best-prepared in the ground forces.[101]

Plans revealed in early 1998 foreshadowed a cut in ground force numbers that year of 120 000 personnel[102] to achieve a force of about 400 000 to 450 000 (although the actual strength at that time was already as low as 400 000). Command and control elements of the ground forces had been cut by about 30 per cent in 1997 in connection with the reorganisation of command structures. Army aviation was to be cut by up to 60 per cent, and only one of the three colleges for air crew and engineers would remain open.[103] In three years to 1998, units of the North Caucasus Military District which formally takes in Chechnia had cut their strengths by a total of 7500 men but claimed more combat readiness as a result.[104] Units involved in training and combat tasks had been brought up to 95–100 per cent of their strength, although officer billets were staffed at slightly lower levels.

In January 1998, Defence Minister Sergeyev claimed that 'formations and brigades' were manned at 90–94 per cent.[105] According to the ground forces Main Directorate in early 1998, the constant readiness units were staffed at 84 per cent (presumably meaning peacetime establishment).[106] But at the same time, there was a shortage of 19 000 junior officers, of which 70 per cent were platoon commanders (below the rank of captain), but with shortages also at the level of company commander and deputy-battalion commander. By early 1999, only 86 per cent of officer billets were filled.[107] There was an especially acute shortage at the lower officer ranks, some 8000 positions. Nevertheless, the military leadership expected this problem to be overcome by 2001 simply by take-up of graduates from military academies. One local initiative to remedy this problem was taken by the Trans-baikal Military District which in 1997 established an innovative program, unique in the army at the time, for the training of warrant officers to be troop commanders, a category for which the MD's deficit was several thousand.[108] In selecting candidates, preference is given to residents of the Military District in an effort to promote retention rates.

In an effort to overcome spiralling crime, increases in other disciplinary offences, and general disaffection among the forces, an experiment to increase the numbers of psychologists or coun-sellors was commenced. In selected units, 24 new posts of deputy troop commander responsible for education were created.[109] In the 3rd Motorised Infantry Division in the Moscow MD, this meant an increase from 7 to 11 psychologists, but the difference about the new posts is that they are unit-specific, and replicate the practice from the Soviet era when the political officers in lower level units were assigned precisely this function—supervision of the personal training and morale of unit members.

The personal health of service personnel, even at the recruit stage, has been serious enough to have a significant impact on readiness. In May 1998, in the Siberian Military District, extra rations were ordered for underweight personnel, and a special unit was set up for soldiers showing signs of dystrophy, who would not be re-assigned to normal units until they had regained a normal body weight.[110]

Women

The ground forces will turn increasingly to women to fill some of the personnel shortfalls. Accounting for 120 000 billets in 1998 (about 10 per cent of the entire armed forces)[111] and suffering many experiences of harassment similar to their counterparts in the US armed services, women have not been accepted as readily in the services in professional capacities as in the USA. The ground forces have however deployed women on operations in air defence units with peacekeeping units.[112]

EQUIPMENT LEVELS AND STANDARDS

After the collapse of the USSR, the takeover of formerly Soviet military assets by newly independent countries on whose territory the assets were located meant that the new countries were getting front-line units which had much more modern equipment than the rear area units that Russia was left with in the formerly internal military districts of the USSR. This resulted in huge deficits in modern equipment for the ground forces. This was particularly the case with artillery command and control and reconnaissance assets, leaving Russian forces able to fire farther than they could 'see'.[113] Mortars and anti-tank missile inventories were affected as seriously as artillery. One estimate for 1998 suggested that only 40 per cent of tanks were of the most recent vintage.[114]

From their 1994–96 engagement in Chechnia, the ground forces learned some sobering lessons about the combat reliability of some of their most important systems. According to press reporting of a Ministry of Defence evaluation, the fire-fighting system in armoured vehicles was completely inoperable and did not extinguish a single fire in vehicles hit by a rocket launcher or making contact with a mine. Some 60 per cent of tank crews and some 34 per cent of BMP crews were disabled completely or partially, with heavy loss of life. Equipment losses were 51 per cent of tanks, 56 per cent of BMPs, and 66 per cent of BTRs. One of the reasons for heavy tank losses was that they were attacked from the side, rear or above, a circumstance not envisaged for missions such as swift frontal or flank assaults on enemy troops.[115] Many guns did not fire, armoured vehicles fell foul of terrain conditions, and helicopters were inoperable.[116] Artillery commanders fighting in Chechnia used armoured fighting vehicles of clearly distinct design from those of troops and were singled out effectively for initial targeting by the enemy.[117] Siberian units fighting in Chechnia had helmets designed prior to 1940, and these could not stop a 5.45-calibre bullet. Even Pacific Fleet naval infantry fighting in Chechnia were inadequately equipped compared with Ministry of Interior troops, which had the latest generation helmets and bulletproof vests.[119]

By 1998, procurement in the ground forces was down to 10–15 tanks and about 30 BMP infantry fighting vehicles per year.[120] One high-level officer suggested in late 1998 that no new tanks had been procured for two years.[121] The newest armoured vehicles (including 120 T-90Ss) have been deployed east of the Urals so that older equipment of the same type in the CFE Treaty area would not have to be destroyed.[122] Repair levels in some tank units have been reported as being quite good.[123] Production of all models of tanks in service (T-72, T-80U and T-90S) was continuing through 1998, but the preferred model is the T-90 as the ground forces need to move toward a single tank.[124] In the mid-

1990s, the expectation was that the T–90 would become the main tank after 2005, but this may not happen because of low procurement rates.

According to the most senior ground forces officer speaking in early 1998, the average age of equipment in the service as a whole was about eight years and about 22 per cent of equipment was the most modern.[125] In March 1998, about 25 per cent of equipment with artillery and missile units was the most modern in the Russian inventory, with some individual units having as little as 4–6 per cent of their equipment in that category. More than 50 per cent of major equipment with the artillery and missile troops was more than 15 years old, and was in a relatively poor state of repair.[126] According to government critics, over 70 per cent of radar systems with ground air defence units had exceeded their service life.[127]

The ground forces had estimated that by 2000 the share of modern equipment in these units would be down to 8–9 per cent. Series delivery of new equipment had practically stopped. While production had dropped off sharply (to one-sixteenth of 1993 levels), the ground forces were not even buying what was available. The lack of new deliveries was imposing heavier burdens on repair and maintenance than normal. The missile and artillery troops considered that a reasonable percentage share for the most modern equipment should be 60 per cent. The ground forces had received only 10–15 new artillery pieces each year between 1995 and 1998, and only one SAM launcher each year. By late 1999, there was considerable expectation that a new missile (probably *Iskandr*) would come into service to replace the *Scud*. An earlier replacement had been identified (*Oka*) but it had been scrapped in compliance with the treaty on theatre nuclear missiles.[128] In 1999, the Ground Forces will receive 30 T–90S, 100 BTR–80A and 24 self-propelled howitzers (probably *Msta–S*). [129]

Army aviation was particularly affected by the collapse of procurement. Nationwide, it had in the five years to 1997 only received four Ka–50, ten Mi–26 and eight Mi–8 helicopters to replace several hundred that had been written off.[130] This represented about 12 per cent of its estimated requirements of 40 transport helicopters and 25–30 combat helicopters per year. Serviceability rates stood at about 30 per cent because of poor availability of spares and failure to meet regular maintenance schedules. Lack of aircraft meant that each pilot was flying about 20–30 hours per year compared with a minimum standard of 120–180 hours per year.

The Russian government had abandoned plans announced in 1994 to develop a new indigenously produced training helicopter. By July 1998, it appeared likely that only three of a scheduled eight Ka–50 helicopters would be delivered to the ground forces that year because of an 80 per cent shortfall in government payments to the factory.[131] (The factory is in Arsenev in the Far East.) In August 1998, the head of the ground forces Main Directorate suggested that the service life of existing army aircraft was minimal.[132] One estimate for 1998 suggested that only 2 per cent of helicopters were of the most recent vintage.[133] East of the Urals, the situation was equally grim. In 1997, a deputy commander of the Far East Military District reported that it had received no new military equipment at all in the previous year.[134] One consequence of the cutbacks to the airborne forces was that they had fallen below the level where it was commercially viable to develop specialised military equipment for them.[135]

To solve the longer-term problem, the government sought to implement a moratorium on purchasing equipment, including weapons, until 2001 in the hope that funds made available could be channelled into research and development of new models.[136] But officials were aware that they could not allow the 2001 re-start date to slip. According to the Head of the ground forces Main Directorate, the normal life of army equipment is about 15–20 years, while most Russian ground forces equipment was on average about 10 years old. To maintain minimal serviceability and competitive technology levels, an annual replacement rate of about 5 per cent of inventory was needed.[137] The Russian ground forces were in that officer's opinion unlikely to reach such replacement rates before 2005.

The ground forces were also placing some store in their capacity to incorporate new regimes of modernisation of sub-systems, given that Soviet practice had placed more emphasis on replacement of entire weapons systems than US practice.[138] There was in fact a backlog of modernisations of ground forces weapons that could be implemented as soon as money became available. The Mi–24 helicopter, the BMP–1 and BMP–2, and old artillery pieces were already being modernised or upgraded in some way.[139] In early 1999, a senior ground forces officer, General Bukreyev, expressed considerable confidence in the capacity of Russian defence industry after 2005 to provide the ground forces with a sharp boost to their combat capability—provided the funding situation had stabilised.[140] The commander of the airborne forces declared his confidence in early 1999 that within 10 years they would be equipped with more than 20 types of new weapons or hardware.[141] Russian engineers have certainly not lost their passion for innovation, as discussion of 'robotised' tanks indicates.[142]

An alternative view of the status of ground forces equipment was given by the head of the General Staff's armaments department, Colonel General Sitnov, in late 1998. He said that the ground forces had never endorsed the official strategy of postponing equipment purchases, a policy set out in 1997 by the former First Deputy Minister of Defence, Andrei Kokoshin. Sitnov said that contrary to the policy, and associated public information, the serial production of weapons has not stopped, and research and development continues on a scale much bigger than officially admitted.[143] Sitnov said that it was not necessary to maintain production lines at full capacity, since the rate of use or purchase of new weapons was so low, but he insisted that all production lines were being maintained. Moreover, he said that the amount of stockpiled weapons would last well beyond 2005. Some new systems development has definitely continued in the ground forces in recent years. For example, in mid-1998 in the Far East MD, missile troops successfully test-fired the *Tochka–U* tactical missile system designed to replace the *Scud* in both conventional and nuclear warhead delivery.[144]

Tactical nuclear weapons

According to the Chief of Staff of the Missile and Artillery Force (a branch of the ground forces) speaking in late 1998, there were no tactical nuclear weapons deployed with his forces since they were all stored at military bases controlled by the General Staff.[145] (He also said that there were no chemical weapons held by troops subordinate to him.) The artillery forces had high-precision conventional weapons, such as the *Krasnopol* and *Centimetre* guided shells which were used mainly against armoured vehicles and tanks. In an interview in December 1998, the Deputy Chief of the Missile and Artillery Troops affirmed that his troops remain a means for using tactical nuclear weapons, but that they are no longer held by them.[146] Reports of 1996 and 1997 indicate exercises in western Russia have included use of tactical nuclear weapons in exercise scenarios and play.[147]

Table 9.3 shows equipment holdings in the military districts east of the Urals as recorded by the USNI Military Database. These equipment estimates[148] correlate fairly closely to information compiled by IISS based in part on Russia's reporting required

Table 9.3 Ground forces equipment holdings east of the Ural Mountains[149]

	Urals MD	Siberian MD	Far East MD	Total Russia
MBT	1 100	4 468	5 600	15 500
ACV	1 500	7 400	7 000	22 000
Art/MRL/mortars	900	5 700	5 800	16 840
SAM	600	–	570	2 300
SSM (Tochka–U)	–	48	48	316
Assault Helos	–	120	190	1 060

Table 9.4 Major ground forces equipment 1998–99[150]

	Total Russia	Non-CFE: Eastern Russia	CFE
MBT	15 500	9 041	5 559
AIFV/APC	26 300	16 461	9 839
Arty	15 700	9 701	5 999

under the Treaty on Conventional Forces in Europe as indicated in Table 9.4.

TRAINING

By 1998, ground forces training had fallen off dramatically from already low levels.[151] The Defence Minister complained in 1997 that no large-scale army exercises of the sort needed to maintain readiness (involving 15 000–20 000 troops) had been held for several years.[152] He said that some army and corps commanders had no experience of live-fire exercises. No divisional exercises were held between 1992 and 1997.[153] In early 1998, his successor complained that there had been no operational–strategic level exercise of the ground forces in 10 years, and that the army even found it difficult to carry out regimental exercises.[154] The units of constant combat readiness seemed to be having more success in achieving normal training levels at lower levels of activity at least, such as range firing drills.[155] By 1998, annual work-rates for drivers of infantry fighting vehicles had fallen to 100–150 km, compared with 1000 km in many Western armies.[156] Personal preparation of officers has also been identified as an area that needed substantial improvement, and individual weapons skills of soldiers remain well below expectations.[157] Through 1998, only 72 per cent of scheduled exercises were held.

The ground forces nevertheless have tried valiantly to keep up appearances and spirit through more limited training. In August 1997, the Defence Minister, Igor Sergeyev, and other VIPs from Moscow attended a field firing exercise at Yurga, 200 km from Novosibirsk, carried out by 2000 men of the 74th Independent Motorised Infantry Brigade of the Siberian Military District. The exercise scenario included a river assault, an airborne assault and defensive operations against such assaults.[158] Sergeyev praised the unit for maintaining a high level of military training despite 'critical underfinancing'.[159] This was the first exercise of the sort conducted by the 74th since it was sent to Chechnia three years previously. In March 1998, a live-fire exercise of the Sevastopol Motorised Infantry Regiment of the Siberian MD was held at Yurga under the command of the MD commander, Colonel General Grigory Kasperovich, and involving a large variety of ground force units, including aviation.[160]

In late March and early April 1999, the Russian armed forces stationed in the Far East conducted the largest strategic command and staff exercise in the past eight years. This exercise was commanded by the Far East MD commander, Colonel General Victor Chechevatov, and involved troops of the MD, the Pacific Fleet, the Far Eastern 11th AF/AD Army, Eastern District of Ministry of Interior troops, and border guards units. More than 4000 personnel were involved, 37 tanks, 50 pieces of SP artillery, 70 artillery pieces, 50 combat aircraft and 25 helicopters.[161] By comparison with the largest exercises of countries like France and the UK, this was not a large exercise.

Fuel shortages have affected training across the board in the ground forces, including in their aviation units. On 15 December 1997, all aviation units of the Transbaikal Military District were grounded for five days except for combat operations or medical emergencies.[162] The exercise at Yurga in August 1997 mentioned above could not have been held without the support of the Siberian Accord Association, which had provided the fuel.[163]

By 1999, with the creation of the constant readiness units, the ground forces attempted to increase the resource flow to these units for training by assigning them the highest priority.[164] The expectation was that each of the constant readiness units would be able to fulfil completely their assigned program of military training.[165] But in these circumstances this was recognised as being a particularly difficult task. As a senior officer of the Volga MD pointed out, his district had only received 30 per cent of its fuel requirements in 1998, and he could not readily see where the additional fuel would come from if the training targets were to be met.

One positive aspect of these shortages in supplies for exercises was that it forced the ground forces to more economical methods than those employed in the Soviet period. Economies achieved through more effective accounting methods and through common-sense approaches have reduced some training costs considerably, by a factor of five in one tank regiment in the Volga MD.[166] Military personnel were undertaking many more activities on foot than previously, a circumstance judged to have improved the effectiveness of the infantry units, who had become somewhat too reliant on their fighting vehicles. A number of range firing exercises involving tanks and infantry fighting vehicles had been conducted by connecting the stationary vehicles to electric power from the civil grid, rather than relying on their fuel-driven motors. More unit training now takes place within the base or the immediate vicinity, rather than in designated firing ranges or training grounds.

The cost pressures meant that simulator training had now become a necessity. In 1998, Russia took a giant step forward with the introduction of the first computerised training exercises for command and control of missile and artillery troops.[167] This training was conducted in the Mikhailovski Artillery University in St Petersburg.

In stark contrast to the shortages of fuel, some ground forces units have been reported to have no restrictions on the ammunition available, except for tank shells.[168] The official allocations of funding for ammunition expended in exercises, though, remains very low.

Training in the airborne forces has been especially weak in terms of their capacity to deal with the operational tasks they were being assigned, especially civil emergencies. As one senior officer put it: 'Skills of individual officers . . . in extreme situations and with an abrupt situation change are especially poor'. This critic, an army colonel, identified battalion commanders as particularly weak because they had received their training in the classroom and not in the field, and most certainly not in operational situations. Noting that some training reforms had been instituted in 1997 on the basis of experience in 'undeclared wars' and local conflicts, the colonel called for a complete overhaul of existing methods of training for the airborne forces.[169] Routine drill training has continued but air drop exercises for the 76th Pskov Guards Airborne Division had been cut to one per year for several years up to 1998. The expectation (or hope) for 1999 was that two such exercises could be held.[170] In the 1998 exercise, seven men landed inside an air-dropped infantry fighting vehicle—the first time this had been done in the Russian Airborne Forces. The scenario for this exercise was reinforcement of border posts, with some attention to crossing strong-current water obstacles.

The ground forces in the Caucasus region (58th Army) give relatively high profile to their training exercises and highlight mountain warfare, particularly lessons learned from the 1994–96 Chechnia campaign. According to some sources in Moscow, there is reason to doubt however that these units are conducting effective training. One newspaper suggested that the publicity given to exercises by them in mid-1998 probably had more to do with politics than with combat readiness: either the ground forces commanders in the region and in Moscow were trying to intimidate separatists or they were trying to convince the Russian government that if it wanted to use force in Dagestan or even Chechnia again, that was an option.[171] But one need not be too cynical about the training of the 58th Army. They have strong interests in keeping on their toes and the political leadership's decision to deploy special forces to work with the army group is some indicator of the seriousness with which the army views the situation there.

Ground forces units exercise regularly with military units of other power ministries, such as the Ministry of Interior troops. This provides valuable experience in coordinating work, which was so visibly absent in the joint operations in Chechnia. It also provides some economies for the ground forces training budget.[172]

The ground forces also hold exercises with foreign armies in Russia. For example, 'Peacekeeper 1999' manoeuvres with NATO forces, principally US forces, were scheduled for the Orenburg region. The scenarios for these exercises were not related to combat but, as their name suggests, to peacekeeping.[173] Russia also participates in exercises in other countries. In May 1998, it joined forces from 17 countries in 'Cooperative Jaguar–98' for peacekeeping training in Belgium.[174] This was Russia's first participation in a multinational training exercise, though Russia's land force involvement in that exercise was with Baltic Fleet naval infantry, not ground forces.

Officially available information on ground forces exercises has been criticised by serving officers because of the lack of an appropriate inspection system to verify the quality of training or even the basic data about it. One case cited is that MoD claims about tactical battalion exercises may be correct as to the total number conducted, but that most of them were conducted only for 24 hours, not for the 48-hour period stipulated in regulations.[175] Similarly, too many live-firing exercises were being conducted in place, rather than on the move as stipulated.

CONCLUSION

A Finnish specialist assessed that by 2015, the Russian ground forces will probably comprise 10 ready divisions, 10–20 under-manned divisions 'with equipment dating back to the present', and then 'another 20–30 divisions that are mobilisation capable'.[176] He expected the Russian government to maintain the airborne forces at high levels of readiness and that the training of large numbers of personnel since discharged to the reserves would give Russia a large and effective mobilisation capacity. From a theoretical per-spective the ground forces may now have an optimal size and shape for contemporary requirements.[177] They will remain hamstrung, however, by deficiencies in funding, training, and equipment.

As long as Russia is prepared to give high priority to getting funds to the units concerned, it will remain able in the coming decade to field significant ground forces in large numbers for the sorts of low-level contingencies it is likely to face. With several months preparation, Russia could deliver powerful conventional ground forces for decisive intervention in mid-level conflicts on its borders. These forces will however face substantial difficulties in meeting the new requirements. It may well take up to a decade for the ground forces to make the adjustments in training, exer-cises and unit structure that are required for Russia's new doctrinal commitments to local war and smaller conflicts. With-out a significant and sustained change in spending priorities, Russian ground forces would soon be routed in conventional warfare if opposed by NATO forces at any distance from Russian borders. But Russian ground forces are not looking for war with NATO nor are they postured for it. They can be expected to make important contributions to peacekeeping operations in the coming decade, either under UN auspices or otherwise.

10

Military industry and regional arms sales

Soviet military industry, once taken for granted by the armed forces and once the foundation stone of that country's aggressive military diplomacy in the Third World, has for the successor state of Russia become the weakest link in national security and the last lifeline of manufacturing exports for an ailing national economy.[1] Domestic orders for military equipment, that is for Russia's own armed forces, have fallen to a level which will not support for much longer a single military industrial factory producing conventional armaments. But some of Russia's defence industries have been scoring good foreign sales, particularly in the richer countries of the Pacific Rim and the Persian Gulf. The degree to which Russia's military industrial sector is able to keep producing profitably will have a profound influence on the strategic posture of the country but will also provide some measure of Russia's capacity to exercise some attraction to other powers, great and small, in global diplomacy. But Russia is not the USSR and the new government in Moscow does not take the same approach to arms sales as its Soviet forebear. In line with a general international strategic posture that is non-offensive, Russia is now an advocate of the need to dampen conflicts when they arise, not exploit them. The big question in this regard is how much Russia's practice matches its preaching. This chapter provides a brief overview of these aspects—all inter-related—of Russia's military industry. It looks first at military industry, foreign arms sales, and proliferation aspects of arms exports, and then provides an overview of Russia's arms trade with India and China. Russia's arms sales to other countries of East Asia, such as Malaysia, South Korea and Indonesia, have been relatively small and are of relatively minor strategic significance. The arms supply relationship with North Korea may take on a sharper strategic significance in the longer term for reasons outlined in chapter 4, but this would probably take a number of years and a fundamental strategic reorientation by Russia.

MILITARY INDUSTRY

Russia was in a far better position than most of its brother republics in the former USSR when it came to defence industry. The RSFSR had a markedly higher proportion of Soviet defence industries on its territory, employing about three-quarters of the workforce in this sector, while having only half of the total population of the USSR.[2] More than 50 per cent of the largest industrial enterprises (those employing upwards of 5000 people) in Russia in 1991 were defence factories—some 267 plants.[3] These military enterprises each employed about 6000 to 8000 workers.[4] The region which employed the most workers in military industry was the Sverdlovsk region, with about 350 000 workers—20 to 30 per cent of the local workforce. Other eastern Russian regions with large military industry workforces included Novosibirsk (20 to 30 per cent), Omsk, Cheliabinsk, Khabarovsk and Krasnoiarsk (each with 10 to 20 per cent of the local workforce), but the most heavily 'militarised' part of the RSFSR with respect to defence industry was the area west of the Urals, not eastern Russia.[5]

The state of defence industry in Russia after 1991 has been severely affected by declining domestic procurement and by a drying up of international demand for Russian weapons for a number of geostrategic and commercial reasons. A number of additional domestic factors also caused severe shocks to military industry enterprises after 1991. There was pressure for privatisation, development of a free labour market drawing people away from remote defence establishments, and the inability of government factories to pay workers and pay for inputs.

By 1991, procurement in the Soviet armed forces had dropped sharply as a result of the declining budgets and the general political and economic turmoil—by 20 per cent according to a US intelligence assessment.[6] By February 1992, work had begun on scrapping the first nuclear-powered aircraft carrier, *Ulianovsk*, which was being constructed in a shipyard in Ukraine.[7] In 1995, the air force took delivery of only two aircraft, compared with 585 in 1991. By 1999, according to the Defence Ministry, procurement was only one-tenth of what it was in 1991.[8] Between 1995 and 1998, the air force had received only two Su–25 TM multi-purpose planes, and naval aviation was supplied with one deck reconnaissance plane at the end of 1998. In 1998, the armed forces did not buy a single tank, aircraft or nuclear submarine. The strategic nuclear forces received only half of their budgeted allocations for R&D. Most other programs received almost no funds at all. The Defence Ministry still owes more than 20 billion roubles to industrial enterprises for procurement or other services, although even the size of the debt is contested—some say 100 billion roubles[9]—and little of this debt is likely ever to be met.[10] According to one estimate, by 2005, the share of the order of battle taken by new weapons would be only about 7 per cent, compared with 60–80 per cent for most industrialised countries.[11]

When the USSR collapsed, the new Russian government did not replace the former defence industry ministries, choosing instead to create one super industry ministry covering civil and military sectors. By 1992, the power of the defence sector reasserted itself and a new Defence Industrial Commission was created. Although it was less powerful than its Soviet predecessor in its ability to dominate economic and industrial resources, it did manage to carve out for itself exemptions from many of the reforms introduced by the Yeltsin administration in the economy at large.[12] By the time a new military doctrine was approved in November 1993, the Russian armed forces and the government accepted that military development, including procurement, had to occur within the context of transition to a market economy and with a radically new sensitivity to the overall potential of the national economy.[13] Under a secret presidential decree of 19 August 1993, Yeltsin allowed for the privatisation of some defence industries (482 enterprises and design bureaus were exempted), but control over the arrangements would lie with the new Defence Industrial Commission, and its powers included the certification of all directors of privatised military industrial enterprises.[14] One example of privatisation has been the plant in Kazan producing Mi–8 helicopters, of which several hundred are in service in the Russian armed forces. This plant has been a listed company since 1993, in which the Russian government held only a 30 per cent stake at the end of 1997.[15] By 1997, the government abolished a new dedicated Ministry of Defence Industry that had been established only in 1996 and subordinated its functions to the Ministry of the Economy.[16] The Defence Industrial Commission eventually became moribund, and was disbanded in 1998.[17]

Conversion of enterprises from military to civil production and other pressures of the transformation and reform processes led to an estimated 50 per cent of the military enterprise workforce leaving the sector between 1989 and 1995, even though this still left some 6 million workers employed in it.[18] (Official estimates put the size of the workforce in military industrial enterprises in 1995 at only 3 million, including in civil production.)[19] By 1998, the conversion process came to be regarded as a complete failure because it had proceeded without the required financial support from the government and eventually resulted in abandonment of military production, with very few enterprises able to begin producing non-military items.[20]

By 1995, according to official statistics, the output of military equipment had shrunk to one-ninth the 1990 level, but the drop in output had not been compensated for in civil production, which also started a sharp decline after some initial successes.[21] By 1997, the production of both civil and military goods from defence factories was 17.8 per cent of the January 1991 levels.[22] By early 1999, according to some reports, the crisis was even deeper, and the arms industries were hit very hard by the August 1998 economic crisis.[23] Although the dollar cost of production fell and good profits were being made in some plants, the gains were more than undermined by the rapid rises in the cost of credit. One observer commented in 1998 that 'the financing of defence in each passing year is having an ever increasing destructive effect on . . . the defence industrial complex'.[24] Another observer reported in 1998 that 80 per cent of all enterprises in the sector were bankrupt, and only 500 of 1746 lead enterprises were operating.[25] Only six fixed-wing aircraft plants remained open in early 1998.[26]

As for eastern Russia, Siberia has been called the 'cradle of the Soviet military-industrial complex'.[27] The Poliot factory in Omsk made *Proton* rockets, communication satellites and boosters for the *Buran* space systems. This history of military production in the region provides both opportunities and penalties in the new economic conditions of Russia. Some efforts at conversion to civil production have been successful. In 1992, officials of the Maritime Territory were attempting to sell non-military versions of some small naval craft, such as shallow-draft amphibious craft, to Japan.[28] By 1994, the Omsk Tank Plant had produced versions of the Belarus tractor.[29] Many military industry enterprises do not lend themselves to such simple or quick conversions, but some military industries were able to keep afloat.

By 1997, Russia was trumpeting the successful design of a new tank, the 'Black Eagle', developed on the basis of the T–80U version, by the Omsk Transport Machinery Plant. The tank is claimed to surpass performance standards of Western equivalents by as much as 70 per cent in mobility, firepower, armour penetration, and protection. It is also said to have a unique turret design which reduces its target profile. The tank has been demonstrated to foreign military observers, but with its turret and weapons covered.[30] The tank was displayed at a military equipment exhibition, which also featured advanced electronic warfare equipment, but Russian officials associated with the exhibition noted that the companies concerned were too badly placed financially to be able to exhibit such equipment abroad.[31]

Industry leaders in Siberia identified an opportunity to marry the demand of the high-income oil and gas industry for machinery with the latent capacity of the defence factories in the region to produce it. In January 1997, representatives of 11 oil companies and directors of 70 military industry factories or research institutes established an inter-regional group to pursue the opportunity. Some groundwork had already been laid for this program in Siberia with several military factories having produced prototype equipment for the oil industry, but the initiative would face problems raising venture capital and competition from other defence industry factories in the Urals and Volga regions which had started similar programs for the oil industry earlier.[32]

The mess that Russian defence industry finds itself in is well represented even in one of the two most successful arms exporters of the decade—the Sukhoi Aviation Military Industrial Combine (AIMC). This firm was established by government edict in August 1996 on the basis of four separate entities all involved in production of Sukhoi aircraft but in different stages of privatisation: the Sukhoi Experimental Design Bureau, and three production plants (Irkutsk, Novosibirsk, and Komsomolsk) each constituted as independent Aircraft Production Associations. The Design Bureau had been privatised as early as December 1992, with the government eventually retaining 50 per cent plus one share, and the rest being held primarily by two banks. The Irkutsk plant had been privatised with only 14.7 per cent remaining in government hands, and a large share going to one of the two banks owning large shares in the Design Bureau. This plant builds a two-seater Su–27, the Su–27B, and the Su–30, and is building an order of 29 Su–27s for India. The Novosibirsk plant remained a state enterprise and has been the least successful. It builds the Su–27IB (or Su–34, Su–32FN) fighter bomber. The Komsomolsk plant also remained

state-owned, but has the greatest capacity, and is fulfilling orders
for China.

The 1996 edict failed to deliver organisational cohesion to the
new Sukhoi hybrid, as it represented some sort of reversal of the
principle of privatisation, and because it threatened returns to
provincial governments from the state-owned components. By
1997, a new edict on the ownership–management regime for the
Sukhoi AIMC was issued offering a softer regime which held out
compromise for the competing interests. Leading personnel were
changed, and by late 1998, the new firm began to settle down.[33]
In a May 1998 interview, the Director General of Sukhoi AIMC
conceded that closure of one or more of the plants was inevitable
if new product lines could not be established.[34]

Simultaneously, other parts of the Sukhoi network, but
not part of Sukhoi AIMC, had been developing their own
privatised mergers, involving Sukhoi component supplier plants in
Belarus, Ukraine and Georgia, and two of the Sukhoi Experimental Design Bureau's five departments—attack aviation and sports
aviation. These elements of the Sukhoi network set about establishing a unified firm, Sukhoi Attack Aircraft, under the 1997 CIS
Convention on Establishing Transnational Corporations. One of
the main production plants in this group is at Ulan Ude and
produces the Su–25TM (Su–39), but there is also one in Tblisi,
Georgia. The leader of this process has vigorously opposed the
government-decreed Sukhoi AIMC merger as anti-competitive and
a return to Soviet-style command economics.[35] Sukhoi Attack
Aircraft have secured a small order for the new Su–25TM from
the RFAF.

Foreign military industrial companies have shown considerable interest in investing in their Russian counterparts and may
make an important contribution to revitalisation of the Russian
defence industry. For example, through 1997 and 1998, the Italian
company Aeromacchi was involved in co-development of a design
for a jet trainer, the YAK–130, to be built in the Sokol factory in
Nizhni Novgorod as early as late 1998. Three of the prototypes
co-designed by the Yakovlev design bureau and Aeromacchi
would be tested in Russia and one would be tested in Italy.
Aeromacchi would provide half of the investment cost, and provide and fit avionics, control systems, and the engine, among
other systems. The Russian partners were hoping for finance from
the Russian Ministry of Defence but declared their intention to
proceed without it if necessary.[36] The aircraft, a two-seater, is
expected be of the same standard and prices as European coun-

terparts. To enhance such cooperative activities or to promote foreign sales, some Russian military aircraft have been modified to accommodate some foreign systems, such as French avionics on the Su–37.[37] There are concerns in Russia, however, that foreign interest in Russia's defence industry is monopolistic in intent and that factories or interests purchased by foreign companies may be closed down by them to reduce competition.

The science and technology base of Russian defence industry has all but collapsed. A 1998 report of the RF Audit Office concluded that if recent trends continue, Russian defence industry would 'lose the capability to develop advanced technologies and world-level industrial models by 2003–2005'.[38] The report found that spending patterns and even allocations for new development work in the military sector did not match the rhetoric of military and political leaders, and had been declining consistently between 1992 and 1998. For example, between 1992 and 1998, the share taken by military R&D of government expenditure allocated to all R&D had declined from 12.8 per cent to 0.5 per cent. (In 1990, the proportion was 79 per cent.) This precipitous fall was the direct result of government policies—encouraged by the IMF—to shift the responsibility for industrial innovation to the private sector.

The above discussion shows that the military industry sector in Russia has not escaped either the chaos and dislocation created by the political reform process or the economic collapse that has gone on in the rest of the country. There is no longer a unified and powerful lobby group as existed in the Soviet era to shape strategic policy for its own purposes. There is little likelihood that a militant and highly-organised military industrial complex will re-emerge to overturn the political order,[39] either by itself or in alliance with a political party or a section of the armed forces.

But these considerations should not disguise the fact that Russian leaders retain a strong commitment to restoration of their military industry for the purposes of national defence and strategic power projection of the traditional great power variety. Military leaders believe Russian military technology is, can be or should be equal to or better than that of other major powers, including the USA. To this end, the military planners have identified priority areas for military R&D which may seem ambitious but which reflect their determination to be part of the latest 'revolution in military affairs'.

FOREIGN ARMS SALES

One of the most important foundations for restoration of the military industrial base of Russia will be its success in making foreign sales. Sukhoi factories have been kept alive by arms exports to the point where one has been able to roll out a new aircraft type (Su–37) without substantial support from domestic orders.[40] The design work for this aircraft began in 1987 and it may enter service about 2006. But without a restoration of domestic procurement, even high success rate in foreign sales will not allow the sort of rejuvenation of defence industry that most in Russia still hope for. Most major arms exporting countries consume about 80–90 per cent of total production domestically.[41] And there are unlikely to be substantial domestic orders for Russian defence industry for many years, even for the Su–37.

In 1993, the government created a new marketing arm for its defence industries, called Rosvooruzhenie [Russian Armaments], which is the major exporter, but not the exclusive one. By 1998, there were eight other firms authorised to sell weapons abroad[42] but Rosvooruzhenie has the right to set prices, most of which are rigid and too high, putting Russian exporters in a non-competitive position.[43] The Russian firms are often in competition with each other, as in trials in 1998 for a new Indian tank in which Promexport, selling T–72 models, was competing with Rosvooruzhenie selling T–90 models.

In 1996, according to early IISS estimates in US dollars, Russia regained its position as the second largest exporter of military equipment.[44] Later figures suggest that this was not the case. The US led the field for all years between 1992 and 1997, and the UK was second ahead of France for all years but one in the same period. Russia has been a distant fourth in all of these years, accounting for between 3 and 10 per cent of 'identified' arms orders in each of those years.[45] Nevertheless, hard currency profits for Rosvooruzhenie in 1998 were US$2.3 billion.[46] In that year, Russia sold weapons to 64 countries, seven of which (China, India, Iran, the UAE, Vietnam, Greece and Algeria) accounted for more than 82 per cent.[47] Air force systems accounted for 49.2 per cent of the 1998 sales, ground forces 25 per cent, navy 15.9 per cent, and air defence 8.1 per cent.[48] The most heavily traded items in 1998 were Su–27 planes, 636-project *Kilo* submarines, armoured personnel carriers, BMP–3 armoured vehicles and *Tunguska*-M missile complexes.

Russia has identified China and India as its most important potential customers.[49] This circumstance is particularly complex for Russia given that India regards China as it most significant long-term threat.

According to the Director General of Rosvooruzhenie, Yevgeny Ananev, speaking in 1998, Russia's share of the US$40 billion annual arms market is probably fairly stable at only about $3 billion.[50] But in early 1999, Russian Defence Ministry officials were looking for an increase in arms exports of 20 per cent in 1999.[51] They thought this could be achieved partly on the basis of the restructuring and rationalisation of defence industry already under way, an intensive marketing campaign directed at restoring arms trade with traditional partners, and an increase in cooperative ventures with foreign producers. By early 1999, Rosvooruzhenie had orders worth US$8.4 bn for the period up to 2004.[52] But the market penetration of Russian arms exporters in most of its markets is very low, with some 50 countries taking a total of US$11 million worth of equipment in 1997.[53]

Efforts by Rosvooruzhenie to move into co-production or joint projects with Western European countries with a view to joint sales in the Third World hold out some prospects for the agency, even though there has been an interruption of this work in response to the NATO bombing of Yugoslavia. The agency is particularly keen to marry its relatively advanced platforms with instruments and software developed in the other European countries.[54] MiG–29 and Su–30MKI have been exported with foreign radars fitted (GEC-Marconi and Thomson CSF respectively).[55] Rosvooruzhenie is also expecting a gradual improvement in military exports to former Warsaw Pact allies, even to those which have joined NATO.[56] This expectation is based on the fairly reasonable proposition that leaders of these countries will see the economic sense in returning to Russian suppliers.

Russia faces a number of obstacles in expanding its arms sales. The policy mechanisms in Moscow for controlling arms exports are rather chaotic, and this produces inconsistent behaviour, often in contravention of international agreements Russia has signed (as discussed in the following section).[57] Rosvooruzhenie has been critical of the time it takes for the government to approve arms sales, of the exaggerated prices set by some Russian producers, and the failure to meet scheduled delivery dates or servicing requirements. Russia faces stiff competition from some former Warsaw Pact states or newly independent states. Ukraine alone has sold about US$800 million of military equipment and weapons, half of which it inherited from the USSR and half of which it manufactured.[58] Many of the countries to which Russia might seem a more natural partner than the USA and its allies are already so heavily in debt to Russia that they can get no new credit from Russia to finance new deals.

One advantage Russia faces is that it does not apply the same tests of political leverage or linkage to good behaviour often applied by NATO countries.[59]

The biggest problem Russia faces in expanding its share of the international arms market is, as discussed above, that the industrial base is not renewing itself. As one 1998 report of the Russian Audit Office found, the 'potential for competitiveness of the main models of weapons and military equipment is close to exhaustion' because the technologies on offer are those developed in the 1970s and 1980s.[60]

NUCLEAR, MISSILE AND WEAPONS PROLIFERATION

Soon after the collapse of the USSR, grave concerns were expressed over the prospect of transfer of its technology or equipment for weapons of mass destruction. China was a particular point of concern[61] but that has become much less the case toward the end of the decade. Some commentators do not believe that Russia has any interest in or commitment to preventing the proliferation of nuclear weapons, and other mass destruction weapons. These opinions have been advanced by incontrovertible evidence that Russian suppliers have been linked to development by Iraq and Iran of weapons of mass destruction (nuclear, chemical or biological).[62]

A counter argument is that there are clear instances where the Russian government has not had full control over the supply arrangement. Such cases have occurred both where the sale might have been judged contrary to Russia's own direct security interests and where the sale was in breach of an international proliferation-related commitment undertaken by Russia. This is especially the case with activities involving Russian organisations and firms active in Iran in the field of missile technology, in a way that breaches Russia's commitments under the Missile Technology Control Regime (MTCR).[63]

An assessment prepared for the Defence Committee of the North Atlantic Assembly concluded that Russian leaders only pay lip service to non-proliferation commitments, and that the Foreign Ministry is too weak in institutional terms to carry through an effective export control regime.[64] This report suggested that even the General Staff has little influence because the government has given 'absolute priority' to boosting arms exports. Even if the General Staff can recognise security threats to Russia in any undermining of the proliferation regimes Russia has agreed to, they might not be inclined to be rigorous in opposing breaches because the armed forces receive, through Russian government policy, some financial spin-offs from the exports. Russian commentators and politicians rail against US and NATO complaints about Russian breaches with accusations that these countries want to monopolise the arms markets.

The record would appear to be that notwithstanding these incidents, the Russian government has moved decisively on most occasions to ensure that arms exporters observe both Russia's own security needs and its international obligations. Russia's commitment to most proliferation goals pursued by the USA and its allies remains firm. A US government assessment in 1997 observed that 'Russia recognises that preventing the spread of destabilising arms and technologies can protect Russian security interests'; that 'Russia has worked constructively with us to reduce the proliferation dangers created by the collapse of the USSR'; and that 'Russia is a strong supporter of the global non-proliferation regime'.[65] The evidence on these points is incontrovertible. The Russian government at the strategic level has made a number of decisions through the 1990s in agreement with the USA and other major powers to limit or prohibit transfers of certain types of systems.[66] This disposition was evident right through the Soviet era, in the USSR's support for the Nuclear Non-Proliferation Treaty and the International Atomic Energy Agency, and in its refusal in the late 1950s to transfer nuclear and missile technology to China. Since the end of the Cold War, Russia has abandoned a number of potentially lucrative weapons deals and technology cooperation arrangements to sign up to new non-proliferation regimes. A senior US official has provided the following as evidence of Russia's commitment:[67]

- Support for the indefinite extension of the NPT and for a strengthening of the IAEA safeguards regime.
- Effective participation in the removal of nuclear weapons from Kazakhstan, Belarus and Ukraine.
- Continued observance of UN arms embargoes against arms sales to Libya and Iraq.
- Support for UNSCOM activities in Iraq to monitor destruction of its weapons of mass destruction.
- Membership of the Nuclear Suppliers Group which controls exports of nuclear weapons-related materials and technologies.

- Abandonment of a sale of missile technology to India in 1993 and subsequent joining in 1995 of the MTCR.
- Agreement in 1995 to end weapons sales to Iran within a few years.[68]

As one Russian commentator has observed, 'it would be naive to think that this is all some kind of front'.[69] There is other evidence of a very strong commitment at the national level to preventing breaches of Russia's proliferation commitments. For example, in 1998 Russian security services, including special forces, have been conducting sustained operations against Iranian agents attempting to acquire Russian military technologies in contravention of Russia's international anti-proliferation commitments. In April 1999, Russia and Belarus signed an agreement for joint export control of militarily sensitive technologies, especially those relating to weapons of mass destruction and their delivery systems.[70] The agreement commits both parties to be sensitive to the national interests of the other, while promoting trade with third countries, as well as being guided by existing international non-proliferation regimes. The agreement was premised on the proposition that proliferation is a threat to both countries. The agreement stipulates that national procedures for controlling these technologies must conform to existing international obligations.

Russia will remain hostile however to US efforts to force Russia to accept arms embargoes against other countries, such as Syria, where these have not been agreed with it.[71] It has powerful economic incentives to maximise its arms sales where it has made no commitment to limit them. But this has been one of the principal points of dissension between the USA and Russia on proliferation issues—Russia simply does not support all of the anti-proliferation regimes that exist, and until it commits formally to such regimes, it has no obligation to observe them. The existence of 'grey areas' in commitments made by Russia or in interpretations of those commitments have also been a source of considerable dispute. For a number of reasons, Russia will probably move toward a single gatekeeper for all military exports (probably an arm of the General Staff)[72] and in those circumstances, the government will be far better placed than it has been to enforce its policies.

INDIA

The main aspect of current Indo–Russian military industrial co-operation is not just collaboration in supplying India with

Table 10.1   Russian/Soviet systems in India's order of battle: selected
categories[73]

Item	Total	Russian/Soviet origin
Main battle tanks	3414	2200
AIFV	1350	1350
Submarines	19	15
Destroyers	6	5
Frigates	18	5
FGA aircraft	367	279
Ftr aircraft	368	333

Russian-made armaments but a transfer of Russian technologies to India, which indicates an allied relationship between partners rather than simple buyer–seller cooperation. India produces significant quantities and types of Russian-designed equipment under licence and a large proportion of its order of battle is from Russian or recent Soviet sources, as Table 10.1 shows.

India established security and military ties with the USSR in the mid-1960s following wars with China in 1962 and Pakistan in 1965. This collaboration reached new levels in September 1971 when the two countries signed a Treaty of Friendship and Cooperation at the height of the civil unrest in East Pakistan, a move almost certainly premised in India's case on its intentions to intervene in this crisis. With Sino–American rapprochement also in progress at the same time, the treaty with the USSR strengthened India's hand to resolve the Bangladesh issue by force in December 1971, and to wage war with Pakistan, against the possibility of military intervention by Pakistan's then allies, China and the USA.

Even though India's main security problems were not directly related to Cold War politics but to Pakistan and China, its fears were compounded by great power intrusions into South Asia that resulted from Cold War politics. Rivalry between the USA and the USSR and between China and the USSR enabled Pakistan to obtain US and Chinese military assistance to counter Indian military capabilities. Meanwhile, India had turned increasingly to the USSR for weapons to counter or pre-empt Pakistani arms procurement, though India continued to buy equipment from countries allied to the USA, such as the UK.

Towards the end of the 1990s, the strategic relationships between India, Pakistan and China at the regional level, and Russia and the USA at the global level, continue to define the security framework of India, although the nature of these relationships has shifted, and the intensity has declined. Indeed, at the end of the Cold War there was a sudden Indian rush towards embracing the USA. New Delhi sought greater military cooperation, but soon ran into several roadblocks. India's refusal to protect American pharmaceutical patents, its decision to buy Russian cryogenic engines for its rocket program, and the testing of the *Prithvi* missile in defiance of American warnings, cooled US interest in establishing closer military ties, and provoked growing suspicions in India about American friendship. Correspondingly, while it has become clear that the Russian Federation has few benefits to offer India, the sudden break in Indo–Russian military collaboration following the end of the Cold War is now being mended. The scale of India's growing collaboration with Russia is invariably mentioned in statements from Russian and Indian politicians. For example, during his visit to Moscow in October 1997, India's Defence Minister Mulayam Singh Yadav, following a meeting with President Boris Yeltsin, said: 'Our relations with Russia are based on trust and understanding. There is commonality of interests between us and our views on all major international issues are the same.'[74]

The mutual attraction of the two countries is further strengthened by the fact that neither accepts the dominant role of the USA in the world as it has emerged through the 1990s. New Delhi once again regards Moscow as its main strategic partner and a dependable ally on the global scene, while Moscow sees New Delhi as its main trade and strategic ally in Asia. India is the only country in the world with which Russia has a long-term program of military technical cooperation (until 2000), a program which is worth more than US$10 billion. While Yadav was in Moscow in 1997, both sides agreed to prolong the program until 2012. Obviously, military–technical cooperation has become the backbone of bilateral relations.

An extended collaboration between the two countries in the military sphere may place India's armed forces on a quite different level compared to their present condition. Traditionally, the Indian military has regarded its land forces as a crucial factor in the conduct of wars and has therefore concentrated on improving the fighting capabilities of its ground troops. However, changes in the nature of modern warfare have influenced decisions of India's military and political leaders. They accept that the massive employment of sophisticated technological combat systems is one of the main characteristics of armed conflict in the 1990s and beyond. They also acknowledge that the technological level of their own armed forces is not equal to that of the leading powers, in spite of their success in absorbing some modern military technologies. Hence, since the beginning of the 1990s, India has invested heavily in new armaments to redress this deficiency.

India's current military modernisation has taken two quite contradictory paths: it involves both the acquisition of weapons from other nations and a modernisation of its domestic armaments industry to reduce dependence on foreign suppliers. As discussed above, India has resumed substantial defence trading with Russia and the Indian armed forces are equipped mainly with Russian military hardware: the navy with about 80 per cent, the air force with about 64 per cent, and the ground troops with about 48 per cent.[75] In the period between 1990 and 1996, India imported Russian arms worth US$3.5 billion.[76] Yet, one of the particular features of contemporary Indo–Russian military industrial collaboration is the shift from supplying India with Russian-made weapons to providing it with weapons assembly capacity, thereby introducing some of Russia's newest technologies into India's military industry. Russian military experts are also actively involved in the research and development for India's indigenous military programs. India has concentrated on modernising its air and naval forces, recognising that they are the main means of power projection in South Asia.

The current friendly relations of the two countries were made possible by a breakthrough in military–technical cooperation in December 1996, when Russia's state arms-export company Rosvooruzhenie signed a large-scale contract—called by the Russians the 'contract of the century'—for the delivery to India of 40 Su–30MKI *Flanker* tactical aircraft, worth US$1.8 billion. Other deals followed, but in December 1998 when Prime Minister Primakov visited India, the two countries signed a massive arms deal and a military industrial cooperation agreement, involving air force, naval and army systems, including T–90 tanks and S–300 PMU1 air defence systems.[77]

In the Indian Air Force (IAF), the plan is to deploy the Su–30MKI aircraft by 2000, a project in which India is helping to fund the design and over which India has acquired veto rights for Russian sales to other countries, such as China.[78] The acquisition of new *Flankers* is not only the largest purchase of foreign combat aircraft by the IAF but also a significant step in improving its strike capabilities. The Su–30MKI has potent thrust-vectoring canard technology. It is equipped with the fourth-generation R–73 *Vympel* and R–77 *Vympel* air-to-air missiles (AAM)[79] which are, according to a number of accounts, superior to practically any

Western-made AAM, including the US AIM–9M and AIM–7M. Designed for a deep penetration role, the Su–30MKI has twice the combat radius of the F/A–18A, higher energy manoeuvrability, higher sustained and instantaneous turn rate, a longer-ranging *Phazotron* radar, substantially larger missile load, and unsurpassed manoeuvre performance. At the end of 1996, the first eight Su–30MKIs had been delivered to the IAF for assembly and Russian test pilots have assisted in bringing them to operational status.

During Yadav's visit to Moscow in October 1997, Russia and India finalised negotiations for a contract for the delivery of four Il–78 aerial refuellers to India, which will increase the range of the Indian Su–30MKIs to 5000 km. Moscow and New Delhi have also concluded an agreement on retrofitting 125 MiG–21B *Fishbed* fighters of the IAF. This significant modernisation of the IAF will boost India's air power potential, thus making the IAF the most potent regional force, superior to all other regional powers.

One of the key goals of the Indian Navy's new modernisation program is enhancing its submarine warfare capabilities. In January 1997, India announced that its navy would purchase four improved *Kilo* class submarines from Russia, with two submarines to be built by the Russian shipyards, while the rest are assembled in India—at a price of US$800 million each. INS *Sindhu Rakshak* of the *Kilo* class (Type 636), was commissioned in the Indian Navy on 25 December 1997. *Kilo* class submarines, codenamed 'Black Hole' by NATO for their silent running capabilities, are considered to be one of the quietest conventionally powered submarines in the world. The Type 636 is the advanced version of the standard *Kilo* (Type 877EKN). It is capable of detecting an enemy vessel at a range three to four times greater than that at which it can be detected by the vessel's aircraft. The low detectability and the capability to fire powerful and accurate rapid-action torpedoes gives it the advantage of being able to deliver a first strike.

It is now clear that Russia is also helping India in creating its own nuclear-powered submarine. With Russian assistance, India has already gained experience in operating nuclear submarines, with a Russian *Charlie–I* submarine being leased for three years (1988–91) by the Indian Navy. But the desire of the Indian government to have its own nuclear submarine fleet came into reality with the establishment of the Advanced Technology Vessel (ATV) project, with facilities in New Delhi, Hyderabad, Vizag and Kalpakkani. Russia is helping India to build a power generator for the ATV and also provides design support. There are rumours that the ATV will be a stretched version of the *Kilo* class conventional submarine, or will even resemble the new Russian *Severodvinsk* class SSN, although the Indian submarine will probably be of the SSGN type.

India is also trying to update its surface fleet with Russian support. The Indian Navy has acquired six *Krivak-III* class guided missile frigates (FFG) from Russia. Designed primarily for antisubmarine warfare (ASW) and air defence of a task force, the Russian FFGs were chosen because the Indian Navy wants to fill the gap created by the decommissioning of the *Leander* class FFG until its own Project 17 FFGs enter service. The first three vessels will be built in Russia and the final three in India. The first *Krivak* will be supplied to the Indian Navy not earlier than 2000. Russia is also involved in a program to build new *Delhi* class destroyers for the Indian Navy. In particular, the first vessel, INS *Delhi*, is equipped with Russian engine components and weapons systems. It can be expected that the follow-on ships of this series will be equipped with domestically developed components based on Russian technologies.

One of the most intriguing issues in Indo–Russian military cooperation has been the negotiations about the possible purchase by India of Russia's last remaining *Kiev* class VSTOL aircraft carrier *Admiral Gorshkov*. For quite some time India has shown interest in leasing or purchasing this vessel and its interest increased after the INS *Vikrant* was decommissioned due to its obsolescence. Moreover, the INA's other carrier, the aging *Viraat*, is at the end of its operational life and should be decommissioned by 2005. It has been reported that the transfer of the *Admiral Gorshkov* to India was part of the December 1998 agreement.[80] If the transfer proceeds, Russia will significantly upgrade *Admiral Gorshkov*. The carrier will probably be adjusted so it can accommodate MiG–29K *Fulcrum* fighters.[81] The flying deck of *Admiral Gorshkov* will be changed to include a ski-jump and aerofinishers, similar to those on the *Admiral Kuznetsov*. The new carrier air wing will comprise 16–18 MiG–29Ks, probably some *Sea Harrier* jets and ASW helicopters. There have been serious doubts that India would purchase the carrier. One highly placed anonymous source in the Indian Ministry of Defence told *The Hindu*: 'In case we induct the *Gorshkov*, it would mean heavy expenditure on related infrastructure because of its large size. The navy has so far not been equipped to handle a carrier of around 40 000 tonnes displacement.'[82] Indeed, the Indian Navy only has experience of operating relatively small carriers: the *Viraat* has 28 700 tonnes displacement, and the retired *Vikrant* 19 500 tonnes. Consequently, there has been a strong view within the Indian military that it will be more efficient for them to operate a smaller carrier of approximately 20 000 tonnes displacement and a range of around 8000 km. Apart from *Admiral Gorshkov,* India has also considered proposals to purchase aircraft carriers from France and the UK. Furthermore, India has also indicated a desire to build its own carrier. Vice-Admiral Sushil Kumar, Vice Chief of the Indian Navy, in presenting a report about the present condition of the navy, said: 'Our first and fundamental priority is to build our own aircraft carrier and we can do it'.[83] Moreover, India has not been entirely happy with Russia's offer of approximately US$2 billion for leasing the carrier. The future of the deal has become even more uncertain since the *Admiral Gorshkov* was reactivated within Russia's Northern Fleet. The December 1998 agreement reportedly involves transfer of the *Admiral Gorshkov* to India at a very cheap price,[84] presumably with the prospect of getting contracts for refitting or upgrading it. Even if India does take the *Admiral Gorshkov,* India may still move toward construction of its own indigenously built carrier.

Traditionally, the Indian Navy could hardly be described as a 'blue water' navy. However, recent Indian naval modernisation may significantly improve its offensive capabilities, well beyond its present potential. Any major expansion of the Indian Navy into a blue water capability has always raised the possibility of a naval response from Indonesia, Pakistan, and even Iran, since India's maritime territorial jurisdiction extends to the Lakshwadeep Islands in the Arabian Sea. For example, Pakistan, in response to India's naval build-up, has already acquired 9 submarines (including 2 Italian *Augusto* class and 4 French *Daphne* class) and 11 surface ships (including 3 ex-US *Gearing* class destroyers and 6 ex-UK *Amazon* class frigates). Russia's support for India's continuous regional naval build-up could eventually alter the regional military balance and lead to a naval arms race in the Indian Ocean region.

By enhancing its military cooperation with Russia, India above all showed the USA and China that it does not intend to accept their strategic plans for South Asia. India is also affirming its status as a regional power. And Russia is the only country which can provide military–industrial backing to the strategic ambitions of New Delhi through comprehensive support in key technologies—modern weapons, missile and space programs, and nuclear-power engineering. Other countries capable of such help cannot establish strategic partnerships with India for various political reasons. The United States and China are cooperating with India's neighbour, Pakistan. Japan has a close alliance with the USA, and would not embark on the distribution of high technology against US interests. European powers are not prepared to collaborate with India on a large scale, since such collaboration would align them with a strong regional power opposed to Pakistan, China and the United States.

As if on cue and against an anti-US backdrop, India extended a hand of friendship to Moscow, as the Russian leaders pondered an 'adequate reply' to the eastward expansion of NATO. Russia is not averse to becoming an ally to India in its confrontation with Pakistan, since there are many problems in Russo–Pakistani relations. Such problems include the role of Pakistan in support of the anti-Soviet rebels in Afghanistan through the 1980s and its support more recently for Taleban victories over Russian-supported forces there. Pakistan's continuing strategic relationship with the USA, though somewhat strained in recent years, is also viewed somewhat cautiously in Russia.

There is also the matter of Ukraine's contract to sell T–80UD main battle tanks to Pakistan. Moscow is convinced that the tank deal between Pakistan and Ukraine is contrary to Russia's national interests. In February 1997, Russia's Minister of Foreign Economic Relations, Oleg Davydov, said in an interview:

> There will be no cooperation with Ukraine in this direction. Ukraine has concluded the contract with Pakistan without consulting Russia. The project contradicts the state interests of our country. Russia is not going to promote the growth of Pakistan's military potential in the region to the detriment of the interests of India, Russia's strategic partner.[85]

Consequently, Russia refused to supply Ukraine with tank engines, electronic equipment and ammunition for the T–80UD MBT, a move which seemed to make the Ukrainian tank sale impossible. However, Ukraine managed to start its own production of necessary spare parts, and by 1998, all 320 T–80 MBTs were delivered to the Pakistani military. Still, Russia's attempts to impose this 'arms embargo' upon Pakistan, through its refusal to supply Ukraine, is the clearest confirmation of allied relations between Russia and India.

This developing alliance can also be seen in advances in operational cooperation between the Russian and Indian navies, which may even lead to a resumption by Russia of a naval presence in the Indian Ocean. This matter was discussed during the official visit in January 1997 of the newly-appointed Commander-in-Chief of the Russian Navy, Admiral Vladimir Kuroyedov, to India. During the visit, the possibility of a long-term naval pact between the two countries to significantly enhance collaboration emerged. So far, it has not been revealed whether Russia and India have actually signed such a pact, though India's naval chief, Admiral Vishnu Bhagvat, described the talks as 'highly successful' and, in revealing that Russia and India will hold a joint exercise in 1997, emphasised that co-operation between the two navies would grow in the immediate future.[86]

Indo–Russian cooperation on many different military aspects will continue to grow. India needs Russian support to strengthen its regional ambitions and to counter strategic pressure or possible threats from Pakistan and China (who are themselves engaged in military modernisation); and with Russian help, India could become one of the world's leading power centres. Russia also needs India. Indian military orders keep Russia's military–industrial complex afloat, and help finance Russia's research and development programs. By arming India, Russia has no fear that it is creating a potential opponent. India and Russia have never been engaged in any kind of hostilities with one another, nor have they suffered territorial disputes or other forms of confrontation which could prevent the development of the alliance ties. On the contrary, via military cooperation, Russia will gain a powerful ally in a strategically important region. Situated in the geostrategic hub of the vast Indian Ocean region, with the second largest population in the world, India can become Russia's valued partner in pursuit of its national objectives not only in South Asia, but in Southeast Asia and the Persian Gulf as well.

CHINA

Compared with the military industrial cooperation between Russia and India, that between Russia and China is still relatively underdeveloped, notwithstanding the volumes of newsprint expended on particular sales since 1992. While such ties with India have been developing quite steadily since 1971, and India and Russia have a history of good bilateral relations, those with China have been developing for less than a decade and China and Russia have had an extremely bitter history of bilateral relations to overcome.

The USSR had abruptly terminated its military and economic aid relationship with China in 1960 as part of a policy of political pressure, and these moves caused severe dislocation in development plans and locked China's armed forces into technological backwardness relative not only to the USSR but also to the USA. In fact, it was this move by the USSR in 1960 which convinced China's political elites that dependence on other powers for military supply would undermine China's long-term ambitions to assert itself as a global power.

This determination to avoid dependence has become an entrenched part of China's arms import policy and colours even today the level and type of purchases that China is making from Russia. This disposition to avoid dependence on foreign supply was reinforced in 1989 when the USA and allied states cut off all military contacts with China in reaction to the Tiananmen Square repressions of that year. At that time, China and the USA were very close to completion of a number of deals for arms sales that China regarded as very important and which had been pursued by Chinese leaders at some domestic political cost. After the suspensions, China once again found key military development programs thrown into chaos by the whims of foreign powers.

Military relations between the USSR and China had already taken a new turn in May 1989 when President Gorbachev visited China, which was alive with the excitement of democratic protest, most visibly in Tiananmen Square. With the collapse in relations between China and the major Western powers after the suppression on 4 June, military relations between China and Russia intensified.

In May 1990, the leading Vice-Chairman of the Central Military Commission of China, General Liu Huaqing, visited Moscow, where he initiated talks on purchasing Russian Su–27 fighter aircraft.[87] In October 1992, China took delivery of the first batch of 24 Su–27 fighters, with another 48 to be delivered in 1994.[88] Between 1992 and the end of 1996, Russia had only transferred, according to Russian sources, 48 Su–27 aircraft of various modifications, and not the 72 agreed.[89] The deal for the first 24 aircraft reportedly cost China more than US$1 billion for the aircraft, related weapons, logistic support and training, although only 35 per cent of the cost would be paid in hard currency, with the remainder to be paid by barter.[90] Russian sources suggest the cost of each batch of 24 aircraft was about US$1 billion.

In December 1996, Russia and China signed a contract allowing China to build 200 Su–27s. The tooling and equipment needed
by China would be transferred from the Sukhoi plant in
Komsomolsk on the Amur.[91] Estimates of the rate of completion
of aircraft under this assembly agreement have varied, with the
initial estimate as high as 200 in five years from commencement.
Another report suggests that 13 years is more likely.[92]

The sale of the Su–27 aircraft has been a very successful
venture for both Russia and China and has given a strong impetus
to the military cooperation relationship. The initial deployment
of these aircraft to the Wuhu base not too distant from Taiwan
(800 km north-west of Taipei) was an indicator of the importance
China placed on this purchase as a means of redressing in part
the substantial gap between its own air attack capability and that
of Taiwan.

In August 1992, a mixed intergovernmental commission on
military cooperation between Russia and China was established.[93]
Between 1992 and 1997, according to one Russian report, Russia
supplied China with 48 Su–27s, eight divisions of ZRK
S–300PMU1 mobile medium-range air defence missile system[94]
(assessed to have some limited ABM capacity), 14 *Tor*-M1 air
defence systems, two Type 877 submarines and one Type 636
submarine. At the end of 1998, projected deliveries were to
include two Type 965E destroyers (*Sovremennyi* class), Ka–28
ASW helicopters, Ka–27 ship-borne helicopters, and further Type
636 submarines.[95] Other deliveries reported by a reliable US
source include more than 40 Mi–17 helicopters, 14 Il–76 aircraft,
and 100 RD–33 engines for F–7 and F–8 Chinese fighter aircraft.[96]
Some of these systems have not been delivered until several
years after being placed, and in 1998, sources were suggesting
that the *Sovremennyi* destroyers were unlikely to be delivered
before 2000.[97]

China has accounted for about 25 per cent of Russian arms
sales in the 1990s.[98] By the end of the 1990s, most deals were
being concluded on a cash basis, a sign of China's growing wealth
and hard currency reserves.[99]

Plans for future sales agreed in late 1998 are reported to
include *Shmel'* flamethrowers, 120 mm self-propelled artillery,
BMP–3 IFVs, 300 mm RS30 *Smerch* multiple rocket launchers,
152 mm *Msta*-S self-propelled rocket launchers [*gaubitsa*], and
ship-borne anti-aircraft systems. There are also plans for production under licence in China of other items.[100] In coming years,
Russian sources expect China to buy additional S–300 and *Tor*-M1

systems, some 20 Su–30 fighter jets off the shelf and a licence to produce them.[101]

There are some reports that Russia and Israel are working together on a joint weapons development project with China. In June 1997, Russia and Israel signed an agreement on the joint production of a long-range radio-location detection plane which is believed to be destined for China.[102]

Russia's arms supply relationship with China has not only coincided with and benefited from warming relations in other areas of the strategic relationship, as indicated in chapter 4, but has directly contributed to this warning. More than 5000 Russian specialists have visited China in support of the arms sales program, and some 1646 Chinese military technicians have been educated in Russia. In April 1996, the two governments signed a long-term contract for Russian training of Chinese technicians. Some 177 Chinese military personnel were in Russian military higher education schools in late 1998.[103] In 1993, there was reported to be a 1500-strong Russian military industry work-force,[104] but according to Russian sources, almost all of these people were there without the knowledge of the Russian government and many were working on highly sensitive technologies that Russia regarded as inappropriate to transfer to China. After applying a substantial amount of pressure of an extra-legal kind on these people, Russia's security services managed to convince most of them to return to Russia.

China's weapons purchases from Russia represent only a modest commitment by China to an arms supply relationship with it.[105] While a large proportion of China's foreign arms purchases in the 1990s have been from Russia, modern Russian weapons account for only 1–2 per cent of Chinese inventories.[106] As of 1998, China had about 4000 combat aircraft of which only 48 in service were modern Russian types. And as Dennis Blasko points out, the regional balance of military capacity between Russia and China in terms of modern military systems is heavily in Russia's favour.[107] The same could be said of the balance between China and Japan, or between China and Taiwan. Both Japan and Taiwan have far more modern aircraft and naval forces than China and they continue to import far more modern military equipment than China. For example, between 1992 and 1997, both Japan and Taiwan imported much more foreign military equipment than China. Cumulative totals for each country for these years were: Japan US$13 bn, Taiwan US$13 bn, and China US$3.5 bn.[108]

The main impact for China of the Russian arms sales is technological and this is its primary motivation. China's leaders have committed themselves to policies aimed at the long-term rejuvenation of the country's industrial and technological base, and they have set themselves a target closer to the middle of the 21st century than the start of it for achieving even a modest catch-up relative to the most technologically advanced countries. All through the 1990s, with only one exception (Su–27 aircraft), China has not sought to buy foreign equipment with a view to kitting out its order of battle in the same way that India has. It has bought very modest numbers with a view to mastering the associated technology, both from the point of view of training its forces to defeat more modern systems and from the point of view of mastering the technology in the systems themselves. China continues to practise the age-old system of reverse engineering of modern systems, rather oblivious to the degree to which such activities lock the country into technological backwardness.[109]

The longer-term strategic significance of these sales is that they have set certain parameters for any expansion of military hardware purchases were the Chinese government to decide that was appropriate and were the Russian government to agree with such a course. There are still powerful reservations on both sides.

There are heated debates in the Russian media, the parliament and the government about the wisdom of building up China's military power. For example, one commentary in late 1997, remarked that the so-called strategic partnership between Russia and China only had one dimension, arms sales, and that China was not helping Russian commercial interests in any other way at all.[110] The view is that Russia is subordinating its long-term national security to short-term commercial gain. In fact, according to a Russian newspaper, the deal for the Su–27 licence production by China was negotiated independently from the government by the director of the Sukhoi Design Bureau, and that when confronted with the deal, the Russian government could not overturn it without fear of offending China.[111] The domestic imperative of keeping the industry alive also influenced immediate Russian responses.

Not all Russian commentators see the future China in a threatening light. For example, a deputy director of the Russian Centre for Analysis, Strategy, and Technology, Konstantin Makiyenko, saw the Chinese purchases as largely defensive in inspiration.[112] He also pointed out that Russia retained the nuclear forces it needed to deter Chinese military adventures. (He identified the main threat coming from China as demographic rather than military—the 'geographic proximity of over-populated China to half-deserted Siberia'). Moreover, the Russian government has increasingly realised that it can sell a number of systems to China without having much impact on the order of battle, and where there is such an impact, this can be spread out over quite protracted periods—15 years in the case of the Su–27s. Until China seeks more expedited delivery rates or the most modern Russian technologies, then the parameters of the arms supply relationship are unlikely to be severely tested. But it is highly unlikely that Russia would be prepared to sell China weapons systems in large quantities relative to the country's order of battle, either on a national scale, or in a specific locality. Russian Foreign Ministry sources have consistently said that the country's arms sales will not be allowed to affect the regional balance of power in East Asia.[113]

As far as China is concerned, the reservation about dependence on foreign arms supply remains quite strong, and even though the number of Su–27 aircraft purchased was the largest purchase by China of a single foreign weapons system for more than three decades, aspects of the deal are not entirely to China's liking. For example, engine overhaul will have to be undertaken in Russia.[114]

In assessing the Russia–China arms supply relationship, two additional points need to be noted. First, the Russian government claims to have honoured its international commitments to limit arms transfers or militarily sensitive technologies. These claims are contested by some commentators. In 1993, Russia supplied China with some missile-related technology, described by some sources in alarming terms—Russia's 'most sensitive missile technology'[115]—and by others as 'upper stage rocket engines'.[116] The original press reports suggested that Russia had sold rocket fuel technology, mobile missile technology, large liquid-fuel engines, guidance and multiple warhead technology, and provided hundreds of missile experts.[117] A reliable US source suggests that the sale of ballistic missiles has not been verified.[118]

The second point is that many sensational or inaccurate reports about Russian arms transfers to China appear in the popular press and are often replayed uncritically in academic and official papers. There are numerous examples, but one is given here. In 1993, *Armed Forces International* reported that the two countries had agreed on the sale and licensed production of up to 150 MiG–31 aircraft and that the first deliveries were due in April 1994.[119] As of early 1999, no such sale has been confirmed. Not only have many of these reports proved inaccurate, most of them assume a near instantaneous impact from the Russian arms sales either on Chinese order of battle and military capacity or on regional military perceptions. But as the above discussion suggests, it takes many years for a country to absorb and effectively employ foreign-supplied hardware, especially if it is of markedly higher levels of technology than that already in service.

The future of the Russia–China arms supply relationship will be profoundly affected by the development of Russia's domestic defence industry. If predictions about the collapse of that capacity prove accurate, then China probably only has a short window for the procurement of Russian systems, probably no more than five to ten years. Moreover, if Russian firms currently supplying China collapse, then China's ability to service and operate those systems it has purchased from Russia will be open to question. The other side of this coin, that a collapsing Russian industry creates special opportunities for China, will remain true, but this will have most strategic significance for making minor contributions to China's general military technological base in the longer term. Neither scenario holds out the prospects for large-scale purchases that would have a dramatic impact on the capabilities of China's forces in the field in the medium term.

CONCLUSION

At the end of the 1990s, Russian arms sales to India and China are tied up with great power ambitions in a way not wholly anticipated at the beginning of the decade. Russia is struggling to hold on to its status as great power, while India and China are both trying to extend the foundations of their great power status. India and China are no longer arms trade clients seeking Russian weapons for a quick victory in a war with a neighbouring state. These two Asian powers are both committed to a long-term strategic ascendancy, not necessarily belligerent, but both have avowedly chauvinistic tendencies. The decline of Russia's military capacities and the decline in its defence industries have suggested that for now, India and China are useful partners in military industrial cooperation.

This picture will almost certainly change in coming years. While India's order of battle is still heavily reliant on systems of Russian origin, it is looking to produce a high proportion of its military equipment indigenously. Russian firms will benefit initially through licence fees and other support from this indigenisation of defence production, but in the next decade, India will not be as good a market for Russian-produced military equipment as it has been in the 1990s. For its part, China is not interested in shoring up the failing Russian defence sector, but in opportunistic purchases of selected items with a view to enhancing its own independent military industrial capacity. As Russian defence industry continues to suffer, its technological foundations will wither and its R&D capacities will evaporate. Within 10 years, India and China would be locking themselves into serious technological backwardness if they continued to buy weapons from Russia at the same rate as they are now.

India or China, or both, may make such a choice. If they do, it will be in the coming decade, rather than in the longer term, that any destabilising effects in regional or global strategic relationships will be felt from their arms supply relationship with Russia. Yet there is little in Russia's current arms supply relationship with India or China that is likely to provoke a threat to regional or global strategic stability in the medium term.

Conclusion

The strategic policies of Russia and the posture of its armed forces are in dynamic transformation. Within one or two years of this book going to print, or even perhaps in the time that it takes to get to print, there could well be radical change in Russia's military position in world affairs. We know the parameters of this change. Some are reassuring but others provide grounds for concern about possible threats in the medium term to regional order in Eastern Europe, in the southern tier, and in East Asia. Some trends in Russian strategic thinking and in Russian domestic politics provide grounds for concern about possible threats in the longer term to global order.

On the one hand, Russia has consistently pursued for this decade a policy of integration into the international community and observance of its norms. There may have been exceptions to the policy dictated in large part by emergency circumstances associated with the collapse of the USSR. There have certainly been important lapses in the attentiveness of the leadership to the principles it was espousing, as in Chechnia. But since Russia was on that occasion facing loss of its own territory, its responses to that were more visceral and neuralgic than one might reasonably expect in strategic policy where Russian territory is not threatened. Notwithstanding these cases, the trend in strategic policy has been a firm and consistent one of cooperative internationalism, even as it has been tinged with shades of great power chauvinism.

The country's conventional military forces will remain small and will in all probability continue to shrink. The military leadership and all shades of political opinion believe that the reductions to date have taken the armed forces to a critical level, and that further cuts will leave the country without adequate defences even for low-level conflict and small wars. But the leaders of Russia have not shown the political will or been able to achieve the degree of political stability necessary to deliver resources at the minimum level to keep the forces either at the desired personnel levels or at suitable levels of readiness, in terms of equipment, training or morale. Russia's military industry is weak, even as some sectors are doing not too badly in their struggle for survival. The NATO war against Yugoslavia in early 1999 may show the need for Russia's political leaders to display more commitment to the country's defence posture by offering substantial assistance not only to maintain the industry but to improve it.

The national economic base does not provide Russia with the range of diplomatic tools it would like to implement its great power aspirations—even in states on its borders. Some states that initially supported the creation of the Commonwealth of Independent States, such as Uzbekistan and Azerbaijan, have drawn closer to the USA and Western Europe because Russia is in decline. The Russian political system offers nothing distinctive that is attractive to other states in terms of cultural appeal—'soft power'. The Russian state is not a powerful core around which other states are likely to coalesce.

On the other hand, Russia remains a nuclear superpower, with more than enough weapons to end life on the planet as we know it. The daily peacetime regime for control of these nuclear weapons has deteriorated and the risks of inadvertent launch or diversion of nuclear weapons material to other states have risen correspondingly. As for war, the armed forces, with the full endorsement of the political leadership, have shifted to military doctrines that give more emphasis to use of nuclear weapons to compensate for weaknesses in conventional force posture. While this doctrinal shift does not represent a substantial change from what was almost certainly the situation in practice in the Cold War, the declining capacities of the armed forces and their low morale, combined with public opinion that Russia has been trodden on and abandoned by the civilised community of states, provide dangerous pressures for fundamentally different strategic calculations compared with those made in Moscow during the Cold War. Russia is a nuclear superpower that is becoming increasingly troubled by its perceptions of US and NATO policies. Social relations within the armed forces are at crisis point. And the relationship between the armed forces and society is also in crisis. Over the longer term, the deteriorating personal standards of recruits in the lower levels of the armed forces will create a military force less amenable to reasoned and civilised behaviour, as the brutality of some Russian troops against civilians in the 1994–96 Chechnia campaign demonstrated. All of these circumstances provide a very explosive mix.

The first explosion—if it occurs—will almost certainly be a contained one, and would be felt largely within the borders of Russia itself. It would involve widespread use of force to install or prop up a dictatorial regime and to maintain the territorial integrity of the Russian Federation. This outcome would in the short term tear apart the armed forces even further, and lead to a more serious degradation of their military readiness for international conflict. It would only be over the longer term that Russia could pick itself up and mobilise its conventional armed forces for sustained military confrontation with other great powers. In the shorter term, the most likely international victims of any new belligerent Russia would be those countries that it can reach most easily, are weak on their own account, and have weak ties with the USA. This means Central Asia, rather than Eastern Europe or East Asia.

But dramatic outcomes are not inevitable, and in fact are less likely than a slow but inevitable restoration of military order and military production. This has been the pattern of reform in the armed forces where, in the face of extremely debilitating personal circumstances, and after five years of political controversy, a clear path for restructuring and cost reductions has been laid out. The unification of the two air forces into one, the unification of the missile and space forces, the creation of units of constant combat readiness, the creation of unified territorial commands, and the large-scale restructuring of military higher education demonstrate that determined hard work and effective leadership do offer some way out of the chaos that resulted from the collapse of the USSR. And the deployment of a new strategic nuclear missile system and the rolling out of a new advanced fighter suggest that there are still untapped reserves of resilience in the armed forces.

The more likely political outcome for the society as a whole is one desired by most Russians, one that flows directly from Russia's political and social history, and one that reflects the abiding seriousness and social responsibility of most Russians. This outcome would be the imposition of a soft authoritarian dictatorship that works consistently to restoration of social order, effective government and economic restructuring. But dictatorship is not necessary. A determined and capable President, with the mandate of election success, could build easily on the post's enormous constitutional power to begin the process of rebuilding that is needed. But the pace of reform would be much slower and the path more uncertain.

The path Russia takes will depend on the outcome of elections for the State Duma in December 1999 and elections for President in 2000. But without an early imposition of dictatorship, which would take several years to bring about stabilisation of economic and social conditions, many in Russia fear that other factors may intervene to provoke a major catastrophe. This view is held even among some of the most liberal-minded political leaders in Russia. It is probably the case that the widespread corruption and incompetence in government will not be reversed within several years without extreme, extra-legal measures.

The sustained political and economic crisis in Russia since 1991 has had the most serious and debilitating effects on the armed forces. The failure of the government to achieve any effective reform of the armed forces until 1997 exacerbated the impact of severe under-financing. Had the armed forces been cut more sharply in 1992 or 1993, more money might have been available for pay, new equipment and exercise costs. But military forces are by nature highly conservative social institutions. It would have been a miracle if any army in any country could have subjected itself to an effective structural reform within a decade of the massive upheaval that the Russian forces faced.

For several years after 1991, the armed forces were forced to deal with massive relocations from Eastern Europe, Mongolia and the newly independent states of the former USSR. At the same time, military emergencies or commitments of one form or another were preoccupying military planners. If that were not enough to delay reform, the armed forces had been drawn into the domestic political battle between Yeltsin and the Soviet-era parliament that survived until 1993. And many military personnel were struggling to cope on a personal basis with daily survival for themselves and their families in terms of food and housing. Then in 1994, the government threw them into civil war in Chechnia with very inadequate preparation, a conflict in which they won the Battle for Grozny at such great cost that they had to surrender in the war.

The inadequacies of the Chechnia campaign proved to be a very powerful catalyst for more determined government efforts to force reform on the armed forces, and for senior military officers who were committed to reform to rise to the top jobs. By 1997, major structural reforms were set in place, and at the time of publication these structural reforms were beginning to have some of the desired effects. Cost savings in particular were noticeable from the eradication of duplicative structures and elimination of many units.

Only time will tell if those reforms finally put in place in 1997 and 1998 will set the armed forces on the path to more balanced and coherent development, and therefore on the path to sustainable military postures relative to Russia's peripheral regions. If the external conditions (defence budget and political order) were to gain some stability, there is every prospect that the structural reforms will give new coherence to military development, although it would still take some years for their full effects to work through the services.

But the structural reforms did not and could not address the chronic problems faced by the armed forces, such as a continuing lack of money for pay, new equipment and exercises, and the consequent collapse in the country's military industry. The fate of Russia's armed forces depends on circumstances over which until now they have had little control. One of the biggest questions about the future of the armed forces is their relationship to the government: will they remain the obedient servants of a government that consistently fails to deliver the budget support and political stability they need to regain a reliable military posture? Or will they step into the breach and use force to install a government that can? They would have to be extraordinarily apathetic and apolitical to avoid taking the latter course. A military coup in Russia is a strong possibility unless a strong, effective President and an effective parliament capable of building social consensus can be installed soon.

Appendix

SUMMARY OF FORCES

In 1999, there were four services: the Strategic Missile Forces (SMF), the Russian Federation Navy (RFN), the Russian Federation Air Force (RFAF), and the Ground Forces. In addition, the Ministry of Defence had about 200 000 personnel, including centrally controlled units for electronic warfare, logistic support and training, and intelligence. Total strength of the Russian armed forces in 1998 was estimated by the International Institute for Strategic Studies as 1.159 million. In spite of efforts to move to a largely volunteer force, in late 1998 there were only 163 000 contract personnel in the forces—a mere 15 per cent. Women in the armed forces in 1998 numbered about 130 000, all of whom were volunteers.

Strategic Missile Forces

Russia remains a nuclear superpower. No other country apart from the USA has the numbers, variety and advanced technology of Russia's nuclear forces. In 1998, Russia had 756 ICBMs, 348 SLBMs and 70 strategic bombers, which under strategic arms limitation agreements with the USA were designated to carry a total of 5972 nuclear warheads. Russia's strategic defence forces (the former Missile Space Forces and Missile Space Defence) have about 21 000 personnel, 100 anti-ballistic missiles, a number of satellites and up to 20 related radar sites, including some sites newly constructed in former Soviet republics (Belarus, Azerbaijan, and Kazakhstan).

Navy

In 1998, the Russian Pacific Fleet had 18 major surface combatants: two Cruisers (one *Ushakov* class and one *Slava* class), 11 Destroyers (6 *Sovremennyi* class; 5 *Udaloi* class); three Frigates (*Krivak*–I). The Submarine fleet comprised 7 SSBNs (one *Delta*–I, 6 *Delta*–III); 6 SSGNs (*Oscar*–II); 7 SSNs (7 *Akula*, 2 *Victor*–III); and 11 SSKs (*Kilo*). The Pacific Fleet air arm consisted of approximately 100 fixed-wing aircraft and 96 helicopters, most of which are based ashore. The fixed wing component comprised 9 Tu–22 strike aircraft; 27 Tu–142 and 19 Il–38 ASW aircraft; 15 Su–24 Fighter-Bombers; 8 Tu–95 and An–12 Reconnaissance/EW aircraft; and 7 Tu–142 communications aircraft. The Fleet air arm had 80 Ka–25/27 and Mi–14 ASW helicopters and 16 other Ka–29 and M–14 helicopters. Pacific Fleet Naval Infantry numbered about 8000 organised into one division, with tracked and wheeled amphibious vehicles including BTR–70 and BTR–80 armoured personnel carriers. It had 329 main battle tanks (T–72 and T–80), 215 pieces of artillery, including eighteen 152-mm 2S3 *Akatsia* self-propelled howitzers. There were about 30 000 personnel in the Russian Pacific Fleet.

Air Force

As of 1 March 1998, the date of amalgamation of the former Air Defence Forces and the Air Forces, the air force comprised 200 000 men with 45 per cent of the enlisted personnel to be reduced as the result of the integration. The combined Russian Air Force had five tactical air armies and three air defence armies, with the following aircraft inventory:

- 725 bombers/tactical aircraft (475 Su–24 *Fencer*, 250 Su–25 *Frogfoot*);
- 1215 fighters/interceptors (100 MiG–23 *Fogger*, 315 MiG–29 *Fulcrum*, 425 MiG–31 Foxhound, 375 Su–27 *Flanker*);
- 200 reconnaissance aircraft (40 MiG–25 *Foxbat*, 160 Su–24 *Fencer*);
- 20 AWACS (Il–76 *Candid*);
- 1760 training aircraft (165 MiG–23 *Flogger*, 10 MiG–25 *Foxbat*, 100 MiG–29 *Fulcrum*, 95 Su–24 *Fencer*, 30 Su–25 *Frogfoot*, 10 Su–27 *Flanker*, 1100 L–39, and 250 L–410/Tu–134); and
- 820 combat helicopters.

In early 1999, the RFAF comprised three AF/AD Armies (headquartered in St Petersburg, Rostov on the Don, and Khabarovsk), three AF/AD

Corps (headquartered in Chita, Ekaterinburg, and Novo-sibirsk), and the Moscow AF/AD District. It had approximately 1850 combat aircraft, out of which 1365 were potent fourth-generation planes: MiG–29 *Fulcrum*, MiG–31 *Foxhound*, Su–25 *Frogfoot*, and Su–27 *Flanker*. Half of Russia's combat aircraft, around 900, were located east of the Ural Mountains. Most combat aircraft have been withdrawn from the Kuril Islands and Sakhalin Island.

Ground forces

By early 1999, the strength of the ground forces was 318 000, or 30 per cent of the armed forces. The ground forces were organised into six tank divisions, 19 motorised infantry divisions, 4 airborne divisions, three artillery divisions, and 5 special forces brigades. Equipment holdings included 15 559 main battle tanks, 26 300 armoured infantry fighting vehicles, 3245 armoured personnel carriers, 15 700 artillery pieces, 316 surface to surface missiles, 1000 attack helicopters and 1300 transport helicopters.

By 1 January 1999, a restructuring of the Airborne Forces had been completed, resulting in the loss of 14 000 personnel (including 2403 officers) to reach a total force strength of 32 000. By July 1998, there were four airborne divisions (106th Division at Tula, 98th Division at Ivanovo, 7th Kaunasskaia Division at Novorossiisk and 76th Svirskaia Division at Pskov) and one independent airborne brigade (31st at Ulianovsk).

Ground forces units east of the Ural Mountains in early 1998 relative to the rest of Russia were as follows:

	Urals MD	Siberian MD	Far East MD	Total all Russia
Airborne	0	1	1	5
Airborne bde	0	0	0	3
Spetsnaz	1	2	1	8
Tank Divisions	l	3 (1 trg)	0	6
Tank Bde/Regt	1	0	0	1
Motor Infantry Div	1	2	10 (2 trg)	19
Motor Infantry Bde/Regt	0	3	0	11
MG/Artillery or Artillery Div	0	2	3	7
Artillery bde/regt	2	10	9	32
ATK Bde/Regt	1	4	1	9
SAM Bde/Regt	0	2	5	21
SSM	1	2	3	13
Helo Regt (assault t'port)	0	1	2	7
(attack)	0	2	2	12
(training)	0	0	0	7

In 1998, ground forces equipment holdings east of the Ural Mountains were as follows:

	Urals MD	Siberian MD	Far East MD	Total Russia
MBT	1100	4468	5600	15 500
ACV	1500	7400	7000	22 000
Art/MRL/mortars	900	5700	5800	16 840
SAM	600	–	570	2300
SSM *Tochka–U*	–	48	48	316
Assault Helos	–	120	190	1060

Notes

Preface

1 As classically defined, and as described in a 1914 book on the Asian parts of Russia, the boundary between Europe and Asia runs along geographical divides or contemporary state borders, 'in the north, along the Kara River from its mouth in the Kara Sea to its source, then along the Ural Mountain Range between the source of the Kara and Ural Rivers, then the Ural River for its entire length to its mouth in the Caspian Sea, then the west shore of the Caspian Sea from the mouth of the Ural River to the city of Baku, and from there along the Caucasus Mountain Range to the Black Sea'. See *Aziatskaia Rossiia* [Asiatic Russia], vol. 1, Izdanie pereselencheskago upravleniia, Glavnago upravleniia zemleustroistva i zemledeliia, St Petersburg, 1914, vol. 1, p. 39.
2 In Russian, the term is *oblast'*, translated in this book as province.

1 Russia: rebuilding the state, reconstituting the nation

1 Urban et al., 1997, p. 119.
2 The word *perestroika* can be translated as reconstruction or restructuring. *Glasnost'* means candour or openness.
3 Urban et al., 1997, pp. 122–3, 147.
4 ibid. p. 201. Yeltsin won the position as Chairman of the Russian Supreme Soviet by only four votes more than the required 531, while 502 members opposed him.
5 Löwenhardt, 1995, p. 93.
6 ibid. p. 185.
7 See Dunlop and Dunlop, 1993, p. 191ff. Chapter Five, 'Anatomy of a Failed Coup', in Dunlop and Dunlop provides an excellent analysis of the implementation and failure of the coup.
8 ibid. p. 199.
9 ibid. pp. 273–4.
10 'Belarus' is the name of the country formed subsequently on the

same territory as the union republic of Bielorussia. The two names in Russian and Bielorussian are only slightly different—perhaps no different—in meaning, although they carry different connotations because of the political history of the term Bielorussia in Tsarist and Soviet days.

11 Löwenhardt, 1995, p. 106.

12 Khasbulatov, 1993, p. 223.

13 An excellent compilation of official documents and commentaries on the transition of the former USSR into the shaky union embodied in the Commonwealth of Independent States, covering the period 1991 to 1995, is provided in Brzezinski and Sullivan (eds), 1997. The volume has over 800 pages of text, commentary, maps, and charts.

14 The five Central Asian union republics were Kazakhstan, Kyrgyzstan, Tajikistan, Turkmenistan, and Uzbekistan. The two Transcaucus union republics were Armenia and Azerbaijan.

15 Löwenhardt, 1995, p. 109.

16 Over the next few years, the people of Russia were to see a collapse in their economy some 100 per cent worse than the great depression of 1929. Between 1990 and 1995, the net decline in GDP of Russia was roughly 50 per cent. See Brzezinski and Sullivan (eds), 1997, p. 811.

17 Silverman and Yanowitch, 1997, p. 17.

18 Sakwa, 1996, p. 77.

19 Rigby, 1994, p. 211.

20 ibid. p. 210.

21 Silverman and Yanowitch, 1997, p. 130.

22 Azerbaijan—284 km; Belarus—959 km; China (two sectors)—3645 km; Estonia—290 km; Finland—1313 km; Georgia—723 km; Kazakhstan—6846 km; North Korea—19 km; Latvia—217 km; Lithuania—227 km; Mongolia—3441 km; Norway—167 km; Poland—432 km; Ukraine—1576 km. See Central Intelligence Agency, *Factbook 1997* (electronic version).

23 Central Intelligence Agency, *Factbook 1997* (electronic version).

24 Estimates for 1995 put the population at 148 million. See Central Intelligence Agency, *Factbook 1997* (electronic version).

25 Mendras, 1992, p. 33.

26 ibid.

27 Guroff and Guroff, 1994, p. 88.

28 Rigby, 1994, p. 208.

29 Sakwa, 1996, p. 85.

30 For English text, see Sakwa, 1996, pp. 395–429.

31 Sakwa, 1996, p. 240.

32 Buchs, 1994, p. 84.

33 Silverman and Yanowitch, 1997, p. 125.

34 Sakwa, 1996, p. 243.

35 Interfax, 'Siberian Business Report', 30 December 1997–12 January 1998, carried in FBIS-SOV–98–013, 13 January 1998: 'Russia: Interfax Siberian Business Report'.

36 Buchs, 1994, p. 84.

37 Interfax, 'Siberian Business Report', 2–8 December 1997, carried in FBIS-SOV–97–343, 9 December 1997: 'Russia: Interfax Siberian Business Report'.

38 The Amnesty International Annual Report covering 1997 reported the following main issues of concern in Russia: 'Two prisoners of conscience were held during the year. Two others released in 1996 were awaiting trial. Conscientious objectors were forcibly conscripted. Torture and ill-treatment by law enforcement officers and within the armed forces continued to be reported. Conditions in penitentiaries and pre-trial detention centres amounted to cruel, inhumane or degrading treatment. At least 846 prisoners remained under sentence of death.' See http://www.amnesty.org/ailib/aireport/ar98/eur46.htm accessed 8 August 1998.

39 The 1993 Constitution guarantees freedom of religion (Article 28), and declares Russia to be a secular state, without a state religion, which gives all religious associations equal status (Article 14).

40 Guroff and Guroff, 1994, pp. 83–5.

41 Nezavisimaia gazeta, March 1997, cited in Krasnov (ed.), 1996, p. 175.

42 McAuley, 1997, p. 298.

43 Sakwa, 1996, p. 45.

44 ibid. p. 85.

45 A. Frolov, 'Kommunisty o perpsektivakh obshchestvennogo protsessa', Svobodnaia mysl', 1995, no. 9, p. 47, cited in Krasnov (ed.), 1996, p. 156.

46 'Programma KPRF', Pravda, 31 January 1995, cited in Krasnov (ed.), 1996, p. 157.

47 Rossiia: partii, vybory, vlast', Krasnov (ed.), p. 153.

48 Tolz et al., 1993, p. 20.

49 Sakwa, 1996, p. 391.

50 Krasnov (ed.), 1996, p. 177. The figures in Table 1.3 for each party are slightly different from the figures in Table 1.2, but not significantly so. The two tables are based on material from different sources.

51 Sakwa, 1996, p. 391.

52 Other authoritarian nationalist parties include the Congress of Russian Societies, 'Empire', and the Govorukhin bloc.

53 McFaul, 1997, p. 52.

54 In 1995, a law was enacted on the manner of election of the President. For text, see Okun'kov, 1995, pp. 163–228.

55 Australia. Department of Foreign Affairs and Trade. East Asia Analytical Unit, 1996, p. 16.

56 A law on the Principles of Local Self Government has been decreed by President Yeltsin, but it is as contentious as the Constitution has proved to be, partly because of the lack of appropriate and detailed regulations across the full range of administrative issues.

57 For example, the Tiumen region in Siberia has two autonomous republics as well as a province.

58 Mendras, 1992, p. 34.

59 Urban et al., 1997, pp. 282–5.
60 ibid. pp. 282–3.
61 Baev, 1996, p. 141.
62 Payin and Popov, 1996 (electronic version).
63 Thomas, 1997 (electronic version).
64 Baev, 1996, p. 147.
65 Kasaev, 1996 (electronic version).
66 ITAR-TASS, 29 September 1996.
67 ITAR-TASS, 26 May 1998.
68 Interfax, 21 May 1998.
69 Jewish Autonomous Province near the Chinese border in the Far East.
70 Moscow and St Petersburg. St Petersburg, established by Peter the Great in 1703 with that name, had been renamed Petrograd (meaning 'City of Peter') by Tsar Nikolai II during the First World War and subsequently became Leningrad ('City of Lenin') under the Communists. The city reverted to its original name after the collapse of the USSR.
71 Sakwa, 1996, p. 221.
72 Daniels, 1997, p. 233; Shlapentokh et al., 1997, p. 12.
73 Peterson, 1997, p. 146.
74 ibid.
75 Philip R. Pryde, 'Russia—An Overview of the Federation', in Pryde (ed.), p. 29. The world rankings for resource endowments are based on 1990 information.
76 Central Intelligence Agency, *Factbook* (electronic version).
77 Silverman and Yanowitch, 1997, New Russia, pp. 129, 137.
78 Matejka, 1994, p. 52.
79 Sakwa, 1996, p. 234.
80 Georgy Arbatov, 'A Neo-Bolshevik Brand of Capitalism', *International Herald Tribune*, 12 May 1992.
81 Sakwa, 1996, p. 234.
82 Kaiser, 1994, p. 7.
83 USIS, 'Bush Asks Congress to Support G–7 Aid Plan for Russia', 2 April 1992.
84 USIS Asia Pacific Wireless File, 'G–7 to Provide New Aid Package for Russia', 1 April 1992.
85 USIS Asia Pacific Wireless File, 'Stabilization Fund for Ruble Several Months Off', 21 April 1992.
86 Matejka, 1994, p. 52.
87 Sakwa, 1996, p. 238.
88 Silverman and Yanowitch, 1997, p. 134.
89 Sakwa, 1996, p. 236.
90 Kaiser, 1994, p. 9.
91 Matejka, 1994, pp. 49, 51.
92 ibid.
93 Silverman and Yanowitch, 1997, p. 85.
94 ibid. p. 95.
95 ibid. p. 47.
96 ibid. p. 24.

97 ibid. p. 26.

98 ibid. p. 67.

99 Interfax, 13 May 1997.

100 Norman Stone, 'Can Russia Survive the Horrors that Lie Ahead?', *The Independent*, 18 August 1997.

101 Arbatov, 1998 (1). Arbatov is the Deputy Chairman of the Committee on Defence of the State Duma, Russia's lower house of parliament. He is Doctor of Historical Sciences, and the son of a former adviser to Soviet leader, Georgyi Arbatov.

102 Michel Camdessus, 'Russia and the IMF: Meeting the Challenges of an Emerging Market and Transition Economy', Address to the US–Russia Business Council, Washington DC, 1 April 1998.

103 Silverman and Yanowitch, 1997, p. 17.

104 See Russian Central Bank Statistics at http://www.cbr.ru/dp accessed 24 May 1999.

105 *IMF Survey*, vol. 27, no. 1, 3 August 1998, pp. 238–9.

106 Kaiser, 1994, p. 9.

107 A vicious cycle had emerged involving non-payment by government agencies for their consumption, coupled with demands from the government for tax based on the profits of firms to which the government was indebted.

108 Interfax, 15 October 1998.

109 Other prominent figures in the poll registered the following results: Moscow Mayor Yuriy Luzhkov (41 per cent), Krasnoiarsk territory Governor Aleksandr Lebed (38 per cent), leader of the Yabloko movement Grigoryi Yavlinskii (36 per cent), Kemerovo region Governor Aman Tuleyev (30 per cent), Communist Party leader Gennadyi Ziuganov (25 per cent), Duma Chairman Gennady Seleznev (17 per cent), Federation Council Chairman Yegor Stroyev (17 per cent), Liberal Democratic Party of Russia leader Vladimir Zhirinovski (8 per cent), former Russian Prime Minister Viktor Chernomyrdin (5 per cent), former USSR President Mikhail Gorbachev (3 per cent) and head of the Unified Energy Systems national utility Anatoly Chubais (2 per cent).

110 See Russian Central Bank Statistics at http://www.cbr.ru/dp accessed 24 May 1999.

111 Shlapentokh, 1998 (electronic version).

112 Shlykov, 1997, p. 3.

113 ITAR-TASS, 5 October 1997, carried in FBIS-SOV-97-278, 5 October 1997: 'Russia: Moscow Mayor Notes Importance of Siberia's Development'. Another source suggests that Moscow's contribution may be about 27 per cent. See Shlykov, 1997, p. 9.

114 Anatoly Kulikov, 'Shadow Covers 60 Million Russians', *Obshchaia gazeta*, 30 July–5 August 1998, no. 30, p. 7, FBIS SOV 98 223, 11 August 1998: 'Russia: Kulikov on Economic Security Issues'.

115 Douglas Stanglin and others, 'Toxic Wasteland', *US News & World Report*, 13 April 1992, p. 42, citing Murray Feschbach and Alfred Friendly, authors of *Ecocide in the USSR*, Basic Books, 1992.

116 Baev, 1996, p. 25.

2 Russia east of the Ural Mountains

1 Mote, 1998, pp. 39–40.
2 Tishkov, 1994, pp. 38–9. See Appendix I for eastern Russia republics and autonomous regions. Tishkov is citing 'Fact Sheet on Ethnic and Regional Conflict in the Russian Federation', Strengthening Democratic Institutions Project, Harvard University, September 1992.
3 Australia. Department of Foreign Affairs and Trade. East Asia Analytical Unit, 1996, p. 13.
4 Stephan, 1994, pp. 289, 297.
5 ITAR-TASS, 23 February 95, FBIS-SOV–95–036, 23 February 95: 'Shakray Warns about Migration from Siberia, Far East'.
6 ITAR-TASS, 18 April 1995.
7 Andrei Korbut, 'Lev Rokhlin and the Officers Movement in Russia', *Nezavisimoe voennoe obozrenie*, no. 33, 5–11 September 1997, p. 3, FBIS-SOV–97–254, 11 September 1997: 'Russia: Article Ponders Chances of Military Putsch'.
8 ITAR-TASS, 19 November 1998.
9 Rumer and Sternheimer, 1982, p. 30.
10 G. I. Filshin interview, *Sovietskaia rossiia*, 24 March 1989, p. 1.
11 Skorokhodov, 1988, p. 7.
12 Filshin interview, *Sovietskaia rossiia*.
13 Kliuchnikov, 1988, p. 9.
14 Fish, 1995, pp. 139–40.
15 Stephan, 1994, p. 293.
16 ibid. p. 294.
17 Ibid. pp. 288–95 gives a good account of this mix of sentiments in the Far East region.
18 ibid. p. 293.
19 Zhdanov, 1995, p. 121.
20 Stephan, 1994, p. 290.
21 Cited in Stephan, 1994, p. 287.
22 ITAR-TASS, 23 February 95, FBIS-SOV–95–036, 23 February 95: 'Shakray Warns about Migration from Siberia, Far East'.
23 Akaha et al., 1997, p. 50.
24 ibid. p. 59.
25 ITAR-TASS, 14 December 1996, FBIS-SOV–96–242, 14 December 1996: 'Russia: Siberian Accord Association Holds Emergency Meeting'.
26 NTV, 3 July 1997, translated in FBIS-SOV–97–184, 3 July 1997: 'Russia: Protesting Doctors Block Trans-Siberian Railway'.
27 Moscow radio, 15 January 1998, translated in FBIS-SOV–98–015, 15 January 1998: 'Russia: Siberian Coal Miners Hold Protest Action in Kemerovo'.
28 Interfax, 4 February 1998, carried in FBIS-SOV–98–035, 4 February 1998: 'Russia: More Siberian Transport Workers Join Hunger Strike'.
29 Moscow radio, 15 January 1998, translated in FBIS-SOV–98–015,

15 January 1998: 'Russia: Siberian Coal Miners Hold Protest Action in Kemerovo'.

30 NTV, 27 January 1998, translated in FBIS-SOV–98–027, 27 January 1998: 'Russia; Trans-Siberian Railway Blockade Lifted; Strike Continues'.

31 ITAR-TASS, 2 July 1997, carried in FBIS-SOV–97–183, 2 July 1997: 'Russia: Siberian Scientists Oppose Program of Layoffs'.

32 *Poisk*, no. 4, 21–27 January 1995, p. 2, JPRS-UST–95–017, 21 April 1995: 'Personnel Reforms Successful in RAS Siberian Division'.

33 Strand, 1995, p. 80.

34 Scherbakova and Monroe, 1995, p. 61

35 ibid.

36 Strand, 1997, p. 80.

37 Scherbakova and Monroe, 1995, p. 63.

38 Strand, 1997, p. 86.

39 Kyoto, 18 August 1994, JPRS-TEN–94–021, 18 August 1994: 'Japanese, Russian Researchers Discuss Siberian Forests'. This report included the opinion of Japanese researchers that global warming, if it occurred, may cause dissolution of the Siberian permafrost, leading to the release of 'tens of billion of tons of methane gas' into the atmosphere, further exacerbating global warming.

40 Strand, 1997, p. 87.

41 Akaha et al., 1997, p. 63.

42 Zhdanov, 1995, p. 121.

43 Kovrigin, 1997, p. 70.

44 Interfax, 'Siberian Business Report', no. 213–214, 30 December 1997–12 January 1998, carried in FBIS-SOV–98–013, 13 January 1998: 'Russia: Interfax Siberian Business Report'.

45 Kellison, 1995, p. 198.

46 ibid.

47 Christensen, 1995, p. 207.

48 Interfax, 'Siberian Business Report', no. 4, 20–26 January 1998, carried in FBIS-SOV–98–026, 26 January 1998: 'Russia: Interfax Siberian Business Report'.

49 Interfax, 'Siberian Business Report', no. 213–214, 30 December 1997–12 January 1998, carried in FBIS-SOV–98–013, 13 January 1998: 'Russia: Interfax Siberian Business Report'.

50 Interfax, 'Siberian Business Report', no. 4, 20–26 January 1998, carried in FBIS-SOV–98–026, 26 January 1998: 'Russia: Interfax Siberian Business Report'.

51 ibid.

52 Interfax, 'Siberian Business Report', no. 213–214, 30 December 1997–12 January 1998, carried in FBIS-SOV–98–013, 13 January 1998: 'Russia: Interfax Siberian Business Report'

53 Interfax, 'Siberian Business Report', no. 4, 20–26 January 1998.

54 Moscow radio, 15 January 1998, translated in FBIS-SOV–98–015, 15 January 1998: 'Russia: Siberian Coal Miners Hold Protest Action in Kemerovo'.

55 Interfax, 'Siberian Business Report', no. 4, 20–26 January 1998.

56 ibid.
57 ibid.
58 Interfax, 'Siberian Business Report', no. 213–214, 30 December 1997–12 January 1998, carried in FBIS-SOV–98–013, 13 January 1998: 'Russia: Interfax Siberian Business Report'.
59 Interfax, 'Siberian Business Report', no. 4, 20–26 January 1998.
60 ibid.
61 Interfax, 'Siberian Business Report', 23–29 December 1997, carried in FBIS-SOV–97–364, 30 December 1997: 'Russia: Interfax Siberian Business Report 23–29 Dec'.
62 Interfax, 'Siberian Business Report', no. 213–214, 30 December 1997–12 January 1998, carried in FBIS-SOV–98–013, 13 January 1998: 'Russia: Interfax Siberian Business Report'.
63 Interfax, 'Siberian Business Report', 16–22 December 1997, carried in FBIS-SOV–97–356, 22 December 1997: 'Russia: Interfax Siberian Business Report 16–22 Dec'.
64 ibid.
65 ITAR-TASS, 27 January 1998, translated in FBIS-SOV–98–027, 27 January 1998: 'Russia: Russia, Japan to Work Together on Trans-Siberian Railway'.
66 ITAR-TASS, 11 June 1997, FBIS-SOV–97–162, 11 June 1997: 'Russia: Nemtsov Discusses Revival of Trans-Siberian Railway'.
67 ITAR-TASS, 2 March 1997, FBIS-SOV–97–041, 2 March 1997: 'Russia, South Korea: Minister on Trans-Siberian Railway Accord Reached in Seoul'.
68 Interfax, 'Siberian Business Report', no. 213–214, 30 December 1997–12 January 1998.
69 Budapest MTI, 31 October 1997, carried in FBIS-EEU–97–307, 3 November 1997: 'Hungary: Trans-Siberian Railway Line to Improve Freight Amount'.
70 ITAR-TASS, 11 June 1997, FBIS-SOV–97–162, 11 June 1997: 'Russia: Nemtsov Discusses Revival of Trans-Siberian Railway'.
71 ITAR-TASS, 3 April 1997, FBIS-SOV–97–093, 3 April 1997: 'Russia: Effect of Union with Belarus on Trans-Siberian Railway'.
72 NTV, 20 March 1997, FBIS-SOV–97–086, 27 March 1997: 'Russia: TV Features Underused Airport Capacity in West Siberia'.
73 Delovaia sibir', no. 16, 27 April–10 May 95, p. 17, FBIS-SOV–95–102, 26 May 95: 'Siberian Accord's Progress Detailed'.
74 ITAR-TASS, 12 September 1997, carried in FBIS-SOV–97–225, 12 September 1997: 'Russia: Siberia–Altai, Kuzbas Implement Cooperation Agreement'.
75 Delovaia sibir', no. 16, 27 April–10 May 95, p. 17.
76 Akaha et al., 1997, p. 67.
77 Pryde, 1995, p. 31.
78 Scherbakova and Monroe, 1995, p. 70.
79 ibid. pp. 72–3.
80 According to publicly released US intelligence information. See Bulletin of the Atomic Scientists, February 1993, p. 56.
81 ITAR-TASS World Service, 13 October 1997, translated in FBIS-TEN–

97–286, 13 October 1997: 'Russia: Scientists Probe Impact on Siberia of Soviet Nuclear Tests'.
82 Scherbakova and Monroe, 1995, p. 74.
83 NTV, 22 December 1997, translated in FBIS-TEN–97–357, 23 December 1997: 'Russia: Siberian Villagers Blighted by 93 Plutonium Plant Accident'.
84 *Atomnaia energiia*, March 1996, vol. 80, no. 3, pp. 201–8, FBIS-UST–96–042, 1 March 1996: 'Russia: Assessment of Impact of Siberian Chemical Combine on Radioactive Environmental Pollution in 1989–1994'.
85 *Spravka*, 1994, JPRS-UST–95–003-L, 21 March 1995: *Report of Working Group of RF Security Council on Results of Verification of Assurance of Radiation and Ecological Safety of Siberian Chemical Combine (Tomsk–7) and Adjacent Territories* (draft).
86 *Atomnaia energiia*, February 1996, no. 2, pp. 71–3, FBIS-UST–96–029, 1 February 1996: 'Russia: Shutdown of Industrial Reactors of Siberian Chemical Combine'.
87 Scherbakova and Monroe, 1995, pp. 68–9.
88 Sergey Rykov, 'One Spark Could Reduce Lake Samotlor to Ashes', *Komsomol'skaia pravda*, 9 April 1997, p. 2, translated in FBIS-SOV–97–108, 9 April 1997: 'Russia: Report on Oil Pollution in Siberia'.
89 Strand, 1995, p. 87.
90 Akaha et al., 1997, p. 63.
91 Leonid Krutakov, 'The Chief of Yamal–Berezovsky?', *Moskovskii komsomolets*, 30 January 1997, p. 2, FBIS-SOV–97–047, 30 January 1997: 'Russia: Berezovsky's Siberian Oil Role'.
92 See Urban et al., 1997, pp. 283–4.
93 Zhdanov, 1995, p. 123.
94 Sakwa, 1996, p. 223.
95 ibid. p. 215.
96 Khasbulatov, 1993, p. 251.
97 Sakwa, 1996, p. 219.
98 The corresponding terms in Russian are *oblast'* and *krai*.
99 For a useful account of the republics see Sheehy, 1993, pp. 34–40.
100 The term governor is used as shorthand for head of administration of one of the territorial units of the Russian Federation.
101 Zhdanov, 1995, pp. 124, 128.
102 Sakwa, 1996, p. 222.
103 Zhdanov, 'Contemporary Siberian Regionalism', pp. 128–9.
104 Sakwa, 1996, p. 222.
105 ibid. p. 227.
106 ibid. p. 223.
107 The information has been extracted from Krasnov (ed.), 1996, pp. 484–501.
108 NTV, 18 December 1997, translated in FBIS-SOV–97–352, 18 December 1997: 'Russia: Yavlinskiy, Lebed Forces Ally for Siberian Elections'.
109 Interfax, 9 February 1998, carried in FBIS-SOV–98–040, 9 February 1998: 'Russia: Lebed to Run for Governor of Russia's Siberian Region'.

110 Interview for TV6, Moscow, 14 September 1998, BBC Monitoring, 17 September 1998: 'Russia: Krasnoiarsk Governor Confirms Support to New Premier'.
111 The percentage share of votes received is a percentage of votes cast, not a share of eligible voters. Voter turnout was very low in some constituencies. For example, Amur Province had 686 145 registered voters but only some 450 000 voted.
112 PWS—Party of Workers' Self-Management, a Social-Reformist party; CRS—Congress of Russian Societies, a nationalist party; CWR—Communists–Working Russia, a communist-aligned party; WOR—Women of Russia, a social-reformist party; EMP—Social Patriotic Movement 'Empire', a nationalist party; PWS—Party of Workers' Self-Management, a social-reformist party; APR—Agrarian Party of Russia, a communist-aligned party; PTP—Power to the People, a communist-aligned party; TOF—Transformation of the Fatherland, a centre-right party; DCR—Democratic Choice of Russia, a liberal democratic party.
113 *Vechernyi Novosibirsk*, 5 November 1996, pp. 1–2, FBIS-SOV–96–223-S, 5 November 1996: 'Russia: Siberia Mayors Protest Oblast Meddling'.
114 *Vostochno-sibirskaia pravda*, 30 January 1996, p. 1, FBIS-SOV–96–032-S, 30 January 1996: 'Russia: Govorin Elected Siberian Cities Chief'.
115 See for example a brief report on a meeting between the President of the Republic of Sakha and the Governor of Irkutsk in December 1998 in ITAR-TASS, 17 December 1997, translated in FBIS-SOV–97–352, 18 December 1997: 'Russia: Siberian Leaders Discuss Integration with Asia–Pacific'.
116 *Rossiiskie vesti*, 11 October 1997, p. 3, translated in FBIS-SOV–97–287, 14 October 1997: 'Russia: Siberian Mayors Welcome Law on Local Self Government'.

3 National strategic policy

1 For extensive coverage of these developments, see Arbatov (ed.), 1993.
2 Rusi, 1998, p. 142.
3 Ashton Carter, Assistant US Secretary of Defense for International Security Policy, 'Protecting US Security during the New Russian Revolution', *Defense Issues*, vol. 10, no. 77 (electronic version).
4 For example, the USA has maintained vigorous political contacts with Ukraine, including high-level military contacts. The President of Ukraine, Leonid Kravchuk, made an official visit to Washington in May 1992.
5 Kozyrev, 1992, p. 13.
6 ibid. p. 9.
7 The CSCE Agreement covers the entire Russian territory.
8 Kozyrev, 1992, p. 11.
9 ibid. p. 8.

10 ibid. p. 15.

11 ibid. p. 177.

12 Löwenhardt, 1995, p. 175.

13 See Arbatov, 1993. In 1999, one of Russia's most respected intellectuals and member of the Presidential Council, Andranik Migranian, blamed Kozyrev for the initiation even before 1991 of destructive tendencies in Soviet foreign policy, based on 'endless unilateral concessions and unconditional support of the USA and western countries'. 'Nuzhno li Nam Pomogat' Iugoslavii' [Should We Help Yugoslavia?], *Nezavisimaia gazeta*, 28 April 1999, p. 1.

14 Moscow Television, 19 December 1995.

15 Lunev, 1996.

16 ibid.

17 Vladimir Yanchenkov, 'Ivan Rybkin: We Cannot and Will Not Take on the Whole World', *Trud*, 10 June 1997, p. 3, FBIS-SOV–97–114, 10 June 1997: 'Russia: Rybkin on Security Blueprint'.

18 ibid.

19 This was a term used to describe an approach to strategic policy, new to the USSR—that a system of common security might replace the traditional European and international order of alliances aimed at protecting one group of states from another.

20 Institute of National Security and Strategic Studies, 1997 (electronic version).

21 Moscow Television, 11 September 1998 (live coverage), BBC Monitoring, 12 September 1998: 'Primakov in Russian State Duma: Questions and Answers'.

22 Arbatov, 1998: 1.

23 Interview with Russian Defence Minister, *Nezavisimoe voennoe obozrenie*, no. 26, 17–23 July 1998, pp. 1, 3, FBIS-UMA–98–204, 23 July 1998: 'Russia: Sergeyev Gives Vision of Reformed Forces'.

24 Interfax, 22 January 1999, FBIS-SOV–99–022, 22 January 1999: 'Russia: Russia's Ivanov: Partnership with US Overrides Irritants'.

25 ITAR-TASS, 26 January 1996, FBIS-SOV–1999–0126: 'Ivanov: Russia, US Have Concurring Strategic Interests'

26 Lunev, 1996.

27 Oleg Falichev and Vladimir Matiash, 'Zadachi 1998 goda vooruzhionnym silam piishlos' vypolniat' v slozhnykh usloviiakh' [The Armed Forces Have Completed their Tasks for 1998 in Difficult Circumstances], *Krasnaia zvezda*, 13 November 1998, p. 1.

28 Dmitry Gornostaev and Aleksandr Reutov, 'Moskva otozvala poslov iz SSHA i Velikobritanii i gotova otpravit v persidskii zaliv boevye korabli' [Russia Recalls Ambassadors from the USA and Great Britain and is Ready to Send Combat Ships to the Persian Gulf], *Nezavisimaia gazeta*, 19 December 1998, pp. 1, 6.

29 Joint Press Conference with US Secretary of State, Madeleine Albright, Moscow, ITAR-TASS, 26 January 1999, FBIS-SOV–1999–0126: 'Russia's Ivanov Calls on US to Avoid Surprises'. Ivanov listed some of the main sources of Russian dissatisfaction with the USA.

30 ITAR-TASS, 24 February 1999, FBIS-SOV–1999–0225: 'Balkan Lessons Make Russia Revise Military Doctrine'.

31 This treaty, signed in 1972 and limiting the deployment of ballistic missile defence to one location, has been seen as a cornerstone of stability in strategic nuclear arms in that it entrenched as common policy the notion of deterrence, thereby allowing the two sides more confidence in dealing with each other and eventually allowing them to reach agreement on significant cuts in strategic nuclear missiles.

32 Interview with Viacheslav Trubnikov, *Nezavisimoe voennoe obozrenie*, 17–23 July 1998, no. 26, p. 8, FBIS-SOV–98–209, 28 July 1998: 'Russia: SVR Chief Trubnikov Interviewed'.

33 Lunev, 1996.

34 Interfax, 31 March 1999, FBIS-SOV–1999–0331: 'Duma Urges Yeltsin to Strengthen Russia's Defence Ties'.

35 Interfax, 7 April 1999, FBIS-SOV–1999–0407: 'Russia: Sergeyev to Revise Military Downsizing Plans'.

36 Xinhua, 5 April 1999, FBIS-CHI–1999–0405: 'Xinhua: Ivanov Says Russia Not to Start Arms Race'.

37 Interfax, 10 April 1999, FBIS-SOV–1999–0410: 'Russia: Luzhkov Warns against Balkan War Involvement'.

38 ITAR-TASS, 29 March 1999, FBIS-SOV–1999–0329: 'Yeltsin Calls for Normalisation of Russia–US Relations''

39 Guroff and Guroff, 1994, p. 96.

40 Staar, 1996, p. 124.

41 Selivanova, 1996.

42 Aleksandr Lebed was the commander of a group of airborne personnel involved in the planning for the August 1991 coup against Gorbachev but as the events evolved refused to obey the orders of the coup leaders and changed sides. His decision was one of the influential turning points in the attempted coup, and he rose to political prominence in subsequent years for this and because of his successful settlement of the fighting in Moldova in 1992.

43 After that operation, Lebed was formally appointed commander of the 14th Army.

44 Zaloga, 1995, p. 297.

45 IISS, *The Military Balance, 1998/99*.

46 Zaloga, 1995, pp. 303–4.

47 Baev, 1996, p. 104. The relevant chapter in Baev's book provides an excellent discussion of the complex influences shaping Russian military interventions in the newly independent states.

48 This was not the national parliament of the USSR, but the parliament of the Russian Soviet Federated Socialist Republic. The parliament had been elected before the collapse of the USSR.

49 Kozhokin, 1996.

50 Dubnov, 1996.

51 Staar, 1996, p. 122.

52 ibid.

53 Khodjibaev, 1997 (Internet Version).

54 IISS, *The Military Balance, 1998/99*.

55 *Nezavisimoe voennoe obozrenie*, 27 November–3 December 1998, pp. 1, 2, FBIS-UMA–98–363, 29 December 1998: 'Russia: Border Troops in Tajikistan Reorganised'.

56 *Neftianik*, Jan-Feb 94, pp. 2–4, FBIS-USR–94–089, 16 August 1994: 'Oil Minister on Siberia's Role in Energy Complex'.

57 Zaprudnik, 1994, p. 143. Eventually the economic pressures for Belarus were too great and, as mentioned above, in 1997 the two countries signed the document of union.

58 Texts of these agreements are included in Brzezinski and Sullivan (eds), 1997.

59 *Sovietskaia rossiia*, 5 November 1998, p. 2, FBIS-SOV–98–309, 5 November 1998: 'Russia: Impeachment Commission Views Army Decline'.

60 *Jane's Defence Weekly*, 11 April 1992, p. 597.

61 *International Defense Review*, 1992, no. 6, p. 491.

62 ibid. p. 493.

63 Garthoff, 1992, p. 50.

64 These included a Declaration on State Borders, 7 August 1993; a Unified Air Defense Agreement, 25 February 1995; and a Treaty on Border Protection between CIS and Non-CIS States, 7 July 1995. For texts, see Brzezinski and Sullivan (eds), 1997, pp. 541–8.

65 One of the advantages for Russia has been that its language remains the common language even in such smaller regions as the Transcaucasus.

66 Interfax, 17 June 1997, FBIS-SOV–97–168, 17 June 1997: 'Russia: Yeltsin to Meet with Leaders of CIS Mini-Union States'.

67 Interfax, 22 January 1998, FBIS-SOV–98–022, 22 January 1998: 'Russia: Seleznev—Tajikistan May Join CIS States Custom Union'.

68 *Nezavisimaia gazeta*, 27 February 1999, pp. 1–2.

69 Interfax, 23 May 1997, FBIS-SOV–97–143, 23 May 1997: 'Russia: Russia–Belarus Union Charter Open to other CIS States'.

70 Interfax, 18 May 1997, FBIS-SOV–97–138, 18 May 1997: 'Russia: Lebed Favors Russia–Belarus Union of Sovereign States'.

71 ITAR-TASS, 2 April 1997, FBIS-SOV–97–092, 2 April 1997: 'Russia: Most Members of State Duma Back Union with Belarus'.

72 Dmitry Shusharin, 'The Danger Comes from the West', *Literaturnaia gazeta*, 20 November 1996, FBIS-SOV–97–022, 4 February 1997: 'Russia, Belarus: Union of States Seems Dangerous'.

73 ITAR-TASS, 28 March 1997, FBIS-SOV–97–061, 1 April 1997: 'Russia: Text of Yeltsin's Speech to CIS Summit'.

74 Interfax, 25 January 1998, FBIS-SOV–98–025, 25 January 1998: 'Russia: Stroyev—Transcaucasus States Need Union with Russia'.

75 Arbatov, 1998:1.

76 Vadim Soloviov, 'Washington is Establishing a New World Order', *Nezavisimoe voennoe obozrenie*, 24 December 1998–14 January 1999, p. 1, FBIS-UMA–99–029, 29 January 1999: 'Russia: Airstrikes Demonstrate Moscow's Weakness'.

77 *Nezavisimaia gazeta*, 25 February 1999, pp. 1, 5.

78 ibid. p. 5

79 See Yury Pankov, 'NATO Primerila mundir mirovo zhandarma' [NATO Tries on the Uniform of World Gendarme], *Krasnaia zvezda*, 28 April 1999, p. 1.

80 Ilia Kedrov, 'Afghan Syndrome: Russian Troops Should Scarcely be Withdrawn from Tajikistan', *Nezavisimoe voennoe obozrenie*, no. 9, 6–12 March 1998, p. 2, FBIS-SOV–98–070, 11 March 1998: 'Russia: Border Guards Pullout from Tajikistan Would Be a Mistake'.

81 Baev, 1996, p. 95.

82 These were members of the Warsaw Treaty Organisation established in 1955 and the Council for Mutual Economic Cooperation (COMECON). They included Czechoslovakia, Poland, Bulgaria, Hungary, Romania and the German Democratic Republic.

83 Vladimir Abarimov, 'Moscow Reconciled to NATO Expansion, But Still Threatens Adequate Reply Measures', *Segodnia*, 1 October 1996.

84 Igor Korotchenko, 'Russian Defence Minister Speaks in Favour of Creating a CIS Defence Alliance', *Nezavisimaia gazeta*, 26 December 1996.

85 For example, Uzbek leader Islam Karimov opposed the idea of creating a politico-military bloc within the CIS as a counterweight to NATO's expansion.

86 See *Izvestiia*, 24 April 1999, p. 2.

87 Vladimir Mukhin, 'Otvet na Agressiu NATO?' [Response to NATO's Aggression?], *Nezavisimaia gazeta*, 28 April 1999, p. 5.

88 *Ria Novosti*, 11 April 1997.

89 Oleg Falichev, 'Ukrepliaia slavianskii souz' [By Strengthening Slavic Union], *Krasnaia zvezda*, 27 April 1999, pp. 1, 3; V. Mukhin, 'Otvet na agressiu NATO?', p. 5. Long-range, early warning radar near Baranovichi is regarded in Russia as a replacement for the similar facility in Scrunda (Latvia), which the Russian military had to abandon and which was subsequently destroyed by Latvian authorities.

90 Ken Delve, 'NATO—Growing Pains', *Air Forces Monthly*, no. 105, December 1996, p. 19.

91 See Tatiana Ivzhenko, 'Ukraina ne Vstupit v NATO v Blizhaishie 10 Let' [Ukraine Will Not Join NATO in the Next 10 Years], *Nezavisimaia gazeta*, 11 February 1999, p. 2.

92 'Ukrainian Foreign, Defence Ministers Visit Disputed Island', Open Media Research Institute, Prague, 11 August 1995.

93 See Makhmut Akhmetovich Gareyev, 'Russia's Military Doctrine', *Nezavisimoe voennoe obozrenie*, no. 29, 9–15 August 1997, pp. 1, 4, FBIS-TAC–97–233, 21 August 1997: 'Russia: Military Academician on New Military Doctrine'. Gareyev is President of the Academy of Military Sciences and a former Deputy Chief of the Soviet General Staff.

94 Valery Gromak, 'Rybkin: Kaliningrad is Russia's Baltic', *Krasnaia zvezda*, 10 June 1997.

95 Lee Hockstader, 'Russian Warns of Attack if NATO Expands East'. *Washington Post*, 16 February 1996.

96 Viktor Barynkin, 'Russia's Stand on Plans for Enlargement of NATO', *Military News Bulletin*, vol. 5, May 1996.

97 See Sergei Baturin, 'Moscow's Spineless Policy Gives NATO Leaders a Free Hand', *Pravda*, 22 May 1997; Valentina Morozova, 'Velvet Deportation', *Nezavisimaia gazeta*, 29 November 1996.

98 On completion of his talks with US Secretary of State Madeleine Albright, Russian Foreign Minister Yevgenyi Primakov stated that 'Russia strongly objects to the Baltic states entering NATO and is ready to give them guarantees of security' (Novosti, 13 July 1997).

99 There were already arguments to this effect as early as 1995. For further discussion, see Aleksandr Liasko, 'Will Grachev Seize the Baltics?', *Komsomol'skaia pravda*, 27 October–2 November 1995; Anton Surikov, 'Staff at a Specialised Institute are Proposing to Russia . . .', *Segodnia*, 20 October 1995.

100 For a discussion of this, see Muraviev, 1998.

101 Sir Brian Barder, 'NATO Enlargement', *The Times*, 6 March 1997.

102 Slovenia, Bosnia-Hercegovina, Croatia, the Former Yugoslav Republic of Macedonia, and the rump state of Yugoslavia (including Serbia, Montenegro and Kosovo).

103 Dr Yelena Guskova (a specialist in the State Duma), 'Russia's Interests in the Balkans', *Delovoi mir*, 6 August 1996.

104 Novosti, 22 May 1997.

105 See the interview with Dimitr Pavlov in 'Bolgaria I Rossiia Vsegda Vmeste' [Bulgaria and Russia Are Always Together'], *Voenny Parad*, N 1 1997, p. 22.

106 *Military News Bulletin*, vol. 8, August 1996.

107 Novosti, 8 April 1997.

108 Macedonia regards Russia as one of Europe's key players, thus it began with an orientation towards Russia in European affairs. Novosti, 18 July 1997.

109 Russia supplied Cyprus with advanced armoury: T–80U MBTs and BMP–3 AIFVs. Also, Cyprus bought Russia's state-of-the-art S–300PMU–1 air defence missile complexes which are superior to the US counterpart, the *Patriot*. This system could effectively neutralise Turkish air superiority on the island. See Mikhail Pogorelyi and Sergei Novozhilov, 'Confrontation on Arms Markets', *Krasnaia zvezda*, 9 January 1997.

110 'Turkey Ups Stakes in Cypriot Dispute', *Western Australian*, 11 January 1997.

111 These eight countries are Georgia, Armenia, Azerbaijan, Kazakhstan, Uzbekistan, Tajikistan, Turkmenistan and Kyrgyzstan.

112 See for example, Aleksey Nikulin, 'Ankara's Spy Games', *Nezavisimoe voennoe obozrenie*, 20–26 February 1998, p. 7, FBIS-SOV–98–054, 23 February 1998: 'Russia: Turks Warned Against Imperial Thinking in Caucasus'.

113 See for example, Sergei Putilov, 'Bosnian Scenario Projected for Caspian', *Nezavisimoe voennoe obozrenie*, 27 February–5 March 1998, p. 8, FBIS-SOV–061, 2 March 1998: 'Russia: US Said Seeking to Draw Caspian into Sphere of Influence'.

114 Vitaly Strugovets, 'Proshchai, bratstvo po oruzhiu?' [Goodbye Brotherhood of Arms], *Krasnaia zvezda*, 5 February 1999 (EV).

115 The Russian armed forces made a major contribution to the creation of the Armenian army. Russia secretly transferred weapons and equipment worth $1 billion. This included practically every type of weaponry, from missiles and heavy artillery to assault rifles and light ammunition. In particular, Russia delivered to Armenia 8 *Scud–B* launchers with 24 missiles, 84 T–72 MBTs, 50 BMIP–2s. See Nikolai Novichkov, 'Russia Details Illegal Deliveries to Armenia', *Jane's Defence Weekly*, 16 April 1997, p. 15.

116 Novosti, 16 April 1997.

117 Aleksandr Vladimirov and Sergei Grigor'ev, 'Otrazit ugrozu s Iuga' [To Repel Threat from the South], *Nezavisimoe voennoe obozrenie*, no. 14 1999, p. 5.

118 ITAR-TASS, 11 February 1999, FBIS-SOV–1999–0211: 'Mayor Luzhkov: Armenia is Russia's Strategic Partner'.

119 For example, in 1996 Russia transferred approximately 30 MiG–29 *Fulcrum* and Su–27 *Flanker* fighters plus some training aircraft to the Kazakh Air Force. Kazakh aircrews were trained at the Russian Air Force training centre at Lipetsk. See 'Military Affairs— Kazakhstan', *Air International*, vol. 50, no. 3, May 1996, p. 260.

120 Tsypkin, 1992, p. 37.

121 ibid.

122 Vladimir Yanchenkov, 'Ivan Rybkin: We Cannot and Will Not Take on the Whole World', *Trud*, 10 June 1997, p. 3, FBIS-SOV–97–114, 10 June 1997: 'Russia: Rybkin on Security Blueprint'.

4 Strategic policy in the Asia–Pacific

1 Kozyrev, 1992, p. 15.

2 Vladimir Misanikov, Deputy Director of the Institute of the Far East, cited in Blank, 1997, p. 16.

3 See *Rossiiskaia gazeta*, 15 October 1997, p. 3, FBIS-SOV–97–290, 17 October 1997: 'Russia: Coordinated Approach Urged to Eastern Russia, Asia–Pacific'.

4 Leonid Ivashov, 'Rossiia i Asiatsko-Tikhookeanskii region: ne pora li meniat orientiry?' [Russia and the Asia–Pacific Region: Is it Time to Change Orientation?], *Voennyi parad*, no. 1, 1997, p. 17.

5 Igor Ivanov, 'Rossiia dolzhna byt' aktivna v ATR' [Russia Must be Vigorous in the APR], *Nezavisimaia gazeta*, 23 February 1999, p. 6.

6 For a discussion of Russia's strategic relations with the Asia–Pacific region in the first half of the 1990s, see Austin and Callan, 1996.

7 *Trud*, 11 March 1997, p. 4, FBIS-SOV–97–048, 11 March 1997: 'Russia, China: G. Karasin on Relations with DPRK, China'.

8 In October 1986, Mikhail Gorbachev, then Secretary General of the Communist Party of the Soviet Union, made a speech in Vladivostok which laid out Russia's hopes for expansion of economic links and improvement of political relations with the USSR's former strategic rivals on the Pacific Rim.

9 This was originally a loose grouping of states that sought to build

new cooperative security mechanisms on the foundations of the successful international negotiations that resulted in the UN-sponsored settlement of the Cambodian conflict.

10 Ivanov, 'Rossiia dolzhna byt' aktivna v ATR'.

11 This form of trade was a primary form of trade for communist economies and less developed countries which had little or no access to hard currencies. It involved exchange of goods rather than payment in cash for exports or imports. For example, in 1992 a Chinese company traded 500 railcar loads of light industrial goods for four Tupolev TU–154M civil airliners in a deal worth about US$321 million. See *International Herald Tribune*, 30 July 1992.

12 Nemets, 1996, pp. 39–40.

13 *Trud*, 11 March 1997, p. 4, FBIS-SOV–97–048, 11 March 1997: 'Russia, China: G. Karasin on Relations with DPRK, China'.

14 Nemets, 1996, pp. 26–30.

15 Ivanov, 'Rossiia dolzhna byt' aktivna v ATR'.

16 For a discussion of the early years of the Sino-Russian relationship after 1991, see Austin, 1995.

17 Emil Pain, 'Problem: Illegals on Amur Shores: On Chinese Immigration in the Russian Far East', *Rossiiskie vesti*, 6 May 1997, p. 3, FBIS-SOV–97–093, 6 May 1997: 'Russia, China: Yeltsin Adviser Views Chinese Immigration'.

18 Yonhap, 25 December 1997, carried in FBIS-EAS–97–349, 15 December 1997: 'South Korea: ROK to Cooperate on Development of Siberian Oil Fields'.

19 Interfax, 'Siberian Business Report', No. 213–214, 30 December 1997–12 January 1998, carried in FBIS-SOV–98–013, 13 January 1998: 'Russia: Interfax Siberian Business Report'.

20 Interfax, 'Siberian Business Report', 2–8 December 1997, carried in FBIS-SOV–97–343, 9 December 1997: 'Russia: Interfax Siberian Business Report'.

21 ibid. Siberia has a large surplus of generating capacity, and China was pushing for a cut in the offered price.

22 Interfax, 'Siberian Business Report', No. 213–214, 30 December 1997–12 January 1998, carried in FBIS-SOV–98–013, 13 January 1998: 'Russia: Interfax Siberian Business Report'.

23 Nemets, 1996, pp. 23–4.

24 Radio Rossii, 27 February 1998, FBIS-SOV–98–058, 27 February 1998: 'Russia: Nemtsov to Inaugurate Russian–Chinese Border Crossing'.

25 *Trud*, 11 March 1997, p. 4, FBIS-SOV–97–048, 11 March 1997: 'Russia, China: G. Karasin on Relations with DPRK, China'.

26 ITAR-TASS, 22 June 1997, FBIS-SOV–97–173, 22 June 1997: 'Russia: Moscow Seeks Strategic Partnership with Japan'.

27 ITAR-TASS, 25 June 1996, FBIS-SOV–96–124, 26 June 1996, cited in Blank, 1997, p. 16.

28 Ivanov, 'Rossiia dolzhna byt' aktivna v ATR'.

29 *International Herald Tribune*, 10 September 1992.

30 Blank, 1997, p. 20.

31 In October 1997, the Russian parliament held special hearings in

Irkutsk to discuss this question as well as more positive aspects of Russia's relations with Asian countries. *Rossiiskaia gazeta*, 15 October 1997, p. 3, FBIS-SOV–97–290, 17 October 1997: 'Russia: Coordinated Approach Urged to Eastern Russia, Asia–Pacific'.

32 Rozman, 1997, p. 543.

33 ibid. p. 559.

34 Nemets, 1996, p. 41.

35 ibid. pp. 39–40.

36 Pain, 'Problem: Illegals on Amur Shores: On Chinese Immigration in the Russian Far East'.

37 ibid.

38 ITAR-TASS, 27 October 1997, FBIS-SOV–97–300, 27 October 1997: 'Russia: Chinese Citizens Violate Russian Border'.

39 *Look Japan*, December 1992, p. 10.

40 Arai, 1997, p. 168.

41 *Defense News*, 4–10 May 1992.

42 *Defense News*, 23 March 1992.

43 *Sydney Morning Herald*, 30 July 1992.

44 *Sydney Morning Herald*, 17 September 1992.

45 Akihiko Tanaka, 'Should We, or Shouldn't We?', *Look Japan*, May 1992, p. 21.

46 Reuter, 20 April 1992.

47 Editorial, *Sankei shimbun*, 3 November 1997, morning edition, p. 3, translated in FBIS-EAS–97–309, 5 November 1997: 'Japan: Japanese Editorial Praises Outcome of Japan–Russia Summit'.

48 *Washington Post*, 31 March 1992.

49 Zagorsky, 1997, p. 38.

50 Yelena Ishkova, 'How to Avoid Discord between Center and Regions', *Rossiiskie vesti*, 7 August 1997, p. 2, FBIS-SOV–97–220, 8 August 1997: 'Russia: Vice Premier Bulgak on Far East Talks'. The article cites an interview with Vice Premier, Vladimir Bulgak.

51 Kyodo, 1 November 1996, FBIS-EAS–96–213, 1 November 1996: 'Japan: Russia to Scrap Curb on Airlines Overflying Siberia'.

52 Nobuo Miyamoto, 'Why Japan–Russia Ties Are Second Only to Japan–US Ties', *Chuo koron*, February 1999, pp. 244–251, FBIS-SOV–1999–0126: 'Ties to Russia 2nd Only to US'.

53 Interfax, 3 January 1997, FBIS-SOV–97–002, 3 January 1997: 'Russia: Deputy Minister on Relations with Japan, China, India'.

54 Kyodo, 10 June 1997, FBIS-EAS–97–161, 10 June 1997: 'Japan: Japan, Russia Seek Cooperation in Siberia Development'.

55 ITAR-TASS, 10 October 1997, FBIS-SOV–97–283, 10 October 1997: 'Russia: Former Envoy on Future Russo–Japanese Cooperation'.

56 ITAR-TASS, 22 June 1997, FBIS-SOV–97–173, 22 June 1997: 'Russia: Moscow Seeks Strategic Partnership with Japan'.

57 Interfax, 'Siberian Business Report', 2–8 December 1997, carried in FBIS-SOV–97–343, 9 December 1997: 'Russia: Interfax Siberian Business Report'.

58 ibid.

59 *Mainichi shimbun*, 30 October 1997, morning edition, p. 5, translated

in FBIS-EAS–97–304, 31 October 1997: 'Japan: Editorial Urges Tokyo, Moscow to Improve Ties at Summit'.

60 Interfax, 'Siberian Business Report', No. 213–214, 30 December 1997–12 January 1998, carried in FBIS-SOV–98–013, 13 January 1998: 'Russia: Interfax Siberian Business Report'.

61 ibid.

62 ibid.

63 ITAR-TASS, 27 January 1998, translated in FBIS-SOV–98–027, 27 January 1998: 'Russia: Russia, Japan to Work Together on Trans-Siberian Railway'.

64 See Austin, 1997:2.

65 See Austin, 1997:1.

66 ITAR-TASS, 10 October 1997, FBIS-SOV–97–283, 10 October 1997: 'Russia: Former Japanese Envoy on Future Russo–Japanese Cooperation'.

67 See for example, Sergei Sokut, 'Washington Revives Star Wars Program', *Nezavisimoe voennoe obozrenie*, no. 3, 29 January–4 February 1999, FBIS-SOV–1999–0215: 'Star Wars Revived, Moscow Prepared to Act'.

68 Ivanov, 'Rossiia dolzhna byt' aktivna v ATR'.

69 Yonhap, 12 March 96, FBIS-EAS–96–049, 12 March 1996: 'ROK, Former Soviet Union Almost Agreed on Far East Siberia Lease'.

70 For details of these moves, see Reese, 1998, pp. 45–6.

71 ITAR-TASS, 17 March 1999, FBIS-SOV–1999–0319, 18 March 1999: 'Initialing of New Russia–DPRK Treaty Viewed'; 'Interview with Deputy Foreign Minister, Grigorii Karasin', Voice of Russia World Service, 24 March 1999, FBIS-SOV–1999–0327: 'Russian Official Viewed on DPRK Situation'.

72 'North Korea Close to New Russian Military Deal', *Jane's Defence Weekly*, 19 February 1997, p. 12.

73 *Choson Ilbo*, 20 January 1999 (Internet Version), FBIS-EAS–99–022, 22 January 1999: 'South Korea: Daily Cites Russian Source on Weapons Smuggling into DPRK'.

74 ITAR-TASS, 4 February 1999.

75 *Choson Ilbo*, 27 January 1999 (Internet Version), FBIS-EAS–99–027, 27 January 1999: 'South Korea: Russian Envoy Warns over DPRK Inspection'.

76 ITAR-TASS, 2 February 1999, FBIS-TAC–99–033, 2 February 1999: 'Russia: Russian Expert: DPRK Incapable of Nuclear Strike on US'.

77 *Korea Herald*, 4 January 1999 (Internet Version), FBIS-EAS–99–003, 3 January 1999: 'South Korea: Russian Envoy Says 1999 Year for Russia–Korea Relations'.

78 Yonhap, 8 April 1999, FBIS-EAS–1999–0408: 'ROK, Russia Initial Pact on Nuclear Energy'.

79 Yonhap, 15 April 1999, FBIS-EAS–1999–0415: 'ROK, Russia to Hold Talks on Maritime Shipping Treaty'.

80 *Choson Ilbo*, 21 March 1999 (Internet Version), FBIS-EAS–1999–0321: 'Column Comments on Russia's Diplomacy with ROK, DPRK'.

81 *Korea Times*, 7 January 1999 (Internet Version), FBIS-EAS–99–007: 'South Korea: Russian Envoy on 6-Party Talks'.
82 *Korea Times*, 31 December 1998 (Internet version), FBIS-EAS–98–365, 31 December 1998: 'South Korea: Government Plans to Set Up Northeast Asia Economic Group'.
83 ITAR-TASS, 14 April 1998, FBIS-UMA–98–104: 'Russia: Military Accord Signed by Transbaykal Military District, Moscow'.
84 Cross-border violations have been an issue with Mongolia, with a six-day exercise in Altai Republic in 1997 netting 125 Mongolians violating migration laws. Radio Rossii, 7 May 1997, FBIS-UMA–97–127, 7 May 1997: 'Russia: Joint Operation Cracks Down on Border Violations'.
85 Oleg Falichev, 'Strategiccheskoe partnerstvo, obrashchennoe v 21 vek' [Strategic Partnership Turned to the 21st Century], *Krasnaia zvezda*, 27 October 1998, p. 1.
86 Igor Korotchenko, 'RF sokhranit voenno-morskoe prisutstvie vo Vietname' [Russian Federation Will Maintain Naval Presence in Vietnam], *Nezavisimaia gazeta*, 22 October 1998, p. 2.
87 Dmitry Gornostaev and Sergei Sokut, 'Karatelnaia akstia protiv Iraka zavershilas krizisom mezhdunarodnykh otnoshenii' [Action Against Iraq Culminated in International Relations Crisis], *Nezavisimaia gazeta*, 22 December 1998, p. 1.
88 Operation 'Desert Fox'.
89 See *Nezavisimoe voennoe obozrenie*, no. 2, 1999, p. 2.
90 See Dmitrii Gornostaev, 'Bol'she poloviny chelovechestva osudilo agressiu NATO' [More than Half of Humankind Condemned NATO's Aggression], *Nezavisimaia gazeta*, 31 March 1999, p. 6.

5 Military doctrine and force posture

1 *International Defense Review*, 1992, no. 6, p. 491.
2 The term in Russian, *velikaia otechestvennaia voina*, can be translated either way, but neither English rendering by itself captures the connotation of the Russian word *otechestvennaia*, the adjectival form of the word for 'fatherland'.
3 *Jane's Defence Weekly*, 16 May 1992, p. 838; *Morskoi sbornik*, no. 7, 1992, p. 20.
4 Novosti, 8 August 1992.
5 In the immediate aftermath of the collapse of the USSR, the other CIS states asserted control over 13 combined-arms armies, 4 tank armies, 2 strategic missile armies, 3 air defence armies, and 5 air armies.
6 Vladimir Georgiyev, 'Iubilei Rossiiskoi Armii' [Anniversary of the Russian Army], *Nezavisimoe voennoe obozrenie*, no. 17, 1999, p. 1.
7 Arbatov, 1997, p. 11.
8 ibid. pp. 12–13.
9 ibid. p. 18.
10 ibid.

11 Arbatov, 1998:2, p. 134.
12 Garthoff, 1992, pp. 46–7.
13 ibid. pp. 47–8.
14 ibid. pp. 52–7.
15 Lunev, 1995.
16 For the officially released version, see 'Osnovnye Polozhenia Voennoi Doktriny Rossiiskoi Federatsii' [Basic Provisions of the Military Doctrine of the Russian Federation], *Krasnaia zvezda*, 19 November 1993.
17 *Defense News*, 21–27 December 1992.
18 Garthoff, 1992, pp. 57–9.
19 'Russia's New Military Doctrine' (Interview with Major General Yurii A. Kirshin), *Perspective*, vol. 4, no. 2, December 1993 (EV).
20 *Sueddeutsche Zeitung*, 12 March 1999, p. 9, FBIS-WEU–1999–0312: 'General Naumann: NATO, Russia Agree on Nuclear Strategies'.
21 Natalya Kuznetsova, 'Voennaia Reforma v Rossii' [Military Reform in Russia], *Nezavisimaia gazeta*, 16 December 1996, p. 2.
22 Trenin, 1997, p. 63.
23 *Mirovaia ekonomika i mezhdunarodnye otnosheniia*, no. 4, 1997, pp. 5–21, FBIS—UMA–97–136-S, 17 July 1997: 'Russia: Arbatov: Military Reform: Doctrine, Troops'.
24 'Kontseptsiia natsional'noi bezopasnosti Rossiiskoi Federatsii' ['Blueprint for National Security of the Russian Federation'], Presidential Edict No. 1300, 17 December 1997.
25 Interfax, 3 August 1998, FBIS-SOV–98–217, 5 August 1998: 'Russia: Kokoshin: Yeltsin Signs Defense Concept 2005 Document'.
26 ITAR-TASS, 24 February 1999, FBIS-SOV–1999–0225: 'Balkan Lessons Make Russia Revise its Military Doctrine'.
27 Interfax 27 April 1999, FBIS-SOV–1999–0427: 'Sergeyev: Russia To Adjust Military Doctrine'.
28 NTV, 22 April 1999, FBIS-SOV–1999–0422: 'More on Russia Adjusting Military Doctrine'.
29 Makhmut Akhmetovich Gareyev, 'War and Modern International Confrontation: National Interests Must be Defended Above All by Non-Military Means', *Nezavisimoe voennoe obozrenie*, no. 1, 9–15 January 1998, p. 4, FBIS-SOV–98–040, 9 February 1998: 'Russia: Gareyev: War, Modern International Conflict'.
30 This service was often called the Strategic Rocket Forces in English.
31 *International Defense Review*, 1992, no. 6, p. 491.
32 Tomas Ries, 'Russia's Military Inheritance', *International Defense Review*, 1992, no. 3, p. 223.
33 *International Defense Review*, 1992, no. 6, p. 491.
34 *International Herald Tribune*, 23–24 May 1992, p. 2.
35 Krasnov (ed.), 1996, p. 168.
36 *Washington Post*, 27 September 1992, citing the report of the Russian investigation into the coup.
37 Sakwa, 1996, p. 317.
38 Lambeth, 1995, p. 87. Lambeth cites the two coup attempts in 1991 and 1993, and operations against political demonstrations in Latvia

and Georgia in the last two years of Soviet rule. He also cited the lack of enthusiasm in the armed forces for operations in Chechnia. The authors of this book believe there was more enthusiasm in the armed forces to use force against Chechens and Georgians than against fellow Russians. Another scholar paints a more ugly picture, referring to the Tblisi massacre of 1989, the brutal occupation of Baku in 1990, and a number of violent events in the Baltic republics in 1991. See Sakwa, 1996, p. 317.

39 Sakwa, 1996, p. 317.

40 The armed forces leadership did attempt a coup in 1991, but the units that were ordered to enforce the take-over baulked at the prospect of use of violence even on a relatively small scale.

41 Ibid. p. 318 suggests that the armed forces and related groups, including family members of voting age, make up 40 million people out of a total electorate of about 110 million.

42 *Defense News*, 21–27 December 1992.

43 On 3 June 1992, Yeltsin set up by decree a National Security Council. This was retained in the 1993 Constitution.

44 According to Article 87, the regime of martial law is defined in federal constitutional law.

45 Okun'kov, 1996, p. 54.

46 Aleksandr Shaburkin, 'Civilian Control over the Armed Forces', *Nezavisimoe voennoe obozrenie*, 28 June–4 July 1997, p. 4, FBIS-UMA–97–184, 3 July 1997: 'Russia: Strong Parliamentary Control over Defense Budget Urged'.

47 Vladimir Yanchenkov, 'Ivan Rybkin: We Cannot and Will Not Take on the Whole World', *Trud*, 10 June 1997, p. 3, FBIS-SOV–97–114, 10 June 1997: 'Russia: Rybkin on Security Blueprint'.

48 Presidential Edict on Several Measures for the Improvement of State Control in the Sphere of Defence and Security, No. 220, 3 March 1998.

49 *Rossiiskaia gazeta*, 26 December 1997, pp. 4–5, FBIS-SOV–97–364, 30 December 1997: 'Russia: Russian National Security Blueprint'.

50 Krasnov (ed.), 1996, p. 168.

51 Russian government estimates suggest less than 4000 soldiers died in Chechnia, but other groups have estimated total killed as 5000. See Sarah Brown, 1997, p. 66.

52 ibid. p. 61.

53 Herspring, 1996, p. 169.

54 Krasnov (ed.), 1996, p. 169.

55 ibid. p. 171.

56 ibid. pp. 171–3.

57 ibid. pp. 172–3.

58 McFaul, 1997, pp. 50–2.

59 IISS, *Strategic Survey 1996/97*, p. 127.

60 IISS, *Strategic Survey 1996/97*, p. 126.

61 Herspring, 1996, pp. 164–5.

62 NTV, 14 August 1997, translated in FBIS-SOV–97–226, 14 August

1997: 'Russia: Sergeyev Observes Training in Siberian Military District'.

63 *Trud*, 11 February 1997, pp. 1, 3, FBIS-SOV–97–029, 11 February 1997: 'Russia: Rodionov: Russia's Defense Almost Breached'.

64 Kipp, 1999:1 (EV).

65 Arbatov, 1997, pp. 7–8.

66 *Mirovaia ekonomika I mezhdunarodnye otnosheniia*, no. 4, 1997, pp. 5–21, FBIS–UMA–97–136-S, 17 July 197: 'Russia: Arbatov: Military Reform: Doctrine, Troops'.

67 TASS, 4 April 1992.

68 Herspring, 1996, p. 175.

69 *International Herald Tribune*, 8 May 1992.

70 Herspring, 1996, p. 169.

71 ibid. p. 170.

72 ibid. pp. 175–6.

73 ibid. pp. 172–3.

74 Mayak Radio Network, 23 January 1997, FBIS-SOV–97–015, 23 January 1997: 'Russia: Siberian Military Commander Cites Catastrophe in Funding'.

75 ITAR-TASS, 29 May 1997, FBIS-UMA–97–149, 29 May 1997: 'Russia: Siberian Military Commander Resigns on Health Grounds'.

76 Moscow TV, 23 November 1997, FBIS-SOV–97–327, 23 November 1997: 'Russia: Prosecutor Surprised at Scale of Abuse in Russian Army'.

77 NTV, 14 August 1997, translated in FBIS-UMA–97–226, 14 August 1997: 'Russia: Sergeyev Continues Inspection of Siberian Troops'.

78 ITAR-TASS World Service, 11 February 1998, translated in FBIS-UMA–98–042, 11 February 1998: 'Russia: Siberian Base Hit by Power Cut During Training'.

79 Moscow NTV, 6 February 1998, FBIS-UMA–98–044, 13 February 1998: 'Russia: Power Cut Leaves Border with China Unprotected'.

80 NTV, 22 January 1998, translated in FBIS-UMA–98–022, 22 January 1998: 'Russia: Russia's NTV on Reaction to Military Reform in Siberia'.

81 Vladimir Nikolaevich Yakovlev, 'Under Conditions of Limited Funding: The Future Look of the Integrated Strategic Missile Troops', *Nezavisimoe voennoe obozrenie*, 22–28 May 1998, No. 19, p. 4, FBIS-SOV 98 188, 7 July 1998: 'Russia. Yakovlev: RVSN under Limited Financing'.

82 Shlykov, 1997, p. 13.

83 Herspring, 1996, p. 170.

84 *Washington Post*, 5 February 1993.

85 *Aviation Week & Space Technology*, 5 October 1992.

86 Herspring, 1996, p 171.

87 ibid. p. 174.

88 Shlykov, 1997, p. 12.

89 Krasnov (ed.), 1996, p. 170.

90 ibid.

91 Herspring, 1996, p. 174.

92 IISS, *Strategic Survey 1996/97*, p. 126
93 *Vooruzhenie, politika, konversiia*, no. 14, 1996, pp. 13–15, FBIS-SOV–97-161-S, 20 August 1997: 'Russia: Russia Lacks Money to Support an Army'.
94 Mikhail Zubov, 'Army Pyramid', *Trud*, 22 July 1997, p. 2, FBIS-UMA–97-204, 23 July 1997: 'Russia: Total Wage Arrears to Military over 8 Trillion Rubles'.
95 Shlykov, 1997, p. 14.
96 *Mirovaia ekonomika I mezhdunarodnye otnosheniia*, no. 4, 1997, pp. 5–21, FBIS-UMA–97-136-S, 17 July 197: 'Russia: Arbatov: Military Reform: Doctrine, Troops'.
97 'Voennyi biudzhet—1999 ostaiotsia nesovershennym' [Defence Budget—1999 Remains Incomplete], *Nezavisimoe voennoe obozrenie*, no. 11, 1999, p. 4.
98 *Krasnaia zvezda*, 20 April 1999, p. 1.
99 Sergei Mikhailovich Rogov, 'Russia and Nuclear Weapons', *Nezavisimoe voennoe obozrenie*, 11–17 December 1998, no. 47, p. 4, FBIS-UMA–98-351, 17 December 1998: 'Russia: Support for SNF Reforms, START–2'.
100 Russian forces were withdrawn from Hungary and Czechoslovakia in 1991, Poland in 1992, Lithuania in 1993, Estonia, Latvia and Germany in 1994. In Moldova, Russian military units were dissolved in 1995 rather than withdrawn. The withdrawals included Cuba in 1992, where a brigade of ground forces (1500 troops) had been stationed since the Cuban missile crisis in 1962.
101 Fiodorov, 1998 (EV).
102 Presidential Edict on Priority Measures for the Reform of the Armed Forces of the Russian Federation and the Improvement of their Structure, No. 725s, 16 July 1997.
103 Interview with Head of the Main Operations Directorate of the General Staff, *Krasnaia zvezda*, 3 November 1998 (EV).
104 NTV, 22 January 1998, translated in FBIS-UMA–98-022, 22 January 1998: 'Russia: Russia's NTV on Reaction to Military Reform in Siberia'.
105 Vadim Makarevsky, 'Phases of Military Reform in Russia', *FSU: 15 Nations: Policy and Security*, November 1997, p. 5.
106 Anatoly Kvashnin, 'Restructuring on Suvorov's Principles', *Nezavisimoe voennoe obozrenie*, no. 26, 17–23 July 1998, pp. 1–2, FBIS-UMA–98-209, 28 July 1998: 'Russia: Kvashnin on Military Reform, Progress'.
107 ibid.
108 Presidential Edict on the Ministry of Defence of the Russian Federation and the General Staff of the Armed Forces of the Russian Federation, No. 1357, 11 November 1998; and an associated protocol on the General Staff of the Armed Forces of the Russian Federation.
109 Reuters, 10 February 1999.
110 Makarevsky, 'Phases of Military Reform in Russia', p. 5.
111 IISS, *The Military Balance 1998/99*, 1997. Unless otherwise indicated, all information in this book on strengths, deployments and

structure of the Russian armed forces is taken from relevant annual issues of *The Military Balance*. The International Institute for Strategic Studies (IISS) takes a number of steps to confirm the accuracy of its information, including where possible checking with intelligence information available to a number of governments. Some data in *The Military Balance* is therefore not up to date or reliable. Where possible, this book has sought other sources of information, and where there are major differences with IISS information, this will be indicated. In the case of numerical strength of the branches of the Russian armed forces, information elsewhere is slightly different. For example, IISS holds the strength of the navy in 1997 at 220 000 while the Japanese Defense Agency (JDA) holds navy strength in 1997 at 190 000. The JDA cites for its source, IISS 'and others'. The difference between the JDA and IISS figures represents a 1.5 percentage difference, which is probably not significant in an estimate of peacetime strength. If the difference was accounted for by lower manning levels in naval strategic nuclear forces, that could be more significant. IISS holds the personnel strength of naval nuclear forces at 13 000.

112 *Mirovaia ekonomika I mezhdunarodnye otnosheniia*, no. 4, 1997, pp. 5–21, FBIS-UMA–97–136-S, 17 July 1997: 'Russia: Arbatov: Military Reform: Doctrine, Troops'. The author said that there were 900 000 civilians employed by the Ministry of Defence.

113 The Russian name is *Ministerstvo vnutrennykh del* (MVD).

114 The Russian name is *Federal'naia Pogranichnaia Sliuzhba* (FPS).

115 IISS, *The Military Balance 1998/99*.

116 Russian name is *Federal'naia Sliuzhba Bezopasnosti* (FSB).

117 IISS, *The Military Balance 1997/98*.

118 Makarevsky, 'Phases of Military Reform in Russia', p. 7.

119 *Vechernyi Novosibirsk*, 30 January 95, p. 4, FBIS-SOV–95–005, 30 January 95: 'Lt-Gen Mayorov on Situation of Siberian Troops Fighting in Chechnia'.

120 ITAR-TASS, 3 August 1998.

121 *Rossiiskaia gazeta*, 23 September 1998, p. 3.

122 ITAR-TASS, 3 August 1998.

123 ITAR-TASS, 30 March 1998, FBIS-UMA–98–089, 30 March 1998: 'Russia: Russia's Orenburg Cossack Troops Now Subordinate to State'.

124 Herspring, 1996, p. 173.

125 Sarah Brown, 1997, p. 62.

126 Interfax, 12 August 1998, FBIS-UMA–98–224, 12 August 1998: 'Russia: Sergeyev Doubts Transfer to Professional Army by 2000'.

127 *Mirovaia ekonomika i mezhdunarodnye otnosheniia*, no. 4, 1997, pp. 5–21, FBIS-UMA–97–136-S, 17 July 1997: 'Russia: Arbatov: Military Reform: Doctrine, Troops'.

128 Makarevsky, 'Phases of Military Reform in Russia', p. 4.

129 Oleg Falichev, 'Boevaia uchioba—Glavnyi kriterii zhizni voisk' [Combat Training—The Main Criterion of Military Life], *Krasnaia zvezda*, 8 December 1998 (EV).

130 Aleksei Arbatov, *Nezavisimoe voennoe obozrenie*, 13–19 March 1998,

p. 5, FBIS-UMA–98–079, 20 March 1998: 'Russia: Economics of Switch to Contract Assessed'.

131 ITAR-TASS, 16 April 1998.

132 *Krasnaia zvezda*, 19 September 1998 (EV).

133 Valdimir Mukhin, 'Rank and File', *Nezavisimoe voennoe obozrenie*, 29 January–4 February 1998, no. 3, p. 1, FBIS-SOV–1999–0215: 'Mukhin: Results of Conscription Drive'.

134 Sergei Sokut, 'Military Scientists Discussed Reform', *Nezavisimoe voennoe obozrenie*, 13–19 February 1998, no. 6, p. 3, FBIS-UMA–98–049, 18 February 1998: 'Russia: Army Paper Welcomes Kulikov Reform Blueprint'.

135 Donnelly, 1995.

136 Tatiana Yermolaeva and Vladimir Georgiev, 'Neprikosnovennyi zapas ili poslednii rezerv?', *Nezavisimoe voennoe obozrenie*, 5 March 1999 (EV).

137 ITAR-TASS, 7 March 1999.

138 Kvashnin, 'Restructuring on Suvorov's Principles'.

139 ibid.

140 *Military News Bulletin*, vol. 6, June 1996 and vol. 10, October 1996.

141 This indicates that new strategic principles were tested in the MDs responsible for the defence of the western districts which could be involved in possible armed conflict with NATO forces. KOR stands for *Kaliningradsky osobyi raion* (Kaliningrad Special District), a special military administrative entity, directly subordinated to the General Staff of the Armed Forces of the Russian Federation.

142 'On the Priority Measures to Reform the Armed Forces of the Russian Federation and Improve Their Structure', *Rossiiskaya gazeta*, 19 July 1997.

143 Mikhail Khodarenko, 'Russia Is Not Prepared for Future Military Challenges', *Nezavisimoe voennoe obozrenie*, 13–19 November 1998, no. 43, pp. 1, 4, FBIS-UMA–98–334, 30 November 1998: 'Russia: High Command Problems Threaten Combat Readiness'.

144 Kvashnin, 'Restructuring on Suvorov's Principles'.

145 ibid.

146 Aleksandr Chukanov, 'Pulse of Reforms', *Armeiiskii sbornik*, March 1998, no. 3, pp. 44–47, FBIS-SOV–98–159, 8 June 1998: 'Russia: Proposals for Improving RF Armed Forces Logistic Systems'.

147 'Rossiia unichtozhit svoi khimicheskie arsenaly' [Russia is Destroying its Chemical Arsenal], *Krasnaia zvezda*, 20 March 1999, p. 1.

148 Barbara Starr, 'USA Projects Conflicting Vision for Russian Forces', *Jane's Defence Weekly*, 21 August 1996, p. 12.

149 Oleg Lisov, 'Khimooruzhie: Rossii nuzhno prodlit' sroki vypolneniia konventsii', Chemical Weapons: Russia Must Extend the Deadline for Implementation *Krasnaia zvezda*, 10 April 1999, p. 3.

150 Vadim Maiatski, 'Higher School: Development and Prospects', *Armeiiskii sbornik*, June 1997 no. 6, pp. 64–8, FBIS-SOV–97–158-S, 1 June 1997: 'Russia: Lt.-Gen. Koriakin on Affairs of Military Academy of Chemical Defense'.

151 See Richard Preston, 'Annals of Warfare: The Bioweaponeers', *New*

Yorker, 9 March 1998, printed in the Record of the US Senate, 12 March 1998.

152 For more information see United States, Department of Defense. *Soviet Military Power 1984*, Washington DC, 1984, p. 73.

153 'Biologicheskogo Oruzhia v Rossii Net' [Russia Does Not Have Biological Weapons], *Krasnaia zvezda*, 15 July 1999, p. 2.

154 Anthrax or *Bacillus anthracis* is the most 'famous' bacterial weapon. See Beckett, 1983, pp. 111–25.

155 Vladimir Mukhin, 'Minoborony sdelalo stavku na grazhdanskie vuzy' [The MOD is Banking on Civil Colleges], *Nezavisimoe voennoe obozrenie*, no. 10, 1999, p. 3.

156 Interfax, 5 August 1997.

157 Interfax, 7 April 1997.

158 Arbatov, 1997, pp. 8–9.

159 *Washington Post*, 2 July 1992.

160 Interview with Sergeyev, *Der Spiegel*, 26 January 1998, pp. 118–19, FBIS-UMA–98–026, 26 January 1998: 'Russia: Defense Minister Views Army Reform, NATO Expansion'.

161 Vladimir Georgiyev, 'Effektivnyi instrument gosudarstva' [Effective Instrument of the State], *Nezavisimoe voennoe obozrenie*, 9 October 1998, No. 38 (EV).

162 IISS, *The Military Balance 1995/96*, p. 104.

163 Makarevsky, 'Phases of Military Reform in Russia', p. 5.

164 Abarinov, 'Moscow Reconciled to NATO Expansion, But Still Threatens "Adequate Reply Measures"', Segodnia, 1 October 1996.

165 *Ria Novosti*, 22 May 1997.

166 On 1 February 1997, the 11th Guards Army of the KOR was formally disbanded. All its units were transferred to the Baltic Fleet. *Morskoi sbornik*, no. 12, 1997, p. 26. See also *Morskoi sbornik*, no. 1, 1998, p. 25; no. 2, 1998, p. 29.

167 Ilia Kedrov and Sergei Sokut, 'Vozdushnyi Most na zapad' [Air Bridge to the West], *Nezavisimoe voennoe obozrenie*, 26 March–1 April 1999, p. 3.

168 Col.-Gen. Piotr Deniekin, 'Reform of the Air Force is a Must', *Military News Bulletin*, vol. 8, August 1996.

169 *Morskoi sbornik*, no. 1, 1996, p. 35; no. 2, 1996, p. 39.

170 See *Jane's Defence Weekly*, 28 March 1992, p. 503.

171 *Jane's Fighting Ships 1997–98*, p. 560.

172 ibid. p. 565.

173 ibid. p. 568.

174 ibid. p. 570.

175 ibid. p. 562.

176 Valentin Kunin, 'Russia Will Never be First to Use Nukes—Unless It Has To', *Ria Novosti*, 14 May 1997.

177 Vladimir Mukhin, 'Minoborony ukrepliaet zapadnye rubiozhi' [The MOD Strengthens the Western Borders], *Nezavisimoe voennoe obozrenie*, no. 14, 1999, p. 1.

178 For details, see Interfax, 3 September 1998, FBIS-UMA–98–246, 3 September 1998: 'Russia: Russia Reduces Army Groups in Northwest'.

179 Interfax, 20 March 1998, citing the Head of the Main Operations Directorate of the General Staff, Colonel General Yurii Baluyevskii.
180 *Military Balance, 1998/99.*
181 Vadim Soloviov, Sergei Sokut, and Nikolai Ivanov, 'Na Severnyi Kavkaz pala ten' vtoroi chechenskoi voiny' [The Shadow of the Second Chechen War is Falling on the North Caucasus], *Nezavisimoe voennoe obozrenie,* 12 March 1999 (EV); Vladimir Mukhin, 'Voisk men'she, a zadachi slozhneye' [The Forces are Smaller, but the Tasks Are More Difficult], *Nezavisimoe voennoe obozrenie,* no. 11, 1999, p. 1.
182 Kvashnin, 'Restructuring on Suvorov's Principles'.
183 ibid.
184 NTV, 22 January 1998, translated in FBIS-UMA–98–022, 22 January 1998: 'Russia: Russia's NTV on Reaction to Military Reform in Siberia'.
185 *Sovietskaia sibir',* 23 February 1996, p. 2, FBIS-UMA–96–060-S, 23 February 1996: 'Russia: Siberian MD Commander Interviewed'.
186 Zagorsky, 1997, p. 39. The other three were Moscow, Leningrad and North Caucasus.
187 Aleksei Popov, 'Okrug rasshiraet vladeniia' [The District Expands its Realm], *Krasnaia zvezda,* 24 November 1998, p. 2.
188 Valeryi Shcheblanin, 'Uchatsia komandiry polkov' [Regimental Commanders Are Learning], *Krasnaia zvezda,* 11 January 1999.
189 Oleg Falichev, 'Privolzhskii I Ural'skii voennye okruga gotoviatsia k ob'edineneiiu' [Trans-Volga and Urals Military Districts Prepare to Unify], *Krasnaia zvezda,* 27 February 1999, p. 1.
190 Admiral I. Kasatonov, 'Kamchatskoe Napravlenie' [Kamchatka Front], *Morskoi sbornik,* no. 7, 1998, pp. 5–6.
191 'No Troop Cuts on Kamchatka Peninsula, Says Gen. Rodionov', *Jane's Defence Weekly,* 23 October 1996, p. 13.
192 Sergei Boeikov, 'Kamchatka: Novaia sistema upravleniia voiskami' [Kamchatka: a New System of Force Management], *Krasnaia zvezda,* 21 March 1998, p. 1.
193 ibid.
194 'Na Kamchatskom napravlenii' [On Kamchatka Front], *Krasnaia zvezda,* 31 January 1998, p. 1.
195 Andrei Kurnaiev, 'Kamchatskii rubezh' [Kamchatka Boundary], *Krasnaia zvezda,* 27 August 1998, p. 2.
196 *Sbor-pokhod* is a new form of naval training discussed in chapter 7 on the navy.
197 Sergei Boeikov, 'Sobrannye v edinyi kulak' [Folded into a Single Fist], *Krasnaia zvezda,* 17 September 1998, p. 1.

6   Nuclear forces

1 This comment was made at a conference on 'The Soviet Estimate, 1950–1984' at Harvard University in December 1994 by a former CIA analyst.
2 For more information see 'Osnovnye polozhenia voennoi doktriny

Rossiiskoi Federatsii' [Basic Provisions of the Military Doctrine of the Russian Federation], *Krasnaia zvezda*, 19 November 1993, pp. 1–2.

3 See Barbara Starr, 'Russia Is Still Preparing For War with USA', *Jane's Defence Weekly*, 16 December 1995, p. 5. While Russia and the USA have reached agreement on detargeting nuclear missiles previously aimed at each other, this is judged by most military analysts to be militarily insignificant because they can be retargeted almost immediately.

4 *Krasnaia zvezda*, 13 March 1998, p. 1.

5 Vladimir Nikolaevich Yakovlev, 'The SMF's Special Mission', *Armeiskii sbornik*, May 1997, pp. 36–41, FBIS-SOV–97–137-S, 1 May 1997: 'Russia: Col-Gen V. N. Yakovlev: Chief on Priority Role of Missile Forces in State Security'.

6 Arbatov, 1997, p. 11.

7 See FitzGerald, 1994, p. 469.

8 'Russia May Use N-Arms First in Fight, Says Official', *Straits Times*, 12 February 1997, p. 1.

9 ibid.

10 Anatoly Pankov, 'Man with a Gun', *Kuranty*, 21–27 May 1997, no. 20, p. 10, FBIS-UMA–97–136, 27 May 1997: 'Russia: Problems of Russian Strategic Missile Troops Command Centre'.

11 NRDC Nuclear Notebook, 'Russian Strategic Nuclear Forces, End of 1998', *Bulletin of the Atomic Scientist*, March/April 1999, p. 63. Counting rules of the Strategic Arms Limitation Treaty (START) are applied.

12 In Russian, *Raketnye Voiska Strategicheskogo Naznachenia*.

13 In Russian, *Voenno-Kosmicheskie Sily*.

14 In Russian, *Raketno-Kosmicheskaia Oborona*.

15 'O pervoocherednykh merakh po reformirovaniu vooruzhennykh sil Rossiiskoi Federatsii i sovershenstvovanii ikh struktury' [On Priority Measures to Reform the Armed Forces of the Russian Federation and Improve Their Structure], *Rossiiskaia gazeta*, 19 July 1997, p. 5.

16 Anatoly Pankov, 'Man with a Gun', *Kuranty*, 21–27 May 1997, no. 20, p. 10, FBIS-UMA–97–136, 27 May 1997: 'Russia: Problems of Russian Strategic Missile Troops Command Centre'.

17 'Integratsia RVSN, VKS i Voisk RKO–ne prosto mekchanicheskoe ob'edinenie sil' [Integration of the SMF, Military-Space Forces and Missile-Space Defence Troops is Not Just Mechanical Unification of Forces], *Krasnaia zvezda*, 18 February 1998, p. 2.

18 Aleksandr Gol'ts, 'Voennaia reforma: god pervyi' [Military Reform: The First Year], www.intellectualcapital.ru, accessed 15 March 1999.

19 'Integratsia RVSN, VKS i Voisk RKO'.

20 *Ria Novosti*, 6 June 1998.

21 Sorokin, 1994, p. 28.

22 Sergei Mikhailovich Rogov, 'Russia and Nuclear Weapons', *Nezavisimoe voennoe obozrenie*, 11–17 December 1998, no. 47, p. 4, FBIS-UMA–98–351, 17 December 1998: 'Russia: Support for SNF Reforms, START–2'.

23 NATO classification SS–18 *Satan*.

24 This table is from NRDC Nuclear Notebook, 'Russian Strategic Nuclear Forces, End of 1998', *The Bulletin of the Atomic Scientist*, March/April 1999, p. 63. Counting rules of the Strategic Arms Limitation Treaty (START) are applied.

25 Vladimir Nikolaevich Yakovlev, 'Under Conditions of Limited Funding: The Future Look of the Integrated Strategic Missile Troops', *Nezavisimoe voennoe obozrenie*, 22–28 May 1998, no. 19, p. 4, FBIS-SOV–98–188, 7 July 1998: 'Russia: Yakovlev: RVSN under Limited Financing'.

26 The division is a single base in the SMF.

27 Vladimir Nikolaevich Yakovlev, 'The SMF's Special Mission', *Armeiskii sbornik*, May 1997, pp. 36–41, FBIS-SOV–97–137-S, 1 May 1997: 'Russia: Col-Gen V. N. Yakovlev: Chief on Priority Role of Missile Forces in State Security'.

28 *Jane's Defence Weekly*, 25 June 1994, p. 32.

29 'Novye orbity "Satany"' [New Orbits of Satan], *Krasnaia zvezda*, 22 April 1999, p. 1.

30 Sergei Mikhailovich Rogov, 'Russia and Nuclear Weapons', *Nezavisimoe voennoe obozrenie*, 11–17 December 1998, no. 47, p. 4, FBIS-UMA–98–351, 17 December 1998: 'Russia: Support for SNF Reforms, START–2'.

31 Mikhail Yumashev, 'K armii XXI veka', *Krasnaia zvezda*, 18 February 1999 (EV).

32 Vladimir Nikolaevich Yakovlev, 'Under Conditions of Limited Funding: The Future Look of the Integrated Strategic Missile Troops', *Nezavisimoe voennoe obozrenie*, 22–28 May 1998, no. 19, p. 4, FBIS-SOV–98–188, 7 July 1998: 'Russia: Yakovlev: RVSN under Limited Financing'.

33 Vladimir Georgiev, '"Topolei" Stanet Bol'she' [There Will Be More Topols], *Nezavisimoe Voennoe Obozrenie*, N 29 1999, p. 3; Yuri Gavrilov, 'Novogo Oruzhia Budet Bol'she' [There Will be More New Weapons], *Krasnaia Zvezda*, 21 July 1999, p. 1.

34 Viacheslav Bezborodov, '12 April—Cosmonautics Day', *Armeiskii sbornik*, April 1997, no. 4, pp. 34–8, FBIS-SOV–97–157-S, 1 April 1997: 'Russia: Today's Problems of Russian Cosmonautics'.

35 'Novye orbity "Kosmos v pogonakh"' [New Orbits: Space in Epaulets], *Krasnaia zvezda*, 14 April 1998, p. 1.

36 'Kliuch k pobede–na orbite', *Nezavisimoe voennoe obozrenie*, 12 February 1999 (EV).

37 'Novye orbity "Satany"'.

38 ibid.

39 Vladimir Nikolaevich Yakovlev, 'The SMF's Special Mission', *Armeiskii sbornik*, May 1997, pp. 36–41, FBIS-SOV–97–137-S, 1 May 1997: 'Russia: Col-Gen V. N. Yakovlev: Chief on Priority Role of Missile Forces in State Security'.

40 Forrow et al., 1998.

41 ibid.

42 Vladimir Nikolaevich Yakovlev, 'The SMF's Special Mission', *Armeiskii sbornik*, May 1997, pp. 36–41, FBIS-SOV–97–137-S, 1 May

1997: 'Russia: Col-Gen V. N. Yakovlev: Chief on Priority Role of Missile Forces in State Security'.

43 Sergei Sokut, 'Novye *Topolia* poluchat iadernye boegolovki' [New Topols Will Receive Nuclear Warheads], *Krasnaia zvezda*, 16 December 1998, p. 2.

44 Anatoly Pankov, 'Man with a Gun', *Kuranty*, 21–27 May 1997, no. 20, p. 10, FBIS-UMA–97–136, 27 May 1997: 'Russia: Problems of Russian Strategic Missile Troops Command Centre'. This report cited the Minister of Defence on this point during a visit for journalists to the SMF command centre at Vlasikha.

45 *Krasnaia zvezda*, 24 January 1998, p. 1.

46 Forrow et al., 1998.

47 ibid.

48 Reuters, 10 February 1999.

49 Sorokin, 1994, p. 28.

50 NATO classification SS–24 *Scalpel*.

51 See Wilkening, 1998, pp. 92–3.

52 Nikolai Poroskov, 'Tri deviatki posle zapiatoi' [Triple Nine after Comma], *Krasnaia zvezda*, 29 May 1998, p. 2.

53 NATO classification SS–27.

54 Colonel Alexandr Dolinin, 'V iadernom karaule' [On Nuclear Guard], *Krasnaia zvezda*, 21 April 1998, p. 2.

55 Igor Korotchenko, 'Zavtra na boevoe derzhurstvo budet postavleny desiat' novykh strategicheskikh raket *Topol-M*' [Ten New Topol-M Strategic Missiles Will be Put on Station Tomorrow], *Nezavisimaia gazeta*, 29 December 1998, pp. 1–2.

56 NRDC Nuclear Notebook, 1999, p. 63. Counting rules of the Strategic Arms Limitation Treaty (START) are applied.

57 Igor Korotchenko, 'Zavtra na boevoe derzhurstvo budet postavleny desiat' novykh strategicheskikh raket *Topol-M*'; and interview with Sergei Rogov, 'Na povestke dnia—stratgeicheskaia stabil'nost' [Strategic Stability is on the Table], *Krasnaia zvezda*, 11 March 1999, pp. 1–2.

58 Dmitry Litovkin, 'Gordost RVSN—Topol-M' [*Topol-M* is the Pride of the SMF], *Krasnaia zvezda*, 24 February 1998, p. 4.

59 *Ria Novosti*, 19 February 1998.

60 NRDC Nuclear Notebook, 1999, p. 63. Counting rules of the Strategic Arms Limitation Treaty (START) are applied.

61 USIS, 'US–Russian Agreement on Reducing Strategic Arms', 7 July 1992.

62 'Nel'zia dal'she zatiagivat' ratifikatsiu Dogovora SNV–2' [It is Wrong to Further Prevent the Ratification of the START-II Treaty], *Krasnaia zvezda*, 29 May 1998, p. 1.

63 NRDC Nuclear Notebook, 1999, p. 63.

64 Sorokin, 1994, pp. 29–33.

65 Muraviev, 1998, p. 5.

66 'Nel'zia dal'she zatiagivat' ratifikatsiu Dogovora SNV–2', p. 3.

67 Interfax, 11 November 1998, citing the Chief of the General Staff.

68 Vladimir Mariukha, 'SNV–2: Vypolniv etot dogovor, Rossiia stanet

silnee' [START–II: Russia Will Become Stronger By Fulfilling This Treaty], *Krasnaia zvezda*, 9 June 1998, p. 3.

69 Igor Korotchenko, 'Funding of Strategic Nuclear Forces Will be Guaranteed by Law', *Nezavisimoe voennoe obozrenie*, 6–12 November 1998, pp. 1, 3, FBIS-UMA–98–313, 9 November 1998: 'Russia: Draft Law on Strategic N-Forces Outlined'.

70 Sergei Mikhailovich Rogov, 'Russia and Nuclear Weapons', *Nezavisimoe voennoe obozrenie*, 11–17 December 1998, no. 47, p. 4, FBIS-UMA–98–351, 17 December 1998: 'Russia: Support for SNF Reforms, START–2'.

71 Arbatov, 1997, p. 4.

72 Forrow et al., 1998.

73 Sergei Mikhailovich Rogov, 'Russia and Nuclear Weapons', *Nezavisimoe voennoe obozrenie*, 11–17 December 1998, no. 47, p. 4, FBIS-UMA–98–351, 17 December 1998: 'Russia: Support for SNF Reforms, START–2'.

74 ibid.

75 In Russian, *dal'niaia aviatsia*.

76 The numerical strength of the LRA in 1998 was approximately 3000 personnel, down from 25 000 in 1992.

77 'Kiev–Moscow Talks Resume on Cash Dispute', *Jane's Defence Weekly*, 18 March 1998, p. 6.

78 *Ria Novosti*, 18 June 1997.

79 'Tochka v spore o sudbe samoletov' [The Final Point in the Argument About the Fate of the Aircraft], *Krasnaia zvezda*, 14 May 1998, p. 2.

80 Sergei Sokut, 'Vzaimovygodnaia Rokirovka' [Mutually Beneficial Exchange], *Nezavisimoe Voennoe Obozrenie*, no. 29 1999, p. 3.

81 Sergei Sokut, 'Szhimaetsia iaderny kulak' [Nuclear Fist is Condensing], *Nezavisimaya gazeta*, 21 October 1998, p. 1.

82 P. L. Podvig, *Strategicheskoe iadernoe vooruzhenie Rossii*, p. 303; 'Vozdushnye ratniki iz engelsa' [Air Warriors from Engels], *Krasnaia zvezda*, 15 May 1998, p. 1. The Tu–160, the world's largest bomber, is named by the Russians *Ilia Muromets* in memory of the famous Russian heavy bomber *Ilia Muromets* from the First World War.

83 IISS, *The Military Balance 1998–99*, pp. 108–12. Piotr Butowski, 'Bear Successor Will Enter Service after 2010', *Jane's Defence Weekly*, 9 September 1998, p. 17. Western military analysts estimate that Russia's current strategic bomber force comprises 70 aircraft, not 75, as Russian sources report.

84 'Perspectivy Dalnei Aviatsii' [The Future of Long-Range Aviation], *Krasnaia zvezda*, 5 March 1998, p. 2.

85 In Russian, *Vozdushnaia Armiia Verkhovnogo Glavonogo Kommandovania (Strategicheskogo Naznachenia)* or VA VGK (SN).

86 In Russian, *Upravlenie Vozdushnoi Armii*. See 'Ne teriat temp reform, zavershit nachatoe', p. 2.

87 Podvig (ed.), *Strategicheskoe iadernoe vooruzhenie Rossii*, pp. 303–304. In more recent sources, the 73rd Division in Ukrainka is identified as the 326th Division. See Ilia Kedrov, 'Vozdushnyi brosok na zapad', *Nezavisimoe voennoe obozrenie*, no. 12, 1999, p. 7.

88 Podvig (ed.), *Strategicheskoe iadernoe vooruzhenie Rossii*, p. 304; Valentin Rog, 'VVS Dolzhnyi ostat'sia edinymi', *Nezavisimoe voennoe obozrenie*, no. 12, 1999, p. 7.

89 Sergei Babichev, 'Strategi pod osobym kontrolem' [Strategists' Under Special Control], *Krasnaia zvezda*, 7 February 1998, p. 1.

90 'Strategic Bomber Numbers Cut in Russian Reshuffle', *Jane's Defence Weekly*, 29 April 1998, p. 13.

91 Dean A. Wilkening, an expert on Russia's strategic forces, estimated that existing Russian strategic aircraft can last for approximately another 20 years (if properly maintained), leaving Russia with a bomber force of 64 aircraft by the year 2015. Wilkening, 1998, pp. 99–101.

92 'Perspectivy Dalnei Aviatsii', p. 2.

93 *Ria Novosti*, 18 June 1997.

94 'Ne teriat temp reform, zavershit nachatoe', p. 2.

95 Due to the chronic shortage of money for R&D, it would be a surprise to see a new strategic bomber deployed within the LRA before 2010. See Butowski, '*Bear* Successor Will Enter Service after 2010'.

96 Podvig (ed.), '*Stratigecheskoe iadernoe vooruzhenie Rossii*', p. 300.

97 V. Georgiev, '"Topolei" Stanet Bolshe', p. 3.

98 Piotr Bukowski, 'Sukhoi Takes Back Seat as "Backfire" is Upgraded', *Jane's Defence Weekly*, 29 January 1997, p. 5.

99 The assumption can be made that ageing *Backfire-B*s will be taken out of service and scrapped. An exception will be made for naval *Backfires*. The plan is to re-equip them with a new-generation air-to-surface missile.

100 The annual average flying hours for pilots in the LRA in 1997 was 30.

101 Sergei Babichev and Nikolai Baranov, 'Armiia "Dolgorukikh" snova v boiu' [Army of the 'Dolgorukhi' Again in Battle], *Krasnaia zvezda*, 9 October 1998, p. 1.

102 'Vozdushnye ratniki iz Engelsa', p. 1.

103 Babichev and Baranov, 'Armiia "Dolgorukikh" snova v boiu', p. 1.

104 Baranov and Babichev, 'VVS: chto udalos za god', p. 1.

105 Name in Russia is *Ob'edinionnoe Glavnoe Komandovanie Strategicheskikh Sil Sderzhivaniia*.

106 'Na povestke dnia—strategicheskaia stabilnost'.

107 Sergei Sokut, 'Prioitctnyi Gosinteres Rossii' [Russia's Priority State Interest], *Nezavisimoe voennoe obozrenie*, no. 17, 1999, p. 1.

108 *Washington Post*, 5 February 1993.

109 'Osnova voennoi moshchi Rossii', *Krasnaia zvezda*, 30 April 1999. See also Igor Korotchenko, 'Otechestvennyi iadernyi kompleks razvalivaetsia' [The National Nuclear Complex is Collapsing], *Nezavisimaia gazeta*, 30 April 1999, p. 2. One of the other two decrees signed concerned development of the experimental base of Russia nuclear complex.

110 'Iz Kremlia. Garant bezopasnosti', *Krasnaia zvezda*, 16 March 1999.

111 Vladimir Semenovich Belous, 'With Robert McNamara and Makhmut Gareyev', *Nezavisimoe voennoe obozrenie*, 30 January–5 February 1999,

p. 4, FBIS-UMA–98–355, 21 December 1998: 'Russia: Role of Nuclear Weapons Viewed'.

112 Sergei Mikhailovich Rogov, 'Russia and Nuclear Weapons', *Nezavisimoe voennoe obozrenie*, 11–17 December 1998, no. 47, p. 4, FBIS-UMA–98–351, 17 December 1998: 'Russia: Support for SNF Reforms, START–2'.

113 *Segodnia*, 20 October 1995.

114 *Ria Novosti*, 24 May 1997.

115 Korotchenko, 'Otechestvennyi iadernyi kompleks razvalivaetsia'.

116 Mikhailov, Vtishin and Chernyshov, 'NATO's Expansion and Russia's Security'.

117 ITAR-TASS, 21 November 1995.

7 Naval forces

1 In the late nineteenth century, Russia's navy maintained a strong and visible presence in the Pacific, prompting concerns as far away as Australia that Russia might use its naval power in anger against the British colony. In 1904–05, Japan was forced to defeat the Russian navy in order to fulfil its expansionist policies in North Asia.

2 In this context, 'maritime activities' includes the merchant marine, fishing industry, research and shipbuilding activities.

3 Booth, 1993, p. 158.

4 Singh, 1993, p. 545.

5 Kelly, 1993, p. 31.

6 Bateman, 1993, p. 37.

7 In 1968, a special naval formation, a squadron, was formed for operations in the Indian Ocean. Subordinated to the Pacific Fleet, this unit was known by the acronym SOVINDRON (Soviet Indian Ocean Squadron) by Western analysts.

8 In 1979, Vietnam granted the USSR access to the naval port of Cam Ranh Bay, where the USSR subsequently developed its largest foreign military installation outside of the Warsaw Pact. At no stage however did this facility compare in size or mission to the US facilities at Subic Bay naval base or Clark Air Base in the Philippines.

9 Soviet and Russian sources described the Pacific theatre as a Maritime Theatre of Military Action (MTVD—*morskoi teatr voennykh deistvii*).

10 Jukes, 1975, pp. 308–9.

11 See *Jane's Fighting Ships 1998–99*, Jane's Information Group, 1998.

12 MccGwire, 1990, p. 212.

13 Kensuke Ebata, 'CIS Spells Out Defensive Plan', *Jane's Defence Weekly*, 20 June 1992, p. 1050.

14 ibid. p. 836.

15 ibid.

16 *Morskoi sbornik* [Naval Digest], no. 6, 1996, p. 7.

17 Rear-Admiral (ret.) G. Kostev, 'Mysli po povodu reform na Flote'

[Thoughts About the Reform of the Navy], *Morskoi sbornik*, no. 4, 1998, p. 9.

18 *Australian Aviation*, no. 126, March 1997, p. 11.

19 After the collapse of the USSR and the establishment of the CIS, about one-third of the naval shipyard capacity of the former Soviet Union became the property of Ukraine.

20 Garthoff, 1992, p. 62.

21 *Morskoi sbornik*, no. 4, 1997, p. 10.

22 For comparison, in 1990 although the Pacific Fleet had a modern and very capable guided missile destroyer for anti-submarine warfare—the *Udaloi* class—it also had at least three other types of major surface combatants which could perform similar tasks: *Kara* class and *Kresta*-II guided missile cruisers, and the *Kashin* class guided missile destroyer.

23 Captain 1st Rank S. Topichev, 'Kakoi flot my imeli i kak ego nado reformirovat' segodnia' [What Fleet We Had and How It Should be Reformed Today], *Morskoi sbornik*, no. 12, 1996, p. 13.

24 Captain 1st Rank U. Poliakov, 'Stoyanka avianosnykh kreiserov na reide' [The Basing of Aircraft-Carrying Cruisers in Harbour], *Morskoi sbornik*, no. 6, 1994, p. 40.

25 This is the calculation offered in the Soviet-era publication *Otkuda iskhodit ugroza miry* [Whence the Threat to Peace], 3rd edn, Moscow, Voenizdat, 1984, p. 80. This publication was first and foremost a propaganda document published in response to the US Defense Department series on Soviet Military Power, a similarly propagandist document. Nevertheless, the calculation that US naval forces were significantly superior to those of the USSR is one that the authors of this book accept easily. It is a judgement shared by a number of US naval officers who had studied the Soviet Navy before the end of the Cold War but who, on seeing its capabilities first-hand after the end of the Cold War, concluded that the USA had significantly overestimated the strengths of the Soviet Navy.

26 Rear-Admiral V. Aleksin, Captain 1st Rank E. Shevelev (ret.), 'Sudby Rossii i flota nerazdelimy' [Destinies of Russia and the Navy are Inseparable], *Morskoi sbornik*, no. 6, 1996, p. 11.

27 V. Aleksin and E. Shevelev, 'O reformirovanii nashego VMF' [About the Reform of Our Navy], *Morskoi sbornik*, no. 3, 1995, pp. 13, 16.

28 *Jane's Defence Weekly*, 20 June 1992, p. 1050.

29 *Tiazhelyi avianesushchii kreiser* (TAKR).

30 'V soglasii flotov—bezopasnost regiona' [The Security of the Region Lies in Agreement between Navies], *Morskoi sbornik*, no. 1, 1997, p. 12.

31 'Pod flagom Rossii' [Under Russia's Ensign], *Morskoi sbornik*, no. 3, 1993, p. 12.

32 Stanley B. Weeks, 'Law and Order at Sea: Pacific Cooperation in Dealing with Piracy, Drugs and Illegal Immigration', in *Calming the Waters: Initiatives for Asia Pacific Maritime Cooperation*, eds Sam Bateman and Stephen Bates, Strategic and Defence Studies Centre,

Research School of Pacific and Asian Studies, ANU, Canberra, 1996, p. 47.

33 ibid, p. 51. See also *Morskoi sbornik*, no. 4, 1994, p. 16.

34 *Jane's Defence Weekly*, 31 July 1993, p. 7.

35 *Morskoi sbornik*, no. 4, 1994, p. 16.

36 *Ria Novosti*, 9 February 1997.

37 *Morskoi sbornik*, no. 7, 1992, p. 21.

38 The first exercise was held in Russia in June 1994. See *Jane's Defence Weekly*, 2 July 1994, p. 10.

39 Vladimir Kuroyedov, 'O morskoi strategii Rossii' [Russia's Naval Strategy], *Voennyi parad*, vol. 2, no. 26, 1998, p. 8.

40 Valery Aleksin, 'The Navy Will Not Let Us Down', *Nezavisimoe voennoe obozrenie*, no. 27, 24–30 July 1998, pp. 1, 3, FBIS-UMA–98–025, 24 July 1998: 'Russia: Kuroyedov on Navy's Current Role, Strength'.

41 ibid.

42 The former practice was to have single-purpose formations, such as ASW.

43 'Sokhranit professionalov i korabli' [To Save Professionals and Ships], *Morskoi sbornik*, no. 4, 1998, p. 17.

44 Over 1000 tonnes in displacement.

45 da Cunha, 1990, p. 13.

46 ibid. pp. 13–14.

47 The ship is the former *Chervona Ukraina* and has the honorific title of 'Guards' which means that a unit of the same name distinguished itself in the Great Patriotic War.

48 *Jane's Fighting Ships 1998–99*, p. 564.

49 The Russian designation is *raketnyi kreiser* (RKR).

50 The capability of the *Slava* to destroy an aircraft carrier gave this series of ships the nickname 'carrier-killer'.

51 The air defence armament of *Variag* comprises multi-layered missile and artillery systems: 8 long-range SA-N–6 *Grumble* vertical launchers, 2 short-range SA-N–4 *Gecko* twin launchers, 2 twin 130 mm dual-purpose guns, and 6 30 mm multi-barrel AA gun systems. The long-range SA-N–6 SAM system operates with a fire-control system, similar to the USN *Aegis* class.

52 The Russian designation is *tiazhelyi atomnyi raketnyi kreiser* (TAKR). The *Lazarev* is the former *Frunze* which was renamed after the demise of the USSR. The *Ushakov* class is a new name given to the former *Kirov* class.

53 Weapons systems include 20 *Granit* lower flight profile surface-to-surface missiles (SS-N–19 or *Shipwreck* in the NATO designation) with 750 kg conventional or 350 kt nuclear warhead, capable of destroying any surface combatant; 2 twin 130 mm dual purpose guns; and 500 SAMs of various classes (SA-N–6 *Grumble*, SA-N–4 *Gecko*, SA-N–9 *Gauntlet*, CADS-N–1. The *Ushakov* class CGN carries 3 Ka–27 helicopters.

54 *Jane's Fighting Ships 1996–97*, Jane's Information Group, 1996, p. 564.

55 Admiral O. Erofeev, 'S uchetom realii, ne vpadaia v krainosti' [Taking

Into Account Realities, Not Going to Extremes], *Morskoi sbornik*, No. 6, 1998, p. 8.

56 'Kreiser "Admiral Lazarev" Budet Vozvrachshen v Stroi' [Cruiser *Admiral Lazarev* Will be Returned Into Operation], *Krasnaia zvezda*, 24 July 1999, p. 1.

57 Da Cunha, *Soviet Naval Power in the Pacific*, p. 16.

58 The Russian designation is ZM–80E *Moskit*.

59 The Russian designation is *bolshoi protivolodochnyi korabl* (BPK) or large antisubmarine ship. The *Kara* and *Kresta*-II class cruisers were also designated as BPK, and this is some indication that the Russian Navy may consider the *Udaloi* class as their successor.

60 *Jane's Fighting Ships 1998–99*, p. 570.

61 They entered service in the mid-1970s.

62 They first entered service in 1984.

63 Vice-Admiral V. Patrushev, 'Nashi podvodnye sily segodnia' [Our Submarine Forces Today], *Morskoi sbornik*, no. 3, 1997, p. 3.

64 The Komsomolsk shipyard began construction of submarines for the Pacific Fleet in the early 1930s. In the 1970s, it became the second-largest submarine-building facility in the world after the Severodvinsk complex.

65 *Jane's Defence Weekly*, 16 May 1992, p. 836.

66 The Russian designation is RSM–40/R–29.

67 The Russian designation is RSM–50.

68 Since late 1987, some *Delta*-III SSBNs have been re-armed with SS-N-23 ballistic missiles, usually carried by the *Delta*-IV class SSBN. See Derek da Cunha, *Soviet Naval Power in the Pacific*, p. 39.

69 Rady Zubkov, 'Uncertain Future of Missile Submarines', *Nezavisimoe voennoe obozrenie*, no. 47, 11–17 December 1998, p. 6, FBIS-UMA–98–351, 17 December 1998: 'Russia: Development of Navy Strategic Forces Viewed'.

70 NRDC Nuclear Notebook, 1999, p. 63.

71 Aleksei Inavnovich Podberezkin, 'A Treaty Giving the United States Advantages', *Nezavisimoe voennoe obozrenie*, 20–26 February 1998, No. 7, p. 6, FBIS-SOV–98–089, 30 March 1998: 'Russia: Podberezkin, Surikov Opposing START–II Ratification'.

72 ibid.

73 *Mirovaia ekonomika I mezhdunarodnye otnosheniia*, no. 4, 1997, pp. 5–21, FBIS-UMA–97–136-S, 17 July 197: 'Russia: Arbatov: military Reform: Doctrine, Troops'.

74 First entered into service in the Soviet Navy in 1982.

75 First entered into service in the Soviet Navy in 1986.

76 Barbara Starr, 'Russian Subs "Not Suffering", Says US Navy', *Jane's Defence Weekly*, 16 April 1997, p 5

77 *Jane's Defence Weekly*, 3 January 1996, p. 6.

78 Herspring, 1996, p. 176.

79 'Razvedka kak ona est' [Reconnaissance As It Is], *Morskoi sbornik*, No. 3, 1995, p. 46.

80 *The Military Balance 1998–99*, IISS, 1998, p. 113.

81 Colonel-General V. Deineka, 'Aviatsia VMF krylia ne skladyvaet' [Naval Aviation Does Not Lay Down Wings], *Morskoi sbornik*, no. 7, 1997, pp. 11–12.

82 The Russian name is *morskaia pekhota*.

83 Andrei Kuzminov, '*Chernye Diavoly* Segodnia i Zavtra' ['Black Devils' Today and Tomorrow], *Soldat udachi*, no. 7, 1997, p. 22.

84 Better known by the Russian designation *spetsnaz* which simply means 'special purpose'.

85 The Russian term here is *divizion*, which is used for a formation of ships of one class.

86 *Krasnaia zvezda*, 11 September 1998, p. 1. Troop lift capacity refers only to a standard schedule of a ship. A considerably larger number of troops can be embarked in all classes of amphibious ships for short transits.

87 The first of this class entered the Pacific Fleet in 1979.

88 V. Patrushev, 'Sostoianie i prioritetnye napravleniia razvitiia VMF Rossii' [The Condition and Priority Directions of the Development of Russia's Navy], *Morskoi sbornik*, no. 11, 1996, p. 4.

89 Captain 1st Rank V. Tymel, 'Kak gotovit korabli' [How to Exercise Ships], *Morskoi sbornik*, no. 5, 1996, p. 42.

90 'Vremia trebuet peremen' [The Times Demand Change], *Morskoi sbornik*, no. 12, 1997, p. 33.

91 *Morskoi sbornik*, no. 5, 1996, p. 34.

92 *Morskoi sbornik*, no. 12, 1997, pp. 4, 33.

93 Captain 2nd Rank A. Khrolenko, 'Strogii ekzamen sdan' [The Hard Test is Over], *Morskoi sbornik*, no. 10, 1997, p. 37.

94 See V. Gutsalov, 'V Liuboi Situatsii—Nadezhda na Luchshee . . .' [In Any Situation There is Hope for the Best], *Morskoi Sbornik*, no. 7, 1999, pp. 38–9; 'Uchenia TOF' [The Pacific Fleet Exercises], *Nezavisimoe Voennoe Obozrenie*, no. 23, 1999, p. 1; Vladimir Mukhin, 'Strategicheskie manevry dostigli tseli' [Strategic Manoeuvres Reached Their Objective], *Nezavisimaia gazeta*, 7 April 1999, p. 2.

95 *Morskoi sbornik*, no. 5, 1998, p. 45.

96 ibid. p. 2.

97 'V soglasii flotov—bezopasnost Regiona' [The Security of the Region Lies in the Agreement Between Navies], *Morskoi sbornik*, no. 1, 1997, p. 13.

98 'Vizhu tikhookeanskii flot obnovlionnym' [I See the Pacific Fleet Restored], *Morskoi sbornik*, no. 9, 1996, p. 18.

99 *Morskoi sbornik*, no. 5, 1998, p. 1.

100 *Krasnaia zvezda*, 29 August 1998, p. 1.

101 Patrushev, 'Sostoianie i prioritetnye napravleniia razvitiia VMF Rossii', pp. 5–6.

102 Admiral N. Khmelnov, 'Rossiiskii VMF: Na poroge chetvertogo stoletia' [The Russian Navy on the Threshold of its Fourth Century], *Morskoi sbornik*, no. 8, 1996, p. 17.

103 Patrushev, 'Nashi podvodnye sily segodnia', p. 4.

104 L. Khudiakov, 'Skolko RPKSN neobkhodimo Rossii v nachale

21 veka' [How Many SSBNs Does Russia Need at the Beginning of the 21st Century], *Morskoi sbornik*, no. 4, 1996, p. 20.

105 Captain 1st Rank (ret.) B. Makeev, 'Perspektivy otechestvennykh MSIaS' [Perspectives of National Maritime Strategic Nuclear Forces], *Morskoi sbornik*, no. 4, 1996, p. 21.

106 Rady Zubkov, 'Uncertain Future of Missile Submarines', *Nezavisimoe voennoe obozrenie*, no. 47, 11–17 December 1998, p. 6, FBIS-UMA–98–351, 17 December 1998: 'Russia: Development of Navy Strategic Forces Viewed'.

107 Aleksei Ivanovich Podberezkin, 'A Treaty Giving the United States Advantages', *Nezavisimoe voennoe obozrenie*, 20–26 February 1998 no. 7, p. 6, FBIS-SOV–98–089, 30 March 1998: 'Russia: Podberezkin, Surikov Opposing START–II Ratification'.

108 NRDC Nuclear Notebook, 'Russia's Strategic Nuclear Forces, End of 1998'.

109 Patrushev, 'Sostoianie i prioritetnye napravleniia razvitiia VMF Rossii', pp. 6–7.

110 Khmelnov, 'Rossiiskii VMF: Na poroge chetvertogo stoletia', p. 17

111 Aleksin and Shevelev, 'O reformirovanii nashego VMF', p. 17.

112 *Krasnaia zvezda*, 4 January 1998, p. 2.

113 *Morskoi sbornik*, no. 9, 1996, p. 20.

114 See *Krasnaia zvezda*, 21 April 1998, p. 1.

115 *Jane's Defence Weekly*, 5 August 1995, p. 14.

116 *Krasnaia zvezda*, 17 September 1998, p. 2.

117 Interfax, 9 July 1997, FBIS-UMA–97–190, 9 July 1997: 'Russia: Payments for Two Nuclear Submarines Remain Uncertain'. It is likely that these are improved *Akula-II* class submarines.

118 Kelly, 'Changing Superpower Maritime Roles', p. 32.

119 *Jane's Defence Weekly*, 18 March 1998, p. 5.

120 *Krasnaia zvezda*, 17 January 1998, p. 5.

121 *Morskoi sbornik*, no. 4, 1998, p. 5.

122 *Jane's Fighting Ships 1996–97*. Note: *Udaloi-II* class DDG *Admiral Chabanenko* was the only capital ship supposed to be commissioned in 1995 but it joined the Northern Fleet only in 1999.

8 Air forces

1 The Defence Ministry is not the only one to control significant air assets, and shares this function with the Ministry of Internal Affairs, the Ministry for Civil Defence, Emergencies and Natural Disasters, Customs, the Federal Border Service, and civil aviation authorities.

2 Many large aviation units and formations, aerodrome infrastructure, command and control, as well as pilot training facilities, ceased to exist. The production ties of aviation industry and aircraft repair facilities were disrupted. As of 1998, around 40 per cent of military airfields need to be repaired.

3 'Russian Air Force Weakness', *Jane's Defence Weekly*, 16 April 1997, p. 14.

4 Jeroen Brinkman, 'Russian Air Force in Turmoil', *Air Forces Monthly*, no. 105, December 1996, p. 2.

5 Colonel-General Anatoly Kornukov, 'Avitsionnaia podderzhka voisk: gospodstvo v nebe—uspekh na zemle' [Air Support of Troops: Air Superiority is Success on the Ground], *Krasnaia zvezda*, 11 November 1998, p. 2.

6 'O pervoocherednykh merakh po reformirovaniu vooruzhennykh sil Rossiiskoi Federatsii' [On Priority Measures to Reform the Armed Forces of the Russian Federation], *Rossiiskaya gazeta*, 19 July 1997, p. 5.

7 Lieutenant-General Vladimir Vasiutin, 'Voenno-vosdushnye sily Rossii na poroge XXI veka' [Russia's Air Force At the Turn of the 21st Century], *Voennyi parad*, no. 1, 1997, p. 56.

8 Natalia Kuznetsova, 'Voennaia reforma v Rossii' [Military Reform in Russia], *Nezavisimaia gazeta*, 12 December 1996, p. 2.

9 *Teatr voennykh deistvii*.

10 Kornukov, 'Avitsionnaia podderzhka voisk: gospodstvo v nebe—uspekh na zemle'.

11 Valentin Rog, 'The Air Offensive and Air Defense', *Armeiskii sbornik*, November 1997, no. 11, pp. 4–9, FBIS-SOV–98–042, 11 February 1998: 'Russia: Role of Air Forces Described'.

12 Anatoly Mikhailovich Kornukhov, 'The Structural Development Theory of the New Air Force', *Nezavisimoe voennoe obozrenie*, 31 March 1998, no. 10, pp. 1, 3, FBIS-UMA–98–341, 7 December 1998: 'Russia: Gen Kornukov on Organizational Changes to Air Force'.

13 Rog, 'Novoi Rossii—Novuiu Voennuiu Aviatsiu', p. 5.

14 These figures are estimates made by the Russian Air Force: Major-General (ret.) Valentin Rog (Doctor of Military Science) and Lieutenant-General Valentin Vasiutin (Professor).

15 *Nezavisimaia gazeta*, 15 October 1997, p. 5; *Voennyi parad*, no. 1, 1997, p. 55.

16 'Ne teriat temp reform, zavershit nachatoe' [Do Not Lose the Tempo of Reform, Finish What Has Been Started], *Krasnaia zvezda*, 12 August 1998, p. 1; see also 'Integratsia voisk VVS i PVO—Ob'ektivnaia neobkhodimost' [Integration of the Air Force and the Air Defence Troops is the Objective Necessity], *Krasnaia zvezda*, 23 January 1998, p. 1.

17 See remarks of Russia's Defence Minister, Marshal Sergeyev, in 'Integratsia voisk VVS i PVO—Ob'ektivaia neobkhodimost', p. 1.

18 Alexandr Drobyshevsky, 'VVS narashivaiut boevoi potentsial' [The Air Force Increases Its Combat Potential], *Krasnaia zvezda*, 4 April 1998, p. 1.

19 IISS, *The Military Balance, 1998/99*.

20 Sergei Babichev and Alexandr Beklich, 'Idiot pereraspredelenie sil i sredstv VVS i voisk PVO' [The Re-distribution of Forces and Means of the Air Force and the Air Defence Troops is Taking Place], *Krasnaia zvezda*, 18 March 1998, p. 1.

21 Yury Gavrilov, 'Bez otryva ot boevoi uchioby' [With no Distraction from Combat Training], *Krasnaia zvezda*, 16 July 1998, p. 3.

22 See the report of the Air Force Commander in Chief, Colonel-General Anatoly Kornukov, in Alexandr Ivanov and Sergei Babichev, 'VVS dolzhny sokhranit vysokuiu nadezhnost' [The Air Force Must Retain High Reliability], *Krasnaia zvezda*, 24 March 1998, p. 1.

23 'Ne teriat temp reform, zavershit nachatoe'.

24 ibid.

25 Ivanov and Babichev, 'VVS dolzhny sokhranit vysokuiu nadezhnost'.

26 'Nagruzka na biudzhet umenshitsia' [Burden on the Budget Will be Reduced], *Krasnaia zvezda*, 9 January 1998, p. 2.

27 These figures are from RFAF C-in-C; it is noted that *The Military Balance 1998–99* reports that only five flying schools were operating in 1998.

28 'Ne teriat temp reform, zavershit nachatoe'.

29 'Nagruzka na biudzhet umenshitsia'.

30 Babichev, 'Plany korrektituet zhizn' [Life Corrects Plans], *Krasnaia zvezda*, 13 March 1998, p. 1.

31 Drobyshevski, 'VVS narashivaiut boevoi potentsial'.

32 'Boevoy Potentsial PVO Budet Sokhranen' [The Air Defence Combat Potential Will be Preserved], *Krasnaia zvezda*, 11 April 1998, p. 2.

33 Gavrilov, 'Bez otryva ot boevoi uchioby'.

34 'Soedinenie PVO Ukrupniaentsia' [The AD Formation is Expanding], *Nezavisimoe Voennoe Obozrenie*, N 24 1999, p. 1.

35 *Dal'niaia aviatsiia*.

36 *Voenno-transportnaia aviatsiia*.

37 Ilia Kedrov and Sergei Sokut, 'Transportirovat diviziu za odin vyliot' [To Transport Division in One Take-off], *Nezavisimoe voennoe obozrenie*, no. 11, 1999, p. 1.

38 Data on the numerical strength is from *The Military Balance 1998–99*, p. 112, and *Asia-Pacific Defence Reporter (Annual Edition)*, 25 (1), 1999, p. 80.

39 Kedrov and Sokut, 'Transportirovat diviziu za odin vyliot', p. 1. There are some 350 civilian An–12/Il–76 transport planes, plus more than 1000 passenger aircraft in Russia. See IISS, *The Military Balance 1998–99*, p. 112.

40 NATO designation SA–10.

41 NATO designation SA–11.

42 NATO designation SA–19.

43 'Novy oblik voiskovoi PVO' [The New Image of Army Air Defence], *Krasnaia zvezda*, 15 August 1998, p. 2.

44 ibid.

45 IISS, *The Military Balance 1998–99*, pp. 112–13.

46 Podvig (ed.), 1998, p. 355.

47 *The Military Balance 1998–99*, pp. 109, 113.

48 Alexandr Ivanov and Sergei Babichev, 'Ob'edinionnye VVS pristupili k resheniu postavlennykh zadach' [The Integrated Air Force Began the Fulfilment of the Set Tasks], *Krasnaia zvezda*, 3 March 1998, p. 1.

49 Babichev and Beklich, 'Idiot pereraspredelenie sil i sredstv VVS i voisk PVO'.

50 ibid.

51 'Vozdushnaia granitsa ne oslabeet' [The Air Border Will Not Be Weakened], *Krasnaia zvezda*, 27 March 1998, p. 2.

52 ibid.

53 Valery Usoltsev, 'Opredelilas Sud'ba "Zolotoi Doliny"' [The Fate of the 'Golden Valley' Has Been Determined], *Krasnaia zvezda*, 7 April 1998, p. 1

54 *Krasnaia zvezda*, 20 August 1998, p. 2.

55 Kensuke Ebata, 'Russia Trims MiG–23 Forces in Kuril Islands', *Jane's Defence Weekly*, 12 June 1993, p. 23.

56 Dmitri Karpov, 'Armeiskaia aviatsia ostaniotsia na ostrovakh' [Army Aviation Will Stay on the Islands], *Krasnaia zvezda*, 15 October 1998, p. 1.

57 Colonel-General Anatoly Kornukov, 'Avitsionnaia podderzhka voisk: gospodstvo v nebe—uspekh na zemle' [Air Support of Troops: Air Superiority is Success on the Ground], *Krasnaia zvezda*, 11 November 1998, p. 1.

58 Kornukov, 'Avitsionnaia podderzhka voisk: gospodstvo v nebe—uspekh na zemle'.

59 Gavrilov, 'Bez otryva ot boevoi uchioby'.

60 'Russia to Ground MiG–31s?', *Australian Aviation*, no. 128, May 1997, p. 8.

61 'Russians Test JASDF', *Aircraft & Aerospace Asia-Pacific*, 75 (10), November 1995, p. 22.

62 'Ne teriat temp reform, zavershit nachatoe'.

63 Nikolai Baranov and Sergei Babichev, 'VVS: chto udalos za god' [The Air Force: What Has Been Achieved During the Year], *Krasnaia zvezda*, 19 November 1998, p. 1.

64 *Novosti*, 6 March 1998.

65 *Krasnaia zvezda*, 4 January 1998, p. 1.

66 Oleg Litvinov, 'Su–30 i MiG–31: Desiat chasov v vozdukhe' [Su–30 and MiG–31: Ten Hours in the Air], *Krasnaia zvezda*, 9 July 1998, p. 1.

67 Sergei Sokut, 'Rybok k severnomu poliusu' [Flash to the North Pole], *Nezavisimaia gazeta*, 9 April 1999, p. 2.

68 Baranov and Babichev, 'VVS: chto udalos za god'.

69 See interview with General Anisimov in 'Boegotovnost Trebuet Raskhodov' [Combat Readiness Requires Expenditure], *Krasnaia Zvezda*, 17 July 1999, p. 2.

70 *Nezavisimoe voennoe obozrenie*, 15–18 December 1997, No. 45, p. 6, FBIS-SOV–98–012, 12 January 1998: 'Russia: Report on Testing of MIG–29SMT'.

71 MAPO is the Russian acronym for the Moscow Aircraft Production Association.

72 IISS, *The Military Balance, 1998–99*.

73 This figure includes civilian production.

74 Valentin Rudenko, 'MiG–29 narashivaet muskuly' [The MiG–29 Builds Up Its Muscles], *Krasnaia zvezda*, 24 April 1998, p. 1.

75 Still, it should be kept in mind that MiG–29 was developed as a front-line fighter to gain air superiority.

76 The main distinctive feature of the MiG–29SMT from its predecessor

is a modernised cockpit with two large, colour multi-function dis-
plays on either side of the conventional instruments, and a new
heads-up display. The new updated airborne radar N-019MP allows
terrain cartography to increase the guidance efficiency. Another
major improvement is the additional fuel tank behind the cockpit
with a capacity of more than 2000 litres.
77 *Krasnaia zvezda*, 4 August 1998, p. 3. As it is expected, only later
   produced models of the MiG-29 will be modernised. The rest will
   be decommissioned or cannibalised for spare parts.
78 Nikolai Novichkov, 'Russian Upgrade Can Only Stretch to Three
   MiG-29s', *Jane's Defence Weekly*, 5 August 1998, p. 16. The MiG-
   29UBT version can also be used for combat operations.
79 Rudenko, 'MiG-29 narashivaet muskuly'.
80 Novichkov, 'Russian Upgrade Can Only Stretch to Three MiG-29s',
   p. 16.
81 Craig Hoyle, 'Russia Receives First MiG-29SMT', *Jane's Defence
   Weekly*, 13 January 1999, p. 12.
82 'Ne teriat temp reform, zavershit nachatoe'.
83 ibid.
84 Piotr Butowski, 'Clearing Skies', *Jane's Defence Weekly*, 29 April
   1998, p. 25.
85 Piotr Butowski, 'Sukhoi Order Set to Boost Russia's Rapid Deployment', *Jane's Defence Weekly*, 8 April 1998, p. 29.
86 ibid.
87 See 'Plotting a Revolution for Russia's Air Force', *Jane's Defence
   Weekly*, 31 July 1996, p. 24.
88 Mike Spick, '*Flanker* Proliferation', *Air Force Monthly*, no. 117,
   December 1997, p. 35.
89 It is confirmed that at least three Su-34s were delivered to the RFAF
   in 1995-96. See Brinkman, 'Russian Air Force in Turmoil', p. 2.
90 'Plotting a Revolution for Russia's Air Force', p. 25.
91 See *Air International*, 50 (4), April 1996, p. 198.
92 'Moscow Airscene', *Air International*, 49(4), October 1995, p. 198.
93 'Rossiia ne mozhet byt bezkryloi' [Russia Cannot Be Without Wings],
   Krasnaia zvezda, 15 August 1998, p. 3.
94 Kedrov and Sokut, 'Transportirovat' diviziu za odin vyliot'.
95 'Ne teriat temp reform, zavershit nachatoe'.
96 Valentin Rudenko, 'Presidenty Rossii i Ukrainy blagoslovili v puliet
   An-70' [Presidents of Russia and Ukraine Blessed the Flight of the
   An-70], *Krasnaia zvezda*, 3 March 1998, p. 1.
97 Kedrov and Sokut, 'Transportirovat' diviziu za odin vyliot'.
98 In Russian, *mnogofunktsional'nyi istrebitel'*.
99 Butowski, 'Clearing Skies', p. 24.
100 Valery Vvedenski, Alexandr Gusev, '*Berkut*-ryvok k sovershenstvy'
   [*Berkut* is a Breakthrough to Perfection', *Voenny parad*, 3 (27), 1998,
   pp. 110-11. S-37 is also known outside Russia as S-32.
101 Igor Korotchenko, 'Sozdan rossiiskii mnogofunktsional'nyi
   istrebitel' piatogo pokolenia' [A Fifth Generation Multirole Fighter
   Has been Created], *Nezavisimaia gazeta*, 24 December 1998, pp. 1-2.

102 See Piotr Butowski and Oleg Panteleyev, 'MiG Finally Rolls Out MFI Aircraft', *Jane's Defence Weekly*, 6 January 1999, p. 4.
103 In Russian, *Liogkii frontovoi istrebitel'*.
104 Butowski, 'Clearing Skies', p. 24.
105 Nick Cook, 'Russian Air Force is Down But Not Out', *Jane's Defence Weekly*, 19 March 1997, p. 23.
106 Kornukov, 'Avitsionnaia podderzhka voisk: gospodstvo v nebe—uspekh na zemle'.
107 ibid.
108 NATO designation *Hocum-A*.
109 Grigory Kuznetsov, 'Ka–50: V konkurse pobezhdaet silneishii' [Ka–50: The Strongest Wins the Competition], *Voenny parad*, 3 (27), 1998, p. 103.
110 Valery Usoltsev, 'Osvaivaiut "Tchernuiu Akulu" [Familiarise with the *Black Shark*], *Krasnaia zvezda*, 7 August 1999, p. 1.
111 Piotr Butowski, 'Russia Rolls Out Light Helicopter Ka–60 Prototype', *Jane's Defence Weekly*, 5 August 1998, p. 15.

9   Ground forces

1 Interfax, 4 November, 1998, FBIS-SOV–98–308, 4 November 1998: 'Russia: Russia Adjusts Tactical Troop Deployment to Counter NATO'.
2 Airborne forces and a number of special forces units were not directly subordinated to the Ground Forces Commander in Chief for most of the post-war period in the USSR. They were however closely identified with the ground forces in terms of basic training and operations.
3 *Nezavisimoe voennoe obozrenie*, 15–21 March 1997, no. 10, p. 2, FBIS-UMA–97–075-S, 21 March 1997: 'Russia: Semenov Offers Defense over His Ouster'.
4 Interfax, 3 March 1999, FBIS-SOV–1999–0303, 3 March 1999: 'Russia's Ground Forces Designed to Rebuff Aggression'; Dmitri Litovkin, 'Perspektivy sukhoputnykh voisk' [Prospects for the Ground Forces], *Krasnaia zvezda*, 5 March 1999, p. 1.
5 Interview with Colonel General Yury Dmitriyevich Bukreyev, Chief of the Main Operational Directorate of the General Staff, *Armeiskii sbornik*, August 1998, pp. 10–13, FBIS-UMA–98–340, 6 December 1998: 'Russia: New Look of Ground Troops'.
6 ibid.
7 Oleg Vladykin, 'Khaki-Coloured Russian Dolls', *Obshchaia gazeta*, no. 11, 19–25 March 1998, p. 3, FBIS-UMA–98–082, 23 March 1998: 'Russia: Army High Command Will Be Resurrected'.
8 Arbatov, 1998:2, p. 130.
9 Interview with Roman Popkovich, Chairman of the Defense Committee of the State Duma, Radio Rossii, 19 February 1999, FBIS-SOV–1999–0219, 19 February 1999: 'Duma Defense Committee Chairman Interview'.
10 Oleg Vladykin, Khaki-Coloured Russian Dolls', *Obshchaia gazeta*,

No. 11, 19–25 March 1998, p. 3, FBIS-UMA–98–082, 23 March 1998: 'Russia: Army High Command Will Be Resurrected'.

11 ITAR-TASS, 12 March 1998. One Russian newspaper was reporting in 1996 that actual strengths that year had fallen to 350 000. See *Segodnia*, 26 April 1996 (USNI Database).

12 Interfax, 3 March 1999, FBIS-SOV–1999–0303, 3 March 1999: 'Russia's Ground Forces Designed to Rebuff Aggressors'.

13 Vladimir Mukhin, 'Sokrashenie sukhoputnykh voisk zaversheno' [Cuts to the Ground Forces Are Complete], *Nezavisimaia gazeta*, 5 March 1999, p. 2.

14 IISS, *The Military Balance, 1998/99*.

15 A statement by a senior Russian military officer in 1998 suggested that Russia had 25 000 tanks. See 'Bronevoi shchit Otechestva', *Krasnaia zvezda*, 12 September 1998, p. 1.

16 Vladimir Leonidovich Suvorov, 'Fire Chief's Hot Spots', *Nezavisimoe voennoe obozrenie*, no. 5, 2–6 Feb 1998, p. 2, FBIS-SOV–98–089, 30 March 1998: 'Russia: Effectiveness of Use of Troops for Domestic Purposes'.

17 For a useful account of how this has played out in the case of the air defence units of the ground forces, see 'Roundtable', *Armeiskii sbornik*, February 1997, no. 2, pp. 12–27, FBIS-UMA–97–093-S, 1 February 1997: 'Russia: Roundtable Discussion of Ground Troops Air Defense Troops Hot Spots'.

18 Aleksandr Alekseyevich Chindarov, 'The Winged Guard', *Armeiskii sbornik*, August 1996, no. 8, pp. 13–16, FBIS-UMA–96–234–3, 1 August 1996: 'Russia: Col-Gen Chindarov on Airborne Troops'.

19 Russia also sent 210 policemen and 30 border guards to be part of the international police force in the troubled province.

20 *Rabochaia tribuna*, 25 April 1995, p. 2, FBIS-SOV–95–081, 25 April 1995: 'Further Reportage on Chechnia–Siberians Puzzled by Appeal'.

21 Novosti, 12 December 1994.

22 *Vechernyi Novosibirsk*, 30 January 1995, p. 4, FBIS-SOV–95–005, 30 January 1995: 'Lt-Gen Mayorov on Situation of Siberian Troops Fighting in Chechnia'.

23 Yuri Baluyevski, 'The Role and Place of Land Forces in Modern Operations', *Military Parade*, 1997 (electronic version).

24 ibid.

25 ibid.

26 ibid.

27 Vladimir Chelyshev et al., 'Equipment and Arms—The T–34 of the 21st Century', *Armeiskii sbornik*, no. 19. October 1998, pp. 60–3, FBIS-SOV–1999–0303, 1 October 1999: 'Specifications of Russian 21st Century Robotized Tanks'.

28 See Makhmut Akhmetovich Gareyev, 'Russia's Military Doctrine', *Nezavisimoe voennoe obozrenie*, no. 29, 9–15 August 1997, pp. 1, 4, FBIS-TAC–97–233, 21 August 1997: 'Russia: Military Academician on New Military Doctrine'.

29 *Nezavisimoe voennoe obozrenie*, 13–19 November 1998, no. 43,

pp. 1, 3, FBIS-UMA–98–336, 2 December 1998: 'Russia: Dep Chief of Missile and Artillery Troops Interviewed'.

30 'Russia: New Look of Ground Troops'.

31 ibid.

32 Valery Mironov, 'Reform of the Armed Forces Implies More than Just Their Reduction', *Military Parade*, May–June 1997 (electronic version).

33 'Voiska meniaiut oblik' [The Forces Are Changing Their Appearance], *Krasnaia zvezda*, 13 June 1998, p. 2. Constant combat readiness units are also to be formed in the navy and air force.

34 Aleksandr Veklich, 'Prioritet—boegotovnost' [Combat Readiness is a Priority], *Krasnaia zvezda*, 20 February 1998, pp. 1–2.

35 For more information about this division, see *Krasnaia zvezda*, 20 February 1998, p. 2.

36 *Nezavisimoe voennoe obozrenie*, no. 19, 13–19 March 1998, FBIS-UMA–98–076, 17 March 1998: 'Russia: Ground Forces Cuts Will Not Affect Combat Capability'.

37 Interfax, 12 August 1998, FBIS-UMA–98–224, 12 August 1998: 'Russia: Sergeyev Doubts Transfer to Professional Army by 2000'.

38 NTV, 14 August 1997, translated in FBIS-SOV–97–226, 14 August 1997: 'Russia: Sergeev Observes Training in Siberian Military District'.

39 Evgeny Shaltsev and Aleksei Popov, 'Liudi v stepi' [People in the Steppes], *Krasnaia zvezda*, 9 June 1998, pp. 1–2; Aleksandr Veklich, 'Sibirskii kharakter' [Siberian Character], *Krasnaia zvezda*, 28 April 1998, pp. 1–2. The unit was already established as a special unit, given its independent status and its access to paratroops and helicopters.

40 *Krasnaia zvezda*, 4 February 1998, p. 2.

41 Mayak Radio Network, 23 February 1998, FBIS-SOV–98–055, 24 February 1998: 'Russia: Russia's Sergeyev on Military Reform'.

42 Leonid Pozdeev, 'Uralskii Variant' [Urals Variant], *Krasnaia zvezda*, 12 March 1998, p. 1.

43 *Krasnaia zvezda*, 9 September 1998, p. 2.

44 Interview with Head of the Main Operations Directorate of the General Staff, *Krasnaia zvezda*, 3 November 1998 (EV).

45 ITAR-TASS, 4 November 1998, FBIS-UMA–98–308, 4 November 1998: 'Russia: Russia to Form 10 Divisions on Constant Combat Readiness'.

46 'Sukhoputnye voiska ukomplektovany pol'nostiu' [Ground Forces Are Fully Manned], *Nezavisimoe voennoe obozrenie*, no. 10, 1999, p. 1.

47 Interfax, 4 November 1998, FBIS-SOV–98–308, 4 November 1998: 'Russia: Funds Shortages Thwart Plan to Reduce Service Numbers'. This report quoted General Yurii Baluyevskii.

48 *Nezavisimoe voennoe obozrenie*, 13–19 November 1998, no. 43, pp. 1, 3, FBIS-UMA–98–336, 2 December 1998: 'Russia: Dep Chief of Missile and Artillery Troops Interviewed'.

49 Dmitri Avanesov, 'Poka vmeshalsia vyshestoiashchii shtab . . .', *Krasnaia zvezda*, 28 January 1999 (EV).

50 Interfax, 3 March 1999, FBIS-SOV-1999–0303, 3 March 1999: 'Russia's Ground Forces Designed to Rebuff Aggression'.

51 Leonid Pozdeev, 'Versiia Polkovnikova Konovalova', *Krasnaia zvezda*, 13 January 1999 (EV).

52 'Sukhoputnye voiska: vchera, segodnia, zavtra', *Krasnaia zvezda*, 9 February 1999 (EV).

53 'Chasti postoiannoi gotovnosti dolzhny byt' khorosho obustroeny', *Krasnaia zvezda*, 25 December 1998 p.1.

54 Aleksandr Bugai, 'Vyzhivi bez boia, polk', *Krasnaia zvezda*, 22 January 1999 (EV).

55 'Sukhoputnye voiska ukomplektovany polnostiu'.

56 Interfax, 3 March 1999, FBIS-SOV-1999–0303, 3 March 1999: 'Russia's Ground Forces Designed to Rebuff Aggression'.

57 Vladimir Mukhin, 'Monitoring: Reform Process Took in the Bulk of Troops', *Nezavisimoe voennoe obozrenie*, no. 19, 22–28 May 1998, pp. 1, 3, FBIS-SOV-98–190, 9 July 1998: 'Russia: Mukhin Summarizing Reductions as of May 1 by District'.

58 ibid.

59 IISS, *Military Balance, 1998/99*.

60 Vladimir Georgiyev, 'Piat let russkogo mirotvorchestva' [Five Years of Russian Peacekeeping], *Nezavisimoe voennoe obozrenie*, no. 15, 1997, p. 2.

61 'Sukhoputnye voiska: vchera, segodnia, zavtra'.

62 *Nezavisimoe voennoe obozrenie*, 26 June–2 July 1998, p. 2, FBIS-UMA–98–197, 16 July 1998: 'Russia: Rotation of Peacekeeping Forces through Southern Ossetia'.

63 ITAR-TASS, 22 February 1998, FBIS-SOV-98–053, 22 February 1998: 'Russia: Minister Sees Peacekeepers as Model for Army Reform'.

64 Valeryi Mironov, 'Reform of the Armed Forces Implies More than Just Their Reduction', *Military Parade*, May–June 1997 (electronic version).

65 USNI Military database, 'Russia–Army', last updated 1 December 1998, www.periscope.ucg.com accessed 14 March 1999.

66 *Krasnaia zvezda*, 14 February 1996.

67 The lower figure of 70 per cent was from a Russian source. See Interview with Lieutenant General Georgii Shpak, Commander of Airborne Troops, *Krasnaia zvezda*, 6 January 1997 (USNI Database). The higher figure of 85 per cent was from a foreign source. See Rafael Estrella, 'The State of the Russian Forces', North Atlantic Assembly, October 1997, p. 8.

68 *Armeiskii sbornik*, August 1997, no. 8, pp. 6–9, FBIS-SOV–97–307, 3 November 1997: 'Russia: Col Gen Shpak on Airborne Troops Reorganisation'.

69 Interview with Lieutenant General Georgii Shpak, Commander of Airborne Troops, *Krasnaia zvezda*, 6 January 1997 (USNI Database).

70 ITAR-TASS, 24 August 1998, FBIS-UMA–98–237, 25 August 1997: 'Russia: Russian Airborne Troops Complete Tactical Exercises'.

71 Ilia Kedrov and Sergei Sokut, 'Vozdushny most na zapad' [Air Bridge to the West], *Nezavisimoe voennoe obozrenie*, no. 11, 1999, p. 3.

72 *Armeiskii sbornik*, August 1997, no. 8, pp. 6–9, FBIS-SOV–97–307, 3 November 1997: 'Russia: Col Gen Shpak on Airborne Troops Reorganisation'.

73 ITAR-TASS, 24 August 1998, FBIS-UMA–98–237: 'Russia: Russian Airborne Troops Complete Tactical Exercises'. Other sources report the losses to have been 16 000, which was the intended size of the cuts. See Vladimir Mukhin, 'Monitoring: Reform Process Took in the Bulk of Troops', *Nezavisimoe voennoe obozrenie*, no. 19, 22–28 May 1998, pp. 1, 3, FBIS-SOV–98–190, 9 July 1998: 'Russia: Mukhin Summarizing Reductions as of May 1 by District'.

74 Sergei Larionov, 'The Big Caucasus Target', *Moskovskii komsomolets*, 9 July 1998, pp. 1–2, FBIS-SOV–98–197, 16 July 1997: 'Russia: Preparations for War in North Caucasus'.

75 'VDV: Stavka na mobilnost' [Airborne: Staking on Mobility], *Krasnaia zvezda*, 16 April 1998, p. 1.

76 ITAR-TASS, 14 January 1999, FBIS-UMA–99–014, 14 January 1999: 'Russia: Official Says Russian Airborne Troops Retain Efficiency'. The report cited the Commander of the Airborne Troops.

77 See the interview with General Shpak in *Krasnaia zvezda*, 19 June 1999, p. 1.

78 Mukhin, 'Monitoring: Reform Process Took in the Bulk of Troops'.

79 ITAR-TASS, 24 August 1998, FBIS-UMA–98–237: 'Russia: Russian Airborne Troops Complete Tactical Exercises'.

80 'Nadezhny li krylia desanta' [Are the Wings of the Airborne Forces Reliable], *Krasnaia zvezda*, 9 December 1998, p. 1.

81 'Russia Seeks Airborne Expansion', *Jane's Defence Weekly*, 27 January 1999. p. 15.

82 *Krasnaia zvezda*, 23 June 1999, p. 1.

83 'Spetsnaz i politik', *Nezavisimoe voennoe obozrenie*, 13 November 1998, No. 43 (EV).

84 Sergei Ptichkin, 'The Partisan Trails of Special Missions', *Rossiiskaia gazeta*, 25 August 1998, pp. 2, 7, FBIS-UMA–98–245, 2 September 1998: 'Russia: Special Antiterrorist Forces Advocated'. Ptichkin was citing an unidentified GRU special forces officer.

85 Lunev, 1996.

86 USNI Military database, 'Russia—Army', last updated 1 December 1998, accessed 14 March 1999.

87 Moscow NTV, 10 April 1997, FBIS-UMA–97–101, 11 April 1997: 'Russia: NTV Reports Special Forces Training'.

88 Pozdeyev, 'Versiia Polkovnika Konovalova'.

89 *Armeiskii sbornik*, August 97, no. 8, pp. 10–13, FBIS-SOV–97–307, 3 November 1997: 'Russia: Col Gen Pavlov on Ground Troops Aviation'.

90 ITAR-TASS, 12 March 1998.

91 Matiash, 'Sukhoputnye voiska meniaiut oblik'.

92 Cossacks are communities based more on acceptance of common traditions than on strict ties of kinship or language. Even in the earliest surviving oral histories of Russia, the Cossacks were borderland communities treated as autonomous as long as they gave strict

loyalty to the princes or tsar. They earned their status based largely on a warrior tradition which is their most defining characteristic.

93 Novosti, 2 February 1993.

94 Novosti, 3 March 1993.

95 ITAR-TASS, 30 March 1998, FBIS-UMA–98–089, 30 March 1998: 'Russia: Russia's Orenburg Cossack Troops Now Subordinate to State'.

96 Evgeny Lisanov, 'Kazaki idut na sliuzhbu' [Cossacks are Going into Service], Krasnaia zvezda, 24 March 1999, p. 3.

97 ITAR-TASS, 1 July 1998, FBIS-UMA–98–182, 1 July 1998: 'Russia: Results of Staff Exercises in Far East District Reviewed'.

98 Lisanov, 'Kazaki idut na sliuzhbu'.

99 In the absence of public information from reliable official sources, manning levels of military units are very difficult to assess.

100 Leonid Peven, '201st Motorized Rifle as a Mirror of the Professional Army', Armeiskii sbornik, June 1997, no. 6, pp. 45–7, FBIS-SOV–97–158-S, 1 June 1997: 'Russia: Survey of Contract Personnel in 201st Motorized Rifle Division'.

101 Vladimir Georgiyev, 'Forpost Rossii v Tsentralnii Azii' [Russia's Forward Outpost in Central Asia], Nezavisimaia gazeta, 26 Decemebr 1998, p. 2.

102 Nezavisimoe voennoe obozrenie, no. 19, 13–19 March 1998, FBIS-UMA–98–076, 17 March 1998: 'Russia: Ground Forces Cuts Will Not Affect Combat Capability'.

103 ITAR-TASS, 12 March 1998, FBIS-UMA–98–072, 13 March 1998: 'Russia: Details of Russian Army Ground Forces Reform'.

104 ITAR-TASS, 29 April 1998.

105 ITAR-TASS, 13 January 1998, FBIS-SOV–98–103, 13 January 1998: 'Russia: Russian Defense Ministry to Work Hard on Reforms'.

106 ITAR-TASS, 12 March 1998, FBIS-UMA–98–071, 12 March 1998: 'Russia: Russian Army to have Permanently Ready Units by 2001'.

107 Dmitry Litovkin, 'Perspektivy sukhoputnykh voisk', Krasnaia zvezda, 5 March 1999 (EV). This report cited an interview with the Chief of the Main Directorate of the Ground Forces, Colonel General Yury Bukreyev.

108 ITAR-TASS, 4 November 1997, FBIS-UMA–97–308, 4 November 1997: 'Russia: Russian Warrant Officers Used to Fill Vacant Officer Posts'.

109 'V chastiakh postoiannoi gotovnosti. Chto pokazal eksperiment', Krasnaia zvezda, 29 January 1999 (EV).

110 ITAR-TASS, 25 May 1998, FBIS-UMA–98–145, 25 May 1998: 'Russia: Underweight Army Recruits in Siberia to be Given Special Treatment'.

111 Pravda, 1 March 1999.

112 Boris Dukhov, 'Building Combat Skills', Military Parade, 1997 (electronic version).

113 Nezavisimoe voennoe obozrenie, 13–19 November 1998, no. 43, pp. 1, 3, FBIS-UMA–98–336, 2 December 1998: 'Russia: Dep Chief of Missile and Artillery Troops Interviewed'. In Chechnia, the main forms of artillery spotting were by binoculars and rangefinders rather than

more modern technologies in which the USSR had made substantial advances.

114 Dick, 1996.

115 Interview with Chief of the Main Armour Directorate of the Ministry of Defense, *Krasnaia zvezda*, 4 October 1996 (USNI Database).

116 Aleksandr Babkin, 'I Rammed the Charge into the Cannon Tightly', *Rossiiskaia gazeta*, 19 August 1998, p. 3, FBIS-SOV–98–233, 21 August 1998: 'Russia: Modernized Tanks, Armored Vehicles Needed'.

117 *Nezavisimoe voennoe obozrenie*, 13–19 November 1998, no. 43, pp. 1, 3, FBIS-UMA–98–336, 2 December 1998: 'Russia: Dep Chief of Missile and Artillery Troops Interviewed'.

118 *Morskoi sbornik*, no. 3, 1995, p. 22.

119 ibid.

120 Nikolai Baranov, 'Weapons Must Serve for a Long While', *Armeiskii sbornik*, March 1998, no. 3, pp. 66–71, FBIS-SOV–98–154, 3 June 1998: 'Russia: Problems of Modernizing Missile and Artillery Equipment'.

121 'Bronevoi shchit Otechestva'.

122 USNI Database, last updated 1 December 1998, www.periscope.ucg.com accessed 14 March 1999.

123 Pozdeyev, 'Versiia Polkovnikova Konovalova'.

124 See 'Bronia i liudi v graiduchshem veke' [Armour and People in the Coming Millennium], *Krasnaia zvezda*, 10 June 1999, p. 1.

125 Litovkin, 'Perspektivy sukhoputnykh voisk'.

126 Baranov, 'Weapons Must Serve for a Long While'. Baranov, a Lieutenant General, was Deputy Chief of Main Missile/Artillery Directorate of the Ministry of Defence at the time of publication.

127 Ibragim Usmanov, 'Impeachment Commission Continues Work', *Sovietskaia Rossiia*, 5 November 1998, p. 2, FBIS-SOV–98–309, 5 November 1998: 'Russia: Impeachment Commission Views Army Decline'.

128 Interfax, 19 November 1999, FBIS-UMA–98–323, 19 November 1998: 'Russia: Russia To Commission New Tactical Missile in 1999'.

129 Vladimir Georgiyev, '"Topolei" Stanet Bolshe', p. 3.

130 Interview with the Commander of Army Aviation, Col. Gen. Vitalii Pavlov, *Armeiskii sbornik*, August 1997, no. 8, pp. 10–13, FBIS-SOV–97–307, 3 November 1997: 'Russia: Col Gen Pavlov on Ground Troops Aviation'.

131 ITAR-TASS, 29 July 1998, FBIS-SOV–98–218, 6 August 1998: 'Russia: Military to Continue Using *Black Shark* Helicopters'.

132 'Russia: New Look of Ground Troops'.

133 Dick, 1996.

134 Interfax, 22 January 1997.

135 *Armeiskii sbornik*, August 1997, no. 8, pp. 6–9, FBIS-SOV–97–307, 3 November 97: 'Russia: Col Gen Shpak on Airborne Troops Reorganisation'.

136 ITAR-TASS, 12 March 1998, FBIS-UMA–98–071, 12 March 1998: 'Russia: Russian Army to have Permanently Ready Units by 2001'.

137 Litovkin, 'Perspektivy sukhoputnykh voisk'.

138 Interview with Colonel General Yury Dmitriyevich Bukreyev, *Armeiskii sbornik*, August 1998.

139 Baranov, 'Weapons Must Serve for a Long While'.

140 ITAR-TASS, 22 October 1998, FBIS-UMA–98–296, 23 October 1998: 'Russia: Russian Army Says Production of New Weapons Continues'.

141 Litovkin, 'Perspektivy sukhoputnykh voisk'.

142 ITAR-TASS, 18 January 1999, FBIS-UMA–99–018, 18 January 1999: 'Russia: Russia's Airborne Troops to Be Rearmed'.

143 Vladimir Chelyshev et al., 'Equipment and Arms—The T–34 of the 21st Century', *Armeiskii sbornik*, no. 19. October 1998, pp. 60–3, FBIS-SOV–1999–0303, 1 October 1999: 'Specifications of Russian 21st Century Robotized Tanks'.

144 ITAR-TASS, 22 October 1998, FBIS-UMA–98–296, 23 October 1998: 'Russia: Russian Army Says Production of New Weapons Continues'.

145 Valery Usoltsev, 'Pobednaia tochka raketchikov', *Krasnaia zvezda*, 24 July 1998, p. 1.

146 Interfax, 19 November 1999, FBIS-UMA–98–323, 19 November 1998: 'Russia: Russia To Commission New Tactical Missile in 1999'.

147 Interview with Lieutenant General Nikolai Nikolaevich Mukhin, *Nezavisimoe voennoe obozrenie*, no. 43, 13–19 November 1998, pp. 1, 3, FBIS-UMA–98–336, 2 December 1998: 'Russia: Dep Chief of Missile and Artillery Troops Interviewed'.

148 *Washington Times*, 8 July 1998; *Krasnaia zvezda*, 26 February 1996 (USNI Database).

149 This source records Russian forces at higher numbers of divisions and other formations, and at higher personnel levels, than the IISS or official Russian sources. While the authors believe that those USNI estimates are probably incorrect, the USNI estimates for equipment holding are probably more reliable.

150 USNI Military database, 'Russia—Army', last updated 1 December 1998, www.periscope.ucg.com accessed 14 March 1999.

151 *Military Balance, 1998/99*

152 When army aviation units went to join combat in Chechnia, supplementary training had to be undertaken in operational areas. *Armeiskii sbornik*, August 1997, no. 8, pp. 10–13, FBIS-SOV–97–307, 3 November 1997: 'Russia: Col Gen Pavlov on Ground Troops Aviation'.

153 *Trud*, 11 February 1997, pp. 1, 3, FBIS-SOV–97–029, 11 February 1997: 'Russia: Rodionov: Russia's Defense Almost Breached'.

154 Estrella, 1997, p. 3.

155 Mayak Radio Network, 23 February 1998, FBIS-SOV–98–055, 24 February 1998: 'Russia: Russia's Sergeyev on Military Reform'.

156 ibid.

157 'Sukhoputnye voiska: vchera, segodnia, zavtra'.

158 Oleg Falichev and Vladimir Matiash, 'Zadachi 1998 goda Vooruzhionnim Silam prishlos' vypolniat' v slozhnykh usloviakh', *Krasnaia zvezda*, 13 November 1998, p. 2.

159 NTV, 14 August 1997, translated in FBIS-SOV–97–226, 14 August 1997: 'Russia: Sergeev Observes Training in Siberian Military District'.

160 Radio Rossii, 14 August 1997, translated in FBIS-UMA–97–226,

14 August 1997: 'Russia: Defense Minister Inspects Siberian Military District'.

161 Taras Rudyk and Aleksandr Veklich, 'Grom nad taigoi' [Thunder above the Taiga], *Krasnaia zvezda*, 31 March 1998, pp. 1–2.

162 Vladimir Mukhin, 'Strategicheskie manevry dostigli tseli' [Strategic Exercises Achieved Their Aims], *Nezavisimaia gazeta*, 7 April 1999, p. 2.

163 ITAR-TASS, 15 December 1997, FBIS-UMA–97–349, 15 December 1997: 'Russia: Military Aircraft in Transbaykal Area Grounded Until 20 Dec'.

164 NTV, 14 August 1997, translated in FBIS-SOV–97–226, 14 August 1997: 'Russia: Sergeev Observes Training in Siberian Military District'.

165 ITAR-TASS, 4 November 1998, FBIS-UMA–98–308, 4 November 1998: 'Russia: Russia to Form 10 Divisions on Constant Combat Readiness'.

166 Aleksandr Bugai, 'Ucheba budet. Zapakhlo by goriuchim', *Krasnaia zvezda*, 13 March 1999, p. 2.

167 ibid.

168 RADEA, 20–27 November 1998 (accessed 14 March 1999).

169 'Sukhoputnye voiska: vchera, segodnia, zavtra'.

170 Ivan Komar, 'Combat Training: Like Commander, Like Subordinate', *Armeiskii sbornik*, August 1998, pp. 30–3, FBIS-UMA–98–340, 6 December 1998: 'Russia: Ways to Improve Officer Training'.

171 ITAR-TASS, 24 August 1998, FBIS-UMA–98–237: 'Russia: Russian Airborne Troops Complete Tactical Exercises'.

172 Sergei Larionov, 'The Big Caucasus Target', *Moskovskii komsomolets*, 9 July 1998, pp. 1–2, FBIS-SOV–98–197, 16 July 1997: 'Russia: Preparations for War in North Caucasus'.

173 'Sukhoputnye voiska: vchera, segodnia, zavtra'.

174 Interfax, 20 October 1998, FBIS-SOV–98–293, 20 October 1998: 'Russia: NATO Inspects Russian Training Area for 1999 Exercises'.

175 ITAR-TASS, 27 May 1998, FBIS-UMA–98–147, 27 May 1998: 'Russia: Russia to Take Part in NATO Peacekeeping'.

176 'Sukhoputnye voiska: vchera, segodnia, zavtra'.

177 Unto Hamalainen, 'Researcher Stefan Forss: Russian Military in Better Shape than West Thinks', *Helsingin Sanomat*, 28 May 1998, p. 7, FBIS-SOV–98–175, 24 June 1998: 'Russia: Russian Military Decline Exaggerated'.

178 'Sukhoputnye voiska: vchera, segodnia, zavtra'.

10 Military industry and regional arms sales

1 Sergei Sokut, 'New Tailor Assigned to Patch Defense Industry', *Nezavisimoe voennoe obozrenie*, 31 July–6 August 1998, pp. 1, 6, FBIS-SOV–98–233, 21 August 1998: 'Russia: Sokut on Problems of Defense Industries'.

2 Gaddy, 1996, p. 18.

3 ibid. p. 25.

4 ibid. p. 27.

5 ibid. pp. 29, 155.

6 *Inside the Navy*, 15 June 1992.
7 *Jane's Defence Weekly*, 2 May 1992.
8 Interfax, 2 February 1999, FBIS-UMA–99–033: 'Russian Defense Ministry Reduces Arms Purchases Since 1991'.
9 Sokut, 'New Tailor Assigned to Patch Defense Industry'.
10 See Aleksei Shulunov, 'Deceptive Accounting', *Nezavisimoe voennoe obozrenie*, 31 July–6 August 1998, p. 1, FBIS-SOV–98–233, 21 August 1998: 'Russia: Conflict over Defense Order Arrears, Remedies'.
11 Herspring, 1996, p. 172.
12 Gaddy, 1996, pp. 69–70.
13 ibid. pp. 73–4.
14 ibid. pp. 83–4.
15 Interfax, 'Siberian Business Report', No. 213–214, 30 December 1997–12 January 1998, carried in FBIS-SOV–98–013, 13 January 1998: 'Russia: Interfax Siberian Business Report'.
16 Vladimir Pimenov, 'The Defense Industry Needs a Leader', *Nezavisimoe voennoe obozrenie*, 13–19 November 1998, no. 43, p. 4, FBIS-UMA–98–335, 1 December 1998: 'Russia: State Commission Needed to Oversee Defense Industry Policy'.
17 Sokut, 'New Tailor Assigned to Patch Defense Industry'.
18 Gaddy, 1996, p. 129.
19 ibid. p. 115.
20 Aleksei Shulunov, 'A Systemic Crisis', *Nezavisimoe voennoe obozrenie*, 16–22 January 1998, no. 2, pp. 4–5, FBIS-SOV–98–049, 18 February 1998: 'Russia: Shulunov: Defense Industry's Systemic Crisis'.
21 Gaddy, 1996, pp. 171–2.
22 Shlykov, 1997, p. 15.
23 Sergei Sokut, *Nezavisimoe voennoe obozrenie*, 4–10 December 1998, no. 46, p. 6, FBIS-UMA–99–004: 'Russia: Options, Need for Reforming VPK Noted'.
24 Vladimir Lukianets and Pavel Zaitsev, 'The Guarantee of Superiority', *Nezavisimoe voennoe obozrenie*, 27 November–3 December 1998, no. 45, p. 6, FBIS-UMA–98–349, 15 December 1998: 'Russia: Defense Industry Must Focus on New Technologies'.
25 Sokut, 'New Tailor Assigned to Patch Defense Industry'.
26 Shulunov, 'A Systemic Crisis'.
27 Scherbakova and Monroe, 1995, p. 75.
28 *Defense News*, 4–10 May 1992.
29 *Trud*, 18 May 1994, pp. 1–2, FBIS-USR–94–057, 18 May 1994: 'Omsk Governor on Siberian Accord, Current Tasks'.
30 ITAR-TASS, 23 September 1997, carried in FBIS-SOV–97–266, 23 September 1997: 'Russia: New *Black Eagle* Tank on Display at Siberian Exhibition'.
31 ITAR-TASS, 28 August 1997, carried in FBIS-SOV–97–240, 28 August 1997: 'Russia: Siberian City to Hold Weapons Exhibition'.
32 *Delovoi mir*, 27 December 1996–2 January 1997, p. 4, FBIS-SOV–97–014, 2 January 1997: 'Russia: Siberian Oil Programs Aid Defense Industry'.

33 Sergei Grigorev, 'War and Peace in the Sukhoi Complex', *Nezavisimoe voennoe obozrenie*, 22–28 May 1998, no. 19, p. 6, FBIS-SOV–98–182, 1 July 1998: 'Russia: Grigoryev on Method of Resolving Problems in MIC'.

34 Interview with Mikhail Aslanovich Pogosian, *Nezavisimoe voennoe obozrenie*, 22–28 May 1998, no. 19, p. 6, FBIS-SOV–98–182, 1 July 1998: 'Russia: Sukhoi's Pogosyan on Current Operations, Plans'.

35 Interview with Vladimir Petrovich Babak, *Nezavisimoe voennoe obozrenie*, 6–12 March 1998, no. 9, pp. 1, 6, FBIS-SOV–98–093, 3 April 1998: 'Russia: General Director on Plans for Sukhoi Reorganisation'.

36 Interfax, 'Siberian Business Report', no. 4, 20–26 January 1998, carried in FBIS-SOV–98–026, 26 January 1998: 'Russia: Interfax Siberian Business Report'.

37 *Vooruzhenie, politika, konversiia*, no. 14, 1996, pp. 13–15, FBIS-SOV–97–161-S, 20 August 1997: 'Russia: Russia Lacks Money to Support an Army'.

38 Vladimir Lukianets and Pavel Zaitsev, 'The Guarantee of Superiority', *Nezavisimoe voennoe obozrenie*, 27 November–3 December 1998, no. 45, p. 6, FBIS-UMA–98–349, 15 December 1998: 'Russia: Defense Industry Must Focus on New Technologies'.

39 Cooper, 1992, pp. 79–80.

40 Cook, 1998.

41 Shulunov, 'A Systemic Crisis'.

42 Cook, 1998.

43 Anatolyi Yanukevich, 'Quest for the Optimum', *Nezavisimoe voennoe obozrenie*, 16–22 October 1998, no. 39, p. 6, FBIS-UMA–98–313, 9 November 1998: 'Russia: Proposal for Further Reform of Arms Sales Sector'.

44 IISS, *Strategic Survey 1996/97*, pp. 126–7.

45 IISS, *The Military Balance, 1998/99*.

46 ITAR-TASS, 21 April 1999, FBIS-SOV–1999–0422: 'Russia Remains Among Five Leading Arms Exporters'.

47 ibid.

48 Interfax, 21 April 1999, FBIS-SOV–1999–0421: 'Russian Arms Trader Receives $2.3 Billion for Exports'.

49 Interfax, 7 May 1998, FBIS-SOV–98–127, 7 May 1998: 'Russia Sees China, India as Key Arms Trade Partners'.

50 ibid.

51 Interfax, 10 March 1999, FBIS-SOV–1999–0310: 'Experts Say Russian Arms Exports To Rise 20% in 1999'.

52 ITAR-TASS, 21 April 1999, FBIS-SOV–1999–0422: 'Russia Remains Among Five Leading Arms Exporters'.

53 Yanukevich, 'Quest for the Optimum'.

54 ITAR-TASS, 31 March 1999, FBIS-SOV–1999–0331: 'Russian Arms Exporter Hopes to Continue Ties With NATO'.

55 Yanukevich, 'Quest for the Optimum'.

56 ITAR-TASS, 31 March 1999, FBIS-SOV–1999–0331: 'Russian Arms Exporter Hopes to Continue Ties With NATO'.

57 Blank, 1997, p. 8.

58 Interfax, 7 May 1998, FBIS-SOV–98–127, 7 May 1998: 'Russia Sees China, India as Key Arms Trade Partners'.
59 ibid.
60 Lukianets and Zaitsev, 'The Guarantee of Superiority'.
61 *Los Angeles Times*, 30 November 1992.
62 Cook, 1998.
63 Statement of the Deputy Assistant Secretary of State For Non-Proliferation, Subcommittee on International Security, Proliferation and Federal Services, US Senate, 5 June 1997, *Proliferation: Russian Case Studies*, p. 9.
64 Cook, 1998.
65 Statement of the Deputy Assistant Secretary of State For Non-Proliferation, Subcommittee on International Security, Proliferation and Federal Services, US Senate, 5 June 1997, *Proliferation: Russian Case Studies*, p. 7.
66 For conventional weapons, Russia contributes to the UN Register on Conventional Arms Transfers and is party to the Wassenaar Agreement on export of dual use or militarily sensitive technologies.
67 Statement of the Deputy Assistant Secretary of State For Non-Proliferation, Subcommittee on International Security, Proliferation and Federal Services, US Senate, 5 June 1997, *Proliferation: Russian Case Studies*, p. 7.
68 In April 1999, Russia announced that within the framework of the Gore–Chernomyrdin Commission it had committed itself to end arms sales to Iran by the end of the year until the international bans were lifted, thus honouring its 1995 commitment. Interfax, 21 April 1999, FBIS-SOV–1999–042: 'Russian Enterprise Not To Sell Arms to Iran After 1999'.
69 Mikhail Kirillin, 'Missile Illusion', *Nezavisimoe voennoe obozrenie*, 3–9 April 1998, no. 13, p. 7, FBIS-TAC–98–099, 9 April 1998: 'Russia: Motives for Alleging Russian MTCR Breached'.
70 ITAR-TASS, 26 April 1999, FBIS-SOV–1999–0426: 'Russia–Belarus Arms Export Control Agreement Signed'.
71 Interfax, 21 April 1999, FBIS-SOV–1999–042: 'Russian Enterprise Not To Sell Arms to Iran After 1999'.
72 Sergei Sokut, *Nezavisimoe voennoe obozrenie*, 4–10 December 1998, no. 46, p. 6, FBIS-UMA–99–004: 'Russia: Options, Need for Reforming VPK Noted'.
73 IISS, *The Military Balance, 1998/99*.
74 'India, Russia to Boost Military Ties', *The Hindu*, 13 October 1997.
75 *Ria Novosti*, 11 July 1997.
76 Sunil Kataria, 'India, Russia to Extend Cooperation Treaty', *India Web Post*, 28 October 1997.
77 Vadim Soloviov, 'Realities: Final Airshow of the Outgoing Year', *Nezavisimoe voennoe obozrenie*, 24 December 1998–14 January 1999, no. 49, p. 6, FBIS-SOV–99–015, 15 January 1999: 'Russia: Russian Aviation VPK in India Viewed'.
78 Interfax, 20 November 1998, FBIS-SOV–98–324, 20 November 1998: 'Russian Official Sees China Remaining Major Arms Buyer'.

79 NATO designations are AA–11 *Archer* and AA–12 *Adder*.

80 Vadim Soloviov, 'Realities: Final Airshow of the Outgoing Year', *Nezavisimoe voennoe obozrenie*, 24 December 1998–14 January 1999, no. 49, p. 6, FBIS-SOV–99–015, 15 January 1999: 'Russia: Russian Aviation VPK in India Viewed'.

81 MiG–29K *Fulcrum* is the navalised version of the MiG–29 fighter. It was rejected by the Russian Navy in favour of the Su–33.

82 Atul Aneja, 'Navy Exploring New Aircraft Carrier Options', *The Hindu*, 9 September 1997.

83 'And Now a Desi Aircraft Carrier', Rediff on the Net, 20 July 1997.

84 Vadim Soloviov, 'Realities: Final Airshow of the Outgoing Year', *Nezavisimoe voennoe obozrenie*, 24 December 1998–14 January 1999, no. 49, p. 6, FBIS-SOV–99–015, 15 January 1999: 'Russia: Russian Aviation VPK in India Viewed'.

85 Vladimir Savin, 'Russia Opposes Ukrainian–Pakistani Tank Deal', *Kommersant Daily*, 21 February 1997.

86 Igor Aleksandrov and Vladimir Georgiyev, 'Yeltsin Postpones Visit to India', *Nezavisimaia gazeta*, 13 January 1998.

87 *Los Angeles Times* (Washington Edition), 13 July 1992.

88 *Armed Forces Journal International*, January 1993.

89 Interfax, 'Siberian Business Report', No. 213–214, 30 December 1997–12 January 1998, carried in FBIS-SOV–98–013, 13 January 1998: 'Russia: Interfax Siberian Business Report'.

90 *Los Angeles Times* (Washington Edition), 13 July 1992.

91 Interfax, 'Siberian Business Report', No. 213–214, 30 December 1997–12 January 1998, carried in FBIS-SOV–98–013, 13 January 1998: 'Russia: Interfax Siberian Business Report'.

92 Interfax, 20 November 1998, FBIS-SOV–98–324, 20 November 1998: 'Russian Official Sees China Remaining Major Arms Buyer'.

93 Igor Korotchenko, 'Diplomatiia Marshala Sergeyeva' [Diplomacy of Marshal Sergeyev], *Nezavisimoe voennoe obozrenie*, 30 October 1998.

94 NATO designation SA–10B *Grumble*.

95 Korotchenko, 'Diplomatiia Marshala Sergeyeva'.

96 Blasko, 1997–98, p. 92.

97 Interfax, 20 November 1998, FBIS-SOV–98–324, 20 November 1998: 'Russian Official Sees China Remaining Major Arms Buyer'.

98 ibid.

99 Interfax, 20 November 1998, FBIS-SOV–98–324, 20 November 1998: 'Russian Official Sees China Remaining Major Arms Buyer'.

100 Korotchenko, 'Diplomatiia Marshala Sergeyeva'.

101 Interfax, 20 November 1998, FBIS-SOV–98–324, 20 November 1998: 'Russian Official Sees China Remaining Major Arms Buyer'.

102 ibid.

103 Korotchenko, 'Diplomatiia Marshala Sergeyeva'.

104 *Armed Forces Journal International*, January 1993.

105 Blasko, 1997–98, p. 92.

106 Interfax, 20 November 1998, FBIS-SOV–98–324, 20 November 1998: 'Russian Official Sees China Remaining Major Arms Buyer'.

107 Blasko, 1997–98.

108 IISS, *The Military Balance, 1998/99*.

109 There has been a report in 1998 that China has designed an air defence system (FT–2000) which is similar in appearance at least to Russia's S–300 system but probably too soon after purchase to expect that process to have borne fruit. See Interfax, 20 November 1998, FBIS-SOV–98–324, 20 November 1998: 'Russian Official Sees China Remaining Major Arms Buyer'.

110 Mikhail Urusov, 'Destroyers in Exchange for Canned Meat', *Moskovskie novosti*, no. 44, 2–9 November 1997, p. 8, FBIS-UMA–97–310, 6 November 1998: 'Russia: Russia Helping China Build War Machine'.

111 Stephen J. Blank, 'The Dynamics of Russian Arms Sales to China', Strategic Studies Institute, US Army War College, Carlisle Barracks PA, 1997, p. 6, citing Kommersant, 18 July 1996, FBIS-SOV–96–140, 19 July 1996, pp. 20–2.

112 Interfax, 20 November 1998, FBIS-SOV–98–324, 20 November 1998: 'Russian Official Sees China Remaining Major Arms Buyer'.

113 For an early public statement of this, see Tai Ming Cheung, 'China's Buying Spree', *Far Eastern Economic Review*, 8 July 1993, p. 26. This has been confirmed to the authors privately by Russian officials on numerous occasions since and is implicit in a number of Russian government actions.

114 *Jane's Defence Weekly*, 18 February 1998.

115 Non-Proliferation Policy Education Centre, 'Reckless Russian Rocket Exports', incorporated in the Congressional Record, Subcommittee on International Security, Proliferation and Federal Services, 5 June 1997, *Proliferation: Russian Case Studies*, p. 30.

116 Blank, 1997, p. 7.

117 *Wall Street Journal*, 14 October 1993, p. A12 and *Washington Times*, 12 November 1993, p. A16.

118 Blasko, 1997–98.

119 *Armed Forces Journal International*, January 1993.

Bibliography

BOOKS AND BOOK CHAPTERS

Akaha, Tsuneo, Minakir, Pavel A and Okada, Kunio, 'Economic Challenge in the Russian Far East', in *Politics and Economics in the Russian Far East—Changing Ties with Asia–Pacific*, ed. Tsuneo Akaha, Routledge, London, 1997, pp. 49–69.

Arai, Nobuo and Hasegawa, Tsuyoshi, 'The Russian Far East in Russo–Japanese Relations', in *Politics and Economics in the Russian Far East*, ed. Tsuneo Akaha, Routledge, London, 1997, pp. 157–86.

Arbatov, Aleksei (ed.), *The Security Watershed: Russians Debating Defense and Foreign Policy after the Cold War*, Gordon and Breach Science Publishers, Amsterdam, 1993

Greg Austin, 'Russian Influences and Mutual Insecurity', in *China as a Great Power—Myths, Realities and Challenges in the Asia–Pacific Region*, eds Stuart Harris and Gary Klintworth, St Martins, New York NY, 1995, pp. 103–30

——(1997:1) 'Economic Rivalry and Security Linkages in US–Japan Relations', in *Asia–Pacific Security: The Economics—Politics Nexus*, eds Stuart Harris and Andrew Mack, Allen & Unwin, Sydney, 1997

——(1997:2) 'The Taiwan Issue in Japanese Domestic Politics', in *Missile Diplomacy and Taiwan's Future—Innovations in Politics and Military Power*, ed. Greg Austin, Canberra Papers in Strategy and Defence, Strategic and Defence Studies Centre, The Australian National University, 1997, pp. 81–110.

Austin, Greg and Tim Callan, 'Russia: Terrier at the Feet of the Great Asian Powers', in *The Asia–Pacific Region: Less Uncertainties, New Opportunities*, ed. Gary Klintworth, St Martins, New York NY, 1996

Aziatskaia Rossiia [Asiatic Russia], Izdanie pereselencheskago upravleniia, Glavnago upravleniia zemleustroistva i zemledeliia, St Petersburg, 1914

Baev, Pavel K., *The Russian Army in a Time of Troubles*, Sage Publications, London, 1996

Bateman, Sam, 'Strategic Change and Naval Roles', in *Strategic Change and Naval Roles: Issues for a Medium Naval Power*, eds Sam Bateman and Dick Sherwood, Canberra: Strategic and Defence Studies Centre, Research School of Pacific Studies, ANU, 1993

Beckett, Brian, *Weapons of Tomorrow*, Plenum Press, New York, 1983

Booth, Ken, 'The Role of Navies in Peacetime: The Influence of Future History on Sea Power', in *Naval Power in the Pacific: Toward the Year 2000*, eds H. Smith & A. Bergin, L. Rienner, Boulder, Colorado, 1993

Brzezinski, Zbigniew and Sullivan, Paige (eds), *Russia and the Commonwealth of Independent States: Documents, Data and Analysis*, M. E. Sharpe, Armonk NY, 1997

Buchs, Thierry D., 'Systemic Transformation: How Far from the Market?', in *Today's Russia in Transition: A First Economic and Political Balance Sheet*, ed. Curt Gasteyger, Geneva Institute of International Studies, Geneva, 1994

Christensen, Paul T., 'Property Free-for-all: Regionalism, "Democratization" and the Politics of Economic Control in the Kuzbas, 1989–93', in *Rediscovering Russia in Asia*, eds Stephen Kotkin and David Wolff, M. E. Sharpe, Armonk NY, 1995, pp. 207–23

Cooper, Julian , 'Defense Industries in Russia and the Other Post-Soviet States', in *State Building and Military Power in Russia and the New States of Eurasia*, ed. Bruce Parrott, M. E. Sharpe, Armonk NY, 1992

da Cunha, Derek, *Soviet Naval Power in the Pacific*, Lynne Rienner Publishers, London, 1990

Daniels, Robert V., 'Democracy and Federalism in the Former Soviet Union and the Russian Federation', in *Beyond the Monolith*, eds Peter J. Stavrakis, Joan De Bardeleben, and Larry Black, with the assistance of Jodi Koehn, Woodrow Wilson Center Press, Johns Hopkins University Press, Washington DC, 1997

Dunlop, John T. and Dunlop, Dorothy W., *The Rise of Russia and the Fall of the Soviet Empire*, Princeton University Press, Princeton NJ, 1993

Feschbach, Murray and Friendly, Alfred, *Ecocide in the USSR*, Basic Books, New York, 1992

Fish, M. Steven, *Democracy from Scratch—Opposition and Regime in the New Russian Revolution*, Princeton University Press, Princeton NJ, 1995

Gaddy, Clifford G , *The Price of the Past Russia's Struggle with the Legacy of a Militarized Economy*, Brookings Institution Press, Washington DC, 1996

Garthoff, Raymond L., 'Russian Military Doctrine and Deployments', in *State Building and Military Power in Russia and the New States of Eurasia*, ed. Bruce Parrott, M. E. Sharpe, Armonk NY, 1992

Guroff, Gregory and Guroff, Alexander, 'The Paradox of Russian National Identity', in *National Identity and Ethnicity in Russia and the New States of Asia*, ed. Roman Szporluk, M. E. Sharpe, Armonk NY, 1994

Herspring, Dale R., *Russian Civil–Military Relations*, Indiana University Press, Bloomington, 1996

Institute of National Security and Strategic Studies, *Evoliutsiia struktur voennoi bezopasnosti: rol' i mesto Rossii (geopoliticheskii aspekt)*, Moscow 1997 (EV).

Jane's Fighting Ships 1997–98, Jane's Information Group, Coulsdon, Surrey, 1997

Jukes, Geoffrey, 'Soviet Policy in the Indian Ocean', in *Soviet Naval Policy: Objectives and Constraints*, eds Michael McGwire, Ken Booth and John McDonnell, Praeger, New York NY, 1975

Michael Kaiser, 'Economic Transition and Political Stability: One or the Other?', in *Today's Russia in Transition*, ed. Curt Gasteyger, Geneva Institute of International Studies, Geneva, 1994

Kasaev, Alan C., 'Ossetia-Ingushetia', *US and Russian Policymaking with Respect to Use of Force*, eds Jeremy R. Azrael and Emil A. Payin, Rand, Santa Monica CA, 1996

Kellison, Bruce, 'Siberian Crude—Moscow, Tiumen and Political Decentralisation', in *Rediscovering Russia in Asia*, eds Stephen Kotkin and David Wolff, M. E. Sharpe, Armonk NY, 1995, pp. 193–206

Kelly, R. J. 'Changing Superpower Maritime Roles', in *Maritime Change: Issues for Asia*, eds Ross Babbage and Sam Bateman, Allen & Unwin, Sydney, 1993

Khasbulatov, Ruslan, *The Struggle for Russia—Power and Change in the Democratic Revolution*, Routledge, London, 1993

Kovrigin, Evgenii B., 'Problems of Resource Development in the Russian Far East', in *Politics and Economics in the Russian Far East*, ed. Tsuneo Akaha, Routledge, London, 1997, pp. 70–86.

Krasnov, Valerii Nikolaevich (General Editor), *Rossiia: partii, vybory, vlast'*, Obozrevatel' Information and Publishing Agency, Moscow, 1996

Löwenhardt, John, *The Reincarnation of Russia, Struggling with the Legacy of Communism 1990–1994*, Duke University Press, Durham NC, 1995

McAuley, Mary, *Russia's Politics of Uncertainty*, Cambridge University Press, Cambridge, 1997

McFaul, Michael, *Russia's 1996 Presidential Election: the End of Polarized Politics*, Hoover Institution Press, Stanford University, Stanford CA, 1997

McGwire, Michael, 'The Soviet Navy and World War', in *The Sources of Soviet Naval Conduct*, eds Philip S. Gillete and Willard C. Frank, Lexington Books, Lexington, 1990

Matejka, Harriet, 'Macroeconomic Equilibrium—Not Without the Market?', in *Today's Russia in Transition*, ed. Curt Gasteyger, Geneva Institute of International Studies, Geneva, 1994

Mote, Victor L., *Siberia: Worlds Apart*, Westview Press, Boulder CO, 1998.

Nemets, Alexander, *The Growth of China and Prospects for the Eastern Regions of the Former USSR*, The Edwin Mellen Press, Lewiston NY, 1996

Okun'kov, L. A., *Prezident Rossiiskoi Federatsii—Konstitutsiia i politicheskaia praktika* [President of the Russian Federation—The Constitution and Political Practice], Infra-M Norma, Moscow, 1995

Peterson, D. J., 'The Regionalization of Russia's Economy and the Impact on its Environment and Natural Resources', in *Beyond the Monolith: the Emergence of Regionalism in Post-Soviet Russia*, eds Peter J. Stavrakis, Joan De Bardeleben, and Larry Black, with the assistance of Jodi Koehn, Woodrow Wilson Center Press, Johns Hopkins University Press, 1997

Podvig, P. L. (ed.), *Strategicheskoe Yadernoe Vooruzhenie Rossii* [Russia's Strategic Nuclear Armament], Moskva: IzdAT, 1998

Pryde, Philip R., 'Russia—An Overview of the Federation', in *Environmental Resources and Constraints in the Former Soviet Republics*, ed. Philip R. Pryde, Westview Press, Boulder CO, 1995

Rigby, T. H., 'Conclusion: Russia in Search of Its Future', in *Russia in Search of its Future*, eds Amin Saikal and William Maley, Cambridge University Press, Cambridge, 1994

Rusi, Alpo M., *Dangerous Peace, New Rivalry in World Politics*, Westview Press, Boulder CO, 1998

Sakwa, Richard, *Russian Politics and Society*, 2nd edn, Routledge, London, 1996

Scherbakova, Anna and Monroe, Scott, 'The Urals and Siberia', in *Environmental Resources and Constraints in the Former Soviet Republics*, ed. Philip R. Pryde, Westview Press, Boulder CO, 1995

Shlapentokh, Vladimir, Levita, Roman and Loiberg, Mikhail, *From Submission to Rebellion—The Provinces versus the Center in Russia*, Westview Press, Boulder CO, 1997

Silverman, Bertram and Yanowitch, Murray, *New Rich, New Poor, New Russia—Winners and Losers on the Russian Road to Capitalism*, M. E. Sharpe, Armonk NY, 1997

Singh, Jasjit, 'Trends in Maritime Security', in *Maritime Security*, ed. Jasjit Singh, The Institute for Defence Studies and Analysis, New Delhi, 1993

Staar, Richard F., *The New Military in Russia—Ten Myths that Shape the Image*, Naval Institute Press, Annapolis MD, 1996

Stephan, John, *The Russian Far East—A History*, Stanford University Press, Stanford, CA, 1994

Strand, Holly, 'The Russian Far East', in *Environmental Resources and Constraints in the Former Soviet Republics*, ed. Philip R. Pryde, Westview Press, Boulder CO, 1995

Tsypkin, Mikhail, 'The Politics of Russian Security Policy', in *State Building and Military Power in Russia and the New States of Eurasia*, ed. Bruce Parrott, M. E. Sharpe, Armonk NY, 1992

Urban, Michael with Igrunov, Vyacheslav and Mitrokhin, Sergei, *The Rebirth of Politics in Russia*, Cambridge University Press, Cambridge, 1997

Woff, Richard, *The Armed Forces of the Former Soviet Union*, 2nd edition, Brassey's, London, 1996, vol. 1

Zagorsky, Alexei V., 'The Security Dimension', in *Politics and Economics in the Russian Far East—Changing Ties with Asia–Pacific*, ed. Tsuneo Akaha, Routledge, New York NY, 1997, pp. 23–48

Zaloga, Stephen J., *Inside the Blue Berets—A Combat History of Soviet and Russian Airborne Forces, 1930–1995*, Presidio, Novato CA, 1995

Zaprudnik, Jan, 'Development of Belarusian National Identity and its Influence on Belarus' Foreign Policy Orientation', in *National Identity and Ethnicity in Russia and the New States of Eurasia*, ed. Roman Szporluk, M. E. Sharpe, Armonk NY, 1994

Zhdanov, Vladimir A., 'Contemporary Siberian Regionalism', in *Rediscovering Russia in Asia—Siberia and the Russian Far East*, eds Stephen Kotkin and David Wolff, M. E. Sharpe, Armonk NY, 1995, pp. 120–132

JOURNAL ARTICLES AND REPORTS

Arbatov, Aleksei G., 'Russia's Foreign Policy Alternatives', *International Security*, vol. 18, no. 2, 1993.

——, 'The Russian Military in the 21st Century', Strategic Studies Institute, US Army War College, Carlisle Barracks PA, 1997

——, 'The National Idea and National Security', *Mirovaia ekonomika i mezhdunarodnye otnosheniia*, no. 5, 1998, pp. 5–21, FBIS-SOV–98–208, 27 July 1998: 'Russia: Arbatov on New National Security Approach' (1998: 1)

——, 'Military Reform in Russia: Dilemmas, Obstacles, and Prospects', *International Security*, vol. 22, no. 4, 1998 (Spring), p. 130 (1998: 2)

Blank, Stephen J. 'The Dynamics of Russian Arms Sales to China', Strategic Studies Institute, US Army War College, Carlisle Barracks PA, 1997

Blasko, Dennis, 'Evaluating Chinese Military Procurement from Russia', *Joint Forces Quarterly*, Autumn/Winter 1997–98

Brown, Sarah, 'Modern Tales of the Russian Army', *World Policy Journal*, Spring, 1997

Carter, Ashton, Assistant US Secretary of Defense for International Security Policy, 'Protecting US Security during the New Russian Revolution', *Defense Issues*, vol. 10, no. 77

Dick, C. J., 'Russian Military Reform: Status and Prospects', Conflict Studies Research Centre, 1996

Donnelly, Christopher, 'The Future of Russian National Security Policy', paper presented at the Tri-Service Conference, London, November 1995

Dubnov, Arkadyi Yu, 'Tadjikistan', *US and Russian Policymaking with Respect to the Use of Force*, Rand, Santa Monica CA, 1996

Fiodorov, Yurii E., 'Voennaia reforma i grazhdanskii kontrol' nad vooruzhionnymi silami v Rossii' [Military Reform and Civilian Control of the Armed Forces in Russia], Centre for Political Studies, Moscow State Institute of International Relations, Moscow, 1998 (EV).

Fitzgerald, Mary C., 'The Russian Military's Strategy For "Sixth Generation" Warfare', *Orbis*, Summer 1994

Forrow, Lachlan et al., 'Accidental Nuclear War: A Post-Cold War Assessment', *New England Journal of Medicine*, 30 April 1998, entered into the record of the US Senate, 30 April 1998

Institute of National Security and Strategic Studies, *Evoliutsiia struktur voennoi bezopasnosti: rol' i mesto Rossii (geopoliticheskii aspekt)* [Evolution of the Structure of Military Security: the Role and Place of Russia (the Geopolitical Aspect)], Moscow 1997

International Institute for Strategic Studies (IISS), *The Military Balance* (various issues)

Jane's Fighting Ships 1996–97, Jane's Information Group, Coulsdon UK, 1997

Khodjibaev, Karim, 'Russian Troops and Conflict in Tajikistan', *Perspectives on Central Asia*, vol. 2, no. 8, November 1997

Kipp, Jacob W., 'Forecasting Future War: Andrei Kokoshin and the Military Political Debate in Contemporary Russia', Foreign Military Studies Office, Fort Leavenworth KS, 1999 (EV)

Kliuchnikov, B. 'The Soviet Far East in the Pacific Century', *Far Eastern Affairs*, 1988, no. 4

Kozhokin, Evgenyi M., 'Georgia-Abkhazia', *US and Russian Policymaking with Respect to the Use of Force*, Rand, Santa Monica CA, 1996

Lambeth, Benjamin S., 'Russia's Wounded Military', *Foreign Affairs*, March/April 1995

Lunev, Stanislav, 'Russia's New Military Doctrine', *Prism*, 1 December 1995

———, 'Future Changes in Russian Military Policy', *Prism*, 9 February 1996

Makarevsky, Vadim, 'Phases of Military Reform in Russia', FSU: 15 Nations: Policy and Security, November 1997

Mendras, Marie, 'Existe-il un Etat russe?', *politique étrangère*, 1992, no. 1

Muraviev, Aleksey, 'Responses to NATO's Eastward Expansion by the Russian Federation', SDSC Working Paper WP323, Canberra, 1998

NRDC Nuclear Notebook, 'Russian Strategic Nuclear Forces, End of 1998', *Bulletin of the Atomic Scientist*, March/April 1999

Payin, Emil A. and Popov, Arkady A., 'Chechnya', in *US and Russian Policymaking with Respect to the Use of Force*, Rand, Santa Monica, 1996

Reese, David, *The Prospects for North Korea's Survival*, Adelphi Paper, no. 323, 1998

Rozman, Gilbert, 'Choices for the Russian Far East', *Journal of East Asian Affairs*, 1997, Summer/Fall, vol. 11, no. 2

Rumer, Boris and Sternheimer, Stephen, 'The Soviet Economy: Going to Siberia', *Harvard Business Review*, January–February 1982

Selivanova, Irina F., 'Trans-Dniestra', *US and Russian Policymaking with Respect to the Use of Force*, Rand, Santa Monica CA, 1996

Sheehy, Ann, 'Russia's Republics: A Threat to its Territorial Integrity?', in *Russia at the Crossroads*, RFE/RL Research Report, vol. 2, no. 20, 14 May 1993, pp. 34–40.

Shlapentokh, Vladimir, 'The Truth about Russia: A Liberal Society Is Not to Be Had in the Future', *Post-Soviet Prospects*, CSIS, Washington DC, vol. VI, no. 4, September 1998

Shlykov, Vitalyi V., 'The Crisis in the Russian Economy', Strategic Studies Institute, US Army War College, Carlisle Barracks PA, 1997

Skorokhodov, Yu, 'Soviet Far East—Problems and Prospects', *Far Eastern Affairs*, 1988, no. 3

Sorokin, Konstantin E. 'The Nuclear Strategy Debate', *Orbis*, Winter 1994

Thomas, Timothy, 'The Caucasus Conflict and Russian Security: The Russian Armed Forces Confront Chechnia. III The Battle for Grozny, 1–26 January 1995', Foreign Military Studies Office, Fort Leavenworth KS, 1997

Tishkov, Valery, 'Nationalities and Conflicting Ethnicity in Post-Communist Russia', United Nations Research Institute for Social Development, March 1994

Tolz, Vera, Slater, Wendy and Rahr, Alexander, 'Profiles of the Main Political Parties', in *Russia at the Crossroads*, RFE/RL Research Report, vol. 2, no. 20, 14 May 1993

Trenin, Dmitri, 'Stratégie russe: une difficile naissance', *politique étrangère*, no. 1, Spring 1997

Wilkening, Dean A., 'The Future of Russia's Strategic Nuclear Force', *Survival*, vol. 40, no. 3, 1998

NEWSPAPERS AND MAGAZINES

Air International
Air Forces Monthly
Armeiskii sbornik [Army Digest]
Australian Aviation
Bulletin of the Atomic Scientist
Chuo koron
Choson Ilbo
Defense News
Delovoi mir [Business World]
Der Spiegel
Helsingin Sanomat
International Defense Review
International Herald Tribune
Jane's Defence Weekly
Jamestown Prism
Komsomol'skaia pravda [Komsomol Truth]
Korea Herald
Korea Times
Krasnaia zvezda [Red Star]
Look Japan
Literaturnaia gazeta [Literature Newspaper]
Mainichi shimbun
Military News Bulletin
Military Parade (English Version)
Morskoi sbornik [Naval Digest]
Moskovskii komsomolets [Moscow Komsomolets]
Neftianik [Oilman]
Nezavisimaia gazeta [Independent Newspaper]
Nezavisimoe voennoe obozrenie [Independent Military Review]
New Yorker

Novosti
Obshchaia gazeta [Social News]
Pravda [Truth]
Rabochaia tribuna [Workers' Tribune]
Rossiiskaia gazeta [Russian Newspaper]
Rossiiskie vesti [Russian News]
Sankei shimbun
Segodnia [Today]
Sovietskaia Rossiia [Soviet Russia]
Sueddeutsche Zeitung
Straits Times
Sydney Morning Herald
Times (London)
Trud [Labour]
Vechernyi Novosibirsk [Evening Novosibirsk]
Voennyi parad [Military Parade]
Vooruzhenie, politika, konversiia [Armaments, Politics, Conversion]
Vostochno-sibr'skaia pravda [Eastern Siberia Truth]
Washington Post
Washington Times
Western Australian

NEWS AGENCIES

Asia Pacific Wireless File
Interfax
ITAR-TASS
Mayak
Novosti
NTV
Radio Rossii
Reuter
Xinhua
Yonhap

ELECTRONIC DATABASES AND ON-LINE NEWS

RADEA
USNI Database

OFFICIAL DOCUMENTS (NATIONAL AND INTERNATIONAL AGENCIES)

Australia, Department of Foreign Affairs and Trade, East Asia Analytical
    Unit, *Pacific Russia—Risks and Rewards*, Canberra, 1996
Camdessus, Michel, 'Russia and the IMF: Meeting the Challenges of an

Emerging Market and Transition Economy', Address to the US–Russia Business Council, Washington DC, 1 April 1998

Carter, Ashton, Assistant US Secretary of Defense for International Security Policy, 'Protecting US Security during the New Russian Revolution', *Defense Issues*, vol. 10, no. 77 (EV)

Cook, Frank (UK), 'The Reform of the Russian Military: Prospects, Possibilities and Dangers', Defence and Security Committee, North Atlantic Assembly, November 1998

Estrella, Rafael, 'The State of the Russian Forces', North Atlantic Assembly, October 1997

'Kontseptsiia natsional'noi bezopasnosti Rossiiskoi Federatsii' [Blueprint for National Security of the Russian Federation], Presidential Edict No. 1300, 17 December 1997.

Kozyrev, Andrei, 'Russia: A Chance for Survival', *Foreign Affairs*, Spring 1992

Law of the Russian Federation on Defence, Passed 24 April 1996 (No. 61-F3)

Law of the Russian Federation on Security, Passed 22 December 1992 (No. 4235-1)

'Osnovnye Polozhenia Voennoi Doktriny Rossiiskoi Federatsii' [Basic Provisions of the Military Doctrine of the Russian Federation], *Krasnaia zvezda*, 19 November 1993, pp. 1–2

Otkuda iskhodit ugroza miry [Whence the Threat to Peace], 3rd edn, Moscow, Voenizdat, 1984

Presidential Edict on Priority Measures for the Reform of the Armed Forces of the Russian Federation and the Improvement of their Structure, No. 725s, 16 July 1997

Presidential Edict on Several Measures for the Improvement of State Control in the Sphere of Defence and Security, No. 220, 3 March 1998

Presidential Edict on the Ministry of Defence of the Russian Federation and the General Staff of the Russian Federation, No. 1357, 11 November 1998; and associated Protocol on the General Staff

Presidential Edict on the Security Council of the Russian Federation, No. 1418, 18 November 1998

Protocol on the Security Council of the Russian Federation, No. 1024, 10 July 1996

United States Senate, Committee on Governmental Affairs, Subcommittee on International Security, Proliferation and Federal Services, 105th Congress, First Session, Hearing, June 5 1997: '*Proliferation: Russian Case Studies*'.

Index

Abakan 272
Abkhazia 75–6, 262, 263
ABM Treaty 71, 72, 112, 141
Academy of Military Sciences 71, 141, 142
Academy of Sciences 43
Aegean Sea 89
Aeromacchi 292
Afanasievski, Nikolai 171
Afghanistan 76–7, 263, 305
 Soviet invasion/occupation 81, 120,
  144, 245, 276
Aga-Buriat Locality 40, 58
Agrarian Party of Russia 16, 17, 58
Air Bridge 99 172
Air Forces xiii, 143, 160, 176, 178,
 194–8, 200–1, 204, 234–56
 capability assessments 234, 238, 249,
  250, 255
 command and control 178, 197,
  200–1, 234, 240, 242, 243, 244
 conditions of service 150, 270
 deployments 155, 174–5
  air defence 74
  post-Soviet redeployments 131, 234
  strike 174
 Eastern Russia 222, 241, 243–4, 245,
  246, 255–6, 274
 equipment/weapons 241, 242, 243–4,
  246, 248–54, 255
  air defence 243
  strike 243–4
 exercises 180, 247, 271
  air defence 180
  airlift 172, 271
  strike 180, 271
 force structure 235–6, 241–5, 316
  air defence 84, 158, 244
  airlift 243
  strike 158, 243–4
 missions 176, 235, 236–8, 243, 245,
  247, 253, 255–6
  air defence 222, 238–9, 243, 244
  airlift 243
  strike 85, 175–6, 239, 243–4, 253
 morale 155
 operations 246
 order of battle 240, 242–3, 244, 241,
  245, 248, 255
  air defence 244, 245
  airlift 243, 270
  strike 243–4, 245
 personnel issues 155, 234–5, 241–2,
  243–4, 246–7
 procurement 242, 247–54, 289
  air defence 243

R&D/technology 71, 248–54, 290, 293
 readiness 238, 241, 246
  air defence 246
  units of constant combat
   readiness 250
 reforms 158, 235–6, 238–45, 237, 255,
  316
 training 234, 242, 245–7, 255
  air defence 246
  airlift 245
  strike 245
Airborne Forces 144, 152, 243, 270–3, 263
 command and control 270
 deployments 269
 Eastern Russia 269
 equipment (maintenance) 280–1
 exercises 172, 225, 271
 force structure 269
 missions 270–1
 operations 23, 74, 75, 263, 271–3
 order of battle 262, 269, 270, 272
 personnel issues 271–3
 procurement 280–1
 R&D 280
 readiness 243, 267, 286
 reforms 271
 training 284–5
Alaska 39, 44
Albania 88
Algeria 294
Alma Ata 262
Alma Ata Declaration 5
Amur Province 50, 58, 106, 197
Amur River 39, 47, 101, 207
Anadyrskii Ostrog 39
Ananev, Yevgeny 295
Anisimov, Nikolai 248
APEC 124
 relations with Russia 69, 98–9, 125
 relations with the USSR 125
Apple 16, 17, 18, 57, 58, 59, 151
Arabian Sea 304
Arbatov, Aleksei 68, 70, 80, 133, 134,
 137, 153, 156, 162, 170
ARF 124
 relations with Russia 99
Armed Forces (*see also* Air Forces,
 biological weapons, chemical
 weapons, General Staff, Ground
 Forces, Navy, Military Doctrine,
 Military Space Forces, Nuclear
 Forces, Paramilitary Forces, strategic
 posture, and named military
 districts/fleets/units)

weapon systems) xiii-xv, 78, 93, 130–4, 143–6, 309
budgets/defence spending 141, 143, 145, 147, 155–7, 158, 174, 179, 180, 189, 228, 247, 270, 190, 293, 315, 317, 318
capability assessments 133, 145, 173, 314
civil–military relations xiv, 36–7, 41, 56, 76, 92, 95, 131, 142, 144–5, 257, 259, 261, 263, 293, 314, 315, 318
command and control 159, 163–6, 178–9, 187, 197, 260, 271
conditions of service 143, 145, 154–5, 156, 315, 318
conscription 143, 154, 162–3
crime 153, 277
deployments 133
post-Soviet redeployments 131, 143, 157, 277, 317
Eastern Russia xiii-xiv, 41, 176–80, 283
equipment 139, 143, 153, 277, 289, 318
exercises (joint) 165–6, 172, 180, 283, 318
force structure (see also Armed Forces-reform programs)158, 159, 160, 316
High Command 146, 148, 157, 163–6, 185, 187, 197, 200, 271, 275, 281
high precision weapons 175
higher education 169–70, 316
information warfare 69, 132, 140, 164, 175–6, 265
maintenance 139
mobilisation 163, 266
morale 139, 153, 315
operations 22, 74–5, 157
peacekeeping 75, 76, 80, 92, 174–5, 180, 269–70, 271
personnel issues 139, 144, 156, 157, 159, 160, 162–3, 186, 277
plans 87, 170, 263
procurement 280, 288–9, 194, 318
R&D/technology (see also Military Industry) 132
readiness 93, 133, 141, 143, 154–5, 159, 163, 174, 258, 265–8, 315
reform programs 134, 143, 148, 152, 157–60, 161, 176–80, 180–1, 259–60, 261, 316, 318
military district merger 158–9, 176–7
unified operational commands 159, 166, 176–80, 261, 269, 316
symbols and ceremonials 130
training 139, 155, 159, 283
women 163, 277
Armenia 9, 75
relations with Russia 83, 90–1
military deployments 91, 262
Armour Academy 170
Arms Sales (see Military Industry)
Arsenev 254, 280
ASEAN 97, 117
relations with Russia 99, 117, 119, 124
Asian Financial Crisis 97

Association of Siberian and Far East Cities 57, 60
Astrakhan xii
Avtovaz 13
Azerbaijan 9, 74–5, 81, 91, 315
relations with Russia 80
military deployments 74–5, 80, 262

Baikonur 118
Baku 22
Balkans (see also Albania, Bosnia, Bulgaria, Greece, Kosovo, Yugoslavia) 63, 71, 88–90, 94, 122, 141
Baltic States (see also Estonia, Latvia, Lithuania)
relations with Russia 83, 86–7, 136
relations with the USSR 261
Baluyevski, Yury 258, 264–5
Bangladesh 120
Barder, Sir Brian 88
Barents Sea 171
Barnaul 269
Bateman, Sam 205
Baturin, Yury 157
Bay of Bengal 120
Bay of Strelok 215
BBC 105
Belarus (Bielorussia) 5, 6, 9, 51, 131, 185, 188, 191, 261
relations with Russia 69, 77, 78, 79, 80, 136, 185, 297, 298
military industrial links 77, 84
Belgium 285
Belovezh Forest Agreement 5
Berdsk 273
Bering Sea 210, 225
Berlin Wall 6, 62, 121
Bhagvat, Vishnu 306
biological weapons 168–9, 296
Black Hundreds 10
Black Sea viii, 85
Blasko, Denis 309
Bondarev, Yury 242
Booth, Ken 204, 211
Bosnia 82
NATO operations 67
Russian views 67
Brezhnev, Leonid 41
Budennovsk 21, 174
Bukreyev, Yury 280
Bulgaria 88–9
Buriat Republic 40, 59, 247

Cam Ranh Bay (see also Vietnam) 118, 119, 210, 223
Cambodia 99
Caspian Sea (see also Navy) xiii, 8
CENTO 120
Central Asia (see also Strategic Posture —Russian Federation; and individual country/republic names) 80, 316
CFE Treaty 78, 126, 134
Eastern Russia 171, 176, 258, 278
Russian compliance 89, 171–2, 174, 198, 257, 258, 278, 281–2

Chechen-Ingush Republic (see also Chechnia) 21, 22
Chechevatov, Viktor 283
Chechnia 21, 22, 23, 24, 36, 55, 197, 259, 176
  1994–96 war xiv, 21–2, 23, 90, 93, 136, 149, 150, 155, 157, 223–4, 257, 262, 314, 315, 317
  evaluation 166, 235, 265–6, 278, 285
  operations 21, 92, 223–4, 235, 250–1, 253, 264, 278,
  units deployed 161, 175, 223–4, 263, 264, 267, 283
  future military option 175
Cheliabinsk xiii, 50, 52, 58, 110, 228
chemical weapons 78, 143, 167–8, 296
Chemical Weapons Convention 126, 167–8
Chernenko, Konstantin 41
Chernobyl 52
Chernomyrdin, Viktor 12, 30–1, 32, 44, 154, 157
Chevron 49
Chile 11, 34–5
China (see also Taiwan) xii, 25, 40, 97, 98, 99, 100–7, 111, 114, 115, 116, 117, 118, 119, 120, 123–5, 257, 295, 305, 306, 307
  military capabilities 110, 111, 199, 203, 231, 306, 308, 309
  relations with Russia 65, 68, 72, 97, 100–7, 121–9, 203, 258, 299
  arms purchases 124, 125–6, 258, 306–12
  border issues 100–6, 133, 258
  licensed military production 308
  military exchanges 103
  military technology transfer 308, 309, 310, 311
  strategic relations 67, 100–7, 309, 310, 311, 312
  relations with the USSR 98, 100, 100–1, 119, 176, 307
Chirkov, Valery 213
Chita 58, 154, 187, 242
Chubais, Anatoly 12, 57, 158
Chukotka Peninsula 177, 178, 179
Chukotsk Locality (Republic) 40, 59
Cold War xv, 37, 62, 88, 100, 104, 107, 113, 124, 128, 135, 183, 210, 300, 315
Commonwealth of Independent States (see also Newly Independent States) 5, 66, 75–6, 83, 139, 237, 315
  forces/military formations 78–9, 153, 206
  military operations 76
  military relations 71, 78–81, 83, 90, 91, 105, 137, 140, 141, 142, 143, 315
  agreements 78–9, 90
  peacekeeping 76
  political relations 78–81, 82, 83, 137
Communist Party of the Russian Federation 15, 33, 37, 58, 76, 151
  election results 16–18, 57–9
  platform 16–17
Communist Party of the Soviet Union 1, 16, 68
  Central Committee 16

Politburo 2, 16, 42
Congress of Russian Societies 16, 58
Constitution, Russian Federation 11, 13, 14, 15, 17, 18–19, 24, 69, 146
  executive government's powers 147–8
  Federal Assembly's powers 19, 147
  Federation Council's powers 19
  defence powers 147
  President's powers 19, 32, 62
  defence powers 146–7
  foreign affairs powers 62, 146
  State Duma's powers 19, 62
  defence powers 19, 147
Constitution, USSR 1977 13
Constitutional Court 16
'Cooperative Jaguar 98' 285
Cossacks 39, 161
  military units 75, 161–2, 274–5
Council of Europe 66
Cramer, Michael 220
Crimea 8, 85
Crimean War 88
Croatia 82
CSCE (see also OSCE) 66, 108
Cyprus 89–90
Czech Republic 69, 82, 85–6, 90
Czechoslovakia 261

Da Cunha, Derek 216
Dagestan 23, 262, 285
Dahlak 223
Dardanelles 88
Defence Council (Russian Federation) 137, 157
  abolition 148
  roles 134, 152
  relations with Security Council 148, 152
Defence Industrial Commission 289
Defense Intelligence Agency (US) 168
Democratic Choice of Russia 16, 17, 18, 58–9
Deneiken, Piotr 195, 198
Deng Xiaoping 104
Dorogin, Valery 179
DPRK (see North Korea)
Dzhida 247

East Siberia (see also Siberia) xiii, 41, 55, 110
elections 3
  RSFSR parliament 1989 1–3
  RSFSR President 1991 3
  Russia President 1996 17–18, 26, 32, 57, 151
  Russia President 2000 28, 34, 73, 123, 141, 317
  State Duma 1993 11
  State Duma 1995 15–17, 56, 58–9, 67–8, 149, 150
  State Duma 1999 34, 73, 123, 141, 317
  USSR Supreme Soviet 1990 2
Engels 196
Ernst & Young 50
Estonia (see also Baltic states) 9, 85, 86–7, 127
  relations with Russia 81

relations with the USSR 3, 5
European Bank for Reconstruction and
    Development 51
European Union 80, 122, 127
Evenk Locality 40, 59
Exxon 49

Far East Military District xiii, 78, 159,
    176, 177, 222, 225, 226, 235, 243, 244,
    254, 267, 272, 275, 280, 281, 282, 283
Far East Region xiii, 40, 41, 42, 43, 47, 52,
    54, 96, 102, 106, 107, 110, 133, 255
Far East Shipping Company 51
Fatherland Party (bloc) 36
Federal Assembly (see also Constitution,
    Federation Council, Russian
    Federation, State Duma) 19, 85, 147
    Law on Local Self-Government 56
    Law on Defence 147, 164
Federal Border Service (see also
    Paramilitary Forces—border troops)
    140, 149, 160–1, 217, 275
Federal Government Communications
    Agency 140, 149, 161
Federal Security Bureau 34, 36, 149, 161, 175
Federation Council (see also
    Constitution) 19, 26
Finland 51
Fiodorov, Viktor 215, 220
Fokino 215, 220
Foreign Intelligence Service 68, 72, 140, 149
Forward Russia 58
France 49, 122, 126, 199, 203, 283, 294, 304
Frunze Academy 170

G–7 30, 69
G–8 69
Gadauta 272
Gaidar, Yegor 30
Gareyev, Makhmut 71, 141, 142
Gargarin Air Force Academy 236
Garthoff, Raymond 134
GEC Marconi 295
General Agreement on Tariffs and Trade
    65–6, 125, 126
General Staff—Russian Federation 87,
    157, 177, 186, 265, 266, 267, 272,
    281, 296, 297, 298
    organisational aspects 148, 157, 158,
        164–6, 170, 259–60
        Chief of GS 157, 164, 200
        role in doctrine 164
Georgia 5, 9, 21, 74, 75–6, 81, 131
    relations with Russia 75–6
        military deployments 74, 75–6,
            262, 272
Germany 8, 49, 51, 82, 83
    relations with Russia 122, 126
    relations with the USSR 82, 100, 130, 261
Gorbachev, Mikhail 1–5, 12, 20, 41, 42,
    62, 63, 68, 71, 98, 101, 107, 113, 134,
    135, 142, 144, 183, 200, 201, 259, 307
Gorbulin, Vladimir 195
Gorno-Altai Republic 40, 59, 269

Gorshkov doctrine 207, 209
Grachev, Pavel 144, 145, 151, 152, 176, 266
Great Patriotic War (see also Second
    World War) 10, 130, 135, 143, 235, 245
Greece 88, 89, 90, 294
Ground Forces (see also Airborne Forces,
    Paramilitary Forces, Special Forces) 78,
    130, 143, 152, 160, 168, 204, 257–86
    budget issues 275, 270, 280, 284, 285,
        286
    capability assessments 163, 286
        artillery 175
    command and control 178, 259–61, 276
        abolition of GF Command 158,
            259–61, 271
    conditions of service 154, 270
    deployments 78, 171, 175
        artillery 171
        infantry 174
        post-Soviet redeployments 131, 257
        tank forces 171
        Eastern Russia 171, 257–8, 261, 263,
            269, 274, 280, 281, 282
    equipment 78, 258, 268, 277–82, 284, 286
        AD/missile troops 269, 278, 279, 282
        artillery 175, 278, 279, 281, 282, 284
        aviation units 254, 279, 282
        infantry 282
        tank forces 277, 282
    exercises 180, 281, 282
    force structure 258, 260–2, 265–9
        AD/missile troops 259, 262
        artillery 262
        aviation units 259, 262
        infantry 262, 267
        tank forces 259, 262
    Main Operational Directorate 158,
        259–61, 266–7
    missions 259, 264–5, 274
        tank forces 274
    morale 154, 263
    operations 74, 75, 76, 257, 262–4
        infantry 23, 75, 76, 263
    order of battle 261–2, 265–9, 286
        AD/missile troops 262, 269
        artillery 262, 269
        aviation units 254, 262, 269
        infantry 262, 269, 270
        tank forces 262, 269
    peacekeeping 269–70
    personnel issues 257, 261–2, 266,
        268, 275–7
        aviation 274, 279
    procurement 254, 257, 277–82, 278,
        279, 280, 289
    readiness 154–5, 165–8, 175, 258,
        263, 275, 276, 281, 282
        'units of constant combat
            readiness' 265–8, 276, 282,
            283, 285, 286, 316
    reforms 158, 259–61, 286
    training 257, 263, 268, 270, 282–92
        aviation units 269, 274, 283
    women 277

Grozny 21, 223, 317
GRU (see Main Intelligence Directorate)
Gulf War (1991) 236

Hainan–Luzon–Hong Kong triangle 212
Harbin 101
Hokkaido 110, 112, 246
Hong Kong 97, 98
Honour and Conscience 18
Hungary 51, 69, 82, 85–6, 90
Hyderabad 302

IAEA 297
IMF 30, 32–3, 65, 125, 126, 293
India 97, 117, 120, 125, 126, 295
    relations with Russia 97, 100, 104,
        117, 119–22, 125–8, 299, 300, 304,
        305, 306, 312–13
    arms purchases 125–6, 287–94,
        298–306, 312–13
    licensed production 299, 300, 301,
        312–13
    military technology transfer
        125–6, 298, 300, 312–13
    relations with the USSR 120, 125, 299
    arms purchases 299
    licensed production 125
Indian Ocean 99, 125, 206, 210, 211,
    223, 306
Indonesia 224, 287, 304
INF Treaty 202
information warfare (see Armed Forces)
Ingushetia (see Chechen-Ingush
    Republic, Chechnia)
Institute for Defence Studies 201
Institute of National Security and
    Strategic Studies 69
Iran 81, 90, 94, 120, 298
    relations with Russia 67, 122, 294, 296
Iraq (see also UN) 67, 70, 71, 80, 91, 94,
    99, 121, 126, 128, 304
    relations with Russia 122, 196
Irkutsk 39, 102, 196, 291
Irkutsk Province 50, 58
Israel 309
Italy 292
Itochu 110
Iuzhmash 170
Ivanov, Igor 70, 72, 97, 105
Ivanovo 272
Ivashov, Leonid 96

Japan 8, 28, 40, 51, 97, 111, 112, 114, 116,
    117, 119, 125, 127, 210, 211, 305, 309
    relations with Russia (see also Kuril
        Islands) 68, 97, 100, 102, 104,
        107–13, 116, 122, 124, 127, 246
    relations with the USSR (see also
        Kuril Islands) 100, 107, 109, 112
Jewish Autonomous Province 40, 55, 58
Jewish nationality 14, 42, 55

Kaliningrad 85, 86–7, 174, 229
Kaliningrad Special District 166, 177, 269

Kalpakkani 302
Kamchatka 58
Kamchatka Peninsula 43, 177, 178–9
Kamchatskaia 214
Kamov Design Bureau 254
Karasin, Grigory 110, 115
Karia Bay 220
Kasatonov, Igor 178
Kasperovich, Georgy 283
Kazakh nationality 8, 10, 103, 106
Kazakhstan xii, xiii, 9, 52, 171, 191
    relations with Russia 65, 97, 83, 103,
        195, 258, 262
    military aspects 91, 171, 185, 188,
        258, 262
    relations with the USSR 10, 176
Kazan aviation plant 198, 289
Kelly, R.J. 205, 231
Kemerovo city 51, 55
Kemerovo Province 58, 265
KGB 15, 68
Khabarovsk (city) 39, 242, 263, 273
Khabarovsk Territory 40, 43, 56, 58, 106, 288
Khakassia Republic 40, 59, 272
Khanti-Mansiisk (Mansai) Locality 28,
    40, 49, 54, 59
Khrushchev, Nikita 194
Kiakhta 273
Kiriyenko, Sergei 32
Kirshin, Yury 135, 136
Kitanovski, Lazar 89
Klebanov, Ilia 216
Kokoshin, Andrei 141, 153, 186, 281
Komsomolsk 207, 217, 291, 308
Korean Energy Development
    Organisation 114
Korean nationality 8, 42
Korean Peninsula (see also North Korea,
    South Korea) xii, 113–16
Korean War 113
Koriak Locality (Republic) 40, 59
Kornukhov, Anatoly 197, 198, 237, 238, 249
Kosovo 71, 73, 90, 116, 127
Kosvinski Mountain 187
Kot, Viktor 247
Kovytka 102
Kozyrev, Andrei 63, 65–6, 68, 73, 93, 96, 108
Krasnaia zvezda 198
Krasnoiarsk City 39, 41, 52, 57, 111, 263
Krasnoiarsk Territory 27–8, 40, 57, 58,
    60, 61, 288
Kuchma, Leonid 251
Kulikov, Anatoly 35
Kumar, Sushil
Kurgan Province xiii, 58
Kuril Islands
    dispute with Japan 107–110, 112
        Habomai Group 108, 112
    military/strategic issues 109, 110,
        210, 220, 244
Kuroyedov, Vladimir 227, 306
Kuzbas 43
Kuznetsk 43
Kuznetsov, Valentin 193

Kvashnin, Anatoly 175–6, 266
Kyrgyzstan 9, 171
  relations with Russia 79, 83, 103,
    171, 262
  relations with the USSR 176

Lake Baikal 25, 53
Lake Karachai 52
Laos 99
Latvia (see also Baltic states) 9, 85, 86–7,
    127
  relations with Russia 81
  relations with the USSR 3, 5
Lavrov, Sergei 122
Lebed, Aleksandr 18, 28, 29, 57, 61, 74,
    79, 151–2, 272
Lenin, Vladimir 3
Leningrad (see St Petersburg)
Leningrad Military District 74, 131, 171,
    174, 268
Liaki 80
liberal democracy 11, 13, 14, 19, 26, 34,
    37, 56, 60, 65
Liberal Democratic Party of Russia 16,
    17, 18, 56–9, 151
Libya 94
Lithuania (see also Baltic states) 9, 10,
    20, 85, 86–7, 174
Liu Huaqing 307
Lugernetskoe 49
Lukashenko, Aleksandr 83
Luzhkov, Yury 27, 35, 36, 72, 85, 91

Macedonia 88, 89, 127
Magadan 40, 43, 50, 58, 98
Main Intelligence Directorate 160, 273
Makachkala 23
Makiyenko, Konstantin 310
Malaysia (see also Military
    Industry—arms sales) 97
Maritime Territory 28, 39, 40, 43, 44, 56,
    57, 58, 60, 105, 106, 218
Marubeni 50, 110
Mayak plant 50
MccGwire, Michael 206
Mediterranean Sea 88, 172, 211
Mexico 98
Middle East (see also Persian Gulf) 65,
    67, 68, 95
Midway 210
MiG-MAPO 248
Mikhailov, Viktor 85
Mikhailovski Artillery Academy 284
Mil Design Bureau 254
Military Doctrine xiii, 63, 71, 72, 131–4,
    146, 157, 167, 175–6, 180–1, 228,
    235, 237, 250–1, 264–5, 266, 270,
    289, 315
  operational 134
  strategic 134–42
    1992 draft 135
    'Basic Provisions' 1993 135–7, 183
    'Blueprint' 1997 69, 137–40, 148,
      213, 237

'Fundamentals' 1998 140–1, 159
  limited nuclear war 182
  local war 135, 136, 139, 142,
    165–6, 180–1, 235, 237, 263, 266
  nuclear aspects 135, 136, 138, 140,
    173, 180, 182–5, 201–2, 203, 315
  threat assessment 69, 72, 135–42,
    170, 180–1
  war scenarios 136, 172, 173, 183,
    237, 263
Military Industry (see also Sukhoi,
    MiG-MAPO) xiii, 150, 207, 217,
    228–9, 248, 253–4, 255, 279, 280,
    281, 287–313, 315, 318
  Eastern Russia 52, 288, 291
  government measures 289, 291–2, 294
  conversion
  government structures 284
  privatisation 289, 292
  NIS aspects 77, 288, 292, 296
  nuclear 53
  R&D/technology 296, 313
  sales xiii, 89, 294–312
    China 124, 125–6, 287, 292, 294,
      297, 301, 306–12, 313
    India 125–6, 287, 294, 298–306
    Malaysia 119, 287
    North Korea 287
    South Korea 116, 287
Military Space Forces (see also Nuclear
    Forces) 51, 143, 158, 185, 187–8, 200, 316
  command and control 200
  deployments 188
  Eastern Russia 51
  equipment 188
  ground stations 84, 185
  launch facilities 51, 185, 188
  order of battle 187–8
  operations 187–8
  procurement 188
  readiness 187–8
  reforms 158, 185, 316
Minister of Defence 144, 149, 151, 152,
    157, 159, 200, 270, 282
  roles 160, 164
Ministry of Defence 131, 155, 157, 159,
    160, 162, 177, 193, 202, 220, 275,
    281, 292, 295
  roles 152, 158
Ministry of Defence Industry 289
Ministry of Emergencies 275
Ministry of Foreign Affairs 93, 149, 296
Ministry of Interior (Internal Affairs)
    13–14, 36, 149, 157, 160, 167
  forces (deployments, operations) 21,
    22, 143, 151, 160, 167, 175, 177,
    224, 264, 266, 275, 278, 283, 285
Ministry of Security 157
Minsk 5, 78
Mitsubishi 110
Mitsui 50, 110
Moldavia (see also Moldova) 3
Moldova 5, 9, 74, 81
  Russian military deployments 74, 262

Mongolia xii, 97, 98, 117–18, 258, 317
    relations with Russia 102, 258
    relations with the USSR 101, 176
Mor'skaia kul'tura 227
Moscow 6, 20, 27, 35, 44, 54, 79, 86, 172, 244
Moscow Military District 74, 133, 134,
    166, 267, 268, 277
Mozdok 197–8
MTCR 296, 298

Nagorno-Karabakh 74–5
Nakhodka 51, 52, 244
National Space Agency 188
Navy xiii, 87, 130, 160, 200–1, 204–33
    budget issues 207, 220, 222, 227–8,
        230, 232
    capability assessments 205, 215, 220,
        224, 231–2
    command and control 177–8, 200–1,
        213, 214, 221, 226, 232, 269
    conditions of service 154, 155
    deployments (see also Cam Ranh Bay,
        South China Sea) 71, 87, 118–19,
        172, 174, 177, 210, 219, 220, 224, 225
        post-Soviet redeployments 79, 85
        ship visits 103, 114, 118
    Eastern Russia 204–33
    equipment 207–9, 210, 213–17, 228–31
        amphibious 223–4
        aviation 208, 221–3
        carriers 208
        submarines 143, 210, 217–21, 228–9
        surface 215–17, 228, 229, 230
    exercises 180, 213, 223, 224–6
    force structure 207–9, 213–27
        Baltic Fleet 172, 173, 214, 223, 228
        Black Sea Fleet 85, 172, 173, 214, 228
        Caspian Sea Flotilla 214, 228
        Kamchatka Flotilla 177–9, 214
        Mediterranean Squadron 172
        Northern Fleet 172, 173, 200, 214,
            216, 219, 223, 228, 230, 232
        Pacific Fleet 71, 155, 173, 177–9,
            200, 204–33, 269, 278
    missions 205–7, 210–13
        amphibious 223–4
        ASW 215, 219, 220, 221
        aviation 219, 221
        submarines 210, 220
        surface 210, 215–17
    morale 155, 226–7
    operations
        amphibious 223–4
        ASW 215
        submarines 178
        surface 208
    order of battle 207–9, 211, 213–27,
        227–31, 232
        amphibious 223–4
        aviation 213, 214, 221–3
        carriers 211
        submarines 177–8, 213, 217–21
        surface 213, 214, 215–17
    personnel issues 226–7, 228, 231

    amphibious 223–4
    aviation 223–4
    procurement 227–31, 289
    readiness 233
        amphibious 224
        aviation 222–3
        submarines 219–20
    training 224–6
        amphibious 224, 226
        aviation 222–3, 225–6
        submarines 224, 225–6
Nazdratenko, Yevgeny 56
Nemtsov, Boris 51, 110
Newly Independent States (see also
    Commonwealth of Independent
    States, Strategic Posture—Russian
    Federation) 73–81
    economic relations 77
Nizhne Kamchatsk 39
Nizhni Novgorod 292
Nizhniaia Tura 52
Non-Aligned Movement 120
North Atlantic Cooperation Council 65
North Atlantic Treaty Organisation
    (NATO) (see also Strategic
    Posture—Russian Federation,
    Yugoslavia–NATO operations) 65, 67,
    78, 80, 81, 82, 86, 87, 88, 89, 90,
    123, 124, 135, 141, 170–4, 180, 183,
    184, 286, 295, 296, 297, 315
    capability assessments 170
    deployments 89, 132, 171
    forces 85
    new strategic concept 141
    operations 63, 88, 99
    Partnership for Peace 90, 171
    plans 84
    relations with Russia 65, 68, 70, 72,
        82, 134, 135, 181, 285
        Founding Act 69, 171
North Caucasus Military District 171,
    172, 174–5, 267, 268, 269, 276, 285
North Korea xii
    relations with Russia 113–16
        military relations 100, 114, 115, 116
    relations with the USSR 113–15
        1961 Treaty 113
Novaia Zemlia 53
Novorossiisk 272
Novosibirsk city 39, 57, 58, 242, 250,
    267, 269, 283, 288, 291
Novosibirsk province 58
Novozhilov, Genrikh 251
NPT 114, 194, 297
Nuclear Forces (see also Military Space
    Forces, Navy, SALT I-II, START I-II-III)
    135, 138, 143, 152, 182–203, 228–9, 269
    budget issues 187, 189, 190, 198, 202, 228
    capability assessments 192, 194
        bombers 189
        ICBM 189, 191, 192, 193, 194
        SSBN/SLBM 189
    command and control 185, 186, 187,
        190, 197, 199–201

launch security 189–90, 201, 203
conditions of service 182
deployments
  bombers 196–8
  ICBM 185, 191
  post-Soviet redeployments 185, 195, 197
  SSBN/SLBM 218
Eastern Russia
  bombers 187
  SSBN/SLBM 177–8, 217–21
equipment/maintenance 182
  bombers 195–9
  ICBM 186, 190–4
  SSBN/SLBM 217–21, 228–9
exercises 170–1, 172, 224
force structure 185–8, 197
  bombers 187, 194–9, 243
  ICBM 185–8, 189–94
  SSBN/SLBM 187, 217–21
missions 196
  bombers 196–7, 243, 245
  ICBM 196
  SSBN/SLBM 196
operations, SSBN/SLBM 178, 224
order of battle
  bombers 187, 192, 195–99, 243, 245
  ICBM 185–7, 189–94
  SSBN/SLBM 187, 192, 217–21, 228–9
personnel issues 185, 187–8, 195, 199
plans 196
procurement 190–1, 197, 198–9
R&D 190, 191, 198, 289
readiness 156, 189, 193, 197, 199, 219, 243
reforms 158, 197, 316
  unified OGK 159, 182, 199–201
  unified SMF 160, 182–3, 185–94, 200, 316
tactical weapons 201–2, 215, 281–2
training 191, 199, 245
nuclear pollution 52–3, 221
Nuclear Proliferation (see Proliferation)
Nuclear Suppliers Group 297

oil and gas industry–Russian Federation 27, 77
  eastern Russia 13, 47–50, 54, 102, 110, 291
Okhotsk 39
Omsk (city) 39, 43, 187, 272, 275, 290
Omsk Province 58, 288, 291
Oparin, Nikolai 196, 199
Orenburg 187, 285
Orthodox Church 88
  Russian Orthodox Church 10, 15, 42, 130
    Christ the Saviour Church 15
OSCE (Organisation for Security and Cooperation in Europe) 90, 122, 136
Ossetia (North and South) 22, 73–4, 262

Pacific Ocean (see also Navy–Pacific Fleet, Russian Federation–borders) xiii, 210
Pakistan 120, 127, 299, 304, 305, 312
Pamiat 10
Paramilitary Forces (see also Federal

Border Service, Federal Government Communications Agency, Federal Security Ministry, Ministry of Interior) 143, 159, 166–7, 175, 177, 273
  border troops 36, 143, 156, 217, 283
  civil defence troops 143
  communication troops 143
  railroad troops 143, 161
  Service for the Protection of the Russian President 36, 143, 149, 152, 161
Paris Declaration (1990) xv
Party of Workers' Self-Management 16, 18
Pavlov, Dimitri 89
Pavlovskoe 218, 220
Peacekeeper 99 285
Perestroika 42
Persian Gulf (see also Middle East) 91, 95, 125, 126, 128, 134, 287
Peru 98
Petropavlovsk 39
Petropavlovsk-Kamchatski 178, 214, 218, 220
Plesetsk 186, 188
Poland 51, 69, 82, 85, 90, 132, 171, 173, 174, 261
Popular Republican Party 57
Portugal 11
Power to the People 17, 58–9
Prigorodny 22
Priluki 195
Primakov, Yevgeny 23, 32, 41, 61, 67, 68, 70, 71, 72, 93–4, 104, 110, 111, 121–2, 301
proliferation (see also biological weapons, chemical weapons, MTCR) 296–8
  missiles 99, 115, 298, 296, 311
  nuclear 99, 114–15, 120, 296–8
Promexport 294
Prudnikov, Viktor 246
Pskov 22, 272
Putin, Vladimir 34

Razumkov, Aleksandr 84
Red Star 131
Redut 95 165
Redut 96 165–6
Referendum, March 1991 3
Riazantsev, Valery 225
Rodionov, Igor 83, 137, 151, 152, 156, 178, 189, 270
Rogov, Sergei 157, 194, 201
ROK (see South Korea)
Romania 74, 85, 90
Rostov 242
Rosvooruzhenie 294, 295
Royal Dutch Shell 50
RSFSR (Russian Soviet Federated Socialist Republic) 18, 60, 131, 176, 288
  flag 14
  politics 1–8
  territory 8, 74
Russia (see also RSFSR, Russian Federation) 14

culture 10
Declaration of Sovereignty 1990 3, 18
geography xii, 29, 44–7
history 10, 39, 63, 66, 83, 98, 130, 204
    pan-Slavism 66, 67, 88
Russia Our Home 16, 17, 18, 58–9
Russian Communist Workers Party 17
Russian Federation (see also RSFSR, Russia)
    administrative units 8, 18–29, 54–5
    nationality-based units 8–9, 40, 55
    borders xii, 8, 64, 74, 75, 78, 81, 85,
        92, 131, 134, 140, 155, 258, 286
    civil aviation 158
    coat of arms 14
    defence industry (see Military
        Industry)
    Eastern Russia (see also Military
        Industry, oil and gas) xii–xiv, 39–61
        administrative units 39, 54–5
        economy 13, 28, 41–54, 60–1, 95,
            97, 101–6, 107–11
        infrastructure 41, 47, 48, 51–2
            101–2, 103, 105, 110–11
        military issues xii–xiv, 41, 109–10,
            176–8
        politics xiii, 41–2, 43, 54–61
        population 25, 39–41, 43, 105–6, 118
        resources 41, 42, 44, 47, 49, 52,
            54, 60, 96, 102, 107
        social conditions 41, 42, 43, 47,
            49, 58
        topography xiii, 44–7
    economy (see also IMF, Military
        Industry, oil and gas) xiii, xv, 6, 12,
        27–37, 41–54, 77, 96, 101, 114, 123,
        132, 138, 180, 255, 261, 315
        black economy 27, 35
        exchange rate 30, 32
        foreign aid 6, 37, 107–8
        GDP growth 6, 32–4, 35
        inflation 30
        poverty 6, 27, 31, 32, 37
        privatisation 12–13, 30
        resources 29, 47, 49–50, 54
        social welfare (pensions) 14, 25,
            27, 31, 32, 42
        state budgets 25, 26, 27, 35, 44, 58
        unemployment 31, 33, 42, 47
        wages 6, 31, 32, 33, 35, 42
    environmental conditions 36, 52–4, 138
    flag 14
    foreign relations (see also Balkans,
        Baltic States, Central Asia,
        country headings for bilateral
        partners and headings for
        multilateral organisations) 5–6,
        36–8, 63, 94, 95, 97, 136, 139
        CIS 66, 75–6, 81, 82, 83
        East Asia/Asia Pacific xiv, 65,
            96–129, 138
        Eastern Europe 65, 81–8, 88–90
        EU 65, 81, 86
        Middle East 67, 68, 95

NIS 64, 65, 73–81, 90–1, 93, 128,
    136, 143
South Asia xiii, xiv, 119–20,
Southeast Asia 65, 119
Transcaucasus 73–4, 75–6, 80, 81,
    90–1, 128, 133
human rights 13–14, 19, 37
internal security 138, 140, 174
    law and order 12–14, 35, 138, 153
    local government 27, 56, 60, 105
    military strategy (see military doctrine)
    ministries (see also Ministry of Defence,
        Ministry of Interior)(Emergencies,
        Security) 148, 149
    national identity xiiii, xv, 8–11, 62, 66–7
    politics (see also Constitution,
        elections) xiii, xv, 10–20, 34–8, 42,
        60–1, 62, 65–6, 92, 94, 105, 106,
        123, 180, 316–18
        nationalism 15–16, 34, 72
        nationalities 8–9, 21–4, 40, 55
        parliamentary politics (see Federal
            Assembly, Federation Council,
            State Duma)
        political parties 15–18
        presidential administration 60, 62,
            92, 146, 149, 153, 162
        role of armed forces 36–8, 41, 56, 76,
            92–3, 95, 131, 142, 144–55, 257,
            259, 261, 263, 293, 314, 315, 318
    population 8–9, 39–40, 105–6, 118
    regionalism 20–9, 36, 41, 42, 54–6,
        60–1, 105–6, 128, 139
        economic aspects 24–9, 60
        Far East Republic 24–5, 56
        regional associations (see also
            Siberian Accord) 24, 55, 56, 57–60
    territory 8, 92, 98, 103, 139
Rutskoi, Aleksandr 145
Rybachi 218, 219
Rybkin, Ivan 85, 184
Ryzhkov, Viktor 211

Sakha Republic (Yakutia) 40, 47, 51, 59,
    110, 177
Sakhalin Energy 50
Sakhalin Island 39, 49, 110
Sakhalin Province 40, 58
SALT II 228, 229
Samovydvizhenie 59
San Francisco Peace Treaty 98
Saratov xii, 191
Saudi Arabia 81
Savosleika 247
Sea of Japan 211, 220, 225, 226
Sea of Okhotsk 102, 107, 178, 211, 219,
    220, 225, 226
Second World War (see also Great
    Patriotic War) 3, 130, 204
Security Council (Russian Federation) 78,
    85, 137, 141, 148–50, 152, 201, 202
    composition 149
    enabling legislation 148
    roles 146, 148

relations with Defence Council
148, 152
Sergeyev, Igor 70, 71, 72, 84, 89, 141, 152,
154, 157, 162, 170, 171, 239, 267, 276
Severodvinsk 173, 228
Shakrai, Sergei 40
Shandong 102
Shpak, Georgy 272
Siberia (see also East Siberia, Russian
Federation–Eastern Russia, West
Siberia) 40, 42, 43, 44, 47, 51, 52, 53,
54, 55, 96, 102, 133, 255
Siberian Accord (see also Russian
Federation–Politics) 24, 55, 56, 283
Siberian Chemical Combine 53
Siberian Military District xiii, 154, 155,
159, 176, 244, 264, 267, 268, 269,
272, 273, 275, 277, 278, 182, 283
Sibneft 13, 49
Singh, Jasjit 205
Sitnov, Anatoly 248, 281
Slovakia 82
Slovenia 263
Smolensk 196
Sobchak, Anatoly 4
South Asia (see Bangladesh, India, Pakistan)
South China Sea 99, 100
South Korea 28, 51
relations with Russia 97, 100, 102, 113–16
relations with the USSR 113–14
South Ossetia (see Ossetia)
South Pacific 99
Special forces 160, 161, 270, 273, 274
capability assessments 224
conditions of service 274
deployments 174, 175
Eastern Russia 269–73
force structure 160, 161, 262, 269, 273
missions 272
operations 22, 75, 223–4, 263
order of battle 262, 269
readiness 224
St Petersburg (formerly Leningrad) 86,
87, 131, 174, 242
Stalin, Iosif 1, 15
START I 191–3, 202
START II 189, 192–4, 202
START III 193–4
Staskov, Nikolai 272
State Duma (see also Constitution–
Russian Federation) 19, 33, 34, 56,
62, 70, 72, 80, 147, 149, 160, 192
committees 12–13, 19, 23, 70, 80,
137, 153, 156, 193
Strategic Posture–Russian Federation
xiii-xv, 1, 62–95, 121–28, 286, 314–18
Central Asia xii, 62, 77, 80, 81, 120
East Asia/Asia Pacific xii, 62, 96–129,
204–6, 252, 309–10, 311, 314, 316
Eastern Russia xiii-xiv, 1, 41, 96–7,
205, 231–3
Europe 62, 65, 68, 70, 72, 81–90, 97,
120, 170–4, 286, 314, 316, 317
Kosovo 71

NATO expansion 64, 67, 69, 70,
71, 72, 81–8, 90–1, 94, 123,
125, 127, 133, 136, 137, 139,
141, 170–4, 180–1, 202, 305
Middle East 67, 68, 95, 306
NIS 64, 65, 67, 70, 131, 136, 143,
174, 317
Baltic 136
Belarus 69, 131, 136
Central Asia 67, 133, 174–5, 258
Kazakhstan 65
Southern Russia 90–1
Transcaucasus 67, 128, 131, 171, 174–5
Ukraine 65, 131, 136
Persian Gulf 70, 71, 95, 306
threat assessments 67, 68, 69, 72, 85,
86, 87, 88, 97, 105–6, 133, 134, 135,
142, 153, 170, 172, 180–1, 183, 310
Suez Canal 51
Sukhoi 198, 291–2
Sukhoi Log 50
Sukhumi 75
Sungari River 101
Surgutneftegaz 49
Sverdlovsk Province xiii, 27, 56, 58, 60,
61, 288
Sverdolovsk (see Yekaterinburg)
Svobodny 51, 188
Sweden 93
Szczecin 171

Taimyr Locality 40, 59
Taiwan 97, 98, 110, 111, 124, 125, 127,
308, 309
Tajikistan 9
relations with Russia 76–7, 79, 80,
83, 103
military aspects 75, 76–7, 91, 92,
262, 276
Tartarstan 3
Tashkent Treaty 78, 80, 83
Tatishchevo 191
Tblisi 22, 250, 292
Thomson CSF 295
Tiumen Oil 13
Tiumen Province 58
TMD 71, 112, 116, 127
Togliatti 13
Tomsk (city) 39, 52
Tomsk Province 58
Trans-Siberian Railway 43–4, 47, 51, 111
Transbaikal Military District 78, 101,
117, 154, 155, 177, 267, 272, 277, 283
merger with Siberian MD 1777, 268
Transformation of the Fatherland 56, 58
Treaty of Nerchinsk 39
Treaty of Peking 39
Trubnikov, Viacheslav 72
Tula 272
Turkey 81, 88, 89, 90, 91, 120, 173
Turkmenistan 9
Tyva Republic 40, 59

Ukraine 5, 8, 10, 65, 74, 87, 90, 123,
131, 185, 191, 261
military industry 190, 207, 251–2, 288, 305
relations with Russia 69, 81, 83,
84–5, 136, 190, 305
military aspects 78, 83, 84–5, 185,
188, 195–6, 251–2, 297, 305
Ukrainian Republic (USSR) 5
Ukrainka 197
Ulan Ude 250, 254, 272, 292
Ulianovsk 272
Union Treaty, draft 4, 142
United Arab Emirates 294
United Kingdom 98, 126, 146, 203, 283,
294, 299, 304
United Nations 136, 165, 263, 270
Russian seat 5
Security Council 6, 66, 67, 71, 95,
121, 122, 138, 141, 170
sanctions against Iraq 70, 126, 297
UNSCOM 70, 297
Ural Mountains xiii, 39, 54, 56, 187
Urals Military District xiii, 133, 159,
177, 242, 267, 268, 282
merger with Volga MD 177, 268
USA xii, 28, 39, 40, 44, 60, 71, 94, 97,
118, 119, 124, 131, 132, 134, 137, 146,
265, 277, 293, 294, 296, 297, 298, 299
foreign relations, Russia 65, 67, 68,
70, 71, 72, 73, 80, 94, 95, 97, 100,
104, 112–13, 121–8, 170, 185,
191–4, 213, 297, 299
navy 107, 112, 118, 204–6, 209–10,
220, 223, 231–2
nuclear forces 100, 189, 194, 196, 203
strategic policy 65, 67, 70, 71, 80, 81,
84, 86, 90, 93, 94, 95, 97, 99, 104,
106, 107, 110, 111, 112, 115, 116,
117, 120, 121–8, 141, 170, 180–1,
300, 305, 307, 315, 316
USSR xii-xv, 18, 23, 103, 180, 206, 209,
211, 232, 288, 289
armed forces 7, 36, 63, 74, 75, 78,
101, 118, 130, 131, 132, 135, 142,
144, 158, 176, 227, 258, 261, 277
air forces 78, 235, 236, 254
biological weapons 168
chemical weapons 167
ground forces 78, 257–8, 259,
261–2, 263
navy 100–1, 118, 172, 204–6, 207,
208–10, 211, 215, 217, 220,
223, 224
nuclear forces 78, 182–3, 201
operations 22, 73, 74, 76, 186, 194
special forces 273
economy 7, 12, 24, 31, 41 49, 77, 113
foreign relations 73–5, 82, 113
nationality policy 9, 10, 55
politics 1–8, 11–12, 18, 31, 36, 55,
130, 131, 144, 153
population 8–9
social conditions 7, 31
strategic policy 7, 62–3, 82, 83, 92,

100–1, 104, 107, 113, 117, 135,
173, 182, 206, 315
territory 86, 107
Ussuri River 102
Ussuriisk 272, 273
Ust-Orda Buriat Locality 40, 59
Uzbekistan 9, 81, 90, 171, 315
relations with Russia 80

Vasiutin, Vladimir 236
Vietnam (see also Cam Ranh Bay) 97,
117, 210
relations with Russia 100, 117,
118–19, 128, 294
relations with the USSR 98–9, 100,
118–19, 206
Vilnius 22
Vizag 302
Vladimir 187
Vladivostok 39, 40, 41, 44, 51, 57, 98,
105, 107, 113, 213, 214, 218, 244
Vlasika 187
Volga Military District (see also Urals
Military District) 133, 177, 268, 283
Volga River xii
Volgograd xii
Voronezh 247
Vozdushnyi most 271

Warsaw Pact 6, 65, 67, 69, 82, 131, 134,
136, 171, 254, 257, 261, 195
West Siberia (see also Siberia) xiii, 41,
49, 55, 291
Women of Russia 16, 17, 18
Working Russia 16
World Bank 65, 126

Xinjiang 103

Yablokov, Aleksei 202
Yadav, Mulayam Singh 300, 302
Yakovlev, Vladimir 183, 190
Yakovlev Design Bureau 292
Yakutia (see Sakha)
Yamalo-Nenetsk Locality 28, 40, 54, 59
Yavlinksi, Grigory 18, 57, 80, 151
Yefanov, Viacheslav 251
Yekaterinburg 39, 42, 52, 242, 267
Yelisovo 235
Yeltsin, Boris 1–4, 11, 12, 15, 20, 25, 37,
76, 123, 144, 151, 317
Eastern Russia 42, 54, 56
economic policies 28, 30, 33, 34
foreign policies 68, 73, 80, 108, 111
impeachment 34, 159–60
presidential campaign 1996 18
strategic/military policies 69, 72, 92, 93,
94, 130, 135, 137, 140, 144, 149, 152,
154, 156, 157, 158, 159, 162, 167,
168, 169, 185, 201, 231, 251, 269, 289
Yenisei River 52
Yokosuka 112
Yugoslavia (see also Bosnia, Croatia,
Kosovo) 82, 88, 90, 121

NATO operations 63, 71, 72, 83, 88, 90, 99, 122, 141, 170, 174, 242, 263, 295, 315
Russian military involvement 72, 88, 90, 263
Yukos 49
Yuksi 49

Yurga 267, 283

Zabaikalsk 103
Zakharenko, Mikhail 207, 226
Zhirinovski, Vladimir 18, 28, 36, 56, 80, 151
Ziuganov, Gennady 18, 151
Zolotaia Dolina 244

Index of weapon systems/platforms

Aircraft

An–12 221, 251
An–22 243, 252
An–70 251, 252
An–124 243, 252
F/A–18A 302
F–22 252
Il–38 221
Il–76 160, 241, 243, 251, 252, 308
Il–78 196, 234, 247
Il–106 251
Ka–25 221
Ka–27 217, 221, 308
Ka–28 308
Ka–29 221
Ka–50 254, 279, 280
Ka–52 254
Ka–60 254
L–39 241
L–410/Tu–134 241
LFI 253
MFI 252–3
Mi–4 194
Mi–8 175, 279
Mi–14 221
Mi–17 308
Mi–24 160, 254, 280
Mi–26 279
Mi–28 254
MiG–21 89, 302
MiG–23 241, 242, 244
MiG–25 241
MiG–27 250
MiG–29 89, 91, 195, 241, 242, 243, 248–9, 295
MiG–31 180, 222, 235, 241, 242, 243, 244, 246, 247, 249, 311
S–37 252–3, 255
Su–17 222, 250
Su–24 221, 222, 241, 247, 250
Su–25 222, 241, 242, 243, 249–50, 292
Su–27 195, 222, 234, 241, 242, 243, 244, 248, 249, 250, 291, 294, 307–8, 310, 311
Su–30 241, 247, 291, 295, 301, 302, 309
Su–34 241, 248
Su–35 116
T–60S 198
Tu–16 222
Tu–22 196, 198–9, 221, 222

Tu–95 187, 194, 195, 196, 198, 199, 221, 222, 234, 247
Tu–142 210, 221
Tu–160 187, 195, 196, 198, 199, 234
Tu–330 251
Yak–38 222
Yak–130 292

Ground Forces

BMP 271, 278, 280, 289
BTR 278, 279
Centimetre 281
Krasnopol 281
Msta-S 279
Shmel' 308
Smerch 308
T–72 89, 223, 278, 294
T–80 223, 278, 290–1, 305
T–90 278, 279, 294

Missiles/Space Vehicles

9K–22 243
9M–38 243
AIM–7M 302
AIM–9M 302
AS–15 ALCM 195
Buran 290
Iskandr 202, 279
Kh–31 249
Kh–59 249
Oka 202, 279
Patriot 86
Pioneer 202
Proton 290
R–73 253, 301
R–77 249, 253
RS–12 Topol 186, 190, 191, 202
RS–20 186, 190
RS–22 190
S–300 89, 91, 116, 180, 243, 269, 308
SA–8 223
SA–9 223
Scud 202, 279, 281
SS–17 191
SS–18 187, 191, 192
SS–19 187, 191
SS–24 187, 191
SS–25 187, 192
SS–26 187
SS-N–8 219

SS-N-12 215
SS-N-14 217
SS-N-18 187, 219
SS-N-19 220
SS-N-20 187
SS-N-22 216
SS-N-23 187
SS-N-28 229
Tochka-U 281, 282
Tomahawk 210, 229
Tor M-1 308
Tunguska-M 294
X-31/A 249

Ships

Amazon 304
Arleigh Burke 231
Gearing 304
Ivan Rogov 224
Kara 208, 213
Kashin 208, 216
Kiev 206, 208, 211, 215, 303
Kildin 216
Kirov 208, 216
Kotlin 208, 216
Kresta 208
Krivak 208, 217, 303
Kynda 173, 208
Leander 203
Neustrashimyi 173
Novik 229
Ropucha 212
Skoryi 216
Slava 208, 215

Sovremennyi 173, 208, 215, 216, 217, 230
Sverdlov 208, 215
Ticonderoga 216
Udaloi 173, 208, 212, 215, 217, 232
Ushakov 173, 208, 215, 216, 230

Submarines

Akula 218, 220, 231, 232
Augusto 304
Borey 228
Bravo 218
Charlie 218, 302
Daphne 304
Delta 218, 219
Echo 218
Foxtrot 218
Golf 218
Hotel 219
India 218
Juliet 218
Kilo (636/877) 218, 220, 294, 302, 303, 308
Los Angeles 231
November 218
Oscar 180, 210, 218, 219, 220, 231
Severodvinsk 229, 303
St Petersburg 229
Victor 218, 220
Whisky 218
Yankee 218, 219

Index of named military units/ships

Air Forces

11th AF/AD Air Army 244, 283
22nd Bomber Div 196, 197, 199
30th LRA Army 196
46th LRA Army 196
37th Strategic Air Army 197, 199, 200, 243
61st Strategic Air Army 243, 251, 271
73rd Bomber Div 197, 200
121st Bomber Rgt 196, 197
123rd Bomber Rgt 197
126th Bomber Rgt 197
182nd Bomber Rgt 195, 197
184th Bomber Rgt 195

Ground Forces/Airborne (AB)/Special Forces (SF)/Naval Infantry (RNI)

4th Army 75
4th Guards Tank Div 267
7th AB Div 272

10th Independent Airborne Bde 263
10th Operational Sqn (SF-naval) 215
11th Air Assault Bde (AB) 272
11th Guards Army 177
14th Army 74
27th Infantry Div 270
31st Indep AB Bde 272
34th Infantry Div 267
45th Indep AB Bde 271
55th Div (RNI) 223
58th Army 175, 285
74th Indep. Infantry Bde 267, 283
76th AB Div 271, 272, 284
81st Infantry Rgt 268
83rd Air Assault Bde (AB) 272
84th Infantry Div 267
98th AB Div 271, 272
100th AB Bde 272
104th AB Div 272
106th AB Div 272
136th Infantry Bde 23
165th Rgt (RNI) 224
201st Infantry Div 76-7, 276
331st AB Rgt 271

336th Infantry Rgt 74, 75
345th AB Rgt 272
Kamchatka Army Corps 269
Sevastopol Infantry Div 283

Ships

Admiral Chabanenko 173
Admiral Fokin 208
Admiral Gorshkov 173, 303, 304
Admiral Kuznetsov 172, 303
Admiral Lazarev 208, 215, 216
Admiral Oktiabrskii 208
Admiral Seniavin 207, 208
Admiral Spiridonov 208
Admiral Tributs 208, 212, 217
Admiral Ushakov 216
Admiral Vinogradov 208, 212
Admiral Zakharov 208
Aleksandr Suvorov 208
Bezboiaznennyi 208
Bezuprechnyi 173
Boevoi 208
Burnyi 208
Bystryi 208
Frunze 206, 208
Gordelivyi 208
Groziashchii 208
INS Sindhu Rashak 302
INS Vikrant 303, 304
INS Viraat 303, 304
Letuchii 208
Marshal Voroshilov 208
Minsk 206, 207, 208, 211
Nikolaev 208
Nikolaevsk 208
Novorossissk 206, 207, 208, 211

Odarionnyi 208
Osmotritelnyi 208
Petropavlovsk 208, 212
Piotr Velikii 173, 230
Poryvistyi 208
Raziashchiskii 208
Razumnyi 208
Retivyi 208
Revnostnyi 208
Sevastopl 208
Simferopl 208
Skrytyi 208
Sposobnyi 208
Steregushchii 208
Stoikii 208
Storozhevoi 208
Tallin 208
Tashkent 208
Ulianovsk 288
USS Abraham Lincoln 220
USS Independence 112, 220
Variag 208, 215, 226
Vasilyi Chapayev 208
Vazhnyi 208
Vladivostok 208
Vozbuzhdionnyi 208

Submarines

K–180, K–211, K–223, K–424, K–433,
   K–441, K–445, K–449, K–490, K–506
   all at page 219
Tomsk 231
Yury Dolgorukii 228